CLAUDE DEBUSSY

COMPOSER RESOURCE MANUALS
(VOL. 27)

GARLAND REFERENCE LIBRARY
OF THE HUMANITIES
(VOL. 771)

GARLAND COMPOSER RESOURCE MANUALS

General Editor: Guy A. Marco

1. *Heinrich Schütz: A Guide to Research* by Allen B. Skei
2. *Josquin Des Prez: A Guide to Research* by Sydney Robinson Charles
3. *Sergei Vasil'evich Rachmaninoff: A Guide to Research* by Robert Palmieri
4. *Manuel de Falla: A Bibliography and Research Guide* by Gilbert Chase and Andrew Budwig
5. *Adolphe Adam and Léo Delibes: A Guide to Research* by William E. Studwell
6. *Carl Nielsen: A Guide to Research* by Mina F. Miller
7. *William Byrd: A Guide to Research* by Richard Turbet
8. *Christoph Willibald Gluck: A Guide to Research* by Patricia Howard
9. *Girolamo Frescobaldi: A Guide to Research* by Frederick Hammond
10. *Stephen Collins Foster: A Guide to Research* by Galvin Elliker
11. *Béla Bartók: A Guide to Research* by Elliott Antokoletz
12. *Antonio Vivaldi: A Guide to Research* by Michael Talbot
13. *Johannes Ockeghem and Jacob Obrecht: A Guide to Research* by Martin Picker
14. *Ernest Bloch: A Guide to Research* by David Z. Kushner
15. *Hugo Wolf: A Guide to Research* by David Ossenkop
16. *Wolfgang Amadeus Mozart: A Guide to Research* by Baird Hastings
17. *Nikolai Andreevich Rimsky-Korsakov: A Guide to Research* by Gerald R. Seaman
18. *Henry Purcell: A Guide to Research* by Franklin B. Zimmerman
19. *G. F. Handel: A Guide to Research* by Mary-Ann Parker Hale
20. *Jean-Philippe Rameau: A Guide to Research* by Donald Foster
21. *Ralph Vaughan Williams: A Guide to Research* by Neil Butterworth
22. *Hector Berlioz: A Guide to Research* by Jeffrey A. Langford and Jane Denker Graves
23. *Claudio Monteverdi: A Guide to Research* by K. Gary Adams and Dyke Kiel
24. *Carl Maria von Weber: A Guide to Research* by Donald G. Henderson and Alice H. Henderson
25. *Orlando di Lasso: A Guide to Research* by James Erb
26. *Giovanni Battista Pergolesi: A Guide to Research* by Marvin E. Paymer and Hermine W. Williams
27. *Claude Debussy: A Guide to Research* by James Briscoe

CLAUDE DEBUSSY
A Guide to Research

James R. Briscoe

GARLAND PUBLISHING, INC. • NEW YORK AND LONDON
1990

Library of Congress Cataloging-in-Publication Data

Briscoe, James R., 1949–
Claude Debussy: a guide to research / James R. Briscoe.
p. cm. — (Garland reference library of the humanities ; vol. 771) (Composer resource manuals; vol. 27)
ISBN 0–8240–5795–3 (alk. paper)
1. Debussy, Claude, 1862–1918—Bibliography. I. Title. II. Series. III. Series: Garland composer resource manuals; v. 27.
ML134.D26B7 1990
016.78'092—dc20 89–23691
CIP
MN

Printed on acid-free, 250-year-life paper
Manufactured in the United States of America

To my mother and father

GARLAND COMPOSER RESOURCE MANUALS

In response to the growing need for bibliographic guidance to the vast literature on significant composers, Garland is publishing an extensive series of research guides. This ongoing series encompasses more than 50 composers; they represent Western musical tradition from the Renaissance to the present century.

Each research guide offers a selective, annotated list of writings, in all European languages, about one or more composers. There are also lists of works by the composers, unless these are available elsewhere. Biographical sketches and guides to library resources, organization, and specialists are presented. As appropriate to the individual composer, there are maps, photographs, or other illustrative matters, and glossaries and indexes.

Claude Debussy by Robert Kastor, with an excerpt by Debussy from the opera **Pelléas et Mélisande** and his signature. By kind permission of The Pierpont Morgan Library, New York. The Frederick R. Koch Foundation Collection. Koch 361.

CONTENTS

Preface xiii
Acknowledgments xv
Introduction
The Past and Future for Debussy Research xvii
How to Use this Book xxi

I. Chronology of Life and Works 3

II. Catalogue of Musical Works 17

Sketch Books 19
Lyric Theater 20
Ballet 26
Incidental Music and Plays 28
Orchestral Works 30
Arrangements
Arrangements by Debussy of His Works 37
Arrangements and Editions by Debussy of Others' Works 39
Works for Chorus and for Soloists with Orchestra 40
Chamber Music 44
Songs for Voice and Piano 46
Piano Solo 65
Duos and Duets for Piano 77
Musical Greetings 80
Exercises for the Paris Conservatory 80

III. Letters, Critical Writings, and Interviews

1. Interpretations of Debussy's Letters and Critical Writings 83
2. Published Collections of Debussy's Letters 86
3. Manuscript Letters in Libraries and Private Collections 98
4. Debussy's Critical Writings and Interviews 130

IV. Index of Letters and Writings 133

V. Reference Books

1. Catalogues of Works 185
2. Bibliographies 187
3. Discographies 189
4. Iconographies 190

VI. Studies of Debussy's Life

1. Books Surveying Debussy's Life and Works 193
2. Surveys Contained within Larger Studies 205
3. Studies of Particular Biographical Issues 211

VII. Collective Volumes and Conferences

1. Periodicals, Collective Volumes, and the Centre de Documentation Claude Debussy 215
2. Catalogues of Expositions 246
3. Catalogues of Important Sales 248
4. Festivals and Conferences 248

VIII. Debussy's Relationships

1. Artistic Climate 253
2. Reception 272
3. Composers 276
4. Performers and Other Musical Figures 324
5. Dancers 328
6. Writers and Literary Movements 330
7. Visual Arts 344

IX. Studies of Style and Aesthetic

1. General Style and Aesthetic 349
2. Programmaticism, Impressionism, and Symbolism 358
3. Structure 363
4. Harmony and Tonality 375
5. Rhythm 385
6. Timbre and Texture 386
7. Melody and Prosody 392

X. Studies of Compositions 395

XI. Addresses

1. Scholars and Others 459
2. Libraries and Institutions 464
3. Publishers 465

XII. Index of Debussy's Works 469

XIII. General Index 478

PREFACE

The compositions and ideas of Claude Debussy comprise one of the most pervasive achievements in Western music. He is arguably the only foremost composer of the twentieth century whose works have acquired a firm place in the public consciousness. His musical thought has provoked a response from virtually every major composer of this era. When one considers as well his interaction with popular music and his encouragement of a global musical perspective, then one can expect future scholarship on Debussy to be even more vigorous than it has been in the past.

Claude Debussy: A Guide to Research seeks to facilitate scholarship of differing interests, whether by musicologists, theorists, performers, or university students. **RILM Abstracts**, **Music Index**, and the bibliography in the yearly **Cahiers Debussy** (entry 123) have been major guides in the preparation of this book.

Concerning primary sources, the **Guide** catalogues all of Debussy's musical works, indicating publication history, main arrangements, text, and current location of manuscripts. It thereby updates François Lesure's **Catalogue de l'oeuvre de Claude Debussy** of 1977 (entry 51). The present guide lists published collections of letters and annotates all manuscript letters in important libraries and private collections, and it indexes all of Debussy's accessible letters for the first time. In like fashion, the collections of his critical writings are annotated and indexed.

Secondary sources annotated here have been selected because they make a unique contribution to the study of Debussy's life, music, and cultural relationships. The present guide annotates 910 books, dissertations, and articles treating Debussy and his artistic environment, in all languages where appropriate research has occurred. It includes all major writings from Debussy's time onward and emphasizes scholarship since 1972, the stopping point for Claude Abravanel's **Claude Debussy: A Bibliography** (entry 53). Although it is not annotated, Abravanel's book remains an indispensable guide to virtually all earlier writings on Debussy. Some of these seemed too limited or outdated to be included here among the core literature, but they still might inform specialized studies. Most of the annotations in the present guide are based upon an examination of the sources themselves. A few inaccessible items are also listed that promise help with particular questions, such as surveys in languages not central to musicological research and studies of topics not discussed elsewhere.

ACKNOWLEDGMENTS

Many people have contributed to this book. Such model scholars as William W. Austin, William S. Newman, and Thomas Warburton have inspired me. Among esteemed colleagues engaged in Debussy studies, I thank David Grayson of the University of Minnesota for advice on **Pelléas et Mélisande** and other sources; Roy Howat of Morden, Surrey, for updating details of the the Catalogue of Works; and Arthur Wenk of the Sedbergh School in Québec Ville for a thoughtful reading of the entire manuscript. Marie Rolf of the Eastman School, and Myriam Chimènes and Yves Lado of Paris, contributed generously to refining sections of the Catalogue of Works. Their efforts have been worthy, and errors that remain are my own.

Librarians, as well, have gone far beyond mere duty in the effort to gather sources. With gratitude I acknowledge the expert and friendly assistance of Phyllis Schoonover and Sheridan Stormes of the Butler University Music Library; J. Rigbie Turner of the Pierpont Morgan Library; Susan T. Sommer of the Toscanini Memorial Archives, New York Public Library; Cathy Henderson of the Humanities Research Center, The University of Texas; Catherine Massip, François Lesure, and Mihnea Penesco of the Bibliothèque Nationale, Département de Musique; and Mlle Nicole Wilde of the Bibliothèque de l'Opéra.

During my fourteen years of Debussy research, I have been supported most generously by private collectors and by publishers. Warmest thanks are extended to Georges Alphandéry of Montfavet, France; Denise Jobert-Georges of the Editions Jobert; François Meyer of Paris; and Odette Vidal of Editions Durand. Henri Thieullent of Le Havre, chief heir of Debussy, similarly is to be thanked for his valuable support. I honor the memory of two great ladies, Dolly de Tinan and Isabel Goüin, who helped me and other Debussy scholars in innumerable ways.

This research project has enjoyed the financial support of Butler University, through its Faculty Academic Grants program. Furthermore, the understanding and flexibility of my department chairperson, Richard Osborne, have permitted the time needed to concentrate on this book. Matt Dickerson provided expert help in researching bibliographic details.

"A _ma_ petite mienne" I offer a devoted appreciation, "pour remercier le mois d'août 1973." Final and lasting thanks go to my parents, whose faith has sustained the journey and to whom I dedicate this book with love.

Indianapolis,
July 1989

INTRODUCTION

1. The Past and Future for Debussy Research

Scholarship on the life, music, and environment of Claude Debussy changes with each generation and parallels his reception in general. In the first two decades of this century, the vogue of Debussy swayed many admirers but also provoked a negative reaction, the misconceptions of both groups vexing Debussy himself. However, a few critics of his time, the foremost of them being Louis Laloy, were able to sound the depths of what his works meant. The generation of scholars between the two World Wars leaned perhaps too heavily upon the significance of national identity and Impressionism. Of these, the pacesetting biographer Léon Vallas is representative and dominant; his work is to be admired for his instinctual love of the music and devoted scholarship but to be faulted for his failure to probe the man, the psychology, and the depths of meaning of the music. This shortcoming, present in Vallas's generation of scholars, was parallel to the public perception, which persisted in an exclusively Impressionistic appreciation of Debussy, and to that of lesser composers, who were more prone to react positively or negatively to the manner of the music while missing the substance. Meanwhile, Debussy's music affected the deep levels of creativity among such leading composers as Schoenberg, Ives, and Stravinsky. Since about 1945, scholars, composers, and to a lesser extent the public have concentrated on Debussy's full message: the new appreciation ranges from Boulez to a few scholars of world music and to modern jazz musicians. This new range was made manifest in the 1960s in the masterful biographies by Dietschy and Lockspeiser (items 68 and 85). Since the equally comprehensive reference tools by Abravanel and Lesure of the early 1970s (53 and 51), a relative profusion of specific studies has brought to light new facts and ideas. The moment is ripe for synthesizing these special studies into a new view that also examines Debussy's reception, multi-faceted style and aesthetic, and psychology.

Much that is exciting remains ahead for scholars of Debussy. Four broad areas and, within those, specific questions call for attention. Work with primary sources has been hampered by the private interests of family, collectors, and on occasion scholars focused too narrowly on their subject. Now that the universal relevance of Debussy is accepted, the elucidation of the primary sources is of paramount importance. The ongoing publication of Debussy's compositions in a critical edition is long overdue, and one trusts that the acumen of Roy Howat's work with the **Préludes** is indicative of a complete thoroughness in the future volumes of the **Oeuvres complètes**. Under François Lesure's direction, the publication of the critical writings and certain letters is a landmark, and scholars await the publication of the complete letters. Such internationalization as Roger Nichols's and Richard Langham Smith's translations of letters and criticism (items 29 and 45) represents a refreshing expansion of Debussy source work, as does David Grayson's careful studies of the **Pelléas** sources (753). However, an interpretation of the whole of Debussy's critical writings has not been attempted since Vallas, and a comprehensive revaluation is called for. Debussy's interests will be served well by a complete discography and, even more, by a careful look at performance practices that the discography might encourage. Debussy, more than most, can be illuminated by a clear and fully annotated iconography.

Marcel Dietschy and Edward Lockspeiser went far to explain Debussy's psychology in their biographies. But it was Dietschy (item 112) who called for a further, sensitive probing of Debussy's complex personality, a call not satisfied in today's terms. Upon the publication of the letters, criticism, and biography, Debussy scholarship now is poised to follow the lines of psychological investigation suggested by Beethoven, Ives, and Schubert biographers.

The kaleidoscope of Debussy's relationships seems infinite in design and thus all the more inviting to exploration. As William Austin has suggested, Debussy's music and ideas may link Western thought to the upcoming global musical consciousness (item 169). Debussy's impact upon popular music and jazz is sketchily traced and is a vastly important area for investigation. A few penetrating studies have shown stylistic interrelationships with the Viennese School, but there is a great need to clarify the exchange with Schoenberg, Berg, and Webern further. Similarly, Debussy's bearing upon the creativity of Ives, Gershwin, Sibelius, and Britten awaits fuller assessment, and such fundamental relationships as those to Wagner and Ravel require further, comprehensive study. German-language scholars such as Claudia Maurer-Zenck are to be commended for their efforts to trace Debussy's reception by modern German composers, while Boulez and certain contemporaries in France have done much to articulate Debussy's relationship to them. However, contemporary links to American, English, and other French composers await full exploration.

The critical reception of Debussy has been discussed perceptively by Theo Hirsbrunner, Eiko Kasaba, Jann Pasler, Johannes Trillig, and others. A fuller picture may be arrived at after scholars consider many further areas of popular impact, including Britain, France, and the United States. Debussy's multi-faceted contacts with arts and literary movements offer numerous possibilities for discussion, as exemplified by the scholarship of Stefan Jarocinski, Langham Smith, and David Hertz (items 564, 481, and 478).

Analysis of the music has not always been penetrating, which is due largely to the outmoded but tenacious urge to explain Debussy simplistically and exclusively as a musical Impressionist or iconoclast. Both approaches have resulted in much incomplete analysis of his "immediate sensuality" or "breaking down" of tradition. Thought concerning Debussy's structures and deeper meanings well might combine with the traditional interpretation of Debussy to recognize the multiple levels on which he speaks. Especially provocative is Howat's work on structure, Wenk's on musico-poetics, Serge Gut's and Jean-Jacques Nattiez's synthetic view of long-range auditory experience, and Jean Barraqué's work on timbral and open-forming processes. Recent scholarship has on occasion misrepresented Debussy when it has relied upon an inflexible Schenkerian approach, on the one hand, or analytic modes more appropriate to nontonal music, on the other. The writings of Richard Parks, however, suggest exciting ways to associate new analytic modes with Debussy and, perhaps thereby, to relate Debussy to the whole of the 20th century.

Whole concepts and major works invite concentrated studies, including Debussy's rhythm, the evolution of his orchestration, the **Nocturnes**, the **Danses** for harp, many of the song sets, and the earlier piano music. Studies such as those by Myriam Chimènes, Robert Orledge, and Marie Rolf on the genesis of certain compositions point the way for much needed work.

The foregoing has only begun to describe the intriguing future that lies before Debussy research. This book seeks as its main purpose to reveal some of the many directions for new thought that may advance the appreciation of Debussy, one of the most pronounced creators in the music of our time.

2. How to Use this Book

Readers should see the **Table of Contents** (p. xi) regarding broad areas of study. The **Chronology** (p. 3) provides the dates of main events and publications. The **Index of Letters and Critical Writings** (p. 133) provisionally indexes materials that are printed or accessible in manuscript collections. The **Index of Debussy's Works** (p. 469) indexes works mentioned throughout this book, except for those discussed in letters and critical writings.

The **General Index** (p. 478) lists proper names and subjects mentioned throughout this book, again excepting those occurring in letters and critical writings. Information about currently active scholars, libraries, and publishers of Debussy's music may be found beginning on p. 459.

The researcher should consider this book as an introduction to the sources of Debussy research. The current author has selected what he views as the foremost writings on Debussy beginning with his time, and he has included most sources written since 1970. The Preface (p. xiii) cites certain reference tools that will update the present guide.

Abbreviations in use throughout:

D - Claude Debussy
DA - **Dissertation Abstracts**, reference set to American dissertations
ISBN - International Standard Book Number
LC - Library of Congress number, whether card or call number, such as ML or MT classes
Martyre - Debussy's composition **Le Martyre de Saint Sébastien**
Pelléas - the opera **Pelléas et Mélisande**

Prélude-faune - the composition **Prélude à l'après-midi d'un faune**
S.N.M. - Société Nationale de Musique

Further abbreviations are indicated concerning the Catalogue of Works, p. 18.

Claude Debussy

I

CHRONOLOGY OF DEBUSSY'S LIFE AND WORKS

This chronology presents only major events and dates of compositions. For more detailed chronologies, see Goubault (item 73), Hirsbrunner (75), and Jarocinski (77). The entry for each year lists biographical events, compositions, and performances. The dates of early songs and many incomplete projects are approximate in some cases. See the Catalogue of Works for particulars.

1862 Birth of Achille-Claude Debussy at 38, rue au Pain, Saint-Germain-en-Laye, near Paris, August 22. Father: Manuel-Achille (bn. Montrouge, May 10, 1836); mother: Victorine-Joséphine-Sophie Manoury (bn. Paris, Oct. 28, 1836). D's parents were married at Levallois, Nov. 30, 1861. At the time of his birth, they were keeping a china shop.

1863 Birth of sister, Adèle-Clémentine (d. 1952).

1864 D is baptised July 31. His godfather is Achille Arosa; his godmother is his aunt Clémentine Debussy (Mme Roustan), who signs her name Octavie de la Ferronnière). In late 1864 the family moves to Clichy, rue des Frères-Herbert.

1867 In May or June the family moves to Paris, 11 rue de Vintimille, 9e arrondissement. Manuel becomes a traveling salesman. Sept. 19: birth of third child, Emmanuel Debussy (d. 1937).

1868 The family moves to 69 rue Saint-Honoré, 1er arrondissement. Manuel is employed by a lithograph printing firm.

1870 Feb. 16: birth of fourth child, Alfred (d. 1937), in Cannes. The family is on a visit to D's aunt Clémentine and returns to Paris in April.

1871 D's second trip to Cannes, where he takes his first piano lessons with an Italian, Jean Cerutti. D's father, Manuel, takes part in the Garde Nationale and the Commune. Upon its defeat he is imprisoned and on Dec. 11 he is sentenced to four years in prison. In October D begins piano lessons with Antoinette-Flore Mauté "de Fleurville," a self-styled former pupil of Chopin and mother-in-law of the poet Verlaine. The family moves to 59bis rue Pigalle.

1872 Oct. 22: D is admitted to the Conservatoire in Paris, in the piano class of Marmontel and the solfège class of Lavignac. D has received some random tutoring by his mother but no formal schooling of any sort. In December, Manuel's sentence is commuted with suspension of civil rights.

1873 Nov. 10: birth of fifth child, Eugène-Octave (d. 1877). Manuel assumes a position as assistant bookkeeper with the Compagnie de Fives-Lille.

1874 Marmontel and Lavignac note D's musicality and artistic temperament in their regular reports at the Conservatoire. D receives the third prize in solfège and a second certificate of merit in piano, performing part of Chopin's Second Concerto. The family moves in with D's grandmother Manoury, 13 rue Clapeyron, 8e arr.

1875 Lavignac and Marmontel again report on D's excellent talent and seriousness as a student. He receives the second prize in solfège and first certificate of merit in piano, playing the Second Ballade by Chopin.

1876 Appears in a concert at Chauny, in a piano trio and as vocal accompanist. Marmontel reports that D is careless in theory. D receives first prize in solfège but no prize in the piano concours, in which he plays Beethoven's Sonata op. 111, first movement.

1877 Marmontel reports a greater seriousness in D's studies. D receives second prize in piano, performing Schumann's Sonata in G minor. Enters the harmony class of Emile Durand.

1878 D's professors observe musicality and excellence in score reading but also blundering in harmony studies. In the public concours D receives no prizes in piano or harmony.

1879 D receives no prize in harmony or piano. Enters Auguste Bazille's class in accompaniment and practical harmony and briefly Franck's organ class. Is recommended by Marmontel as pianist for Mme Pelouze-Wilson at the Château de Chenonceaux, for service during the academic vacation.
Composes the songs **Ballade à la lune** and **Madrid, princesse des Espagnes**.

1880 Bazille praises his facility at keyboard harmony and reading; D receives first prize in the practical harmony class. At Marmontel's suggestion, D becomes pianist in the entourage of Mme von Meck. Travels with her to Interlaken, Arcachon, and Florence. Perhaps in 1880 he also visits San Sebastian, Spain. In November-December in Paris, is engaged as pianist for the private singing class of Mme Moreau-Sainti. There he meets Mme Marie-Blanche Vasnier and later Mr Vasnier, the major benefactors of his youth. On December 24 enrolls in the composition class of Ernest Guiraud at the Conservatoire.
Composes **Symphonie en si mineur**, **Danse bohémienne**, **Premier trio en sol**, and the songs **Souhait**, **Nuit d'étoiles**, **Fleur des blés**, **Caprice**, and **Beau soir**.

1881 Guiraud reports on D's intelligence and potential as a composer. First visit to Moscow, then to Gurievo, in Mme von Meck's company.
Composes for Mme Vasnier (a soprano **léger**) the songs **Pierrot**, **Rondel chinois**, **Souhait**, **Tragédie**, **Zéphyr**, **Aimons-nous et dormons**, **Jane**, and **Séguidille**. Composes **Diane-ouverture** and ca. 1881 the cantata **Daniel**.

1882 Attends the first performance of Lalo's ballet **Namouna**, his enthusiasm for which causes him to be removed from the concert. Receives second merit at the Conservatoire in counterpoint and fugue but fails to pass the preliminary exam in composition with his **Le printemps (Salut Printemps)**. Joins Mme von Meck in Moscow, then Plechtcheyvo, and develops a youthful infatuation for her daughter Sonia. Succeeds Paul Vidal as piano accompanist of the choral society La Concordia, directed by Widor. Meets Gounod there.
First publication 1882 (date of legal deposit at Bibl. nat.), of **Nuit d'étoiles**. Composes the songs **Fantoches** (first version); **Le lilas**; **Fête galante**; **Les roses**; **Flots, palmes, sables**; **Rondeau ("Fut-il jamais")**; **Mandoline**; **Clair de lune** (first version); **Pantomime**; **La fille aux cheveux de lin**;

Sérénade; **En sourdine** (first version); **Hymnis**; **Beau soir**; **Nocturne et scherzo** (cello and piano); **Printemps (Salut Printemps**, chorus); **Intermezzo** (cello and orch./piano); **Triomphe de Bacchus** (orch.(piano 4-hands)); **Andante Cantabile**, **Divertissement**, and **Intermezzo** (the latter three works for piano 4-hands).

Gives first public performance on May 12 of his compositions (**Les roses**, **Le lilas**, **Nocturne et scherzo**) at the salons Flaxland, with Mme Vasnier and the violinist Thieberg.

1883 Guiraud observes that D has a bizarre but intelligent nature in a report to the Conservatoire. D receives fourth place in composition trial for the choral work **Invocation**, then second prize for the cantata **Le gladiateur**.

Composes the songs **Coquetterie posthume**; **Romance (Silence ineffable)**; **Paysage sentimental**; **Chanson espagnole**; **Musique**; **Chanson triste**, **Fleur des eaux**; **L'archet**; the duo **Eglogue**; **Première suite d'orchestre**.

1884 Passes the preliminary trial in composition at the Conservatoire with the choral work **Le printemps** ("L'aimable printemps"). On June 27 wins the first place in the Prix de Rome competition with the cantata **L'enfant prodigue**.

Composes the songs (Romance) **Voici que le printemps** (subtitled "musique pour éventail"), **Regret**, **La Romance d'Ariel**, **Apparition**. Ca. 1884: the song **Les baisers**.

1885 Leaves Paris for Rome Jan. 27, on Prix de Rome stipend at the Villa Medici. Visits Count G. Primoli at Fiumicino near Rome. Returns to Paris on vacation in July. Back in Rome remains dissatisfied, but Mr Vasnier dissuades him from renouncing the Prix and tenure in Rome. Reads widely and meets Liszt, who plays for him and counsels D to listen to Palestrina and Lassus. Hears their music at the church of Santa Maria dell'Anima.

Works intently on **Diane au bois** and begins the cantata **Zuleima**. Composes songs **L'ombre des arbres** (in set **Ariettes oubliées**) and **Barcarolle**. Also ca. 1885: **Chevaux de bois (Ariettes)**.

1886 Takes a leave to go to Paris in February, returning to Rome April 26. Another leave to go to Paris in July, returning to Rome in September. Studies Wagner and Mozart, reads Shakespeare and plans a collaboration on **As You Like It**, and reads Baudelaire, Rossetti, Berlioz's **Memoirs**, and the

English Romantics. Studies **Tristan**.
Composes **Green (Ariettes)**. Completes the single extant scene from **Diane au bois**.
The Académie des Beaux-Arts sponsors a performance of **Zuleima**, but it is judged "incomprehensible."

1887 Returns to Paris permanently, his stay in Rome (the minimum of 2 years) completed. Moves in with his parents, 27 rue de Berlin (now rue de Liège). Hears **Lohengrin** and befriends Paul Dukas and Etienne Dupin, who suggest a trip to Bayreuth to hear Wagner's music dramas.
Composes **Printemps** (in version for chorus and 2 pianos); **C'est l'extase** (in **Ariettes**), **La mort des amants (Cinq poèmes de Baudelaire)**. Begins **La damoiselle élue**.
At first performance at the Académie des Beaux-Arts, **Printemps** is criticized for its "vague Impressionism."

1888 First visit to Bayreuth, where he hears Wagner's **Parsifal** and **Meistersinger**. Becomes lifelong friends with writer and scholar Robert Godet.
Composes **Le balcon (Cinq poèmes de Baudelaire)**. Ca. 1888 works on a scene for the opera project **Axel**. Completes **La damoiselle élue**. Begins **Petite suite** and **Deux arabesques** (piano). Publication of **Ariettes oubliées**.

1889 Becomes a member of the Société Nationale de Musique (S.N.M.). Attends Universal Exposition in Paris and hears the Javanese gamelan in the Dutch exhibit; visits the Annamite theater. Vacations in Brittany. Attends a concert of Russian music (Glinka, Borodin, Rimsky-Korsakov, Tchaikovsky, and Glazunov) at the Trocadéro under the direction of Rimsky-Korsakov. Second visit to Bayreuth; hears **Parsifal** and **Meistersinger** again and also **Tristan**. Returns disenchanted to Paris. Famous conversations with Guiraud on aesthetics and Wagner, noted down by Maurice Emmanuel. Ca. 1889, first contact with Musorgsky's opera **Boris Godunov**.
Composes **Harmonie du soir, Le Jet d'eau,** and **Recueillement (Cinq poèmes de Baudelaire)**. Completes **Petite suite** (piano duo). Begins the **Fantaisie pour piano et orchestre** and the opera **Rodrigue et Chimène**. Envisions a setting of Poe's **Fall of the House of Usher**.

1890 Breaks with the Académie des Beaux-Arts by refusing to write a required overture. Attends the poet Mallarmé's gatherings. Meets the innovative artistic personalities Moréas, de Régnier, Gide, Narcisse Lebeau. Frequents the Chat Noir cabaret and the Taverne Pousset.

Completes the **Fantaisie** but withdraws it from a concert after d'Indy decided to conduct only the first part. Composes **La Belle au bois dormant**, **Mazurka**, **Tarentelle styrienne**, **Valse romantique**, and early version of **Suite bergamasque**. Begins the opera **Rodrigue et Chimène**. About 1890 collaborates with René Peter on the drama **Les frères en art**. **Cinq poèmes de Baudelaire** published.

1891 Breaks off a relationship with an unidentified woman. Requests Maeterlinck's permission to set **La Princesse Maleine** but is refused. Friendship with Erik Satie in 1891 or before.

Composes the **Trois mélodies de Paul Ver laine**, **Fêtes galantes** set I, **Dans le jardin** (song), **Deux romances** (songs on texts by Bourget). Publication of **Rêverie** (piano), **Paysage sentimental** (song), **Deux arabesques** (piano), **Marche écossaise** (piano 4-hands), **Les angelus** (song), **Beau soir** (song).

1892 Signs his name "Claude Debussy" for the first time (heretofore Achille and then Claude-Achille). Meets Gabrielle Dupont and moves out of his parents' home and into an attic with her, 42 rue de Londres, 8e arr. Forms close friendship with Chausson, H. Lerolle, Stevens, and Louÿs. Plans to visit the U.S. at the instigation of Prince Poniatowski.

Publishes the **Nocturne** (piano). Works on **Trois scènes au crépuscule**. Begins the **Proses lyriques** and the **Prélude, interlude et paraphrase finale pour "L'Après-midi d'un faune" de Mallarmé**. Abandons **Rodrigue et Chimène**.

1893 Hears Wagner's **Die Walküre** and later performs a 4-hand version of **Das Rheingold** at a lecture by Mendès, both at the Opéra. Moves with Gaby Dupont to 10, rue Gustave-Doré, 17th arr.

Works on **Rodrigue et Chimène**. Attends the play **Pelléas et Mélisande**, obtains Maeterlinck's permission to set it, and begins work. Completes the **Proses lyriques**. Publication of **La damoiselle élue** and completion of the **Quatuor**, which is premiered by the **Quatuor Ysaÿe**.

First performance of **La damoiselle élue** at the S.N.M.

1894 Becomes engaged to the singer Thérèse Roger, whom he accompanies in a performance of **De fleurs** and

De soir (**Proses lyriques**) at the S.N.M. Plays Act I of **Parsifal** in a private gathering. Plans marriage to Thérèse Roger on April 16 but breaks the engagement and returns to Gaby Dupont. Georges Hartmann, collaborator of the publisher Fromont, grants a monthly stipend.

Continues arduous work on **Pelléas**, playing excerpts in a private gathering at the home of H. Lerolle. Plans **Amphion** with the poet Paul Valéry. Composes **Images [oubliées]** for piano. Completes and sells rights for the **Prélude à l'après-midi d'un faune** to the editor Fromont.

The premiere of **Prélude** at the S.N.M. is received favorably. First concert devoted wholly to D's works, in Brussels (**La damoiselle élue**, **Quatuor**, and two of the **Proses lyriques**).

1895 Asks for the hand of Catherine Stevens, daughter of the painter Alfred Stevens. Frequents the Taverne Weber and Reynold's Bar, often in the company of the writers Toulet and Louÿs.

Completes first version of **Pelléas et Mélisande** and plays parts of it in a private gathering. **Nocturnes** in second version (for violin and orch.) nearing completion. A project to perform the work at the Théâtre de L'Oeuvre is aborted. Publication of **Prélude à l'après-midi d'un faune** and **Proses lyriques**.

1896 Works on two projects never completed, the ballet project **Daphnis et Khloé** (on a scenario by Louÿs adapted from Oscar Wilde) and the cantata **La saulaie**. Orchestrates **Proses lyriques** (only **De grève** and **De soir**) and the **Gymnopédies** 1 and 3 by Satie.

1897 Violent scenes with Gaby, who attempts suicide. Encounters serious financial woes and asks for Hartmann's assistance.

Works on a projected pantomime, **Le chevalier d'or**, and plans the **Chansons de Bilitis**. Of that set, **La chevelure** is completed and performed.

1898 Hears Ravel's **Habañera**, is impressed, and asks for a loan of the score. States to Louÿs that he is haunted by thoughts of suicide. Meets Rosalie (Lilly) Texier, an haute-couture model. Plagued by debts, D gives piano, harmony, and singing lessons.

Hopes for an agreement with the Opéra-Comique regarding **Pelléas** and is disturbed to learn that Maeterlinck already has approved incidental music by Fauré for the play. Composes **"Dieu!"** and

"Yver" of the **Trois chansons de Charles d'Orléans**. Completes the **Chansons de Bilitis**.

1899 Financial worries require a loan from Hartmann. Separates from Gaby Dupont and becomes closer to Lilly Texier. Later in 1899 inscribes to Gaby the 2-piano manuscript of **Prélude à l'après-midi d'un faune**. Marries Lilly Oct. 19 in a civil ceremony, having given a piano lesson that morning to pay for the wedding meal. Satie, L. Fontaine, and Louÿs are witnesses. The couple moves into 58, rue Cardinet, 17 arr.

The singer Jeanne Raunay refuses to premiere the **Chansons de Bilitis** on moral grounds. They are published by Fromont. Completes the **Nocturnes** and composes the **Berceuse pour La tragédie de la mort**.

1900 After Hartmann's death (April 22), D counts on Louÿs and other friends for assistance with debts. Lilly Debussy loses the child she is carrying in August. **L'Echo de Paris** names Debussy "the Verlaine of music, the equal of the other Verlaine."

Works on the **Nuits blanches** and considers the play **L'herbe tendre** by René Peter. Performs **Pelléas** at home for friends, including Ravel. Its appearance is announced for 1901 in **Le Ménestrel**.

Blanche Marot and D perform the **Chansons de Bilitis** at the S.N.M. (Salle Pleyel). At the Universal Exposition of 1900, **La damoiselle élue** and the **Quatuor** are performed (Aug. 23). **Nuages** and **Fêtes** (**Nocturnes**) are premiered at the Concerts Lamoureux.

1901 Maeterlinck indicates a preference for his wife, Georgette Leblanc, to sing the role of **Mélisande**. Later, Mary Garden is selected. First article of music criticism, which appears in the **Revue blanche**. On July 1 D's critical personnage (nom de plume) Monsieur Croche appears in the **Revue blanche**.

Pelléas and **Pour le piano** are completed. Composes **Lindaraja** (2 pianos).

Albert Carré agrees to perform **Pelléas** at the Opéra-Comique in 1902. **Chansons de Bilitis** (musique de scène) are performed. First complete performance of the **Nocturnes**.

1902 Hartmann's heirs sell all D's works in their possession to the publisher Fromont. D is prosecuted to repay debts. Maeterlinck enters a formal and public dispute over the choice of Mary Garden instead of Georgette Leblanc in the role of Méli-

sande. First visit of D to London.
Works on **Diable dans le beffroi** (Poe) and projects settings of **As You Like It** (Shakespeare), now with Paul-Jean Toulet, and **King Lear** (Shakespeare).
Pelléas et Mélisande premiered at the Opéra-Comique, April 30. 1st performance by the pianist R. Viñes of a work by D, **Pour le piano**, January 11.

1903 Writes music criticism for **Gil Blas** and **Mercure de France**. Is decorated Chevalier de la Légion d'Honneur. Enthusiastic hearing and review of Rameau's **Castor et Pollux**, but later in 1903 D repudiates Gluck. Second voyage to London to review the **Ring**. Meets Emma Bardac in October, upon giving piano lessons to her son Raoul Bardac.
Composes **Estampes** (piano). Begins **La mer**, **Images** for piano (first series), and **Rapsodie** for saxophone. Turns again to **Le diable dans le beffroi**. Collaborates with René Peter on the satirical comedy **Les frères en art**. Agrees to complete Chabrier's opera **Briséis** for the publisher Enoch.
Concert of D's works at the Schola Cantorum (**Pour le piano**, **Chansons de Bilitis**, **Quatuor**, and 2-piano version of **Nocturnes**).

1904 Leaves Lilly for life with Emma Bardac, July. Moves with Mme Bardac to 10 Avenue Alphand and then to 80 Avenue du Bois de Boulogne. Lilly attempts suicide. Many friends desert him. End of friendship with Louÿs. Third voyage to London.
Composes **Fêtes galantes** set II, **L'isle joyeuse**, piano score of **La mer**, **Danses** (harp and strings), and sections of **Le Roi Lear**. Completion and publication of **Trois chansons de France** and **Masques** (piano).
First performance of **Estampes**. Records on the early phonograph the first five **Ariettes** with Mary Garden, along with "Mes longs cheveux" from **Pelléas**, Act III beginning.

1905 Divorce of Emma Bardac from her husband granted May 4; that with Lilly granted on August 2. Claude-Emma Debussy ("Chouchou") born October 30. Signs a contract with Durand granting exclusive rights to publish all future works.
Completion and first performance of **La mer**, and publication by Durand. New orchestration of **L'enfant prodigue** and revision of **Suite bergamasque**. Completion and publication of **Images** for piano series I.

First performances of **Masques** and L'isle joyeuse by R. Viñes.

1906 The critic Pierre Lalo writes in **Le Temps** that "The religion of Debussyism has replaced the religion of Wagnerism." Meets Richard Strauss. Befriends Victor Segalen and plans to collaborate on the Buddhist drama **Siddharta**. **Le Mercure Musical** announces the collaboration of D as a contributing writer.

Works on **Le diable dans le beffroi**. First sketches for **Preludes** for piano, book I.

Viñes premieres **Images** book I.

1907 Is concerned about losing his inspiration. Others imitate his style, to his dismay. Hears Paul Dukas's **Arianne et Barbe-bleue** with enthusiasm; also attends performance of Richard Strauss's **Salome**. Meets de Falla. Begins friendship with André Caplet. Emma's uncle dies and disinherits her in his will, undercutting a projected financial security.

Composes the **Images** for piano series II. Projects **Histoire de Tristan** in collaboration with Gabriel Mourey.

First German performance of **Pelléas** in Frankfurt, April 17.

1908 Marries Emma in a civil ceremony, Jan. 20. Concert on Jan. 30 devoted to his works, organized by Jane Bathori and Emile Engel. A second "Festival Debussy" occurs Feb. 13. Fifth voyage to London, conducts **Prélude à l'après-midi d'un faune** and **La mer**. Hears Rameau's **Hippolyte et Aricie** and Musorgsky's **Boris Godunov** at the Opéra. First biography appears, by Louise Liebich (item 83).

First performance and publication of **Images** for piano set II. Completes **Children's Corner**, **Ibéria** (piano score), the **Rapsodie** for saxophone, and **Quand j'ai ouy**, the last song completed of the **Trois chansons de Charles d'Orléans**.

Signs a contract with the Metropolitan Opera of New York for first performance of **La chute de la maison Usher** and **Le diable dans le beffroi**, with an option for **La légende de Tristan**. **Pelléas** performed in Lyon, New York, Prague, Milan, Berlin, and Munich.

1909 Visits London twice, to conduct the **Prélude-faune** and the **Nocturnes** and then to supervise the London premiere of **Pelléas**. Publication of **Le cas Debussy** (item 228) and the biography by Laloy (81).

Projects ballet **Masques et bergamasques**, for which he writes the scenario, and the vocal work **Orestie**. Continues to struggle with the Poe projects, **La chute de la maison Usher** and **Le diable dans le beffroi**. Completes **Hommage à Haydn** and some of the **Préludes** for piano book I.

Pelléas is also performed in Rome, Boston.

1910 Dines with Mahler and attends the performance of Mahler's second symphony, but D leaves during the second movement. Plans a voyage to the United States. Is in financial straits. Meets Toscanini. Hears Stravinsky's **L'oiseau de feu** at the Opéra with great interest, meets the composer, and writes of him in letters. D's father dies Oct. 28. Conducts in Vienna and plays in Budapest. Meets the conductor Ernest Ansermet.

Completes **Préludes** for piano book I, **La plus que lente**, **Hommage à Haydn**, **Rapsodie for clarinet**, **Trois ballades de François Villon**, and the **Promenoir des deux amants**. Works diligently at **La chute de la maison Usher**. Signs contracts with the dancer Maud Allan to compose the ballet **Khamma** and the impresario G. Astruc for **Le martyre de Saint Sébastien**.

First performances of **Ibéria** and **Rondes de printemps** (orchestral **Images**), **D'un cahier d'esquisses** (by Ravel as pianist). Caplet premieres the orchestral version of **Children's Corner** in New York; Mahler conducts **Rondes de printemps** there.

1911 Considerable financial difficulties and renewed thoughts of suicide. Refuses Caplet's invitation to visit Boston, citing personal reasons.

Begins the composition of **Khamma** and continues working on **Chute de la maison Usher** and **Diable dans le beffroi**. L'Opéra-Comique programs both works for the following season, but D cannot bring himself to complete them.

Premiere of **Le martyre**, despite a declaration by the Archbishop of Paris repudiating the work as offensive to Christian sensibilities. Premiere of the **Rapsodie pour clarinette et piano** and **Trois ballades de Villon**. Conducts **Prélude-faune**, **Children's Corner**, and **Ibéria** in Turin. Mahler conducts **Ibéria** in New York, and **Pelléas** is heard in Vienna.

1912 The **Prélude-faune** is danced by the Ballets Russes with Nijinsky, provoking a scandal in the press. Receives a score of **Petruchka** from Stravinsky and reads **Le Sacre du printemps** with him at the piano.

Completes the piano score of **Khamma**, begins the

orchestration, and leaves to Charles Koechlin the remaining orchestration. Composes **Jeux** and returns to his "old labors" of **Chute** and **Diable**. Begins the **Préludes** for piano book II and **Gigues**, and with that completes the three **Images pour orchestre**. The Opéra announces as forthcoming D's opera **Crimen amoris**, on a text by Charles Morice after Verlaine.

100th performance of **Pelléas** at the Opéra-Comique and a dinner in D's honor.

1913 Conducts in Moscow and St. Petersburg at the invitation of Serge Koussevitzky. Attends the premiere of Stravinsky's **Sacre du printemps**. A concert "Gala Claude Debussy" is given at the Comédie des Champs-Elysées.

Composes **Trois poèmes de Stéphane Mallarmé**. Completion and publication of **Preludes** for piano book II. Collaborates with André Hellé on the ballet **La Boîte à joujoux** and completes the piano score. Considers a ballet in collaboration with Louis Laloy, entitled **Fêtes galantes**; begins the ballet **No-ja-li**.

First complete performance of the **Images** for orchestra, including the premiere of **Gigues**. Premiere of **Printemps** for orchestra, as orchestrated by Henri Büsser. Premiere of **Jeux** by the Ballets Russes, produced by Diaghilev with Nijinsky's choreography. **Syrinx (Pièce pour Psyché)** premiered at performance of Mourey's play **Psyché**.

1914 Conducts in Rome, The Hague, and Amsterdam, which tires him greatly. In July writes of his inability to work and thinks of suicide. Travels to London for a private concert. World War I conflict disturbs him; he regrets being able to do little for the war effort. Discusses a trip to the United States with the violinist Arthur Hartmann.

Recomposes the musique de scène **Chansons de Bilitis** as the **Six épigraphes antiques**. Composes the **Berceuse héroïque** in honor of King Albert I of Belgium for his wartime valor. Revises **Le martyre** for a performance in operatic form. Works on **No-ja-li (Le palais du silence)** and discusses its orchestration with Koechlin.

1915 Lassitude and insecurity over the direction of his music and music in general. His mother dies on March 23. Regains his determination to compose in July. In October states that illness prevents him from completing **Chute de la maison Usher**. In November rectal cancer is diagnosed; undergoes surgery in December.

Composes **Pièce pour piano (Pour le vêtement du blessé)**, **En blanc et noir**, **Sonata for Violoncello**, **Sonata for Flute, Viola, and Harp**, **Etudes for Piano**, **Noël des enfants**, **Elégie** (piano). Completes the edition of the works of Chopin for Durand.

1916 Begins the year with painful recovery from cancer surgery; further radium treatments are administered. Litigation between D and his ex-wife disturbs him considerably. Writes to his friend and editor Durand that only the the duty of completing the Poe projects (**La chute de la maison Usher** and **Le diable dans le beffroi**) prevents him from committing suicide.

Completes libretto in final version for **La chute de la maison Usher**.

Premiere of **En blanc et noir**, with D and Roger-Ducasse as pianists.

1917 Declines an invitation to perform the **Etudes** in a concert proposed by Fauré, stating that his piano playing is no longer adequate. Attends the premiere of Satie's ballet **Parade**.

Completes the **Sonata for Violin**. Sketches the beginning of **Ode à la France** and the musique de scène for **As You Like It**. Edits the sonatas for violin and for cello of Bach for Durand.

First performance of the sonatas for cello and for violin (both with D as pianist) The performance of the violin sonata, May 5, is his last concert in Paris. D's last performance is of the same, at St.-Jean-de-Luz in September.

1918 Widor and Marcel Baschet nominate D to the Institut de France. Debussy dies at home on March 25. He is buried temporarily on March 28 in the Père-Lachaise cemetery and removed to Passy cemetery in 1919.

Chouchou Debussy died July 16, 1919. Emma Debussy died in 1934.

II

CATALOGUE OF MUSICAL WORKS, complete or fragmentary

Note on the order and numbering

The catalogue is arranged by genre and thence alphabetically. The order of the genres and page where each begins are as follows:

Page		
19	S:	Sketch Books
20	T:	Lyric Theater
26	B:	Ballet
28	I:	Incidental Music
30	O:	Orchestral Works
37	A:	Arrangements by Debussy of his Works
39		Arrangements by Debussy of Others' Works
40	V:	Vocal Works
44	C:	Chamber Music
46	M:	*Mélodies*
65	P:	Piano Solo
77	D:	Duos and Duets for Piano
80	G:	Musical Greetings
80	E:	Exercises for the Paris Conservatory

Example of a catalogue number:
T1 - Item 1 of the Lyric Theater works.

General order of each entry

Title.
Genre or scoring (where explanation is needed).
Lesure number. L 82 = item 82 in Lesure Catalogue.
Date of composition.
Author of text.
Dedication.
Publication information for the composition, giving first edition and important further editions.
Manuscript source or sources (MS).
Performance. First and important further performances.
Further commentary at the end of the entry.

Abbreviations

acc.	- accompanied, accompanist
auto.	- autograph manuscript
ARR	- arranged, arrangement
Bibl.	- Bibliothèque
B.n.	- Bibliothèque nationale, Département de Musique, Paris
c.	- copyright
ca.	- circa
coll.	- collection of manuscripts
comp.	- complete, completed
ded.	- dedicated to
ed.	- edition, edited by
Eng.	- English
f., ff.	- folio, folios. Music on recto only unless noted.
facs.	- facsimile
Fr.	- French
Ger.	- German
HRC	- Harry Ransom Humanities Research Center, University of Texas
incl.	- includes, including
incomp.	- incomplete
LC	- Library of Congress, Division of Music, Washington, DC
m., mm.	- measure, measures
Morgan	- Pierpont Morgan Library, New York
MS, MSS	- manuscript, manuscripts
mvt.	- movement
NY Publ.	- New York Public Library
orch.	- orchestra, orchestral, orchestrated
p., pp.	- page, pages
perf.	- performance (first, unless so stated)
pl.	- plate, plates
pn.	- piano, pianos
publ.	- published
r.	- recto of page
rev.	- revised, revision
sax.	- saxophone
sc.	- scene
son.	- sonata, sonatas
sop.	- soprano
trans.	- translated
Univ.	- University
v.	- verso of page
vcl.	- violoncello
vln.	- violin

See the List of Scholars, Publishers, and Institutions, page 000, for addresses of libraries and publishers mentioned in the catalogue.

See the <u>Index of Debussy's Works</u>, page 469, for writings concerned with specific works or groups of works, such as songs, piano music, or **Pelléas et Mélisande**.

See Cobb, **The Poetic Debussy** (item 48), for details of literary texts.

The Catalogue of Musical Works is indebted to Lesure's earlier **Catalogue** and to Goubault's biography for details of source locations and first performances. Researchers may consult those sources (annotated items 51 and 73) for commentary. The present catalogue updates the Lesure catalogue where further information has been available.

1. Sketch Books

Other sketches are listed under pertinent works.

S1 Sketchbook, 110 p. MS Lehman coll., formerly on deposit Morgan. Contains sketches for **Images** (orch.), **Ibéria**, **Préludes** for piano Book I (**La fille** and **Cathédrale engloutie**), other works.

S2 B.n. Ms. 15380. 13-p. sketches of vln. son.; other sketches unidentified.

S3 B.n. Ms. 17726 (ca. 1916-17). P. 1 has note to Emma Debussy concerning vln. son. Various sketches.

S4 B.n. Ms. 17729. 9 ff.; unidentified sketches.

S5 B.n. Ms. 17730. 8 ff.; sketches for **No-ja-li** and for unidentified vocal works.

S6 B.n. Ms. 17731. 1 f., incl. musical greeting "Noel pour la p'tite Mienne." Other sketches.

S7 B.n. Ms. 17732. Sketches for finale of vln. son. Ca. 1916-17.

S8 B.n. Ms. 17678. Sketches for vln. son.

S9 B.n. Rés. Vmc. Ms. 51. "Six sonates..." Notebook p. without music, ca. 1915, in Debussy's hand outlining the projected series of sonatas.

S10 B.n. Ms. 20632 (1). Sketchbook, provenance Lilly Debussy and André Meyer, 56 p. Includes the songs **L'archet** and **Fleur des eaux** in unfinished state.

S11 B.n. Ms. 20632 (2). Sketchbook, provenance André Meyer, 68 p. Includes sketches for **Scènes au crépuscule**.

2. Lyric Theater

T1 **Axel** (L 63). (opera project)
ca. 1888. Text by Villiers de L'Isle-Adam, which appeared in **La jeune France** from Nov. 1885 to June 1886. According to Vallas, 1 scene was completed (unpubl.). Auto. MS location unknown.

T2 **La chute de la maison Usher** (L 112). (opera)
1908-17. Libretto by Debussy after Edgar Allen Poe.
MS of music:

1) B.n. W.54(2), 22 p. notebook containing sketches. on p. 7-8, ca. 1909.
2) B.n. MS 14520, 1 p., 18 m. presented as birthday greeting to Emma, June 11, 1909, with indication "ce qui sera peut-être le prélude à La chute de la maison Uscher [sic]"
3) Coll. André David, 1 p., ca. 1909, 9 m. of the end.
4) B.n. MS 17726. Sketches on f. 1v-8r of **No-ja-li** sketchbook.
5) B.n., formerly coll. Mme de Tinan. 1 p.
6) B.n. MS 9885. Short score of 1916. Facsimile in Lockspeiser **Poe**, item 486.
7) Coll. Henry Prunières, 1 p.
8) B.n. MS 17727. Sketches for first part of scene 2.
9) Coll. Marc Pincherle. 1 p. Facsimile in Lockspeiser (486) pl. 26-27.
10) Coll. Arthur Hoérée, 1 p., first part of scene 2.
11) B.n. MS 17727, 18 m. for middle of sc. 2.
12) British Library, Reference Division, London. Add. MS 47860 (3). Sketches for scene 2, apparently ff. 25-28. Meyerstein Bequest Vol. XX. Inscribed by Emma Debussy to the pianist Marcelle Meyer. Sotheby and Quaritch sales, both 1940.
13) B.n. MS 17727. Sketches for end scene 2.
14) B.n. MS 9885. 8-m. sketch for end, found on p. 21 of MS. Also contains libretto.

For further details see Orledge, item 843.
MSS of the libretto:

1) working draft of 27 p., in three scenes (prologue and two scenes), HRC.
2) 14 p. dated August 1909-June 1910, first version in three scenes, B.n. Rés. Th.b.143, formerly coll. Mme de Tinan.
3) B.n. Ms. 9885, 17 p., final version in two scenes, completed 1916, publ. Lockspeiser (item 486).
4) B.n. Rés. Vmd. 41: D's annotated copy of Baudelaire trans.
5) Gimbel estate (private coll., New Hampshire), 1 p. of prose scenario.
6) 1 p. of end of libretto, dated "VIII 09", coll. A. David.

Publ. version by Juan Allende-Blin. Paris: Jobert, 1979. Perf. Yale Univ., New Haven, Conn., Feb. 25, 1977, in version by Carolyn Abbate. 1st perf. of version by Allende-Blin on Hessischer Rundfunk, Frankfurt, Dec. 1, 1977. Stage perf. of version by Allende-Blin Oct. 5, 1979, by Berlin Opera.

T3 **Le diable dans le beffroi** (L 101). (opera, or music drama)
1902-1911 or 1912. Libretto by D after Edgar Allen Poe. Unpubl. Sketches for scenario and music publ. in Lockspeiser, **Debussy et Edgar Poe** (item 486). 2 tableaux planned by D.
Music MSS: 1) 3 p. of sketches, B.n. Ms. 20634, formerly coll. Meyer, dated "25 août 1903," reprod. in Lockspeiser **Poe** (item 486). See also Orledge, p. 316 (item 843) concerning the related **Morceau de concours**. 2) 4 p. incl. vln. solo (or whistling part for the devil?), description of scenery, and a song (?); MS location unknown.
Libretto MS: "Notes pour le Diable dans le beffroi," 6 p. dated Aug. 25, 1903, B.n. Vm. micr. 21, formerly coll. Meyer, publ. in Lockspeiser **Poe**.

T4 **Diane au bois** (L 51). (opera scene)
1881-86. Text by Théodore de Banville. Unpubl., vocal score for sop. and ten. with 3-staff short score acc., and related score **"Diane...Ouverture."** Forthcoming ed. in **Oeuvres complètes**, Durand-Costallat, by Paul Meecham. The extant vocal score is the complete final scene,

adapting Banville's text of Act II, scenes iii and iv.

MSS 1) Morgan Library, Cary Coll. (vocal score), 29 p. music (15 f.), f. 16 bears text in D's hand of **Chanson espagnole**; 2) B.n. Ms. 17999, **"Diane..Ouverture,"** for 2 pianos, 29 p., signed "Corso. Rome. 27 Novembre, 1881"; main theme relates to vocal scene, ded. "à mon cher maître Mr Ernest Guiraud."

Perf. of vocal score: 1968 over British Broadcasting Corporation, under auspices of E. Lockspeiser; Cleveland, Ohio, American Musicological Soc., Nov. 8, 1986, under direction of J. Briscoe.

* **The Fall of the House of Usher.** See above, **La chute...**

T5 **Hymnis** (L 37). (operatic sections)

ca.1882. Text by Théodore de Banville. Unpubl. vocal score for two voices and piano.

MSS 1) 4 p., the song **Il dort encore,** setting the opening strophe of Banville's play, MS in Geneva, Fondation Martin Bodmer. Publ. Jobert 1985 (c. 1984), in **Debussy: Sept poèmes de Banville**. Perf. April 1982, Romantic Music Festival, Indianapolis, by Laura Niemeier, soprano, and Anna Briscoe, pianist.

2) 11 p., final scene **Ode Bachique,** ded. "à Mme Vasnier." MS Koch Foundation, on deposit Morgan Library, provenance A. Toscanini. Perf. of final scene 1986 as **Diane au bois**.

3) 29 p., voice and piano, relating to scenes i, ii, vii, and an unnumbered scene; location unknown.

T6 **Mais il ton chant son luth** [Mais il touche son luth?]. MS fragment: Stanford Univ., A Memorial Library of Music. 1 f. (1 p.). Words and music with auto. corrections, inserted in a copy of **Pelléas** first ed.

T7 **Orphée-roi**. (opera project; only libretto extant)

1909. A collaboration between D and Victor Segalen. MS libretto: in private coll. Annie Joly-Segalen. Facs. of p. showing D's criticisms publ. in **Segalen et Debussy** (item 35). Revised by Segalen as a play, publ. Paris: Crès, 1915, which is republ. in item 35.

T8 **Pelléas et Mélisande** (L 88). (opera) 1893-1902 (with revisions 1902-05). Text by Maurice Maeterlinck (1st ed. Brussels: Paul Lacomblez, 1892); abridged and adapted by Debussy (libretto publ. as "**Pelléas et Mélisande**, drame lyrique en cinq actes, tiré du théâtre de Maurice Maeterlinck, musique de Claude Debussy, nouvelle éd., modifiée conformément aux représentations de l'Opéra-Comique" (Brussels: Paul Lacomblez, 1902)).

Ded. "A la mémoire de Georges Hartmann et en témoignage de profonde affection à André Messager."

Publ.: vocal score Fromont, 1902; rev. Durand 1905 and 1907. Full score Fromont 1904 [repr. New York: Dover, 1985]; Durand 1905; new rev. ed. Durand 1966; Kalmus, [196-?]. The **Oeuvres complètes** edition is in preparation by David Grayson.

Further trans. and arrangements: German trans. Durand 1906; Italian trans. Durand 1908; arr. complete for piano solo, extracts for pn. solo, and complete opera arr. for 4 hands by L. Roques, Durand 1906 and 1907; piano trio based on themes by H. Mouton, Durand 1909; extracts arr. for small orch. by R. Branga, Durand 1930; **Pelléas et Mélisande Symphonie** (based on excerpts) by M. Constant, Durand 1981.

See Grayson **Genesis** (item 753) for a detailed catalogue of the MS sources. The following lists all unchanged aspects of, additions to, and revisions of Grayson's catalogue as suggested by him.

Preliminary Drafts (Sketches)

1) B.n. Ms. 20631. 52 f., preliminary draft June-July 1895, "Meyer MS" formerly A. Meyer coll. Fragments of Act I/scenes 1-2 and IV/3, and complete scenes II/1-3 and V. Signed at the end "pour H. Lerolle...juin-juillet 1895."
2) B.n. Ms. 20703. 4 f., preliminary draft of IV/3 (bought at auction 17 June 1987).
3) HRC, 1 p. 3 staves, 16 m. of sketch for an interlude [?] and thus dating perhaps from 1902.

Developed Draft (Short Score)

4) Coll. Robert Owen Lehman, formerly on deposit Morgan. Act IV scene iv, "Une fontaine dans le parc," dated "Septembre-Octobre [18]93", 12 f., incl. sketches on versos 7-10 and 12; the sketch on f. 12v belongs to Act 4/sc.1. Known as "Legouix MS," formerly Legouix coll.

5) B.n. Ms. 1206, 20 f. (the last blank) of developed draft (short score) of Act IV, scenes i and iv; "Bréval MS" formerly coll. Lucienne Bréval; dated Sept.-Oct. 1893, May 1895.
6) Coll. Frederick R. Koch Fdn., on deposit Morgan; formerly New Eng. Cons. of Music, known as "New England Conservatory MS"; auto. short score of entire opera, 1893-1901, 131 f. (with music on 11 facing versos and with f. 1 verso of Act IV containing an outline of a projected orch. score).

<u>Piano-Vocal Score</u>

7) Private coll., Basel, 7 f., Act IV, scenes i-ii (preliminary version).
8) B.n. Ms. 17686, piano-vocal score "Stich-vorlage": 25 f. of Act IV sc. i and ii and Act V, prov. Denise Jobert-Georges.
9) B.n. Ms. 17683, piano-vocal score "Stich vorlage", 13 f., Act IV, scenes iii and iv, on deposit from Françoise Prudhomme coll.
10) B.n. Res. Vma. 237, corrected proofs of piano-vocal score, first ed. (Fromont 1902); "Périer proofs," former coll. Jean Périer, currently coll. Françoise Prudhomme, on deposit at B.n. This source involves two different sets of proofs: 1 set of Acts I-III (corresponding to p. 2-169 of the vocal score), the other of Acts II-IV (pp. 48-242). Thus there are 2 different copies of Acts II-III and one each of I and IV.
11) Private coll., London. Piano-vocal score (Durand 1907) having belonged to Maggie Teyte, with auto. corrections by Debussy.

<u>Full Score</u>

12) B.n. Mss. 961-965, fair copy of full score. (Ms. 961 is Act I, etc.).
13) HRC. Act I, scenes i and iii. 3 f. recto only, 2 p. containing orchestral writing; other p. of vocal-orch. score containing Geneviève's text "vite...Il y a longtemps...[to] vous avez la clar-"[end of p.]. Corr. in blue pencil. These f. were rejected from B.n. Ms. 961, listed above.
14) B.n. Ms. 1029, first corrected proofs of Act I and second corrected proofs of Act III, with extra and missing pages.
15) present location unknown: 1 f. containing 2 corrections to the publ. orch. score (vio la, m. 4-5 p. 391; and strings, harp, 4th horn m. 1-2 p. 385). Facs. in auction cat. "Succession van Parys," March 7-8, 1979, item 399ter.
16) Lehman coll., formerly on deposit Morgan.

Various corrected proofs of 1st ed. full score, Fromont 1904: Act I (2nd proofs), Act II (2nd proofs), Act III (1st proofs), Act IV (1st proofs?), Act V (1st proofs). With extra and missing pages.
17) present location unknown: Act I (3rd proofs?), pp. 65-68, described in Coulet et Faure sale catalogue, Spectacles (1972), p. 175. no. 1045.
18) Set of proofs, Archives Durand, Asnières-sur-Oise. Used by Messager to conduct 1903-04 performances at Opéra-Comique, with Messager's annotations.
19) B.n. Rés. Vma. 281, final proofs marked "bon à tirer," ded. to Emma Bardac and formerly in the coll. of Dolly de Tinan, dated 29 June 1904, 409 p.
20) Bibl. François Lang, Royaumont. Full score Fromont 1904 having belonged to Debussy, with many corrections and changes by him.
21) Coll. of Editions Durand, Paris. Durand 1905 score with corrections and revisions by Debussy and copyist as basis for correction of parts (Aug. 1905) and full score (pl. corr. Apr. 1949, used to create new plates for study score printed in 1950, and used for imprint of full score only in 1966).
22) B.n. Cons. Rés. 2729, printed orch. pocket score Durand 1908, Debussy's copy with auto. corrections dated 1908, includes 1 p. music MS, ded. to Emma Bardac and dated April 1908.
23) B.n. Rés. Vms. 338. 41 orch. parts relating to Durand 1905 ed., prov. Opéra-Comique, with auto. performance indications by various persons.

Perf. of **Pelléas et Mélisande**: Paris, Opéra-Comique, Apr. 30, 1902, cond. André Messager.

T9 **Rodrigue et Chimène** (opera) (L 72).
1890-92. Text by Catulle Mendès, after G. de Castro and Corneille. Ded. on title p. of Act I "A Mademoiselle Gabrielle Dupont, Avril 90." Unpubl. vocal score (part in incomp. sketch) of Acts I-III. MS coll. Lehman, formerly on deposit Morgan. Forthcoming realization of sketched sections and ed. by R. Langham Smith, Durand, **Oeuvres complètes**.

3. Ballet

B1 **La boîte à joujoux** (ballet pour enfants) (L 128).
1913. André Hellé. Piano score Durand 1913; Full score Durand 1920 (beginning of orch. by D, the remainder by André Caplet from D's sketches); piano and full scores, ed. R. Zimmermann, Peters 1978. ARR: 4-hand, by L. Roques, Durand 1914; piano trio, H. Mouton, Durand 1914.
MSS: 1) B.n. Ms. 976 is autograph piano score. 2) B.n. Ms. 979 is orch. score and contains 7 p. by D, the remainder in Caplet's hand. 3) B.n. Ms. 19910, 3 p., which completes p. 8 of B.n. Ms. 979. 4) 1 p. in a sketchbook of 1913, formerly coll. Meyer, currently B.n. 5) B.n. Fol. Vm6.45A is annotated MS by A. Caplet. 6) B.n. Vm7.18648A is 1913 Durand piano score, with annotations in Caplet's hand. 7) Orledge reports existence of second proofs with auto. corr. by Debussy and with Hellé's MS scenario, in an unidentified coll.
Perf. Théâtre Lyrique du Vaudeville, Dec. 10, 1919. Dir. Désiré-Emile Inghelbrecht, decor and costumes by A. Hellé, scenic design by R. Quinault.

B2 **Fêtes galantes** (originally titled **Crimen amoris**) Opera-ballet, on a text by Charles Morice, after Verlaine's **Crimen amoris**. Intended for the Opéra; never realized. 1912-1915.
MSS: 1) typed libretto of **Fêtes galantes**, with corrections in hand of Louis Laloy (?), who had replaced Morice as collaborator. Bears indication in D's or Laloy's hand: "F.g. Ballade en trois tableaux d'après Paul Verlaine. Par Claude Debussy." Argument of the ballet, 14 folios, B.n., Res. Vmb. 33; 2) B.n. Ms. 17730, 7 p. sketches, according to Orledge, of **Fêtes galantes** ballet.

B3 **Jeux** (poème dansé) (L 126).
1912-13. libretto by Nijinsky, or on his idea by Diaghilev. Ded. Mme Jacques Durand. Piano score Durand 1912; full score Durand 1914, repr. 1947; orch. score, ed. by Max Pommer, Peters, 1971. ARR: 4-hands, L. Roques, Durand 1914.
MSS: 1) Orch., B.n. Ms. 966; 2) Orch. sketch dated Apr. 1913 and at end 28.III.[19]13 [to] 24.IV.[1913], Lehman coll., formerly on deposit at Morgan; 3) Stadtbibliothek Winterthur, Rychenberg-

Stiftung 11/3, orch. draft dated "23,28,29 aout 1912-1,[2 sept.]", formerly Legouix coll.; 4) printed proof set [3rd?] with many autograph corrections, Coll. Fr. Lang, Royaumont; 5) copyist's MS with annotations by Diaghilev, Nijinsky, Debussy, formerly coll. Serge Lifar, currently Koch coll. on deposit Morgan; 6) MS piano red., B.n. Ms. 1008, title p. and 22 f. incl. f. 14a, 14b, 21a, 21b; 7) MS piano score bound with 2-piano score of **La mer**, B.n. Ms. 1022 [this source not verified].

Concert perf. Concerts Colonne, Feb. 28, 1914, dir. Gabriel Pierné. First ballet perf. May 15, 1913, Théâtre des Champs-Elysées, Ballets russes (de S. Diaghi lev), dir. by Pierre Monteux, Choreog. by V. Nijinski, decor and costumes by Léon Bakst.

B4 **Khamma** (légende dansée) (L 125).

1911-12. W.L. Courtney and Maud Allan. Piano score by Debussy, Durand 1912 (placed on sale in 1916); full score Durand, beginning of orch. by D, remainder orch. by Chas. Koechlin under Debussy's supervision. ARR: 4-hand, L. Garban, Durand 1918.

MSS: 1) copy at B.n., Gr. Vma. 289, of MS 3 (HRC) below; 2) B.n. Ms. 15470 orch. draft of 41 p. indicated as "1re version," in hands of D and Koechlin; 3) HRC orch. fair copy [stamped "matériel appartenant à Durand et Fils"], 80 p. (1-10 in D's hand, 11-80 in that of Koechlin), certain extra leaves and fragments laid in; 4) B.n. Ms. 17728, short score, 1 f., of sketches for the "Khamma" theme; 5) MS formerly in coll. Maud Allan with revisions by D, dating from 1912, sold at auction 1956 and present location unknown; 6) MS of scenario: B.n., Rés. Th. b.126. 9 p. in D's hand.

Perf. projected but not realized New York 1916, to have been dir. Ernest Bloch; first perf. Paris, Concerts Colonne, dir. Gabriel Pierné, Nov. 15, 1924, in concert performance; Paris, Opéra-Comique, March 26, 1947, in stage perf. dir. Gustave Cloez, choreog. J.J. Etcheverry.

B5 **Masques et bergamasques** (only a ballet scenario extant)

Auto. scenario of 4 p., dated VII [19]09 and signed, at HRC. Scenario by D publ. Durand 1910, 8 p. Orledge (item 843, p. 322) states that 1 measure marked "Angélus" of the score exists in the **Images** sketchbook, Lehman coll. formerly on deposit at Morgan.

B6 **No-ja-li (Le palais du silence.** Incomplete ballet project).
1913-14. Georges de Feure [Georges van Sluijters]. Unpubl. MSS: B.n. MS 17726, **No-ja-li** sketchbook, sketches for prelude and scene 1; 2) B.n. MS 17730, 8 p.; 3) B.n. Ms. 17726, sketchbook with sketches only; 4) MS scenario dated Nov. 2, 1913, in archives of Editions Durand.

* **Le palais du silence**. See **No-ja-li**.

4. Incidental Music and Plays

I1 **Berceuse pour "La tragédie de la mort"** (music to accompany a play) (L 93).
1899. Text by René Peter, to whom the MS is ded.: "Cher René, excuse-moi de prendre momentairement l'accent 'poitevin' pour t'assurer une fois de plus de ma sincère amitié!...Avril 1899, Claude Debussy." MS: 2 p. of unacc. melody setting a single verse of scene 1, "Berceuse pour la 'Tragédie de la mort' sur une vieille chanson poitevin: Il était un' fois une fée qui avait un beau sceptre blanc", at LC, Washington. An unpubl. excerpt in Orledge (item 843).

I2 **Chansons de Bilitis** (music to acc. readings of poems by Pierre Louÿs, with reciter and tableaux vivants) (L 96).
Sections: I Chant pastoral, II Les Compa raisons, III Les contes, IV Chanson, V La partie d'osselets, VI Bilitis, VII Le tombeau sans nom, VIII Les courtisanes égyptiennes, IX L'eau pure du bassin, X La danseuse aux crotales, XI Le souvenir de Mnasidica, XII La pluie au matin.
1900-01. Ded. intended perhaps for P. Louÿs. Publ. Jobert, 1971, with preface and celesta part realized by A. Hoérée. MS B.n. 16280, 3 separate part books. Scored for 2 flutes, 2 harps, celesta (lost). Celesta part reconstructed by P. Boulez 1954, for a concert of Domaine musical, Théâtre Marigny, Apr. 10, 1954. D used certain material of the work in **Six epigraphes antiques**.

Premiered Paris, private concert of **Le Journal**, Feb. 7, 1901.

I3 **Esther et la maison de fous** (play).
Farce by Debussy in collab. with René Peter [see Orledge item 843]. MS: location unknown, formerly in coll. Mme R. Peter (4 f.), which is a synopsis by D, undated. See Dietschy (item 68), p. 136.

I4 **Les Frères en Art** (play; also known as **F.E.A.**).
1903. Satirical comedy planned by D and René Peter; only the play completed by Debussy in 1903.
MS: B.n. Rés. Vma. ms. 1062, prov. André Meyer, 39 pp. of 3 tableaux.
Publ.: 1) tableau 2, sc. 1-3 (1897-98 version) in Peter (item 88); 2) Meyer coll. catalogue (item 49) reprints a list of scenes and characters in D's handwriting; 3) excerpts from final version publ. in Lockspeiser, **Revue de musicologie** 56 (1970): 165-176.

I5 **Le martyre de St. Sébastien** (mystère) (L 124).
Feb.-May 1911. Text by Gabriele D'Annunzio. Publ.: Orch. score Durand 1911; vocal score transcribed by André Caplet, Durand 1911. ARR: extracts for pn., A. Caplet, Durand 1911; extracts 4-hands, L. Roques, Durand 1912; version in French and English with piano acc. of voice, Durand 1914.
MSS: 1) B.n., Opéra, Rés. 2004, auto. orch. score in hands of D, Caplet and 3 other copyists; 2) Priv. coll. Sheridan Russell, London. 1 p. of D's corrections of harp and cymbals parts; 3) Priv. coll. Sheridan Russell, London. 4 m. in short score, end Act 2 no. 3. Facs. of 2) and 3) are in Caplet **Lettres** (item 11); 4) according to Lesure's **Catalogue**, sketch of prelude to Act IV with indications of orch., location unknown, which is possibly the same as MS source 2; 5) printed orch. score with corrections and some modifications by Caplet, at Bibl. de l'Opéra, Paris; 6) partial full score in coll. Mlle Astruc, microfilm at B.n. Vm. micr. 21, contains Acts I-IV in part, with orch. in hands of D and Caplet.
Orch. by Debussy and Caplet as described above. Perf. Théâtre du Chatelet, cond. André Caplet (organized G. Astruc), May 22, 1911.

I6 **Pièce pour Psyché**; orig. title **Flûte de Pan**; publ. as **Syrinx** (L 129)
1913. Ded. Louis Fleury. MS not extant.

Projected originally as incidental music for the play **Psyche** by Gabriel Mourey. The extant flute solo represents the song of Pan in his final moments. Publ. as **Syrinx** [publisher's title], Jobert 1927; Peters 1969. ARR: alto sax., J. Londeix, Jobert 1971.
Perf. by Louis Fleury, Dec. 1, 1913.

I7 **Roi Lear, Le** (incidental music for Shakespeare play in trans. by Pierre Loti and Emile Vedel) (L 107).
1904-06. Ded. intended for Georges Jean-Aubry. Incomplete: 7 sections are listed as sketched in an unrecovered MS sold at Hôtel Drouot 1933.
MSS: 1) B.n. Rés. Vmf. Ms. 53 lists 7 mvts.: "Prélude, 3 Interludes, Le sommeil de [Lear]," "Le roi Lear dans la lande," and "Fanfare"; 2) coll. Daniel Ericourt, sketch; 3) 4 m. of the MS Prelude is given in Boucher, item 64, pl. 43/2; 4) according to Lesure's **Catalogue**, an extract of the MS "Prélude" (possibly same as Boucher) publ. in facs. in **Images de France**, Noël 1941.
Pub. Jobert 1926 in piano and in orch. versions by Jean Roger-Ducasse: two movements: **Fanfare d'ouverture** and **Le sommeil de Lear**. Perf. Oct. 22, 1926, in a piano version by Léon Vallas at the Salle Gaveau. The 1st perf. of orch. version Concerts Pasdeloup, Oct. 30, 1926, cond. by Albert Wolff.

* **Syrinx**. See **Pièce pour Psyché**.

5. Orchestral Works

* Unidentified orch. sketch, 1 f. HRC.

* **De l'aube à midi sur la mer**. See **La mer**, I

O1 **Danse sacrée et danse profane** (otherwise entitled **Deux danses pour harpe, pour harpe chromatique ou piano avec accompagnement d'orchestre d'instruments à cordes**) (L 103).
April-May 1904. Ded. Gustave Lyon. Publ. Durand 1904; arr. for 2 pn. by Debussy, publ. Durand 1904. Re-ed. for pedal harp, H. Renié, Durand 1910, repr. 1957. Also publ. Peters 1972.

ARR: for vln. and pn., L. Roques, Durand 1904; for vcl. and pn., L. Roques, Durand 1907; for pn. solo, J. Durand, Durand 1907.
MS of orig. version B.n. Ms. 1012; autograph MS of arr. by D for 2 pn. B.n. Ms. 1011. Perf. Concerts Colonne Nov. 6, 1904, dir. E. Colonne, soloist Mme Wurmser-Delcourt.

* **Dialogue du vent et de la mer.** See **La mer**, III.

02 **Fantaisie pour piano et orchestre** (L 73).
1889-90. Ded. René Chansarel. Publ. in full score Fromont 1920; corrected ed. Jobert 1968; Moscow: Editions musicales d'état, 1963; Peters 1976. ARR: 2 pianos, G. Samazeuilh, Fromont 1919; Peters 1975.
MSS: 1) formerly coll. Jobert-Georges, currently coll. Lehman, formerly on deposit Morgan, 125 p., dated "Octobre 89-Avril 90," ded. to R. Chansarel; 2) British Library, Zweig MS 31, former coll. Marguerite Long, 32 p. of sketches of solo part with pn. red. of orch.; 3) coll. F. Lang, Royaumont, 2nd and 3rd proof sets with corrections considered in 1968 Jobert ed.; 4) coll. Dr. Vacher, Malakoff, red. for 2 pn. [this latter relates to the final proofs of the 2-piano arr., completed and with corrections by G. Samazeuilh, preserved at HRC].
Perf. Royal Philharmonic Soc. with Alfred Cortot, Nov. 20, 1919.

* **Fêtes.** See **Nocturnes**, II.

* **Gigues.** See **Images** (orch.), I.

* **Ibéria.** See **Images** (orch.). **Ibéria** consists of 1) **Par les rues et par les chemins**
2) **Les parfums de la nuit**
3) **Le matin d'un jour de fête.**

03 **Images pour orchestre** (L 122).
1905-12. Ded. Emma Debussy. Publ. as set Durand 1913; Eulenburg, 1977; Peters 1978. Perf. as set Concerts Colonne, Jan. 26, 1913, dir. Debussy.

Gigues, 1909-12. Publ. full score Durand 1913. MSS: 1) B.n. Ms. 1010; 2) coll. Lehman, formerly on deposit Morgan; provenance coll. Jobert-Georges, short score (orch. draft) on 4 staves, 7 leaves. 1st perf. as above. ARR: 4-hands and 2 pn., A. Caplet, Durand 1912; pn. solo, L. Garban, Durand 1952.

Ibéria, 1905-08.
1) **Par les rues et par les chemins**
2) **Les parfums de la nuit**
3) **Le matin d'un jour de fête.**

Publ. full and pocket scores Durand 1910. MSS: 1) B.n. Ms. 1009, 73 p.; 2) coll. Lehman, formerly on deposit Morgan, short score of **Les parfums** and **Le matin**, dated 1908, title p. and 11 ff.; 3) Bn. Ms [unnumbered], formerly de Tinan coll, 19 f. of sketch; 4) B.n. Ms. 10931, 2 f., sketches of 1st theme of **Par les rues**; 5) B.n. Ms. 14518, 1 p., "Fin réelle d'Ibéria," dated 1908; 6) coll. R. Lehman, formerly on deposit Morgan, several pp. of sketches in a sketchbook; 7) proof set [3rd?] with corrections, concerning 1910 Durand ed., in Coll. Lang, Royaumont; 8) former coll. G. Samazeuilh, 1 p. sketch, reprod. in cat. Coulet et Faure, p. 36 [this is probably the fragment now preserved at the HRC]. Perf. Feb. 20, 1910, Concerts Colonne, dir. G. Pierné. ARR: 2 pn. and 4-hands, A. Caplet, Durand 1910; pn. solo, L. Garban, Durand 1952.

Rondes de printemps, 1905-09.
Publ. full score Durand 1910. MSS 1) B.n. Ms. 994, 38 p.; 2) B.n. Fol. Vm15.160A, corrected proofs; 3) 3rd proofs corrected by D, Coll. Lang, Royaumont. Perf. Mar. 2, 1910, Concerts Durand, Salle Gaveau, dir. Debussy; version for 2 pianos perf. Théâtre des Champs-Elysées, June 19, 1913, perf. by D and R. Viñes. ARR: 2 pn. and 4-hands, A. Caplet, Durand 1910; pn. solo, L. Garban, Durand 1952.

O4 **Intermezzo** (L 27).
June 1882. Inspired by a passage by Heine. According to MS indication, planned as 4th part of a suite for cello and orch. MSS: 1) former coll. R. Legouix, location unknown, 28 pp. orch. score; 2) coll. G. Piatigorsky, currently Coll. Drachman [copy of MS at LC], for cello and pn. but with the indication "Suite pour violoncelle Solo et Orchestre / Intermezzo 4 [intended as 4th movement of multi-movement suite?]," title p. and 4 p. music. The Piatigorsky MS was publ. by Elkan-

Vogel 1944.
Note: see **Intermezzo [4-hands]** under Piano 4-Hands concerning another composition with this title, reported incorrectly as a version of the present work.

* **Jeux.** See under Ballet Works.

* **Jeux de vagues.** See **La mer**, II.

* **Le matin d'un jour de fête.** See **Images**, part II **Ibéria**, 3.

O5 **La mer. "Trois esquisses symphoniques"** (L 109)
1) **De l'aube à midi sur la mer**
2) **Jeux de vagues**
3) **Dialogue du vent et de la mer.**

August 1903-March 5, 1905. Ded. Jacques Durand. Pub. full score Durand 1905, rev. ed. Durand 1909; full score Peters, 1972; Dover, 1983 (in **Three Great Orchestral Works of Debussy**, repro. of 1905 ed.), Eulenburg (pocket score, n.d.); Kalmus (n.d.); pn. 4 hands arr. D, Durand 1905; version for 2 pn. 6 hands by A. Caplet 1908, performed in concert by D and others. ARR: 2 pn., A. Caplet, Durand 1909; pn. solo, L. Garban, Durand 1938.

MSS: 1) B.n. Ms. 967, orch. full score, 97 p.; 2) Rochester, Eastman School of Music, orch. draft; 3) B.n. Ms. 1022, autog. transcr. for 2 pn., 31 p.; 4) Proof set [3rd?] with corrections, coll. F. Lang, Royaumont; 5) Durand ed. with auto. [?] corrections, Conservatoire de Genève or E. Ansermet, now lost; 6) 1905 Durand ed. with auto. corrections and ded. to E. Varèse, coll. Louise Varèse; 7) British Library (Music Library) K.5.d.16, 1905 Durand ed. with auto. corrections, most of which were incorporated into 1909 Durand ed.; 8) B.n. Rés. Vma 288, proof set of 1st mvt. with auto. corrections; 9) B.n. Vm7 18281, corrected proof set of mvts. 1-3; 10) B.n. Res. Vmf. ms. 53, sketches; 11) HRC, Texas, 1-p. sketch with heading "Mer belle aux îles sanguinaires." Contains key signature and 4/4 meter signature but no music.

Perf. Concerts Lamoureux, Oct. 15, 1905, dir. C. Chevillard; Jan. 19, 1908, Concerts Colonne, dir. Debussy.

06 **Nocturnes.** **"Triptyque symphonique pour orchestre et choeurs"** (L 91)
1) **Nuages**
2) **Fêtes**
3) **Sirènes** [with female voices]
Dec. 1897-Dec. 1899. Ded. Georges Hartmann. Publ. full score Fromont 1900, 1909; Jobert 1930 and 1964, in editions rev. according to D's autograph corrections of Fromont ed.; Peters 1977/78; Dover 1983 (in **Three Great Orches tral Works**, reprint of 1900 ed.); Boosey and Hawkes (n.d.); International (n.d.); Kalmus (n.d.). ARR: 2 pn., M. Ravel, Fromont 1909 [MS coll. Koch, on deposit Morgan]; pn. solo and 4-hands versions, 3 mvts. in ARR publ. separately: 1) **Nuages**, G. Samazeuilh, Jobert 1923; 2) **Fêtes**, L. Borwick (2 pn.), Jobert 1914 and G. Samazeuilh (4-hand), Jobert 1923; 3) **Sirènes**, G. Samazeuilh, Jobert 1923; **Sirènes** for vln. and pn., Samazeuilh, Jobert 1925. **Fêtes** publ. in a "partition analysée," Heugel 1977.

MSS: 1) coll. Jobert-Georges, 49 f.; 2) LC, orch. draft, 22 f., dated "Vendredi, 15 D. 3h du matin," with auto. ded. to Lilly Debussy; 3) Coll. Monteux, Hancock, Maine, corrected proofs, ded. to P. Louÿs; 4) coll. F. Lang, Royaumont, printed score [Fromont] with autograph corrections [copy in microfilm at B.n., Vm. micr. 824 et 826]. Perf.: **Nuages** and **Fêtes** Dec. 9, 1900, Concerts Lamoureux, dir. C. Chevillard; entire set by the same, Oct. 27, 1901.

Possibly a revision of the **Trois scènes au crépuscule** (project of 1892-93, see below).

* **Nuages.** See **Nocturnes**, I.

* **Par les rues et les chemins.** See **Images** part II, **Ibéria**, 1.

* **Les parfums de la nuit.** See **Images** part II, **Ibéria**, 2.

07 **Prélude à l'après-midi d'un faune** (L 86).

1892-94. Symphonic commentary on poem by Mallarmé. Ded. Raymond Bonheur. Publ. 2 pianos Fromont 1895; full score Fromont 1895; arr. M. Ravel pn. 4 hands, Fromont 1910. Repr. of 1895 Fromont full score by Dover, 1983 (in **Three Great Orchestral Works**); Kalmus 1948; M. Baron (New

York, n.d.); Boosey and Hawkes (n.d.); Eulenburg Pocket Score (n.d.). Facsimile reprod. of auto. score, preface by R. Manuel, Paris, Ed. Rombaldi, 1943. Color facsimile of pre-orchestral version, preface R. Manuel, Washington, R.O. Lehman Fdn., 1963 (MS 2 below). New editions: Norton 1970 (critical ed. with commentary by William Austin); Peters 1970.

ARR: 4-hands, M. Ravel, Fromont 1910 [MS coll. Koch, on deposit Morgan]; solo pn., L. Borwick, Fromont 1914; flute and pn., G. Samazeuilh, Jobert 1925; vln. and pn., Jobert 1925.

MSS: 1) B.n. Ms. 17685, prov. coll. Jobert, 26 p. orch. score, dated at end "Septembre 1894" with ded. "à Raymond Bonheur"; 2) coll. R. Lehman, formerly on deposit Morgan Library, 6 f. orch. short score, signed "à...Gaby...Octobre 1899"; 3) coll. Jobert, trans. for 2 pianos, 6 pp.; 4) Rochester, Eastman School, proofs with auto. corr.; 5) Geneva, Switzerland, Bibl. publique, score inscribed to Godet but with no auto. indications; 6) Bibl. F. Lang, Royaumont, orch. score (Fromont) having belonged to Debussy with auto. corr.; 7) Cary coll., on deposit Morgan Library, score with revisions and annotations used by S. Diaghilev for the 1912 production by the Ballets russes; 8) British Library Add 47215, choreographic score of the ballet by V. Nijinsky, Budapest, Aug.-Sept. 1915, 28 f.

Perf. Salle d'Harcourt, Société nationale de musique, Dec. 22, 1894, dir. Gustave Doret. Choreographed by Nijinsky, perf. Théâtre du Châtelet, May 29, 1912.

Ravel red. for piano 4 hands, MS Koch coll., Morgan Library.

* **Première rapsodie** [clar.]. See under Arrangements by Debussy.

O8 **Première suite d'orchestre** (L 50).

ca. 1883. **Fête, Ballet, Rêve, Bacchanale.** Unpubl. MS: 1) red. for pn. of mvts. I, II, and IV, former coll. Mme. Jean Lerolle, location unknown; 2) Mvt. III, 26 p., sold in New York, Walter Schatzki, 1958, location unknown. The 1942 exposition cat. by Auguste Martin (no. 37) suggests that there were both orch. and 2-piano scores in MS.

O9 **Printemps** (L 61).

1887. Symphonic suite for orchestra, piano, and chorus. Inspired by a painting by Marcel Baschet, who had been inspired by Botticelli's "Primavera."

Publ.: 1) first mvt., for 2 pn. and textless voices, **Revue musicale, supplément musical** in three installments: February 15, March 1, and March 15 1904; 2) the same but with the voices reduced onto a single staff and with revisions for piano 4-hands, Durand 1904.

None of the following eds. and arr. contain the original chorus: 3) red. by H. Büsser (under Debussy's supervision?) for pn. 4 hands, Durand 1912, ded. "à la mémoire d'Auguste Durand"; 4) orch. by H. Büsser under Debussy's very general supervision in 1912, publ. Durand 1913; the latter republ. Budapest, Musica, 1974. ARR: arr. for 4-hands of 1904 ed., by H. Benfeld, Durand 1907; paraphrase for vln. and pn., J. Durand, Durand 1910; for vcl. and pn., L. Roques, Durand 1910; for pn. solo, H. Büsser, Durand 1930.

MS: 1887 score for two pn. and textless chorus, containing title page and 37 p. fair copy, with emendations, signed "Ach. Debussy [18]87," at HRC.

Perf. of Büsser orchestration Apr. 18, 1913, Soc. Nationale, Salle Gaveau, dir. Rhené Bâton. Premiere of original version Oct. 26, 1989, Univ. of Texas Chamber Choir under P. Gardner, in ed. by J. Briscoe, for American Musicological Soc.

O10 **Rapsodie** (L 98).

1903. For saxophone and orchestra. Ded. Elisa Hall, President of Orch. Club of Boston, who commissioned the work. First written as an orch. particell for alto sax. and orch., sketched by D and completed by Roger-Ducasse. Publ. Durand 1919 in Roger-Ducasse's realization for sax. with pn. and sax. with orch. ARR: pn. 4-hands, L. Garban, Durand 1919; for English horn and pn., Durand 1923.

MSS: 1) Boston, New England Cons., 14 f., orch. draft [microfilm at NY Public Lib. Lincoln Ctr., Special Coll. Music]; 2) B.n. Ms. 1001, 35 f. Perf. Salle Gaveau, Soc. nationale de musique, May 14, 1919, dir. André Caplet, saxophonist Mayeur.

Further see **Rapsodie** under Chamber Music concerning the version with pn. acc.

* **Rapsodie, Première** [clar.]. See under **Première rapsodie** in Arrangements by Debussy.

* **Rondes de printemps.** See **Images** (orch.), III.

* **Scènes au crépuscule, Trois.** See **Trois scènes au crépuscule.**

* **Sirènes.** See **Nocturnes**, III.

O11 **Symphonie en si mineur** (L 10).
1880. Ded. "A Madame de Meck de la part de son dévoué serviteur Ach. Debussy." For pn. 4-hands, score publ. Moscow 1933, ed. N. Gilaiew, and republ. Moscow 1965; also see Blumenthal (item 701), where the 1st and 2nd Soviet eds. are reprinted with editorial commentary. MS at Tchaikovsky Museum, Klin, USSR, 11 p. Arr. for orch. by Michael Schelle, for premiere orch. performance in Indianapolis, Butler University, Romantic Music Festival, Apr. 22, 1982.

O12 **Le triomphe de Bacchus** (L 38).
2 extant movements: Allegro, Andante cantabile. Ca. 1882. Suite inspired by Banville; complete suite (if it existed) is lost. Publ. of Allegro mvt. only, arr. by M.F. Gaillard for pn., Choudens 1928; orch. by Galliard, publ. Choudens 1928. MS (containing both Allegro and Andante cantabile) formerly coll. M. Cobb, currently Morgan, 8 p., for pn. 4 hands. Perhaps relates to de Tinan fragment for pn. 4 hands, which see. A new edition of both the first and second movements is given in Blumenthal (see item 701).

O13 **Trois scènes au crépuscule** (L 83).
1892-93. Unpubl. MS: B.n. Ms. 20632 (2), 2 p. in a sketch notebook, provenance A. Meyer. Originally intended apparently for solo vln. and orch., and for Eugène Ysaÿe specifically. Possibly sketches leading to the **Nocturnes**. See Vallas (96), p. 146, 149.

6. Arrangements

Arrangements by Debussy of His Works

Further see the original works as indicated.

A1 **Berceuse héroïque** (L 132).
1914. Orch. of original piano work. Publ.

Durand in full score 1915. MS Paris, Bibl. de l'Opéra, Rés. 56, 7 pp. Perf. Oct. 26, 1915, Concerts Colonne-Lamoureux, dir. C. Chevillard.

A2 **Le jet d'eau** (No. 3 of **Cinq poèmes de Baudelaire**, L 64).
1907. Orch. (revised by André Caplet) of orig. song, for 1 voice and orch. Full score publ. Durand 1907. MS of D's orch. version is B.n. Ms. 1016; Caplet's MS version is B.n. Rés. Vma. Ms. 992.; a preparation score in Caplet's hand is Rés. Vma 322. Perf. Concerts Colonne, Feb. 24, 1907.

A3 **Marche écossaise sur un thème populaire** (L 77).
1894-96, completed 1908. Orch. of original pn. work (1891; see under Piano solo). Ded. General Meredith Read. Publ. Jobert 1911. MS former coll. R. Legouix, location unknown. Perf. Theatre des Champs-Elysées, Apr. 19, 1913, dir. D.E. Inghelbrecht. 1911.

A4 **Minstrels** [no. 12 of Preludes, Book I].
Arr. 1914 "Pour piano et Hartmann" [vln. and pn.]. Publ. Durand 1914. MS: Sibley Library, Eastman School of Music, Rochester, New York.

A5 **La plus que lente** (L 121).
1912. Orch. of original pn. work. Publ. full score Durand 1912. MS of orch. score, 18 p., B.n. Ms. 1026.

A6 **Première rapsodie pour clarinette en si bémol** (L 116).
1910-11. Arr. for clar. and orch. of original work for piano and clar. Ded. "A P. Mimart, en témoignage de sympathie." Publ. for clar. and orch., Durand 1911; Pe ters 1976; Musica Rara 1977. MS B.n. Ms. 1003 A, 33 p. Perf. May 3, 1919, Concerts Pasdeloup, clar. soloist G. Hamelin. ARR: solo pn., J. Charlot, Durand 1912. REARR E. Rousseau, Etoile Publ., 1975.

A7 **Trois ballades de Villon** (L 119).
1910. Arr. of orig. song set (voice and pn.) for voice and orch. Full score publ. Durand 1911; with French and English texts (the latter by Nina Cox), Durand 1912. MSS: 1) B.n. Ms. 975, 36 p.;

2) 2 p. autograph corrections, sold Hôtel Drouot 1933, location unknown; 3) HRC, full score with auto. corrections; 4) 1911 Durand orch. score with corrections in Debussy's hand, preserved in the Coll. F. Lang, Royaumont. See below under Songs for additional autograph sources of the orch. arrangement. Perf. Concerts Sechiari, March 5, 1911, dir. Debussy, Chas. W. Clark, baritone.

Arrangements and Editions by Debussy of Others' Works

A8 Bach, J.S. **Six sonates pour violon et clavecin** and **Trois sonates pour piano et violoncelle** [sic]. Edition revised by Debussy. Durand, Edition classique, 1923.

A9 Chopin, Frédéric. **Oeuvres complètes pour piano.** Ed. revised by Debussy, 12 vol., Durand 1915-17.

A10 Raff, Joachim. **Humoresque en forme de valse.** Trans. 1893 by D for pn. Hamelle 1903.

A11 Rameau, Jean-Philippe. **Les fêtes de Polymnie.** Rev. and for pn. by Debussy. B.n. score D.16506 is D's corrected proof copy. Publ. Durand 1908.

A12 Saint-Saëns, Camille. **Caprice pour piano sur les airs de ballet d'Alceste de Gluck.** Trans. 1889 for pn. 4 hands. Durand 1891.

A13 ------. **Introduction et rondo capriccioso** [for vln. and orch.], op. 28. Trans. for 2 pn., 1889. Durand 1889.

A14 ------. **Airs de ballet d'"Etienne Marcel".** Trans. for two pn. Durand 1890.

A15 ------. **Deuxième symphonie en la mineur, op. 55.** Trans. for two pn. Durand 1890.

A16 Satie, Erik. **Deux gymnopèdies (1896).** Orch. of original **Trois gymnopédies**, nos. 1 and 3. Publ. full score Paris: Baudoux, 1898; Bellon, Ponscarme et Cie.; Rouart-Lerolle, 1911. MS private coll., Basel, formerly coll. Darius Milhaud. Perf. Salle Erard, Feb. 20, 1897, dir. Gustave Doret.

A17 Schumann, Robert. **Six études en forme de canon, op. 56.** Trans. for 2 pn. Durand 1891.

A18 _______. Am Springbrunnen (A la fontaine), from 12 pieces op. 85 for two pianos. Arr. for solo pn. Fromont 1904, then Jobert.

A19 Tchaikovsky, Peter. **Three dances from "Swan Lake."** Trans. for piano four hands. 1880. Publ. Moscow, Jurgenson [reprint 1965].

A20 Wagner, Richard. **Le vaisseau fantôme, Ouverture.** Trans. for 2 pn. 1890. Durand et Schoenewerk, 1890.

7. Works for Chorus and for Soloists with Orchestra

V1 **Choeur des brises** (L 35).
ca. 1882. Sketch for soprano and 3 female voices. MS at Stanford U., Memorial Lib. of Music, 4 p. Extract publ. in N. Van Patten, **Cat. of the Mem. Library of Music**, Stanford, California, 1950.

V2 **La damoiselle élue** (L 62).
1887-88, reorch. 1902. Ded. Paul Dukas. **Poème lyrique** for soprano, female chorus, and orch. Text by Dante Gabriel Rossetti; trans. Gabriel Sarrazin.
Publ. vocal score Librairie d'art indépendant, 1893; vocal score Durand 1902 [with French and German text Durand 1908; with Fr. and English Durand 1908]; full score Durand 1903; Prelude alone trans. by D for pn., Durand 1909. ARR: by others for organ, vln. and pn., pn. solo, and pn. 4-hands, all publ. by Durand.
MSS: 1) B.n. Ms. 984, orch. short score of 14 pp.; 2) B.n. Ms. 985, Debussy's revised 1902 orch.

(possibly 1888 score with 1902 revisions), 60 p.; 3) coll. Cary in Morgan, 15 p. piano-vocal score, dated May 1893 in ded. of MS as gift to Bailly; 4) red. for pn. with contralto part, 4 p., location unknown; 5) B.n. Rés. Vma.330, D's score with annotated corr., formerly coll. A. Caplet.

Perf. in concert Salle Erard, Soc. Nationale de Musique, Apr. 8, 1893, dir. Gabriel Marie. The new orch. first perf. Dec. 21, 1902 by Mary Garden, Orch. Colonne. A concert (or stage?) perf. Opéra-Comique, Feb. 4, 1904, cond. André Messager with Mary Garden.

V3 **Daniel** (L 20).

ca. 1881. Cantata for 3 solo voices and orch. Text by Emile Cicile. Apparently only scene i and part of scene 2 completed. Unpubl. MSS: 1) coll. G. Piatigorsky [currently Drachman; copy at LC], 38 p.; 2) formerly Legouix coll., MS of 9 p., air of Balthazar, location unknown.

V4 **L'enfant prodigue** (L 57).

May 24-June 18, 1884. Scène lyrique (cantata) for solo voices and orch. Text by Edouard Guinand. Ded. Ernest Guiraud.

Publ. Durand, Schoenewerk et Cie 1884, 61 p. vocal score, with indication "Académie des Beaux Arts, Premier grand Prix de Rome." Rev. 1906-08, orch. score and piano score (with French and English text and rev. possibly with assistance of A. Caplet) publ. Durand 1908 Vocal score with Italian and German texts, Durand 1910. Extracts (Récit. et Air de Lia) Durand 1906. Prelude for pn. 4-hands arr. by Debussy, Durand 1907. ARR: Prelude for solo pn., Durand 1908; Récit. and Air de Lia, with acc. of small orch., R. Branga, Durand 1926.

MSS: 1) B.n. Ms. 968, 88 f., D's orig. orch.; 2) B.n. Ms. 1013, 12 p., recit. and air of Azaël, leading to 1908 ed.; 3) B.n. Ms. 1021, 14 p., Cortège and Air de danse with rev. orch., dated both 1884 and 1906. B.n. Vm7.18648A and Vm7.18648B are printed piano-vocal scores (Durand 1908) annotated by A. Caplet.

Perf. Conservatoire June 27, 1984; then Institut de France, June 28, 1884. The 1st perf. of the revised Cortège and Air de Danse on Dec. 12, 1907, by the Concerts Séchiari at the Salle Gaveau. Complete stage perf. London, Feb. 28, 1910, in French.

V5 **Le gladiateur** (L 41).
May 19-June 13, 1883. Cantata for 3 solo voices and orch. Text by Emile Moreau. Unpubl. MSS: 1) B.n. Ms. 969, 118 p.; 2) formerly coll. de Tinan, 9 p. of scene 11, MS at B.n. (currently unnumbered). Perf. Académie des Beaux-Arts, June 23, 1883.

V6 **Hélène** (L 20 bis).
Ca. 1881-82. Scène lyrique for sop., SATB chorus, and orch. Text Leconte de Lisle. Unpubl. MS former coll. de Tinan, 17 f., incomp., orch. score, current location unknown (possibly transferred for a time from de Tinan coll. to B.n.). Score begins in midst of chorus, "Franchis les mers icariennes...", proceeds to orch. interlude, and ends with fragment of sop. solo, "Vierges ceintes de laurier..."

V7 **Invocation** (L 40).
May 5-11, 1883. For male chorus TTBB and orch., auto. indication "Concours d'essai 1883." Text by Lamartine. Vocal score with pn. 4-hands publ. Choudens 1928; full score publ. Choudens 1957; vocal score with acc. arr. for solo pn. by M.F. Gaillard, Choudens 1928. MSS: 1) red. [1st version?] for voices and pn. 4-hands or 2 pn., 11 p., former coll. M. Cobb, currently Morgan Library; 2) orch. score, 18 p., B.n. Ms. 969. Perf. Salle Pleyel, Apr. 2, 1928, Société des Concerts du Conservatoire, dir. M.F. Gaillard.

V8 **Ode à la France** (L 141).
1917. Text by Louis Laloy. Exists only as an incomplete pre-orchestral sketch of 15 p., B.n. Ms. 17673. Laloy collaborated with M.F. Gaillard to establish a piano-vocal score, which Gaillard published through Choudens (1928) and also orchestrated. Perf. Société des Concerts du Conservatoire et Choeur mixte de Paris, Apr. 2, 1928, Gaillard cond.

V9 **Le printemps** ("L'aimable printemps," L 56)
May 10-16, 1884. For SATB chorus and orch. Text by Jules Barbier. Unpubl. MSS: 1) B.n. Ms. 968, "Concours d'essai 1884," 20 p. orch. score; 2) formerly coll. M. Cobb, currently owned by Morgan, 7 p. incomplete vocal score with 2-piano red.; 3) coll. Serge Lifar, 4 p. of vocal score

with 2-piano reduction of acc.; this fragment is the ending of and completes the Morgan score. First modern perf. of orch. version by Orange County Pacific Sym. with Pacific Chorale, Keith Charles dir., C. Leonard Coduti organizer, Orange Co., California, March 23, 1985. First perf. of 2-pn. version same as **Printemps** (orch.), first version.

V10 **Le printemps** ("Salut, Printemps," L 24)
May 1882. For female chorus and orch. Text by Comte de Ségur. Publ. Choudens 1928 with Debussy's original 4-hands acc., and another version with acc. arr. for pn. solo by M.F. Gaillard, also 1928. Full score Choudens 1956 [orch. by Gaillard?]. MSS: 1) B.n. Ms. 973c, 19 pp., orch. score; 2) formerly Cobb coll., currently Morgan Library, 8 pp. red. [1st version?] for 2 pn. (or 4 hands) and voices. Perf. Salle Pleyel, Apr. 2, 1928, Soc. des Concerts du Conservatoire, dir. M.F. Gaillard.

* **Salut, Printemps.** See **Le printemps (Salut, Printemps)**.

V11 **La saulaie** (L 89).
1896-1900. For baritone voice and orch. Text by D.G. Rossetti, trans. Pierre Louÿs. Incomplete. 1 p. publ. in Lockspeiser **Debussy et Edgar Poe** (item 486). MSS: 1) Stanford Univ., Memorial Lib. of Music, 1 p. of sketches; 2) B.n., Rés. Vmb ms. 19, 4 p. of text in D's hand.

V12 **Trois chansons de Charles d'Orléans** (L 92).
For chorus SATB unaccompanied.
Three movements:
1) Dieu! qu'il la fait bon regarder! 1898.
2) Quant j'ai ouy le tabourin. 1908.
3) Yver, vous n'estes qu'un villain. 1898.
Ded. Lucien Fontaine. Text Charles d'Orléans. Publ. as set of three by Durand 1908; publ. with Fr. and English texts Durand 1910. ARR: for solo voice and pn. (texts in Fr. and Eng.), L. Roques, Durand 1923.
MSS: 1) B.n. Ms. 982, 10 p., version of 1908, songs 2 and 3 only; 2) song 1, earlier version different from publ. version, B.n. Ms. 17689, dated 1898; 3) MS of songs 1 and 3 formerly in

coll. Fontaine, 5 p. dated Apr. 1898, present location unknown.

Perf. Concerts Colonne, Apr. 9, 1909, dir. Debussy.

V13 **Zuleima** (L 59).

1885-86. Probably for voice and orch. Unpubl., MS lost. Text by Georges Boyer, after Heine. Perf. Académie des Beaux-Arts, Dec. 1886.

8. Chamber Music

Also see the section on Piano Duos and Duets.

C1 **Intermezzo pour violoncelle solo et orchestre** (L 27). Ca. 1882. Further see **Intermezzo** under orchestral music.

C2 **Morceau à déchiffrer pour le concours de clarinette de 1910** (L 120).

July 1910. Publ. as **Petite pièce** [for cl. and pn.] Durand 1910. ARR: vln. and pn., L. Roques, Durand 1910; for pn. solo, J. Charlot, Durand 1911. MS at Archives nationales AJ37/198.2, 3 pp., formerly B.n. Ms. 1003B. Perf. July 10, 1910.

C3 **Nocturne et scherzo** (L 26).

"14 juin 1882." For cello and piano. Unpubl. MS B.n. Ms. 20635, prov. coll. André Meyer, 7 p. pn./vcl. and 6 p. vcl. part. Perf. in version [now lost] for vln. and pn., Salons Flaxland, May 12, 1882, by Maurice Thieberg and D as pianist. Vcl. version perf. Jan. 1969, ORTF, cellist M. Rostropovitch.

* **Petite pièce pour clarinette et piano.** See **Morceau à déchiffrer**, above.

C4 **Première rapsodie** (L 116).

"Dec. [19]09-Jan.10". For clar. and pn.; then clar. and orch. Ded. "A P. Mimart, en témoignage de sympathie." Publ. Durand 1910 in version with pn.; Durand 1911 with orchestra; Peters 1971 with pn. acc. MSS: 1) B.n. Ms. 1002, 7 p. with pn. acc.; 2) B.n. Ms. 1003A, 33 p. with orch. by Debussy.

Perf. at Conservatoire concours July 14, 1910;

at Salle Gaveau, Soc. Musicale Indépendante, Jan. 16, 1911.

C5 **Quatuor à cordes, Premier**, op. 10 (L 85).
1893. String quartet in G minor. Ded. to Quatuor Ysaÿe [ded. 1st planned for Ernest Chausson]. Publ. Durand 1894, rev. ed. 1904; International 1950; Peters 1971; Kalmus (n.d.). ARR: 4-hand, Durand 1904; 2 pn., G. Samazeuilh, Durand 1915.
MSS: 1) B.n. Ms. 1004, 38 p.; 2) corrected proofs, formerly coll. A. Meyer, currently B.n. Rés. Vmb. 70; 3) printed score (Durand, no date, plate no. D. & F. 4778) with auto. corr., coll. F. Lang, Royaumont. Perf. Soc. Nat. de Musique, Salle Pleyel, Dec. 29, 1893, by the Quatuor Ysaÿe.

C6 **Rapsodie** (L 98).
1901-08. Conceived for saxophone and orchestra. (See above under Orchestra.) Alto saxophone and piano red. publ. Durand 1919. MS B.n. Ms. 1001bis is Debussy's reduction (or first version? for sax. and pn.).

C7 **Sonate [2ème] en trio pour flûte, alto, et harpe** (L 137).
Sept.-Oct. 1915. Ded. Emma Debussy. Publ. Durand 1916 (score and parts); pocket score Durand 1950; Peters 1970 (score and parts). ARR: pn. 4-hands, L. Garban, Durand 1919.
MSS: B.n. Ms. 991, 28 p. dated "été 1915"; 2) another, unspecified MS of the 3 sonatas sold at Hôtel Drouot 1933, location unknown; 3) B.n. Rés. Vmc, ms. 51, D's auto. outline for a projected set of six sonatas.
Perf. Durand et Cie., Dec. 10, 1916. Further perf. Salle Laurent, Mar. 9, 1917.

C8 **Sonate [3ème] pour violon et piano** (L 140).
Oct. 1916-Apr. 1917. Ded. Emma Debussy. Publ. Durand 1917; Peters 1969. ARR: pn. 4-hands, L. Garban, Durand 1919.
MSS: 1) B.n. Ms. 992, 19 p. dated "hiver 1916-1917" with corrected proofs; 2) another, unspecified MS of the 3 sonatas sold at Hôtel Drouot 1933, location unknown; 3) notebook with sketches, formerly de Tinan coll, currently B.n. unnumbered; 4) sketchbooks containing portions: B.n. Ms. 15380 (9 p. of sketches), 17726, 17732,

and 17768.
Perf. Salle Gaveau, May 5, 1917, by Gaston Poulet and Debussy.

C9 **Sonate [1ère] pour violoncelle et piano** (L 135).
July-Aug. 1915. Ded. Emma Debussy. Publ. Durand 1915; Peters 1969. MSS: 1) B.n. Ms. 990, 14 p. dated "été 1915"; 2) another, unspecified MS of the 3 sonatas sold at Hôtel Drouot 1933, location unknown; 3) coll. W. Reinhart, at Winterthur, Switzerland, sketch. Perf. Mar. 24, 1917, by Joseph Salmon and Debussy.

* **Syrinx** (L 129). See Incidental Music, **Pièce pour Psyché**.

C10 **Trio en sol, Premier** (L 3).
1880. Piano trio. Ded. "Beaucoup de notes accompagnées de beaucoup d'amitié, offert par l'auteur à son professeur, Monsieur Emile Durand...Ach. Debussy."
MSS: 1) formerly Lehman coll., currently Morgan, full score of 1st mvt. (21 p.) and vcl. part of all 4 movements (14 p.); 2) formerly coll. of Maurice Dumesnil, currently Univ. of Michigan, School of Music, full score of last three movements but involving a revision of the original version, as judged by the Morgan Library vcl. part. Publ. Henle 1986, preface and critical remarks by E. Derr. Perf. Oct. 20, 1985.

9. **Mélodies**: Songs for Voice and Piano

Two collections of the songs are relevant:
1) **43 Songs**, ed. Sergius Kagen. New York: International, 1951. Version for low and medium voice and another for high voice.
2) **Mélodies de Debussy**, in 2 vols. Tokyo: Zen-on, 1971, 1984.
The Zen-on collection is more reliable editorially and more extensive but gives only French text underlay and Japanese translations apart. The International edition gives French underlay and English translations in a preface. The contents of the International edition:

Nuit d'étoiles
Beau soir
Fleur des blés
Mandoline
La belle au bois dormant
Voici que le printemps
Paysage sentimental
Cinq poèmes de Baudelaire
Ariettes oubliées
Romance (L'âme évaporée)
Les cloches
Les angélus
Dans le jardin
La mer est plus belle
Le son du cor s'afflige
L'échelonnement des haies
Fêtes galantes I
Proses lyriques
Chansons de Bilitis
L'enfant prodigue (Lia's recit. and Aria; Siméon's recit. and aria)
Fêtes galantes II
Trois chansons de France

The Zen-on edition omits the extracts from **L'enfant prodigue** but includes in addition to the above:

Zéphyr
Rondeau (Fut-il jamais)
Aimons-nous et dormons
Calmes dans le demi-jour (En sourdine, early version)
Pantomime
Clair de lune (early version)
Pierrot
Apparition
Le promenoir des deux amants
Trois ballades de François Villon
Trois poèmes de Stéphane Mallarmé
Noël des enfants qui n'ont plus de maison.

M1 **Aimons-nous et dormons** (L 16).
Ca. 1881. Text Théodore de Banville. Publ. Presser, in **The Etude**, Feb. 1933, pp. 110-11. MS coll. Alphandéry, Montfavet. 2 f. (verso blank): 2 p. of score, no title p.

M2 **Les angélus** (L 76).
1891. Text Grégoire Le Roy. Publ. Hamelle 1891, 1926; Peters 1975. ARR: for orch., F.

Salabert, Salabert 1927. MS in unidentified private coll., New York.

M3 **Apparition** (L 53).
Feb. 8, 1884. Text Stéphane Mallarmé. Ded. "à Madame Vasnier. P.F.A. / Ville d'Avray. 8.2.84." Publ. **Revue musicale**, supplement of May 1, 1926; modern ed. in **Quatre chansons de jeunesse**, ed. A. Hoérée, Jobert, 1969; Peters 1975. MSS: 1) LC, 3 f. (3rd blank), ded. and dated as above; 2) sketches in notebook, former coll. de Tinan, currently at B.n. Perf. May 17, 1926.

M4 **L'archet** (L 46).
Ca. 1883. Text Charles Cros. Unpubl. 1 p. facs. publ. in **Collection musicale André Meyer**, item 49, pl. 33-34. MS in a sketch notebook (of which 5 f. are of **L'archet**), B.n. Ms. 20632 (1), 76 p. The sketches apparently for **L'archet** are on three staves without text. Provenance coll. Lilly Debussy then A. Meyer.

M5 **Ariettes oubliées** (L 60).
1) C'est l'extase langoureuse
2) Il pleure dans mon coeur
3) L'ombre des arbres
4) Paysages belges. Chevaux de bois ("Tournez, tournez")
5) Acquarelles, 1, Green ("Voici des fruits")
6) Acquarelles, 2, Spleen ("Les roses étaient toutes rouges").

1885-1903 [1 and 2: March 1887; 3: Jan. 6, 1885; 4: 1885; 5: Jan. 1886]. The Fromont ed. of 1903 ded. to Mary Garden. Publ. separately by Veuve Girod 1888; Fromont 1903 with changes; later Jobert; Peters 1973. Song 1 appeared in **Courrier musical**, supplement, Nov. 15, 1903. ARR: song 2 for vln. and pn. by Arthur Hartmann (publ. Fromont 1908) and perf. in concert by Hartmann and Debussy Feb. 5, 1914; song 2 for vcl. and pn., F. Ronchini, Durand 1912; song 1 for vln. and pn., Jobert 1927. **Il pleure** for orch., H. Mouton, Jobert 1927; for pn. solo by D. Ericourt, Jobert 1933; for vcl. and pn., Fromont 1912.

MSS: songs 1 and 2 provenance coll. Arthur Honegger, presently B.n. Ms. 20695 (1-2), 7 p.; and song 1 in coll. Lang, Royaumont;

song 3 in Koch Coll. 113, on deposit Morgan Library, 2 p. dated "Paris le 6-1.[18]85," a slightly different version from publ.

song 4: 1) B.n. Rés. Vma ms. 33, with ded. "Souvenir amico musical à mon ami Bachelet...Paris..85," according to Cobb (item 48) this is a version distinct from the following MS 2 and is unpubl.; 2) Koch Foundation coll., no. 1138, box 119.3f (5 p.), on deposit Morgan, a version different from publ. ; 3) coll. Lang, Royaumont;
song 5: 1) last sold publicly Hôtel Drouot 1958, location unknown; 2) coll. Lang, Royaumont;
song 6: 1)formerly in Legouix coll, location unknown; 2) coll. Lang, Royaumont.

The HRC preserves a copy of the Girod 1888 ed. of the entire set with corrections in Debussy's hand [bound together with proof copy of song "Fantoches"]. Perf. of 2 songs (which 2 unidentified) by Bagès and Debussy, Société Nationale, Feb. 2, 1889.

* **Auprès de cette grotte sombre.** See **Promenoir des deux amants**, I.

M6 **Les baisers** (L 55bis).
Ca. 1884. Text Théodore de Banville (**Amé thystes**, vol. 1). MS came to light in Germany, 1984, now owned by unknown private collection. Copy of MS is at Centre de Documentation Claude Debussy.

* **Le balcon.** See **Cinq poèmes de Baudelaire**, I.

M7 **Ballade à la lune** (L 1).
Ca. 1879. Text Alfred de Musset. Unpubl.; MS not found. Known only by recollection of Paul Vidal, **Revue musicale**, May 1, 1926, p. 12-13.

* **Ballade de Villon à s'amye.** See **Ballades de Villon**, I)

* **Ballade des femmes de Paris.** See **Ballades de Villon**, III.

* **Ballade que Villon feit à la requeste de sa mère.** See **Ballades de Villon**, II.

* **Ballades de François Villon, Trois.** See **Trois ballades de François Villon.**

M8 **Barcarolle** (L 58).
Ca. 1885. Text Edouard Guinand. Unpubl. MS location not known; listed in the catalogue of the dealer Simon Kra, May 1931, MS of 3 p.

M9 **Beau soir** (L 6).
Ca. 1883. Text Paul Bourget. Publ. Veuve Girod 1891 [date of legal deposit at B.n.]; Fromont 1919; Jobert [n.d.]. ARR: for vln. and pn. by A. Bachmann, Jobert 1923 [1909]; for orch. by H. Mouton, Jobert 1926; for vcl. and pn., Jobert 1923. MS location not known.

M10 **La belle au bois dormant** (L 74).
July 1890. Text Vincent Hyspa. Publ. Soc. nouvelle d'Editions musicales (Paul Dupont), Dec. 1902; Sirène musicale (n.d.); Eschig 1950; Peters 1975. MS coll. M. Cobb, formerly on deposit Morgan.

* **Calmes dans le demi-jour.** See **En sourdine.**

M11 **Caprice** (L 5).
1880. Text Théodore de Banville. Ded. Mme Vasnier. Publ. in item 872, p. 167-68. MS B.n. Cons. Ms. 14523, 2 p. and title p., bearing indication "Fait en l'an 1880."

* **C'est l'extase langoureuse.** See **Ariettes oubliées, I.**

M12 **Chanson espagnole** (L 42).
1883. Duo for two voices and piano. Text Alfred de Musset (**Oeuvres posthumes**, Paris, 1860). Ded. Mme Vasnier. Publ. Salabert 1980. MS B.n. Ms. 17716/3, "Recueil Vasnier," which see. MS of 10 p., pn. part incomplete.

M13 **Chanson triste** (L 47).
Ca. 1883. Text Maurice Bouchor. Unpubl. MS formerly coll. André Meyer, currently at B.n. Ms. 20632 (1), 7 p. in a sketchbook.

M14 **Chansons de Bilitis** (L 90).
1) La flûte de Pan
2) La chevelure
3) Le tombeau des naïades.
June 1897-March 1898. Text Pierre Louÿs. Publ. Fromont 1899, then Jobert; **La chevelure** appeared in review l'Image Oct. 1897, with ded. to Mme Alice Peter. ARR: **La chevelure**, for orch., H. Mouton, Jobert 1926.
MSS: 1) songs 1 and 2 B.n. Ms. 1007, 6 p.; 2) song 1 formerly A. Meyer coll., currently at B.n. Ms. 20636, 3 p. dated June 22, 1897; 3) song 3 formerly in coll. Lucien Fontaine, 3 p., location unknown; 4) corrected proofs, given to Louÿs, dispersed in sale of his library 1927, location unknown. Perf. March 17, 1900, Salle Pleyel, Soc. Nat. de Musique, by Blanche Marot and Debussy.

* **Chansons de Charles d'Orléans, Trois**. See under Choral Music.

* **Chansons de France, Trois**. See **Trois chansons de France**.

* **Chansons de jeunesse, Quatre**. See **Pantomime**, **Clair de lune** 1st version, **Pierrot**, and **Apparition**.

* **Chevaux de bois**. See **Ariettes oubliées**.

* **La chevelure**. See **Chansons de Bilitis**, II.

M15 **Cinq poèmes de Charles Baudelaire** (L 64).
Ded. Etienne Dupin. Publ. by subscription in 1890 and sold by Librairie de l'Art indépendant (Bailly); republ. Durand 1902; publ. with French and English texts Durand 1906; Peters 1972.
MSS and dates of composition:
1. Le balcon. Jan. 1888. MS B.n. Ms. 1017, 8 p. Another MS is reported in an unidentified private coll.
2. Harmonie du soir. Jan. 1889. B.n. Ms. 1018, 6 p.
3. Le jet d'eau. Mar. 1889. B.n. Ms. 1015, 7 p. Sketches in Meyer Sketchbook, B.n. Orch. by Debussy (further see this title under Orchestrations, above).
4. Recueillement. 1889. B.n. Ms. 1019a, title p. and 3 p. with indication "première"; B.n. Ms.

1019b, 2 p. and title p. bearing indication "2e rédaction."

5. La mort des amants. Dec. 1887. B.n. Ms. 1020, 3 p.; B.n. Ms. 13071.

First perf. no. 3 by Mme Camille Fourrier with acc. M. Delacroix, Thèâtre des Mathurins, May 15, 1905; no. 3 and 4 by Jeanne Raunay, Soirées d'Art, Dec. 7, 1905; no. 3 in orch. form by Concerts Colonne and Hélène Demellier, Feb. 24, 1907; Complete set by G. Paulet, June 19, 1913.

M16 **Clair de lune** (1st version) (L 32).

Ca. 1882. Text Paul Verlaine. Ded. Mme Vasnier. Publ. **Revue musicale**, supplement of May 1, 1926; also in **Quatre chansons de jeunesse**, Jobert 1969; Peters 1974. MSS: 1) B.n. Ms. 17716/4, "Recueil Vasnier" (see below), 4 pp.; 2) Newberry Lib., 3 p. See also the letter at the Newberry Library from the manuscript dealer Kra concerning provenance.

* **Clair de lune** (2nd version). See **Fêtes galantes** 1st set, III.

* **Les cloches**. See **Deux romances**, II.

* **Colloque sentimental**. See **Fêtes galantes** 2nd set, III.

M17 **Coquetterie posthume** (L 39).

Mar. 31, 1883. Ded. "A Madame Vasnier." Text Théophile Gautier. Publ. Salabert 1980. MS B.n. Ms. 17716/6, "Recueil Vasnier," 6 p. Perf. Mar. 14, 1939, concert of the **Revue musicale**.

* **Crois mon conseil, chère Climène**. See **Promenoir des deux amants**, II.

M18 **Dans le jardin** (L 78).

MS date: 1903. Text Paul Gravollet. Publ. Hamelle 1905 separately and in coll. **Les Frissons: 22 mélodies [de différents au teurs]...Gravollet**; Peters 1975. ARR: for orch., F. Salabert, Salabert 1928. MS in unidentified private coll., USA. Morgan Lib. preserves a title p., "Les frissons...Dans le jardin...," dated 1903.

* **De fleurs.** See **Proses lyriques**, III.

* **De grève.** See **Proses lyriques**, II.

* **De rêve.** See **Proses lyriques**, I.

* **De soir.** See **Proses lyriques**, IV.

M19 **Deux romances** (L 79).
1891 [date of publ.]. Texts Paul Bourget.
1) Romance ("L'âme évaporée et souffrante")
2) Les cloches ("Les feuilles s'ouvraient")
Publ. Durand 1891; Peters 1977; **Les cloches** publ. with Eng. and Fr. texts, Durand 1906; **Les cloches** with Ger. and Fr. texts, Durand 1913. MS B.n. Ms. 995. Possibly composed well before publ.; Cobb (item 48) suggests the date 1886.

* **Dieu! qu'il la fait bon regarder.** See **Chanson de Chas. d'Orléans**, I.

* **L'échelonnement des haies.** See **Trois mélodies**, III.

M20 **Eglogue** (L 49).
Ca. 1881-3. Vocal duo for soprano and tenor with piano acc. (in essence short score), with indications of orchestration. Text Leconte de Lisle. Unpubl.; 1 p. of MS in facs. in Lesure cat. (51), facing p. 50. MS B.n. Ms. 15377, title p. and 15 p. score.

M21 **En sourdine** (early version; L 28).
Ca. 1882. Text Paul Verlaine. Publ. as "Calmes dans le demi-jour" Elkan Vogel 1944 [based on the Piatigorsky MS 1 below]. Facsimile of MS 4 publ. in item 132. MSS: 1) coll. Piatigorsky, 3 p., dated and signed "Vienne, 16 Sep. 82" (currently Coll. Drachman, copy on deposit LC); 2) B.n. Ms. 17716/1, "Recueil Vasnier," song 2; 3) formerly coll. Margaret Cobb, currently Morgan Library, 4 p., at end MS contains 1st 9 measures of Mandoline; 4) provenance coll. Denise Jobert-Georges, currently coll. Lehman [formerly on deposit Morgan], 2 pp., incl. ded. "à Mademoiselle C. Stevens./En sourdine./(Fêtes galantes, P. Verlaine)/Claude Debussy"; 5) Houghton Library, Harvard Univ., 4 p., contains music for 2 songs

(incomplete) and 3 Verlaine poems. Perf. March 14, 1939, concert of **Revue musicale**, by Mme Blanc-Audra.

* **En sourdine** (second version). See **Fêtes galantes**, first set, I.

* **Eventail**. See **Poèmes de S. Mallarmé, Trois**, III.

M22 **Fantoches** (early version; L 21).
Jan. 8, 1882. Text Paul Verlaine. Ded. Mme Vasnier. Unpubl. Facs. of p. 1 of MS 2 in M. Boucher, C. **Debussy**, 1930, pl. ix. MSS: 1) coll. Toscanini, 4 p. (copy at NY Public); 2) B.n. Ms. 17716/1, "Recueil Vasnier" (see below), 4 p.

* **Fantoches**. See **Fêtes galantes**, first set, II.

* **Le faune**. See **Fêtes galantes**, second set, II.

M23 **Fête galante** [single song] (L 23).
1882. Ded. Mme Vasnier. Text Théodore de Banville. Publ. Jobert 1985 (c. 1984), in **Debussy: Sept poèmes de Banville**. MSS: 1) coll. F. Lang, Royaumont, 3 f. (title p. and 2 p. score); 2) B.n., Coll. Morssen [not catalogued at time of writing]. Perf. [of which version not known] May 12, 1882, Salons Flaxland, by Mme Vasnier and Debussy; version 1 perf. Apr. 23, 1985, Indianapolis, Butler Univ. Romantic Music Festival, by Laura Niemeyer and Anna Briscoe.

M24 **Fêtes galantes**, first set (L 80).
1) En sourdine (2nd version)
2) Fantoches (2nd version)
3) Clair de lune (2nd version)
[Further see the above separate titles concerning earlier versions.]
1891. Texts Paul Verlaine. Ded.: song 1 to Mme Robt. Godet, 2 to Mme Lucien Fontaine, 3 to Mme Arthur Fontaine. Publ. Fromont 1903, then Jobert 1924. ARR of Fantoches: solo pn., Jobert 1925; vln. and pn., Jobert 1927; orch., Jobert 1927.
MSS: 1) song 1, provenance coll. Jobert-Georges, 3 p., dated 1891, ded. "à Mademoiselle [Catherine] Stevens," currently coll. Lehman,

(formerly deposited Morgan); 2) song 1 in a slightly different version is at HRC, ded. "à Mademoiselle Catherine Stevens/ en Hommage...," 4 p., dated "Mai 92." Perf. no. 2: Dec. 6, 1905 by Mme C. Fourrier, Salle de Géographie.

M25 **Fêtes galantes**, second set (L 104).
1) Les ingénus
2) Le faune
3) Colloque sentimental
1904. Texts Paul Verlaine. Ded. Emma Bardac, "pour remercier le mois de juin 1904. A.L.P.M. [A la Petite Mienne]." Publ. Durand 1904; Peters 1973. ARR of **Le faune** for voice and orch., Roland-Manuel, Durand 1929.
MSS: 1) B.n. Ms. 996, 10 p.; 2) B.n. Ms. 17734, 10 p., provenance coll. de Tinan; 3) MS sold Hôtel Drouot, Dec. 14, 1979, location unknown, provenance colls. Martin and Legouix; 4) MS of "Colloque sentimental" [possibly the same source as MS 3], a version distinctly different from publ. version, acquired 1986 by Koch Foundation coll., item 1138 (box 119) on deposit Morgan.
Perf. June 23, 1904, at a private reception of Mme E. Colonne.

M26 **La fille aux cheveux de lin** (L 33).
1882-84. Text Leconte de Lisle. Ded. Mme Vasnier; MS bears exuberant inscription (see Cobb item 48). Unpubl. MS: provenance coll. Salem. MS now in Koch coll., on deposit Morgan, 6 p. music, p. 7 is a draft for part of the song, and p. 8 contains unidentified sketches in piano score without voice. MS prov. Sotheby's-London, Nov. 29, 1985. Copy of MS at Centre de documentation C. Debussy.

M27 **Fleur des bles** (L 7).
Ca. 1880. Ded. Mme Emile Deguingand. Publ. Veuve Girod 1891; Leduc 1921; Peters 1975. Arr. for 4-part male chorus, Leduc 1934. MS not recovered.

M28 **Fleur des eaux** (L 48).
Ca. 1883. Unpubl. MS: textless draft of 4 p. in a notebook, identified only by title; prov. Lilly Debussy then André Meyer coll.; currently B.n Ms. 20632 (1), notebook of 76 p. This song occurs on p. 40-43, although p. 32-39 and 65-67

might be related. Facs. in item 49 (Coll. **Meyer**), vol. II, pl. 29-30.

M29 **Flots, palmes, sables (Mélodie persane)** (L 25). June 2, 1882. Ded. Mme Vasnier. Text Armand Renaud. Unpubl. MSS: 1) coll. Alphandéry, Montfavet, contains only a harp part with title "Mélodie Persane," 3 p.; 2) coll. Stanley Seeger, 4 p.

* **La flûte de Pan.** See **Chansons de Bilitis**, I.

* **Green.** See **Ariettes oubliées**, I.

* **La Grotte.** See **Trois chansons de France**, II.

* **Harmonie du soir.** See **Cinq poèmes de Baudelaire**, II.

* **Il dort encore.** See **Hymnis** under Operas.

* **Il pleure dans mon coeur.** See **Ariettes oubliées**, II.

* **Les ingénus.** See **Fêtes galantes**, second set, I.

M30 **Jane** (L 19).
1881 or 1882. Text Leconte de Lisle. Ded. Mme Vasnier. Publ. Presser 1982, ed. R. Howat; also in item 872, p. 169-70. MS in coll. Hollanders, copy B.n. F.S. 197, 3 f. (title p. and 2 p. score). Perf. Salle Gaveau, June 29, 1938, by Claire Croiza. A report in **Monde musical**, July 1938, p. 162, describes the first performance of **Jane**, **Le lilas**, **Sérénade**, and **Souhait** by Croiza and the pianist Jean Doyen.

Le jet d'eau. See **Cinq poèmes de Baudelaire**, III.

* **Je tremble en voyant ton visage.** See **Promenoir des deux amants**, III.

M31 **Le lilas** (L 22).
Apr. 12, 1882. Text Théodore de Banville. Pub. 1985 (c. 1984) Jobert (ed. J. Briscoe). MS coll. Alphandéry, Montfavet. Perf. Salle Gaveau, June 29, 1938, by Claire Croiza (further see Jane concerning 1st performance); Modern perf. as **Fête galante**, 1985.

M32 **Madrid, princesse des Espagnes** (L 2).
MS dated 1880, but probably not dated by Debussy. Text Alfred de Musset. Ded. "à mes bons amis P. Vidal et Passerieu...Ach. de Bussy." Unpubl. MS of 2 p. in coll. Koch item 14, on deposit Morgan, prov. J.A. Stargardt sale, June 8-9, 1982. On title p. are unidentified musical sketches possibly in another hand. At 18 m. in length, probably Debussy's shortest composition, excluding musical greetings.

M33 **Mandoline** (L 29).
1882. Ded. Mme Vasnier. Publ. **Revue illustrée**, Sept. 1, 1890; Durand et Schoenewerk 1890; Durand 1905 [with Fr. and Eng. texts]; Durand 1907 [with Fr. and Ger. texts]; Peters 1974. ARR for voice with orch., L. Beydts, Durand 1930. MSS: 1) Harvard Univ. Lib., MS ded. to Mme Vasnier; 2) Bibl. nat. Ms. 17716/1, "Recueil Vasnier" (which see), 4 p.; 3) 1st 9 m. appear on MS of En Sourdine (early version), coll. Lehman, formerly on deposit at Morgan. Perf. Bagès, 1904. MS 1 [?] contains New Year greeting to Mme Vasnier "Je vous la souhaite...", see under Musical Greetings.

* **Mélodie persane**. See **Flots, palmes, sables**.

* **Mélodies, Trois**. See **Trois melodies**.

* **La mer est plus belle**. See **Trois mélodies**, I.

* **La mort des amants**. See **Cinq poèmes de Baudelaire**, V.

M34 **Musique** (L 44).
1883. Text Paul Bourget. Ded. Mme Vasnier. Publ. Salabert 1980. MS Bibl. nat. Ms. 17716/5, "Recueil Vasnier" (see below), 4 p. Perf. Mar. 4, 1939.

M35 **Noël des enfants qui n'ont plus de maison** (L 139).
Dec. 1915. Text by Debussy. Publ. Durand 1915 for voice and piano. (with Fr. and Eng. texts); Durand 1916 in a version for piano and 2 soprano voices (Fr. and Eng. texts). MSS: 1) B.n. Ms. 1023, 5 p., for 1 voice and pn.; 2) B.n. Ms. 1024, 6 p., for children's choir and pn. Facs. in Boucher (64), plate LVII. [In a letter Debussy

indicated that he had sketched an orchestration, currently not located.] Perf. Apr. 9, 1916, by Jane Monjovet.

M36 **Nuit d'étoiles** (L 4).
Ca. 1880. Text Théodore de Banville. Ded. Mme Moreau-Sainti. Publ. 1880 in review **Fantaisie artistique et littéraire** [of which copy not found]; Soc. artistique (E. Bulla) 1882 [date of legal deposit; date of publ. not indicated]; Coutarel, 1907 and 1910; Peters 1975. Debussy's first published work. ARR vln. and pn., Coutarel 1923. MS coll. Lily Pons (location not known at present).

M37 **Nuits blanches** (L 94).
1899-1902. Projected 5 songs as 2nd set of **Proses lyriques**. Text by Debussy. Unpubl. MS of 9 m., Bibl. de l'Opéra, dated "Juillet 1900" [facs. in Lesure item 51, p. 99]. Facsimile of final 3 measures of the preceding in Octave Séré, **Musiciens français d'aujourd'hui**, Paris: **Mercure de France**, 1911 and 1921, p. 130. Vallas observed the texts in a notebook, since disappeared, having belonged to D.

* **O floraison divine des lilas**. See **Le lilas**.

* **L'ombre des arbres**. See **Ariettes oubliées**, III.

M38 **Pantomime** (L 31).
Ca. 1882. Text Paul Verlaine. Ded. Mme Vasnier. Publ. **Revue musicale**, supplement, May 1, 1926; in **Quatre chansons de jeunesse**, Jobert 1969; Peters 1974. MS B.n., Ms. 17716/1, 5 p. Further see "Recueil Vasnier."

M39 **Paysage sentimental** (L 45).
1883. Text Paul Bourget. Ded. to Mme Vasnier on MS, then to Jeanne Andrée on 1st ed. Publ. **Revue illustrée** April 15, 1891; publ. as song 3 of **Trois mélodies**, Société nouvelle d'éditions Musicales (Paul Dupont), 1902; Eschig 1907, 1947; Peters 1977; Salabert 1980. ARR for vln. or vcl. and orch., F. Salabert, Salabert 1929. MS B.n. Ms. 17716/7, "Recueil Vasnier" (see below), 7 p.

M40 **Pierrot** (L 15).
Ca. 1881. Text Théodore de Banville. Ded. Mme Vasnier. Publ. **Revue musicale**, supplement, May 1, 1926; in **Quatre chansons de jeunesse**, Jobert 1969; Peters 1977. MS at LC, 4 p.

* **Placet futile**. See **Trois poèmes de Mallarmé**, II.

* **Poèmes de Banville, Sept**. See **Sept poèmes de Banville**.

* **Poèmes de Baudelaire**. See **Cinq poèmes de Charles Baudelaire**.

* **Poèmes de S. Mallarmé, Trois**. See **Trois poèmes de S. Mallarmé**.

* **Pour ce que plaisance est morte**. See **Trois chansons de France**, III.

M41 **Promenoir des deux amants, Le** (L 118).
1) Auprès de cette grotte sombre. 1904 (also in **Trois chansons de France**, II).
2) Crois mon conseil, chère Climène. 1910.
3) Je tremble en voyant ton visage. 1910.
Ded. Emma Debussy. Text Tristan Lhermite. Publ. Durand 1910 (with Fr. and Eng. texts); Peters 1972. MSS: song 1, B.n. Ms. 981 [together with MSS of **La grotte** and **Rondel: Pour ce que plaisance**]; songs 2 and 3, B.n. Ms. 1027. Perf. of no. 1 Salle Erard, Soc. Nat. de Musique, Jan. 14, 1911, by Jane Bathori and Ricardo Viñes.

M42 **Proses lyriques** (L 84).
1892-93. Texts by Debussy. Publ. Fromont 1895, then Jobert; Peters 1973. Perf. songs 3 and 4 Feb. 17, 1894, Soc. Nat. de Musique, by Thérèse Roger and Debussy.
1) De rêve. 1892. MS formerly coll. Marcel Labey, 6 pp., unidentified private coll. Ded. Vital Hocquet [Narcisse Lebeau].
2) De grève. 1892. MS not found. Ded. Raymond Bonheur.
3) De fleurs. 1893. MSS: 1) B.n. Ms. 8642. Ded. "à Madame M.A. Fontaine, en hommage à sa/voix si délicieusement musicale. Claude Debussy," 20 pp.; 2) in former coll. Mme Jean Lerolle, currently in unidentified private coll. in Austria, with ded. Mme E. Chausson.
4) De soir. 1893. MSS: 1) B.n. Ms. 8642 [see

description of song 3]; 2) coll. Jean-Marie Martin, sketch in 2 p.; 3) B.n. Ms. 19183, dated at end "à la fin juillet [18]93."

* **Quant j'ai ouy le tabourin.** See **Trois chan sons de Charles d'Orléans**, II.

* **Recueil Vasnier** (Vasnier Songbook).

B.n. Ms. 17716 (1-9). Ded. "à Madame Vasnier. Ces chansons n'ont jamais vécues que par elle, et qui perdront leur grâce charmeresse, si jamais plus elles ne passent par sa bouche de fée mélodieuse, l'auteur éternellement reconnaissant, Ach. Debussy. Chantons...." 41 p. Provenance Henry Prunières. Further see **Chanson espagnole, Clair de lune, Coquetterie posthume, En sourdine, Fantoches, Mandoline, Musique, Paysage sentimental, Regret, Romance "Voici que le printemps," Romance "Musique pour eventail," Romance d'Ariel, Romance "Silence ineffable."**

The grouping of the MS, precise titles, dates if any, and pagination of Ms. 17716 as follows:

[1.] Fêtes galantes:
- 1o Pantomime [title p. and 4 p.].
- 2o En sourdine [4 p.].
- 3o Mandoline [4 p.].
- 4o Clair de lune [4 p.]
- 5o Fantoches [4 p., dated in unidentified hand "8 janvier 1882"]

[2.] Coquetterie posthume. Dated "31 Mars 83." 6 p. Begins "Quand je mourrai..."

[3."] Chanson espagnole. Duo pour deux voix égales." 10 p. Incomplete piano part.

[4.] "Romance." Begins "Silence ineffable de l'heure..." title page and 3 p. Dated "Septembre 83."

[5.] "Musique.... poésie de P. Bourget." Begins "La lune se levait..." title p. and 3 p. music.

[6.] "Paysage sentimental...poésie de P. Bourget." Dated "Novembre 83." Begins "Le ciel d'hiver..." Title p. and 6 p.

[7.] "Romance...musique pour éventail...poésie de P. Bourget." Dated "Janvier 1884." Begins "Voici que le printemps..." Title p. and 4 p.

[8.] "La romance d'Ariel...poésie de P. Bourget." Dated "Février 1884." Begins "Au long de ces montagnes..." Version apparently not finalized: consists of 5 p.

and 2 extra p., including a short melodic sketch that appears to be an alternative melody.

[9.] "Regret...poésie de P. Bourget." Dated "Février 84." Begins "Devant le ciel..."; title p. and 3 p. music.

* **Recueillement**. See **Cinq poèmes de Baudelaire**, IV.

M43 **Regret** (L 55).
Dated "Février 84." Text Paul Bourget. Ded. Mme Vasnier. Publ. Salabert 1980. MS B.n. Ms. 17716/9, "Recueil Vasnier" (see above), 4 p. Perf. salon of the **Revue musicale**, Mar. 14, 1939.

M44 **Rêverie** (L 8).
Ca. 1882. Text Théodore de Banville. Publ. same as **Fête galante**. MS in coll. Denise Jobert-Georges. Premiered in 1985 same as **Fête galante**.

* **Romance** ("L'âme évaporée"). See **Deux romances**, I.

M45 **Romance** ("Silence ineffable"; L 43).
Sept. 1883. Ded. Mme Vasnier. Text Paul Bourget. Publ. Salabert 1980. MS. B.n. Ms. 17716/4, "Recueil Vasnier" (see above). Perf. concert of **Revue musicale**, Mar. 14, 1939, by Mme Blanc-Audra.

M46 **Romance** ("Voici que le printemps"; L 52).
Jan. 1884. Text Paul Bourget. Ded. Mme Vasnier. Publ. in **Trois mélodies**, song 2, Soc. Nouvelle d'éditions musicales (Paul Dupont), 1902; Sirène musicale (n.d.); Max Eschig 1947; Peters 1977; Salabert 1980. ARR for orch., F. Salabert, 1928. MS B.n. Ms. 17716/7, "Recueil Vasnier" (see above).

M47 **La romance d'Ariel** ("Au long de ces montagnes douces;" L 54.)
"Février 1884." Ded. Mme Vasnier. Text Paul Bourget. Publ. Salabert 1980. MS B.n. Ms. 17716/8, "Recueil Vasnier" (see above), 5 p. and 2 p. of incomp. sketches.

* **Romances, Deux.** See **Deux romances.**

M48 **Rondeau** ("Fut-il jamais;" L 30).
Ca. 1882. Text Alfred de Musset. Ded. Alexandre de Meck. Publ. Schott 1932; Peters 1975. MS not located.

* **Rondel (Pour ce que plaisance).** See **Trois chansons de France.**

* **Rondel (Le temps a laissie).** See **Trois chansons de France.**

M49 **Rondel chinois** (L 17).
Subtitled "Musique chinoise d'après des manuscrits du temps." Ca. 1881-82. Ded. "à Madame Vasnier, la seule qui peut chanter et faire oublier tout ce que cette musique a d'inchantable et de chinoise." Text by unknown writer, possibly Debussy. Unpubl. MS at LC, 4 f., incl. title p., 2 p. score, final f. blank.

M50 **Les roses** (L 13).
Ca. 1882. Text Théodore de Banville. Ded. Mme Vasnier. Publ. Jobert 1985 (c. 1984), in **Sept poèmes de Banville.** MS formerly in coll. R. Nydahl, currently Stiftelsen Musikkulturens främjande, Stockholm, 3 f. (title p. and 2 p. score). Perf. May 12, 1882, Salons Flaxland, by Mme Vasnier and Debussy; Modern perf. as **Fête galante**, 1985.

* **Sept poèmes de Banville.** See individual song titles **Fête galante, Il dort encore** (see **Hymnis** under Lyric Theater), **Le lilas, Rêverie, Les roses, Sérénade, Souhait.**

M51 **Séguidille** (L 14).
Ca. 1881. Text Théophile Gautier. Ded. Mme Vasnier. Unpubl. MS Piatigorsky coll. [now Drachman, copy on deposit LC], 6 f. (title p., 4 p. score, 1 p. sketches).

M52 **Sérénade** (L 34).
Ca. 1882. Text Théodore de Banville. Ded. Mme Vasnier. Publ. Jobert 1985 (c. 1984), in **Sept poèmes de Banville.** MS in coll. Alphandéry,

Montfavet. Perf. Salle Gaveau, June 29, 1938, by Claire Croiza. Further see **Jane** concerning 1st perf. and **Fête galante** concerning modern performance in 1985.

* **Le son du cor s'afflige.** See **Trois mélodies**, II.

M53 **Souhait** (L 11).
1881. Text Théodore de Banville. Publ. Jobert 1985 (c. 1984), in **Sept poèmes de Banville.** MS in coll. Alphandéry, signed at end "Florence. Ach. Debussy." Perf. Salle Gaveau, June 29, 1938, by Claire Croiza. See **Fête galante** concerning modern perf., 1985.

* **Soupir.** See **Trois poèmes de Mallarmé**, I.

* **Spleen.** See **Ariettes oubliées**, II.

* **Le temps a laissié son manteau.** See **Trois chansons de France**, I.

* **Le tombeau des Naïades.** See **Chansons de Bilitis**, III.

M54 **Tragédie** (L 18).
Ca. 1881. Text Léon Valade after Heine. Ded. Mme Vasnier. Unpubl. MS in coll. Max Reis, 3 pp.

* **Triolet à Philis.** See **Zéphyr**.

M55 **Trois ballades de François Villon** (L 119).
1) Ballade de Villon à s'amye
2) Ballade que Villon feit à la requeste de sa mère pour prier Nostre Dame
3) Ballade des femmes de Paris

Dated May 1910. Text François Villon. Publ. Durand 1910, 1912 (with Fr. and Eng. texts); Peters 1972. MSS: 1) B.n. Ms. 974, 14 p.; 2) HRC, Durand ed. of 1910 with auto. corrections and inscribed to A. Messager.

Perf. by Marguerite Babaïan and A. Delacroix, Jan. 16, 1911, and by Paule de Lestang, Feb. 5, 1911; in orch. version Mar. 5, 1911, by Charles W. Clark and the Orchestre Séchiari, dir. by Debussy. Orchestrated by Debussy (see under Arrangements).

* **Trois chansons de Charles d'Orléans.** See under Choral Works.

M56 **Trois chansons de France** (L 102).
1) Rondel (text Charles d'Orléans. "Le temps a laissié")
2) La grotte (Tristan Lhermite. "Auprès de cette grotte")
3) Rondel (Charles d'Orléans. "Pour que la plaisance")

1904. Ded. Mme S. Bardac (later Mme Emma Debussy). Publ. Durand (1904). Song 2 republ. 1910 in set **Promenoir des deux amants**. MS: B.n. Ms. 981, title p. and 7 p, containing all 3 songs.

Perf. no. 2: May 27, 1904, by Rose Féart and Debussy; nos. 1 and 2: May 15, 1905, by Camille Fourrier with M. Delacroix at Théâtre des Mathurins; nos. 1-3: Feb. 6, 1906, by J. Périer at Salle des Agriculteurs.

* **Trois mélodies.** See **Belle au bois, Paysage sentimental,** and **Romance ("Voici").**

M57 **Trois mélodies** [Verlaine]. (L 81)
1) La mer est plus belle que les cathédrales
2) Le son du cor s'afflige vers les bois
3) L'échelonnement des haies moutonne à l'infini.

Dec. 1891. Texts Paul Verlaine. Ded. Ernest Chausson (song 1), Robert Godet (songs 2 and 3). Publ. Hamelle 1901 (all 3), 1909 (song 1); Fromont 1907 (song 3); Jobert 1924 (songs 2 and 3 with Fr. and Eng. texts); Peters 1974. ARR of song 1 for orch., Salabert 1928.

MSS: 1) formerly Meyer coll. currently at B.n., Ms. 20633; 2) coll. Ria Wilhelm, Bottmingen, W. Germany, 7 p., ded. to Lucien Fontaine, signed Apr. 1895. Perf. of songs 1 and 2 Jan. 16, 1904, by Marthe Legrand; song 3 perf. Dec. 6, 1905, by Mme C. Fourrier and M. Delacroix.

M58 **Trois poèmes de Stéphane Mallarmé** (L 127).
1) Soupir
2) Placet futile
3) Eventail.

1913. Ded. "à la mémoire de Stéphane Mallarmé et en très respectueux hommage à Madame E. Bonniot (née G. Mallarmé)." Publ. Durand (1913), Peters

1972. MSS: 1) B.n. Ms. 1028; 2) a sketch of song 1 in a notebook, provenance coll. de Tinan, currently B.n. unnumbered. Perf. Mar. 21, 1914, by Ninon Vallin and Debussy at the Salle Gaveau.

* **Trois poèmes de Tristan Lhermite.** See **Prome noir des deux amants.**

* **Voici que le printemps.** See **Romance** ("Voici").

* **Yver, vous n'estes qu'un villain.** See **Trois chansons de Charles d'Orléans**, III.

M59 **Zéphyr (Triolet à Philis)** (L 12).
Signed "Rome. Novembre 1881, Ach. Debussy." Text Théodore de Banville. Publ. Schott (Mainz, with Ger. and Eng. texts), 1932; Peters 1975. MS coll. Alphandéry, Montfavet, 1 f., no title p. Debussy gives on MS same title of Banville, "Triolet à Philis;" the title "Zéphyr" appeared on the 1st ed.

10. Piano Solo

P1 **Arabesques, Deux** (L 66).
1888-91. Publ. Durand et Schoenewerk 1891; rev. ed. Durand 1904; Elkan-Vogel 1956; Peters 1969; Dover 1972; Lemoine 1984 "révision pédagogique"; Henle "Urtext" 1983; Universal (Wiener Urtext). ARR (all publ. Durand except as specified): for harp, H. Renié, 1906; pn. trio, J. Roberts, 1912; pn. 4-hands, J. Durand, 1907; 2 pn., L. Roques, 1910; 2 pn. 8 hands, L. Roques, 1911; clarinet and pn., 1912; fl. and pn., 1908; organ, 1911; vln. and pn., 1907, 1909. ARR for woodwind quintet Elkan-Vogel 1956.
MS B.n. Ms. 978, 7 p. Perf. of no. 2 on May 23, 1894. First perf. of no. 1 not traced.

P2 **Ballade slave** (L 70).
1890. Ded. Mme Ph. Hottinguer. Publ. Choudens 1891 (legal deposit at B.n.) with subtitle "Pièce pour piano, no. 2"; republ. as "Ballade" by Fromont 1903; Dover 1972. ARR pn. 4-hand, Jobert 1923; for vcl. and pn. Jobert 1924. MS not traced.

P3 **Berceuse héroïque** (L 132).
1914. With extended title "Pour rendre hommage à S.M. Le Prince Albert 1er de Belgique et à ses soldats." Publ. Durand 1915. MS B.n. Ms. 980, 3 p. Further see B.n. Ms. Op. Rés. 36, an orch. probably in Debussy's hand. Also see this Catalogue under Orchestrations. First appeared under Durand copyright in **King Albert's Book** (Hall Caine, preface), London: Daily Telegraph, 1914. This source shows the context of the work as a tribute, alongside art works, poems, and music by Messager, Maeterlinck, and others.

* **Boîte à joujoux.** See under Ballets.

* **Brouillards.** See **Préludes, Livre II.**

* **Bruyères.** See **Préludes, Livre II.**

* **Canope.** See **Préludes, Livre II.**

* **La cathédrale engloutie.** See **Préludes, Livre I.**

* **Ce qu'a vu le vent d'Ouest.** See **Préludes, Livre I.**

P4 **Children's Corner** (L 113).
1) Doctor Gradus ad Parnassum
2) Jimbo's Lullaby
3) Serenade for the Doll
4) The Snow is Dancing
5) The Little Shepherd
6) Golliwogg's Cake-walk

1906-08. Ded. "A ma chère petite Chouchou..." Publ.: "Serenade for the Doll" publ. separately Durand 1906 as "Sérénade à la poupée." Full set publ. Durand 1908; Peters (n.d.); Polskie Wyd., Krakow, 1970; Henle 1983; Universal (Wiener Urtext) 1984. ARR, all publ. Durand: complete set for orch., A. Caplet, 1911; "Golliwogg" for guitar (A. de Belleroche, 1909), for alto sax (R. Branga, 1934), for vln. and pn. (G. Choisnel, 1908,-10); "Jimbo's Lullaby" for alto sax., (arr. by R. Branga, 1934); "Little Shepherd" for fl. and pn. (1910), for vln. and pn. (J. Durand, 1908), for vcl. and pn. (F. Ronchini, 1910); "Serenade for the Doll" for vln. and pn. (arr. by G. Choisnel, 1908, 1910). Numerous other arr. of individual movements. B.n. Rés. Vma Ms. 1066 is an arr. in MS by J. Heifetz of "Golliwogg," ca. 1930.

MS B.n. Ms. 983 (excludes "Serenade"). Perf. Cercle musical, Dec. 18, 1908, by Harold Bauer. Orch. 1910 by André Caplet, Durand. Orch. 1st perf. New York Nov. 10, 1910.

* **Clair de lune.** See **Suite bergamasque**.

* **Cloches à travers les feuilles.** See **Images**, second set.

* **Les Collines d'Anacapri.** See **Préludes, Livre I**.

* **Danse, pour piano.** See **Tarentelle styrienne**.

P5 **Danse bohémienne** (L 9).
1880. Publ. Mainz: Schott, 1932. According to Lesure (51), MS formerly in coll. of Alexander von Meck, who sold it to Schott. MS presently not traced.

* **La Danse de Puck.** See **Préludes, Livre I**.

* **Danseuses de Delphes.** See **Préludes, Livre I**.

* **Des pas sur la neige.** See **Préludes, Livre I**.

* **Deux arabesques.** See **Arabesques, Deux**.

* **Doctor Gradus ad Parnassum.** See **Children's Corner**.

P6 **D'un cahier d'esquisses** (L 99).
1903. Publ. with this complete title in **Paris illustré**, album of music no. 11, Feb. 4, 1904; Schott, Brussels, 1904; Dover 1972; Chester (n.d.); **Oeuvres complètes**, série I vol. 3, Durand-Costallat 1989, ed. R. Howat. MS not located. Perf. Soc. musicale indépendante, Apr. 20, 1910, by Maurice Ravel.

P7 **Elégie** (L 138).
1915. Publ. in facsimile in **Pages inédites sur la femme et la guerre...par Paul Alexander Mellor**, 1916; Jobert, 1978. MS not traced.

* **Epigraphes antiques, Six.** See under Piano Duos and Duets. Note that the work was arr. by D for

pn. solo virtually simultaneously with the 4-hand version.

* **Esquisse.** See **D'un cahier d'esquisses.**

P8 **Estampes** (L 100).
1) Pagodes
2) La soirée dans Grenade
3) Jardins sous la pluie.
1903. Ded. J.E. Blanche (ded. on MS of "La soirée" is to Pierre Louÿs). Publ. Durand 1903; Polskie Wyd., Krakow, 1968; Dover 1972; Peters 1973; Henle 1988; Durand-Costallat 1989, **Oeuvres complètes**, série I, vol. 3, ed. R. Howat. ARR of no. 3 for harp, A. Lautemann, Durand 1928; of no. 1 and 2 for 4-hands, J. Durand, Durand 1907; of no. 3 for 4-hands, L. Roques, 1910.
MS: 1) B.n. Ms. 988, 14 p.; 2) HRC preserves a fragment of 1 p. beginning no. 2; 3) Coll. Lehman, formerly on deposit Morgan Library, "**Pelléas** proofs" contain a 1-p. fragment of opening of no. 1. Perf. Salle Erard, Soc. nationale, Jan. 9, 1904, by Ricardo Viñes.

* **Et la lune descend.** See **Images**, second set.

P9 **Etude retrouvée. Pour les arpèges composés.**
1915. Presser 1980, with facs., ed. and realization by Roy Howat. A first version of, but distinct from, Etude 11. MS: coll. M. Cobb, on deposit Morgan. 6 p., of which 1-3 are complete and 4-6 are in rough draft.

P10 **Etudes, Douze, pour le piano** (L 136).
Livre I:
1) Pour les cinq doigts
2) Pour les tierces
3) Pour les quartes
4) Pour les sixtes
5) Pour les octaves
6) Pour les huit doigts
Livre II:
7) Pour les degrés chromatiques
8) Pour les agréments
9) Pour les notes répétées
10) Pour les sonorités opposées
11) Pour les arpèges composés
12) Pour les accords

1915. Ded. "A la mémoire de Frédéric Chopin." Publ. Durand 1916; Polskie wyd., Krakow, 1967; Peters 1970. MSS: 1) B.n. Ms. 993, 38 pp; 2) sketches of Etudes 7 and 12, B.n. Ms. 17733, former coll. de Tinan; 3) sketch of no. 1 at Musée municipal, St.-Germain-en-Laye; 4) B.n. Ms. 17973, auto. MS variant (discarded page?) of no. 10, former coll. de Tinan; 5) different version of no. 11, 6 folios, formerly coll. Cobb, currently Morgan Library, signed "A Marius François Gaillard/23 mars 1921./Emma Claude Debussy" [see **Etude retrouvée** above]; 6) Coll. F. Lang, Royaumont, contains working drafts of "Les Tierces," Les Quartes," "Les Octaves," "Sol bémol maj." ["Pour les 8 doigts"], "Pour les degrés chromatiques," "Fa majeur ["Pour les agréments"], "Les Notes répétées," "Pour les sonorités opposées, "Pour les arpèges composées," and "Pour les accords"; 7) sketch of no. 9 on D's wartime passport (Sept. 1914), of which a facs. appears in **Etude**, March 1933, p. 156; 8) complete MS draft of no. 4 formerly in coll. de Tinan and present location unknown, but complete facsimile in **L'Approdo musicale**, 1959, pp. 98-102.

Perf. Dec. 1916 by Walter Rummel.

* **Les fées sont d'exquises danseuses.** See **Préludes, Livre II.**

* **Feuilles mortes.** See **Préludes, Livre II.**

* **Feux d'artifice.** See **Préludes, Livre II.**

* **La fille aux cheveux de lin.** See **Préludes, Livre I.**

* **"General Lavine," eccentric.** See **Préludes, Livre II.**

* **Golliwogg's Cake-walk.** See **Children's Corner.**

P11 **Hommage à Haydn** (L 115).

1909. Publ. in the review **S.I.M.**, "Hommage à Haydn, centenaire d'Haydn (1909)," p. 20, Jan. 1910; Durand 1910. MS in coll. Claude Ecorcheville, 3 f. Perf. March 11, 1911, by Ennemond Trillat, Soc. Nat. de Musique, Salle Pleyel.

* **Hommage à Rameau.** See **Images**, first set.

* **Hommage à S. Pickwick, Esq.** See **Préludes, Livre II**.

P12 **Images** ("Images oubliées," 3 pieces) (L 87).
1) (Lent)
2) (Sarabande; occurs with slight revisions as no. 2 of **Pour le piano**); tempo indication "Dans le mouvement d'une sarabande"
3) "Quelques aspects de 'Nous n'irons plus au bois'"

1894. Ded. Yvonne Lerolle. Publ. of no. 2 in **Grand Journal**, supplement of Feb. 17, 1896; all 3 publ. **Piano Quarterly** (June-July 1978), then by Presser 1978 (ed. by A. Hoérée and R. Howat). MS provenance Alfred Cortot, currently coll. Lehman (formerly on deposit Morgan Library), 13 pp. No. 3 bears thematic resemblances to no. 3 of **Estampes**. B.n. Ms. 18484 is the beginning of no. 1 in hand of Raoul Bardac; f. 2 bears the inscription: "Que ces 'Images' soient de Mademoiselle Yvonne Lerolle avec un peu/de la joie que j'ai de lui dédier./Ces morceaux craindraient beaucoup 'Les Salons brillament illuminés' ou se réunissent habituellement/les personnes qui n'aime pas la musique./Ce sont plutôt 'Conversations' entre le Piano et Soi,/il n'est pas défendu d'ailleurs d'y mettre sa/petite sensibilité des bons jours de pluie!"

First performed as a set by Paul Jacobs, 1978, Minneapolis conference of the American Musicological and College Music Societies. Recorded 1960s-early 1970s by Jörg Demus and Noël Lee, and possibly performed publically by them prior to Jacobs's performance.

P13 **Images** (première série) (L 110).
1) Reflets dans l'eau
2) Hommage à Rameau
3) Mouvement

1901-05. Publ. Durand 1905; Dover 1972; Peters 1970 [1975?]; Durand-Costallat, **Oeuvres complètes de Debussy**, série 1 vol. 3, 1989 (ed. R. Howat). ARR for 4-hands, J. Durand, Durand 1907. MSS: 1) B.n. Ms. 998 **Reflets dans l'eau**, 4 pp.; 2) B.n. Ms. 999, **Hommage à Rameau**, 3 pp. dated 1905; 3) B.n. Ms. 1000, **Mouvement**, 4 pp. Perf. of no. 2 by M. Dumesnil, Dec. 14, 1905; perf. as set R. Viñes, Feb. 6, 1906, Salle des Agriculteurs.

No. 2 trans. by D for pn. 4-hands, Durand 1905.

P14 **Images** (deuxième série) (L 111).
1) Cloches à travers les feuilles (ded. Alexandre Charpentier)
2) Et la lune descend sur le temple qui fut (ded. Louis Laloy)
3) Poissons d'or (ded. Ricardo Viñes).
1907. Publ. Durand 1908; Krakow, Polskie wyd., 1967; Durand-Costallat, **Oeuvres complètes**, série 1 vol. 3, 1989. MS B.n. Ms. 1005, 11 pp., dated "Octobre 1907." Perf. Cercle musical, Feb. 21, 1908, by Ricardo Viñes.

P15 **L'isle joyeuse** (L 106).
1903-04. Publ. Durand 1904 [but previously advertised by Fromont 1903-04, as 3rd piece of **Suite bergamasque**, along with **Masques** and 2nd **Sarabande**]; Krakow, Polskie wyd., 1957; Dover 1972; Peters 1973; Henle 1986; Durand-Costallat, **Oeuvres complètes**, série 1 vol. 3, 1989. ARR for orch., B. Molinari, Durand 1923.
MSS: 1) B.n. Ms. 977, 7 pp.; 2) sketches Berlin, Staatsbibliothek Preussischer Kulturbesitz, N. Mus. ms. 136 (reprod. in facs. in **Katalog J.A. Stargardt**, no. 577, Marburg, Nov. 1966, pl. 12); 3) 1-p. sketch in coll. Lemoine; 4) sketch in B.n. Ms. 17729, p. [5] recto and verso. Perf. Jan. 13, 1905 (private perf.) and Feb. 10, 1905, Salle Aeolian, R. Viñes.

* **Jardins sous la pluie**. See **Estampes**.

* **Jimbo's Lullaby**. See **Children's Corner**.

P16 **Little Nigar, The** ("Danse nègre dite Danse du gâteau") (L 114).
1909. Publ. in Théodore Lack, **Méthode élémentaire de piano**, Leduc 1909; separately publ. Leduc 1934. ARR, all publ. Leduc: pn. 4-hands and solo, 1935; fl. and pn., 1936; vcl. and pn., 1935; vln. and pn., 1936; cl. and pn., 1936; alto sax. and pn., 1937; 4 saxophones, 1943; bassoon and pn., 1946; wind quintet, 1946; guitar, 1949. MS not traced.

* **Little Shepherd, The**. See **Children's Corner**.

* **Marche écossaise**. See under Duos and Duets for Piano.

P17 **Masques** (L 105).
1903-04. Publ. Durand 1904 [but see note for **L'isle joyeuse** regarding Fromont publ. plans]; Dover 1972; Durand-Costallat, **Oeuvres complètes**, série 1 vol. 3, 1989. MSS 1) B.n. Ms. 997, 7 pp. and title p., indicates "juillet 1904" but not "Images no. 1"; 2) B.n. Rés. Vma 287, proofs corr. by Debussy for 1904 ed. Perf. Salle Aeolian, Feb. 10, 1905, by Ricardo Viñes.

P18 **Mazurka** (L 67).
Ca. 1890. Publ. Hamelle 1904; Fromont 1905, then Jobert; Dover 1972. ARR for orch. by H. Mouton, Jobert 1923; 4-hands, Jobert 1923. MS not located.

* **Menuet**. See **Suite bergamasque**.

* **Minstrels**. See **Préludes, Livre I**.

P19 **[Morceau de concours]** (L 108, where entitled **Pièce pour piano**).
1904. Publ. in **Album musical**, supplement to revue **Musica**, Jan. 1905, as "Morceau anonyme" no. 6, p. 9. Republ. Durand 1980, with title **Morceau de concours**, ed. R. Howat. Based on sketches from opera project **Le diable dans le beffroi**. MS not located.

* **Mouvement**. See **Images**, first set.

P20 **Nocturne** (L 82).
1892. Publ. in **Le figaro musical**, fascicle 11, Aug. 1892; Paul Dupont, 1892; Société nouvelle d'éditions musicales, 1908; Eschig (ed. Isidor Philipp). ARR for vln. or vcl. and pn., P. Bazelaire, **La sirène musicale**, 1927; for harp, M. Jacquet, **La sirène musicale**, 1927. MS not located.

* **Ondine**. See **Préludes, Livre II**.

* **Page d'album**. See **Pièce pour piano**.

* **Pagodes**. See **Estampes**.

* **Passepied**. See **Suite bergamasque**.

* **Petit nègre, Le.** See **Little Nigar, The.**

* **Petite suite, La.** See under Duos and Duets for Piano.

P21 **Pièce pour piano (pour l'oeuvre du "Vêtement du blessé")** (L 133).
June 1915. Ded. Emma Debussy. Publ. with title **Page d'album, Etude** supplement (Mar. 1933), p. 169, then Presser 1933; corrected ed. Presser 1980 (ed. R. Howat). MS B.n. Ms. 14522. Perf. on a concert the benefits of which went to benefit war wounded, March 24, 1917.

P22 **La plus que lente** (Valse pour piano) (L 121).
1910. Publ. Durand 1910. ARR for alto sax. and pn., J. Viard, Durand 1931; for 4-hands, Durand 1910; for vln. and pn., L. Roques, Durand 1910. MS B.n. Ms. 1025, 4 pp. Debussy orchestrated the work, publ. Durand 1912, MS B.n. Ms. 1026, 18 pp.

* **Poissons d'or.** See **Images**, second set.

P23 **Pour le piano** (L 95).
1) Prélude (ded. Mlle Worms de Romilly)
2) Sarabande [see also **Images oubliées no.2**] (ded. Mme E. Rouart (Yvonne Lerolle))
3) Toccata (ded. Nicolas G. Coronio)

1894-1901. Sarabande [final version] publ. in **L'illustration**, Nov. 9, 1901, no. 3063, musical supplement, p. 155-157; set of 3 pieces publ. Fromont 1901; International 1957; Polskie wyd., Krakow 1963; Dover 1972; Peters 1973; Schirmer (n.d.); Henle 1984. MS in coll. Dr. R. Grumbacher, 11 pp. Perf. Salle Erard, Soc. nationale, Jan. 11, 1902, by Ricardo Viñes.
M. Ravel orchestrated **Sarabande**, MS in coll. Koch (on deposit Morgan), publ. Jobert.

* **Pour les accords, Pour les agréments**, etc. See **Etudes**.

P24 **Préludes, Livre 1** (L 117)
Titles and dates on the autograph: 1) Danseuses de Delphes, 7/XII/1909; 2) Voiles, 12/XII/1909; 3) Le Vent dans la plaine, 11/XII/1909; 4) "Les sons

et les parfums tournent dans l'air du soir [after Charles Baudelaire]," 1/I/1910]; 5) Les collines d'Anacapri, 26/XII/1909; 6) Des pas sur la neige, 27/XII/1909; 7) Ce qu'a vu le Vent d'Ouest; 8) La fille aux cheveux de lin, 15-16/I/1910; 9) La sérénade interrompue; 10) La Cathédrale engloutie; 11) La danse de Puck, 4/XI/1910; 12) Minstrels, V/1/1910.

Date of composition: ca. 1907-Feb. 1910. Publ. Durand 1910; no. 8 separately in **Figaro**, literary supplement, Apr. 30, 1910; no. 12 transcribed by Debussy for vln. and piano, publ. Durand 1914, of which the MS is at Sibley Music Library, Eastman School of Music. Book I further publ. Warsaw, Polskie wyd. 1965; Peters 1969; Musica (Budapest) 1972; Durand-Costallat 1985 (ed. R. Howat and C. Helffer in **Oeuvres complètes**, série I vol. 5); Henle 1986 (ed. Heinemann); Universal (Wiener Urtext) 1985 (ed. M. Stegemann); Alfred (ed. M. Hinson); G. Schirmer 1989 (ed. J. Briscoe); Lea Pocket Scores (n.d.).

ARR, all Durand except as noted: Cathédrale (organ 1910; also orch. by H. Büsser, unpubl. MS for orch. at B.n.); Puck (orch. in MS at B.n. by Grovlez, 1920); Fille (harp 1931, alto sax. and pn. 1931, vln. and pn. 1910, organ 1931); Minstrels (orch. in MS at B.n. by Grovlez, 1920), alto sax. 1934, guitar, A. Hartmann, 1953); Danseuses and Fille (fl. and pn., publ. Billaudot 1983). Debussy arr. Minstrels for vln. and pn., about which see under Arrangements.

Primary sources: 1) complete auto. MS coll. R. Lehman, formerly on deposit Morgan Library, 31 pp., dated 1909-1910, provenance Alfred Cortot (facs. of which MS publ. New York: Dover, 1988, with an intro. by R. Howat); 2) the second proofs with autograph corrections in the archives of Editions Durand; 3) a sketchbook (ca. 1907-09) containing sketches of Voiles and La Fille is in coll. R. Lehman; 4) Debussy's copy of first corrected ed., issued 1913 in a deluxe ed., with inscription to Emma Debussy but with no auto. corr. is at Centre de Documentation Claude Debussy, Paris.

Perf.: preludes 1, 2, 10, 11 by D, May 5, 1910, Société Musicale Indépendante; preludes 5, 8, 9 by Ricardo Viñes, Jan. 14, 1911, Soc. Nationale de Musique; preludes 3, 4 by Franz Liebich, Jan. 16, 1911, Salle des Agriculteurs; prelude 12 by R. Viñes, Feb. 10, 1911; preludes 4, 3, 6, 12 by Debussy Mar. 29, 1911, Concert Durand at Salle Erard. The premiere of prelude 7 is untraced. On Feb. 5, 1914, Debussy and the violinist A.

Hartmann performed no. 8 in an arr. by Hartmann (publ. Durand 1910).

P25 **Preludes, Livre 2** (L 123).
Contains: 1) Brouillards; 2) Feuilles mortes; 3) La Puerta del Vino; 4) "Les fées sont d'exquises danseuses"; 5) Bruyères; 6) General Lavine--eccentric; 7) La terrasse des audiences du clair de lune; 8) Ondine; 9) Hommage à S. Pickwick Esq. P.P.M.P.C.; 10) Canope; 11) Les tierces alternées; 12) Feux d'artifice.
Composed 1911-13. Publ. Durand 1913. Other recent eds. as above Book I.
ARR, all publ. Durand except as noted: Bruyères (vln. and pn. 1926); Lavine (orch. in MS at B.n., by Grovlez, 1920); Ondine (orch. in MS as Lavine); Nos. 2, 3, 5 (fl. and pn. publ. Billaudot 1983).
Primary sources: 1) B.n. Ms. 1006, 40 pp.; 2) coll. Mme D.F. Lamy, Paris, copy of 1st ed. with auto. corrections by Debussy; 3) coll. O.W. Neighbour, 2 pp. sketch of no. 1; 4) coll. G. Piatigorsky-Mrs. D. Drachman (copy on deposit LC), 3 pp. sketch of no. 2; 5) Debussy's copy of first, corrected ed. (1913) with further auto. corrections, Centre de Documentation Claude Debussy, Paris, prov enance coll. de Tinan.
Perf.: preludes 1, 2, 3, March 5, 1913, by Debussy at Salle Erard; preludes 4, 7, 12, Apr. 5, 1913, by R. Viñes, Soc. Nationale de Musique; preludes 5 and 6, Apr. 8, 1913, by Norah Drewett, Salle Erard; preludes 7, 10, 9, June 19, 1913, by Debussy at the "Gala Claude Debussy," Théâtre des Champs-Elysées; preludes 2, 3, 6, 8, 10, Dec. 5, 1913, by Jane Mortier. Premiere of prelude 11 is not known.

* **Prélude**. See **Pour le piano** and **Suite bergamasque**.

* **La puerta del Vino**. See **Préludes, Livre II**.

* **Reflets dans l'eau**. See **Images**, first set.

P26 **Rêverie** (L 68).
1890. Publ. Choudens 1891; **L'illustration**, musical supplement Nov. 16, 1895; Fromont 1905, then Jobert 1925; Dover 1972. ARR for 4-hands, H. Woollett, Fromont 1913; for organ, Jobert 1924; for alto sax and pn., M. Mule, Jobert 1946; for vln. and pn., A. Bachmann, Fromont 1912; for vcl. and pn., Fromont 1914.

MS not located. Perf. possibly for 1st time by Germaine Alexandre, Feb. 27, 1899.

* **Sarabande.** See **Images oubliées** and **Pour le piano, Suite.**

* **Sérénade à la poupée.** Incorporated in **Children's Corner** as **Serenade for the Doll.**

* **La sérénade interrompue.** See **Préludes, Livre I.**

* **The Snow is Dancing.** See **Children's Corner.**

* **La Soirée dans Grenade.** See **Estampes.**

* **Les sons et les parfums tournent.** See **Préludes, Livre I.**

P27 **Suite bergamasque** (L 75).
1) Prélude
2) Menuet
3) Clair de lune
4) Passepied
1890, rev. 1905. Publ. Fromont 1905; Peters [1969]; Dover 1972; Henle 1983. ARR: of entire suite for 4-hands, E. Nérini, Jobert 1914, 1928; of Menuet and Passepied for vln. and pn., Jobert 1926; of Clair de lune, all Jobert: clar. and pn. 1948, harp 1929, 2 pn. (H. Dutilleux) 1947, alto sax. and pn. 1946, vln. and pn. 1924, women's chorus with pn. (on a text by P. Louÿs) 1938, big band 1956.

MS not located; proofs with auto. corr. B.n. Rés. Vma. 286, for 1905 ed.

* **Suite pour le piano.** See **Pour le piano.**

P28 **Tarentelle styrienne** (Danse) (L 69).
1890. Ded. Mme Ph. Hottinguer. Publ. Choudens, dated 1890, legal deposit 1891; republ. as **Danse** by Fromont 1903; then Jobert; also publ. New York, E.B. Marks, 1935. ARR: for vln. and pn., Fromont 1912; for pn. 4-hands, H. Woollett, Durand 1913. MS not located. Perf. Salle Pleyel, Soc. nationale, Mar. 10, 1900, by Wurmser.

Danse (Tarentelle styrienne), arr. for orch. by M. Ravel, publ. Jobert 1923. Ravel's auto.: Koch coll., on deposit Morgan, signed "Maurice Ravel/December 1922."

* **La terrasse des audiences du clair de lune.** See **Préludes, Livre II.**

* **Les tierces alternées.** See **Préludes, Livre II.**

* **Toccata.** See **Pour le piano.**

P29 **Valse romantique** (L 71).
1890. Ded. Mlle Rose Depecker. Publ. Choudens 1890; Fromont 1903, then Jobert; Dover 1972. ARR for orch. by H. Mouton, Jobert 1925; for vln. and pn., Jobert 1924. MS not located.

* **Le vent dans la plaine.** See **Préludes, Livre II.**

* **Voiles.** See **Préludes, Livre I.**

11. Duos and Duets for Piano (two pianos, and one piano four hands)

D1 Sketches for 2 pianos or 4 hands.
Former coll. de Tinan, currently at B.n. Vmg. 19769, which reunites a single MS previously divided: 1 p. Cobb coll. (in photocopy), 2 p. former coll. de Tinan.

D2 **Andante cantabile** (4 hands).
Ca. 1880. Publ. in Blumenthal diss. (item 701). MS Morgan. Formerly coll. Margaret Cobb. The second movement of the **Triomphe de Bacchus**, regarding which see above under Orchestral Works.

D3 **Andante cantabile** (4 hands, L. 36 bis).
Ca. 1882. MS of 8 pp.; sold at a Paris auction in 1979 to an unknown private collector. Publ. in Blumenthal diss. (see item 701).

* **Diane. Ouverture** (2 pianos). See under Operas, **Diane au bois.**

D4 **Divertissement** (2 pianos or 4 hands, L 36).
Ca. 1882. Unpubl. MS B.n. Ms. 19182, 21 pp. without date or signature. Ends on an incomplete cadence. Perhaps relates to Mme de Tinan sketches

D1, to **Triomphe de Bacchus**, or to **Andante cantabile** item D3.

D5 **En blanc et noir** (2 pianos, L 134).
1) [beginning of poetic epigraph:] "Qui reste à sa place...," from Barbier and Carré, **Roméo et Juliette**.
2) "Prince, porté soit des serfs Eolus...," from F. Villon, **Ballade contre les ennemis de la France**
3) "Yver, vous n'estes qu'un vilain," from Chas. d'Orléans.

1915. Ded.: no.1 to A. Koussevitsky; no. 2 to Jacques Charlot; no. 3 to Igor Stravinsky. Publ. Durand 1915; International 1944; Polskie wyd. 1967; Peters 1978; Durand-Costallat 1986 in **Oeuvres complètes**, série I vol. 8.

MSS: 1) B.n. Ms. 989, 22 pp., bears orig. title "Caprices en blanc et noir," word "Caprices" lined through by Debussy; 2) an unlocated MS, 32 pp., sold at Hôtel Drouot 1935. Perf. home of Princesse E. de Polignac, Jan. 22, 1916, by Walter and Thérèse Rummel; home of Mme Georges Guiard, Dec. 21, 1916, by Debussy and Roger-Ducasse.

D6 **Epigraphes antiques, Six** (piano 2 or 4 hands, L 131).
1) Pour invoquer Pan
2) Pour un tombeau sans nom
3) Pour que la nuit soit propice
4) Pour la danseuse aux crotales
5) Pour l'égyptienne
6) Pour remercier la pluie au matin

1914. Publ. Durand 1915, in versions for 2 and for 4 hands; Peters 1973. ARR for orch., E. Ansermet, Durand 1939.

MSS: 1) B.n. Ms. 986, 20 pp., for piano 4 hands; 2) B.n. Ms. 987, 10 pp., MS transcription by Debussy pn. hands. Perf. March 17, 1917 [?].

In part derived from **Chansons de Bilitis** (which see under Incidental music).

D7 **Intermezzo** (composition for four hands)

Ca. 1882. Unpubl. MS Collection Koch, on deposit Morgan. Consists of a single movement, 11 f. (11 p. music and title p.). Is completely different from "Piatigorsky" **Intermezzo** (see Chamber Music above).

D8 **Lindaraja** (2 pianos, L 97).
Dated "Avril 1901." Publ. Jobert 1926; Peters [1969-?]; Durand-Costallat in **Oeuvres complètes**, série I vol. 8, 1986. MS sold Hôtel Drouot 1933 and exhibited at Opera Comique 1943 currently not located. Perf. Concert S.M.I., Salle des Agriculteurs, Oct. 28, 1926, by Roger-Ducasse and Marguerite Long.

D9 **Marche écossaise sur un thème populaire (Marche des anciens comtes de Ross)** (pn. 4 hands, L 77).
1891. Ded. General Meredith Read. Publ. Choudens, legal deposit 1891; Fromont 1903, repr. Jobert 1976; Peters 1973. ARR for orch., H. Mouton, Jobert 1924; for solo pn., Roger-Ducasse, Jobert 1926. MS 1-p. draft of 1st 7 m. only, Koch coll., on deposit Morgan, facs. in Gauthier (item 58), plate 32. Orch. by Debussy 1908 (see under Orchestrations above). Piano premiere [?] Jan. 16, 1909.

D10 **Petite suite** (piano 4 hands, L 65).
1) En bateau
2) Cortège
3) Menuet
4) Ballet

1888-89. Publ. Durand 1889; Peters 1973. ARR of Ballet for solo pn., J. Durand, Durand 1906; for pn. trio, L. Roques, Durand 1904, 1910. En bateau, Menuet, and Ballet arr. for solo pn., J. Durand, Durand 1906; arr. for 2 pn., I. Philipp, International 1954; entire suite for orch., H. Mouton, Durand 1909; entire suite for 2, 4, and 8 hands By H. Büsser, Durand [n.d.], 1908, 1910. Numerous other arr. publ. Durand for pn. and fl., vln., vcl., and clar., and arr. for harp and for organ.
MS B.n. Ms. 1014, 18 pp. Perf. in private hearing Mar. 1, 1889, by Jacques Durand and Debussy.

* **Prélude à l'après-midi d'un faune.** 2-piano version by Debussy, as publ. in **Oeuvres complètes**, série I, vol. 8, Durand-Costallat, 1986. See above under Orchestral works.

* **Symphonie en si mineur.** See above under Orchestral works

* **Triomphe de Bacchus** (4 hands). (L 38)
See above under Orchestral works.

12. Musical Greetings

G1 "Les accords de septième regrettent!" 9 measures for piano. Greeting for birthday of Emma Debussy, 1905. MS B.n. Ms. 14517.

G2 "Chant des matelots du vaisseau qui ne veut rien savoir." Dec. 25, 1911. 3 measures on a greeting card, for 1st and 2nd basses. B.n., Lettres autographes Debussy, no. 20.

G3 "Je vous la souhaite bonne et heureuse. Achille Debussy." For voice and piano. Ca. 1882 New Year's greeting to Mme Vasnier. Publ. in Vallas (item 96) and in **Musica** I/4 (Jan. 15, 1938), p. 157. MS formerly in coll. Cornuau, location unknown.

G4 "Marche nuptiale pour le mariage de Pierre Louÿs." June 1899. Piece for voice and organ. MS location unknown.

G5 "La neige sur le village. Poème symphonique en 5 mesures." For bells. Greeting card for Emma Debussy. Dec. 25, 1916. MS B.n., Lettres autographes Debussy, no. 29.

G6 "Noël pour célébrer Pierre Louÿs pour toutes les voix y compris celle du peuple." Dec. 25, 1903. MS Stanford Univ., Memorial Library of Music, "Partition pour Petites filles, Filles, Femmes du monde et le Peuple."

G7 "Noël pour 1914...." Dec. 25, 1914, for voice and piano. B.n. Ms. 14521.

G8 "Petite cantate sur grand papier pour le jour de sa fête Emma." For voices, bells and piano. June 4, 1907. B.n. Ms. 14519.

G9 Piano fragment ded. to Emma Bardac, for her birthday, dated "Dimanche 4 juin 1905." B.n. Ms. 14517, 1 p.

13. Exercises for the Paris Conservatory

NOTE: all AJ numbers indicate manuscripts housed at the Archives nationales, Paris. B.n. Vm. micr. 791

[not examined] is a microfilm of all the Archives nationales MSS of the student exercises by Debussy.

E1 1878. Melody and realized bass, for harmony exam. 8 pp., AJ37 204,77. Copy B.n. Ms. 970. Includes Debussy's first preserved signature.

E2 1879. "Chant donné" [1 f.] and "basse donnée" [3 f.]. Dated on folder "1879, 7 juillet. A. Claude Debussy, 16 ans 10 mois, 1er concours d'harmonie et accompagnement en 1878 [?], non mentionné." 8 pp., AJ37 204,67. Copy B.n. Ms. 971.

E3 1879. Melody for harmonization, in class of Emile Durand, April 8, 1879, 1 p., not located.

E4 1880. "Chant donné; basse donnée." Melody and bass for harmony exam. 3 pp., AJ37 204,67, copy B.n. Ms. 972.

E5 1880. "Leçon" for harmony class of Emile Durand, 3 pp., not located.

E6 1881. Fugue. Indication in another hand: "Fugue pour le concours de fugue 1881, âge 18 ans, 10 mois, 1er concours, élève de Guiraud, non mentionnè." AJ37 204(26).

E7 1882. Fugue in 4 voices on a subject by Gounod, for exam leading to Prix de Rome competition. B.n. Ms. 973a, 7 p.

E8 1882. Fugue in 4 voices for final concours in Prix de Rome competition. 7 pp., AJ37 204,16, copy at B.N. Ms. 973b. Bears indication "2ème accessit (1) Concours 1882" and "Contrepoint et fugue."

E9 1883 [?]. Fugue for the exam leading to Prix de Rome competition, 2 pp., coll. Jean-Marie Martin.

E10 1883. Fugue. Indication "Concours de Fugue de 1883. Sujet de M[assenet?]." 8 pp., AJ37 204,23; copy B.n. Ms. 8648.

E11 1884. Fugue in 4 voices for exam leading to Prix de Rome competition, 7 pp., coll. Jean-Marie Martin.

E12 1884. Fugue à 4 voix. 7 pp., bound in B.n. Cons. Ms. 968. Preparatory fugue composed in 1884 prior to **Le printemps** and **L'enfant prodigue**.

E13 AJ37 319,4D has indication: "dons, 18 avril 1889-10 dec. 1925. Pièces sans date. Partitions de Debussy donné par J. Durand." [not examined]

E14 B.n. Vmg. 17559 is a photocopy of an unfinished auto. MS, 4 pp., with indication "Fugue d'école sur un thème de Th. Dubois." Date unknown.

III

DEBUSSY'S LETTERS, CRITICAL WRITINGS, AND INTERVIEWS

I. Interpretations of Debussy's Letters and Critical Writings.

1. Briscoe, James R. "Debussy Through his Letters: the University of Texas Collection." **Library Chronicle** (forthcoming 1990).

Discusses the 138 autograph letters and a number of other manuscript sources at the Harry Ransom Humanities Research Center, Austin, Texas. About half of these letters are not published. For brief descriptions of contents see the list "Texas" among Manuscript Letters below. Article includes in an appendix the complete letters to Georges Hartmann and Emile Vuillermoz both at Texas and at the Pierpont Morgan Library.

2. Cobb, Margaret G. "Debussy in Texas." **Cahiers Debussy** (nouvelle série) 1 (1977): 45-46.

A brief mention of and excerpts from the letters by Debussy owned by the Humanities Research Center, University of Texas, Austin. See the list and annotations below under Manuscript Letters-Texas.

3. "Eléments de la bibliothèque de Debussy dans la vente de 1933." **Cahiers Debussy** (nouvelle série) 1 (1977): 38-40.

Description of the sales catalogue concerning Debussy's library, when it was sold by his widow at the Hôtel Drouot auction rooms in 1933. This sale of Debussy's manuscripts was by far the most important to the dispersion of these primary materials. Brief mention of books from his library and a number with dedications handwritten to D from others. A summary account of 29 letters from composers and 15 by literary figures to him.

* Goubault, Christian. **La critique musicale dans la presse française de 1870 à 1914.** Geneva and Paris: Slatkine, 1984. ISBN 2051005427; LC 84-150444/MN;ML 3880.G69 1984.

Pages 89 ff. place Debussy as critic within the context of music criticism in the France of his day.

4. Kushner, David Z. "Claude Debussy as music critic." **American Music Teacher** 33, no. 2 (Nov.-Dec. 1983): 14, 16, and 18-19.

A general but responsible overview, emphasizing D's unswerving interest in French music and values, which personal viewpoint did not diminish his critical acumen. D's criticism calls for abandonment of long-held notions. Relates D as critic to George Bernard Shaw.

5. Laichterova, Marie. **Debussy, Claude; Barvy a rytmus.** Prague: Statni hudebni vydava tilstvi, 1962. 188 pp., Facsim., music, portraits. LC 76-245558; ML 410.D28A126. In Czech.

A study of D through his letters and critical writings, citing entire documents. Consists of many important letters given in chronological order, with extended annotations. Facsimile of letter to E. Chausson (1893) and an inscribed drawing to P. Louÿs. A very interesting approach to biography, parallel to Lesure, item 23, but with more extensive commentary and interpretation than Lesure.

6. Lesure, François. "Une interview romaine de Debussy (février 1914)." **Cahiers Debussy** (nouvelle série) 11 (1987), 3-8.

The interview appeared in **La tribuna** in Rome, written by Alberto Gasco. Not republished previously in any modern edition of D's critical writing and interviews. Mentions the work D was preparing to conduct, **Prélude-faune**, **La mer**, the Poe projects **Chute** and **Diable**, and Stravinsky. Also mentions the project **Histoire de Tristan**.

* ------. "Les leçons de Monsieur Croche." Chapter VIII, pp. 193-207, in item 65.

A somewhat simplified but quite useful overview of Debussy as a music critic, his values and preoccupations.

7. Palache, John G. "Debussy as Critic." **Musical Quarterly** 10, no. 3 (July 1924): 361-68.

Remains a useful, brief overview for the reader not needing an in-depth exploration. Requires amplification by Vallas and by the primary documents (items 45 and following) for serious research. Based on 1921 **Monsieur Croche anti-dilettante** (42) and thus does not consider the several articles and the interviews omitted from that first collection of criticism.

8. Vallas, Léon. **Les idées de Claude Debussy, musicien français.** Paris: Librairie de France, 1927. 189 p.; list of articles by Debussy, index of names. English trans. as **The Theories of Claude Debussy, Musicien français,** by Maire O'Brien. London: Oxford University Press, 1929. Repr. New York: Dover, 1967. LC card no. of repr. 67-16703; ML 410.D28 V165.

A selection and interpretation of main ideas expressed in the articles, organized by topics: outlook on criticism, definition of music as a free art, musical education, composition and form, nationalism, the works of Wagner, etc. By a path-breaker in Debussy studies, this book remains of considerable interest as a distillation of Debussy's critical writings, even when Vallas' early view now appears short-sighted. For example, Vallas views Debussy too narrowly as a critic virtually absorbed by an interest in French music and aesthetics.

2. Published Collections of Debussy's Letters [Index identifies these by L]

Below are the primary collections of letters to, from, and about Debussy that have been published. Further see Section 3, Collections of Manuscript Letters [Index M].

Annunzio

9. Annunzio, Gabriele D'. **Claude Debussy et Gabriele D'Annunzio. Correspondance inédite.** Preface by Guy Tosi. Neuchâtel: Les Editions du Griffon, and Paris: Les Editions Denoël, 1948. 129 p. ML 410.D28 A122.

Sixty letters by D'Annunzio (librettist of **Le martyre de Saint Sébastien**), Debussy, Emma Debussy, Chouchou Debussy, and Gabriel Astruc, with important preface and notes on the letters. Most were written 1910-14 and concern **Le martyre** and its period. Index of names; illustrations of relevant persons and designs by Léon Bakst for **Le martyre**.

Baron

10. Ambrière, Francis. "La Vie romaine de Claude Debussy." **Revue musicale** 15, no. 142 (Jan. 1934): 20-26.

Excerpts of correspondence with the bookseller Emile Baron, dating from 1886-87 and written while D was in Rome. Dates of the letters are: no date, 6 Nov. 1886, 23 Dec. 1886, winter 1887, 9 Feb. 1887. Subjects discussed include Rome, Villa Medici, **Diane au bois**, Manet, Offenbach, **Printemps** (orch.), J. Moréas, Shelley, the Symbolist publications **Revue Indépendante, La Vogue**, and **La Nouvelle Revue**, Verlaine, Albert Jounet, Charles Morice, Charles Vignier, J.K. Huysmans, Wagner, Flaubert, Tolstoi, and Richepin. An important primary document on the Rome period and thus an adjunct to the Vasnier letters, item 39.

Caplet

11. Debussy, Claude. **Lettres inédites de Claude Debussy et André Caplet (1908-14).** Edited with an introduction by E. Lockspeiser; preface by A. Schaeffner. Monaco: Editions du Rocher [28 rue Comte Félix Gastoldi, Monaco], 1957. 105 p. ML410.D28 A16.

Contains letters to the conductor Caplet concerning **Pelléas**, whose interpretation D considered definitive. Letters also concern Caplet's essential collaboration in **Le martyre**, the **Images**, **Jeux**, the Poe projects **Diable** and **La chute**, and other works. Offers insights into Debussy's preferred performance practices and orchestral thinking. Also contains letters from 1910-14 to the British impresario Henry Russell, who had connections to D and Caplet.

Caplet/Lockspeiser

12. Lockspeiser, Edward. "New Letters of Debussy." **Musical Times** 97 (Aug. 1956): 404-06.

Lockspeiser gives in French additional letters to A. Caplet, the subjects of which are indexed below. Cites in full the letter from Chouchou (D's daughter) to her half-brother Raoul Bardac following her father's death.

Chausson, Ernest.

13. "Correspondance inédite de Claude Debussy et Ernest Chausson." **Revue musicale**, année 7, tome 1 (Dec. 1, 1925; Numéro spécial consacré à E. Chausson): 116-26.

Contains letters:

1) by CD, 26 Aug. 1893. Artist's life.
2) by EC, 6 Sept. 1893. Beethoven and Chopin are models.
3) by CD, 2 Oct. 1893. Genesis of **Pelléas**, influence of Wagner, ideas of Franck and Massenet.
4) by CD, "Lundi" [no date]. on Wagner, Mallarmé, and Bach.
5) by EC, no date. 3rd act of **Pelléas**.
6) by CD, no date. **Pelléas**; visit with P. Louÿs to see Maeterlinck concerning setting his play.
7 and 8) by EC, short greetings.
9) by CD. Relates Ysaÿe's appreciation of **Pelléas** project and contains a lengthy discussion of D's and Chausson's friendship.

Further see "Dix lettres d'Ernest Chausson à Claude Debussy (1893-94)." **Revue de musicologie** 48 (July-Dec. 1962): 49-60. Illustrates the further exchange of ideas.

Further see Oulmont, Charles. "Deux amis: Claude Debussy et Ernest Chausson: documents inédits." **Mercure de France** no. 256 (Dec. 1, 1934): 248-269. Almost entirely reprinted in **Musique d'amour: E. Chausson et la "bande à**

Franck." Paris: Desclée, 1935. Quotes from letters by Chausson, D, and P. Louÿs written in the period 1893-94. All key letters have been reprinted subsequently. Topics include Maeterlinck, **Pelléas**, and Wagner.

Chansarel

14. Lesure, François. "Quatre lettres de René Chansarel à Debussy." **Cahiers Debussy** (nouvelle série) 4-5 (1980-81): 51-56.

Publishes letters from 1889 now at the B.n. The letters testify to a deep friendship and comment on Debussy's projects and mind set. Topics mentioned include J.K. Huysmans, J. Laforgue, Verlaine, the Prix de Rome, Alfred Bachelet, and Massenet's **Esclarmonde**. Indirect references to the **Cinq poèmes de Baudelaire**, Rimsky-Korsakov, and the **Petite suite**.

Cobb

* Cobb, Margaret G. **The Poetic Debussy.**
Further see main entry 48. Prints the following letters for the first time:
1) p. 188. To Mme Arthur Fontaine, "samedi fin 1893." From a private collection. Thanks her and Mr Fontaine for the gift of candlesticks.
2) p. 190. To Pierre Louÿs, "'Dimanche sur les villes' et aussi sur Séville (mars 1895)."
3) From a private coll. Has been ill; asks for a letter; missed the performance of a piece by Lebey, which made little impact.
4) p. 196. To Georges Hartmann, Dec. 18, 1899. From a private collection. Asks for financial assistance.
5) p. 198-201. To Raoul Bardac, Feb. 24 and 25, 1906. MS in the B.n., Paris. Observes rehearsals of music by Rimsky-Korsakov and d'Indy, conductors Chevillard and Colonne. Comments at length on R. Bardac's talents as composer and on aesthetics.
6) p. 206. To Alexandre Charpentier, Sept. 27, 1908. From a private collection. Short note inviting Charpentier to dinner, with a paraphrase from the **Ariettes oubliées**.
7) p. 208. To Jacques Durand, July 27, 1910. Printed in letters to Durand (1927) but here given with Debussy's short musical inscription.
8) p. 230. To Paul Dukas, Sept. 10, 1916. From the collection of M. Cobb. Speaks of his declining health, referring to Charles d'Orléans' expresion concerning melancholia.

9) p. 236. To Paul Dukas, May 19, 1917. From the collection of M. Cobb. Quotes Jules Laforgue and mentions the **Noël des enfants** and the **Sonata for Violin**, which was just performed by G. Poulet.

10) p. 238. To Serge Diaghilev, May 20, 1917. From a private collection. Congratulates him on the "special beauty" of the Ballets russes, which he has just witnessed.

11) p. 240. To Walter Rummel, June 22, 1917. Formerly in the collection of Pasteur Vallery-Radot, current ownership not identified. Poetic congratulations to Rummel for his performance of Bach and Debussy, quoting from Debussy's song **La mer est plus belle**.

Doret

15. Doret, Gustave. "Neuf lettres et billets inédits de C.A. Debussy, commentés." **Lettres romandes** (Geneva) (Nov. 23, 1934). Not examined.

Durand

16. Durand, Jacques. **Lettres de Claude Debussy à son éditeur: publiées par Jacques Durand.** Paris: Durand, 1927. 191 p. ML410.D28 A16.

A highly valuable publication of letters by D to Durand, his principal publisher and close friend, 3 from 1894 and over 200 from 1902-17. Durand took over from Fromont in 1902 as D's exclusive publisher. In publishing the letters, Durand states that he expurgated certain passages having an intimate character, and he replaced certain names of persons of whom D was critical by the letters X, Y, and Z. Sparse annotations by Durand; no index. See Grayson (item 753, p. 3) concerning errors of dating.

Emma

17. Debussy, Emma. **Lettres de Claude Debussy à sa femme Emma.** Preface by Pasteur Vallery-Radot. Paris: Flammarion, 1957. 145 p. ML 410/.D2 A17.

74 letters and telegrams principally to Emma Debussy; some to his daughter Chouchou. Dated Nov. 29, 1910, to April 29, 1914. Certain of these are also listed separately as B.n. autograph letters. Vallery-Radot, a physician and friend of the period, published the letters in accord with Mme Gaston de Tinan (née Hélène Bardac, nickname Dolly), Emma's daughter by her first marriage to

Sigismond Bardac. The letters were written by Debussy during five extended trips away from Paris. Vallery-Radot's extended introduction reviews the events surrounding Debussy's divorce from Rosalie (Lilly) Texier and the fulfilling marriage to Emma. Sparse annotations; no index.

Fauré

18. "Deux lettres de Gabriel Fauré à Debussy (1910-1917)." Edited by F. Lesure. **Revue de musicologie** 48 (numéro spécial, 1962), 75-76.

Godet

19. Godet, Robert and Georges Jean-Aubry. **Lettres à deux amis.** Paris: Librairie José Corti, 1942. 195 p. ML 410.D28 A125.

78 letters by D to Godet, a Swiss journalist and musicologist, and Jean-Aubry, a writer, critic, and editor of the British journal **The Chesterian**. Compiled by the recipients and prefaced by a dialogue reminiscence about D. The letters encompass the period January 1889 to October 1917 and are annotated. Index. [Both the Godet and Jean-Aubry letters are indexed below as L Godet.]

See D's letter to Godet in Godet's article "Le Lyrisme intime de Debussy, I" (item 143).

See "Cinq lettres de R. Godet à Claude Debussy (1917-1918)" (item 141). Contains a preface by F. Lesure discussing the problem of letters from others to Debussy, most of which are lost.

Guéritte

* Guéritte, T.J. "Some Recollections of Debussy." **Musical Times** 59, no. 903 (May 1918).

Contains a letter to Guéritte; see item 134.

Gui

20. Gui, Vittorio. "Debussy in Italia." **Musica d'Oggi** 11, no. 12 (Milan) (Dec. 1932): 463-73.

Discusses D's early reception in Italy and concerns his his voyage there in 1911. Gives in full (in French and Italian) 2 letters to the orchestral conductor V. Gui, dating from Feb. 25, 1912, and Feb. 8, 1914. Subjects include **Children's Corner** (orchestral version), **Ariane et Barbe-bleue** (Dukas), Debussyism, and songs by Gui.

D projects a trip to Rome on 22 Feb. 1914 to conduct.

Hartmann

21. Hartmann, Arthur. "Claude Debussy as I Knew Him." **Musical Courrier** (May 23, 1918): 6-8. Republished in **Canadian Journal of Music** 5, no. 10 (Apr.-May 1919): 151-55.

Discusses the origins of the violinist Hartmann's transcription of **Il pleure dans mon coeur**. Reminisces about D's reports of seeing Wagner and Liszt. Gives in facsimile a short letter from D to Hartmann of June 3, 1910, of a friendly character. Gives 1 page in facsimile of D's transcription of **Minstrels** "pour piano et Hartmann." Cites a letter of 1915 or 1916 concerning the war. Gives in facsimile D's 1910 Christmas greeting, a musical riddle.

Jean-Aubry, Georges. See item 19.

Laloy

22. "Correspondance de Claude Debussy et de Louis Laloy (1902-1914)." Introduction by F. Lesure. **Revue de musicologie** 48 ("Claude Debussy 1862-1962; Textes et documents inédits, July-Dec. 1962): 3-40.

Contains 82 letters from D to Laloy.

Lesure

23. Lesure, François, ed. **Claude Debussy: lettres 1884-1918.** Paris: Hermann, 1980. xv, 294 p. ISBN 2-7056-5918-8; ML 410.D28 A42 1980.

Contains a careful selection of some 250 of D's letters from the approximately 1600 that are extant. Many are published for the first time, and Lesure plans to release the complete correspondence. Virtually all main figures and projects are represented. Lesure regrettably does not include letters from others to D, arguing that their inclusion might have unbalanced or distorted the image of the composer. Illustrated copiously and at times in color, with a table of illustrations. Introduction by Lesure and index of names cited in letters and of addressees. Annotations and identifications of persons and projects are cryptic but still useful. The editor exercizes some freedom in altering D's spelling and punctuation, which on occasion is necessary for understanding. However, emendations are not noted.

Lesure includes many letters from the other published collections and from shorter articles. The index to the letters in the present book cites the selfsame reference in two sources. The researcher nonetheless is advised to explore all citations below and observe the dates of letters. Indexed below as L Lesure.

Lesure/Concordia

24. Lesure, François. "Debussy et la Concordia (1883-85)." **Cahiers Debussy** 3 (première série, 1976): 1-5.

Describes D's role as accompanist to the Concordia Choral Society, which was organized by Henriette Fuchs. Gives 3 letters and 2 concert programs, all previously unpublished. Also see the preceding source, in which a letter of Jan. 15, 1885, is published.

Lockspeiser

25. Lockspeiser, Edward, compiler. **The Literary Clef**. London: Calder, 1958. ML 90.L8.

Contains a sampling of letters to D that first were published elsewhere, including letters to Vasnier, E. Baron, Godet, E. Chausson, Ysaÿe, Louÿs, R. Bardac, Messager, Toulet, Laloy, Jean-Aubry, H. Russell, Caplet, Durand, and Emma Debussy. Valuable for sensitive English translations.

Louÿs

26. Louÿs, Pierre. **Correspondance de Claude Debussy et Pierre Louÿs (1893-1904)**. Edited by Henri Borgeaud, with an introduction by G. Jean-Aubry. Paris: Librairie José Corti, 1945. 206 p. ML 410.D28 A14.

The introduction reviews D's relationship to Louÿs. Contains 216 letters from D to Louÿs and vice versa; appendix containing texts of Louÿs' **Cendrelune** scenario, the romance **L'adieu**, his translation of **La saulaie** (D.-G. Rossetti). Reprints Louÿs's article on D's **Nuages** and **Fêtes** (**La vie parisienne** Dec. 15, 1900), a review in Le

journal (Feb. 8, 1901) of the recited version of **Chansons de Bilitis**, and an article in **Musica** (March 1911) reporting the responses of D and Louÿs to a journalist's inquiry about the interaction of poetry and music.

Further see "Neuf lettres de Pierre Louÿs à Debussy (1894-98)." Edited by E. Lockspeiser. **Revue de musicologie** 48 (numéro spécial, July-Dec. 1962): 61-70. 5 of the 9 letters given were excerpted in the preceding and here are given in their entirety.

<u>Louÿs 1971</u>

27. Lesure, François, ed. "Lettres inédites de Claude Debussy à Pierre Louÿs." **Revue de musicologie** 57, no. 1 (1971): 29-39.

Contains 12 letters previously unpublished and 6 letters published only in part by Borgeaud, in the preceding source.

<u>Messager</u>

28. Messager, André. **L'enfance de "Pelléas": Lettres de Claude Debussy à André Messager.** Ed. by Jean André-Messager, with preface by Emile Vuillermoz. Paris: Dorbon-Ainé, [1938]. 83 p. ML 410/.D2 A15.

19 letters to Messager, dated May 9, 1902 through Sept. 19, 1904, and 2 letters of Apr. 2, 1910, and Nov. 4, 1910. Messager was music director of the Opéra-Comique for the first performance of **Pelléas**. The letters discuss concerns of the production and aspects of their close friendship, which ended abruptly in 1904 when Debussy left his first wife Rosalie (Lilly) for Emma Bardac. The identity of persons and precise dates of events mentioned in the letters are explained in the annotations.

Further see Henri Borgeaud, ed., "Lettres d'André Messager à Albert Carré relatives à **Pelléas et Mélisande.**" **Revue de musicologie** 48 (numéro spécial, 1962): 101-04.

<u>Nichols</u>

29. Nichols, Roger, translator and reviser. **Debussy Letters**. Selected and edited by F. Lesure and R. Nichols. London: Faber, and Cambridge, Mass.: Harvard University Press, 1987.

ML410.D28A42 1987; ISBN 0-674-19429-2 [Harvard ed.] and 0-571-14720-8 [London ed.]. xxvi, 355.

Adds 56 letters to the 255 in Lesure (item 23), retaining Lesure's annotations and annotating the new letters. Of those, 6 are published for the first time. Translations are sensitive but the French original letters are not given alongside. The serious scholar therefore must consult the French originals in Lesure, in the published collections, or at private libraries. This revised and translated collection is quite valuable for the English-speaking scholar, for the additional letters, and for its general index as well as its index of works. Lesure's index, by contrast, is an index only of names and of D's works.

Paoli

30. Paoli, Rodolfo. **Debussy.** Florence: Sansoni, 1947. 2nd ed. 1951. 236 pp. LC a52-10302; ML410.D28 P2 1952.

Outdated as a biography but highly important for its inclusion of letters by D:

1) p. 235, to Alfredo Casella, June 20, 1915. Mentions the **Trois ballades de Villon** in a concert directed by Casella.

2) pp. 235-36, to Marchese di Casafuerte, May 7, 1917. Thanks him for his appreciative remarks regarding the violin sonata.

3) pp. 230-32, 2 letters to Vittorio Gui: a) Feb. 25, 1912. Is pleased he will conduct **Children's Corner** in Rome. Discusses Debussyism. b) Feb. 8, 1914. Thanks Gui for sending his song compositions. D plans to be in Rome Feb. 20, 1914.

4) pp. 232-34, 2 letters to Bernardino Molinari: a) Jan. 9, 1915. Discusses **Martyre** and thanks him for his appreciative remarks. b) Oct. 6, 1915. Speaks of the genesis of **Etudes**, the violin sonata, and the "trio" (sonata for flute, viola, and harp), "sans la grandiloquence des sonates modernes." Intends to orchestrate **L'Isle joyeuse** and to visit Rome again.

Peter

* Peter, René. **Claude Debussy.** Ed. rev. [et] augmentée de plusieurs chapitres et de lettres inédites de Claude Debussy. See main entry 88. ML410.D28 P37 1944.

Poniatowski

31. Poniatowski, André. **D'un siècle à l'autre.** Paris: Presse de la Cité, 1948. 669 pp. LC a50-1984; DC342.8.P65 A3.

Contains 2 letters from D to Poniatowski. These are reprinted in **Rassegna musical** 1, anno XXI (Jan. 1951): 56-59; also both in Lesure (23). a) Sept. 9, 1892. Speaks of Bailly, America and his reception there, A. Rubinstein, **Trois scènes au crépuscule**, and the **Fantaisie**. b) "Jeudi, Fev. 1893." Speaks of P. Bourget, G. Charpentier, Berlioz, Gounod, A. Thomas, Massenet, Palestrina, **Proses lyriques**, and the **Quatuor**.

Popelin

See the article described on page 117, which appeared too late for inclusion here.

Queen's Hall

32. Debussy, Claude. "Letter to the Queen's Hall Orchestra." **Musical Times** (March 1, 1908), 163.

Refers to a concert at Queen's Hall on Feb. 1, 1908, at which D conducted certain of his works. In English. Congratulates the orchestra and Mr. Henry J. Wood for their fine performance.

Ravel

* Lesure, François. "L'affaire Debussy-Ravel." Contains correspondence between D and Ravel. See item 333.

Romilly

33. Romilly, Mme. Gérard de. "Debussy professeur, par une de ses élèves (1898-1908)." **Cahiers Debussy** (nouvelle série) 2 (1978): 3-10.

Extracts from a previously unpublished article by Mme de Romilly of 1933. She was a voice and piano student and recalls aspects of his personality. Includes 2 letters.

Satie

34. Borgeaud, H., ed. "Trois lettres d'Erik Satie à Claude Debussy (1903)." **Revue de musicologie** 48 (numéro spécial, July-Dec. 1962): 71-74.

Segalen

35. Joly-Segalen, Annie and André Schaeffner, eds. **Segalen et Debussy.** Monaco: Editions du Rocher, 1962. 343 p. LC 62-5432; ML 90.J56.

21 short letters from D to Segalen, numerous letters from Segalen to D and to others concerning him, reminiscences in dialogue form written by Segalen concerning their discussions, and reprints of 3 literary works by Segalen that relate to Debussy: "Voix mortes, musique maori," "Dans un monde sonore," and **Orphée-Roi**.

Segalen was a navy doctor and writer who cultivated D's friendship and aesthetic advice from 1906 until D's death, although the attraction was not as compelling for Debussy. Their chief collaboration was the drama **Orphée-Roi**, which Debussy termed "une conception fausse" in 1916 and finally rejected as a libretto. Reprints Debussy's corrections in the margins of **Orphée** as footnotes. Letters are thoughtfully annotated by Schaeffner and show the importance of non-Western culture in Debussy's circle, since Segalen was stationed in China and travelled throughout the East. See also G. Jean-Aubry. "V. Segalen et C. Debussy," **Les Cahiers du Sud** no. 288, 1948.

Stravinsky

36. [Stravinsky, Igor.] **Avec Stravinsky: lettres inédites de Claude Debussy [et altri].** Commentary by R. Craft. Monaco: Editions du Rocher, 1958. 210 p. ML 410.S932 A4.

Contains a discussion by R. Craft (pp. 103-17) of 2 works by Stravinsky written for D: the cantata **Roi des étoiles (Zvezdoliky**, composed in homage in 1911) and **Symphonie pour instruments à vent** (a memorial tribute of 1921, rev. 1947). Contains 7 newly-published letters by D to Stravinsky of 1912-15. Also see item 406.

Toulet

37. Debussy, Claude. **Correspondance de Claude Debussy et P.-J. Toulet.** Edited with a preface by Henri Martineau. Collection Saint-Germain-des-Près No. 10. Paris: Le Divan, 1929.

Contains 63 letters from Debussy to Toulet, 31 from Toulet to Debussy, letters from Toulet to Emma Debussy and Chouchou, and letters from Emma to Mme Toulet. The writer Toulet was an intimate friend of D for a period of 18 years. He collaborated with D on an adaptation of **As You Like It**, planned over 16 years but never completed. That Toulet's letters to Debussy survive permits a valuable view of the exchange of ideas. Further see the entry <u>Lang</u> in section "Manuscript Letters" below.

<u>Vallery</u>

38. Vallery-Radot, Pasteur. **Tel était Claude Debussy, suivi de lettres à l'auteur.** Paris: Julliard, 1958. 156 p. ML 410.D28 V27mlc.

Debussy's friend of later years and admirer since the **Pelléas** premiere, Vallery-Radot contributes a series of biographical essays as a reply to and repudiation of V. Seroff's biography **Debussy, Musician of France** (New York: Putnam's Sons, 1956; also London and Paris editions). Vallery-Radot perpetuates the perhaps unfounded story of a youthful infatuation with Sonia von Meck, but he clarifies the relationship to Blanche Vasnier as that of an "amoureux" rather than an "amant." He calls for historians to deal with documents of proven authenticity.

The letters of Debussy to Vallery-Radot began in 1910 and are included here in their entirety.

<u>**Vasnier**</u>

39. **Prunières, Henry.** "A la Villa Médicis." **Revue musicale** 23 (numéro spécial, May 1 1926): 23 (119)-42 (138).

Letters concern Prix de Rome sojourn 1885-86, impressions and compositions worked on while there.

<u>Vidal</u>

40. "Debussy de 1883-1885 d'après la correspondance de P. Vidal à H. Fuchs." **Revue de musicologie** 48 (numéro spécial, 1962): 98-100.

Describes D in the Prix de Rome years, his relation to his parents, to Guiraud, and to Mme Blanche Vasnier.

Ysaÿe

41. Samazeuilh, Gustave. "Lettres inédites de Claude Debussy à Eugène Ysaÿe." **Les annales politiques et littéraires** no. 2458 (Paris) (Aug. 25, 1933).

Ysaÿe and the string quartet he founded premiered the **Quatuor**. Gives 2 letters by D of Sept. 22, 1894, and Oct. 13, 1896. Both are reprinted in Lesure (item 23). Samazeuilh gives a letter not reprinted in Lesure of Dec. 30, 1903, thanking Ysaÿe for his plans to conduct the **Nocturnes**.

3. Manuscript Letters in Libraries and Private Collections [Index M]

Bn

Bibliothèque nationale, Département de musique. The following numbering is that of the B.n. and should be used for inquiries. The collection of Debussy letters bears the name "Lettres autographes Claude Debussy." The following states all particulars of addresses, date, and topic that the letters cover.

1. "à Monsieur le Directeur [A. Thomas], Dimanche." Inside address of Debussy 27 rue de Berlin. Requests permission to borrow the score of **L'enfant prodigue** from the Conservatoire library.
2. Debussy's [?] ticket stub from the first performance of **Pelléas**.
3. 15 Nov. 1909. Debussy's notes while hearing admissions concours in piano to the Conservatoire. Mostly doodling.
4. June 1915. Notes while hearing exams in "déclamation lyrique" at the Conservatoire. "Mr. X chante faux...ne sait rien."
5. To Vincent d'Indy. 15 Nov. 1908. Acquisition 1154. Placates d'Indy with diplomatic praise.
6. To Lalo. 27 Aug. 1900. Acq. 5561. Praises **Namouna**, which he had heard previously.
7. To René Peter. 15 Feb. 1898. Acq. 9070. Suggests the tune to adapt as the **Berceuse héroïque**.
8. To G. [N.?] Coronio. 27 Jan. 1902. Acquisition 9330. Reflections on Maeterlinck.
9. To Mme Emma Bardac [later Mme C. Debussy].

No place or date. Don 249-62. Calling card with Christmas greeting.

10. To Mme Emma Bardac [later Debussy]. [Paris] no date. Don 249-62. Small greeting card accompanying a gift of flowers.

11. To Mme Emma Bardac [later Debussy]. No place or date. Asks her to pass the afternoon with him.

12. To Raoul Bardac [from Bichain, Yonne] 31 Aug. 1901. Don 252-62. Advice as Bardac composes **Hérodiade**.

13. To R. Bardac [?]. [Paris] 30 March 1902. Don 252-62. Announces a publication by subscription, rue d'Anjou.

14. To R. Bardac. Bichain, Yonne [1903?]. Don 252-62. Consoles him because he was forced by his father to travel.

15. To Mme Sigismond Bardac. Paris, no date [9 June 1904]. Don 249-62. Asks for a rendez-vous. [B.n. note: very likely the first letter to Emma Bardac].

16. As above, dated 31 March 1905. Love letter accompanying the gift of a ring.

17. As above, dated Dec. 1906. Don 250-62. Noël greetings.

18. To R. Bardac. [Paris] 24 and 25 Feb. 1906. Don 252-62. 7-page letter. Has heard Ravel's **Shéhérazade** and d'Indy's **Un jour d'été à la montagne**. Critique of Chevillard. Advice on composition: rigor, patience. Aesthetic reflections.

19. To Emma Debussy. [Paris] 6 June 1911. Don 249-62. Card accompanying a gift of flowers.

20. To Emma Debussy. [Dec.] 1911. Don 255-62. Illustrated Yuletide card with musical autograph in 4-voice texture.

21. To Emma. No place or date [1913]. Don 250-62. Illustrated Yuletide card. Announces a series of 12 pieces of which this is the first, referring to the 12 months of the year.

22. To D.E. Ingelbrecht. Paris, 15 Sept. 1913. Don 247-62. Recommends Raoul Bardac and his work. Regrets the abandonment of **La salamite**.

23. To Emma Debussy. No place, 1 Jan. 1915. Don 250-62. Illustrated Yuletide greeting card.

24. To Raoul Bardac. [Paris] 10 March 1915. Don 252-62. Thanks him on behalf of Chouchou for sending **Une semaine musicale**. In turn sends bad news about his [Debussy's] mother.

25. To Emma Debussy. [Paris] 1 May 1915. Don 249-62. Calling card, perhaps accompanying flowers.

26. To Emma. No place, 4 June 1915. Don 249-62. Flower gift card [for her birthday].

27. To Emma, Paris, 22 Aug. 1915. Small card joined to the gift of the manuscript of **Etudes**, "pour me souhaiter mon anniversaire."

28. To Emma, [Paris], 6 Dec. 1915, "11 heures du soir." Farewell letter [from the hospital?] on the evening before his surgery.

29. To Emma, [Dec.] 1916. Don 255-62. Yuletide greeting card with musical signature "La neige sur le village...poème symphonique...en 5 mesures (état préorchestrale)."

30. To Emma, 24 Dec. 1916. Don 250-62. Yuletide illustrated greeting card, with allusions to his illness.

31. To Emma. No date [8 Jan. 1917]. Don 249-62. Deplores that she is ill and is not doing well himself. Reports that Satie played badly.

32. To Emma. [St. Jean de Luz] July 1917. Don 249-62. Anniversary greetings. Recognition of her goodness.

33. To Léon Kufferath et Guide, directeurs de la Théâtre de la Monnaie, Brussels. No place, 15 Dec. 1905. Acq. 589-63. Asks when and for how long he will be needed at the Théâtre de la Monnaie for the preparation of **Pelléas**.

34. To Antonin Lugnier. [Paris] 23 March 1916. Acq. 589-63. With thanks for sending his book.

35. To Gaston Poulet. [Paris] 14 March 1917. Acq. 589-63. Thanks Poulet for coming to his home to rehearse the **Quatuor**.

36. To G. Poulet. St. Jean-de-Luz [Sept. 1917]. Acq. 589-63. At the announcement of Poulet's coming, he notes that he does not feel "en mesure" for playing. Asks for information concerning Mlle Noelle Cousin.

37. To G. Poulet. [Paris] 18 Oct. 1917. Acq. 589-63. Asks him to come to his home to play the vln.-pn. for André Caplet.

38. To Mme M.A. Fontaine. Paris 24 June 1901. Acq. 634-63. Accepts her invitation.

39. To Gabriel Astruc. No date or place. Don 1031-66. He accepts the bid to work for the Théâtre des Champs-Elysées.

40. To Astruc. Paris, no date. Don 1031- 66. Inopportune time to mount a Debussy festival.

41. To Astruc. Paris, 12 June 1909. Don 1031-66. With thanks for and impressions of the previous evening.

42. To Astruc. Paris, 22 Nov. 1912. Don 1031-66. Suggests a meeting.

43. To Astruc. Paris, 11 Aug. 1902. Don 1031-66. Happiness about the project to build a theater.

44. To Astruc. Paris, 3 Aug. 1913. Don 1031-

66. Apprehensions about their project.

45. To Astruc. Paris, 5 Aug. 1913. Don 1031-66. Those "howling dogs" the merchant-creditors are after him.

46. To Astruc. Paris, 21 Aug. 1913. Don 1031-66. Asks that Astruc not forget him.

47. To Astruc. Paris, 31 Aug. 1913. Don 1031-66. His situation worsens and fears the predicament of "hommes noirs."

48. To Astruc. Paris, 7 Sept. 1913. Don 1031-66. Anguish and discouragement.

49. To Astruc. Paris, 1 Nov. 1914. Don 1031-66. With appreciation; is in an unsettled state.

50. To Astruc. Paris, 25 Nov. 1916. Don 1031-66. Is awaiting a letter from Astruc.

51. To Astruc. Paris, 18 Oct. 1916. Don 1031-66. He remembers Philippe Bertholdt.

52. To Astruc. Paris, no date. Don 1031- 66. Asks for a loge for the performance of **Prélude-faune**.

53. To Astruc. No place, 19 Oct. 1913. Don 1031-66. Concerts that he is conducting. Advantages of the Théâtre des Champs-Elysées over the Opéra.

54. To Astruc. Paris, no date. Don 1031- 66. [On Microfilm 21 at B.n.] Details of staging for the ending of **Martyre**.

55. To Astruc. No place or date. Don 1031-66. [On Microfilm 21 at B.n.] Asks for a meeting on the subject of **Martyre de St. Sébastien**.

56. To Astruc. 23 May 1907. Photocopy of original. Gift 1031-66. Discusses the Concerts russes, **Boris**, **Salome** as "rare as the appearance of a comet."

57. To A. Messager. ca. 1902-03. Frag ments of 11 letters in photocopy. Don 1031- 66. Praises Messager's performance of **Pelléas**; their friendship; work on libretto for **Diable dans le beffroi**; **La mer** and **Estampes** in progress.

58. To Florent Schmitt. No place or date. Don 10466 bis. Is sending Schmitt a letter attached [now missing, possibly a recommendation].

59. To Florent Schmitt. [Paris] 11 Dec. 1911, with envelope. Don 10466 bis. Congratulates Schmitt for his quintet, which greatly interests him.

60. To Pierre de Bréville. "mardi" [ca. 1893], no place. Don 1521, Dossier Bréville. Wishes him well on his upcoming voyage; thanks him for his sympathy toward **La damoiselle élue**.

61. To Bréville. No place, [February 1894]. Don 1521. Announces his engagement to Thérèse Roger.

62. To Bréville. No place, [1894]. Don 1521. Suggest that one play the second movement of the Borodin symphony and inquires whether Mlle Sidner will sing in forthcoming performance.

63. To Bréville. [Paris], "jeudi 24 mars 1898." Don 1521. Still has noone arranged to sing **Chansons de Bilitis**. States his decision not to augment the work with an orchestral "fracas."

64. To Bréville. No place. "mardi, 14 mai 1899." Don 1521. Continued difficulty finding a singer for "Bilitis."

65. To Bréville. No place. 12 April 1901. Don 1521. Regrets that he must retract the **Proses lyriques** from the upcoming performance.

66. To Bréville. No place or date except "dimanche." Don 1521. Has examined the "Joyeuseté d'Avril," a "curious piece" that unites the influence of Chabrier and Sallaniak [illegible].

67. To Bréville. No place or date except "vendredi." Don 1521. He appreciates Bréville's writings for **Mercure** cannot promise anything on the subject of songs.

68. To Bréville. No place or date. Dossier 1521. Concerns with the **Proses lyriques**.

69. To Bréville. No place [1897?]. Dossier 1521. Thanks Bréville for charming letter; announces his appointment to committee of the Société Nationale.

70. To Guy Ropartz. No place or date. Visiting card. Don 729-64. Thanks and greetings.

71. To the Marquis de Casafuerte. Paris, 7 May 1917. Don 114-68. Appreciates his kind remarks concerning the violin sonata.

72. To Ernest Chausson. No date or place. Don 76-68. With envelope in Emma Debussy's hand. Extended letter discussing his relationship to Pierre Louÿs; his visit with Ysaye in Brussels, who received him warmly. He read over the **Cinq poèmes de Baudelaire**, **Damoiselle élue**, **Pelléas**, and Chausson's quartet. Visited Maeterlinck, spoke with him at length and received permission for **Pelléas**. Publ. letter.

73. Visiting card. Don 72-68(325). No addressee or message.

74. To D.E. Ingelbrecht. Typed copy of 18 letters dated 1912-17. Don 77-68.

22 May 1912. Argument with d'Annunzio over Ida Rubinstein.

2 June 1912. Thanks for efforts on behalf of **Martyre** performance.

11 June 1913. Calls attention to R. Bardac's work, regrets that **La salamite** was abandoned.

[1913]. Postcard of 4 German military

figures. "Si vous les trouvez beaux, c'est que vous êtes bien difficile."

24 Feb. 1914. Deplores so much traveling.

26 March 1915. Sadness over the death of his mother the previous day.

30 Sept. 1915. Praises the beauty and quietness of Luxembourg Gardens.

75. To Henriette Fuchs. "Mardi." [1880's] Don 1153-75. Apologizes for the concerns at La Concordia [choral society for which he was accompanist]. Signs "Ach. Debussy."

76. To an unidentified performer. 21 Nov. 1903. Acq.222-74. Flatters the performer.

77. To his daughter Claude-Emma. Vienna, 2 Dec. 1910. Short postcards numbered 1, 2, 3, 5, 6. Don 1-78. Small pleasantries on postcards of German or Austrian soldiers in pompous poses.

78. To his daughter. Paris, 4 Oct. 1910. Don 1-78. Dispatched from England.

79. To his daughter. St. Petersburg, 11 Dec. 1913. Don 1-78. Charming and affectionate letter; he misses Chouchou. Has taken up with Koussevitzky in Moscow.

80. To his daughter. Moscow, 3 Feb. 1913. Don 1-78. Greetings on a short postcard.

81. As above. From St. Petersburg 28 Nov. 1913. Card arrived in Paris 3 Dec. 1913.

82. As above.

83. As above.

84. To his daughter. Berlin, 16 Dec. 1913. Don 1-78.

85. To his daughter. Amsterdam, 28 Feb. 1914. Don 1-78.

86. To his daughter. Rome, 21 Feb. 1914. Don 1-78.

87. To Emma [Mme. S. Bardac]. St. Rémy les chevreuse, 1904. This and all letters to Emma are indicated "Don 1-78." Contains brief musical fragment not identified.

88. To Emma. St. Rémy les chevreuse. 20 June 1904. Short card with greeting "Bonjour Mme Bardac."

89. To Emma. To Emma. Paris. 6 June 1904. Warm greetings upon her gift of flowers to him.

90. To Emma. No place or date. Numbers 90-101 contain affectionate and very brief greetings.

91. As above.

92. As above.

93. As above.

94. As above, with date "1e mai 1911."

95. As above, no date or place.

96. As above.

97. To Emma. 22 Aug. 1911.

98. To Emma. July 1912.

99. To Emma. No date or place.

100. As above.

101. As above.

102. Envelope only. "A Madame C. Debussy."

103. Calling card to Emma. "De la tendre part de ton jeune amant Claude et ton vieux mari Debussy. Total Claude Debussy."

104. Letter to Emma. No date or place. Speaks of "la vieille maison Usher" in a familiar way.

105. As above. His strong affection and appreciation of her constancy.

106. As above.

107. As above. Chides her gently to come see him [hospitalized?].

108. As above.

109. As above. Short note to "chère petite mienne."

110. As above. [Nov. 1913?] Trip to Prefecture of Police; anticipates trip to Ministry of Foreign Affairs and the Russian Consulate.

111. As above. Friendly greeting.

112. As above. Pensive; refers to "une prélude de Bach."

113. To Manuel de Falla. "Dimanche 13 janvier 1902" [photocopy]. Don 163-78. Gives advice on composition.

114. To De Falla. No place. July 1908. Photocopy. Don 163-78. Cordial greeting.

115. To De Falla. No place. 6 Dec. 1907. 2 ff. Photocopy. Don 163-78. Invitation for three days hence.

116. To De Falla. No place. 23 Oct. 1909. 2 ff. Photocopy. Don 163-78. Advises waiting to publish his songs, following discussion between Debussy and Durand.

117. To De Falla. No place. 23 Oct. 1913. 2 ff. Photocopy. Don 163-78. Invites De Falla to visit.

118. To De Falla. No place. 28 Sept. 1913. 2 ff. Photocopy. Don 163-76. Asks to postpone Friday's visit.

119. To De Falla. "Dimanche 9/10/19" [date uncertain]. Photocopy. Don 163-78. Asks De Falla to delay his visit by a day.

120. To Arthur Dandelot. 1 June 1915. Don 81-477.

<u>Note</u>: Letter 120 and all succeeding letters were unavailable for consultation.

121. To Claire Croiza. Paris. 3 June 1915. Don 83-167(27).

122. To Claire Croiza. 27 Jan. 1917. Photocopy. Don 83-167(27).

123. To Claire Croiza. 17 March [1917]. With envelope. Don 83-167.

124. To André Caplet. 10 June 1916. Don 83-266(69).

125. To Caplet. 22 July 1916. Don 83-266(69).

Unnumbered. To Raphael Martenot. [Paris] 29 Jan. 1905. W.46 (76). See below, in section Various Literary manuscripts.

Unnumbered. To Martenot. [Paris] 4 Feb. 1916. W.46 (77). See below, in section Various Literary Manuscripts.

Unnumbered. To Martenot. [Paris] 25 June 1903. W.46 (78). See below, in section Various Literary Manuscripts.

Unnumbered. To Martenot. [Paris. 15 Jan. 1900] W.46 (79). See below, in section Various Literary Manuscripts.

Unnumbered. To Martenot. [Paris] 9 Feb. 1916. W.46 (82). See below, in section Various Literary Manuscripts.

Unnumbered. To Paul Dukas. Visiting card. W.48 (185).

Unnumbered. Notebook. W.54 (1).

Unnumbered. Notebook. W.54 (2).

Unnumbered. Debussy's copy of "The Novel Lover's Calendar for 1915", with manuscript notes. W.54 (3).

<u>Bn Var.</u>
Various Literary Manuscripts of Debussy at the Bibliothèque nationale, Département de musique.

Vm. micr. 557 (microfilm), 5 images. Don 1965. Letter to A. Caplet. Paris. 19 Nov. 1912. 1 p. with article of 2 pp. on Rameau. Deliverable to H. Barron, London. Printed in **Lettres à A. Caplet**, item 11 [19 Nov. 1912].

Rés. Vma. ms. 1063 (1). 5 p., article having appeared April 1, 1901, in **Revue blanche**. Provenance A. Meyer coll.

Rés. Vma. ms. 1063 (2). 4 p., article having appeared June 1, 1901, in **Revue blanche**. Provenance Meyer coll.

Rés. Vma. ms. 1063 (3). 3 p., article having appeared Dec. 1, 1901, in **Revue blanche**.

Provenance A. Meyer coll.

Rés. Vmd. ms. 32. Carnet de notes de C. Debussy. Ms. auto. 3 p.; 110 x 180 mm. Don 123-80. Only the first p. contains notes.

Rés. Vmf. ms. 53. Carnet de notes et d'esquisses de Debussy. Ms. auto., 23 ff., 185 x 70 mm., ff. 9-13 unused. Don 80-123.

Rés. Vmf. ms. 54. Agenda de Debussy. Ms. autographe 1916, 69 ff. 150 x 90 mm. In ink and pencil. Don 123-80.

Rés. Vmf. ms. 55. Carnet de notes et d'adresses de C. Debussy. Ms. auto., ca. 1917, 15 ff. 145 x 75 mm. "Sans indication de date 1917." Don 123-80.

Open letter to the Archbishop of Paris, with G. d'Annunzio as joint signatory. Concerns the performance of **Le martyre** and reacts to the decision of the Archbishop of 1911. Shelved in Lettres autographes Annun zio (G. d'.) 8.

Letter to Raphael Martenot. [Paris] 29 Jan. 1905. Asks if a glissando is feasible on the harp. With a fragment of music by example of his question. Shelved under W. 46 (76).

Letter to R. Martenot. [Paris] 4 Feb. 1916. He has just had surgery and then radium treatment. Shelved under W. 46 (77).

Letter to Raphael Martenot. [Paris] 25 June 1903. Awaits the modifications by Martenot for the harp part of **Pelléas**. Shelved under W. 46 (78).

Letter to Raphael Martenot. [Paris] 15 Jan. [1900?]. Visiting card with thanks for Martenot's sympathies. Shelved under number W.46 (79).

Letter to Raphael Martenot. [Paris] 9 Feb. 1916. Does not sense repugnance at the Negro's state. Acq. 7456. Shelved under number W. 46 (82).

Letter to unknown addressee. Paris, 21 Feb., 1904. 209 x 224 mm., 1 page. Appreciation of the grammophone. Shelved under Cote F.S. 164.

Bn Chouchou

Letters by Claude-Emma Debussy [Chouchou] at the Bibliothèque nationale, Département de musique.

1. To Raoul Bardac. [Paris] 8 April 1918. Don 253-62. Important, innocent recounting of Debussy's death. Published in Lockspeiser biography.
2. To unknown recipient. Don 1-78.
3. To her mother. With envelope. Don 1- 78.
4. To her mother. 25 Dec. 1911. Don 1- 78.
5. To her father. Paris. 1913. With envelope. Don 1-78.
6. Photocopy of a poem by Chouchou that appeared in the newspaper of St. Jean de Luz, 11 Sept. 1918. Typed copy.
7. To her father or mother. Typed copy.

Bn Emma

Letters by Emma Debussy at the Bibliothèque nationale, Département de musique.

1. To R. Brussel. Montpensier. 7 March 1920.
2. To Ricardo Viñes. From St. Jean de Luz [3 July 1918]. 2 folios with envelope. Acq. 4.481 BN 1-50.
3. To Loïe Fuller. No place or date [1913/14?]. Acq. 590-63.
4. As above. Regarding a representation of **Boîte à joujoux**.
5. To Gabriel Astruc. Paris, 31 May 1932. Don 1031-66. Card inviting him to the inauguration of the Debussy monument.
6. To Astruc. No date [1932]. Don 1031- 66. Repeated invitation, as above.
7. To Astruc. No date [1932]. Don 1031- 66. Invitation to attend the Debussy festival.
8. As above.
9. As above.
10. To Astruc. No place or date [1932?]. 2 ff. Don 1031-66. Concerns invitations [to others] regarding the Debussy festival.
11. To Pierre de Bréville. [Paris, 27 April 1916]. Don 1521. Dossier Breville.
12. To Roger Long [spelling unclear]. [3 Dec. 1932]. With envelope. Don 78-68.
13. As above, dated 7 Dec. 1931.
14. As above, dated 27 June 1933.
15. As above, dated 31 Oct. 1933.
16. To L'association d'expansion artistique.
17. As above, dated 20 June 1927.
18. As above, dated 1 June 1927.
19. As above, dated 19 Aug. 1927.

20. As above, dated 2 Oct. 1927.
21. As above, dated 6 Oct. 1927.
22. As above, dated 22 Oct. 1927.
23. To Mme Léon Boellmann. Signed E. Bardac. Paris, 13 Oct. 1897. Don 199-78.
24. To Jane Rodrigues. St. Jean de Luz. Don 80-503.
25. To Jane Rodrigues. 8 p. Don 80-503.
26. To Jane Rodrigues. No date or place.
27. As above. 4 p.
28. To Jane Rodrigues. Ste. Adresse.
29. To Jane Rodrigues. Toulon. 11 Aug. 1932. 2 folios in pencil with envelope.
30. To Jane Rodrigues. Paris, 23 June 1924. With envelope.
31. To Claire Croiza. Don 83-67 (27)
32. To Claire Croiza. Paris, 23 May 1929. Don 83-167 (27).
33. To Claire Croiza. Don 83-167 (27).
34. As above [1923?].
35. To Claire Croiza. 2 ff. Don 83-167 (27).
36. As above. Unnumbered. To Paul Dukas. [1918]. W.48 (186).

<u>Bn main</u>
Letters and Scrapbook Signature at Bibliothèque nationale, Département des manuscrits [main library]

1. To unknown addressee. No place or date. Ms. 24839 (Nouv. Acq. Fr.) ser. 4, no. 2406. Thanks him for his article on **Pelléas** and his impressions, which he refrains from discussing, since his views are as valuable as Debussy's own. [Probably a subtle reaction to an unfavorable press review.]
2. To Paul Nadar [photographer]. 19 June 1909. Ms. vol. 24267, item no. 2705 (Nouv. Acq. Fr.). Thanks Nadar warmly for the quality of his photographic work and expresses desire that posterity will refer above all to Nadar's photographs of his likeness.
3. Ms. 14695 Nouv. Acq. Fr. Scrapbook destined for the photographer P. Nadar, with Debussy's signature along with those of P. Viardot, Th. Dubois, C. de Bériot, and others, mostly from period 1893-95.

Lang
Collection Musicale François Lang, Royaumont. Contains autograph musical materials as listed in the present Catalogue of Works as well as numerous autograph letters by Debussy to the following:

Alfred Lang. Congratulating him on the birth of his daughter Isabel.

Emile Baron. Written from Villa Médicis, Rome, on Dec. 23, 1886. Famous letter on distractions caused by a female.

Pierre Louÿs. "21 juillet 1894" postmark; addressed to Louÿs in Biskra, Algeria.

P.J. Toulet. Letters dated by Debussy "5 mai [19]06, 9 mai [19]06, 22 mai 06, 20 juillet 06, 26 aout 06, 14 mai 1907, 10 juillet 1907, [postmark] 27-8-1907, 22 jan. 08, [postmark] 14-3-1908, 23 III 09, [postmark London] May 22, 09, 8 IX 09, 17 X 09, 4 XI, 09, 16 V 10, 1 juin 1910, 14 VI 10, 24 VIII 10, 3 X 10, 29 X 10, 8 XI 10, 7 XII 10, [postmark] 5 avril 1911, [postmark] 11 V 1911, 19 VII, 11, 5 sept. 1911, 20 nov. 1911, [postmark] 20 2 1912, 20 juin 1917, 5 juillet [1912], 7 juin 1917," [postmark unclear] 1917, 9 juillet 1917, [n.d.] "Mon Cher Toulet, Ma femme pensait...," [n.d.] "Cher Toulet, ceci est écrit..."

The Lang Collection also possesses a MS article and review, "La Chambre d'enfants de Moussourgsky...," first published in **La Revue blanche** April 15, 1901.

LC

Library of Congress, Washington, D.C., USA

Letter from Batchelder Collection:
Not dated, addressee unidentified [ca. 1893, possible to Chausson]. Begins "Cher Ami!" Misses his friendship. Has completed first act of **Pelléas**. Call no. ML31.B4.

Letters to Theodore Szánto. 4 letters, call number ML94.S97 case.

1. 16 IX [19]10. Pneumatique. Asks Szánto to visit him to discuss urgent matters.

2. 18 juin [19]11. Is leaving the following day for Turin but will return the 27th. Asks him to visit him thereafter.

3. 6 VI [19]10. Has seen his brother and Dr. Hubay. Requests his visit.

4. 11 août [19]11. Written from Orgeval, Seine-et-Oise. Diplomatic letter, apparently refusing an invitation to a concert tour. Acknowledges no obligation to Rózsavölgyi, despite cordial relationship.

The Szánto collection also contains 3 envelopes without letters, cancelled 14-10-11, 19-juin-11, and 7-8-10.

Letter to [Pierre Louÿs], no date. Call no. ML95.D3 case. 1 leaf. Short note suggesting dinner at Louÿs's home the next day.

To Jenó Hubay:

1. 26 IX [19]10, 80 Ave, du Bois de Boulogne. Call number ML95.D3 case. Refers to D's business arrangements with the Maison Rózsavölgyi in Budapest, repudiating rival arrangements for performances that Hubay proposed to make for him. A long, carefully worded letter exemplary of D's social and diplomatic skills.

2. 1 novembre 1910. Call number, content and interest as in the preceding.

Letter to Jean Marnold. 29 juillet/[19]02, Bichain, par Villeneuve la Guyard, Yonne. Addressed to "Cher Monsieur" with envelope addressed to J. Marnold. 2 leaves. Call no. ML95.D3 case.

Speaks of complete fatigue and his surroundings, which have a "natural aesthetic" of chickens and roosters. Famous letter, including remark that Wagner's music is only "a beautiful sunset." Perhaps what he has just written [Pelléas] has little importance.

Morgan

Letters of Debussy in the Cary Collection and Koch Foundation Collections, Pierpont Morgan Library. The following list and annotations have graciously been provided by J. Rigbie Turner, Curator of Music Manuscripts.

1. To Em[ile] Baron in Paris. Villa Medici, 5 Jan. 1887. Chides Baron for not writing, suggests that the monogram is somewhat large for the small paper and asks that it be changed to white and reduced in size. Requests a copy of Jean Ajalbert's **Paysage des femmes**. 3 pp. 16o, with envelope. Koch Collection 558, box 89. Publ. in Francis Ambrière, item 10.

2. To Mme Dansaert [?], no place or date. Explanation by way of apology, stating that "l'u-tile aventure" must not become "la noire aventure." Asks her to tell René [Peter] that there has been no tragedy, adding that he [Debussy] has the perhaps disagreeable habit of

saying things a bit harshly, etc. 3 pp. 12o. Publ. in René Peter, Claude Debussy [item 88] (Paris: Gallimard, 1952), 220. Morgan Library collection.

3. To [Dr.] Abel Desjardins [Paris, 5? September 1899]. Invites Desjardins to come the following Wednesday to meet "ma petite Lilly" [i.e. Rosalie Texier], saying not to hesitate in telling her if her case is serious. 2 pp. 16o with envelope. Publ. in Lesure Lettres, 99. Morgan Library coll.

4. To [Serge] Diaghilev. [Paris] 20 May 1917. Concerns the Ballets Russes, describing his impressions of a performance he attended the previous Wednesday [16 May], etc. 2 pp. 12o. Koch collection 302 (box 60).

5. To [Serge] Diaghilev. Paris, 26 May 1917. Congratulates Diaghilev and Massine on their use of Fauré's **Pavane** [in **Las meninas**] and states that Stravinsky's **Petruchka** is definitely a **chef d'oeuvre**. 1 p. 8o with envelope. Koch 303 (box 60). Publ, in Lesure and Nichols.

6. To Paul Dukas. [Paris] 13 Mar. 1901. Asks if Dukas received his letter, mentions some music they heard together, etc. 1 p. 8o with envelope. Koch 558.

7. [To Edwin Evans in London.] [Paris] 28 August 1908. Regrets that he cannot accept the invitation made by Evans on behalf of the Philharmonic Society, explaining that he has been engaged for three months to conduct a concert with H.J. Wood's orchestra at Queen's Hall on 27 February 1909 and that Wood justifiably has asked for the premiere of Debussy's **Images**, adding that it would be impossible to give Evans a new work, etc. 2 pp. 8o. Koch 1076.

8. To E[dwin] Evans in London. [Paris] 18 April 1909. Concerns in its entirety the aesthetic principles of **Pelléas**, saying that Evans should eliminate from discussion whether or not there is melody in it, that there is no "guiding thread" in **Pelléas** and no use of leitmotivs. The simplicity of **Pelléas** must be insisted upon: "I have endeavored to prove that people who sing can yet remain human and natural, without ever needing to resemble madmen and puzzles...", etc. 2 pp. 8o

with envelope. Publ. in English in item 753, p. 231. Koch 1019 (box 112).

9. [To Eugene Fromont.] [Bichain] 28 August 1901. Acknowledges late receipt of the piano pieces; criticizes the design of the title page of **Pour le piano**. Asks Fromont to send a copy of his **Nocturnes** to G. Longy, adding "Parlez-moi de **Pelléas**," etc. 2 pp. 8o. See Grayson, **Genesis of "Pelléas"** [item 753], 53 and 296. Koch 847 (box 106).

10. To [Eugène] Fromont. [Paris?] 30 March 1905. Concerns the transfer of the rights to **Pelléas** to Durand, expressing regrets over what has happened but adding that "we have had a bit of happiness with **Pelléas**. Let this console you for the pain of having to relinquish it." States that he will have the **Suite bergamasque** on Saturday. 2 pp. 16o. Koch Coll. 848 (box 106). See item 753, p. 109 and 311, n. 26.

11. To Mme [Eugène] Fromont. [Paris?] 21 April 1905. States that she will have the **Suite bergamasque** the following day, that she is wrong to have allowed **Rêverie** to appear--a piece without importance written for Hart mann-- and saying that he agrees to the transfer of **Pour le piano** only if no mention is made of the **Mazurka**: "Je n'ai vraiment aucun goût pour ce genre de morceau," etc. 2 pp. 12o. Koch 849 (box 106).

12. To P.B. Gheusi. 5 letters dated [Paris] 27 April 1914-2 December 1915. Discusses a number of musical matters, certain performances of **Pelléas**. Mentions Henri [i.e., Henry] Russell, [Vanni-]Marcoux, Higgins, and others, etc. 5 pp. 24o with 4 integral address leaves. Morgan Library collection.

13. To [Georges] Hartmann. [Paris] 15 Jan. 1899. Is sending one of his **Nocturnes**. Apologizes for the delay and asks Hartmann to keep the first page to serve as the cover. 2 pp. 24o. Koch 16 (box 1).

14. To M. [Georges] Hartmann. Two letters [Paris? both] , one dated 13 June 1899, the other not dated. Concerns the binding of the **Trois nocturnes** for orchestra; asks him to change the date of a meeting with Debussy. 4 pp. 16o with one integral address leaf. Morgan Library collection.

15. To D.-E. Inghelbrecht. [Paris, 13 June 1912]. States that it is agreed for tomorrow evening at 6 p.m. 1 p. 24o with envelope. Cary collection.

16. [To Louis Laloy]. Paris, 8 April 1907. Concerns Maurice Ravel. 3 pp. 16o. Koch 161 (box 23).

17. To Pierre Louÿs in Constantine, Algeria. [Paris, 27 July 1894]. Mentions work on **Pelléas** and states that he dined with André Gide and [Paul] Valéry. Mentions F.A. Hérold, Gaby [Gabrielle Dupont], etc. 2 pp. obl. 24o with envelope. Printed in part in item 811. Koch 423.

18. To Pierre [Louÿs]. [Paris?] 24 Sept. 1898. Apologizes for something from the previous evening and reaffirms his affection for Louÿs. 1 p. 16o. Koch 245 (box 57).

19. To P[ierre] Louÿs. Two letters [Paris, 26 October 1910, and n.p., n.d.]. Apologizes for not visiting since his [Debussy's] return to Paris, stating that his **Trois nocturnes** will be played the next day chez Lamoureux, etc. 2 pp. 2o with one integral address leaf. Koch 839 (box 106).

20. [To Jean Marnold]. [Paris?] 8 Aug. 1904. Stating that it was not right to have responded so badly to such affectionate statements, explaining that he had been encumbered with music and promising to see Mlle Burgoin without delay. 1 p. 12o. Cary collection.

21. To [Gabriel] Mourey. [Paris] 17 Nov. 1913. "All artifice is plainly visible as the melodic line cannot help support it with coloristic effects." After numerous trials, Mourey must be content with a solo "flûte de Pan" without any other accompaniment. 2 pp. 16o. Koch 152 (box 22).

22. To Mme M.V.A. Peter. [Paris?, no date, perhaps early 1898]. Is sending the preface; he thinks it is "un joli coup de trompette." Asks her to tell René [Peter] that the letter to Valette is unnecessary: the manuscript has been received by a committee of five, of whom four are personal friends of Pierre [Louÿs]; adds that "je ne mets pas 'mes mains dans les vôtres'" [V. Hugo, Correspondance), etc. 1 p. 24o with integral

address leaf. Morgan Library collection.

23. To René Peter, 12 letters. [Paris, 1897-98 and n.d.]. Makes appointments. Mentions Augusta Holmès; the "pantomime si esthétique" by Mme [J.-L.] Forain [**Le cheva lier d'or**]; asks him to burn a letter--"il y a des mains indiscrètes chez toi"--mentioning Pierre Louÿs and his preface [to **La tragédie de la mort**], etc. 14 pp. various sizes with one envelope and several integral address leaves. Eight publ. (three incom pletely) in René Peter, **Claude Debussy** [item 88] (Paris: Gallimard, 1952), p. 202, 205, 208-09, 213, and 215. Morgan Library collection.

24. To René Peter, signed "Hamlet." [Paris] 10 August 1899. Tells Peter to be very rich when he comes on Sunday, and apologizes for his role of "master borrower," hoping it will be the last time. 1 p. 24o. Publ. in item 23, p. 99. Cary collection.

25. [To André Poniatowski]. [Paris?] February 1893. Confides his parents' disappointment at his failure to establish himself, describing how one's worries can develop a Cult of Desire. States that in **Werther** Massenet showed himself to be a master in the art of pandering to stupid ideas and amateur scandals, sentimentalizing a fine subject. The same thing happened in Gounod's **Faust** and Thomas's **Hamlet**. Praises G. Charpentier, a follower of Berlioz ("a tremendous humbug"), etc. 10 pp. 8o. Publ. in item 23, p. 38-41; in item 29 (Nichols) no. 77; and in part in E. Lockspeiser item 85 vol. I, 170-72. Koch collection 160 (box 23).

26. [To Adolfo Salazar]. [Paris] 18 April 1916. When he heard of the death of poor Granados he was ill and about to be operated on. Since the operation he is still not well. Comments on Granados's music. 1 p. 120. Cary collection.

27. To Rosalie ("Lilly") Texier (Debussy). Mostly Paris, 1899-1905 [and no date]. Some 50 letters, largely of a personal and affectionate nature. ca. 210 pp. 8o (and other sizes) with envelopes or integral address leaves. Koch collection 197 (box 25). 2 publ. in Nichols, nos. 76 and 118.

28. To E[mile] Vuillermoz. [Paris] 24 June 1913. States that if he has been satisfied he

would be ungracious not to do his share; he has to fight against himself; his fear of boredom is like a canker; he has received an anonymous letter, evidently written by a German, demanding a refund for a ticket, etc. 1 p. 24o. Koch 500 (box 84).

29. To an unidentified friend. No place, "Jeudi" Feb. 1893. Koch 160.

30. To an unidentified friend. [Paris?, 1894] "Vendredi." States that today he has rehearsed Mlle Sidner, who will sing three Grieg songs; mentions his concert in Brussels on March 1. 2 pp. 16o. Koch 286 (box 59).

31. To an unidentified recipient. Paris, 30 Dec. 1903. The recipient will receive a corrected copy of the **Nocturnes**; asks that in performance the chorus be placed in the orchestra, not in front of it. 2 pp. 240. Koch 5 (box 1).

32. To an unidentified recipient. "près Dieppe," 19 August 1906. Agrees to modifications in the role of Pelléas. 1 p. 12o. Koch 285 (box 59).

33. To "Mon cher Maître" [otherwise unidentified]. [Paris] 27 July 1916. The Nationale will not reinstate their engagement since he has not paid his premiums for six years, that nothing remains for them except a guaranteed prize regarding the author's rights--"after my death, of course"--but will the adversary be content with the meager meal? Mentions **Pelléas**: "the masterpiece written in misery is a very old legend," etc. 2 pp. 12o. Cary collection.

34. To an unidentified recipient. No place, 25 Dec. 1916. States that the book has not yet appeared: having been ill, he has not worked on it; hence the postponements. 1 p. obl. 24o. Koch 470 (box 83).

35. To an unidentified recipient. [Paris, no date]. Is sending two seats and apologizes that he does not have more. 1 p. 24o. Cary collection.

36. Autograph statement [letter?] No place or date. Refers to the invitation to Grieg to conduct a Concert Colonne, stating that it was at the time of "L'Affaire" [i.e., the Dreyfus affair] and that Grieg said in a letter that he did not wish to set foot in country where liberty was

understood so poorly. 1 p. 8o. See the opening of Debussy's article on Grieg in **Monsieur Croche** (ed. F. Lesure) [item 47], 149.

NY Public

Letters at the Toscanini Memorial Archives, New York Public Library, Lincoln Center, New York.

1. To an unidentified friend. No place or date. 1 p. Short note beginning "Ami, d'abord merci."

[the following not examined:]

2. To the Marquis de Casafuerte. Paris, May 7 1917. 1 p.

3. To Mons. Dandelot. 10 Mar. 1917. 1 p.

4. To Eva Gauthier. 12 Apr., 1910. In Gauthier Collection.

5. To Pierre Louÿs. April 1888. 2 p., with envelope.

6. To Jean Marnold [postmarked 1902]. 1 p., with envelope.

7. To Jean Marnold. 22 Jan., 1908. 2 p. with envelope.

Opéra

Letters at the Bibliothèque de l'Opéra, Paris. In the Collection Jacques Rouché [director of the Opéra 1914-44].

1. Claude Debussy to J. Rouché. 26 March 1915. 1 f. Announces to Rouché the death of Debussy's mother.

2. Debussy to Rouché. Paris, without date. "Très touché de votre affectueuse présence, cher Monsieur Rouché."

3. Debussy to Charles Malherbe. No place or date. 2 ff. States that Debussy is sending Malherbe the manuscript for the Universal Exposition of 1900 [of the **Nuits blanches**, the projected second set of the **Proses lyriques**].

4. Emma Debussy to Tugal. No place or date. 5 ff. Proposes sending documents on **Boîte à joujoux** and a photo of Debussy.

5. Emma Debussy to Jacques Rouché. No place or date. 3 ff. Serge Lifar has discussed his desire to perform **Prélude-faune**.

6. Emma Debussy to Rouché. No place or date. 1 f. Brief thanks.

7. Emma Debussy to Rouché. Paris, without date. 2 ff. Requests authorization for Mlle

Laval to sing in **Pelléas** at the Royal Opera of Madrid.

8. Emma Debussy to Rouché. No place or date. 1 f. Requests permission for Thilu to participate in the gala festival of homage to Debussy, for the performance of **Ode à la France**.

9. Emma Debussy to Rouché. No place or date. 1 f. Indicates performance lengths of various sections of **Pelléas** as conducted by Debussy.

Popelin

Nine letters to Claudius Popelin and his son Gustave, written from Rome in 1885-87, are in the collection of Margaret Cobb. See the article by Cobb, "Claude Debussy to Claudius and Gustave Popelin: Nine Unpublished Letters." **Nineteenth-Century Music** XIII/1 (Summer 1989), 39-48. Also contains full texts of two letters published previously, one in part. The letters comment on the relationship of D to the Vasnier family and the biography during the Rome period generally.

Stockholm.

Stiftelsen Musikkulturens Främjande; Riddargatan 35-37; S-114 57 Stockholm, Sweden. [None of the following examined:]

1. Debussy to Anton Zelling, La Haye. 22 May 1916. Speaks of an article [in a periodical?] and of Zelling's compatriot J. Salmon.

2. Debussy, Claude. Autograph article entitled **Une sonate pour piano de Paul Dukas**. Publ. in **La revue blanche** 15 April, 1901. Repr. in Monsieur Croche (items 45 and 47).

3. Debussy, Emma to A. Carré. 25 May, 1905. Begins "J'aurais beaucoup aimé vous voir hier soir, cher Monsieur..."

4. Debussy, Emma to A. Carré. [25 May, 1905?] Begins "Cher Monsieur, Un accident au bras droit m'interdisant..."

Texas

Letters and related materials at the Harry Ransom Humanities Research Center, the University of Texas.

Autograph Letters-Texas

1. To unidentified lawyer. July 21, 1916. Deep concerns over a legal matter, mentioning "Madame Texier" [Lilly Texier Debussy] and entertaining suicide as an escape.

2. Letters to unidentified recipients.

1. August 2, 1916. [written at] Grand Hotel, Le Moulleau, Arcachon (Gironde). Recommends an artistic director for the Casino municipal de Cannes.

2. August 16, 1899. Has been in bed with rheumatism. Is sending two songs, one with its bass and the other "que vous ferez complètement."

3. "Mardi" [no date]. A note concerning work on **Pelléas** written apparently to a close friend. Mentions Jusseaume, who now understands him, and Rousin [?].

4. Nov. 8, 1901. Remarks on a criticism by Pierre Lalo, whom Debussy terms "critique avisé mais faible philosophe."

5. No date, written from 58 Rue Cardinet. Is occupied by the reprise of **Pelléas**. Intends a meeting with Carré concerning the evening concert in Brussels. Hopes that Carré will release Mary Garden for the single evening concert there.

6. August 13, 1908. Arranges a meeting.

7. Oct. 29, 1907. Is glad to add his name to the homage to Grieg.

8. Dec. 31, 1907. New Year's wishes. Is leaving for London next month.

9. Feb. 25, 1914. Has just returned from Rome and is leaving for Amsterdam this evening. Has read the scenario of **Tania** and is persuaded that it will become a fine representation. However, the press of time hinders him from taking it up and urges a collaboration with another composer.

10. March 19, 1916. Continues to believe that **Tania** has much interest but argues that a musical treatment would require a Musorgsky or another Russian. He does not possess that disposition, and his illness distracts him. He finally will return the manuscript [scenario] of **Tania**.

3. To André Antoine. September 20, 1904. [Published in Antoine, **Souvenirs**, item 167] Important letter concerning the incidental music for **King Lear** by D. Asks Antoine for additional time and specifies that an orchestra of at least 30 players is needed.

4. Letters to Gabriel Astruc.

1. May 22, 1911. Concerns seating of guests at the premiere of **Le martyre de St. Sébastien**.

2. No date. Concerns the audition of singers, probably for **Martyre**. Mentions Mlle Martyl, Mr Dutilloy, Mr Priddez, Bourbon (engaged by Mr Higgins), and Mr Hubardeau.

5. Letters to Bertault.

1. Jan. 8, 1913. Postpones an unidentified event from March to April 25.

2. Nov. 13, 1913. Has received a legal notice from the attorney J. Gillet concerning a certain withdrawal ("mainlevée"). Asks Bertault for advice.

3. Nov. 25, 1913. Legal wrangles, described in excited terms and written in a code of initials. Asks for Bertault's advice.

4. Dec. 23, 1913. Things are still going badly. Has not received the loan of 25,000 francs. Mr Crevel has just telephoned, but Debussy refused to take the call.

5. March 12, 1914. Has received another telephone call from "le vieux bandit." Might he receive Bertault and "la personne en question" Saturday afternoon, concerning the 4800 francs?

6. To Raymond Bonheur. July 28, 1901. Unfortunately the planned visit with Bonheur in Magny has been delayed by a slight illness, and Debussy soon will leave for Burgundy on a visit. Expresses friendly affection for Bonheur.

7. To Albert Carré. October 30, 1909. Has just heard the audition of Mr Coulomb for the part of Pelléas. Praises his voice as pretty and intelligent.

8. To Albert Carré. October 31, 1909. Short greeting including the quotation "Qu'il en soit comme il a voulu." Note in unidentified hand: "removed from the piano-vocal score of **Pelléas**."

9. To Ernest Chausson.

1. October 2, 1893. Quite important and expressive letter concerning struggles in the composition of **Pelléas**, in which he meets the spectre of old Klingsor, alias R. Wagner. Is discovering silence as an agent of expression. [publ. in Lesure [item 23], p. 55-57.

2. "Lundi" [October 24, 1893 on envelope.] Speaks on Chausson's hard work on **Le roi Arthus**. Remarks on Wagner, Mallarmé, and Bach vis-à-vis

Pelléas. Publ. in Lesure [item 23], pp. 57-59.

10. To Nico Coronio. No date. Appreciates the frankness of his letter, even if Coronio is not different from his other friends. At least he has the courage to speak "à la bête fauve."

11. To Dr. V. Crepel. July 15, 1913. Notes that Mme Debussy has need of Crepel's visit as soon as possible.

12. To V. Cyril. June 23, 1914. Does not believe it advisable to announce their intentions, which would indicate "une source aux librettistes altérés."

13. To Dandelot. May 18, 1917. Asks for the address of Diaghilev. Has been unable to speak to him personally to congratulate him on the particular beauty of the Ballets russes.

14. To Dorbon-Ainé, bookseller.

1. March 23, 1910. Asks Dorbon to stop by his home, for he has a group of books that he wishes to sell.

2. March 9, 1913. Again asks for Dorbon to visit concerning the sale of some books. Notes that Debussy and Dorbon may discuss **Monsieur Croche** [the proposed edition of D's critical writings] at that time.

3. May 28, 1914 [postmark]. Work on correcting the proofs of **Monsieur Croche** for publication by Dorbon. Promises his revisions within the week.

15. To Enaux. August 3, 1909. Has just written to Mr Lyon to learn the precise time allowed for writing the piece promised to J. Risler.

16. To Félix Fénéon. No date. Requests another issue, "un autre numéro en plus de mon service."

17. To Raymond Geiger. July 13, 1915. Questions the veracity of a report of appendicitis affecting Mary Garden. Comments on the horrors of the war.

18. To Georges Hartmann.

1. No date. Delivers **Sirènes** [**Nocturnes**] to Hartmann, which required twelve days of hard effort.

2. Jan. 6, 1897. Is it understood that Colonne is to play **La saulaie**? Is unable to have

the score ready until somewhat later. Is enclosing a score that Hartmann had given him.

3. Sept. 14, 1897. The musical plan for **Le chevalier d'or** is complete and the composition will require two and a half months. One can be assured of the Forains' agreement.

4. Dec. 31, 1897. Important letter stating goals for the **Trois nocturnes**, describing difficulties with them, and regretting that they are not completed.

5. Feb. 24, 1898. Letter torn off and incomplete. Does not want the concert season to end without having heard the **Nocturnes**.

6. May 15, 1898. Again regrets that his hands are "vides de musique." Mentions a forthcoming reading [of the **Nocturnes**] by Carré.

7. June 16, 1898. Asks Hartmann to invite him to dinner, when he may discuss an urgent matter.

8. No date; not signed; perhaps last page missing. Has completed the **Nocturnes** excepting the orchestration. Describes the cover of the **Chansons de Bilitis**. Speaks of "complications sentimentales." A treaty involving Carré and Messager might be fortuitous for **Pelléas**. He anticipates **Pelléas** to be something new in art and exciting for the contemporary sensibility.

9. July 23, 1898. Attributes the fumbling of the last letter to neuralgia; has had a crisis of confidence. Reports nightmares, in one of which Golaud was transformed into a bailiff.

10. Nov. 16, 1898. Flatters Hartmann that he is not a publisher "pour un sou." The orchestration of **Nocturnes** goes forward. Asks for an advance of 200 francs.

11. No date ["Fév. 1899" on postmark]. Promises to submit the **Nocturnes** by Saturday. People ask forcefully for the **Chansons de Bilitis**.

12. Jan. 1, 1899. Mlle Dupont, "mon secrétaire," has cancelled her engagement. Many troubles. The **Nocturnes** are en route.

13. Feb. 3, 1899. Asks for an invitation to dinner Wednesday next, when he will bring the **Nocturnes** augmented by several reworkings that will please Hartmann.

14. Feb. 16, 1899. Hartmann will have the **Nocturnes** by next Wednesday without fail.

15. April 20, 1899. List in outline form works in progress or recently completed: **Nocturnes, Images pour piano, Nuits blanches, La saulaie.**

16. June 2, 1899. Arranges a meeting with Hartmann.

17. Jan. 12, 1900. Has withheld the proof of the last **Nocturne** because of many errors. Complains of material difficulties. Requests an advance of 250 francs.

18. March 1, 1900. He and Mme Debussy will come to dinner Saturday. Is troubled that he has not received the proofs of **Sirènes**.

19. "Mardi soir. Mars 1900." General frustration concerning the preparation of the **Nocturnes** by Colonne. The chorus is not prepared, the rehearsal time too brief.

19. To Georges Jean-Aubry. 21 letters and one printed notice of the death of Debussy's father, contained in a large envelope bearing the return address of the **Mercure de France** and dated Nov. 15, 1952.

1. [postmarked Jan. 8, 1911]. Speaks of trip to Geneva, Brussels, Nancy and happiness in returning to Paris. In Budapest he read Jean-Aubry's article in the **Revue de Hongrie**; heard a "tzigane" named Radics.

2. Nov. 30, 1916. No news from England and thus cannot give certain indications. Speaks of Count Zeppelin and his "sinistres joujoux."

3. Nov. 3, 1916. Asks Jean-Aubry to exert some influence concerning an arrangement with the military on behalf of Raoul Bardac. Invites Aubry to dinner to discuss details.

4. March 20, 1917. To Aubry in England. Responds to several questions concerning the price of registered mail [for scores?], a concert involving a fine harpist, and brief personal messages. Requests Aubry's assistance for an indigent Swiss violinist in London named Notweg.

5. May 19, 1917. To Aubry in England. Has an article [in English] by him, which in Mme Debussy's translation is charming. G. Poulet premiered the violin sonata. The big book on Debussy will have to await better times, which are still far off.

6. March 3, 1917. Economic difficulties. Asks for clarification concerning the "Orchestrelle Co." and the piano rolls brought out by Aeolian.

7. Printed notice of the death of Debussy's father, "Monsieur Achille Debussy," died Oct. 28, 1910, at the age of 74.

8. March 2, 1910. Is sorry for his slowness in writing. His health hinders him. Will see him in Paris at the performance of **Ibéria**.

9. March 25, 1910. Notes that his brother is very nice but accustomed to music halls.

Recollections at Aubry's behest of Mallarmé concerning the **Prélude-faune**. Describes a meeting at Debussy's and the short poem Mallarmé wrote on a score.

10. March 7, 1909. Complains of daily hemorrhages.

11. April 30, 1909. Has met Aubry's friends the Liebigs, who are charming. Is planning a trip to London in May for the final rehearsals of **Pelléas**.

12. Dec. 31, 1909. Are the recent news concerning Caplet true? He wrote of his unhappiness to Debussy's wife.

13. Contains a margin note by Aubry that Debussy wrote this note in 1910 or 1911 to indicate the minimum number of instruments necessary to the performance of **Prélude-faune**. In Debussy's hand, an outline of the number of instruments.

14. Jan. 22, 1908. Must take to the sea to hear **La mer**. The London concert is fixed for Feb. 1 at Grosvenor Hotel.

15. Jan. 3, 1908. Responds to Aubry's questions concerning biographical information. Cannot remember certain dates. He recalls writing for **Gil Blas** in 1903 as well.

16. March 6, 1908. Philosophizing on likes and dislikes among audiences and on lack of enthusiasm among performers. Speaks of Caplet's good arrangement of La Mer for two pianos. Asks for the return of the book by Mme Liebich. The binding of **Pelléas**.

17. [postmark April 1, 1908.] Asked **Musica** for the article on Gounod but received no reponse; bad administration. Yesterday heard two songs by Caplet, which he liked.

18. [postmark April 11, 1908.] Is unable to supply the dates Aubry requested for the period of Debussy's life in question. Concerning the **Images** [piano], Viñes gently must be persuaded to work hard on them, for he does not understand their architecture, in spite of his virtuosity. Difficulties finding a player of the chromatic harp.

19. [Postmark April 24, 1908.] Has read his article, which Debussy finds comprehensive and well written. Caplet has brought him cigarettes.

20. Sept. 29, 1908. Short greeting.

21. Feb. 24, 1909. Is leaving for London the following day to conduct **Nocturnes** and **Prélude-faune** on the 27th.

20. To Jacqueline and Lacombe.

1). To Jacqueline, Dec. 7, 1912. Hopes that the accident sustained by Mr Lacombe will have no serious results.

2). To Lacombe, Dec. 18, 1912. Hopes for his recovery and requests Lacombe to establish a date for Debussy.

21. To Lindenlaub. Nov. 23, 1903. Thanks him for his gracious words on **Prélude-faune** and contrasts his remarks to those of unsympathetic critics.

22. To Pierre Louÿs. June 1, 1898. Has been ill. Requests his visit the next day.

23. To Pierre Louÿs.

1). No date. M. Peter has sent his "Nouvelle" to the "concours du Journal." Asks for clarification.

2). Dimanche [no date]. Invites him and presents a ticket to the rehearsal of **Pelléas**.

24. To Vanni Marcoux. May 22, 1909. Written from London. Thanks him for his fine performance of Arkel but subtly suggests a greater expressivity and proper intonation.

25. To Blanche Marot.

1). Aug. 6, 1900. Projects the first performance of **Damoiselle élue** on 23 Aug. If she will be able to sing, can she go to work immediately?

2). Aug. 14, 1900. Will she meet with him and Taffanel?

3). August 24, 1900. Warm thanks for her performance of the **Damoiselle**. A beautiful letter still unpublished.

4). Sept. 13, 1900. He and Mme Debussy hope to see her tomorrow.

5). Dec. 8, 1900. Apologizes that the three concert seats were refused flatly by Chevillard.

6). Aug. 13, 1901. Concerns **Proses lyriques** and regrets that the Société nationale has not allowed more rehearsal time.

26. To Catulle Mendès. Dec. 9, 1897. Thanks him for supervising the performance of the **Quatuor** but cannot go ahead with the song performance.

27. To Gabriel Mourey. 9 letters.

1). Jan. 6, 1909. Is struggling between desire to please the public and his reluctance to finish.

2). Jan. 22, 1908. Concerns his anticipation

of **Damoiselle élue** performance but disagrees with choice of Théâtre des Arts.

3). Nov. 4, 1908. Too busy to pursue the project now: **Pelléas** again at the Opéra-Comique: Chevillard is playing **La mer**. Remarks on Maurice Denis.

4). Oct. 3, 1909. Remarks on the **Opinion** and the **Salon d'Automne**.

5). No date. Brief response.

Letters 6-9 to Mourey not examined.

28. Typed copy of original letter to the Metropolitan Opera, New York. July 5, 1908. Makes firm arrangements for the proposed performance of the two Poe operas.

29. To René Peter.

1). From Lilly Debussy to Peter. No date. Brief note of friendship.

The following from Claude Debussy to Peter:

2). No date. "Cher ami, c'est aujourd'hui..."

3). "Mon cher René, remettons notre rendez-vous..."

4). "Vieux René. Bonheur est venu..."

5). Dec. 9 [1908?] Poem beginning "Par cet après-midi de Décembre..."

6). May 6 [1898?] "Mon cher René. Tu dois..."

7). Aug. 2 [1897?] "Je reçois..."

8). [1900?]. "Merci pour la Guerre"

9). May 19, 1917. "Si tu veux bien..."

10). Sept. 20, 1901. "Je sens incontestablement..."

30. To Claudius Popelin. June 24, 1886. Written from Rome. Outpouring of youthful feelings for a certain lady. Reproduced in part by Vallery Radot in **Revue des deux mondes** (item 97). Also see Radot's interpretation of the letter in **Tel était Claude Debussy** (item 98).

31. To G. Rabani. Oct. 2, 1916. Apologizes for lateness in responding to Rabani's request for information.

32. To Roger-Ducasse. July 20, 1911. Not examined.

33. To Russell. May 15, 1910. Not examined.

34. To J. Schurmann. April 11, 1917. Not examined.

35. To R. Schwartz. July 10, 1912 [postmark]. Will send him the sum in question.

36 and 37. Letters to Emile Vuillermoz, 1912-1916.

1). Jan. 25, 1916. Discusses the piece **Berceuse héroïque**, defending it despite the apathy of the audience. Relates it to the war. Thanks him for the relationship Vuillermoz expressed between Debussy and Monet.

2). Feb. 14, 1915. Nothing has changed. Reaffirms friendship.

3). March 23, 1915. Regrets news of Ecorcheville's death. Announces the death of D's mother this early morning.

4). Oct. 19, 1912. Anticipates word concerning a performance in concealed terms, possibly of **Le martyre**.

5). No date. Short calling card with statement that he his what he could. Reaffirms friendship.

6). No date. Mentions an article to follow this brief note.

7). March 6, 1912. Is finally sending the article, which caused him more difficulty to write than a symphony. Refers to the disposition of his notes on the Concerts Colonne [probably Casals review], which ought be respected.

8). March 17, 1912. Speaks of proofs of his article [Casals review?] and disparages the cover of the **S.I.M.** journal.

9). Jan. 27, 1913. Concerns the forthcoming celebratory dinner after the 100th performance of **Pelléas** [Jan. 28, 1913, Opéra-Comique]. Dinner at Café Riche.

10). Feb. 9, 1913. Fears a gulf forming between himself and Maeterlinck.

11). March 18, 1913. Wishes to describe to the charitable work "des pianistes abandonnés." Has a new Bechstein that gives him high hopes.

12). No date [Jan. 1913]. Delivers the article herewith. Best wishes for the new year 1913.

13). No date. Rehearsals of **Jeux** begin today. The errors in orchestral parts made by Durand's copyist trouble him.

14). March 27, 1913. "There are no errors." Again mentions the Bechstein.

15). April 16, 1913. Is very harried; Durand takes pages from him one by one to get them to Diaghilev.

16). April 10, 1913. Cannot help him; is too busy to write even a few lines.

17). April 29, 1913. Cannot understand what

Ecorcheville is referring to. Mentions **Prélude-faune** as being written long ago.

18). May 10, 1913. Concerns a wording involving trumpets.

19). July 20, 1913. Cannot write for the **S.I.M.** Has been ill with influenza.

20). June 2, 1913. Remarks about old singers and women pianists whom heretofore he has been able to refuse. Calls Vuillermoz a "man of bronze with words of honey."

21). No date. Has just returned from a fatiguing voyage.

<u>Other Material Relating to Debussy</u>
Harry Ransom Humanities Research Center, Univ. of Texas.

<u>Autograph Literary Materials by Debussy</u>

1. Article in manuscript [not Debussy's hand] of 3 p. Begins "La douceur hypocrite d'Avril..." and concerns the "Cas Rust." Ends "Nous n'y manquerons pas dans la suite." Publ. in **Monsieur Croche** (Lesure, ed., item 46), pp. 233-35.

2. Article "Pourquoi j'ai écrit **Pelléas**.". Preserved in a typed copy, unsigned. Begins "Ma connaissance de **Pelléas** date de 1893." Ends "Cela représente douze ans de ma vie." Publ. in **Monsieur Croche** (Lesure, ed., item 46). pp. 61-63.

3. Article in Debussy's hand. 4 p. **A propos de'Hippolyte et Aricie**. Ends "longtemps, à l'Opéra." Publ. in **Monsieur Croche** (Lesure, ed., item 46), pp. 197-200.

4. **Masques et bergamasques**. Ballet scenario. Dated July 1909 and signed by Debussy. 4 p. Begins "A Vénise. Un coin de la piazetta San Marco." Contains autograph emendations in the margins.

5. Article **Notes sur Gounod**, 4 pp. Signed by Debussy, no date. Begins "Beaucoup de gens sans parti pris..." Ends "nul ne songera a nier que Gounod s'y employa genereusement." Published in **Monsieur Croche** (Lesure, ed.), pp. 192-94.

6. **Notes sur les Concerts Colonne**. 1 p. Begins "Monsieur Pablo Casals..." Ends "...vibrante à souhait." Publ. in **Monsieur Croche** (Lesure, ed., item 46), p. 225.

7. Article **Pour la musique.** 3 pp. Begins "Dans ce dernier mois..." Ends "...sans peur et sans reproches." Publ. in **Monsieur Croche** (Lesure, ed., item 46), pp. 255-58.

8. **La chute de la maison Usher.** MS libretto containing prologue and scenes I and II, all in two versions. Working copies with many emendations in ink and pencil.

9. **La damoiselle élue.** Proof copy of original [?] cover.

<u>Letters</u> <u>Texas--others</u>
Letters by others concerning Debussy.
Harry Ransom Humanities Research Center, Univ. of Texas

1. Maurice Maeterlinck to Albert Carré.
   1). No date. Discusses matter of **Pelléas** and Georgette Leblanc.
   2). Jan. 15, 1902. Thanks him for the performance of **Pelléas**.

2. Lilly Debussy to Pierre Louÿs. No date. Asks him to visit to discuss a very serious matter.

3. Emma Debussy to Dorbon ainé, bookseller and publisher.
   1). Dec. 7, 1921. Thanks Dorbon for the dedicatory copy [of **Monsieur Croche**].
   2). Sept. 4, 1920. Is sending him a photograph of Debussy.

4. Author unknown. To C.A. Ellis, General Manager of the Boston Symphony. Dispatched Paris, Aug. 2, 1910. Preserved in a typed, mimeographed copy. Recommends Debussy to the Metropolitan Opera for a first performance and to the Boston Symphony to conduct orchestral works. Also recommends Paul Dukas.

5. Georgette Leblanc to unknown recipient. No date. Asks for permission to give a single benefit performance of **Pelléas**.

6. Charles Fuchs to Debussy. No date; dispatched to 58 rue Cardinet. Rather pushy letter telling of the writer's vocal "Quintette de Paris," requesting Debussy to suggest his works

suitable and to direct their rehearsals. Might he consider writing for them?

7. Edouard Colonne to Debussy. Aug. 23, 1903. Speaks of programming the **Damoiselle élue**.

8. Raoul Bardac to Debussy. Aug. 27 [1903]. Still hopes to study with Debussy, despite Bardac's father dispatching him on a trip to Greece and Turkey. Conveys greetings from his mother [the future Emma Debussy] to Debussy and his wife Lilly.

9. Paul Valéry to Debussy. "Mardi" [no date]. Describes a possible ballet scenario for their collaboration on the Orpheus myth.

10. Series of letters from E. Vuillermoz, Dorbon, and Louise Liebich. The latter recalls Laloy's permission that she might translate his book into English. [Apparently Dorbon, to whom the letter is addressed, had refused her translation in his capacity as original, French-language publisher.]

11. Société Musicale checklist of needs for Festival Debussy. Emendations in Debussy's hand, including suggestion to perform the **Quatuor** (performed by Quatuor Haupt), **Fêtes II**, **Cinq poèmes de Baudelaire**, and the **Chansons de France** (performed by L. Bréval), and the **Estampes** for piano (performed by Risler). Also suggests possibility of performing **Nuages** and the **Danses pour harpe**.

12. Chronology of Debussy's songs. Incorrect and in an unidentified hand.

4. Debussy's Critical Writings and Interviews

In the index to letters and critical writings, "W" refers to names and topics cited in the collected writings by Debussy; "WL" refers the edition by Lesure; "WL/rev." refers to the revision of Lesure's edition; and "WS" refers to the edition by Langham Smith.

42. Debussy, Claude. **Monsieur Croche antidi lettante.** Paris: Dorbon-Ainé, 1921. 145 p. ML410.D28 A2. Republ. Paris: Gallimard, 1921, 1926, 1950.

The first collection of Debussy's critical writings, although only partial. Updated by Lesure and Langham Smith (items 45-47). See the following for an English translation.

43. Debussy, Claude. **Monsieur Croche the Dilettante Hater.** In **Three Classics in the Aesthetic of Music**, pp. 1-71. New York: Dover, 1962. 188 pp., index. ISBN 0-486-20320-4; ML 90.T47.

A translation of item 41 (the 1926 Gallimard reprint) by B.N. Langdon Davies, first publ. London: Douglas, 1927 and New York: Viking, 1928. This translation is superseded by Langham Smith's important one (item 45), which like Lesure (item 47) and subsequent research brings all of D's criticism together. The present may be read alongside Langham Smith for another interpretation in English of D's French. The preface properly admits Langdon Davies's "boldness in rendering [D's] thought." Also contains Charles Ives's **Essays before a Sonata** and F. Busoni's **Sketch of a New Esthetic of Music**.

44. Dietschy, Marcel. "Une interview de Claude Debussy passée inaperçue." **Schweizerische Musikzeitung/Revue musicale suisse** 121/3 (1981): 175-78.

Reprints and comments on an interview in the **London Daily Mail** of May 28, 1909, entitled "The Newest Music: An explanation from M. Debussy." D makes general comments on the direction of modern music. Dietschy also signals the interview of D by Paul Toulet in **Notes de littérature**, Paris 1926 [originally in **Les marges**, 1912, repudiated as false by Debussy] and the interview by Frances Emilie Bauer in **Harper's Weekly**, August 29, 1908. The latter two interviews are published in vol. 2 (première série, 1975) of the **Cahiers Debussy**. The first and third are reprinted in Lesure's revised **Monsieur Croche** (item 47).

WS

45. Langham Smith, Richard, ed. and trans. **Debussy on Music.** New York: Alfred A. Knopf, 1977. xxv, 353 p. ISBN 0-394-48120-8; ML 410/.D28 A333.

An English translation of D's critical writings and "a selection of the more interesting journalistic interviews," as collected and introduced in Lesure. Also contains a foreward by Smith relating D's **nom de plume**, Monsieur Croche, to the writer Paul Valéry's Monsieur Teste; and three interviews and a few phrases not found in Lesure. Two of these interviews previously had appeared in the **Cahiers Debussy**. Includes Lesure's introduction in translation, helpful notes on each writing, a list of lesser-known persons with brief identification, and an index of names, compositions, and subjects mentioned in the writings.

Translations are sensitive but not word-for-word. Does not include the original French texts, so that critical researchers must examine Lesure's edition alongside Langham Smith's and must use the 1987 revised edition of Lesure, item 47.

WL:

46. Lesure, François, ed. **Claude Debussy: Monsieur Croche et autres écrits.** Edition complète de son oeuvre critique. Paris: Gallimard, 1971.

An invaluable edition of D's critical writings from the three periods of his life in which he was active as critic (1901-03, 1906- 08, and 1911-14). Also contains nearly all interviews with D printed in the press. Lesure's brief editorial notes identify persons and compositions, and he indicates the appearance of an article or portion thereof in D's own compilation **Monsieur Croche antidilettante** (Paris: Dorbon, 1921), 25 writings from the period of his criticisms, 1901-1906, which he selected more or less arbitrarily and had reprinted. The index of the complete critical writings is of proper names only, so that the researcher must seek index references to specific compositions and ideas in Langham Smith. Trans. into German by E. Klemm as **Einsame Gespräche**. Leipzig: P. Reclam jun., 1971. Trans. into Spanish by A.M. Alvarez as **El Señor Corchea**. Madrid: Alianza, 1987.

WL/rev.
47. Lesure, François, ed. **Claude Debussy: Monsieur Croche et autres écrits**. Revised and enlarged ed. Paris: Gallimard, 1987. 362 p.; notes and index. ISBN 2-07-071107-2.

This edition adds to the previous collection six interviews given by Debussy to English, American, Hungarian, and Italian journalists, which were gathered since the 1971 edition by Lesure. The index is only of proper names.

* Vallas, Léon. **Les idées de Claude Debussy** (trans. as **The Theories of Claude Debussy**). See item 8.

WS. Denotes the abbreviation used in the following index to the collection of writings edited by Langham Smith, item 45.

IV

INDEX OF LETTERS AND WRITINGS

The following is an index of virtually all of Debussy's letters and writings available to scholars, whether published or in accessible manuscript collections. It is provisional, however, awaiting a publication of the complete letters. Such a publication is in preparation by François Lesure.

Note that many of the manuscript letters and all the extant critical writings described above and indexed here have been published. In general researchers may consult the published collections first before turning to the manuscript sources, particularly when an apparently reliable publication is at hand. Further note that **L Lesure** (item 23) and **L Nichols** (29) are thoughtful selections of the most important letters.

Compositions and other writings by Debussy and other authors should be sought under both the title and the author's name, in the index below and in indexes to published collections. Below, proper names are in capital letters; other entries are in lower case.

<u>Abbreviations</u>

L - letter found in a published collection annotated in Section 2 above, beginning on p. 83.

L Annunzio - letter found in the published collection of letters to D'Annunzio, annotated in Section II above. See the index to that published collection for page reference.

L Emma 137 - refers specifically to p. 137 in the collected letters to Emma, annotated above in Section 2. Such an indication is used when a printed collection of letters contains no index.

(abbreviations continued next page)

M - indicates that a letter is found in a manuscript collection annotated in Section 3 above, p. 96.

M Bn Deb 39 - refers to manuscript letter 39 written by Claude Debussy, housed at the Bibliothèque nationale, as listed in Section 3 under _Bn_.

M Bn Emma 4 - refers to letter 4 by Emma Debussy at the Bibliothèque nationale, listed in Section 3 above under _Bn, Emma Debussy_.

W - refers to names and topics indexed in the collected writings by Debussy, referred to in Section 4 above, p. 127.

- _WL_ - refers to the 1971 edition by Lesure.
- _WL/rev._ - refers to the 1987 revised edition by Lesure.
- _WS_ - refers to the edition by Langham Smith.

A reader should consult the indexes in _WL_ and _WS_ for page reference.

Académie de France. WS
Académie de Sainte Cécile [also see Accademia below]. L Annunzio
Académie de Saint-Pétersbourg. L Annunzio
Académie des Beaux-arts (also see Conservatoire). L Nichols
Accademia Santa Cecilia. L Nichols
Achille (bar). L Godet
ACKTE, A. WL/rev.
ADALBERT, J., **Paysages des femmes**. L Lesure; L Nichols
ADAM, Adolphe. WL; WL/rev.; WS
ADENIS, E. WL; WL/rev.
ADERER, A. L Lesure; L Nichols
ADONIS. L Annunzio
ADORJAN, André. L Emma 92; WL/rev.
Aeolian Co. M Texas 19/6. Further see Grammophone below.
AESCHYLUS. L Laloy; L Nichols. See also Eschyle
aesthetics (as named topic). L Laloy 19
AFFRE. WS/rev.
Africa. L Toulet 5
AGAUNE, Gerard d'. L Annunzio
AICARD, Jean. L Segalen 97
AJALBERT, Jean. M Morgan 1
AKTE, Mlle Aino. L Louÿs
ALAMANNI, Luigi, or Aleman, Loys. L Annunzio
ALBENIZ, Isaac. L Louÿs; WL; WL/rev.; WS
ALBERT. WL; WL/rev.
ALBERT, Henri. L Louÿs
Algeria. L Nichols
ALENÇON, Mlle. Emilienne d'. L Louÿs
Alhambra Theatre, London. L Nichols
ALHEIM, Pierre d'. L Godet; L Lesure; L Nichols; WL/rev.
ALIOTH, Mons. L Lesure; L Nichols; L Toulet 10
ALLAIS, Alphonse. L Godet
ALLAN, Maud. L Annunzio; L Durand 105, 108; L Emma 89; L Godet; L Lesure; L Nichols
ALLARD, André. WL; WL/rev.
ALMANO, Mme. L Toulet 49
ALMANZ. L Laloy; L Lesure; L Nichols
Alpes Dinariques. L Annunzio
ALVAREZ (real name A.-R. Gourron). WL; WL/rev.
AMABLE. L 60.
AMATI L Annunzio
AMBRIERE, Francis. L Louÿs
America, customs, projects relating to [also see particular cities and Metropolitan Opera]. L Caplet 49, 54, 57, 58, 60, 68, 83; L Durand 98, 100, 106, 164; L Laloy 15, 16, 20, 37; L Nichols; L Poniatowski; L Toulet 38; M Texas 28; M Texas Letters by others 4
AMETTE, Monseigneur. L Annunzio

Amsterdam [also see Holland]. L Nichols; M Bn 85
AMYOT. L Louÿs
ANELY, Max. see MAX-ANELY
ANDRE, General. L Lesure; L Nichols
ANDRE-FAIRFAX, Mlle C. WL; WL/rev.
ANGENOT. L Louÿs
ANGYAN, Béla von. L Emma 78, 80, 94; L Lesure; L Nichols
ANHALT-DESSAU (Prince of). WL/rev.
Annales politiques et littéraires, Les. WS
Annamite Theater. L Nichols
ANNUNZIO, D', Gabriele [also alphabetized under D'Annunzio in some indexes]. L Annunzio [see also titles of specific writings in index]; L Caplet 50, 51; L Durand 170; L Emma 88ff; L Godet; L Lesure; L Nichols; M bn 74; M Bn Var.; WL; WL/rev.; WS
ANSERMET, Ernest. L Caplet 16; L Lesure; L Nichols; L Stravinsky
Antibes. L Nichols
ANTOINE, A. L Lesure; L Nichols; L Peter 221; WL/rev.
ANTONGINI, Tom. L Annunzio
ANTONI, André. M Texas 3
ANTONIOTTI, Mary. L Nichols
Anvers, Musée d'. WS
Aphrodite. L Louÿs
Apollo. L Annunzio
Apparition. L Louÿs
Arabesque (as musical device). WS
Arabesques (piano compositions by Debussy). L Louÿs
ARBOS, E.-F. WL; WL/rev.
Arcachon. L Annunzio; L Nichols
ARCHIMEDES. L Nichols
ARDRE, Guy d'. L Annunzio
ARETHUSE. WS
Ariane. L Louÿs
Ariane et Barbe-bleue (Dukas). L Durand 60
Ariettes oubliées. L Caplet; L Cobb; L Godet; L Louÿs; L Nichols
Arkel (Debussy's porcelain toad and mascot) L Durand 135; L Godet; L Vallery
L'art et la vie. L Nichols
Art Indépendant (Librairie de l'). L Louÿs
L'art moderne. L Nichols
ARTHUS [Artus], Louis. L Durand 37; L Laloy 31; L Lesure
ARTON. L Louÿs
ARTUS, Louis. L Segalen 81
Austin (bar). L Godet
As You Like It (project). L Toulet 4-5, 13, 15-21, 103-4, 108, 112, 114, 124
Asnières. L Nichols
Association Chorale de Paris. L Nichols

Association chorale professionale. WS
Association des Chanteurs de St.-Gervais. WS
Association d'Expansion Artistique. M Bn Emma 16- 22
Astarte. L Louÿs.
ASTRUC, Gabriel. L Annunzio; L Durand 60; L Lesure; L Nichols; L Toulet 69; M Bn 39-56; M Bn Emma 5-10; M Texas 4; WL; WL/rev.; WS
Athlète du Christ. L Annunzio
Au ménestrel. L Nichols
Augerge du Clou. L Nichols
AUBERT, Charles. L Louÿs
AUBRY, G.J. L Lesure
AUBRY, Raoul. L Annunzio
AUER, Leopold. WL; WL/rev.; WS
Austria. L Nichols
Auteuil. L Nichols
Autour du martyre de St. Sébastien (E. Vuillermoz). L Annunzio
Avant le martyre de St. Sébastien (L. Handler). L Annunzio
AVELLAN, Admiral. L Lesure; L Nichols
Aventures du roi Pausole. L Louÿs
Azest, interview of Debussy in Budapest. WS

BABAIAN, S. L Nichols
BACCARA [or BACCARIS], Luisa. L Annunzio
BACH, C.P.E. WL; WL/rev.
BACH, J.S. L Annunzio [see also **Passion, St. Matthew**]; L Chausson 4; L Durand 55, 134, 135, 179; L Godet; L Laloy 38; L Lesure; L Louÿs; L Louÿs 1971; L Nichols; L Segalen 107, 137; M Bn 112; M Texas 9/2; WL; WL/rev.; WS
BACH-SISLEY, J. WL/rev.
BACHELET, Alfred. L Chansarel; L Lesure; L Nichols; WL; WL/rev.; WS
BACKER-LUNDE, Johan. L Nichols
BAILLY, Edmond. L Lesure; L Louÿs; L Nichols; L Poniatowski
BAKST, Léon. L Annunzio; L Caplet 51, 96; L Durand 159; L Lesure; L Nichols; WL; WL/rev.
BALAKIREV, Mili. WL; WL/rev.; WS
Balkans. L Laloy 31
Ballades de Villon, Trois. L Durand 84, 89, 91; L Godet; L Louÿs
ballet (as general subject). WS
Ballets russes [also see Diaghilev]. L Cobb; L Nichols; M Morgan 4, 5; M Texas 13
BALZAC, Honoré de. L Durand 130; L Lesure; L Louÿs; L Nichols
Bambara tribe. L Nichols
BANVILLE, Théodore de. L Godet; L Lesure; L Louÿs; L Nichols; L Toulet 83; L Vasnier

BARBIER, J. WL/rev.
BARCZY. L Lesure; L Nichols
BARDAC, Dolly [Mme Gaston de Tinan]. L Caplet 35, 87; L Lesure; L Nichols; L Toulet 36, 38, 131; also see Tinan, Mme below.
BARDAC, Emma (Mme Claude Debussy). See Debussy, Emma below.
BARDAC, Raoul. L Annunzio; L Caplet/Lockspeiser; L Cobb; L Godet; L Lesure; L Lockspeiser; L Nichols; M Bn 12-14, 18, 22, 24, 74; M Bn Chouchou 1; M Texas 19/3; M Texas Letters by others 8
BARDAC, Sigismund. L Nichols
BARET, Ch. L Toulet 38
BARING, Harriet. L Nichols
BARON, Mons. L Durand 157
BARON, Emile. L Baron; L Lang; L Lesure; L Lockspeiser; L Louÿs; L Nichols; M Lang; M Morgan 1
BARRAULT, Jean-Louis. L Annunzio
barrel organs. WS
BARRES, Maurice. L Annunzio; L Godet; WL; WL/rev.
BARTOK, Béla. L Caplet 26, 29, 94; WL/rev.
Basques. L Nichols
Bassano, Rue de. L Annunzio
BASSIANO, Prince Caetani de. L Annunzio
BATAILLE, Henry. L Annunzio
BATCHELDER, William. M LC
BATHORI, Jane. L Godet; L Lesure; L Nichols
BATON, Rhené. L Laloy; WL; WL/rev.
BAUDELAIRE, Charles. L Godet; L Lesure; L Louÿs; L Nichols; L Toulet 128, 130, 132; WL; WL/rev.
BAUDRY, P. L Lesure; L Nichols; L Vasnier
BAUER, Miss Emily Frances. L Durand 65; L Nichols; WL/rev.
BAUER, Henry. L Lesure; L Nichols; WL; WL/rev.; WS
BAUMANN, Emile. L Godet
BAX, Arnold. L Nichols
Bayreuth. L Annunzio; L Louÿs 1971; L Nichols
BAZIN, F. L Caplet 59, 98; L Lesure; L Nichols
Beauce. L Annunzio
Bechstein piano, Debussy's. L Durand 134; M Texas 36/11, 13.
BECQUE, Henri. L Godet; L Lesure; L Nichols
BEDIER, Joseph. L Godet; L Laloy; L Lesure; L Nichols; L Segalen 74-81; L Toulet 75
BEETHOVEN, Ludwig van. L Annunzio [also see Variations]; L Caplet 42; L Chausson 2; L Laloy 13, 19; L Lesure; L Nichols; L Louÿs; L Segalen 137; L Toulet 38; WL; WL/rev.; WS
Bel-Ebat, L Nichols
BELLAIGUE, Camille. L Annunzio; L Godet; WL
BENDA, Julien. L Annunzio
BENFELD, A. L Durand 53
BENOIT, Camille. L Godet

Belgium [also see Brussels and Ghent]. L Laloy 23, 24; L Nichols
BELLAIGUE, C. WL/rev.
Bellamy Co. music paper. L Durand 149; L Nichols
Bellevue. L Nichols
BELLINI. L Louÿs
BEN BRAHIM, Zorah. L Nichols
BENNETT, Gordon. L Laloy 21
BENOIS, A. L Lesure; L Nichols
BENOIT, Camille. L Godet; L Lesure; L Nichols; WS
BERARD. L Peter p.206
Berceuse héroïque. L Godet; L Nichols; M Bn 7; M Texas 36/1
BERG, Alban. L Caplet 29
BERGERAT, Emile. L Godet
Berlin. L Nichols
Berlin Philharmonic Orchestra. WS
BERLIOZ, Hector. L Godet; L Lesure; L Louÿs; L Nichols; L Poniatowski; M Morgan 25; WL; WL/rev.; WS
Berlitz, Ecole. L Annunzio
BERMOND, Adolphe. L Annunzio
BERNAC, Jean. L Nichols
BERNARD, Gabriel. L Louÿs
BERNARD, Robert. L Annunzio
BERNHEIM, A. WL; WL/rev.; WS
BERNSTEIN, Henri. L Laloy 40.
BERRY, Jean de. L Annunzio
BERTAULT, Mons. M Texas 5
BERTHIER, General. L Louÿs
BERTHOLDT, Philippe. M Bn 51
BERTRAND. WL/rev.
BERUTTI, Arturo. L Louÿs
BERYS, J. de. WL; WL/rev.
BEYLE, Léon. WL; WL/rev.
Biarritz. L Nichols
Bibliothèque nationale. L Annunzio
Bichain. L Nichols
BIDEL. L Louys
BIDOU, Henri. L Godet; L Lesure; L Nichols
BIHARI, Janos. L Nichols
BILITIS. L Annunzio
Bilitis, Chansons de. See **Chansons de Bilitis**
BINET-VALMER. WL; WL/rev.
Biskra. L Nichols
BISSON, Alexandre. WL; WL/rev.
BIZET, Georges. L Caplet 9, 50; L Lesure; L Louÿs; L Nichols; WL; WL/rev.; WS
BIZET, R. L Annunzio; WL; WL/rev.
BLANCHE, Jacques-Emile. L Laloy 8; L Lesure; L Louÿs; L Nichols; WS
BLOCH, Ernest. L Godet; L Lesure; L Nichols
BLOY, L. L Lesure; L Nichols
BLUM, Léon. L Annunzio; WL; WL/rev.; WS

BLUMENBERG. L Laloy 37
BOCKLIN, Arnold. WL; WL/rev.; WS
BODINIER. L Louÿs
BOELLMANN, Léon. M Bn Emma 23
BOIELDIEU, François Adrien. L Lesure; L Nichols
BOIS, Jules. L Lesure; L Nichols
Bois-de-Boulogne, Avenue and Square du. L Annunzio; L Nichols; L Segalen 50
Boilesve (restaurant). L Louÿs
Boîte à joujoux. L Caplet 23, 25; L Durand 115, 116, 117-8, 121, 133, 190; L Nichols; M Bn Emma 4; WS
BOITO, Arrigo. L Caplet 39, 90; L Lesure; L Nichols; WL/rev.
BOLDINI. L Toulet 87
BOLO. L Toulet 124, 125
BOLSKA, Adelaida. WL; WL/rev.
BONAPARTE, Napoléon. See Napoléon.
BONAPARTE, Princesse Charlotte. L Nichols
BONAPARTE, Princesse Mathilde. L Nichols
BONHEUR, Raymond. L Caplet 10, 11; L Godet; L Lesure; L Louÿs; L Nichols; L Peter p. 202, 209, 212; M Texas 6, 29/4
BONMARIAGE, Sylvain. L Louÿs
BONNAMY, Emile. L Louÿs
BONNARD, Pierre. WS
BONNARD, Sylvestre. L Toulet 84
BONNAT. L Toulet 87
BONNET, Joseph. L Annunzio
BONNIERES, Robert de. L Lesure; L Louÿs; L Nichols; WL/rev.
BONNIOT, Dr. L Lesure; L Nichols
BONNOT [of the Apache group]. L Durand 139; L Toulet 124
Bordeaux. L Nichols
BORDEAUX, Henri. L Toulet 123
BORDES, Charles. L Godet; L Lesure; L Louÿs; L Nichols; WL; WL.rev.; WS
BORGEX. WL; WL/rev.
Boris Godounov (also see Musorgsky). L Emma 102
BORODINE, A. L Godet; L Louÿs; M Bn 62; WL; WL/rev.; WS
Bostock. L Laloy
Boston, City and Opera. L Annunzio; L Caplet 58, 75, 76, 93; L Nichols; M Texas Letters by others 4
BOUCHARDY, Joseph. L Lesure; L Nichols
BOUCHET, Henri. WS
BOUCHOR, Felix. L Godet
BOUCHOR, Maurice. L Lesure; L Nichols; WL/rev.
BOUCHUT, H. WL/rev.
BOUGUEREAU, W. WL; WL/rev.
BOULANGER, Lili. WL; WL/rev.; WS
BOULEZ, Pierre. L Nichols
BOULOGNE, M. L Nichols
BOUR, Armand. L Annunzio; L Nichols

BOURBON, Jean. L Durand 72; L Lesure; L Nichols; WL; WL/rev.
BOURDEAU. L Louÿs
BOURGAULT-DUCOUDRAY, L.-A. WL; WL/rev.; WS
BOURGEAT. L Caplet 48; L Godet; L Lesure; L Nichols
BOURGEOIS, Mlle. L Durand 37
BOURGEOIS. L Lesure; L Nichols
BOURGES, E. L Segalen 72
BOURGET, Paul. L Durand 182; L Lesure; L Louÿs; L Nichols; L Poniatowski; L Vasnier; WL; WL/rev.; WS
BOURJAT, General. L Louÿs
BOYER, Georges. L Lesure; L Nichols
BRAHMS, Johannes. L Godet; L Lesure; L Nichols; WL; WL/rev.; WS
BRANCOVAN, Prince Constantin de. L Louÿs
BRAYER, Jules de. L Godet; L Lesure; L Nichols
Breitkopf und Härtel. L Durand 130
BREMA, Marie [actual name M. Fehrmann]. WL; WL/rev.; WS
BRET, Gustave. L Laloy; WL; WL/rev.; WS
BREVAL, Lucienne. L Nichols; WL; WL/rev.
BREVILLE, Pierre de. L Lesure; L Nichols; M Bn 60- 69; M Bn Emma 11
BRICE, Mlle Germaine. L Louÿs
bridge, game of. L Laloy 19
BRIEUX, Eugene. L Annunzio; L Louÿs
BRILLAT-SAVARIN. L Toulet 62
Briséis. M Texas 18/2
BRIZEUX, Auguste. WL; WL/rev.
BRUCKNER, Anton. L Caplet 94
BRUERS, Antonio. L Annunzio
BRUNEAU, Alfred. L Lesure; L Louÿs; L Louÿs 1971; L Nichols; WL; WL/rev.; WS
BRUNETIERE, Ferdinand. L Louÿs
BRUSSEL, R. M Bn Emma 1
Brussels, city and voyage to. L Emma see table of contents; L Nichols; L Toulet 32; M Bn 72; M Morgan 30; M Texas 2. Also see Belgium.
BUCCI (operatic tenor). L Nichols
Budapest. L Caplet 49, 50, 94; L Durand 93-4; L Nichols; L Toulet 59;
M LC Szanto and Hubay
Buddhism. L Segalen 55
BULLIER. L Louÿs
BURGER, M. L Lesure; L Nichols
BURGOIN, Mlle. M Morgan 20
BUSONI, Ferruccio. L Emma 108; L Nichols
BÜSSER, Henri. L Caplet 37; L Lesure; L Messager 15ff; L Nichols
BUSSY, Abbé de. L Lesure

Ca'd'oro. L Annunzio
CABAT, Louis. WL; WL/rev.
Café de Paris. L Annunzio
Café Pousset. L Nichols
Café Weber. L Nichols
café-concerts. WS
CAHEN, Albert. WL; WL/rev.
Cahiers (Maurice Barrès). L Annunzio
Cahiers de la Quinzaine (Ch. Peguy). L Annunzio
CAILLARD, C.F. WL; WL/rev.
CAILLAVET, G. de. WL; WL/rev.
CAIN, Georges. L Segalen 97
CAINE, Hall. L Nichols
CALLOT sisters. L Nichols
CALVE, Emma. WL; WL/rev.
CALVOCORESSI, M.-D. L Durand 85; L Laloy 24, 26; L Lesure; L Nichols; WL; WL/rev.; WS
CAMPANINI, Cleofonte. L Durand 71, 72, 74; L Laloy 32; L Lesure; L Nichols; L Toulet 50
CAMPBELL, Mrs. Patrick. L Lesure; L Nichols
CAMPO, Conrado del. WL; WL/rev.
Cannes. L Durand 59; L Nichols
Canope [also see **Préludes**]. L Godet
CANTIE. L Louys
CAPET, Lucien. WL; WL/rev.
CAPLET, André. L Annunzio; L Caplet 16, 17, 23, 87, 93 [as subject]; L Durand 57, 61, 75, 92, 152; L Godet; L Lesure; L Lockspeiser; L Louÿs; L Nichols; M Bn 37, 124-125; M Bn Var.; M Texas 19/12, 19/16, 19/17, 19/19; WL; WL/rev.; WS
Capponcina, La. L Annunzio
Cardiff. L Nichols
CARJAT, Etienne. L Godet; L Lesure; L Nichols
CARLTON. L Caplet 82
CARLYLE, Thomas. L Caplet 39; L Durand 45; L Lesure; L Nichols; WL; WL/rev.; WS
CARNOT, Sadi. L Godet; L Lesure; L Nichols
CARON, Rose. L Nichols; WL; WL/rev.
CARRAUD, Gaston. L Laloy 16, WL; WL/rev.; WS
CARRE, Albert. L Caplet 68; L Durand 27, 79, 80; L Godet; L Lesure; L Lockspeiser; L Louÿs; L Messager 26, 29, 31, 35, 54; L Nichols; L Toulet 47; M Stockholm 3-4; M Texas 2, 8, 18/6, 18/8; M Texas Letters by others 1; WL; WL/rev.; WS
CARRE, Marguerite. L Caplet 13; L Nichols; WL; WL/rev.
CARRE, Michel. WL; WL/rev.; WS
CARREÑO, Teresa. WL; WL/rev.
CARRIERE, E. L Lesure; L Nichols
CARRIES, Jean. L Godet
CARUSO. L Caplet 26, 100; L Durand 121
CARVALHO. L Louÿs; L Nichols
Cas Debussy, Le (Bérys and Caillard). WS
CASAFUERTE, Marchese di. L Paoli 2; M Bn 71; M NY

CASALS, Pablo. M Texas 36/7-8; WL; WL/rev.; WS
CASAS, Perez. WL; WL/rev.; WS
CASAZZA, Mons. G. L Durand 49; WL/rev.
CASELLA, Alfredo. L Paoli 1
Casetta Rosa. L Annunzio
Casino St. Pierre, Geneva. L Nichols
CASTERA, René de. L Laloy 29; WL; WL/rev.
CAVALIERI. L Durand 49
CAZE, Robert. L Godet
CAZENEUVE, Maurice. WL; WL/rev.
Cendrelune. L Louÿs; L Nichols
CHABRIER, Emmanuel. L Godet; L Lesure; L Louÿs; L Nichols; M Bn 66; WL; WL/rev.; WS
CHADAIGNE, Marcel. L Annunzio
CHAGNON, Pierre. WL; WL/rev.
CHAILLEY, Jacques. L Annunzio
CHALIAPINE, Fedor. L Annunzio; L Lesure; L Nichols
chamber music. WS
CHAMBERLAIN, Houston Stewart. L Nichols
CHAMBERLAIN, Joseph. L Lesure; WL; WL/rev.
Chambre magique (Le martyre de St. Sébastien). L Annunzio
CHANSAREL, René. L Godet; L Chansarel
Chanson de la mère. L Nichols
Chansons de Bilitis. L Emma 79; L Godet; L Laloy 9; L Louÿs; L Louÿs 1971; L Nichols; L Segalen 85, 87, 137; M Bn 63-64; M Texas 18/8, 18/11
Chansons de Charles d'Orléans. See Charles D'Orléans, Chansons.
Chansons de France, Trois. L Durand 18; M Texas Letters by others 11
CHANTARD. L Peter pp. 218. 219. 220
CHANTAVOINE, J. WL/rev.
CHARAVAY. L Louÿs
CHARLES D'ORLEANS [including Chansons de]. L Godet; L Lesure; L Nichols
CHARLOT, A. [Dir. of Alhambra, London]. L Caplet 83; L Lesure; L Nichols
CHARLOT, Jacques. L Durand 110, 119, 122, 128, 129, 159; L Lesure; L Nichols
CHARPENTIER. L Caplet 42 [also see the following entry]; L Cobb
CHARPENTIER, Gustave. L Lesure; L Louÿs; L Louÿs 1971; L Nichols; L Poniatowski; M Morgan 25; WL; WL/rev.; WS
CHARPENTIER, V. WL/rev.
Chartres. L Annunzio
CHASSAIGNE, Anna-Marie [also see Liane de Pougy in other indexes].
Chat noir, Cabaret du. L Godet; L Louÿs; L Nichols
CHATEAUBRIAND, François-René, Vicomte de. L Emma 78, 95; L Lesure; L Nichols; L Segalen 101
Châtelet, Théâtre du [see also Théâtre du Châtelet

below]. L Toulet 69
CHAUMET, William. WL; WL/rev.; WS
Chaumié. L Laloy 7
CHAUSSON, Ernest. L Caplet 12, 26; L Chausson 2; L Godet; L Lesure; L Lockspeiser; L Louÿs; L Nichols; M Bn 72; M LC Batchelder; M Texas 9; WL; WL/rev.; WS
CHAUSSON, Mme [also see the preceding]. L Lesure; L Nichols
CHAUVET, René. L Nichols
CHAVANNES, Edouard. L Segalen 144
CHAVANNES, Puvis de. L Louÿs
CHENIER, André. L Nichols
Chesterian, The. L Godet
CHESTERTON; G.K. L Nichols
Chevalier d'or, Le (project). M Morgan 23; M Texas 18/3
CHEVILLARD, Camille. L Cobb; L Durand 15, 26, 35, 39, 106, 112; L Laloy 16; L Lesure; L Louÿs; L Messager 54; L Nichols; M Bn 18; M Texas 25/5, 27/3; WL; WL/rev.; WS
CHEVRIER, André. L Durand 158
Chicago, city of. L Caplet 48; L Nichols
Children's Corner. L Caplet 24, 49, 93; L Caplet/Lockspeiser; L Durand 62, 64, 92; L Gui; L Louÿs; L Nichols; L Paoli 3; WS [where see Golliwog]
China, customs and culture. L Nichols; L Segalen 113ff.
Chinese Exhibition (1910). L Nichols
CHOCOLAT. L Godet
CHOISNEL, Gaston. L Durand 25, 32, 62, 77, 81, 83, 92, 103, 107, 115, 116, 130, 134, 143, 179, 181, 190; L Emma 81; L Godet; L Lesure; L Nichols
CHOPIN, Frédéric [including Debussy's edition of]. L Chausson; L Durand 33, 130-31, 132, 134, 135, 137, 140, 143, 146, 148-9, 150, 151, 154; L Godet; L Lesure; L Nichols; L Segalen 107; L Toulet 47; WL; WL/rev.; WS
Choral societies [also see names, such as Concordia]. WS
CHOUCHOU (Claude-Emma Debussy, daughter of Debussy, which also see). L Annunzio; L Caplet/Lockspeiser; L Durand 103, 127; L Godet
CHOUDENS. L Lesure; L Nichols
CHRIST. L Annunzio
CHRISTEN, Jules. L Lesure; L Nichols
Chrysis. L Louÿs
Chute de la maison Usher, La. L Annunzio; L Caplet 30-31, 38; L Caplet/Lockspeiser; L Durand 61- 2, 76, 77, 79, 81, 85, 88, 89, 91, 98, 111, 168; L Godet; L Nichols; L Segalen 127; M Bn 104; M Texas 28; M Texas Other materials
Cinq poèmes de Baudelaire [also see **Poèmes de Baudelaire** and Baudelaire]. L Chansarel; L Nichols; M Bn 72;

M Texas Letters to others 11
Cinematography. WS
Circus, the. WS
CLAPIERS, Comte de. L Louÿs
CLAPISSON, Louis. WL; WL/rev.
Clarens. L Nichols
CLARK. L Louÿs
CLAUDEL, Mlle Camille. L Godet
CLAUDEL, Paul. L Segalen 132-33; WL; WL/rev.
CLEMENCEAU, Georges. L Lesure; L Nichols; L Toulet 125
CLEMENT. L Durand 42; WL; WL/rev.
CLEO DE MERODE. L Louÿs
CLEOPATRE. L Annunzio
CLERMONT-TONNERE, E. de. L Annunzio
Cloches à travers les feuillages [also see **Préludes**]. L Godet
Clou, Auberge du. L Louÿs
Clouet. L Godet
Clowns. WS
COCTEAU, Jean. L Annunzio; L Louÿs
COHEN, Gustave. L Annunzio
COINDREAU, P. WL; WL/rev.
COLETTE (Claudine novels and other topics). L Nichols; WS
COLIN, Raphael. L Godet
Cologne, City of. L Toulet 32
COLOMBE, Michel. L Annunzio
COLONNE, Ed. [including Orchestre Colonne]. L Cobb; L Durand 15, 26, 32, 33, 39, 40, 45; L Laloy 6, 21; L Nichols; M Morgan 36; M Texas 18/2, 18/19; 36/7; M Texas Letters by others 7; WL; WL/rev.; WS
COMBARIEU. L Laloy 8, 9
COMBE, Edouard. L Godet
Comédie des Champs-Elysées. L Nichols
Commune. L Nichols
Comoedia, general references and interview of Debussy in. L Annunzio; L Lesure; L Segalen 129-30; WS
Comme il vous plaira [also see **As You Like It**]. L Godet
Compagnie Fives-Lilles. L Nichols
Concertgebouw Orchestra. L Nichols
Concerts Colonne [see also Colonne]. L Segalen 105, 106; L Louÿs 1971; WS
Concerts Lamoureux. L Nichols; L Segalen 106, 142; WS
Concerts spirituels (Good Friday Concerts). WS
Concordia Choral Society. L Lesure/Concordia; L Vidal; M Bn 75
conductors, Debussy on. see WS
CONFUCIUS. WL/rev.
CONRAD, Joseph. L Caplet 17; L Durand 85; L Lesure; L Nichols
Conservatoire de Paris. L Caplet 42, 48, 92; L Laloy 36; L Nichols; M Bn 1, 3, 4; WS

COOLUS, Romain. L Louÿs
COPEAU, Jacques. L Annunzio
COPPEE, François. L Louÿs
COPPIER, André. L Nichols
COQUELIN, the younger. L Godet
COQUELIN, Constant. L Louÿs
Coran. See Koran
CORNEAU, André. WL; WL/rev.; WS
CORNELIUS, Mme Marie. L Laloy 11
CORNEILLE, Pierre. WL; WL/rev.
CORONIO, Nicolas. L Lesure; L Nichols; M Bn 8; M Texas 10
CORTOT, Alfred. L Caplet 90; L Louÿs; L Nichols; WL; WL/rev.; WS
COSSIRA, Emile. WL; WL/rev.
COSTALLAT. L Nichols
COSTES, Mme. WL; WL/rev.
Côte-d'Or. L Nichols
COULOMB. L Lesure; L Nichols
COUPERIN, François. L Durand 146, 148; L Laloy 38; L Nichols; L Toulet 67; WL; WL/rev.; WS
Courrier musical. L Nichols
COURTELINE, Georges. L Louÿs
COUSIN, Noelle. M Bn 36
Covent Garden. L Durand 74; L Nichols; WS
COWEN, Sir Frederick. L Nichols
COZANET, Albert. L Nichols
CRANE, W. L Louÿs
CRAPONNE, Mlle. de. WL; WL/rev.
CRAS, Jean. L Durand 136
Crédit Lyonnais. L Durand 152
CRESPEL, Dr. L Lesure; L Nichols; M Texas 11
CREVEL, Mons. M Texas 5/4
CRICKBOOM. L Louÿs; L Nichols
Crimen amoris [theater project by Debussy]. L Segalen 135
Croche, Mons. (as topic and related material; also see relevant journal titles). L Laloy 16, 18, 19, 23, 40; M Texas 14, 36; M Texas Other materials; WL; WL/rev.; WS
CROIZA, Claire. L Durand 177; M Bn 121-123; M Bn Emma 31-36; WL; WL/rev.
CROS, Charles. L Godet; L Lesure; L Nichols
CROZE, J.-L. WL/rev.
CRUSOE, Robinson. L Durand 136
CUI, César. L Louÿs
CULP, Mlle Julia. L Louÿs
CURNONSKY, (Maurice Sailland) [also see Kurne]. L Lesure; L Louÿs; L Nichols; L Toulet 14, 38, 52, 62
CYRIL, V. M Texas 12
CYSTRIA, Princesse de. L Laloy 6, 7, 8
Czechoslovakia. L Laloy; L Nichols

CZERNY, Carl. L Emma 119; L Lesure; L Nichols

DA VINCI, Leonardo. L Durand 107
Daily Telegraph. L Nichols
DALCROZE, Emile Jacques. L Godet; L Lesure; WS
DALIMIER, Mons. L Durand 125; L Nichols
DALLIES. L Durand 177

Damoiselle élue. L Caplet 23; L Durand 6, 7, 66, 117; L Godet; L Laloy 6; L Louÿs; L Messager 54, 81; L Nichols; L Segalen 112; M Bn 60, 72; M Texas 25, 27/2; M Texas Other materials; M Texas Letters by others 7; WS
DAMROSCH, Walter. L Lesure
DANDELOT, A. M Bn 120; M NY; M Texas 13
D'ANNUNZIO, G. See ANNUNZIO, G. D'.
DANSAERT, Mme. M Morgan 2
Danses, Deux, pour harpe. L Durand 18, 40, 176; L Godet; L Laloy 13, 14; L Nichols; M Texas Letters by others 11; WS
Danseuses de Delphes. L Annunzio; L Godet [also see **Préludes**]
DANTE ALIGHIERI. L Annunzio [see also Purgatoire]; WL; WL/rev.
Danube river. L Nichols
Daphnis et Chloe (project). L Louÿs
DAQUIN, C. WL/rev.
DARDEL, Otto de. L Godet; L Lesure; L Nichols
DAS, Mlle. L Durand 37; L Lesure
DAUDET, Alphonse. L Segalen 72; L Toulet 2; WL; WL/rev.
DAUDET, Léon. L Louÿs
DAVIES, Fanny. WL; WL/rev.
DE BUSSY, Abbe. see Bussy, De in L Nichols
DE FALLA, Manuel. L Lesure; L Nichols [see those indexes under Falla]; M Bn 113-119
DE QUINCEY, Thomas. WL; WL/rev.
Debussy (biography by L. Laloy). L Annunzio
Debussy, Achille-Claude (biography by L. Vallas). L Annunzio
DEBUSSY, Alfred. L Godet; L Lesure; L Nichols
DEBUSSY, Chouchou (Claude-Emma). L Caplet 35, 37, 49, 51, 53, 58, 62, 83, 87; L Emma; L Lesure; L Nichols; L Segalen 97, 99, 123, 127ff.; L Toulet 38, 39, 42, 52, 67, 78, 82, 84, 87, 101, 109, 119, 127, 130; M Bn 77-86; M Bn Chouchou. Also see Chouchou above.
DEBUSSY, Claude (as subject and his opinions). See WS under Debussy. Also see L Lesure, L Nichols (Index of works) and WS under Debussy for index to his works discussed.

DEBUSSY, Claude. Commemorative concert 1904. L Laloy 8 [Further see Debussy Festival]
DEBUSSY, Mme Emma Bardac (née Moyse). L Annunzio; L Caplet 35, 49, 65, 77; L Durand; L Emma; L Godet; L Laloy 10, 33; L Lesure; L Lockspeiser; L Messager; L Nichols; L Segalen 86, 99, 123, 127ff.; L Toulet 38, 43, 49, 63, 68, 76, 77, 84, 86-8, 90ff, 106ff, 125-26; M Bn 9-11, 15-17, 19-21, 23, 25-32, 87-112; M Stockholm 3-4; M Texas 11; M Texas Letters by others 3, 8.
DEBUSSY, Manuel-Achille (father). L Durand 89; L Laloy 39; L Messager 83; L Nichols; L Vallery; M Texas 19/7
DEBUSSY-MANOURY, Victorine (mother) L Durand 133; L Louÿs; L Nichols; L Segalen 134; M Bn 24, 74; M Texas 36/3
DEBUSSY, Rosalie Texier (Lilly) [also see Rosalie Texier below]. L Emma; L Godet; L Laloy 12, 15; L Lesure; L Louÿs; L Louÿs 1971; L Messager 17, 41 ff, 43, 49, 75; L Nichols; L Peter; M Morgan 3, 27; M Texas 1, 29/1; Texas Letters by others 2, 8
Debussy Festival (Gala) and commemorative concerts. L Caplet 66, 68, 101; L Durand; L Laloy 8; M Bn Emma 7-10; M Texas Letters by others 11
Debussy Monument. M Bn Emma 5-6
Debussysme [Debussyism], as topic. L Caplet 18-19; L Godet; L Gui; L Nichols
DECARIS, Germaine. L Annunzio
DECOURCELLE, Pierre. WL; WL/rev.
DEGAS, Edgar. L Godet; L Lesure; L Louÿs; L Nichols
DE GROUX, H. L Lesure
DELACROIX, Eugène. L Louÿs.
DELAFOSSE, Henri. L Louÿs
DELAQUYS, Georges. WL; WL/rev.
DELIBES, Léo. L Nichols; WL/rev.
DELIUS, Frederick. WL; WL/rev.; WS
DELMAS, Marc. L Louÿs; WL; WL/rev.
DELMET, Paul. L Lesure; L Louÿs; L Nichols; WL; WL/rev.; WS
DELNA, Mlle Marie. L Louÿs; WL; WL/rev.
DELPEUCH, Edouard. L Louÿs
DELVOYE. WL; WL/rev.
DEMEST, Désiré. L Lesure; L Louÿs; L Nichols
DEMETS. L Louÿs
DENIS, Maurice. L Lesure; L Nichols; M Texas 27/3; WS
D'ENNERY, Adolphe. See Ennery,D
DEPANIS, Giuseppe. L Lesure; L Nichols
DESCHANEL, Emile. L Louÿs
DESCHANEL, Paul. L Louÿs
DESJARDINS, Dr. Abel. L Annunzio; L Lesure; L Nichols; M Morgan 3
DESROUSSEAUX, Mme. L Lesure; L Nichols
DESTOUCHES, A.-C. WL; WL/rev.; WS

DETHOMAS, Maxime. L Louÿs
DETROYAT, L. WL; WL/rev.
DEUTSCH, M. [possibly same as the following]. L Nichols
DEUTSCH DE LA MEURTHE. L Durand 117
DEVRIES, David. WL; WL/rev.
DIABELLI. L Annunzio
Diable dans le beffroi. L Caplet/Lockspeiser; L Durand 43, 81, 98; L Godet; L Messager 22, 70, 74; L Nichols; L Toulet 21; M Bn 57; M Texas 28

DIAGHILEV, Serge. L Annunzio; L Caplet 87, 98; L Cobb; L Durand 77, 78, 85, 110, 111; L Emma 108; L Laloy 34-35; L Lesure; L Nichols; M Morgan 4-5; M Texas 13; WL; WL/rev.; WS
Diane au bois. L Baron; L Nichols; L Prunières; L Stravinsky; L Vasnier; WS
DICKENS, Charles. L Godet; L Nichols
DIERX, Léon. L Godet
DIETSCHY, Marcel. WS
DIEULAFOY, Jane. WL; WL/rev.; WS
D'INDY see INDY, V. D'.
Dives. L Nichols
DIVOIRE, Fernand. L Louÿs; WL; Wl/rev.
DOCQUOIS, Georges. WL; WL/rev.
Doctor Gradus ad Parnassum. WS
DODERET, André. L Annunzio
DOIRE, René. L Lesure; L Nichols; WL; Wl/rev.
DOMREMY. L Annunzio
DONATELLA (Nathalie de Goloubeff). L Annunzio
DONNAY, Maurice. L Louÿs
DORBON, Mons. L Laloy 40; M Texas 14; M Texas Letters by others 10; WL; WL/rev.
DORET, Gustave. L Doret; L Lesure; L Nichols
DOUCET, Camille. L Louÿs
DORGERE, Mme. L Louÿs 1971
DORET, Gustave. L Emma 136
DOSTOIEVSKY. L Annunzio [see under **Frères Karamazov**]; WL; WL/rev.
DOUMIC. L Toulet 76
DOUNAY, Mme. L Louÿs 1971.
Douze études. See **Etudes**.
DRANEM (Armand Menard). L Durand 60; L Lesure; L Nichols
Dresden. L Annunzio
DREYFUS, Alfred [including L'Affaire Dreyfus]. L Louÿs; M Morgan 36; WS
DROEGHMANS, Maurice. WL; WL/rev.
DUBOIS, Théodore. L Louÿs 1971; L Nichols; WL; WL/rev.; WS
DUBOUT, Alfred. L Louÿs.
DUBUS, Edouard. L Lesure; L Nichols
DUCASSE, Roger [also see Roger-Ducasse below and in

other indexes]. L Annunzio; L Caplet 35, 76; L Lesure; L Louÿs; L Nichols
DUFRANE [or Dufranne], Hector. L Lesure; L Messager 19; L Nichols; WL; WL/rev.
DUFY, Raoul. L Godet
DUJARDIN, Edouard. L Durand 21; L Lesure; L Nichols
DUKAS, Paul. L Annunzio; L Cobb; L Durand 87, 124, 162; L Gui; L Lesure; L Louÿs; L Nichols; L Segalen 61; M Bn (unnumbered); M Bn Emma (unnumbered); M Morgan 6; M Stockholm 2; WL; WL/rev.; WS
DULAC, Edmond. L Godet; L Lesure; L Nichols
DUMAS, Alexandre. L Lesure; L Nichols
DUMAS (fils). L Lesure
DUMUR, Louis. L Louÿs
DUNCAN, Isadora. L Caplet 88; L Laloy 13; WL; WL/rev.
DUPARC, Henri. L Godet; L Nichols; WL; WL/rev.
DUPIN, Etienne. L Godet; L Laloy 22; L Lesure; L Louÿs; L Nichols
DUPONT, Mlle Gabrielle [Gaby]. L Lesure; L Louÿs; L Nichols; L Peter 224; M Morgan 17; M Texas 18/2
DUPUIS, Sylvain. L Lesure; L Nichols; WL; WL/rev.; WS
DURAN, Caolus. L Louÿs
DURAND [father of Jacques]. L Durand 27
DURAND, Emile. WS
DURAND, Jacques. L Annunzio; L Caplet 41, 43, 48, 57, 70; L Cobb; L Durand; L Godet; L Laloy 24; 34 [firm of Durand], 35; L Lesure; L Lockspeiser; L Messager 81; L Nichols; M Bn 116; M Texas 13; WL/rev.
DURAND RUEL. L Nichols
DUSE, Eleonora.
DUVAL, Paul (Jean Lorrain). L Nichols
DUVERNOY, A. WL; WL/rev.
DVORAK, Antonin. WL; WL/rev.; WS

Eastbourne (sojourn there). L Durand 29; L Nichols
Echo de Paris. L Nichols
Echo de Paris illustré. L Nichols
Ecole alsacienne. L Louys
ECORCHEVILLE, J. M Texas 36/3, 36/17; WL; WL/rev.
Edinburgh. L Nichols
EDVINA, Mme. L Caplet 67
EDWARDS, Mme. L Annunzio
Eglantin, L'. L Toulet 120
ELGAR, Sir Edward. L Nichols; WL; WL/rev.
ELIOT, George. L Lesure; L Nichols
EMERY. L Lesure; L Nichols
EMMANUEL, Maurice. L Laloy 36
EMILIENNE (Emilienne d'Alençon). L Louÿs
En blanc et noir. L Caplet 14; L Durand 134, 135, 137, 138, 140, 152, 155, 156, 157, 163, 187; L Godet; L

Nichols
En ecoutant Gabriele d'Annunzio (Raoul Aubry). L Annunzio
ENAUX, Mons. M Texas 15
Enfant prodigue. L Caplet 48, 93; L Durand 48, 49, 51, 61, 62, 64, 87, 88; L Louÿs; L Nichols; M Bn 1
ENGEL, Emile. L Godet; L Lesure; L Nichols
England and the English. L D'Annunzio [see that index under Angleterre]; L Caplet 64, 65, 66, 73, 87, 100; L Godet [letters to Jean-Aubry]; L Nichols; L Queen's Hall; L Segalen 68; L Toulet 41; M Bn 78; M Morgan 7-8; M Texas 2, 19/2, 19/4ff.
ENNERY, d'. L Lesure; L Nichols; L Peter 208.
ENOCH, Messrs, and Co. L Nichols
ENOCH, Wilhelm. L Lesure; L Nichols
Epigraphes antiques. L Durand 6, 122, 132; L Louÿs
ERB. L Nichols
ERLANGER, Camille. L Laloy 10; L Louÿs; L Nichols; WL; WL/rev.; WS
ERNST, Alfred. L Lesure; L Nichols; WL; WL/rev.
EROS. L Annunzio
ESCHYLE [also see Aeschylus]. L Laloy; WL; WL/rev.
ESCOBEDO. WL; WL/rev.
Est-ce une renaissance de la musique réligieuse? (H. Malherbe). L Annunzio
Estampes. L Durand 10, 11, 12, 13, 15, 166; L Godet; L Louÿs; L Nichols; M Bn 57; M Texas Letters by others 11
Et la lune descend sur le temple qui fut. See **Images** (2nd series)
Etienne Marcel. L Godet
Etude, The, music magazine. WS
Etudes. L Caplet 14; L Durand 132, 143, 144-45, 146, 147, 148, 150, 152, 155, 156, 157, 163, 187; L Godet; L Nichols; L Paoli; L Stravinsky; M Bn 27
EURIPIDES. L Annunzio; WL; WL/rev.
Eusellugvar. L Nichols
EVANS, Edwin. M Morgan 7-8
Excelsior, Debussy's interviews in. L Annunzio; L Nichols; WS

FABRICE, D. WL/rev.
FALLA. See De Falla above.
Falstaff (Verdi). L Annunzio
FANELLI, Ernest. WL; WL/rev.; WS
Fanfare. L Nichols
Fantaisie pour piano et orchestre. L Godet; L Louÿs; L Nichols; L Poniatowski
FANTIN-LATOUR, Théodore. L Godet; WL; WL/rev.
Fashoda affair. L Nichols
FAURE, Gabriel. L Caplet 92; L Fauré; L Godet; L

Lesure; L Louÿs; L Nichols; L Toulet 69; M Morgan 5; WL; WL/rev.; WS
FAYET, Gustave. L Segalen 61
FEART, Mlle Rose. L Caplet 52; L Durand 176; L Emma 92; L Lesure; L Nichols
Femme et le pantin, La (P. Louÿs). L Annunzio; L Louÿs
FENEON, Félix. M Texas 16; WL; WL/rev.; WS
FERRER, Paz. L Annunzio
FERRIER, Paul. L Nichols
Festin, Le. L Nichols
Fêtes galantes (ballet project). L Durand 134; L Laloy 39, 40
Fêtes galantes (song sets). L Durand 19, 21; L Godet; L Louÿs; L Nichols; WS
FEUILLADE, L. WL/rev.
FEURE, Georges de. L Nichols
FEVAL. L Lesure; L Nichols
FEVRIER, Henry. L Segalen 111; WL; WL/rev.; WS
FEYDEAU, Georges. L Godet; L Laloy 21; L Louÿs.
Figaro, Le. L Emma 91; L Laloy 18, 28; L Nichols; interviews of D indexed WS
Fils du ciel (Segalen). L Segalen 126
FIUME. L Annunzio
Fiumicino. L Nichols
Fiumiselino. L Nichols
"Five, The Russian." L Nichols
FLAT, Paul. WL; WL/rev.
FLAUBERT, Gustave. L Annunzio; L Baron; L Lesure; L Nichols; L Segalen 101
FLERS, Robert de. L Caplet 14; L Godet; WL; WL/rev.; WS
FLEURVILLE, Antoinette Mauté de. L Nichols
FLON, Philippe. L Durand 59, 60; L Lesure; L Nichols
FLOURY. L Louÿs
FOCILLON, H. WL/rev.
FODOR, M. de. L Lesure; L Nichols
FOKINE, Michel. L Annunzio; L Nichols
Folies Bergères. L Nichols
FONTAINAS, André. L Louÿs
FONTAINE, Mme Arthur. L Cobb; M Bn 38
FONTAINE, G. L Nichols
FONTAINE, Lucien. L Lesure; L Louÿs; L Nichols
FONTENAILLES, Hercule de. L Lesure; L Nichols; L Toulet 10
FOOTIT (clown). L Godet; L Peter 214
FORAIN, Jean-Louis, Mr et Mme. L Lesure; L Louÿs; L Nichols; L Peter 204, 205; L Toulet 76; M Morgan 23; M Texas 18/3
FORDYCE. L Louÿs
FOREAU-ISNARDON, Mme. L Durand 49
FORGES, H. de. L Louÿs 1971.
FOUCHER, Paul. L Louÿs
FOUQUIERES, André de. L Emma 91
FOURCAUD, Gabrielle de. L Segalen 135

FOURCAUD, L. de. L Godet; WL; WL/rev.; WS
FOURNIER, P. L Nichols
FRAGEROLLE, Georges. L Lesure; L Louÿs; L Nichols
FRANCE, Anatole. L Godet
France and French life. L Durand 98, 100, 138ff., 141; L Nichols; L Segalen 100
FRANCHETTI, A. WL/rev.
Francis of Assisi, Saint [see under François d'Assise]. L Annunzio; L Godet
FRANCK, Alphonse. L Louÿs; L Peter 219, 221.
FRANCK, César. L Chausson; L Godet; L Laloy 22; L Lesure; L Louÿs; L Nichols; L Segalen 137; L Vasnier; WL; WL/rev.; WS
FRANC-NOHAIN. L Louÿs
FRANÇOIS II, duc de Bretagne. L Annunzio
Frederick II, of Hohenstaufen. L Annunzio
Frères en art (F.E.A.). L Nichols
FRIEDMAN, Ignaz. L Nichols
FREILIGRATH. WL; WL/rev.
FRIESZ, Othon. L Godet
FREUDER. L Emma 77
FRICHE, Mlle. WL; WL/rev.
FRIEDMANN, I. L Durand 130-32; L Lesure
FROMONT, Eugène (editor). L Durand; L Godet; L Lesure; L Messager 21, 30, 33, 36, 57, 73; L Nichols; M Morgan 9-10. Also see the following.
FROMONT, Mme Eugène. M Morgan 11
FUCHS, Charles. M Texas Letters by others 5
FUCHS, Henriette. L Lesure; L Lesure/Concordia; L Nichols; L Vidal; M Bn 75
FUGERE, L. WL; WL/rev.
FULLER, Loie. L Caplet 37, 88; M Bn Emma 3-4
Futurism. WS

GABY. See Dupont, Mlle Gabrielle.
GAILHARD, P. WL; WL/rev.; WS
GALLET, Louis. WL; WL/rev.; WS
Gallois, Le. WL/rev.
GANNE, Louis. L Lesure; L Messager 57; L Nichols
GARDEN, Mary. L Caplet 61; L Laloy 9; L Lesure; L Louÿs; L Messager 15, 19, 39, 39, 46, 51, 66; L Nichols; L Segalen 83-4; M Texas 2, 16; WL; WL/rev.; WS
GARDONE. L Annunzio
GATTI-CASAZZA, Giulio. L Lesure; L Nichols
GAUGUIN, Paul. L Godet; L Lesure; L Nichols; L Segalen 56, 58, 61, 82
GAULTIER, Jules de. L Segalen 86, 92, 99, 101, 102, 111, 123, 135, 139
GAUTHIER, Eva. M NY
GAUTHIERS-VILLARS, Henry [see also WILLY, pseudonym]. L Louÿs; L Lesure; L Nichols; WL; WL/rev.; WS

GAUTIER, Mme Judith. L Lesure; L Louÿs; L Nichols
GAUTIER, Théophile. L Lesure; L Nichols; L Toulet 40; WL; WL/rev.
GAVIOLI. WL; WL/rev.
GEDALGE, André. L Louÿs; WL; WL/rev.
GEIGER, Dr. Raymond. M Texas 17
GEMIER, Firmin. L Lesure; L Nichols; L Toulet 5, 11, 107-8, 111, 113
Geneva, city and conservatory. L Nichols
GEORGE, King. L Godet
GEORGES, Alexandre. L Godet
GEORGES, Mlle Léone. L Nichols; L Toulet 43
GEORGES-MICHEL. WL/rev.
GERARD, General. L Nichols
GERBAUT or GERBAND, Mr. L Emma 94; L Lesure; L Nichols
GERMAN, Edward. L Nichols
Germany (also see War, World, I). L Nichols; M Bn 74, 84
GEVAERT. L Durand 17-18
Ghent. L Nichols
GHEON, Henri. L Annunzio; L Laloy 34
GHEUSI, P.-B. L Durand 121; L Lesure; L Nichols; M Morgan 12; WL; WL/rev.
GIDE, André. L Lesure; L Louÿs; L Nichols; M Morgan 17; WL; WL/rev.; WS
GIGOUT, Eugène. L Nichols
Gigues [also see **Images** for orch.]. L Caplet 24, 44, 57-8, 69, 91, 92-3; L Godet; L Nichols
Gil Blas, Le. L Godet; L Messager 62; L Nichols; M Texas 19/15; WS (Debussy's articles in)
GILBERT DE VOISINS, Louise. L Segalen 143, 144
GILLET. L Louÿs; M Texas 5/2
GILMAN, Lawrence. L Laloy 26
GIORDANO, Umberto. L Lesure; L Nichols
GLUCK, C.W. von. L Caplet 63; L Laloy 22; L Lesure; L Nichols; L Segalen 67, 100; WL; WL/rev.; WS
GOBLOT, E. WL/rev.
GODARD, Benjamin. L Caplet 88; L Louÿs
GODET, Robert. L Annunzio; L Caplet 17; L Godet; L Laloy 23; L Lesure; L Lockspeiser; L Louÿs; L Louÿs 1971; L Nichols; WL; WL/rev.; WS
GOETHE, Johann Wolfgang von. L Godet; L Lesure; L Nichols; WL; WL/rev.
Golliwog's Cakewalk, from **Children's Corner** [which also see]. WS
GOLOUBEFF (Donatella), Countess. See Donatella.
GONCOURT. L Segalen 72
GORKY, Maxim. WL; Wl/rev.
Gougy (bookstore). L Peter 215.
GOÜIN, Isabel. See LANG, F.
GOULUE [L. Weber, called La Goulue]. L Lesure
GOUNOD, Charles. L Godet; L Lesure; L Louÿs; L Louÿs 1971; L Nichols; L Poniatowski; L Vasnier; M

Morgan 25; WL; WL/rev.; WS
GOURMONT, Rémy de. L Louÿs; L Peter 217
GOYA, Francisco. L Durand 137; L Nichols
GOZZOLI, Benozzo. L Annunzio
grammophone (also see Aeolian Co.). M Bn Var.; M Texas 19/6
Granada. L Nichols
GRANADOS. M Morgan 26
Grand Guignol. L Nichols
Grande revue. L Annunzio; L Nichols
GRANDMOUGIN, Charles. L Louÿs
GRAVOLLET, Paul. L Nichols
Greece. L Nichols; L Segalen 82-3
GREEF, A. de. WL; WL/rev.
GREGH, Fernand. L Louÿs
GREFFULHE, Countess. L Laloy 18; L Lesure; L Nichols
GREY, Lady. L Nichols
GRIEG. E. L Durand 119; L Godet; L Lesure; L Nichols; M Morgan 30, 36; M Texas 2; WL; WL/rev.; WS
GRIMM. L Louÿs
GROUX, Henri de. L Godet; L Nichols
GROVLEZ, Gabriel. L Laloy 40; WL; WL/rev.; WS
GRUET, Charles. L Lesure: L Nichols
GUADAGNINI. L Annunzio
GUARNERI. L Annunzio
GUERIN, Charles. L Messager 32
GUERITTE, T.J. L Godet; L Guéritte
GUI, Vittorio. L Caplet 26, 97; L Gui; L Lesure; L Nichols; L Paoli 3
Guide musical. L Nichols
GUILBERT, Mlle Yvette. L Louÿs
GUILLAMAT. WL; WL/rev.
GUILLAUME II. WL/rev.
GUIRAUD, Ernest. L Lesure; L Nichols; L Vidal; WS
GUIRAUDON, Mlle. WL; WL/rev.
GULBRANSON, Ellen. WL; WL/rev.
GULON (engraver of **Pelléas**). L Lesure; L Messager 73; L Nichols
GUNSBOURG, R. WL; WL/rev.; WS

HABRARD, Adrien. L Louÿs
Hague, The. L Nichols
HAHN, Reynaldo. L Annunzio; L Laloy 38; L Lesure; L Louÿs; L Nichols
HALEVY, M. WS
HALEVY, J.-F.-F. WL; WL/rev.
HALL, Mrs. Elisa. L Durand 33; L Lesure; L Louÿs; L Messager 61; L Nichols
HALS, F. WL/rev.
Hamelle (publishers). L Godet; L Nichols
HAMMERSTEIN, Oscar I. L Durand 88; L Nichols
HANDEL, George Frideric. L Godet; L Nichols; WL;

WL/rev.; WS
Handler, Louis. L Annunzio
Hansel und Gretel (Humperdinck). L Messager 36
HARCOURT, Edmond d'. WL [see entry below]; WL/rev.
HARCOURT, Eugène d'. L Godet; WS
Harper's Weekly. L Nichols; WS
HARTMANN, ARTHUR. (violinist). L Durand 119 L Emma 90ff.; L Hartmann
HARTMANN, Dr. L Durand 89
HARTMANN, Georges (editor). L Cobb; L Godet; L Laloy 40; L Lesure; L Louÿs; L Nichols; M Morgan 11, 13-14; M Texas 18; WL; WL/rev.
HASSELMANS, Marguerite. WL; WL/rev.; WS
HATTO, Jeanne. WL; WL/rev.
HAUPTMANN, Gerhart. L Lesure; L Nichols
HAUTSTOUT, J. L Laloy 24
Havre, Le. L Nichols
HAWKINS. L Godet
HAYDN, Joseph. L Godet; WL; WL/rev.
HAYOT. L Laloy 9; L Lesure; L Nichols
Hébert, Ernest. L Lesure; L Nichols; WL; WL/rev.; WS
HEGLON, Mme. WL; WL/rev.
HEINE, Heinrich. L Lesure: L Louÿs; L Nichols; WL; WL/rev.; WS
HELLE, André. L Durand 118; 121; L Lesure; L Nichols; WL/rev.
HELLMANN [HELMANN]. L Lesure; L Nichols
HENDERSON, David-G. WL; WL/rev.
HENRI IV, King of France. L Toulet 68
HEREDIA, José de. L Lesure; L Louÿs; L Nichols
HEREDIA (Mme Pierre Louÿs, née Louise de Hérédia). L Louÿs; L Nichols
HERELLE, Georges. L Annunzio
HERMANT, Abel. L Louys
HEROLD, Ferdinand. L Lesure; L Louÿs; L Nichols; L Peter 216, 217; M Morgan 17; WL; WL/rev.
HEROLD, Louis. L Nichols
HERVE. L Lesure; L Louÿs; L Nichols; WL; WL/rev.
HETTANGE, M. WL/rev.
HEUGEL, H.G. L Lesure; L Nichols
Heure espagnole, L (Ravel). L Annunzio
HEWLETT, Maurice. L Godet
HIGGINS. L Durand 72; L Lesure; L Messager 42; L Nichols; M Morgan 12
Histoire de Tristan, L'. L Durand 51, 54, 55; L Segalen 87
HOCHON, M. L Lesure; L Nichols
HOCQUET, Vital. L Nichols
HOECKEL. L Toulet 76
HOFMANN, Josef. L Nichols
HOKUSAI. L Godet
Holland, voyage to and impressions [also see specific cities]. L Emma; L Durand 120; L Nichols; L

Stockholm 1
HOLMES, Augusta. L Peter; M Morgan 23; WL; WL/rev.; WS
HOMER (**Odyssey**). L Toulet 76
Hommage à Haydn. L Durand 76
HONEGGER, Arthur. L Annunzio
Hôtel Gonnet. L Nichols
Hôtel Hungarian. L Nichols
Houlgate. L Nichols
HOUSTON-CHAMBERLAIN, S. L Louÿs
HROSWITHA. L Godet
HUBAY, Jeno. M LC Szanto and Hubay
HUE, Georges. L Louÿs; L Nichols; WL; WL/rev.; WS
HUGO, Victor. L Lesure; L Louÿs; L Louÿs 1971; L Nichols; L Durand 144; L Segalen 101; WL; WL/rev.
HUMMEL. L Godet
Hungary and its music [also see Budapest]. L Emma 90; L Nichols; L Segalen 85; M LC Szanto and Hubay; M Texas 19/1
HURE, Jean. WL; WL/rev.
HURET, Jules. L Godet; L Lesure; L Nichols
HUVELIN, P. WL; WL/rev.
HUYSMANS, K.-J. L Baron; L Chansarel; L Segalen 49, 61, 72

Ibéria. L Annunzio; L Caplet 15, 16, 19, 44-46, 68, 91, 93, 101; L Godet; L Emma 80 ff; L Nichols; L Segalen 123; WS. [also see **Images** for orch.]
IBSEN, Henrik. L Lesure; L Nichols; WL; WL/rev.
Ièna, Hôtel d'. L Annunzio
Il pleure dans mon coeur. L Hartmann
Ile de France. L Annunzio
Images (orchestra). L Caplet 26, 41, 91; L Durand 26, 28, 40, 43, 45, 48, 51, 55, 58, 63, 68, 70, 77, 80, 81, 83, 93, 104, 105, 109, 112, 117, 164; L Louÿs; L Nichols; L Segalen 50, 102; M Morgan 7; M Texas 19/8; WS
Images (Oubliées, piano). M Texas 18/15
Images (première série, piano). L Durand 28, 30, 31, 32, 33, 34, 188; L Messager 70; L Nichols; WS
Images (deuxième série, piano). L Durand 47; L Godet [also see **Et la lune**]; M Texas 19/18; WS
IMBERT. WL; WL/rev.
Immémoriaux, Les (Segalen). L Segalen throughout
Impressionism. L Durand 58
India and its music. L Segalen 59, 60, 68
INDY, Vincent d'. L Cobb; L Godet; L Laloy 7; L Lesure; L Louÿs; L Segalen 55; L Vasnier; M Bn 5, 18; WL; WL/rev.; WS [also alphabetized d'Indy in some indexes]
INGHELBRECHT, D.-E. L Annunzio; L Caplet 16; L Durand 116; L Godet; L Laloy 40; L Lesure; L Nichols; L Toulet 67; M Bn 22, 74; M Morgan 14; WL; WL/rev.;

WS
INGRES. L Durand 12, 66
Initiation, L'. L Nichols
INJALBERT, Jean-Antoine. L Godet
Intransigeant, L'. [Debussy's article in] WS
Iran. L Annunzio
IRRIBE, Paul. L Toulet 109
ISELIER, Paul. L Louÿs
Isle joyeuse, L'. L Durand 20, 21; L Nichols; L Paoli 4; L Segalen 85, 137
ISNARDON, Mme Jacques. WL; WL/rev.
Italian opera. WS
Italy, voyage to and impressions [also see particular cities]. L Emma [see that table of contents]; L Gui; L Nichols; L Toulet 41, 45; M LC Szanto

JACOB, J. L Louÿs
JACQUELINE, Mons. M Texas 20
JACQUES-DALCROZE, Emile. L Nichols
JAELL, Marie. L Durand 150; L Nichols
JAMET, Pierre. L Durand 176-77; L Godet
JAMMES, Francis. L Godet; L Lesure; L Nichols
JANNEQUIN, Clément. WL; WL/rev.; WS
Japan. L Durand 153; L Godet [see Japon]; L Laloy 15; L Nichols; L Segalen 124-5, 131
Jardins sous la pluie. L Durand 10; L Louÿs; WS
JARECKI. L Godet
Java and Javanese art. L Godet; L Nichols
JEAN, Albert. L Nichols
JEAN-AUBRY, G. L Godet [see letters to Jean Aubry]; L Lockspeiser; L Nichols; M Texas 19; WL; WL/rev.; WS; see under Aubry in L Lesure
JEMAIN, J. WL/rev.
JEHIN. L Lesure; L Nichols
JENPAIN. WL; WL/rev.
Jersey. L Nichols
JESSLER, Count. L Annunzio
JESUS. L Annunzio [see also CHRIST]. L Nichols
Jet d'eau. L Caplet 25; L Godet
Jeux. L Annunzio; L Caplet 13, 16, 27, 50, 98, 99; L Durand 110, 111, 114, 119, 178, 180; L Emma 141; L Godet; L Nichols; L Stravinsky; L Toulet 84, 89; M Texas 36/13-16; WS
JOAN OF ARC. L Nichols
JOLY, Charles. WL; WL/rev.
JOBERT. L Nichols
JOFFRE, Marshal. L Nichols
Joinville. L Nichols
JONCIERES, V. WL; WL/rev.; WS
JOSERE. L Toulet 44
JOSQUIN DES PRES. WL/rev.
JOUB, Romuald. L Annunzio

JOUMET, Albert. L Baron
Journal, Le. L Nichols
JULLIEN, AD. WL; WL/rev.
Jurançon. L Toulet 36, 37
JUSSEAUME, L. L Lesure; L Nichols; M Texas 2; WL; WL/rev.

KANT, Immanuel. L Laloy 35; L Nichols
KARATEGUINE. L Durand 159
KARSAVINA, Tamara. L Annunzio; L Laloy 35; L Nichols; WL; WL/rev.
KEATS, John. L Godet; L Lesure; L Nichols
KERPELY. L Nichols
KERST, L. WL/rev.

Khamma. L Annunzio; L Caplet 27, 88; L Caplet/Lockspeiser; L Durand 105, 108, 116; L Emma 89; L Godet; L Nichols; L Segalen 134
King Albert's Book. L Nichols
King Lear. See **Roi Lear, Le**.
KIPLING, R. L Laloy 35
KIRKBY-LUNN, Mme. WL; WL/rev.
Kléber, Avenue. L Annunzio
KOCHNITZKY, Léon. L Annunzio
KODALY, Z. WL/rev.
KOECHLIN, Charles. L Caplet/Lockspeiser; L Godet
KOPFF. L Durand 53
Koran. L Annunzio [see Coran]
KORSOFF, Mlle. WL; WL/rev.
KOUSSEVITZKY, Serge. L Caplet 26 L Emma 102ff.; L Godet; L Lesure; L Nichols; L Stravinsky; M Bn 79; WL; WS
KRAUSS. WL; WL/rev.
KROPOTKINE, Prince. L Louÿs; L Louÿs 1971
KRUGER. L Louÿs
KUFFERATH, Maurice. L Durand 120; L Lesure; L Nichols; M Bn 33; WL/rev.
KUNC. L Nichols
KURNE [also see Curnonsky and Kurnonsky]. L Toulet 14, 20, 22, 24
KURNONSKY. L Louÿs 1971
KURSAAL, Montreux. L Nichols
KUSSEWITZKY. WL/rev. [also see Koussevitzky above and in other indexes]

LA FONTAINE, Jean de. L Durand 142; L Nichols; WL; WL/rev.
LA JEUNESSE, Ernest. L Lesure; L Louÿs; L Nichols; L Peter.
LA POUPLINIERE. WL; WL/rev.

LA PUCE. L Toulet 90
LA TOUR. L Laloy 27
La Scala. L Nichols. Also see Scala, La
Labergement Sainte-Marie. L Nichols
LABOUNSKAYA. L Louÿs
LACERDA, Francisco de. L Laloy 17, 18, 19, 21, 22, 26; L Lesure; L Nichols
LACOMBE. M Texas 20
LACOMBLEZ. L Louÿs
LADMIRAULT, Paul. WL; WL/rev.
LAFFITTE. WL/rev.
LAFLER BURCKARD, Mme. WL; WL/rev.
LAFORGUE, Jules. L Chansarel; L Cobb; L Godet; L Lesure; L Louÿs; L Peter; L Nichols; WL; WL/rev.; WS
LAGOANIERE (de). L Louÿs
LALO, Edouard. L Lesure; L Nichols; M Bn 6; WL; WL/rev.; WS
LALO, Pierre. L Annunzio; L Caplet 17, 18, 39, 47, 90, 93; L Laloy 18, 26; L Lesure; L Louÿs; L Nichols; L Segalen 74, 92; M Texas 2/4; WL; WL/rev.; WS
LALOY, Louis. L Annunzio; L Durand 88, 145, 160, 162; L Godet; L Laloy 36 [together with all Laloy letters]; L Lesure; L Lockspeiser; L Louÿs; L Nichols; L Segalen 59, 60, 63, 74, 106, 109, 129, 131; L Stravinsky; L Toulet 67, 88; L Vallery; M Morgan 16; WL; WL/rev.; WS
LAMOUREUX [see also Concerts Lamoureux]. L Godet; L Lesure; L Nichols; L Toulet 10; M Morgan 19; WL/rev.
LANDORMY, Paul. L Laloy; L Lesure; L Nichols; WL; WL/rev.
LANE, T. WL/rev.
LANG, Alfred, François, and Isabel Lang-Goüin. M Lang
LANGE-MUELLER, Peter. L Nichols
LANSON, Gustave. L Annunzio
LAPARRA, Raoul. L Lesure; L Nichols
LARA, Mons. Isidore de. L Durand 118
Larousse. L Nichols
LARTIGUE, Jean. L Segalen 138-9
Larue (restaurant). L Annunzio; L Nichols
LASSUS, O. de [Orlando di Lasso]. L Lesure; L Nichols; L Vasnier; WL; WL/rev.; WS
LASVIGNES, Henri. WL; WL/rev.
LATINI, Brunetto. L Annunzio
LATOUR, Contamine de. L Louÿs
LAUDET, Fernand. L Annunzio
Laudi (d'Annunzio). L Annunzio
Lauriston, Rue. L Annunzio
Lausanne. L Nichols
LAVEDAN, Henri. L Annunzio; WL; WL/rev.
LAVISSE, Ernest. L Peter

LAW, J. WL/rev.
LAZZARI, Sylvio. L Louÿs
LE BARGY. L Nichols
LE CARDONNEL, Louis. L Godet
LE FLEM, Paul. L Annunzio.
LE GRIX, Francois. L Annunzio
LE NOTRE, André. L Durand 136; L Nichols
Lear, King. See **Roi Lear, Le**.
LEBEAU, Narcisse (pseudonym of Vital Hocquet). L Louÿs
LEBEY, André. L Cobb; L Louÿs
LEBLANC, Georgette [also see Maeterlinck]. L Godet; L Lesure; L Nichols; M Texas Letters by others 5
LECLERCQ, Maurice. WL; WL/rev
Leda. L Louÿs
LEFEVRE, Frédéric. L Louÿs
Légion d'honneur, Debussy's reception of. L Laloy 6
LEHMANN, Liza. L Nichols
LEJEUNE, Claude. WL; WL/rev.; WS
LEKEU, Guillaume. L Louÿs; WL; WL/rev.
LEMAIRE, Gaston. L Louÿs; L Messager 70
LENORMAND, René. L Lesure; L Nichols; WL; WL/rev.; WS
LEONARDO DA VINCI. L Nichols; Also see Da Vinci
LEONCAVALLO, Ruggerio. L Lesure; L Louÿs; L Messager 66; L Nichols; WL; WL.rev.; WS
LEROLLE, Henry. L Lesure; L Louÿs; L Nichols
LEROUX, Xavier. WL; WL/rev.
LESUEUR, J.-F. L Godet; WL; WL/rev.
LETELLIER, Henri. L Louÿs
LEUDET, Maurice. WL; WL/rev.
LEVADE, Charles. L Lesure; L Louÿs; L Nichols
LEVINSON, André. L Caplet 88
LEVY, Hermann. WL; WL/rev.
LHEUREUX. WL; WL/rev.
LIADOW, A. L Louÿs
LIANE DE POUGY, Mlle. L Louÿs 1971; L Peter. Also see Chassaigne, Anna-Marie.
LIAPUNOV. L Nichols
Librairie de l'art indépendant. L Nichols
Libre esthétique. L Nichols
LIEBAN. WL; WL/rev.
LIEBICH, Franz and Louise. L Godet; L Laloy 37; M Texas 19/11, 19/16; M Texas Letters by others 10
LIEBSTOECKEL, Hans. L Louÿs
LILLIAZ. L Toulet 125
LINDENLAUB. M Texas 21
LINOR, G. WL; WL/rev.
LISZT, Franz. L Caplet 95; L Durand 150, 188; L Godet; L Hartmann; L Lesure; L Louÿs; L Nichols; L Segalen 108; WL; WL/rev.; WS
liturgical music. WS
LITVINE, F. L Durand 35; WL; WL/rev.
LOCARD, E. WL/rev.
LOCKSPEISER, Edward. L Nichols; WL/rev.

LOLIEE, M. WL rev.
London, Debussy's visits to and opinions of. L Annunzio; L Emma; L Laloy 15, 28, 32, 22; L Nichols; WS
London, visits and impressions. See England.
LONG, Marguerite. L Durand 182; L Lesure; L Nichols
LONG, Roger. M Bn Emma 12, 15
LONGUS. L Louÿs
LONGY, G. L Messager 61
LORET, V. WL/rev.
LORIN, Georges. L Godet
LORRAIN, Jean (Paul Duval). L Lesure; L Louÿs; L Louÿs 1971; L Nichols; L Peter; WL; WL/rev.
LOTI, Mlle. Manon. L Louÿs 1971
LOUBET, Emile. L Louÿs; L Messager
LOUIS, Georges. L Godet; L Louÿs
LOUIS, Rudolf. L Lesure; L Nichols
LOUIS IX, Saint. L Caplet 55, 97; L Nichols
LOUIS XIV. L Durand 183; L Toulet 57
LOUIS-PHILIPPE. WL/rev.
LOUYS, Louise (née Hérédia). L Nichols
LOUYS, Pierre. L Caplet 9; L Chausson 6; L Cobb; L Godet; L Lesure; L Lockspeiser; L Louÿs; L Louÿs/1971; L Nichols; L Peter; L Segalen 50, 64, 98; M Bn 72; M Lang; M LC Louys; M NY; M Morgan 17-19, 22-23; M Texas 22-23; M Texas Letters by others 2; WL; WL/rev.; WS
LOWE, Ferdinand. L Caplet 94
LUCIAN of Samothrace. L Nichols
LUDWIG II, King of Bavaria. L Nichols; WL/rev. (where see Louis II)
LUGNE-POE. L Louÿs; L Nichols
LUGNIER, Antoine. M Bn 34
LUIGINI, A. L Laloy 17; WL; WL/rev.; WS
LULLY, Jean-Baptiste. L Caplet 63; WL; WL/rev.
LUQUIN. L Laloy 10, 11
LUTHER, Martin. WL; WL/rev.
Luxembourg Gardens. L Nichols; M Bn 74
LUZZATI, Arturo. L Louÿs
LYON, G. M Texas 15; WL; WL/rev.
Lyon Opera. L Nichols

Ma première rencontre avec G. d'Annunzio (Ida Rubinstein). L Annunzio.
MACHOU, Arthur. L Toulet 8
MACKENZIE, Sir Alexander. L Nichols
Madrid Symphony Orchestra. WS
MAETERLINCK, Maurice. L Annunzio; L Godet; L Lesure; L Nichols; L Segalen 63, 64, 111; WL; WS
MAETZEL (metronome). L Durand 139, 158
MAETERLINCK, Maurice. L Caplet 89; L Chausson 6; L Durand 117, 183; L Louÿs; L Peter; L Segalen 63,

64, 111; M Bn 72; M Texas 36/10; M Texas Letters by others 1; WL; WL/rev.; WS
MAGNIER, Maurice. L Louÿs
MAGUENAT. L Caplet 68; L Lesure; L Nichols
MAILLART, Aimé. L Caplet 92; L Lesure; L Nichols
Maison de l'Oeuvre, la. L Nichols
MALHERBE, Henry. L Annunzio; WL; WL/rev.
MALLARME, Stéphane. L Chausson 4; L Godet; L Lesure; L Louÿs; L Nichols; L Durand 115; M Texas 9/2, 19/9; WL/rev.; WS
MALVY. L Toulet 114
MANCERON, Henry. L Segalen 103-04, 133, 140, 141
MANCERON, Mme. L Segalen 92
Manchester. L Nichols
MANET, Edouard. L Baron; L Godet; WS
MANFRED. L Annunzio
Manon (opera by Massenet). L Durand 19
MANOUVRIER. L Godet
MANTEGNA. L Annunzio
MAQUET. L Lesure; L Nichols
Marche écossaise [**Marche des anciens comtes de Ross**]. L Emma 111, 137; L Godet; L Laloy 14; L Nichols [where see both titles]
Marche nuptiale. L Louÿs
MARCOUX, Vanni. L Caplet 76; L Durand 72; L Lesure; L Nichols; M Morgan 12; M Texas 24
MARECHAL, Alph. WL; WL/rev.
MARIE, Gabriel. L Louÿs
MARIE-ANTOINETTE. WL/rev.
MARIVAUX. WL; WL/rev.
MARLBOROUGH, Duke of. L Nichols
Marmontel. L Nichols
MARNOLD, Jean. L Laloy 16, 39; L Lesure; L Nichols; L Segalen 74; M LC Marnold; M NY; M Morgan 20; WL; WL/rev.
MARONI, Gian Carlo. L Annunzio
MAROT, Mlle Blanche. L Laloy 9, 10; L Lesure; L Louÿs; L Nichols; M Texas 25
MARTENOT, M. L Messager 19
MARTENOT, R. [also see the above]. M Bn (unnumbered); M Bn Var.
MARTIN IV, Pope. L Annunzio
MARTY, Georges. L Lesure; L Nichols; L Vasnier
Martyre de Saint Sébastien. L Annunzio [see names of specific sections]; L Caplet 13, 14, 18, 23, 24, 26, 27, 50-52, 55-6, 75, 96; L Durand 96, 97, 99, 103, 112; L Godet [see St. Sébastien]; L Nichols; L Paoli; L Segalen 127, 129, 131, 137; L Vallery; M Bn 54-55; M Bn Var.; M Texas 4, 36/4; WS
MASCAGNI, Emi. L Annunzio
MASCAGNI, Pietro. L Louÿs 1971; L Nichols; WL; WL/rev.; WS
Masques. L Durand 19, 21; L Nichols

Masques et bergamasques. L Caplet 88; L Durand 78, 83, 84; L Laloy 34-35, 37; L Nichols; M Texas Other materials
MASSENET, Jules. L Chausson 3; L Chansarel; L Durand 66, 99; L Lesure; L Louÿs; L Nichols; L Poniatowski; L Vallery; M Morgan 25; WL; WL/rev.; WS
MASSINE, Léonide. L Nichols; M Morgan 5
MASTIO, Catherine. WL; WL/rev.
MATHILDE, Princess. L Lesure
Matin, Le, Debussy's article on Massenet. L Laloy; WS
MATTHISON, F. von. WL/rev.
MAUCLAIR, Camille. L Lesure; L Nichols; WL/rev.
MAUPASSANT, Guy de. L Caplet 9; L Lesure; L Louÿs; L Nichols; L Segalen 112
MAUS, Octave. L Lesure; L Nichols; WS
MAUTE DE FLEURVILLE, Mme. L Durand 131, 150; L Godet; L Lesure; L Segalen 107 [also see the following]
MAUTE DE FLEURVILLE, Mathilde. L Godet
MAX-ANELY [pseudonym of V. Segalen]. L Segalen 68
Maxim (restaurant). L Godet
MAYEUR. L Louÿs
Mazurka (piano). M Morgan 11
Meck, Mme N. de. L Caplet 16; L Lesure; L Nichols
Meck, Sonia von. L Vallery
MEHUL. WL; WL/rev.
MELBA, Nelly. L Annunzio
MELLOT-JOUBERT, Mme. L Godet; L Nichols
MELTZER, C.H. WL/rev.
Melun. L Nichols
MEMLING, Hans. L Annunzio
MENARD, Armand (Dranem). L Nichols
MENDELSSOHN, Felix. L Louÿs; WL; WL/rev.; WS
MENDES, Catulle. L Godet; L Laloy 10; L Lesure; L Louÿs; L Nichols; M Texas 26; WL; WL/rev.; WS
Mer, La. L Caplet 57, 87, 90-1; L Durand 10, 14, 15, 21, 23, 24, 25, 26, 30, 32, 35, 36, 39, 40, 44, 48, 57, 70, 93, 180; L Emma 81, 104; L Godet; L Laloy 16, 17, 26, 28; L Messager 74; L Nichols; L Peter; L Segalen 87, 89, 90, 91-2, 106; M Bn 57; M Texas 19/14, 19/16, 27/3; WS
Mer est plus belle que les cathédrales, La. See **Trois mélodies de Verlaine**
Mercédès-Hotel. L Annunzio
MERCIER, Henry. L Godet; L Lesure; L Nichols
MERCIN. L Nichols
Mercure de France, Debussy's article in. L Annunzio; L Nichols; M Bn 67; M Texas 19; WS
Mercure musical (review). L Laloy 12, 13, 15, 16, 19, 20, 22, 23, 27; L Nichols; L Segalen 49, 57, 59, 129
Mère Michel. L Toulet 54
MEREDITH, G. L Toulet 113

MERIEM BEN ATALA. L Louÿs
MERODE, Mlle. Cléo de. L Durand 18; L Louÿs
MEROLLE, Mme. L Nichols
MESMAECKER, P.-J. de. WL; WL/rev.
MESSAGER, André. L Caplet 12, 13; L Godet; L Lesure; L Louys; L Laloy 10; L Lockspeiser; L Messager; L Nichols; L Segalen 99; L Toulet 11; M Bn 57; M Texas 18/8; WL; WL/rev.; WS. See Operetta title **Véronique** L Messager 58.
MESSAGER, Madeleine. L Messager 17; L Nichols
METENIE, O. WL/rev.
METERIE, Alphonse. WL; WL/rev.
METRA, Olivier. L Louÿs
Metropolitan Opera, New York. L Nichols; M Texas 28
METTERNICH, Mme de. WL; WL/rev.
Meurice, Hotel. L Annunzio
MEURIS, Mlle. L Louÿs
MEYER, Milly. L Durand 60
MEYERBEER, Giacomo. L Lesure; L Louÿs; L Nichols; WL; WL/rev.; WS
MEYERHOLD. L Annunzio
MICHEL, Louise. L Caplet 61, 99; WL/rev.
MICHEL, Paul-Henri. L Annunzio
MICHELANGELO [see Michel-Ange in French indexes]. L Godet; L Vasnier
Midi. L Nichols
MIKHAEL, Ephraïm. L Nichols
Milan. L Annunzio; L Nichols
Military music. WS
MILLET, Jean François. L Nichols
MILTON, Mlle. L Louÿs
MILY-MEYER, Emilie. L Lesure; L Nichols
Minstrels. L Hartmann (also see **Préludes**)
MIRBEAU, Octave. L Peter; L Segalen 72, 87; WS
MIRY. L Louÿs
MISSA, Edmond. L Lesure; L Nichols; WL; WL/rev.; WS
MLYNARSKI, E. WL; WL/rev.
MOCKEL, Albert. L Louÿs
MOLINARI, Bernardino. L Durand 180; L Lesure; L Nichols; L Paoli
MOLNAR. L Nichols
MOMIGLIANO, Eucardio. L Annunzio
MONET, Claude. L Lesure; L Nichols; M Texas 36/1; WS
MONFREID, Agnès de. L Segalen 61, 125
MONFREID, G.-D. de. L Segalen 140
Monsieur Croche, anti-dilettante. L Laloy 40; L Nichols [see M. Croche]; WS [also see Croche, Mons., above and in several other indexes.]
Mont-St.-Michel. L Toulet 53, 54
MONTABRE, Maurice. WL; WL/rev.
MONTAIGNE. L Annunzio
MONTAMET, Pierre. WL; WL/rev.
MONTEPIN, Xavier de. L Lesure; L Louÿs; L Nichols

MONTESQUIEU, Robert de. L Annunzio
MONTEVERDI, Claudio. L Annunzio
Montreux. L Nichols
MORALES, C. WL; WL/rev.
MOREAS, Jean. L Baron; L Godet; L Lesure; L Nichols
MOREAU, Léon. WL; WL/rev.; WS
MOREAU-SANTI, Mme. L Lesure; L Nichols
MORENO, Mlle. L Louÿs
MORET, Ernest. L Louÿs
MORHARDT, Mathias. L Godet
MORICE, Charles. L Baron; L Godet; L Nichols; L Segalen 135; WL; WL/rev.
MORLAND, Jacques. WL; WL/rev.
MORS, Mme. L Nichols
MOSCHELES, Ignaz. L Durand 132; L Nichols
Moscow. L Laloy 39; L Nichols. See also Russia.
MOTTL, Félix. L Durand 53, 66; WL; WL/rev.; WS
Moulleau, Le. L Annunzio; L Nichols
MOUNET-SULLY. L Louÿs
MOUREY, Gabriel. L Annunzio; L Durand 52, 56; L Laloy; 27n, 31; L Lesure; L Nichols; L Segalen 74, 75, 77; M Morgan 21; M Texas 27; WL/rev.; WS
MOUSSORGSKY, Modest. See Musorgsky
MOUTON, Henri. L Lesure; L Nichols
MOZART, Wolfgang Amadeus. L Durand 156, 164; L Nichols; L Segalen 107; WL; WL/rev.; WS
MUHLFELD, Lucien. L Louÿs
MUNCH, Charles. L Annunzio
Murano. L Annunzio
MURATORE, L. WL; WL/rev.
Musica, Debussy's articles in. L Godet; L Nichols; M Texas 19/17; WS
Musique en Suisse, La. L Nichols
MUSORGSKY (also see Mussorgsky and Moussorgsky in other indexes). L Annunzio; L Emma 109; L Godet; L Lesure; L Louÿs; L Nichols; L Stravinsky; M Bn 56; M Lang; M Texas 2; WL; WL/rev.; WS
My Apprenticeship (Colette). WS

NADAR, Paul. L Nichols; M Bn Main 2-3
NAPOLEON I, Emperor. L Godet; L Nichols; L Toulet 83; WL/rev.
NATANSON. WL; WL/rev.; WS
NATANSON, Alexandre. L Louÿs
NATANSON, Louis-Alfred. L Louÿs
NATANSON, Thadée. L Louÿs; WS
NATANSON, Mme Thadée, née Missia Godebska. L Louÿs; L Peter; WS
NEUFELDT, Ernst. WL; WL/rev.; WS
Neuilly. L Nichols
New York [See also America]. L Nichols
NEY. L Godet

Nice. L Nichols
NICHOLAS, Grand Duke. L Nichols
NICOL [Nicoll], Colonel A.L. L Godet; L Toulet 111
Niedermeyer, l'Ecole. L Godet
NIETZSCHE, Friedrich Wilhelm. L Caplet 9, 98; L Lesure; L Louÿs; L Nichols; L Peter; L Stravinsky; WL; WL/rev.
NIJINSKY. L Annunzio; L Caplet 98; L Durand 85, 180; L Emma 109; L Godet; L Laloy 35; L Lesure; L Nichols; L Toulet 72; WL; WL/rev.; WS
NIKISCH, Arthur. WL; WL/rev.; WS
NIN, Joaquin. L Nichols
No-ya-li [see also **Palais du silence**]. L Nichols
Nocturnes, Trois. L Caplet 14, 18, 36, 88; L Durand 39-40, 69, 93, 118; L Louÿs; L Louÿs 1971; L Emma 106, 137; L Godet; L Nichols; L Segalen 54, 105, 106; L Stravinsky; L Toulet 10; L Ysaye; M Morgan 9, 13-14, 19, 31; M Texas 18, 19/21; M Texas Letters to others 11; WS
Noël des enfants. L Cobb; L Durand 161; L Godet
Noirmoutiers. L Nichols
NORDAU, M.S. WL/rev.
NORDRAAK, Richard. WL; WL/rev.; WS
Normandy. L Nichols
NOSKOWSKY, Sigismund. WL; WL/rev.; WS
NOTE. L Louÿs
NOTWEG. M Texas 19/4
Nouvelle revue. L Baron; L Nichols
Nouvelle revue française. L Annunzio; L Nichols; L Segalen 143
NOVAES, Guiomar. L Nichols
Nuit d'étoiles. L Godet; L Louÿs
Nuits blanches, Les. L Nichols; M Texas 18/15
OBERLEITHNER. L Louÿs
Ode à la France. L Durand 145
OFFENBACH, Jacques. L Baron; L Lesure; L Louÿs; L Nichols; WL; WL/rev.; WS
OHNET, Georges. L Lesure; L Louÿs 1971; L Nichols
Oiseau bleu, L' (Maeterlinck). L Annunzio
Oiseau de feu, L' (Stravinsky). L Annunzio
OLENINE, Marie. L Godet; L Lesure; L Nichols; WL; WL/rev.; WS
OLLENDORF. L Nichols; WL; WL/rev.
OLLONE, Max d'. L Nichols; WL; WL/rev.; WS
Ombres chinoises. L Toulet 43
ONIDA. WL; WL/rev.
ONNEN, Frank. WL/rev.
Open-air music. WS
Opéra de Paris. L Annunzio; L Nichols; L Segalen 99; L Toulet 57; M Bn 53; WS
Opera buffa, renaissance for. WS
Opéra-Comique. L Annunzio; L Caplet 52, 68; L Durand 6, 15, 80, 121; L Laloy 27, 30; L Messager 15, 26; L

Nichols; L Segalen 105, 127; L Toulet 47-51; WS
Opinion, The. M Texas 27/4
ORLEANS, Charles d' (also see **Chansons de...**). L Annunzio; L Cobb; L Emma 103; L Laloy 29-30; L Messager; L Nichols
Orphée-roi (project with Segalen). L Nichols; L Segalen throughout; specifics 67ff.

PADEREWSKI. WL; WL/rev.
Pagodes. L Godet; L Segalen 137
Palais du silence (ballet project; also see **No-ya- li**). L Durand 120, 128; L Nichols
PALESTRINA, Giovanni Pierluigi da. L Lesure; L Nichols; L Poniatowski; L Vasnier; WL; WL/rev.; WS
Pan. L Nichols
PANATELLA. L Toulet 66
PAOLI, R. L Paoli
Paris Universal Exhibition (1889). L Nichols
Paris-Midi. L Annunzio
PARMA, Ildebrando da (PIZZETTI). L Annunzio; L Nichols
PASCAL, B. L Caplet 53, 97; L Godet
PASSAMA, Jeanne. WL; WL/rev.
PASTEUR VALLERY-RADOT. L Annunzio [also see Valery]
Pau. L Nichols
PAWLOWSKI, G. de. WL; WL/rev.
PEGUY, Charles. L Annunzio
Pintures (Segalen). L Segalen throughout
PELADAN, Joseph. L Nichols; WL; WL/rev.
Pelléas et Mélisande L Annunzio; L Caplet 11-14, 16, 19, 24, 57, 64, 65, 67, 68, 75-77, 91, 103-4; L Chausson 3, 5, 6, 9; L Durand 5, 6, 13, 16, 27, 37-8, 44, 53-55, 60, 66, 71, 73, 75, 79, 80, 88, 101, 107, 136, 169, 160, 171; L Godet; L Louÿs; L Louÿs 1971; L Emma 110, 113, 141; L Laloy 9, 21, 23, 26, 30, 32, 36; L Messager (numerous references); L Nichols; L Segalen 61, 71, 75-6, 90, 96, 97, 99, 104, 105, 106, 107, 110, 111, 125; L Toulet 4, 11, 12, 14, 23, 47, 89, 90, 106; L Vallery; M Bn 2, 33, 57, 72; M Bn Var.; M Bn Main 1; M LC Batchelder; M LC Marnold; M Morgan 8-10, 12, 17, 32-33; M Texas 2, 8, 9/1-2, 18/8-9, 19/11, 23/2, 24, 36/9; M Texas Other materials; M Texas Letters by others 1/1-2, 5; WS
PELLEGRIN, Abbé. WL; WL/rev.
PENABLE. WL; WL/rev.
PEQUIN. L Annunzio
PERDRIEL, Mme. See VAISSIERE.
Performance of Debussy's music. L Caplet 12-16
PERIER, Casimir. L Caplet 68; L Lesure; L Nichols
PERIER, Jean. L Caplet 13; L Durand 61; L Laloy 9, 37; L Messager 15, 19, 25; L Lesure; L Nichols. Also see L Caplet 68 and L Segalen.

PERIVIER. WL; WL/rev.
PERRET, Mme. WL; WL/rev.
PERRON, Louis. L Nichols
PETER, Alice. L Lesure; L Nichols [see the folowing]
PETER, Mme M.V.A. M Morgan 22-24 [also see the above]
PETER, René. L Caplet 10-12; L Lesure; L Louÿs; L Louÿs 1971; L Nichols; L Peter; M Bn 7; M Morgan 2, 22-24; M Texas 23/1, 27/3, 29; WL; WL/rev.; WS
Peters Edition. L Durand 130
PETIT. L Lesure
Petite suite L Chansarel; L Durand 93; L Godet; L Louÿs; L Nichols; L Segalen 87
Petrograd. L Nichols
PHILIPPE, Isidor. L Caplet 94: L Nichols
PHILIPPE D'ORLEANS. WL/rev.
PICCINNI, Nicola. WL; WL/rev.
PICQUARD, Lieutenant-Colonel. L Louÿs
PIERNE, Gabriel. L Caplet 93; L Durand 83, 106, 112, 118, 119; L Laloy 30; L Lesure; L Nichols; L Vasnier; WL; WL/rev.; WS
PIERNE, P. WL/rev.; WS
PIERRON, Juliette. WL; WL/rev.
PINCHERLE, Marc. WL/rev.
PINSON, M. WL/rev.
PIODI, Mlle. WL/rev.
Pisa. L Annunzio
PISSARO, Camille and Lucien. L Nichols; WS
PISTER, M. WL/rev.
PITT, Percy. L Caplet 65; L Durand 72; L Messager 32; L Lesure; L Nichols
PIZZETTI. See PARMA
PLANCHET. L Nichols
PLANQUETTE, Robert. WL; WL/rev.
PLANTE, Francis. L Durand 60, 166, 188; L Lesure; L Nichols
PLATO. L Durand 10; L Nichols; L Stravinsky
PLEIADE, LA. L Annunzio
Pleyel piano. L Durand 17, 140
Plume, La Debussy's inquiry in. WS
Plus que lente, La L Caplet 83; L Durand 90; L Nichols
POE, Edgard. L Caplet 30-31, 41, 50, 57, 89, 90; L Caplet/Lockspeiser; L Godet; L Laloy 38; L Lesure; L Louÿs; L Nichols; L Segalen 135; L Vallery; WL; WL/rev.; WS [see also **hute de la maison Usher** / and **Diable dans le beffroi**]
Poèmes de Baudelaire, Cinq. L Godet; L Louÿs
Poetry and music. WS
POINCARE, Henri. L Toulet 100; WS; WL/rev.
POICTEVIN, Francis. L Lesure; L Nichols
POINCARRE, Raymond. L Nichols
POIRET. L Toulet 101
Poissons d'or. L Godet
POLIGNAC, Armand de. L Laloy 15; L Nichols

POLIGNAC, Edmond de. L Lesure; L Louÿs; L Nichols
POLLONNAIS, André. L Louÿs
PONCHON, Raoul. L Godet; L Louÿs
PONIATOWSKI, Prince André. L Nichols; L Poniatowski; M Morgan 25
PONSON DU TERRAIL. WL; WL/rev.
POPELIN, Claudius. L Lesure; L Nichols; M Texas 30
Popular music. L Caplet 95
Porte Saint-Martin. L Nichols
PORTO-RICHE, G. de. L Annunzio
POTHIER. L Caplet 83; L Lesure; L Messager 21; L Nichols
POUGIN, Arthur. L Godet; WL/rev.
POUGY, Liane de. See Chassaigne, Anna-Marie.
POUJAUD, Paul. L Louÿs
POULENC, Francis. L Lesure; L Nichols
POULET, Gaston. L Caplet 13; L Cobb; L Durand 178, 180, 187; L Godet; L Nichols; M Bn 35-37; M Texas 19/5
Pour le piano. L Louÿs; L Durand 188; L Nichols; M Morgan 9, 11
Pourville. L Laloy 26; L Nichols
Pousset (tavern). L Godet
Prager Tageblatt. L Nichols
Prague [see also Czechoslovakia]. L Nichols
PRAT, Max. L Segalen 106
PRATELLA, Francisco Balilla. WL/rev.; WS
Prélude à l'après-midi d'un faune. L Caplet 14; L Durand 48, 69, 93; L Emma 137; L Godet; L Louys; L Nichols; L Segalen 89, 91, 92; L Toulet 48, 68; M Bn 52; M Texas 19/9, 19/13, 19/21, 21, 36/17; WS
Préludes, piano. Book I: L Durand 83, 95, 113, 119, 169; L Hartmann [concerning **Minstrels**]; see WS under particular titles. Book II: L Durand 113. See also L Annunzio; L Caplet 17, 24, 27, 101; L Godet; L Laloy 37; L Nichols; L Segalen 99, 131; see WS under particular titles.
Primitive music. WS
PRESSENSE, Francis de. L Godet
PRIMOLI, Giuseppe. L Lesure; L Nichols; L Vasnier
Prince of Wales Theatre. L Nichols
Printemps, Le (orch., 1887). L Baron; L Durand 65, 112; L Emma 106; L Godet; L Laloy 8, 30; L Louÿs; L Nichols
Prix de Rome. L Baron; L Chansarel; L Durand 42, 48; L Nichols, L Vasnier; L Vidal; WS
Promenoir des deux amants. L Caplet 67
PROSERPINA. L Annunzio
Proses lyriques. L Caplet 67; L Godet; L Louÿs; L Nichols; L Poniatowski; M Bn 65, 68; M Texas 25/6
PROUST, Marcel. L Annunzio; L Louÿs; L Nichols
PRUNIERES, Henri. L Annunzio
Puccinelli. L Annunzio
PUCCINI, Giacomo. L Godet; L Laloy 22; L Lesure; L

Nichols; WL; WL/rev.; WS
PUGNO, Raoul. L Lesure; L Nichols; WL; WL/rev.; WS
PUJET, Théophile. L Louÿs
PUJO, Maurice. L Louÿs; L Nichols
PUVIS DE CHAVANNES, Pierre. L Godet; L Lesure; L Nichols
PYTHAGORAS. L Caplet 63; L Lesure; L Nichols

Quatuor, Premier, pour cordes. L Caplet 14; L Durand 5, 20, 21, 22, 80, 95; L Emma 89; L Godet; L Louÿs; L Nichols [where see String Quartet]; L Poniatowski; L Ysaye; M Bn 35; M Texas 26; M Texas Letters by others 11
Queen's Hall Orchestra, London. L Nichols; L Queen's Hall; M Morgan 7
QUILLARD, Pierre. L Louÿs; L Nichols; WL; WL/rev.
QUINAULT, Pierre. L Louÿs
QUITTARD, Henri. L Lesure; L Nichols

RABANI, G. M Texas 31
RABAUD, Henri. L Louÿs
RABBE, F. L Godet
RABELAIS. L Toulet 123
RACINE, Jean. L Annunzio; WL; WL/rev.
RACHMANINOV, Sergei. L Nichols
RACKHAM. L Godet
RADICS, Béla. L Caplet 50, 94-95; L Godet; L Lesure; L Nichols
RAITIF DE LA BRETONNE. L Louÿs; L Louÿs 1971
Rahon par Chaussin. L Nichols
RAKOCZI. L Lesure
RAMEAU, Jean-Philippe. L Caplet 26, 60, 61, 62-4, 99; L Durand 8, 106; L Godet; L Laloy 22, 26, 28, 38, 39; L Lesure; L Messager 66; L Nichols; L Segalen 99; L Vallery; M Bn Var.; WL; WL/rev.; WS
RANGER GULL, Cyril (Guy Thorne). L Nichols
Rapsodie pour clarinette. L Durand 86, 87, 98, 99, 101, 104, 105, 106; L Emma 113; L Godet; L Nichols [where see Clarinet Rhapsody]
Rapsodie pour saxophone. L Louÿs; L Louÿs 1971; L Messager 61-63; L Nichols
RARA. L Toulet 94
RAUGEL. L Godet
RAUNAY, Mme Jeanne. L Messager 29, 31, 35; WL; WL/rev.
RAVEL, Maurice. L Annunzio [where see **Heure espagnole**]; L Caplet 19; L Godet; L Laloy 19, 24, 25; L Lesure; L Louÿs; L Nichols; L Ravel; L Segalen 137; L Toulet 53; M Bn 18; M Morgan 16; WL; WL/rev.; WS
REDON, Odilon. L Lesure; L Nichols; L Toulet 80
REGNIER, Henri de. L Lesure; L Louÿs; L Nichols; L

Peter; WL; WL/rev.; WS
Reims, Cathedral of. L Annunzio
REMBRANDT. L Godet
RENAN, Ernest. L Lesure; L Nichols; L Peter 202; WL; WL/rev.
RENARD, Jules. L Caplet 37; L Lesure; L Nichols
RENAUD, M. WL; WL/rev.
RENAUDEL. L Toulet 100
RENOIR, Auguste. L Godet; L Nichols
RESZKE, Jean de. L Lesure; L Louÿs; L Messager 16; L Nichols; WL; WL/rev.
Rêverie (piano). M Morgan 11
Revivals, opinions of. WS
Revue blanche, La, articles in and questions concerning. L Nichols; M Bn Var.; M Lang; M Stockholm 2; WS
Revue bleue. L Laloy 9, 10; L Nichols
Revue des deux mondes. L Annunzio; L Segalen 143
Revue hebdomadaire. L Annunzio; L Nichols
Revue indépendante. L Baron; L Nichols
Revue musicale. L Annunzio
Revue wagnérienne. L Nichols
REYER, Ernest. L Louÿs; WL; WL/rev.; WS
Reynold's Bar. L Nichols
Rhapsodie pour clarinette. See **Rapsodie...**
Rheims. L Nichols
RHENES. L Laloy 8
RHODES, Cecil. L Nichols
RICHARD, Marius. L Louÿs
RICHEPIN, Jean. L Baron; L Godet; L Lesure; L Nichols
RICHTER, Hans. WL; WL/rev.; WS
RICHTER, Janos. WL; WL/rev.
RICOU, Georges. WL; WL/rev.
RIDLY, Mr. L Laloy 37
RIEMANN, Hugo. L Lesure; L Nichols; L Segalen 67
RIGAUD, de. L Annunzio; L Lesure; L Nichols
RIGAUX. L Messager 54
RIMBAUD, Arthur. L Lesure; L Nichols; L Segalen 50
RIMSKY-KORSAKOV, Nicolai. L Annunzio [also see **Coq d'or**]; L Caplet 102; L Chansarel; L Cobb; L Lesure; L Louÿs; L Nichols; WL; WL/rev.; WS
RISLER, Ed. WL; WL/rev.; WS
RISLER, Jean. L Durand 17
RIST, Dr. Edouard. L Godet; L Nichols
RIVARDE, A. WL; WL/rev.
RIVIERE, Henri. WS
RIVIERE, Jacques. L Lesure; L Nichols; WL; WL/rev. [also see entry above]
ROBERT, Mlle Julia. L Louÿs
ROBERT, Paul. L Lesure; L Louÿs; L Nichols
ROBINE, René. WL; WL/rev.
ROCHEGROSSE. L Godet; L Louÿs
RODENBACH, Georges L Louys
RODIN, Auguste. L Annunzio; L Godet; L Lesure; L

Nichols; L Segalen 55; L Toulet 87; WL; WL/rev.
Rodrigue et Chimène. L Godet [see Chimène]; L Louÿs; L Nichols
RODRIGUES, Jane. M Bn Emma 24-30
ROGER, Mlle Thérèse. L Lesure; L Louÿs; L Nichols; M Bn 61
ROGER-DUCASSE [also see Ducasse, Roger above and in other indexes], L Durand 67, 96, 115; L Segalen 142; M Texas 32
Roi des Aulnes, Le. L Louÿs; L Louÿs 1971
Roi d'Ys, Le. L Messager 25
Roi Lear (project). L Durand 33, 36, 45; M Texas 3
ROLAND, C. WL/rev.
ROLAND-MANUEL. L Annunzio; L Caplet 17, 27
ROLLAN-MAUGER, Mme. L Godet; L Lesure; L Nichols
ROLLAND, Romain. WS; L Annunzio
ROLLET, Mme. L Segalen 94
ROLLINAT, Maurice. L Godet; L Louÿs
Roman de Tristan (Bédier). L Laloy 27; L Messager 62, 64, 74
Rome, city of and Concours de. L Annunzio; L Baron; L Laloy 40; L Messager 65; L Nichols [where also see Augusteo]; L Vasnier; M Bn 86
ROMILLY, Mme Gérard de. L Lesure; L Nichols; L Romilly
Rondes de printemps. L Caplet 40, 46, 93 [also see Images for orch.]
RONSIN, Eugène. L Lesure; L Nichols
ROPARTZ, Guy. M Bn 70; WL; WL/rev.; WS
ROQUES, Mons. L Durand 81
ROSOOR, Louis. L Lesure; L Nichols
ROSSETTI, D.G. L Godet; L Lesure; L Louys; L Nichols
ROSSINI, Gioacchino. L Louÿs; WL; WL/rev.; WS
ROSTAND, Edmond. L Lesure; L Louÿs; L Nichols
ROUCHE, Jacques. L Annunzio; L Durand 152; L Godet; L Laloy 40; L Toulet 43; M Opéra
ROUQUAIROL, Mme. L Lesure; L Nichols
ROUSSEAU, Jean-Jacques. WL; WL/rev.
ROUSSEL, Albert. L Godet; L Nichols
ROUSSELIERE. WL; WL/rev.
Royal Philharmonic Society. L Nichols
Royan. L Nichols
ROZSAVOLGI. M LC Szanto; M LC Hubay
RUBINSTEIN, Anton. L Lesure; L Nichols; L Poniatowski
RUBINSTEIN, Ida. L Annunzio [throughout]; L Caplet 50; L Emma 89; L Lesure; L Nichols; L Segalen 142; L Toulet 71; M Bn 74
RUMBOLD. L Lesure
RUMMEL, Walter Morse. L Cobb; L Godet; L Lesure; L Nichols
RUEL. L Toulet 28
RUSKIN, John. WS
RUSSELL, Henry. L Annunzio; L Caplet 23-4, 61, 73- 77, 93, 103; L Durand 88, 107; L Lesure; L

Lockspeiser; L Nichols; M Morgan 12; M Texas 33
RUSSELL, Nina. L Caplet 23, 25
RUSSELL, Sheridan. L Caplet 24, 25
Russia, Russian people and music [also see Moscow and St. Petersburg]. L Caplet 66, 73, 99; L Durand 110, 113, 114, 115, 142, 152, 159, 188; L Emma 102ff.; L Laloy 15, 39; L Nichols; L Segalen 77; L Stravinsky; L Toulet 100; M Bn 79, 110; M Texas 2; WS
RUSSOLO, Luigi. WL/rev.; WS
RUST, Friedrich Wilhelm. WL; WL/rev.; WS
RUST, Wilhelm. WL; WL/rev.
RUYSBROECK. L Louÿs

SAILLAND, Maurice. L Lesure; L Louÿs; L Nichols (See also Curnonsky and Kurnonsky)
Saint-Dominique, châlet. L Annunzio
Saint-Eustache, church. L Annunzio
Saint-Germain-en-Laye. L Annunzio; L Nichols
Saint-Gervais. L Nichols
Saint Graal, Le. L Nichols
Saint Jean-de-Luz. L Nichols
Saint-Loubès. L Nichols
SAINT-MARCEAUX, Mme René de. L Messager 53; L Nichols
Saint-Requier, L. WL; WL/rev.
Saint Petersburg. L Emma 116-117ff; L Nichols
SAINT-SAENS, Camille. L Caplet 57; L Durand 150; L Godet; L Lesure; L Louÿs; L Nichols; WL; WL/rev.; WS
SAINT SUAIRE. L Annunzio
SAINTE-BEUVE, Charles-Augustin. WL; WL/rev.
SAINTE-CROIX, Camille de. L Godet; WL; WL/rev.; WS
SAKOUSKY. L Godet
SALAZAR, Adolfo. M Morgan 26
Salammbo. L Nichols; L Vasnier
SALIS, Rodolphe. L Louÿs
Salle d'Harcourt. L Nichols
Salle Gaveau. L Nichols
Salle Pleyel. L Nichols
SALLES, A. WL/rev.
SALMON, J. M Stockholm 1
Salon d'Automne. L Durand 66; L Nichols; M Texas 27/4
Salon de la Rose-Croix. L Nichols
Salon des Beaux-Arts, Brussels. L Nichols
Salon du Champs de Mars, Paris. L Nichols
SALVAYRE, Gaston. L Lesure; L Nichols
SAMAIN, Albert. L Godet; L Lesure; L Nichols
SAMAZEUILH, Gustave. WL; WL/rev.; WS
SAMUEL, Fernand. L Louÿs
SAN MARTINO, Count Enrico di. L Emma 128 ff.; L Lesure; L Nichols
SAN MARTINO VALPERGA, Count Enrico di. L Annunzio

SAND, George. WL; WL/rev.
SANDOW, E. WL/rev.
Santa Maria dell'Anima, Rome. L Nichols
SANTOS-DUMONT. L Louÿs
SAPHO. L Durand 80; L Toulet 51
Sarabande. L Louÿs
SARDOU, Victorien. WL; WL/rev.; WS
SARRAZIN, Gabriel. L Louÿs; L Peter 200
SARRINE. L Emma 110
SATIE, Erik. L Caplet 15, 58; L Louÿs; L Durand 124; L Lesure; L Nichols; L Satie; M Bn 31; WS
Satory. L Nichols
SAUER, Emile. WL; WL/rev.; WS
Saulaie, La (project). L Godet; L Louÿs; L Nichols; M Texas 18/2, 18/5
SAVARD, Augustin. WL; WL/rev.; WS
Savoy. L Nichols
Scala, La. L Annunzio; L Nichols [see La Scala]
SCARLATTI, Alessandro. WL; WL/rev.; WS
SCARLATTI, Domenico. WL; WL/rev.
Scènes au crépuscule. See **Trois scènes...**
SCHAEFFNER, André. WL/rev.; WS
SCHEFFER. WL/rev.
SCHILLER. WL; WL/rev.
Schirmer, G. (publisher). L Durand 50
SCHMID, Willy. L Godet
SCHMITT, Florent. L Annunzio; L Nichols; M Bn 58- 60
SCHNEIDER, Louis. L Annunzio; WL; WL/rev.
SCHOENBERG. See SCHÖNBERG.
Schola Cantorum. L Nichols; L Toulet 27; WS
SCHOLL, Aurélien. L Godet
SCHOLLAR, Ludmila. L Nichols; WL; WL/rev.
SCHOLTZ, Hermann. L Durand 132, 134; L Lesure; L Nichols
SCHÖNBERG, Arnold. L Caplet 29, 94, 102; L Caplet/Lockspeiser; L Godet; L Lesure; L Nichols; WL; WL/rev.; WS
SCHOPENHAUER, Arthur. L Godet; L Lesure; L Nichols
Schott (publisher). L Nichols
SCHUBERT, Franz. L Louÿs; WL; WL/rev.; WS
SCHUMANN, Robert. L Durand 33, 130; L Lesure; L Louÿs; L Nichols; WL; WL/rev.; WS
SCHURMANN, J. M Texas 34
SCHWARTZ, R. M Texas 35
SCOTTI. L Messager 43
SCRIABIN, Alexander. L Nichols
SECHIARI, Pierre. L Lesure; L Nichols
SEGALEN, Victor. L Caplet 11, 36, 88; L Laloy 30, 32; L Lesure; L Nichols; L Segalen; WS.
SEGARD, Achille. L Lesure; L Louÿs; L Nichols
SEIDL, Anton. L Lesure; L Nichols
SELVA, Blanche. L Caplet 46; L Laloy 14; L Lesure; L Nichols

SENECA. L Annunzio
Sens. L Nichols
SERGINE, Vera. L Annunzio
SERPETTE, Gaston. L Louÿs; L Messager 70; WL; WL/rev.; WS
Settignano. L Annunzio
SETTIGNANO, Desiderio da. L Annunzio
SEVERAC, Déodat de. L Laloy 15; L Lesure; L Nichols
Seville. L Nichols
SHAKESPEARE, William. L Caplet 55; L Durand 139, 190; L Godet; L Lesure; L Messager 27; L Nichols; L Toulet 4, 5, 106 [also see **As You Like It**, above in this index]; L Vallery; WL; WL/rev.; WS
SHELLY, Percy B. L Baron
Sicily. L Annunzio
Siddhartha (Segalen). L Nichols; L Segalen 54, 66, 68
SIDNER, Mlle. M Bn 62; M Morgan 30
SIECHIARI. L Toulet 48 [also see Séchiari above]
SIGNAC, Paul. L Nichols
SIGNORET, Henri. L Godet
SILVESTRE, Armand. WL; WL/rev.
S.I.M. (Société Internationale de Musique), Bulletin. L Godet; L Laloy 24, 28, 37; L Nichols; M Texas 36; WS (D's articles in)
SIMON, Jules. L Laloy 21; L Lesure; L Louÿs; L Nichols
SIMONE. Mme. L Annunzio
Sirènes. L Emma 137 [also see **Nocturnes**]
SISLEY, Alfred. L Nichols
SIVRY, Charles de. L Godet; L Lesure; L Nichols
SIVRY, Mlle. Claudie de. L Louÿs
Six, Les. L Nichols
Six épigraphes antiques. L Nichols [also see **Epigraphes**]
Smareglia. L Nichols
Société de la Musique Actuelle. L Stravinsky
Société de Musique. WS
Société des Amis de C. Debussy. L Annunzio
Société des Auteurs, Compositeurs, et Editeurs. L Nichols; L Stravinsky
Société des Auteurs et Compositeurs Dramatiques. L Annunzio
Société des Concerts du Conservatoire. L Annunzio
Société des Grandes Auditions Musicales de France. L Annunzio; L Nichols; WS
Société Internationale de Musique. see SIM above.
Société Musicale Indépendante. L Annunzio; L Nichols
Société Nationale de Musique. L Laloy 37-38; L Nichols; M Bn 69; M Morgan 33; M Texas 25/6; WS
Société des Nouveaux Concerts. WS
Society of English Composers. L Nichols
SOCRATES. L Durand 149; L Nichols
SODINI, Angelo. L Annunzio
Soirée dans Grenade. L Durand 13; L Louÿs 1971; L

Segalen 85
Soissons. L Nichols
Sommeil de Lear [also see **Roi Lear**]. L Nichols
Sonate, flûte, alto, et harpe. L Caplet 14; L Durand 154, 156, 164, 167, 172; L Godet; L Nichols; L Paoli 4
Sonate, violon [early plan]. L Durand 5
Sonate, violon [late work]. L Caplet 13; L Cobb; L Durand 171, 173-4, 175, 178, 180; L Godet; L Nichols; L Paoli 2, 4; M Bn 37, 71
Sonate, violoncelle. L Caplet 14; L Durand 141, 142, 155, 176; L Godet; L Nichols
Sonates [all in general]. L Stravinsky
SONZOGNO, Edoardo. L Durand 54; L Lesure; L Nichols
SOPHOCLES. WL; WL/rev.
SORG, Roger. L Louÿs
SOUDAY, Paul. L Godet
SOUDRY, G. WL; WL/rev.
SOUSA, John Philip. WL; WL/rev.; WS
Spain and Spanish music. L Nichols; L Toulet 40; WS
SPEYER, Sir Edgar and Lady. L Caplet 64, 65, 99, 100; L Durand 121; L Godet; L Nichols
SPINOSA, Baruch. L Durand 53, 170; L Nichols
SPONTINI, Gasparo. WL; WL/rev.
Square du Bois de Boulogne. See Bois de Boulogne, Square de
STANFORD, Sir Charles. L Nichols
STEINLEN, T.A. L Lesure; L Nichols
Stèles (Segalen). L Segalen throughout
STENDHAL. L Toulet 130, 132
STERNE, L. WL/rev.
STOECKLIN, P. de. L Lesure; L Nichols
STOJOWSKI, Sigismund. WL; WL/rev.
STRADIVARIUS. L Annunzio
STRARAM, Walter. L Caplet 94
STRAUSS, Richard. L Annunzio; L Caplet 26; L Durand 36 [**Salome**], 60, 129; Emma 108; L Lesure; L Louÿs; L Nichols; L Peter; L Segalen 107; L Toulet 71; M Bn 66; WL; WL/rev.; WS
STRAVINSKY, Igor. L Caplet 2-6, 64, 68, 70, 89, 101-3; L Caplet/Lockspeiser; L Durand 85; L Godet; L Lesure; L Nichols; L Stravinsky; L Toulet 84, 89; M Morgan 5; WL; WL/rev.; WS
STREET, George. L Lesure; L Nichols
SUARES, André. L Annunzio; L Nichols; WS
SUE, E. WL/rev.
Suite bergamasque. L Louÿs; M Morgan 10-11
SULLIVAN, Arthur. L Godet; L Nichols
SULLY-PRUDHOMME. L Durand 154
SULZBACH, Mme. L Lesure; L Nichols
SVENDSEN, Johan. L Lesure; L Nichols
SWINBURNE, Charles. L Annunzio; L Nichols; L Peter 200; WL/rev.

Switzerland. L Caplet 59; L Nichols
SYLVESTRE, A. WL/rev.
Symbolists [also see particular names]. R Baron; L Nichols
Symphonisches Chor. L Nichols
Syrinx. L Nichols; M Morgan 21
SZANTO, T. M LC Szánto; WL/rev.

TAFFANEL. M Texas 25/2; WL/rev.
TAILHADE, Laurent. L Lesure; L Nichols
TAINE, Hippolyte. WL; WL/rev.; WS
Tania (project). M Texas 2
TAPIE DE CELERAN, Dr. Gabriel. L Louÿs
TASKIN. L Nichols
TAVAN. L Louÿs
TCHAIKOVSKY, Peter. L Caplet 16, 37, 87; L Durand 169; L Lesure; L Nichols; WL; WL/rev.; WS
Teatro de la Comedia. L Nichols
TECLA. L Toulet 95
Temesváry. L Nichols
Temps, Le. L Annunzio; L Nichols
TERRASSE, Claude. WL; WL/rev.; WS
Terrasse des audiences (prelude). L Godet
TEYTE, Maggie. L Caplet 100; L Segalen 105; WL; WL/rev.
TEXIER, Mlle Rosalie (Lilly). L Lesure; L Louÿs; L Nichols. See also Debussy, Rosalie (Lilly) above.
TEYTE, Maggie. L Durand 61; L Emma 119; L Lesure; L Nichols
THALBERG. WL; WL/rev.; WS
Théâtre Antoine. L Nichols
Théâtre d'Art. L Nichols
Théâtre de Claude Debussy (Laloy). L Annunzio
Théâtre de Fête. L Annunzio
Théâtre de la Monnaie, Brussels. L Durand 37; L Laloy 23; M Bn 33
Théâtre de la Porte Saint-Martin. L Annunzio [see under Porte St.-Martin]
Théâtre des Arts. M Texas 27/2
Théâtre des Bouffes-Parisiens. L Nichols
Théâtre des Champs-Elysées. L Annunzio [see Champs-Elysées, Théâtre]; L Caplet 37, 76, 98; L Durand 117, 118; L Nichols; L Segalen 81-2; L Stravinsky; M Bn 53; WS
Théâtre du Châtelet. L Annunzio [where see Châtelet, Théâtre du]; L Nichols
Théâtre du Peuple. WS
Théâtre Elizabéthain. L Godet [see Elizabéthain]
Théâtre libre. L Nichols
Théâtre Populaire. WS
Théâtre Réjane. L Annunzio [see under Réjane]
Théâtre Royale de la Monnaie [also see above Théâtre de la Monnaie]. L Nichols

Théâtre Sarah Bernhardt. L Caplet 56
THEBES, Mme. de. L Durand 147
THIELE, Ivan. L Nichols
THIERS, Mons. L Peter; WL/rev.
THIERY, Marie. WL; WL/rev.
THOMAS, Ambroise. L Lesure; L Louÿs; L Nichols; L Poniatowski; M Bn 1; M Morgan 25; WL/rev.
THOME, Francis. L Lesure; L Nichols
Thommen (café). L Godet
THOMMEN, Mlles. L Godet
THORAILLER. L Durand 159
THORNE, Guy. L Lesure; L Nichols [where see Ranger Gull]
TIERSOT, J. L Lesure; L Nichols
TINAN, Jean de. L Lesure; L Louÿs; L Louÿs 1971; L Nichols; L Toulet 94
TINAN, Mme G. de (née Hélène Bardac, "Dolly"). L Annunzio; L Emma; see under Bardac (Dolly) in L Lesure; L Segalen 123, 132
TINCHANT, Albert. L Godet
TIPHAINE, Jeanne. WL; WL/rev.
TOLSTOY, Count Leo. L Baron; L Godet; L Lesure; L Nichols; WL; WL/rev.
TOMMASINI. L Nichols
TOSCANINI, Arturo. L Annunzio; L Caplet 16; L Segalen 104
TOULET, J.-B. L Louys
TOULET, Mme Marie. L Toulet 127, 129, 130
TOULET, Paul-Jean. L Godet; L Laloy 35; L Lockspeiser; L Lesure; L Nichols; L Segalen 90; L Toulet 1-6 [as subject]; L Vallery; M Lang; WL; WL/rev.
TOULOUSE-LAUTREC, Henri de. L Louÿs; L Nichols; WS
TRACOL, A. WL/rev.
Tragédie de la mort (project). L Morgan 23
TRARIEUX, Gabriel. L Annunzio
TRAVERSI, C.-A. L Annunzio
Trente ans de théâtre (Bernheim). WS
Trianon Palace, Versailles. L Annunzio
TRILLAT, Mr. L Laloy 40
TRINCHERI, Maître. L Annunzio
Tristan et Iseut (theatre project of Debussy). L Nichols; L Toulet 75
Tristan Lhermitte songs. L Laloy 37
Trocadéro. L Nichols
Trois ballades de Villon. L Annunzio; L Nichols; L Paoli 1 [also see **Ballades...,Trois** above]
Trois chansons de Charles d'Orléans. L Caplet 18, 87, 90
Trois chansons de France. L Nichols [also see **Chansons, Trois** above]
Trois mélodies [de Verlaine]. L Cobb; L Nichols
Trois poèmes de S. Mallarmé. L Nichols
Trois scènes au crépuscule. L Nichols; L Poniatowski
TROUHANOVA, N. L Lesure; L Nichols; L Toulet 67

TURBAN, Mme H. L Annunzio
Turin. L Durand 97; L Nichols
TURINA, Joaquin. WL; WL/rev.; WS
TURNER, J.M.W. L Durand 58; L Godet; L Lesure; L Nichols

UDINE, Jean d' (Albert Cozanet). L Laloy; L Lesure; L Nichols; WL
ULLMANN, Constantin. L Peter
ULYSSES. L Annunzio
URBINO, Seconde. L Emma 136
USHER, Roderick. L Godet [see also **Chute de la maison Usher** above]

VACHETTE (café). L Godet
VAISSIERE, Jeanne Perdriel. L Segalen 103-04
VALERY, Paul. L Lesure; L Louÿs; L Nichols; M Morgan 17; M Texas Letters by others 9; WL; WL/rev.; WS
VALETTE, Mons. M Morgan 22
VALLAS, Léon. L Annunzio; L Louÿs; WL/rev.; BWS
VALLERY-RADOT, Pasteur. L Emma; L Toulet 95, 97
VALLETTE, Alfred. L Louÿs; L Peter; L Segalen 54
VALLIN, Mlle. [also see the following]. L Caplet 52, 67
VALLIN, Nino. L Lesure; L Nichols
Valois. L Annunzio
VAN DONGEN. L Godet; L Louÿs
VAN DYCK, Anthony. L Annunzio; WL; WL/rev.
VAN DYCK, Ernest. L Annunzio; L Nichols
VAN HOUT. L Louÿs;
VAN ROOY, A. WL; WL/rev.
VANDERCRUYSSEN. L Durand 87; L Nichols
VANIER, Léon. L Lesure; L Nichols
VANOR, Georges. L Louÿs
VAN REES. L Emma 141
VAN ZANDT, Amelie. L Louÿs
VARESE, Edgard. L Nichols; WL/rev.
Variations, as genre. L Godet
variétés. L Nichols
VASNIER (family circle; also see the ff.). L Louÿs
VASNIER, Eugène. L Baron; L Lesure; L Lockspeiser; L Nichols; L Vallery; L Vasnier; L Vidal; M Texas 30. Also see Vasnier, Marie-Blanche.
VASNIER, Marguerite. L Nichols
VASNIER, Marie-Blanche. L Lesure; L Nichols; L Vasnier. Also see Vasnier, Eugène.
VASNIER, Maurice. L Nichols
Vatican. L Annunzio
VAUCANSON, de. WL; WL/rev.
VAUCORBEIL WL; WL/rev.
VELAZQUEZ, Diego de Silva y. L Godet; L Lesure; L Nichols; L Toulet 100

Venice, city of. L Annunzio; L Laloy 34; L Nichols
VENTURINI, Countess. L Annunzio
VERDI, Giuseppe. L Annunzio; L Lesure; L Louÿs; L Nichols; WL; WL/rev.; WS
Verdun. L Nichols
VERLAINE, Paul. L Baron; L Chansarel; L Godet; L Laloy 39, 40; L Lesure; L Louÿs; L Louÿs 1971; L Nichols; L Segalen 135; WL; WL/rev.; WS
Vent dans la plaine, Le. WS
VERHAEREN, Emile. L Annunzio
VERLAINE, Paul. L Caplet 16; L Lesure
Versailles. L Annunzio
VICAIRE, Paul. L Godet
Vichy. L Nichols
VICTORIA, T. L Lesure; WL (where see Vittoria); WL/rev.
VIDAL, Paul. L Godet; L Lesure; L Nichols; L Vasnier; L Vidal
VIELE-GRIFFIN, Francis. L Lesure; L Louÿs; L Nichols
Vienna and Viennese. L Annunzio; L Caplet 9, 49, 50, 94; L Emma 85; L Nichols; L Toulet 59
VIERNE, Louis. L Annunzio; WL; WL/rev.; WS
VIEUILLE, Félix. L Lesure; L Nichols
VIGNIER, Charles. L Baron; L Godet
VIGUIE. WL; WL/rev.
Villa Medici. L Baron; L Nichols; WS. Further see references to Rome and to Prix de Rome.
Villacidro. L Annunzio
VILLIERS de L'ISLE-ADAM, Comte de. L Godet; L Lesure; L Nichols; L Segalen 112; WS
VILLON, Francois. L Godet; L Nichols; WL; WL/rev.
VINCI, Leonardo da [also see Da Vinci above]. WL; WL/rev.
VIÑES, Ricardo. L Caplet 101; L Godet; L Laloy 9, 10; L Lesure; L Nichols; L Segalen 107-8; M Bn Emma 2; M Texas 19/18
VISEAU. L Caplet 82
VITAL-HOCQUET. L Louÿs
VITRY, Paul. L Segalen 144
VITTORIA, T.-L. da. L Nichols; WL [see also Victoria)
Vittoriale. L Annunzio
VIVIANI, René. L Durand 148; L Nichols
VIZENTINI, Paul. L Caplet 55; L Nichols
Vogue, La (revue). L Baron
VOISINS, Gilbert de. L Louÿs
Voix mortes, musique maori (Segalen). L Segalen throughout
VOLLENHAUPT [also see Wollenhaupt below]. L Caplet 42, 92
Voûte des planètes, La (Martyre de St. Sébastien). L Annunzio
Voyage du Roi Pausole, Le. L Louÿs

VUILLEMIN, Louis. WL; WL/rev.
VUILLERMOZ, Emile. L Annunzio; L Caplet 66; L Lesure; L Nichols; M Morgan 28; WL; WL/rev.

WAGNER, Cosima. WL; WL/rev.; WS
WAGNER, Eva. L Nichols
WAGNER, Richard. L Annunzio [see that index under **Tristan** as well as Wagner]; L Baron; L Caplet 9, 24, 60, 63, 66, 76-7, 95-6, 104; L Chausson 3, 4; L Durand 35, 129, 131; L Godet; L Hartmann; L Laloy 22, 27; L Lesure; L Louÿs; L Louÿs 1971; L Nichols; L Segalen 55, 61, 62-3, 107; L Stravinsky; L Vasnier; M LC Batchelder; M Texas 9/1-2; WL; WL/rev.; WS
WAGNER, Siegfried. WL; WL/rev.; WS
WAILLY, P. de. WL; WL/rev.
WALDBAUER, E. L Lesure
WALDBAUER, Imre. L Nichols [also see the preceding entry]
WALDECK-ROUSSEAU. L Nichols
Wales. L Nichols
WALLANDRY, Mlle. L Laloy 27 [correct name: Vallandri, Mlle.]
War, World, I. L Durand 123ff.; L Hartmann; L Nichols [where see First World War]; L Segalen 138, 144; L Stravinsky; L Vallery; M Texas 36/1
WARNERY, Edmond. L Durand 72, 79; L Nichols
WATTEAU, Jean Antoine. L Godet; L Nichols; WL; WL/rev.
WEBBER, Amherst. WL; WL/rev.; WS
WEBER, Brasserie. L Godet; L Louys; L Toulet 1, 101
WEBER, Carl Maria von. L Godet; L Lesure; L Nichols; WL; WL/rev.; WS
WEBER, Louise (La Goulue). L Nichols
WEBERN, Anton. L Caplet 29
Weimar. L Nichols
WEINGARTNER, Felix. WL; WL/rev.; WS
WENZEL, Leopold de. WL; WL/rev.; WS
WHISTLER, James. L Nichols; WL/rev.
WIDOR, Charles Marie. L Louÿs; L Nichols; WL/rev.
WILDE, Oscar. L Caplet 17
WILDER, Victor. L Lesure; L Nichols
WILLETTE, Adolphe. L Godet
WILLETTE, Henriette. L Godet
WILLY. L Godet; L Louÿs; L Messager 25, 46; see under Gauthier-Villars in L Lesure; WS
WILSON. L Laloy 5; L Toulet 129
WITKOWSKI, G.M. WL; WL/rev.; WS
WOLLENHAUPT, Heinrich Adolf [also see Vollenhaupt above]. L Lesure; L Nichols
WOOD, Henry J. L Caplet 26, 100; L Durand 48, 64; L Lesure; L Nichols; L Queen's Hall; L Segalen 90-91; M Morgan 7

WUILLAUME-FEUILLARD (quartet). L Godet
WYZEWA, Théodore de. WL; WL/rev.

X, letter from Debussy to. L Nichols
Xantho (Chouchou's collie dog). L Emma 119; L Nichols

Yonne. L Nichols
YSAYE, Eugène. L Caplet 12; L Chausson 9; L Lesure; L Lockspeiser; L Louÿs; L Nichols; L Ysaÿe; M Bn 72; WL; WL/rev.; WS

ZAGON, Geza Vilmos. L Lesure; L Nichols
ZAMOISKA, Countess. L Nichols
ZELLING, Anton. M Stockholm 1
ZEPPELIN, Count. L Godet; M Texas 19/2
ZILOTI. L Durand 113, 114-15
ZIMMER, Brasserie. L Annunzio; L Nichols
ZIMMERMANN, Mlle. WL; WL/rev.
ZOHRA. L Louÿs
ZOLA, Emile. L Lesure; L Louÿs; L Nichols; WL; WL/rev.; WS
ZUCCALA, G.G. WL/rev.
Zuleima. L Nichols; L Vasnier; WS
Zurich. L Annunzio

V

REFERENCE BOOKS

1. Catalogues of Works

48. Cobb, Margaret G., ed. **The Poetic Debussy: A Collection of His Song Texts and Selected Letters.** Translations by Richard Miller. Boston: Northeastern University Press, 1982. xxii, 315 p. ML 54.6.D42C62 1982; ISBN 0-930350-28-6.

Preface by the editor, foreword by François Lesure, 12 illustrations (title pages, texts, letters, music manuscripts). Divided into three sections: (1) texts of all songs with English translations, and invaluable information on textual and musical sources of songs; (2) selected letters containing references to poetry, with English translations and bibliographic notes; and (3) descriptions of 26 compositions other than songs that are based on literature. Underscores the literary basis of much of D's thought and assists singers and listeners with excellent translations of Debussy's songs. Most valuable for Miller's translations and for Cobb's careful tracing of literary sources of song texts. Valuable also are the previously unpublished letters, indexed in the present Index of Letters.

49. Lesure, François, ed. **Collection musicale André Meyer.** Abbeville: Imprimerie F. Paillart, 1960. 118 p.; 291, x p.

A catalogue of one of the last, great private collections of music materials in France. These have now converted to government ownership and are housed at the B.n. All Debussy materials are accounted for in the present Catalogue of Works.

50. Durand et Cie. [publishers]. **Catalogue de l'oeuvre de Claude Debussy.** Paris: Durand, 1962. 133 p.

Begins with a brief biography in French and in English translation. Provides a separate entry for each work published by 1962, whether by Durand or another publisher. Entries indicate dedicatee, first performance, and date of publication. Some information is inaccurate and is corrected by Lesure (item 51) and in the present Catalogue of Works. The Durand catalogue is unique in indicating the roles and specific casts of premieres, complete instrumentation of scores, and approximate duration of works. Also indicates published extracts and arrangements by others of Debussy, some of which the present Catalogue of Works does not list, although annoyingly Durand does not indicate the dates of arrangements. A discography also is included.

51. Lesure, François. **Catalogue de l'oeuvre de Claude Debussy.** Publications du Centre de Documentation Claude Debussy III. Geneva: Editions Minkoff, 1977. 167 p. LC 77-566454/MN; ML134.D26 L5; ISBN 2-8266-0657-3.

The first comprehensive catalogue of Debussy's works, which number 141 items including sets. Lesure acknowledges the need for revision of the catalogue as more on the sources is learned. The present Catalogue of Works does revise Lesure, and he projects a further revision. Lesure's catalogue contains an introduction to editorial procedure, the catalogue proper set forth in chronological order of composition, and appendices of (1) conservatory exercises; (2) musical greetings to friends and family; (3) editions, orchestrations, and transcriptions of works by other composers; and (4) unrealized projects. It includes indexes of dedicatees, genres, incipits for vocal works, and titles of works or items in sets. Each catalogue entry indicates performing medium, incipit (for vocal works), date of composition, location of the autograph manuscript, dedicatee,

source of the text, first and on occasion subsequent editions, selective commentary, bibliography, and, frequently, mention of first performances. Concludes with a table of contents and includes facsimiles of single pages from **Caprice**, **Eglogue**, **Nuits blanches**, and the **Violin Sonata**.
Its provisional character and certain factual inconsistencies do not disqualify the catalogue as a primary guide to research but suggest verification. The present Catalogue of Works seeks to update Lesure's catalogue while deriving many, still-valid facts from it.

52. Turner, J. Rigbie. "Nineteenth-Century Autograph Music Manuscripts in the Pierpont Morgan Library: A Check List." **Nineteenth-Century Music** 4, no. 1 (Summer 1980): 49-69.

Lists and describes 20 music manuscripts by D in the holdings at the date of the article, which qualifies Morgan as the most important holder of original D sources other than the B.n. in Paris. Important holdings of autographs by D's contemporaries and predecessors also are described, here and in the second part of this article (same journal, 4, no. 2 [Fall 1980], 157-83).
Since the publication of Turner's article, the Morgan Library has acquired additional manuscripts. See the Catalogue of Works of the present study, which updates the holdings housed at and owned by the Morgan Library.

2. Bibliographies

53. Abravanel, Claude. **Claude Debussy: A Bibliography**. Detroit Studies in Music Bibliography 29. Detroit: Information Coordinators, Inc., 1974. 214 p. LC 72- 90430/MN; ML 134.D26A2; ISBN 911772-49-9.

The most complete bibliography of D to date, listing 1854 items written up to 1972. The present book updates Abravanel by citing and annotating all significant writings since 1972 and by annotating earlier main sources. Categories of entries in Abravanel include bibliographical works; periodicals (issues devoted to D); literature on relations (musicians, poets, national schools); technique and style; musical works (with helpful subdivision by genres); correspondence, interviews, and writings; and critical and literary works. Provides indexes to authors, reviewers, names and compositions mentioned in text, critical and literary works, individual chapters of **Monsieur Croche Antidilettante**, and periodicals cited. Bibliographic entries are from throughout the West, Japan, Israel, and the USSR.

The bibliography remains a foundation of Debussy research, even though it is not annotated and lists writings only up to 1972. A second edition of Abravanel is anticipated.

* **Cahiers Debussy.** Première série 1-3 (1974-1976) and Nouvelle série 1-11 (1977-87 ongoing).

The annual journal devoted to Debussy contains valuable, yearly bibliographies and discographies of each year's activity, although the bibliography is only a partial one. Further see the annotation, item 123.

* Danckert, Werner. **Claude Debussy.** Berlin: De Gruyter, 1950. xvi, 248 p. LC 51-22061; ML 410.D28 D26.

Contains an especially thorough bibliography of writings on Debussy before 1950. Danckert thus complements Abravanel (item 53) as a guide to the earlier bibliography. Further see the annotation of Danckert (67).

54. Lesure, François. "Bibliographie Debussyste." **Revue de musicologie** (numéro spécial Claude Debussy, 1962): 129-35.

Of primary importance for a bibliography of writings in the press concerning Debussy in his day. Concerning the critical reception, further see Trillig (item 240). Lesure's general bibliography has been incorporated into Abravanel (53) and, for the most significant entries, the present Guide. Neither this book nor Abravanel's include certain of Lesure's entries concerning earliest writings in the press.

3. Discographies

* **Cahiers Debussy.** An annual journal devoted to Debussy research. Contains yearly discographies, many by M. Cobb. Further see the annotation in item 123.

55. Cobb, Margaret G. **Discographie de l'oeuvre de Claude Debussy.** Publications du Centre de documentation Claude Debussy I. Geneva: Editions Minkoff, 1975. 127 p. LC 76- 461578/MN; ML156.5.D4 C6; ISBN 2-826-60535-6.

A valuable guide to all 78-rpm recordings. Separate entries for each recorded work list all known recordings and reissues, information on interpreters, date of issue, record company and number, composition on reverse of the recording, and location in selected sound archives. Includes recordings of arrangements by D, works not recorded during the period covered (1902- 50), indexes of works and interpreters, and table of contents. Further see items 73 and 123 regarding modern recordings.

56. Cobb, Margaret G., and Stephen E. Lundgren. **The Debussy Recordings.** In preparation.

A much-needed, comprehensive discography of all the audio recordings of Debussy's works, from 1885 to the time of publication. Planned for two volumes, the first is concerned with vocal, orchestral, and chamber works; the second with piano works. Promises to fill a glaring gap in the reference literature on Debussy.

* Durand et Cie., eds. **Catalogue de l'oeuvre de Claude Debussy.** Contains a discography current in 1962. See item 50.

* Goubault, Christian. **Claude Debussy.**

The "Discographie sélective," pages 253-59 in the section **Dictionnaire**, is by Goubault and Jean-Paul Roussilhe. It is the most useful discography of modern recordings of Debussy to date. Until the appearance of the Cobb-Lundgren discography of modern recordings (item 56),

Goubault's list may be supplemented by the yearly discographies in the **Cahiers Debussy** (123) and by Morse (57). Further see annotation of Goubault's biography, item 73.

57. Morse, Peter. **Debussy and Ravel Vocal Music.** Discography Series XI. Utica, New York: J.F. Weber [1 Jewett Place, Utica, NY 13501], [1973]. LC ML156.5.D26 M6.

A working list of phonograph recordings that is valuable because it extends Cobb's work on the vocal music. Lists all recordings by title of song or cycle up to the early 1970's, so unfortunately it is not current. Gives basic information on performers, label and number, date of recording, poet. Includes recordings of opera excerpts and considers both 78-rpm and long-playing LPs. Also lists recordings made by Debussy himself.

4. Iconographies

58. Gauthier. André. **Documents iconographiques. Avec une préface et des notes.** Geneva: Pierre Cailler, 1952. 31 p.; 205 plates. LC a53-699; ML88.D3 G4.

The first comprehensive iconography and still very useful, considering the unsatisfactory quality of photographic reproduction of the Lesure iconography (59). Photos from 1867 (D at age 5) to his death are given, including the composer, his family, and associates. Falls short by not indicating the sources of the photos and locations of paintings and sculptures. Notes relating to the plates place them in biographical context, however.

59. Lesure, François. **Claude Debussy: Iconographie musicale.** Geneva: Editions Minkoff, 1975. 179 p. ISBN 2-8266-0598-4. Bilingual edition (Fr. and Eng.) Geneva: Minkoff-Lattès, and Paris: Congdon-Lattès, 1980. LC 81-144899/MN/r86; ML88.D3L47.

Compendium of 165 photos, paintings, stage sets, etc., of which six are in color. Introduction, chronology of life, reproduction of ten signatures throughout life, selective bibliography of iconographies, table of illustrations, index. Treats related persons as well as D. Not satisfactory often, because of an indistinct photographic reproductions, sometimes unfocused and darkened by the tan paper on which it is printed.

Also see "Exposition Catalogues" in the section "Compilations," which are particularly important sources for iconography.

60. Cobb, Margaret G. "The Centre de Documentation Claude Debussy." **Fontes artis musicae** 24, no. 4 (1977): 249-52.

The Centre was established by Cobb and Lesure as a place for serious research on Debussy. This article lists the major collections of the Centre as of 1977, including photocopied manuscripts from private collections, books, scores, special recordings, and articles. The Centre collections include important iconographic works. The original Centre was housed at 11 rue d'Alsace, St. Germain-en-Laye, the city of Debussy's birth. The collection of the Centre is out of circulation at present, although new accommodations are being planned at the Centre Pompidou in Paris. For current address see Chapter XI, Sources.

VI

STUDIES OF DEBUSSY'S LIFE

1. Books Surveying Debussy's Life and Works

61. Alexandrescu, Romeo. **Claude Debussy, viata si opera.** Bucharest: Editura Muzicala, 1967. 214 p. In Romanian. Not examined.

62. Balzer, Jurgen. **Claude Debussy: En kritisk studie.** Copenhagen: Jespersen og Pios Forlag, 1949. 208 p.; index, list of works, bibliog. In Danish. Not examined.

63. Barraqué, Jean. **Debussy.** Paris: Editions du Seuil, 1962. 191 p. ML 410.D28 B36; ISBN 2-02-000242-6.

Valuable for its focused line of thought from Debussy's first "masterpiece," **Prélude-faune**, through **Pelléas** and **La mer**, and to **Jeux**. In the **Prélude-faune** Debussy dispenses with the idea of form as a given, in **La mer** and **Jeux** he creates the concept of "open form," and throughout his career he progresses with sureness toward a new aesthetic. Also valuable as the interpretation of a contemporary composer. Barraqué reviews the phases in the critical reception of Debussy, beginning with the nationalists, proceeding to those who viewed Debussy as over-refined (Cocteau, Satie), and ending with critics after World War II, who stressed his universal character and structuralist nature. For Barraqué, Debussy becomes the essential precursor of Boulez, Messiaen, and many contemporaries who value innovative structures alongside sonorous beauty.

64. Boucher, Maurice. **Claude Debussy.** Maîtres de la musique ancienne et moderne, no. 4. Paris: Les Editions Rieder, 1930. 87 p. ML 410.D28 B7.

As a biography, outdated, but the iconography and facsimiles contained among the 60 illustrations remain basic. Certain of these are not available elsewhere.

65. Boucourechliev, André, et al. **Debussy.** Collection génies et réalités. Paris: Hachette, 1972. 263 p. LC 73-320508/MN; ML 410.D28 D36.

A collection of popular essays by various authors on several aspects: "Influences et rencontres musicales," "L'Art et l'esprit fin de siècle," "La bataille de Pelléas et Mélisande," "Interpréter Debussy," etc. Most important for its lavish iconography often in color: main photos and paintings of D from infancy until death and of contemporary artists and stage designs, iconography of related artists Redon, Whistler, Monet, etc. Commentary on specific works; discography grouped by genre.

66. Chennevière, Daniel (pseud. for Dane Rudyar). **Claude Debussy et son oeuvre.** Paris: Durand, 1913. 45 p. LC 14-621; ML410.D28 C3.

Although outdated, is valuable as a contemporary view of Debussy's main tendencies. Finds his oeuvre falling into two periods, dividing at **Pelléas**. In the first, D initiates Symbolism as a movement in music, applying the concepts of Hegel, Mallarmé, and the painter Eugène Carrière. After 1902, Debussy turns from Symbolism as his main tendency and leans toward "naturism" (**Ibéria**) and "une tendence nouvelle" (**Martyre**). Oversimplifies the question, especially as regards the later music, but provides valuable commentary on the general development of Symbolist thought.

67. Danckert, Werner. **Claude Debussy.** Berlin: Walter de Gruyter, 1950. 248 p. LC 51- 22061; ML 410.D28 D26.

Contains an outstanding bibliography of earliest writings on D, many not considered in the present book. Recognizes an incipient polytonality in **Brouillards** and **Puerta del vino**. Contains in facsimile a letter of D to his daughter, written St. Petersburg Dec. 11, 1913. Divides into four sections: Life and Works, Style, Historical Position, and Analyses (of piano and large works). A pioneering biography in its systematic approach to analysis and periodization: 1) Childhood, 2) Period of Schooling (1873-84), 3) Period of Transition (1885-93), 4) The Symbolist Early Period (1894-1902), 5) The Middle Period (1903-1911), 6) The Late Classicizing Period (1912-18).

68. Dietschy, Marcel. **La passion de Claude Debussy**. Neuchâtel, Switzerland: Editions de la Baconnière, 1962. xviii, 287 p. LC 63-35661/L/MN; ML 410.D28 D55.

Contains significant iconography, name index, bibliography, and catalogue of works. An English translation was in press at the time of this writing: **A Portrait of Debussy**. Oxford: Oxford University Press, forthcoming 1989. Translated by William Ashbrook with updated end material by Margaret Cobb.

Alongside Lockspeiser's and in some regards Vallas's work, this is the most important biography to date. Conceives D's art to be the whole substance of his life, qualifying him as one of the four or five most complete musicians of all time. Having accomplished spade-work on many particulars, Dietschy is particularly useful for biographical details and references to further readings. He draws insightful relationships between the composer's life and musical creativity. Includes many photos of persons related biographically and artistically.

69. Dumesnil, Maurice. **Claude Debussy, Master of Dreams.** New York: Ives Washburn, 1940. 326 p. LC 40-32738; ML410.D28 D8.

A popularized biography, drawing generally and loosely upon Vallas. Useful for citations of certain letters and reminiscences by Dumesnil, who knew Emma Debussy after D's death.

70. Ferchault, Guy. **Claude Debussy.** Paris: La Colombe, 1948. 130 p. LC a49-7354; ML410.D28 F4.

First traces the works by genre before passing to valuable essays on aesthetics. Distinguishes the "objective given" (pictorial and programmatic associations) from the "subjective given" (interpretations of nature, psychology, etc.).

The concluding chapter, "Debussy's Aesthetic," centers on the quality of mystery.

71. Gál, György Sándor. **Egy faun délutánja: Claude Debussy élet regénye.** Budapest: Zeneműkiádo, 1974. 598 p. ML410.D28 G24 1981x; ISBN 963-330-3613.

In Hungarian. An up-to-date biography and discussion of the compositions.

72. Goléa, Antoine. **Claude Debussy; "Pelléas et Mélisande."** Preface by Jean Roy. Paris: Slatkine, 1983. 266 p. LC ML 410.D28 G6 1983; ISBN 2-05-000215-7.

A welcome paperback reprint of two books in one, **Claude Debussy** (1966, 190 p.) and **Pelléas et Mélisande** (76 p.). The biography traces main themes of D's life in a direct fashion, although it has been superseded in details by Lockspeiser and Dietschy (items 85 and 68). Pages 165-71 are important for citations of the critical reception. The **Pelléas** book, likewise clear, is a scene-by-scene discussion of plot and themes.

73. Goubault, Christian. **Claude Debussy.** Musichamp l'essentiel. Paris: Champion, 1986. 305 p., paperback. ML 410.D28 G64 1986; ISBN 2-85203-013-6.

Approaches Debussy by three main sections: the biography, career, and chronicle of his life; analytic description of each major work; and a critical synthesis treating in turn such topics and concepts as "Debussysme," rhythm, modality, the Conserva toire, correspondance, and nationalism. This latter section, "Dictionnaire," names and places in context many important secondary writings. Addresses both the amateur and the researcher who seek to learn the current state of Debussy scholarship. The clear, outline form is helpful but necessarily does not achieve a comprehensive narrative of the composer. A most useful, new overview, complementing Lockspeiser's one-volume biography as revised by R. Langham Smith (84).

74. Gourdet, Georges. **Debussy.** Paris: Hachette, 1970. 95 p. LC 79-560610; ML 410.D28 G65.

A brief survey in French for the general reader, engagingly written. Sees D's main works and life in three phases: "Les années d'apprentissage," "La queste de **Pelléas**," and "De **La mer** aux sonates." Consults Dietschy (item 68), but apparently not Lockspeiser or anything more current than Vallas 1958 (item 96). Many details thus have been superseded, although Gourdet maintains a balanced approach that does not overwork such clichés as "Debussy the Impressionist."

75. Hirsbrunner, Theo. **Debussy und seine Zeit.** Laaber: Laaber-Verlag, 1981. 263 p. ML 410.D28 H669; ISBN 3-9215-1861-X.

Proceeds by chapters on aspects of Debussy and his times: salon music, Ravel, De Falla, the Orient and Antiquity, Wagnerian opera, **Pelléas et Mélisande** and **Ariane et Barbe- bleue** [Dukas], "La Musique du silence," Debussy as Poet. Views A. Guiraud's **Pierrot Lunaire** (1884) as a paradigm of artistic life in fin-de-siècle Paris. Debussy was deeply influenced by that atmosphere and by the aristocratic salon. But in the author's terms he was less malleable than Ravel, who was more susceptible to current sentiment. Argues that D joined with Mallarmé in comprehending and further developing Wagner's general intentions more than anyone up to Boulez. Strong, timely approach to D by opening windows on his world. Probably the most important biographical treatment since Lockspeiser's **Debussy: His Life and Mind** (item 85) and Dietschy's **La Passion de Claude Debussy** (68). Warrants English and French translations.

76. Jakobik, Albert. **Claude Debussy oder die lautlose Revolution in der Musik; Analysen von "Prélude à l'après-midi d'un faune," "Les nocturnes," "Pelléas et Mélisande," "La mer," "Jeux."** Würzburg: Trittach, 1977. xii, 164 p. LC 80-469333/MN; MT92.D3 J5; ISBN 3878520320.

Debussy's "silent revolution" is founded on his new sense of timbre as basic to structure. Presents tables concerned with sonorous architecture. Points to D's influence on Penderecki and Ligeti. Points of analysis, centered on timbre, and works considered are limited in number, but the analysis is insightful and frequently cited throughout the recent D literature.

77. Jarocinski, Stefan. **Debussy: Kronika zycia, dziela, epoki.** Krakow: Polski Wydawnictwo Muzyczne, 1973. 633 p. LC 74-205254; ML 410.D28 J4.

Contains useful lists of works and writings, bibliography, and iconography. A chronicle proceeding by years or months, accounting for events in related arts, the appearance of major musical works by others, a biographical sketch for the period in question, and a description of D's compositions and projects. Provides important annotations of writings that concern particular compositions or points of biography. The absence in the D literature of a thorough-going chronicle of this sort strongly calls for a translation into a more international research language than Polish.

78. Kounitskaia, Raisa Ivanova. **O romantitcheskoi i poetike v tvortchestve Debussy.** Moscow: Muzyka, 1982. 87 p.

In Russian. Not available to this study but of potential value to Russian-language researchers if up-to-date.

79. Kremlev, T.A. **Claude Debussy.** Moscow: Muzyka, 1965. 792 p.

Contains a chronicle, bibliography, indexes of names and works. To date the most extensive study of D in Russian, centering on biography.

80. La Mure, Pierre. **Clair de Lune; a Novel Based on the Life of Claude Debussy.** New York: Random House, 1962. 467 p. LC 62-18363.

A sensationalized, popularist biography. Fictionalizes main sections, such as D's childhood, Mme von Meck, the Vasnier family (in the chapter "Love comes too soon"), and so on. Advantages of such an approach include the popularizing of D, but greater responsibility must be taken to avoid sensa tionalism not based on fact. See as a dia metrically opposite, careful interpretation

Dietschy's article on the early childhood (item 112).

81. Laloy, Louis. **Claude Debussy.** Paris: Dorbon, 1909. 113 p. ML 410.D28.L212.

The first comprehensive biography, although preceded by Liebich (83). D appreciated Laloy's biography and his other writings on him, exhibiting a rare approval of critics. Ends with a stylistic commentary on the **Images** (those for piano and for orchestra) and on **Pelléas**. Laloy foresees a new phase beginning with **La mer**. He already distinguishes between Impressionist and Symbolist tendencies in D's music, which he sees as complementary. This is an essential study by a friend and critic, in the latter role perhaps the most perceptive of D's time. A revised edition appeared Paris: Aux Armes de France, 1944, 141 pp. It brings the previous up to the end of D's life, speaking of his "Oeuvres de foi" and observing a faith in nature, the public and its sensibilities, and in God. In some regards, the revised version is romanticized and therefore less perceptive than the first.

82. ------. **La musique retrouvée, 1902-1927.** Paris: Desclée de Brouwer, 1928. Repr. 1974. LC75-508997/MN; ML270.L3 1974.

Contains quite important essays on Laloy's friendship with D, **Printemps** (orch.), the "Debussystes," and **La mer**. Essays on other music of the period also contain numerous references to D. Cites a letter in which D refers to Laloy as almost alone [among music critics] in understanding **Pelléas**. May be read alongside Laloy's biography (item 81) for its invaluable contemporary view. Useful index of names.

83. Liebich, Louise [Mrs. Franz]. **Claude-Achille Debussy.** London and New York: Lane, 1907 [1908]. 92 p. LC 08-8847; ML410.D28 L7.

The earliest biography of D, the list of works indicating **King Lear**, **"Willowwood"** [**La Saulaie**], and the **Histoire de Tristan** as being in preparation. Wishing to "respect the sanctuary of the soul," leaves the personal but also artistic relations as a mystery. Analysis relies largely upon pictorial descriptions. About **Nuages**, "...solemn movement of the clouds dissolving in grey tints lightly touched with white." A number of inaccuracies distinguish Liebich's from Laloy's vitally important early biography, and Liebich lacks his insights as one inside D's circle. Liebich nonetheless is quite pertinent as a document of D's reception in England and the U.S. in D's lifetime. Is first as well in a mode of popular appreciation that remains mostly in effect today.

84. Lockspeiser, Edward. **Debussy.** 5th ed., rev. with preface by R. Langham Smith. London: Dent, 1980. 421 p. LC 80-491637; ML 410.D28L8 1980; ISBN 0-460-02192-2.

The finest one-volume biography in English, first published in 1936 and updated thoroughly. First discusses the life and then the work. Langham Smith's revision incorporates main findings from Lockspeiser's two-volume **Debussy: His Life and Mind** and Dietschy's **La passion de Claude Debussy**. Research in depth still will require consulting these latter two volumes on biography and sources.

85. ------. **Debussy: His Life and Mind.** Volume I: 1862-1902; Volume II: 1902-1918. London: Cassell, 1962 (vol. I) and 1965 (vol. II). Both volumes reprinted Cambridge: Cambridge University Press, 1978. 1978 reprint: ML 410.D28L85; Vol. I ISBN 0-521-22053-X [paperback 0-521-29341-3]; Vol. II ISBN 0- 521-22054-8 [paperback 0-521-29342-1].

French translation by Léo Dilé. Paris: Fayard, 1980. Analysis by Harry Halbreich. Italian translation by Domenico de Paoli. Rome: Rusconi, 1983.

Chronology, bibliog., index of works, general index, exx., illus., appendices concerning letters and other artists. This two-volume study remains the central one in any language of D's life, psychology, and general aesthetic. In such questions it ought to be read alongside Dietschy (item 68), and subsequent studies of particular topics have updated Lockspeiser. Lockspeiser supersedes Vallas significantly by dealing frankly with D's personal and artistic relations and by assessing more objectively the influences of Wagner and nationalism. He notes that "If the style is the man, so is the achievement," exploring brilliantly the unity of D's psychology and creative output. His comprehensive account is backed by a mastery of the primary sources and the related arts, which perhaps cannot be achieved again by a single scholar in today's atmosphere of narrow specialization. Hirsbrunner (item 75) augments helpfully by relating D to society and other artists.

Volume I considers the period from childhood up to **Pelléas**, including D's family, education, the impact of Wagner and other artists, the fertile friendship with Louÿs, and the relationships with Gabrielle Dupont and Rosalie Texier Debussy. Volume II is divided into two parts: "The Years of Debussyism," including his music criticism written under the pseudonym of Monsieur Croche, relations to Romain Rolland, Proust, Strauss, and Mahler; and "The Later Years," including the experience of Poe, d'Annunzio, Diaghilev, and Stravinsky. Volume II concludes by tracing D's declining health and the impact of nationalism and World War I.

86. Nichols, Roger. **Debussy.** Oxford Studies of Composers, 10. London: Oxford, 1973. 86 p. ML 410/.D2 N62. ISBN 0-19-315426-9.

Valuable as an experienced if brief survey of Debussy's musical technique. Recommended for the researcher beginning any study of D's style. See also item 107 for a further description of Nichols's general approach.

87. Paoli, Rodolfo. **Debussy.** Biblioteca sansoniana musicale, no. 2. Florence: Sansoni, 1940. xi, 259 p. 2nd ed. 1952. vii, 239 p. LC 952-10302; ML 410.D28 P21952.

An important Italian-language survey of life and works, relating to Vallas in biography but more helpful in interpretive matters. The final chapter, "L'artista," stresses the concepts of impressionism, intimate lyricism, D as architectonic composer, and D as a synthesizer of forces at the turn of the century (romantic and classic, the interior and exterior modes of expression). Appendices review the writings of Mr Croche and give letters to d'Annunzio, [29/1/1911, 11- 12/2/1911, and 12/6/1913], V. Gui [25/2/1912, 8/2/1914], B. Molinari [9/1/1915, 6/9/1915], A. Casella [20/6/1915], and Marchese di Casafuerte [7/5/1917].

88. Peter, René. **Claude Debussy.** Paris: Gallimard, 1931. Revised 1944. 226 p. LC 47-195; ML 410.D28 P37 1944.

An account of Debussy's personality and character as related to the years of Peter's acquaintance, from 1890 through to about 1910. At times name-dropping and chatty; may be used cautiously as a study of a friendly relationship as viewed by Peter. Includes letters to Peter, some complete and others partial, from 1893-1911. Peter aims in the book to illustrate the course of their friendship.

89. Rootzen, Kajsa. **Claude Debussy.** Stockholm: Wahlstrom & Widstrand, 1948. 229 p. In Swedish.

Progresses by genre following a biographical essay. Index of names and works.

90. Rutz, Hans. **Claude Debussy: Dokumente seines Lebens und Schaffens.** Munich: C.H. Beck, 1954. 264 p. LC 55-20254; ML410.D28 R86.

Fine iconography and useful, liberal quotations from the letters. Otherwise, appears to be based on Vallas and does not equal the analytic interest of Danckert (item 67) among earlier German studies.

91. Sabaneyev, Leonid. **Claude Debussy.** Moscow, 1922. English translation by S.W. Prinz, in **Music and Letters** 10 (1929), 1-34.

Earliest biography in Russian and thus an important document in the study of critical reception outside France. Proceeds in mosaic-like fashion by short sections on biographical and stylistic concepts. The interpretations of D's relation to Russian composers are flavored by post-Revolutionary thought: the Five are seen as not particularly influential, excepting Musorgsky. Stravinsky is "the negative of Debussy."

92. Strobel, Heinrich. **Claude Debussy.** Zurich: Atlantis, 1940. 295 p. ML410.D28 S8.

Dependent upon Vallas but apparently a main communicator of ideas on Debussy to German-speaking audiences and composers until recent times. Repeats Vallas's insistence on Debussy as "musicien français," but with no reverse-nationalistic distortion even when emphasizing the relation to Wagner. May be used to advantage alongside such writers as Hirsbrunner (item 75). Perhaps a main early influence for methodical analysis of Debussy.

93. Thompson, Oscar. **Debussy: Man and Artist.** New York: Dodd, Mead, 1937. xi, 394 p. Repr. New York: Dover; London: Constable; Toronto: General Publ. Co., 1967. ML410.D28 T47 1967; ISBN 486-21783-3.

The first comprehensive U.S. study of life and works, drawing upon Vallas's 1932 and Lockspeiser's 1936 books. In three parts: the man and artist, the life, and the music. The first part contains useful interpretations of biography with illustrations, useful bibliography of earliest writings on D, and index.

94. Tiènot, Yvonne, and Oswald d'Estrade-Guerra. **Debussy, l'homme, son oeuvre, son milieu.** Paris: H. Lemoine, 1962. 258 p. LC 63- 27075; ML 410.D28 T54.

A broad overview discussing first the man and artist and then the compositions. Contains a useful, clear catalogue of the works in the form of a chart. Copious quotations from the letters and critical writings of D recommend this book to serious researchers. May be supplemented by Lockspeiser's, Dietschy's, and Hirsbrunner's biographies (items 85, 68, and 75).

95. Ujfalussy, József. **Achille-Claude Debussy.** Budapest: Gondolat Kiadó, 1959. 302 p. ML 410.D28 U4.

Contains no index but has a detailed table of contents, list of works, bibliography, and illustrations. In Hungarian.

96. Vallas, Léon. **Claude Debussy et son temps.** Paris: Alcan, 1932. 396 p., lxxxiii. Revised Paris: Albin Michel, 1958. 443 p. English translation (of 1932 version) **Claude Debussy: His Life and Works.** Translated by Maire and Grace O'Brien. London: Oxford University Press, 1933. Repr. New York: Dover, 1973 [ML410.D28.V1673 1973; ISBN 0-486-22916-5].

Before Lockspeiser and Dietschy, Vallas's was the leading study of D's life and works. Vallas remains important for insights into the mature works, although his brief attention to the early music is colored by his desire to substantiate D's path-breaking originality. He gained access to works and letters in manuscript that now are inaccessible, and he interviewed many relatives and colleagues. However, his closeness to relatives caused him to "avoid all biographical details the publication of which might be deemed premature and indiscreet." Vallas mostly avoids what Lockspeiser termed the "dark side of Debussy, like Gauguin's and Verlaine's." The 1932 version concludes with appendices on Whistler and the **Nocturnes**, Ysaÿe's interest in **Pelléas**, and the **Sarabande** from **Pour le piano**. Also in the 1932 version there is a thematic catalogue of works published by D and certain unpublished works, which now is outdated. The 1958 version is preferable for its enriched discussion of several main developments, such as the "bohemian" years and particularly **Rodrigue et Chimène**, and for its reassessment of the relation to Stravinsky. Serious researchers should seek out the 1958 version, even though it is not available in an English translation as is the 1932 version. The 1958 book also contains an index of names and works.

Further see Léon Vallas. **Achille-Claude Debussy.** Paris: Presses Universitaires de France, 1944. 255 p. A revision of the 1932 biography in a methodical, simpler format. Proceeds not biographically (as in the 1932 study) but by genre, once the life is surveyed. This version of Vallas is notable for its clarity of presentation and interpretation.

97. Vallery-Radot, Pasteur. "Claude Debussy: Souvenirs." **Revue des deux mondes** (May 15, 1938): 390-418. ML410.D2 V3.

Fervent admirer and friend, the physician Vallery-Radot was close to D from 1910 until D's death. Discusses with clarity the **Pelléas** premiere and initial reception, that of **La mer**, Debussy's personality, and his appreciation of earlier composers (Rameau, Bach). Discusses biographical aspects surrounding the Poe projects and **Le martyre**. Quotes from several letters received from Debussy, which touch on World War I, Rameau, and French musical tradition. Radot's description of Debussy's views of the war is the most complete that is extant. Radot is marked by pronounced enthusiasm and devotion but remains in essence objective. Quite valuable in the study of biography, critical reception, and personality.

98. ------. **Tel était Claude Debussy. Suivi de lettres à l'auteur.** Paris: Julliard, 1958. LC a58-5901; ML410.D28 V27.

Includes a reply **in extenso** to the biography by Victor Seroff. Publishes 17 letters.

99. Vuillermoz, Emile. **Claude Debussy.** Geneva: Kister, 1957. 2nd ed. Paris: Flammarion, 1962. 159 p. LC 59-45006; ML410.D28 V93.

A document of the phase in Debussy criticism that stressed his Impressionist side, nearly to the exclusion of the formal integrity of the music. Is parallel to Vallas in viewing D as "musicien français." Valuable as the writing of a contemporary and an associate of D.

* Weber, Edith, ed. **Debussy et l'évolution de la musique au XXe siècle.** See item 127.

2. Surveys Contained Within Larger Studies

100. Austin, William W. **Music in the Twentieth Century.** New York: W.W. Norton, 1966. 708 p. LC 65-18776/MN/r84; ML 197.A9.

A masterful survey of D's place in the 20th century. Chapters I-III are devoted to D as an originator of new idioms: I) "The Adventure and Achievement of Debussy" (pp. 1-23); II) "Catchwords and Issues of 20th Century Music" (24-41); and III) "Debussy's 20th- Century Music: History in the service of 'recruiting unknown friends'" (42-53).

Furthermore, all of Part I of the book ("...on the edge, trembling with emotion") is conceived around D's achievement: Chapters IV-X discuss his contemporaries in national schools. Finds no one figure after the middle of the century who corresponds to D in influence.

Austin's premise remains a call to thought and action for musicians, who ought to know D better: "...everyone who grows up hearing and making music in the 20th century learns to imagine, dimly or vividly, sounds and sequences of sounds like those Debussy imagined for the first time." Analyzes **Syrinx** in depth. In Ch. II discusses the plurality of D's aesthetic tendencies, including Im pressionism, Symbolism, and Neoclassicism, and traces related tendencies in Bartók, Schoenberg, and Stravinsky. Ch. III centers on the late works **Jeux**, the **Etudes**, the chamber music, and the **Ballade de Villon à s'amye**. A fundamental reading for any student of D. Contains extensive and useful bibliographic sections.

101. Grout, Donald Jay, and Claude Palisca. **A History of Western Music**. 4th ed. New York: Norton, 1988. 910 p. ML 160.G87 1988; ISBN 0-393-95627-X.

Grout includes D in the discussion "new currents in France" (Fauré, Debussy, Satie, and Ravel). Is abreast of current scholarship in recognizing that Impressionism is only one of several tendencies contributing to D's aesthetic. In the 5 pages he devotes to D, Grout writes the strongest brief survey among those reviewed here. **Nuages** (from the **Nocturnes**) is described in some depth and related to Musorgsky's song **Les jours de fête**. Declines to trace with any enthusiasm music since 1950 and D's role in it, a main shortcoming of the treatment of D and of the book in general. Nor does Grout explore except in passing the influence of non-Western music in D.

The companion score anthology, edited by Palisca, is the **Norton Anthology of Western Music** (New York: Norton, 1980. M1.N825 M1495 M5; ISBN 03939-51510, v.2). Volume 2 contains **Nuages**.

102. Lang, Paul Henry. **Music in Western Civilization.** New York: Norton, 1941. 1107 p. LC 41-9128/MN/r70; ML 160.L25 M8.

Represents the scholarly assessment in the generation following D: he is the first great master of the new era. Stops short of interpreting D's influence on subsequent music and ends with the discussion "'The Decline of the West'?" Terms **Pelléas**, for example, a faithful adaptation of a poetic work which in essence is dated and transitory. One is unclear whether the author views D as one who has helped initiate the "new outlook on life" and the coming global society, which Lang projects. Owing to the scope and importance of Lang's study, it challenges D researchers to take up where Lang leaves off and to situate D within the continuing evolution of a global music. Further see Austin, item 169.

103. Machlis, Joseph. **Introduction to Contemporary Music.** 2nd ed. New York: Norton, 1979. 694 p. ISBN 0-393-09026-4; ML 197.M11 1979.

This widely-read survey testifies to the tenacity, in the popular literature on D, of clichés proven outmoded by D scholarship. Machlis is representative of many other music appreciation textbooks. One still awaits a complete overhaul of popular but misleading simplifications such as "for Debussy, harmony is primarily for color rather than for functional value," and "The **Nocturnes** show Debussy in his most pictorial vein." The too-easy tag "Impressionist" similarly persists, despite its decisive challenge by Jarocinski (item 564). While a popular writer is required to capture the general imagination, one also would hope that he or she might vigorously support D's central role in the development of 20th-century music and suggest his imposing structures beyond the merely picturesque. Moreover, D's role in turning serious musical attention outside the West is an idea of vital importance to the general reader.

104. Mason, Daniel Gregory. **Contemporary Composers.** New York: Macmillan, 1918. 290 p. Repr. New York: AMS Press, 1973. ML 390.M383; ISBN 0-404-08327-7.

Contains essays by a widely cited writer on Strauss, Elgar, Debussy, d'Indy, and Music in America. The D essay (pp. 133-51) profoundly misunderstands his achievement: D "has become the idol of the amateur" and "tho prime musical fad of the 20th century...the musician most beloved by the unmusical." A blatant Germanophile, Mason finds Strauss's imagination to be "primarily musical," while D's is "literary, dramatic, pictorial." This essay is a monument to the early misconception of D as an insubstantial "Impression ist," who makes little reference to structure and inherent musical processes. Such an attitude has persisted in veiled forms up to the present.

105. Myers, Rollo H. **Modern French Music from Fauré to Boulez.** New York: Praeger, 1971. 232 p. LC 77-154606/MN/r84; ML270.5 M9M6; ISBN 0-631-13020-9.

A survey of musical developments as seen against the cultural backdrop. Emphasizes the impact of Impressionism, Symbolism, and Surrealism on the new music launched by D. Helpful for placement of D in the musical continuum, although many aspects of the discussion invite an examination of specific studies.

106. **New Oxford History of Music.** Vol. X, "The Modern Age 1890-1960." Edited by Martin Cooper. London: Oxford University Press, 1974. 764 p. LC 74-182275/MN/r84; ML160.N44/vol.10 ML197; ISBN 0-19-316310-1.

Gerald Abraham is the author of 2 sections centrally concerned with D, "The Apogee and Decline of Romanticism: 1890-1914" and "The Reaction ?????" In the first section D is held up as "the very ideal of the late-19th-century artist," but the author does not provide the necessary qualification of such a statement. In the second section, the author more helpfully explores the evolution of D's style. Based perhaps more on Vallas than on Lockspeiser. Elsewhere the **New Oxford History** refers to D and his relation to other composers, although a general overview of his influence is not presented.

107. Nichols, Roger, with work list by Robert Orledge. "Debussy, (Achille-) Claude." **The**

New Grove Dictionary of Music and Musicians. Ed. Stanley Sadie. London: Macmillan, 1980. Volume 5, pp. 292-314. ML100.n48; ISBN 0-333-23111-2.

A comprehensive and clear summary of modern thought and the state of research in the 1970s. Remains a primary point of departure for any research on D, because its thoughtful overview informs any investigation of particular issues. Written in a fluid and experienced fashion, this article falls short only by its improper allocation of adequate space for D. A fuller, more forceful case might be made for D's role as one of the most influential Western composers of the 20th century, for his decided link with and epoch-making evolution from the past, and for his most important contribution to a world view.

Nichols proceeds by discussing 1) D's life, presenting the main works within a chronological narrative; 2) the vocal dramatic works; 3) orchestral and choral works; 4) chamber music; 5) songs; and 6) the piano works. These sections on genres flesh out the biographical context and stylistic advances. Nichols's concluding sections are on 7) musical ideals and 8) D and the musical world. They help promote a view of D's general standing. The works list, like the discussion, is a useful survey that now requires some updating, which Nichols and his collaborator Orledge do in part in **The New Grove Twentieth-Century French Masters**. "Claude Debussy," pp. 41-125. New York: W.W. Norton, 1986. ISBN 0-393-02284-6 (hardcover); ISBN 0-393-30350-0 (paperback).

108. **Schirmer History of Music.** Léonie Rosenstiel, general editor. New York: Schirmer Books [Macmillan], 1982. xviii, 974 p. ISBN 0-02-872190-X; ML160.S32.

Suggests the contemporary assessment of D as a structural composer with the chapter title "New Uses of Timbre: Impressionism and its Outgrowth." Continues to rely on the label Impressionist (without qualifying it as does Grout), but points to the formal role of timbre and neo-classic tendencies. Recalls past analyses with such remarks as "Debussy lacks traditional development procedures," and like them does not always show what took the place of those procedures. Refers to D in discussions of general 19th-century trends, conveying the attitude of Debussy as end development. Helpfully relates him to jazz. The discussions of music since 1950, American music, and popular music do not refer to D's influence as they might have. For instance, D is not cited in the sections "Now Principles of Form" or "Non-Western Influences," areas in which he is a pathbreaker.

109. Slonimsky, Nicolas. **Music since 1900.** 4th ed. New York: Charles Scribner's Sons, 1971. 1595 p. SBN 684-10550-0.

A chronological account of main musical events, in three sections: 1) Tabular View of Stylistic Trends; 2) Descriptive Chronology; and 3) Letters and Documents. Indicates the premiere of **Pelléas** as the initial landmark of modern music and lists and describes briefly the premieres of **Nocturnes**, **Estampes**, **La mer**, and **Ibéria**. Quaint and even humorous characterizations (the **Estampes** show "exotic imagism"), but a keen observation and establishment of perspective. The fourth edition adds a dictionary of terms that aids in understanding the author's peculiar remarks.

Also see Slonimsky's **Lexicon of Musical Invective** (New York: Coleman-Ross, 1953, pp. 89-103) for criticism of Debussy's **Prélude-faune**, **Pelleas**, and **La mer** [**New York Times** 1907: "**The Sea**...is more of barnyard cackle..."]

110. Watkins, Glenn. **Soundings; Music in the Twentieth Century**. New York: Schirmer Books (Macmillan), 1988. 728 p. ISBN 0-02-873290- 1; ML 197.W44.

The section on Debussy (chapter 5, pp. 64-103) orients him to Impressionism, Symbolism, Baudelaire, and Wagner. Discusses the **Ariettes oubliées** and **Pour le piano** in light of Satie. Insights into the literary relationships and musical style of **Prélude-faune** and **Pelléas** are particularly alert, and includes ample sections of the **Pelléas** libretto. Suggests further repertory and readings. Watkins's is an excellent survey well aware of current scholarship. He points to parallels between D and later composers in the course of surveying the century.

3. Particular Studies

111. Dietschy, Marcel. "Pour un portrait de Debussy: Eléments de graphologie." **Revue inter nationale de musique française** 2, no. 5 (June 1981): 93-98.

Reprints in its entirety and comments on the analysis of D's handwriting by Mme R. Schuler (in **Portraits graphologiques contemporains**, 1916). Schuler points to D's anxiety over finances, his "wildness," economy of thought, morality, and attitude toward the physical. Reproduces a letter in facsimile of Jan. 31, 1906, to an unknown addressee as the basis for the handwriting analysis. Dietschy comments on subsequent writing analyses and interpretations of D's personality and morality, concluding that the "moi" of D awaits careful analysis.

112. ------. [Trans. E. Lockspeiser] "The Family and Childhood of Debussy." **Musical Quarterly** 46, no. 3 (1960): 301-14.

Points to Vallas's "sketchy geneology" in both the 1932 and 1958 editions, proposing to remedy this by approaching the childhood fully and frankly. Draws directly upon information included in the author's **Passion de Claude Debussy** (item 68). Views D's childhood as not the idyllic one depicted by earlier biographers, but one fraught with restlessness and apprehension, with shame and destitution in his family. Concludes that the formative years were dark and terrifying, reinforcing Dietschy's call in the preceding for a careful study of D's personality.

113. Prunières, Henry. "Autour de Debussy." **Revue musicale** 15, no. 146 (May-Sept. 1934): 349-58.

Presents the most heated scholarly exchange in published Debussy studies. Prunières begins by criticizing Vallas's **Claude Debussy et son temps** (item 96), which for Prunières is too timid in interpreting D's personal life and his relationships with Lilly Texier and Emma Bardac. Prunières appears irked by Vallas's repudiation of his publication of four early songs (**Revue musicale** 1926, item 145).

Revue musicale 15, no. 147 (1934): 21-26. Continues the attack. Vallas's formal response (pp. 27-33) terms Prunières inaccurate and thus repugnant, citing specific passages. Prunière's "Epilogue" (pp. 34-35) deteriorates unfortunately into an **ad hominem** attack. Robert Godet contributes a note (pp. 35-36) that is more polite but supports Prunières, terming Vallas's biography not an image but a caricature.

Revue musicale 15, no. 149 (Sept.-Oct. 1934). Vallas gives in extenso his defense of biographical questions, against Prunières's attacks. Prunières and Godet respond, although the latter remains high-minded and terms Vallas "an eminent rival."

114. Siohan, Robert. "Pour un cinquantenaire: Images de Debussy." **Revue des deux mondes** 11-12 (June 1968): 362-70.

Reminiscences of Mme de Tinan (née Hélène Bardac), D's stepdaughter. Concerns the composer's personality in later life and in a period of relative quietness.

115. Tinan, Mme Gaston de [née Hélène Bardac]. "Memories of Debussy and his Circle." **Recorded Sound**, no. 50-51 (April-July 1973): 158-63.

Publication of a lecture given on Dec. 18, 1972. The daughter of Emma Bardac Debussy by her first marriage, Mme de Tinan (nicknamed Dolly) recounts the six years of her life at home with D. Notes his sensitive, timid nature that sought a mask in apparent indifference; but he could have violent fits of temper. Notes personal likes, his working habits, conducting, and piano playing, the latter most closely reproduced by Walter Gieseking. Recalls visits to the home by Laloy, Toulet, Caplet, Satie, Roger-Ducasse, Godet, Viñes, Stravinsky, Varèse, Falla, and Fauré. Ends by describing Emma and Chouchou Debussy. Valuable as the recollection of a first-hand witness, although more for general impressions than for perfect recall of facts.

116. Vallas, Léon. "Debussy jugé par ses professeurs au Conservatoire." **Revue de musicologie** 34, nos. 101-102 (July 1952): 46-49.

Expands upon the account of D's Conservatoire experiences given in his earler book (96). Cites primary documents from the Conservatoire of 1874-84, Vallas having combed through the documents from the period. May be read alongside Dietschy's careful documentation of the period (item 68).

117. Vallery-Radot, (Joseph) Pasteur. "Amours de Debussy." **Cahiers de marottes et violons d'Ingres** 54 (1961): 26-43.

Concerns the relationships with Mme Vasnier ("une chaste aventure amoureuse"), with an unidentified woman known only through an 1891 letter to R. Godet, with Gabrielle Dupont, Lilly Texier Debussy, and Emma Bardac Debussy. Somewhat popular in tone but apparently an accurate account by a close friend of D in his later years.

118. Vuillermoz, Emile. "Claude Debussy." **Le ménestrel** 82, no. 24 (June 11, 1920): 241-43; and 83, no. 25 (June 18, 1920): 249-51.

Rather sentimental but sincere praise of D two years after his death, observing him not only as beloved but also as profoundly admired. Observes that many critics of the time found it difficult, following D's death, to "forgive" him for his constant evolution and stylistic surprises. Contributes to a perspective on Debussysme at the end of D's life and the period just following.

119. Wu Yiwei. "The French[man] Claude Debussy, the Man and his Music." **The Art of Music** (Shanghai Conservatory) 1 (1986): 12-19.

Not available to the present study but included as a rare study in Chinese.

VII

COLLECTIVE VOLUMES AND CONFERENCES

1. Periodicals, Collective Volumes, and the Centre de Documentation Claude Debussy

Note that many items annotated elsewhere in this book are simply listed here and cross-referenced.

120. All'ombra delle fanciulle in fiore; la musica in Francia nell'età di Proust. Edited by Carlo de Incontrera. Trieste: Cassa di Risparmio [published Stella, Trieste], 1987. 446 p.

A collective volume exploring music in France at the time of the writer Marcel Proust. It derives from a 1987 festival and conference in Monfalcone, Italy, and includes new writings alongside reprinted ones translated from French. Valuable for tracing D and his times. Contents:

Prefazione, 6-11.

Gli autori e le musiche della rassegna, 12- 20.

Lesure, François. "La musica francese al tempo di Marcel Proust," 21-32.

Chimènes, Myriam. "La principessa Edmond de Polignac e la creazione musicale," 33-58 [reprinted].

Minardi, Gian Paolo. "Les bijoux poètiques du petit Bunibrels," 59-76. Concerns Reynaldo Hahn.

Giubertoni, Anna. "Proust e la cattiva musica," 77-88.

Volta, Ornella. "Du côté de chez Satie," 89-110.

Nectoux, Jean-Michel. "Musica, Simbolismo ed 'Art nouveau'; annotazioni per un'estetica della musica francese 'fin de siècle'," 111- 132 [reprinted].

Rattalino, Piero. "Idee e mito della classicità nella musica pianistica francese della 'Belle Epoque'," 133-58.

Nectoux, Jean-Michel. "Ravel/Fauré e gli inizi della Société Musicale Indépendante," 159-80 [reprinted].
Boucher, Maurice. "L'estetica di César Franck," 181-190 [reprinted].
Bos, Charles du. "Chausson et la Consolation par le Coeur," 191-200.
Fauré, Gabriel. "Ricordi," 201-06 [reprinted].
Ravel, Maurice. "Le 'mélodies' di Gabriel Fauré," 207-14 [reprinted].
Fauré, Gabriel. "Camille Saint-Saëns," 215-218 [reprinted].
Petazzi, Paolo. "Une sonore, vaine et monotone ligne," 219-30. Influence of Mallarmé upon Debussy.
Fargue, Léon-Paul. "Lettera ad Auguste Martin," 231-32 [reprinted].
Romilly, Mme Gérard de. "Debussy professore visto da un'allieva," 233-42 [reprinted].
Rauss, Denis-François. "'Ce terrible Finale': le fonti manoscritte della Sonata per violono di Debussy," 243-74 [reprinted].
Villatico, Dino. "I suoni delle parole," 275-302. D's songs, emphasizing those on Baudelaire and Mallarmé texts.
Castaldi, Paolo. "A Claude Debussy," 303-48. Homage in prose to his standing.
Marnat, Marcel. "Boléro," 349-60. On Ravel.
Gil-Marchex, Henri. "La tecnica di pianoforte," 361-70 [reprinted]. New techniques in the piano music of D and Ravel.
Fubini, Enrico. "Vladimir Jankélévitch e l'estetica dell'ineffabile da Debussy alle Avanguardie," 371-94.
Collaer, Paul. "I 'Sei': Studi sull'evoluzione della musica francese dal 1917 al 1924," 395-443.

121. Analyse musicale 12. Barraqué-Debussy. Textes fondamentaux et grandes analyses d'hier et d'aujourd'hui. Paris, June 1988.

An important representation of contemporary analysis in France, this periodical volume has as its centerpiece Barraqué's previously unpublished analysis of **La mer**. Contents:
Presentation--Introduction, p. 5. Includes abstracts of articles in French and English.
Poirier, Alain. "L'histoire toujours recommencé: Introduction à la pensée analytique de Jean Barraqué," pp. 9-14 (item 370).
Barraqué, Jean. "**La mer** de Debussy, ou la naissance des formes ouvertes," pp. 15-62 (item

693).

Charru, Philippe. "Les 24 **Préludes pour piano** de Debussy: Le mouvement musical au rythme de la forme," pp. 63-88 (item 718)

Mataigne, Viviane. "Le **Prélude à l'après-mid-d'un faune** de Debussy: La dialectique du contraste et de la continuité," pp. 89-102 (item 820).

Chimènes, Myriam. "**La mer, Les préludes pour piano, Le prélude à l'après-midi d'un faune**: Orientations bibliographiques et discographiques," pp. 102-07 (item 719).

Rubrique pratique:

Streletski, Gérard. "Le chef d'orchestre face à **La mer** de Debussy," pp. 108-14 (item 551).

Further notices on the First European Congress on Music Analysis. Summaries of contents, **Analyse musicale** nos. 1 to 12.

122. Bulletin des amis de Jaques Rivière et d'Alain Fournier. Numéro spécial: Debussy. Vol. 38 (3e-4e trimestre 1985). 92 p.

Contains articles by Maxime Jacob, Roger Delage, B. de Schloezer, and André Schaeffner. Also contains texts by J. Rivière and A. Fournier. Not examined.

123. Cahiers Debussy.

The only periodical devoted to Debussy and closely related questions, the **Cahiers** was planned at the formation of the Centre de Documentation Claude Debussy in 1973. Yearly from 1974 through 1976, the Centre published a modest "première série" to link together direct supporters of the Centre. When the Centre flourished under to leadership of François Lesure and Margaret Cobb, a more substantial "nouvelle série" was developed. The "nouvelle série" proposed to publish three sorts of studies:

- musicological studies concerning the career, analysis, manuscripts, and interpretation of Debussy.
- chronicles of the diffusion of the music, new publications and recordings, and the Centre itself and its plans.
- studies of the background of Debussy that enlarge the understanding of his artistic connections, friends, and time.

The "nouvelle série" has been published once yearly beginning in 1977. Its importance to research of depth in Debussy is primary, even when a complete consistency among articles and of editorial policy is wanting. The ISBN number for the entire "nouvelle série" is 2-8266-0434-1. To subscribe or order particular issues, address Les Editions Minkoff, Rue Eynard 8; case postale 377; 1211 Geneva 12, Switzerland. Telephone 022-/204660. For editorial communications address Mr François Lesure at the address given in the List of Scholars at end of this book.

Première série, Cahiers Debussy

No. 1, 1974.

Lesure, F. "Editorial," p. 1.

Cobb, Margaret. "Compte-rendu de l'activité du Centre," 3-7. Lists materials available for study at the Centre, such as copies of manuscripts, books, and recordings.

Lesure, F., ed. "Une interview 'inédite' de Debussy (1910)," 7-9. Interview of Dec. 6, 1910, in **Azest**, Budapest. Flatters Debussy, discusses his contemporaneous trips to Vienna and Budapest, young Hungarian composers, and the Poe opera projects.

Guichard, Léon. "Debussy et les occultistes," 10-14. Original version of article published as appendix of Lockspeiser (item 85).

Cobb, M. "Discographie 'historique' de Debussy (1902-1918)," 14-16.

"Chronique: Une somme debussyste en polonais" [A review of S. Jarocinski **Debussy kronika**, item 77].

" In memoriam Edward Lockspeiser."

"Les Prix Debussy" [piano awards made yearly 1968-73].

No. 2, 1975.

Dietschy, Marcel. "A propos d'une interview inédite de Debussy," 1-6. Interview with Frances Emilie Bauer, published in **Harper's Weekly**. See item 44. Discusses **Pelléas** and the ongoing Poe projects.

Cobb, M. "Compte-rendu de l'activité du Centre," 7.

Nichols, Roger. "Debussy en Angleterre," 8. Recent publications and performances.

Abravanel, Claude. "Debussy en Israel," 8-9.

"Debussy aux Etats-unis" [no author cited], 10.

Hamilton, D. [Recent discography] 11-12.

Hirashima, M. "Debussy au Japon," 13-14.

"Ouvrages publies récemment et sous presse."

No. 3, 1976.
Lesure, F. "Après trois années [du Centre]," 1.
------. "Debussy et La Concordia (1883- 1885)," 1-5. Gives programs of the Concordia amateur choral society when accompanied by Debussy and 3 unpublished letters to Henriette Fuchs, its organizer. Further see item 24.
------. "Debussy à travers le journal de Madame de Saint-Marceaux (1894-1911)," 5-10. Diary entries by a renowned salon hostess, including a letter to her from P. Louÿs concerning the broken engagement of Debussy and Thérèse Roger.
------. "Chopin--Debussy, par Robert Godet," 11-13. Extracts of an unpublished article comparing the two composers. "Recent performances and publications."

Nouvelle série, **Cahiers Debussy**

No. 1, 1977.
Edited by F. Lesure, Kurt von Fischer, and Stefan Jarocinski. Contents:
McKay, James R. "The Bréval Manuscript: New Interpretations," 5-15. Discusses the compositional method and chronology of this early sketch of **Pelléas**, currently B.n. Ms. 1206. B.n. 1206 is a sketch of Act IV, scenes 1, 2, and 4. Transcribes related passages from the Bréval manuscript and the published Durand score. See item 821.
Howat, Roy. "A Thirteenth **Etude** of 1915: The Original Version of **Pour les arpèges composés**," 16-23. Further see item 785.
Devriès, Anik. "Les musiques d'Extrême-Orient à l'exposition universelle de 1889," 25-37 (item 182).
[Editors.] "Eléments de la bibliothèque de Debussy dans la vente de 1933," 38-40.
[Editors.] "Chronique," 41-44. Concerns performances of **Pelléas** in France and Italy and of the **Chute de la maison Usher**. Announces winners of the Concours international de piano de Claude Debussy. Describes performances of Debussy's music in Poland.
Cobb, Margaret G. "Debussy in Texas," 45-46. Brief mention of Debussy's 150 or more letters at the Harry Ransom Humanities Research Center, University of Texas, Austin. See item 2; updated by Briscoe, item 1.
"Bibliographie," 47-48. "Divers," 49-50. "Thèses en cours," 51.

No. 2, 1978.
Romilly, Mme Gerard de. [ed. F. Lesure]. "Debussy professeur, par une de ses élèves (1898-1908)," 3-10. See item 33.
Chimènes, Myriam. "Les vicissitudes de **Khamma**," 11-29. See item 720.
Rauss, Denis-François. "'Ce terrible finale,'" 30-62. See item 862.
Chronique. "Représentations de **Pelléas**; **La chute de la maison Usher**; Concours Debussy à St. Germain-en-Laye [annual piano competition]"; Bibliographie; Thèses; Discographie.

No. 3, 1979.
Jarocinski, Stefan. "Debussy et le groupe des Six," 3-12. See item 314.
Nectoux, Jean-Michel. "Debussy et Fauré," 13-30. See item 355.
Rosen, Charles. "Where Ravel Ends and Debussy Begins," 31-38. Republication of item 375.
Jacobs, Paul. "On Playing the Piano Music of Debussy," 39-44. Republished from **Keynote Magazine**, Sept. 1979, see item 791. Various remarks by an thoughtful interpreter.
Chronique: Recent performances; Nécrologie [of Paul Hollanders de Ouderaen]; Debussy in Minneapolis (item 160); Bibliographie.

Nos. 4-5, 1981.
Edited by F. Lesure, Kurt von Fischer, and Arthur Wenk.
Langham Smith, Richard. "La Genèse de **La damoiselle élue**," [in English] 3-18. See item 807.
Kasaba, Eiko. "**Le martyre de Saint Sébastien**: Etude sur la genèse," 19-37. See item 798.
Nadeau, Roland. "**Brouillards**: a Tonal Music," 38-50. See item 834.
Lesure, François. "Quatre lettres de René Chansarel à Debussy," 51-56. See item 14.
Wenk, Arthur B. "A Debussy Meeting at Denver," 57-62. Paper topics listed in item 161. This article describes the content of the papers.
Lesure, F., ed. "Deux Documents," 63-65. Reprints two short articles from a Debussy commemorative number of **Chantecler** (March 24, 1928): by Serge Prokofiev, "Debussy à Moscou"; and by Paul Vidal, "Debussy à Rome."
Chronique, 65-66. Nécrologie [of the Debussy scholars Stefan Jarocinski, André Schaeffner, and Marcel Dietschy], 67-69.
Bibliographie, 70-72. Discographie (M. Cobb), 72-75.

No. 6, 1982.
Edited by F. Lesure, K. von Fischer, and A. Wenk.
Lesure, François. "Les Oeuvres complètes de Debussy," 3-4. Further see item 128.
Warburton, Thomas. "Bitonal Miniatures by Debussy from 1913," 5-15. See item 648.
Zenck, Claudia Maurer. "Debussy: Prophet and Seducer," 16-21. See item 428.
Friedmann, Michael L. "Approaching Debussy's **Ondine**," 22-35. See item 747.
Lesure, F. "Le' "Jeune Prix de Rome' de Catulle Mendès," 36-40. See item 485.
Chronique, 41-42.
Wenk, Arthur. "Claude Debussy and Twentieth-Century Music," 42-53. See item 226.
Briscoe, James R. "Debussy at Butler University," 44-45. See item 165.
Howat, Roy. "English National Opera's **Pelléas et Mélisande** at the London Coliseum," 45-46.
Bibliographie, 47-48.

No. 7, 1983.
Edited by F. Lesure, K. von Fischer, and A. Wenk.
Koechlin, Charles. "Souvenirs sur Debussy," 3-6. See item 321.
Howat, Roy. "Dramatic Shape and Form in **Jeux de vagues**, and its Relationship to **Pelléas**, **Jeux**, and Other Scores," 7-23. See item 592.
Martins, Jose Eduardo. "Quelques aspects comparatifs dans les languages pianistiques de Debussy et Scriabine," 24-37. See item 347.
Allen, Judith Shatin. "Tonal Allusion and Illusion: Debussy's **Sonata for Flute, Viola, and Harp**," 38-48. See item 614.
Chronique, 49.
Bibliographie, 50.
Discographie 1982-83 (by Margaret Cobb), 51-57.

No. 8, 1984.
Edited by F. Lesure with the assistance of Myriam Chimènes.
Lesure, François. "Debussy, le symbolisme et les arts plastiques," 3-12. See item 156.
Starr, Lawrence. "The 'Modern' Composer, the Conservative Audience...and Debussy," 13- 17. See item 218.
Lang-Becker, Elke. "Aspekte der Debussy-Rezeption in Deutschland zu Lebzeiten des Komponisten," 18-41. See item 233.
Chronique, 42-45. Omaggio a Claude Debussy, Prix de Rome 1884 [summarizes the 1984 festival in

Rome of concerts, talks, and an exhibition, which was organized by the City of Rome and the Académie de France a Rome.]; Publication [Recueil Vasnier, Editions Salabert]; Représentations de **Pelléas et Mélisande**; Communications; Ventes aux enchères; Radio; Concours Debussy; **Trio en sol**; Atelier.
Bibliographie, 46-47. Discographie, 51.

No. 9, 1985.
Edited by F. Lesure, with M. Chimènes.
Martins, Jose Eduardo. "La Vision de l'univers enfantin chez Moussorgsky et Debussy," 3-16. See item 348.
Grayson, David A. "Debussy in the Opera House: an Unpublished Letter Concerning Yniold and Mélisande," 17-28. See item 752.
Chronique, 29-33: Nécrologie [Mme Gaston de Tinan]; **Oeuvres complètes de Claude Debussy**; **Trio en sol majeur**; Trois **Pelléas** [performances]; Festival de Tokyo; Debussy chez les universitaires américains [Debussy papers read in America (see item 166)].
Bibliographie, 34-35. Discographie (by Margaret G. Cobb), 40.

No. 10, 1986.
Edited by F. Lesure with Myriam Chimènes, editorial secretary.
Guillot, Pierre. "Claude Debussy et Déodat de Sévérac," 3-16. See item 289.
Lesure, F. "**Crime d'amour** ou **Fêtes galantes**, un projet verlainien de Debussy (1912-1915)," 17-23. See item 812.
Cobb, Margaret G. "The Several versions of **Trois mélodies** de Claude Debussy," 24-27. See item 724.
Kasaba, Eiko. "La musique de Debussy au Japon," 28-44. See item 232.
Chronique, 45-47. Concerns a Debussy festival at La Scala in Milan in 1986, the acquisition of the collection of Marcel Dietschy by the Centre de Documentation Claude Debussy, a production of **Le martyre** at Milan and Brussels, and the future Musée Debussy at St. Germain-en-Laye.
Bibliographie, 48-49.
Discographie (by M. Cobb), 50-53.

No. 11, 1987.
Lesure, François. "Une interview romaine de Debussy (février 1914)," 3-8.
Rolf, Marie. "Mauclair and Debussy: the Decade from **Mer belle aux îles sanguinaires** to **La mer**," 9-23. See item 501.

Timbrell, Charles. "Walter Morse Rummel, Debussy's 'Prince of Virtuosos'," 24-33. See item 440.

Chronique, 34-35. Concerns **Rodrigue et Chimène** and **Pelléas**. Necrology of Andreas Liess.

Bibliographie, 36-37; Discographie, 38-45, by Margaret G. Cobb.

124. Centre de Documentation Claude Debussy.

Inaugurated on February 9, 1973, as a center for Debussy research in the city of his birth, St. Germain-en-Laye. François Lesure served as director and Margaret Cobb as **animatrice**. It served from its founding as a center for study and repository of recordings, books, and copies of manuscripts by Debussy. Further descriptions of the Centre in **Cahiers Debussy**, première serie, no 1 (1974), by Margaret Cobb, "Compte-rendu." The Centre receives communications addressed to its director: Myriam Chimènes, Centre de Documentation Claude Debussy, IRCAM, 31 rue St. Merry, 75004 Paris.

Further see Cobb, Margaret G., "The Centre de Documentation Claude Debusy." **Fontes artis musicae** 24, no. 4 (1977): 249-52. This article lists the major collections of the Centre as of 1977, including photocopied manuscripts from private collections, books, scores, special recordings, and articles. The original Centre was housed at 11 rue d'Alsace, St. Germain-en-Laye.

The Centre de Documentation has sponsored a series of publications. The address of the publisher and list of publications follows: Publications du Centre de Documentation Claude Debussy. Editions Minkoff, 8 rue Eynard, 1211 Geneva 12, Switzerland.

The publications to date:

1) Cobb, Margaret G. **Discographie de l'oeuvre de Debussy (1902-50)**. See item 55.

2) Debussy, Claude. **Esquisses de "Pelléas et Mélisande."** Facsimile edition with introduction by F. Lesure. See item 811.

3) Lesure, F. **Catalogue de l'Oeuvre de Claude Debussy**. See item 51.

4) Lesure, F. **Iconographie Claude Debussy**. See item 59.

5) Debussy, Claude. **Etudes pour le piano: Fac-simile des esquisses autographes (1915)**. Introduction by Roy Howat. 96 p. ISBN 2-8266-0020-6. Publication projected for 1989.

6) **Dossier de presse de "Pelléas et Mélisande."**

Compiled by F. Lesure. ISBN 2- 8266-0020-6. In preparation.

125. Courrier musical de France (Paris) no. 24 (1968): 224-35. "Cinquante ans après la mort de Debussy."

Barraqué, Jean. "Hommage à Debussy," 224-25. A prefatory statement emphasizing D as the first modern composer, who opens new possibilities.

Guézer, Jean-Pierre. "A propos de **Jeux**," 226-28. The character and progression of timbres and densities relates to Kodály and Bartók.

Gueulette, Alain. "Une forêt obscure, pourtant sans mystère," 229-32. Highlights central figures in D's life, especially women, who shed light on issues of his personality.

Petit, Françoise. "L'oeuvre pour clavier de Couperin et de Debussy," 233-34. Relates D to Couperin in taste, a feel for nature, response to visual stimulus, and flexibility.

Discographie sélective, 235.

126. Debjussi i muzyka XX veka. Sbornik state [Debussy and the music of the twentieth century. A collection of articles]. Leningrad: Muzyka, 1983. 247 p.; music exx. In Russian. Not examined. Contains:

Gurkov, Vladimir. "Impressionizm Debjussi i muzyka XX veka" [Impressionism in Debussy and music of the 20th century].

Laul, Rudolph. "Principy formoobrazovanija v simfoniceskih proizvedenijah Debjussi" [Principles of formal structure in the symphonic works of Debussy].

Cytovic, Vladimir. "Fonizm orkestrovoj vertikali Debjussi" [Phonics in Debussy's orchestral texture].

Pecerskij, Petr. "O foretepiannoj muzyke Debjussi" [On Debussy's piano music].

Bykov, Viktor. "Novatorskie certy fortepiannogo tvorcestva Debjussi" [Novel features in the piano works of Debussy].

Vladimirova, Anna. "Francuzskaja poezija v vokal'nom tvorcestve Debjussi" [The French poetry in Debussy's vocal compositions].

Filenko, Galina. "Vokal'naja lirika kloda Debjussi v svete razvitija zanra" [The development of genre and Debussy's vocal lyricism].

127. <u>Debussy et l'évolution de la musique au XXe siècle</u>. Edited by Edith Weber. Paris: Editions du Centre National de la Recherche Scientifique [15 Quai Anatole France, 75007 Paris], 1965. 365 p.; ML 410/.Dr F82.

Proceedings of the international colloquium on the same subject as the book, 24-31 October 1962, organized by J. Chailley at the Sorbonne. Contains introductory speeches and valuable papers dealing with style, aesthetic, influence in various national schools, and D's relation to the modern figures R. Godet, Schoenberg and Webern, and Varèse. General discussions, synthesis and conclusions, table of musical examples, index of names. A very important compendium of international thought on Debussy. Contents:

Weber, Edith. Avant-propos. 7-10.

Chailley, Jacques. Discours inaugural. 11-14.

Programme. 15-19.

<u>Debussy et l'évolution de la musique au XXe siècle</u>:

Sauguet, Henri. "Debussy, révolution permanente." 23-25.

Roland-Manuel. "Debussy, tradition permanente." 27-30.

<u>Le langage de Debussy</u>:

Ansermet, Ernest. "Le langage de Debussy." 33-45.

Chailley, Jacques. "Apparences et réalités dans le langage de Debussy." 47-76.

Barraqué, Jean. "Debussy: ou l'approche d'une organisation autogène de la composition." 83-95.

Gervais, Françoise. "Debussy et la tonalité." 97-106.

Almendra, Julia d'. "Debussy et le mouvement modal dans la musique du XXe siècle." 109-26.

<u>L'esthétique de Debussy</u>:

Souris, André. "Poètique musicale de Debussy." 133-38.

Lockspeiser, Edward. "Quelques aspects de la psychologie de Debussy." 141-50.

Schaeffner, André. "Debussy et ses rapports avec la peinture." 161-62.

Jarocinski, Stefan. "Quelques aspects de l'univers sonore de Debussy." 167-85.

Kremlev, Jules. "Les tendances réalistes dans l'esthétique de Debussy." 189-98.

Fédorov, Vladimir. "Debussy vu par quelques russes." 199-09.

L'influence de Debussy:

Raad, Virginia. "L'influence de Debussy: Amérique (Etats-Unis)." 215-30.

Correa de Azevedo, Luiz Heitor. "L'influence de Debussy: Amérique latine." 233-37.

Lockspeiser, Edward. "L'influence de Debussy: Angleterre. 239-40.

Stuckenschmidt, Hans-Heinz. "L'influence de Debussy: Autriche et Allemagne." 241-59.

Almendra, Julia d'. "L'influence de Debussy: Espagne et Portugal." 263-66.

Gervais, Françoise. "L'influence de Debussy: France." 269-70.

Bartha, Denès. "L'influence de Debussy: Hongrie." 273-87.

Mantelli, Alberto. "L'influence de Debussy: Italie." 289-90.

Onnen, Frank. "L'influence de Debussy: Pays-Bas (Belgique, Hollande)." 291-99.

Rovsing Olsen, Poul. "L'influence de Debussy: Pays Nordiques." 301-10.

Jarocinski, Stefan. "L'influence de Debussy: Pologne." 313-14.

Kremlev, Jules. "L'influence de Debussy: Russie." 339-40.

Austin, William. "Quelques connaissances et opinions de Schoenberg et Webern sur Debussy." 319-29.

Lesure, François. "Debussy et Edgard Varèse." 333-37.

Ansermet, Ernest. "Debussy et Robert Godet." 339-40.

[Discussion:] "A Propos de la publication des lettres de Debussy." 341-43.

Discussion générale. 345-47.

Weber, Edith. "Synthèse et conclusions." 349-50.

128. Debussy, Claude. Oeuvres complètes.
Paris: Editions Durand and Editions Costallat, jointly. Ongoing.

Two articles concerning this series:

Lesure, F. "Les Oeuvres complètes de Claude Debussy." **Cahiers Debussy** (nouvelle série) 6 (1982): 3-4. Announces the beginning of the complete works publication, jointly by the publishers Durand and Costallat. Discusses the editorial problems such as the dispersion of manuscripts, corrected printer's proofs, and Debussy's personal copies of editions that he corrected. Lesure is the editor-in-chief of the **Oeuvres complètes**.

Howat, Roy. "The New Debussy Edition: Approaches and Techniques." **Studies in Music** 19 (Australia) (1985): 94-113. Howat is an insightful member of the editorial board and recent co-editor with Claude Helffer of the **Piano Preludes** in the **Oeuvres complètes**. Outlines the editorial organization and procedure. Sees parallels with the approach of the new Josquin edition. Illustrates source problems with reference to **Nocturnes**, **Pelléas**, **La mer**, and the **Préludes**. Explores the question of source conflation, co-ordinating variants by Debussy himself or, at least, among the extant sources. Concludes that "the object of all editorial treatment is to keep the debate open." Howat articulates policies that are not firm but changeable according to varying situations.

The series as projected by Durand will consist of 33 volumes:
First Series: Piano Works. 10 volumes.
Second Series: Songs. 3 volumes.
Third Series: Chamber Music. 3 volumes.
Fourth Series: Choral Works. 3 volumes.
Fifth Series: Orchestral Works. 9 volumes.
Sixth Series: Theatrical Works. 4 volumes, and a volume of critical notes relating to **Pelléas et Mélisande**.

Inquiries or subscriptions should be addressed to Edition Claude Debussy, Durand S.A., 215 rue du Faubourg St. Honoré, 75008 Paris, France.

129. Echo musical (Paris). (Numéro spécial, Nov. 1919). For contents see Abravanel (item 53), no. 313.

Important for appreciation of Debussy immediately following his death. H. Roussel's article "Debussy et l'école moderne" is representative of that perspective. M. Pincherle's article "Claude Debussy écrivain" analyzes Debussy's comments on Musorgsky and Wagner. This special periodical number contains selected, important press reviews of the 1902 premiere of **Pelléas**.

130. Education musicale (Paris) 17, no. 89 (June 1962): 3 (231)-36 (264).

Aimed at readers concerned with music education. Contains short surveys primarily:
Machuel, D. "Claude Debussy," 231-35. A chronology of life and works.
Cusenier, S. "Impressionisme," 236-38. A survey of the movement in the visual arts.
Corbiot, O. "Debussy et le gamelan," 239-43. Refers to 1889 Paris Exposition and D's orientation to Javanese music.
Morin, S. "**Quatuor à cordes** Op. 10," 244-46.
Guiomar, Michel. "**Nocturnes** pour orchestre," 247-51.
Bryckaert, Raymond. "**La mer**," 252-54.
Kopff, René. "**Ibéria**," 255-56.
Machuel, D. "La musique de chambre de Claude Debussy," 257-58.
"Oeuvres de Claude Debussy," 259-60.
Discographie, 261-61; Bibliographie, 264.

131. Feuilles musicales (Lausanne) 15, nos. 4-5 (June-July 1962): 63-94. Illus. [Note that **Feuilles musicales** merged with **Revue musicale de Suisse romande** in 1962].

The article by Bryr reviews the theater projects in concise fashion. That by Meylan terms the song **Colloque sentimental** a mature masterpiece that subordinates music to poetry. The other articles are either too brief to permit in-depth discussions or are reprints of writings cited elsewhere in this book. Contents:
Ansermet, Ernest. "Le langage de Debussy," 63-67.
Buenzod, Emmanuel. "Anniversaires," 67-68.
Feschotte, Jacques. "A Claude Debussy," 69-72.
Cortot, Alfred. "Sur le génie de Debussy," 74.
Bruyr, José. "Rêves et projets de Debussy," 75-79.
Chamfray, Claude. "Debussy dans l'art actuel," 80-82.
Meylan, Pierre. "**Colloque sentimental**," 84-86.
Tiénot, Yvonne. "Debussy et Erik Satie," 86.
Dietschy, Marcel. "Debussy et Wagner," 87- 88.
Meylan, Pierre. "Les livres nouveaux," 89- 91.
[Debussy]. "Les réponses à une enquête du 15 février 1889," 92.
Boucherle, Alain. "Courrier suisse du disque," 93-94.

132. <u>Inédits sur Claude Debussy</u>. Collection Comoedia-Charpentier. Paris: Les Publications Techniques, 1942.

Contents:

Peter, René. "Ce que fut le 'Générale' de **Pelléas et Mélisande**," 3-10. Describes the open rehearsal on April 30, 1902 and describes the contrasting sentiment between the Debussystes and the old guard. Quotes a short letter from D to Peter concerning Maeterlinck and the latter's disavowal of the opera in **Le Figaro** (April 14, 1902). Reprints the printed synopsis of scenes distributed at the open rehearsal and quotes press reviews.

Facsimiles, 11-12: 1) Letter from d'Annunzio to D; 2) an opening excerpt from the full score of **Prélude à l'après-midi d'un faune**; 3) an excerpt from **Rodrigue et Chimène**, Act III opening, struck out by D in the manuscript.

Cortot, Alfred. "Un drame lyrique de Claude Debussy," 13-16. Recalls two legends concerning the genesis of **Rodrigue et Chimène**, which more recently have been shown to have no basis in fact (see Lockspeiser, item 85). Refers to documents in Martin's catalogue (see next).

Martin, Auguste. "Commentaires sur un visage," 17-24. 18 photographs with commentary on D.

Hoérée, Arthur. "Entretiens inédits sur Claude Debussy: Ernest Guiraud et Claude Debussy; notes par Maurice Emmanuel (1889- 1890)," 25-33. Gives a literal transcription of the notes from Emmanuel's notebook and the musical excerpts Debussy played to illustrate his points on Wagner and new tonality, at least as Emmanuel recalled them. These notes are republished in **Avant-scène opèra--"Tosca"** (item 416), perhaps more carefully edited by Hoérée in the later publication.

Samazeuilh, Gustave. "La première version inédite de **En sourdine**." Short commentary followed by the MS facsimile of the version of **En sourdine** that is signed and dated "91."

133. <u>Melos</u> [merged in 1975 with <u>Neue Zeitschrift für Musik</u>] 29, no. 11 (Nov. 1962).

Boulez, Pierre. "Général Debussy--eccentric," 341-43. Argues that D is more than "musiçien français" or Impressionist; his music launches into improvisational compositorial methods. Relates Debussy to Cézanne and Mallarmé in outlook.

Strobel, Heinrich. "Claude Debussys Persönlichkeit und Werk," 344-46. States that D stood alone among musicians but drew close in spirit to Baudolaire and Poe and opened the window to a free, spontaneous creativity. His example was followed with personal adaptations by Schoenberg, Webern, Stravinsky, and Boulez.

Debussy, Claude. "Briefe an Strawinsky," 347-50. Letters to Stravinsky dated 13 Apr. 1912, [undated], 15 May 1913, 18 Aug. 1913, 9 Nov. 1913, 17 Nov. 1913, 24 Oct. 1915. These also given in item 405.

Stralet Rostand, Claude. "Debussy gestern--Debussy heute," 350-58. Compares the biography by Vallas (item 96) to that by H. Strobel (92), the latter of whom dwells upon stylistic development while the former stresses the documentation and D's musical Impressionism.

134. Musical Times. "Claude Achille Debussy." May 1, 1918, 198-209.

Valuable for views of contemporaries:

Newman, Ernest. "The Development of Debussy." A man of the 19th century, Newman views D's late works as the products of a "faded dandy...trying to impress his older contemporaries." Criticizes D's "lamentable restriction of resources [in the late works], instead of the expansion we are familiar with in the later styles of men of genius."

Jean-Aubry, Georges. "Some Recollections of Debussy." Valuable observation of D at the end of his life. Describes his plans for a tour of England. Quotes from letters by D to Jean-Aubry of 1907-09 concerning the trips to England. Also quotes (in English, as everywhere) a letter of 1909 to the conductor T.J. Guéritte.

Concludes with selections from the French press on the occasion of D's death by H. Quittard, A. Jullien, P. Landormy, and M. Laurent-Tailhade.

135. Musical Times. Portrait of Debussy [a series of articles in successive numbers of the journal].

Provides quite fine summaries and points of departure for the study of Debussy's relation to composers. To be supplemented by studies of greater depth on particular composers and national schools. Commemorates the 50th anniversary of D's death. Is thus an important adjunct to the discussions of Debussy and the several national schools in Weber (item 127). The series:

Noble, Jeremy. "Debussy and Stravinsky." Jan. 1967, 22-25.

Cross, Anthony. "Debussy and Bartók." Feb. 1967, 125-31.

Henderson, Robert. "Debussy and Schoenberg." Mar. 1967, 222-26.

Carner, Mosco. "Debussy and Puccini." June 1967, 502-05.

Pirie, P.J. "Debussy and English Music." July 1967, 599-601.

Myers, Rollo. "Debussy and French Music." Oct. 1967, 899-901.

O'Loughlin, Niall. "Debussy and Koechlin." Nov. 1967, 993-96.

Smalley, Roger. Debussy and Messiaen." Feb. 1968, 128-31.

Waterhouse, J.C.G. "Debussy and Italian Music." May 1968, 414-18.

Hopkins, G.W. "Debussy and Boulez." Aug. 1968, 710-14.

Lockspeiser, Edw. "Debussy in Perspective." Oct. 1968, 904-06.

136. <u>Musik-Konzepte</u> 1/2. Claude Debussy (Dec. 1977). Ed. by H.-K. Metzger and Rainer Riehn. Munich: D. Vollendorf [Postfach 800529, 8000 Munich 80].

Contents in 4 sections:

I. Allende-Blin, Juan. "Debussy und Poe, eine Dokumentation." Outlines Debussy's attraction to Poe and presents Debussy's complete French libretto of **La chute...Usher**.

Faye, Jean Pierre. "'Musique de l'open air' zwischen drei Sprachen." Relates Debussy's and Poe's **Usher** to Mallarmé's theory of "open air."

II. Allende-Blin, Juan. "Claude Debussy: Scharnier zweier Jahrhunderte." Relates Debussy's **Chute-Usher** to Baudelaire's call for the bizarre in art. Discusses Debussy's pathbreaking declamation, new cyclic form, and sense of theater.

III. Schnebel, Dieter. "Sirènes oder der Versuch einer sinnlichen Musik." Discusses innovative aspects of the early orchestral works **Prélude-faune** and **Nocturnes**.

The ff. 4 essays investigate the works named:

Spies, Markus. "**Jeux.**"

Zeller, Hans Rudolf. "Von den **Sirenen** zu **La sérénade interrompue**."

Hoérée, Arthur. "**Images oubliées**."
Metzger, Heinz-Klaus. "**Khamma**."
IV. Riehn, Rainer. "Verzeichnis der Werke Claude Debussys." Gives list of works, citing first performances and the current publishers.
Riehn, Rainer. "Verzeichnis der von Debussy eingespielten Aufnahmen." Lists Debussy's recordings of nine of his piano works on Welte Music Rolls, and lists his recording with soprano Mary Garden of five of the **Ariettes oubliées** and **Pelléas** Act III, scene 1.
Lesure, François. "Auswahlbibliographie." Expertly chosen general bibliography of Debussy's collected writings, letters, biography, and musicological studies of him.

137. Neue Zürcher Zeitung [newspaper].
"Claude Debussy zum hundersten Geburtstag (22 August)." In special section "Literatur und Kunst." Zurich: **Neue Zürcher Zeitung**, August 19, 1962.
Strobel, Heinrich. "Persönlichkeit und Werk."
Lockspeiser, Edward. [Untitled.] Presents overview of D's orientations and points to **Jeux** as initiating the "cult of the new." Points to Schoenberg as D's successor.
Schuh, Willi. "Debussy, Yvonne Lerolle, Renoir." D's friend Yvonne Lerolle was a prototype for the character Mélisande. Refers to Renoir's drawings and paintings of the sisters Yvonne and Christine Lerolle.
Fischer, Kurt von. "Debussy und die Sonate." Surveys the particular works and the sonata idea as D conceived it.
Stravinsky, Igor. "Erinnerung an Claude Debussy." Recollections of a lunch with Debussy in the company of Satie, after the premiere of **Petrouchka**. They discussed Rimsky-Korsakof and Musorgsky. Excerpted from Stravinsky's **Expositions and Developments**, London 1962.
Proust, Marcel. "Eine **Pelléas et Mélisande** Parodie." Gives in German a letter from Proust to R. Hahn of 1911, containing a parody of an exchange between Pelléas and Arkel in the opera.

138. Nineteenth-Century Music.
Volumes 10, no. 3 and 11, no. 1 (Spring 1987 and Summer 1987) are devoted to musical life 1880-1900. Vol. 10, no. 3, p. 207, contains a précis of all the articles. A significant collection for

the understanding of D's environment, if not systematically referring to him.

Vol. 10, no. 3 contains:
Forte, Allen. "Liszt's Experimental Idiom and Music of the Early 20th Century," 209-28.
Kramer, Lawrence. "Decadence and Desire: The Wilhelm Meister Songs of Wolf and Schubert," 229-42.
Pasler, Jann. "**Pelléas** and Power: Forces Behind the Reception of Debussy's Opera," 243-64. (see item 853)
Taruskin, Richard. "Chez Petroushka: Harmony and Tonality chez Stravinsky," 265-86.

Vol. 11, no. 1 contains:
Burkholder, J. Peter. "'Quotation' and Paraphrase in Ives's **Second Symphony**," 3-25.
Lewis, Christopher. "Mirrors and Metaphors: Reflections on Schoenberg and 19th-C. Tonality," 26-42.
Youens, Susan. "**Le Soleil des morts**: A Fin-de-siècle Portrait Gallery," 43-58.
Lewin, David. "Some Instances of Parallel Voice-Leading in Debussy," 59-72. (see item 666)
Somfai, Laszlo. "19th-C. Ideas Developed in Bartók's Piano Notation in the Years 1907-1914," 73-91.

139. [Peters Edition, Leipzig.]
Zimmermann, Rainer. "Debussy-Werkausgabe in der Edition Peters Leipzig." **Musik und Gesellschaft** 22, no. 4 (1972): 241-45.

Discusses the organization and presentation of materials and the editorial policies of the extensive Debussy publications by Edition Peters. Gives in facsimile p. 1 of the MS of **Pour les cinq doigts (Etudes)**, further discussing the work as an example of editorial procedure. For a reconsideration of the Edition Peters, see Lesure (**Cahiers** item 123). A number of compositions are not included in the Peters catalogue.

140. Revue belge de musicologie 16 (1962), fasc. 1-4, pp. 43-149. "Souvenir et présence de Debussy."

Souris, André. "Debussy et Stravinsky," pp. 45-56. Reviews and extracts Debussy's correspondence about and to Stravinsky. Argues that

Stravinsky inherited a sense of static harmony from Debussy, who first expressed a misunderstanding of and then a profound appreciation for **Le Sacre**.

Ruwett, Nicolas. "Notes sur les duplications dans l'oeuvre de Claude Debussy," 57-70. Explores Debussy's characteristic gesture of repeating phrases nearly literally. Denies that such a device is a cliché and proposes a view of the trait that considers many facets, among them multiple thematic relationships and varying structural functions.

Deliege, Célestin. "La Relation forme-contenu dans l'oeuvre de Debussy," 71-96. Debussy's art is in equilibrium between form and content, such that each aspect confirms the other. A thoughtful study of the song **Le balcon** illustrates the point.

Vander Linden, Albert. "**L'enfant prodigue** de Debussy au Théâtre Royal de la Monnaie en 1913," 97-106. Reviews comments in the press, which for Vander Linden show that D had advanced in positive critical reception since the 1884 first performance in Paris.

------. "Claude Debussy, Octave Maus et Paul Gilson," 107-16. Correspondence and relationship with the Belgian critic Maus; cites 2 extended letters by the composer Gilson relative to Debussy.

Kecskemeti, Istvan. "Claude Debussy, musicien français: His Last Sonatas," 117-49. Debussy's nationalistic and classicizing tendencies surface in the sonatas; that for cello exhibits neo-Romantic effects. The associations and inspiration for the sonatas are explored carefully.

141. <u>Revue de musicologie</u>. Claude Debussy, 1862-1962. Textes et documents inédits. Vol. 48 (numéro spécial, July-Dec. 1962). 219 p.

A collection of primary documents with commentaries by leading authorities. Commemorates the centenary of D's birth.

Lesure, F., ed. "Correspondance de Claude Debussy et de Louis Laloy (1902-1914)," 3-40. 82 letters, apparently the complete extant correspondence. These are indexed in the Letters section of the present book.

"Trois textes de Claude Debussy" [a reprint], 41-48.

1. "Considérations sur le Prix de Rome au point de vue musical" (**Musica**, May 1903, p. 118). D's article on the topic in **Gil Blas** (June 10,

1903) is completely different.

2. "Une 'déclaration arrangée' de Debussy en 1904." A "doctored" interview as reported by Paul Landormy, which D dismissed as inaccurate in a letter to Laloy.

3. "A propos de Charles Gounod" (**Musica**, July 1906, p. 99). High praise for Gounod.

"Dix lettres d'Ernest Chausson à Claude Debussy (1893-94)," 49-60. Apparently the entire extant correspondence, some of which was published previously. These indexed in Letters section.

Lockspeiser, Edward, ed. " Neuf lettres de Pierre Louÿs à D (1894-98)," 61-70. Five of these were excerpted in Borgeaud's ed. of the Louÿs letters (see item 26). The present nine are given in their entirety.

Borgeaud, H., ed. "Trois lettres d'Erik Satie à Claude Debussy (1903)," 71-74.

Lockspeiser, Edward, ed. "Deux lettres de G. Fauré à Claude Debussy (1910-17)," 75-76.

Lesure, François, ed. "Cinq lettres de R. Godet à Claude Debussy (1917-1918)," 77-95. With preface by Lesure concerning the letters, mostly lost, from others to D.

Notes et documents

pp. 96-97. "Deux concerts à Chauny (Aisne) in 1876 avec M. de Bussy." A report by H. Borgeaud of Debussy as pianist at age 14.

pp. 98-100. "Debussy de 1883-85 d'après la correspondance de P. Vidal à Henriette Fuchs." D's youthful relationship to his parents, to Guiraud, and to Mme Vasnier.

pp. 101-03. "Lettres d'André Messager à Albert Carré relatives à **Pelléas et Mélisande**."

pp. 104-06. "...Les fées sont d'exquises danseuses..." Memoirs by Paul Hooreman of his childhood friend Chouchou (D's daughter), and of their mutual interest in the Rackham watercolor that might have inspired the prelude.

pp. 107-08. "Debussy et Stravinsky." Recollections de G. Jean-Aubry of a conversation with D.

pp. 109-20. "Claude Debussy (1918)," by R. Godet. Previously published (Geneva, **La semaine littéraire**, 1918) reflections by a cherished friend, penned the day after D's death.

pp. 121-28. "Coup d'oeil historique sur l'oeuvre de Claude Debussy." A conference paper by Constantin Brailoiu, thoughtfully relating D to tradition and to musical ethnology, the author's field of expertise.

pp. 129-43. "Bibliographie." Important

bibliography up to 1962, by François Lesure.
pp. 144 and following. "Addendum Debussyanum."

142. Revue internationale de musique française. Geneva and Paris: Slatkine.

Vol. 2 (June 1980) contains "Le journal de Ricardo Viñes." Intro., trans. [into French], and notes by Nina Gubisch.

Viñes was an important piano performer of D and Ravel. His diary contains important recollections of first performances and collaboration with D.

Vol. 2/5 (June 1981), "L'impressionisme musical."

A generally useful collection of papers read at the festival "Printemps musical" in Poitiers in 1980. These interpretations may be read alongside Jarocinski (item 564), who calls into question the interpretation of D as an Impressionist.

Contents:

"Eléments de bibliographie," 6.

Gut, Serge. "Introduction," 7-8.

Gervais, Françoise. "Qu'est-ce que l'impressionisme musical?" 9-12.

Pistone, Danièle. "L'impressionisme musical et l'esprit fin-de-siècle," 13-19.

Pasquet, Yves-Marie. "Mouvements multiples," 20-22.

Suter, Louis-Marc. "Quelques aspects du rythme dans la musique de Claude Debussy," 23-30.

Gut, Serge. "Les techniques d'harmonie impressionistes chez Debussy," 31-42.

Durney, Daniel. "L'eau dans la musique impressioniste," 43-50.

Holstein, Jean-Paul. "Le renouveau de la symphonie française à la fin du XIXe siècle et l'appel de l'impressionnisme," 51-60.

Marschall, Gottfried. "Signes avant-coureurs des techniques impressionistes dans la musique de Jules Massenet," 61-72.

Lelouch, Emile. "Le langage impressionniste de Fauré dans son **Requiem**," 73-74.

Beltrando, Marie-Claire. "L'impressionnisme dans les mélodies de Fauré," 75-80.

Gorog, André. "Ravel au piano: Impressionnisme ou expressionnisme," 81-83.

Rayon, Jean-Paul. "Impressionnisme et architecture métallique: L'éclairage zénithal ou La mort de l'ange," 84-85.

Spieth-Weissenbacher, Christiane. "Le récitatif debussyste," 86-93.

Dietschy, Marcel. "Pour un portrait de Debussy: éléments de graphologie," 93-98.
Goubault, Christian. "Les chapelles musicales françaises ou la querelle des 'gros- boutiens' et des 'petits-boutiens,'" 99-112.
Scherer, Colette. "Documentation théâtrale et musicologique à la Bibliothèque Gaston Baty," 113-15.
Boschot, Henriette. "Le Musée Hector Berlioz," 116-19.
Associations; Nouvelles diverses; etc.

143. Revue musicale, 1, no. 2 (Dec. 1, 1920). Numéro spécial consacré à la mémoire de Claude Debussy.

Central to the study of Debussy's appreciation immediately following his death, and also for recollections of facts of biography by close associates. Contents:
Suarès, André. "Debussy," 98-126. Views him in terms representative of the times: Suarès does not approach the music critically or structurally, he seems perplexed by D's innovations, and he resorts to ethereal and nationalist thought to acclaim him as a renewing genius of French music.
Cortot, Alfred. "La musique pour piano de Claude Debussy," 127-50. Interpretive remarks in the broader sense of color and attitudes, recalling Cortot's book on piano music (item 725).
Laloy, Louis. "Le théâtre de Claude Debussy," 151-54. A brief overview only, but as always in the case of Laloy, thoughtful.
Vuillermoz, Emile. "Autour du **Martyre de Saint-Sébastien**," 155-58. Comments on the genesis, production, and performance of a work Vuillermoz terms "Debussy's **Parsifal**."
Peter, René. "Du temps d'Achille," 159-64. Recollections of D during his first enthusiasm for Wagner, his work on **Rodrigue**, and the collaboration with Peter on **Frères en art**.
Godet, Robert. "Le lyrisme intime de Debussy," 167-90. Important insights into the songs by someone who was on the scene during their genesis.
Jean-Aubry, Georges. "L'oeuvre critique de Debussy," 191-202. Thoughtful, balanced survey that observes D's critical views of Wagner in the context of the times.
Chroniques et notes: "L'oeuvre de Debussy en France et à l'étranger." Among the earliest essays on D's reception and hence in valuable:
Vuillermoz, Emile. "France," 203-04.
Lesbroussart, Henri. "Debussy et la Belgique,"

205-06.
Falla, Manuel de. "L'Espagne dans l'oeuvre de Debussy," 206-10.
Dunton-Green, L. "Les anglais et Debussy," 210-12. English music.
Casella, Alfredo. "Debussy et la jeune école italienne," 213-15.
Saminsky, Lazare. "Russie: Debussy à Petrograd," 216.

144. Revue musicale, Supplément musical (Nov. 1, 1920).

Musical compositions in homage to Debussy, for piano except as noted:
Dukas, Paul. **La plainte, au loin, du faune**, 1-5.
Roussel, Albert. **L'accueil des Muses**, 6-7.
Malipiero, G. Francesco. **Hommage**, 8-9.
Goossens, Eugene. [untitled] 10-11.
Bartók, Béla. [untitled] 12-13.
Florent Schmitt. **Et Pan, au fond des blés lunaires, s'accouda**, 14-21.
Stravinsky, Igor. **Fragment** [arr. piano solo] des **Symphonies pour instruments à vent**, à la mémoire de Claude Achille Debussy, 22-23.
Ravel, Maurice. **Duo pour violon et violoncelle**, 24-29.
Falla, Manuel de. **Homenaja** (guitar), 30- 31.
Satie, Erik. **Que me font ses vallons...paroles de Lamartine** [voice and piano], 32.

145. Revue musicale, Numéro spécial (May 1926). "La Jeunesse de Claude Debussy."

Basic to the study of the young Debussy. Especially important are the reminiscences of Marguerite Vasnier (containing a copy of Debussy's first recital of his music in 1882), M. Emmanuel (detailing the youthful relations with Delibes and Guiraud), and Godet (concerning the period 1889 through that of **Pelléas**). Also valuable is Prunières' discussion of the Prix de Rome trip and his citation of extant pertinent letters to E. Vasnier and others. The Chausson letters concern **Pelléas** [one in Lesure, item 23: 8 Jan. 1894]. Régnier deals with the Librairie Bailly [Librairie de L'Art Indépendant] and Debussy's progressive literary tastes of about 1890. Brussel discusses Debussy's having met Dukas in 1885 and relates their relations to the atmosphere of the times. Koechlin gives a pertinent analysis of **Pantomime**, **Clair de lune** [1st version], **Pierrot**, and

Apparition. The musical supplement contains the first publication of these. Table of contents:

Bonheur, Raymond. "Souvenirs et impressions d'un compagnon de jeunesse," 3-9 (alternately paginated 99).

Pierné, Gabriel. "Souvenirs d'Achille Debussy," 10.

Vidal, Paul. "Souvenirs d'Achille Debussy," 11-16.

Vasnier, Marguerite. "Debussy à dix-huit ans," 17-22.

Prunières, Henry. "A la Villa Médicis," 23-42.

Emmanuel, Maurice. "Les ambitions de Claude Achille," 43-50.

Godet, Robert. "En marge de la marge," 51-86.

[Debussy.] "Deux lettres à Chausson," 87-88.

Régnier, Henri de. "Souvenirs sur Debussy," 89-91.

Brussel, Robert. "Claude Debussy et Paul Dukas," 92-109.

Messager, André. "Les premières représentations de **Pelléas**," 110-14.

Koechlin, Charles. "Quelques anciennes mélodies inédites de Debussy," 115.

146. Revue musicale 210 (Jan. 1952). "La littérature française et la musique."

Ramuz, C.F. "Sur Debussy," 31-33. Observes that one must seek Debussy's roots not only in Wagner but also in the French traditions of Rameau and Franck.

Koechlin, Charles. "Claude Debussy et le Debussysme dans l'époque," 55-64. Views D's coming to maturity in the "post-Franckist" decade 1890s. Traces the works from **Prélude-faune** through to **Pelléas** as a synthesis of the aesthetic of that decade.

Onnen, Frank. "Debussy et l'esprit du temps," 65-71. A quite useful survey of mid-century literature (the Goncourt brothers, Baudelaire) and its relation to music. Then discusses D's literary connections after the return from Rome (Mallarmé, Louÿs). Sees a continuous evolution in musico-poetic thought of D: he progresses from a liberal Wagnerism to an integral "francisme."

147. Revue musicale 234 (1957). Numéro spécial illustré, "**Le martyre de Saint-Sébastien**."

This issue was instigated by the revival of **Le martyre** at the Opéra de Paris in 1957, which adapted and abbreviated D'Annunzio's spoken text while leaving Debussy's music intact. Essays reconsider the intent, structure, and genesis of the 1911 work.

Cuttoli, Raphael. "**Le martyre de St.-Sébastien**: Création et reprises," 9-28. Includes valuable illustration of original costumes and press notices; discusses the performance of 1911 and those subsequently.

Cohen, Gustave. "Gabrielle D'Annunzio et **Le martyre de St.-Sébastien**," 29-39. Recollections of D'Annunzio in light of the premiere.

Devillez, Hubert. "L'adaptation du poème D'Annunzio," 41-48. The author defends his 1957 adaptation of the text, the original of which appeared too rich in images and prone to drown the music in a flood of words. The overall length is reduced from the original 5 hours to 1 3/4.

"Témoignages," 49-54: S. Lifar (on choreography); Ludmilla Tcherina (who performed the Saint); F. Labisse (stage decor); and L. Fourestier (conductor). These concern the 1957 performance.

Jacquemont, Maurice. "Notes sur la mise en scène," 55-58.

Vuillermoz, Emile. "La naissance du **Martyre de St.-Sébastien**," 59-63. On the genesis and first performance, comparing original artistic intentions to those of the 1957 production.

Vuillermoz, Emile. "Revue de presse," 64- 80. The critical reception of the 1957 reprise.

"Discographie," 81.

148. <u>Revue musicale</u>, numéro spécial no. 258, 176 p.; Carnet critique no. 259, 56 p. "Claude Debussy, 1862-1962, Livre d'or." [Centenary volume]. Paris: Richard-Masse, 1964.

This issue publishes statements of homage delivered at a centenary celebration at the Sorbonne, April 6, 1962. Also contains special studies, letters, and other documents. These letters are now at the University of Texas-Austin (see Ch. III under Manuscript Letters). A final section of this commemorative issue is devoted to such centennial events as the Colloque International [see item 127], various salutatory addresses, a description of concerts, and press reviews.

The Carnet critique discusses the centennial year's radio and television broadcasts devoted to

D and the many performances of **Pelléas**. Contents:

Godet, Robert. "Debussy," 5-6 [repr. from item 143].
Richard, Albert. "Avant-propos," 7-10 [repr. from item 143].
Mollat du Jourdin, Guy. "L'Année Debussy," 11-16.
Première partie: Hommage de la France à Claude Debussy, "Le 6 avril 1962 à la Sorbonne. Allocutions de L. Paye, Pasteur Vallery-Radot, and E. Bondeville," 17-32.
Deuxième partie: Travaux autour de Debussy
Emmanuel, Maurice. "Les ambitions de Claude Debussy," 33-40. [repr. item 145]
Sauguet, Henri. "Claude Debussy, musicien français," 41-56.
Messager, André. "Les premières représentations de **Pelléas**," 57-60 [repr. from item 145].
Boll, André. "La mise en scène de **Pelléas**," 61-74.
Vallery-Radot, Pasteur. "Présentation du **Martyre de Saint-Sébastien**," 75-76.
Gervais, Françoise. "Structures debussystes," 77-88. See item 587.
Jankélévitch, Vladimir. "L'immédiat chez Debussy," 89-98.
Barbier, Jean-Joel. "Notes sur Debussy," 99-106.
Troisième partie: Correspondance inédite de Claude Debussy
Vallery-Radot, Pasteur. "Claude Debussy et le culte de l'amitié," 107-08.
Vallery-Radot, Pasteur and James N.B. Hill. "Lettres inédites de Debussy à divers," 109- 16. Letters to N. Coronio, A. Hartmann, B. Marot, Lindenlaub, and an anonymous journalist. These at University of Texas (see Texas among Manuscript Letters, Ch. III).
Roy, Jean. "Trois lettres inédites de Debussy," 117-21. Letters to 1) R. Bonheur (Oct. 5, 1890), referring to the **Cinq poèmes de Baudelaire**; 2) A. Hartmann (July 6, 1898), on the Opéra-Comique and its architecture; and 3) A. Hartmann (Sept. 16, 1898), on the genesis of the **Nocturnes**. These now at University of Texas (see Ch. III, Manuscript Letters Texas).

Quatrième partie: Documents sur Debussy
"Calendrier des principales manifestations organisées en 1962," 122.
Weber, Edith. "Debussy et l'évolution de la musique au XXe siècle," 123-28. [précis of item

127]

"Programme du Colloque International," 129- 32.

Cain, Julien. "L'exposition Debussy à Lisbonne," 133-36.

Lesure, François. "Les expositions consacrées à Debussy en 1962," p. 137-42.

Lenoir-Fischer, Jeanne. "La Discothèque et le Musée Claude Debussy à Saint-Germain-en-Laye," 143-46.

Vallery Radot, Pasteur. "Allocution prononcée le 7 juillet 1962," 147-52.

Blancpain, Marc. "Le centennaire de Debussy et l'Alliance Française," 153-56.

MacReady, Alexandra. "Debussy et la sensi bilité de son temps," 157-60.

"Hommage de la **Revue musicale** à Debussy (cycle de concerts)," 161-68.

"Regard sur la presse française," 169 and ff.

Portrait, etc.

149. Revue musicale. Individual articles on Debussy not listed elsewhere:

Bernard, Robert. "A propos du [livre] Claude Debussy d'A. Suarès" no. 171 (Jan. 1937), 141ff.

Annunzio, G. d'. "Un hommage à Claude Debussy" (Oct. 1, 1921), 279ff.

Coeuroy, André. "Debussy et l'harmonie romantique" (May 1, 1921), 117-24.

Liess, Andreas. "L'harmonie dans l'oeuvre de Claude Debussy" (Jan. 1931), 37-53.

Prunières, Henry. "Debussy," no. 146 (May 1934), 349ff.

Vallas, Léon. "Debussy," no. 147 (June 1934), 21ff.

Godet, Robert. [no title] no. 149 (Sept. 1934), 189ff.

150. Ruch muzyczny (Warsaw) 6, no. 16 (Aug. 15, 1962).

A centenary commemorative issue on Debussy, particularly valuable for the views of D expressed by contemporary composers.

Jarocinski, Stefan. "Debussy odnowiciel" [Debussy renewer], 1-2.

Mycielski, Zygmunt. "Niedopowiedzenia i aluzje" [Veiled suggestions and allusions], 3-4.

Dallapiccola, Luigi. [Dallapiccola on Debussy], 4-5.

Boulez, Pierre. "Skazone kadzielnice" [La corruptions dans les encensoirs], 5-6.

Xenakis, Yannis. "Debussy a sformalizowanie muziki" [Formalization and music], 7.

Dutilleux, Henri. [Dutilleux on Debussy], 8.
Poulenc, Francis. [Poulenc on Debussy], 8.
Modrowska, Maria. "Wspomnienia 'Melizandy'" [Mélisande's Recollections], 9.
Pociej, Bohdan. "Debussy i tradycije francuskiej tragedii lirycznej" [Debussy and the French tradition of lyric tragedy], 10-12.
Macierakowski, Jerzy. "**Peleas i Melizandi** w wiedenskiej Staatsoper" [**Pelléas et Mélisande** et the Vienna Stadtsoper], 13.
Schaeffer, Boguslaw. "**Jeux** Debussy'ego" [Debussy's **Jeux**], 14-15.
Porebrowiczowa, Anna. "Krytyka muzyczna we Francji i "Monsieur Croche" Debussy'ego" [Music Criticism in France and Debussy's **Monsieur Croche**], 16.
[additional articles on Alfred Cortot and J.J. Rousseau.]

151. <u>Silences</u>, 4. "**Debussy**." May 1987. Paris: Editions de la Différence [103 rue Lafayette, 75010 Paris], 1987. 288 p. ISBN 2-7291-0249-3.

This number of the revue **Silence**, which apparently devotes each issue to a different composer or concept, is a mixture between articles of scholarly and general interest. It consists of surveys of representative genres or ideas and discussions that are quite current. It is aptly illustrated by graphic art and modernistic sketches by the editor Thierry de la Croix, often incorporating pages from scores or manuscripts by Debussy. The articles by Hirsbrunner, Jameux, Rattalino, Stoianova, Ujfalussy were first presented at a Symposium Claude Debussy in Milan, June 2-4, 1986.

Croix, Thierry de la. "Ni sujet, ni finalité," [editor's preface], p. 3.
Rouard, Isabelle. "Pour en finir avec Docteur Gradus," 7-25. Reviews D's **Etudes** and relates them to Maurice Ohana's **Douze Etudes d'interprétation** and André Boucourechliev's **Etudes d'après Piranèse**, a valuable comparative study.
Ducarsin, François. "La formulation du thème," 27-35. Discusses D's reference to both the French tradition of "figural" form, based on closed melody, and motivic form of German music. Relates him to Schoenberg, Webern, Boulez, and Stockhausen.
Cohen Levinas, Danielle. "Pour une voix instrumentée," 37-41. Discusses the role of the

voice, its timbre and prosody, in **Pelléas**. The work and even orchestration springs from the voice.

Bonnaure, Jacques. "De Banville à Mallarmé," 43-55. An overview of the songs, attending closely to the poets and the literary movements to which they relate.

Rattalino, Piero. "Quelques aspects du piano de Claude," 57-79. Places the piano works in context of musical sociology and performers, discussing piano sonority and interpretation.

Leblanc, Georgette. "Souvenirs (1895- 1918)," 81-85. Republication of an extract from Leblanc's **Souvenirs** (publ. by Grasset, 1931), recounting the relations of Debussy and Maeterlinck and Leblanc's early intentions to premiere the role of Mélisande.

Rosso, François. "**Pelléas et Mélisande**, symbolique de la damnation," 87-97. Important symbols in **Pelléas** relate to the obscure forest, to human blindness, and to the role of darkness in human life as dictated by fate.

Faure, Michel. "**Pelléas**: La trahison sociale au château," 99-111. An insightful examination of the social milieu of **Pelléas**, pointing to the tendency of Maeterlinck, Satie, D and others to take refuge from volatile social conditions in mysticism. Offers sociologic interpretations of the opera: Golaud defends the establishment, while Mélisande and Pelléas are alienated from and ultimately bring down the "château." The case might be overstated but can lead to a wider understanding of the opera.

Maurer, Philippe. "Méditerraniser la musique," 113-17. Traces the Mediterranean aesthetic from Bizet's **Carmen**, through **Pelléas**, and finally to Milhaud. An important effort to link D to Bizet aesthetically.

"Motus; Citations sur Debussy," 118-19. Quotations from Jules Renard, Schoenberg, P. Dukas, Jean Cocteau, E. Grieg, and Michel Sartor on Debussy and particularly **Pelléas**.

Antoni, Eric. "Le neveu de Monsieur Croche," 121-29. An imaginary dialogue concerned with aesthetics, chance meetings on the street, etc.

Stoianova, Ivanka. "Saint-Sébastien, mythe et martyre," 130-155. Explores the religious myth of St. Sebastian and defends the d'Annunzio-Debussy treatment as a valid piece of musical theater evoking the tradition of medieval sacred drama. As a new sacred drama, the work was ahead of its time: recalls Vuillermoz's belief that Debussy had written his **Parsifal** [Wagner] in **Le martyre**, a

Parsifal still awaiting its Bayreuth. Refers to several revisions of **Martyre** that reduce its unacceptable length. An excellent study of the work.

Hauel, Sylvie. "Compositeur de chevalet," 157-62. "Debussy of the painter's easel" unites the urges of painter, poet, and musician. A thought-provoking interpretation of Debussy as artist who responds to several sensibilities, including that of Impressionism.

Ujfalussy, József. "Debussy et Bartók," 165-69. Maintains that Bartók's encounter of D's music was of capital importance in his development. Although brief, this is thoughtful and is valuable as a too-rare comparison of the composers.

Hirsbrunner, Theo. "La rupture du cercle d'occident," 171-79. A major reflection on Boulez's critical appreciation of and reference as a composer to Debussy. Improvisation, timbre, rhythm, the extemporaneous/aleatoric, and scalar uses form parts of the circle that connects both of them to the Orient. Refers to Boulez's work in realizing D's "Musique pour scène, **Chansons de Bilitis**."

Roudier, Patrick. "L'illusion retrouvée," 181-89. The publication of two radio discussions of Debussy's influence on avant-garde music "de plein air...," music of the "mille bruits de la Nature." Composers joining the discussion are François Bayle, Michel Chion, Luc Ferrari, François-Bernard Mâche, and Pierre Schaeffer.

Jameux, Dominique. "Mallarmé: Debussy, Boulez," 191-201. Discusses D's **Trois poèmes de Mallarmé**, Boulez's **Trois improvisations**, and relates Ravel's **Miroirs** to Mallarmé as source of inspiration. D's last works, including the **Etudes** and sonatas as well as the **Trois poèmes** relate to that aesthetic and are particularly timely today.

Lesure, François. "Les oeuvres complètes," 203-5. A short précis of the ongoing publication, its challenges and schedule.

Vial, Mireille. "Du ciel de naissance de Achille-Claude Debussy," 207-29. A reading of the astrological signs informing Debussy's character and music. The richness and complexity of his makeup, as interpreted by the horoscope, permit both Impressionism <u>and</u> Symbolism to have a place in the psyche of the composer. A serious article, despite the point of departure.

Fabiani, François. "Proust: La recherche du temps debussyste," 231-235. Considers Proust's understanding of Debussy in light of passages from his writings. Cites 16 passages that comment on

Proust's close sympathies with Debussy's thought. Issues include social situation, aesthetics, style, sensation and sensuality, and the evocation of Debussy's universe.

Another article deals with Jean Barraqué as composer. The volume also gives record and book reviews.

2. Catalogues of Expositions

152. Bordeaux

Claude Debussy (1862-1918). Ville de Bordeaux. Exposition mai 1962. Rédigé par F. Lesure. Bordeaux: Ville de Bordeaux, 1962. 47 p., 4 plates.

A centenary exposition consisting of 159 items from the Bibl. nat., Institut de France, and several private collections. Includes music manuscripts, photos, letters, etc. Some entries in the catalogue are annotated briefly following the bibliographic listing. There are rather too few illustrations and facsimiles to make the catalogue of lasting use.

153. Lisbon

Claude Debussy. Lisbon: Teatro Nacional de Maria II, 1962. In Portuguese.

Contains a number of portraits and a facsimile of the **Pelléas** pre-orchestral sketch, Act IV, p. 11. Illustrations include that of the opening set of **Pelléas** by Jusseaume, a letter of Sept. 5, 1908, to Francisco de Lacerda concerning Satie and other matters, and reproductions of 4 of D's signatures. Gives a chronology of his life and annotates the 328 items in the exposition, naming their location and giving brief descriptions. The items were lent to this exposition by many public and private collections. The catalogue thus describes an array spanning all of D's life and work.

154. Paris

Claude Debussy. Bibliothèque Nationale 1962. Paris: [Bibl. Nat.], 1962. 72 p. LC 67-53338; ML141.P18 D4.

Celebrating D's centenary. Preface by Julien Cain; list of lenders; chronology of D's life. Catalogues 335 items, many of which are from the B.n. (MSS, photos) and are repeated from the 1942 Martin catalogue. The value of this catalogue is reduced by the absence of illustrations or facsimiles, but the annotations helpfully place items within biographical and musical context.

155. Martin, Auguste. **Claude Debussy: Chronologie de sa vie et de ses oeuvres. Catalogue de l'exposition organisée du 2 au 17 mai 1942 au foyer de l'Opéra-Comique.** Paris: Réunion des Théâtres Lyriques Nationaux, 1942. 86 p.

Prefatory remarks by Henri Büsser, Jean Cocteau, L.P. Fargue, and Francis Poulenc. Exposition catalogue of 485 items including photos, manuscripts, and other iconographic material. Highly valuable annotations listing the owners of materials as of 1942. Some illustrations and facsimiles are of documents no longer accessible otherwise.

156. Rome
Debussy e il simbolismo: Omaggio a Claude Debussy, prix de Rome 1884. Rome: Palombi, 1984. 297 p. Bilingual text in French and Italian.

The most lavish catalogue to date in terms of illustrations and visual representation of D's artistic relationships. The exposition celebrated the centenary of his receipt of the Prix de Rome and was held at the Villa Medici. A thoughtful introduction by F. Lesure traces D's artistic development, relationships, and aesthetics. Contains many color reproductions of paintings by Burne-Jones, Rossetti, Redon, Monet, Hokusai, Turner, Puvis de Chavannes, and Vuillard. Proceeds by chronological phases: "A la recherche d'un style" [1890's]; "La conquête d'un nouveau monde sonore"; "Debussy au risque du théâtre"; and "Le théâtre intérieur."

3. Catalogues of Important Sales

157. **Catalogue Nicholas Rauch**, nos. 20 and 24. Geneva: Rauch, 1958. Lists letters to G. Mourey.

158. **Catalogue de la Collection Walter Straram.** Manuscrits de Claude Debussy. Rambouillet, 1961. Not examined.

159. **Collections Jules Huret et Claude Debussy.** Paris: M. Georges Andrieux, expert. Paris, 1933.

68 p., of which pp. 32-41 [items 174-224] concern the sale of Debussy's autograph materials in the estate of his wife Emma, upon her death. The auction sale advertised in this catalogue was the most significant one in the dispersion of primary documents including manuscripts, letters, and iconographical materials.

4. Festivals and Conferences

160. American Musicological Society. 1978 National Meeting, Minneapolis, Minnesota, Oct. 19-22. Session on Debussy's dramatic music, chaired by Arthur Wenk:

Lawrence Berman (Univ. of Massachusetts-Boston). "**Prelude to the Afternoon of a Faun and Jeux**: Debussy's Summer Rites." See item 699.

Arthur Wenk (Univ. of Pittsburgh). "The Harmonic Structure of **Pelléas et Mélisande**."

Robert Orledge (Univ. of Liverpool). "The Fortunes and Structures of **Khamma**."

Carolyn Abbate (Princeton University). "Preliminary remarks Ron Debussy's Working Method in the Operas" [emphasizing Act IV, scene 4 of **Pelleas**].

William Austin (Cornell University). "A Chord from **Pelléas** Act V and its Reverberations in Stravinsky, Janácek, Berg, and Others."

Papers presented on other sessions of this conference:

Paul Jacobs (Brooklyn College). Lecture-Recital: "Performance Practice Problems in the

Piano Music of Debussy."
Richard Parks (Wayne State Univ.) "Pitch Organizations in Debussy: Unordered Sets in Three Piano Pieces."

161. American Musicological Society. 1980 National Meeting, Denver, Colorado, Nov. 6-9. Session on the future of Debussy research, chaired by Arthur Wenk:

François Lesure (Bibliothèque nationale, Paris, delivered in absentia). "Debussy in 1980."
William Peterson (Pomona College). "The Sources of **Douze études**."
Jean-Jacques Nattiez (Université de Montréal). "Report on the Groupe de Recherches en Sémiologie Musicale de Montréal."
Arthur Wenk (Univ. of Pittsburgh). "A Descriptive Grammar for the Music of Claude Debussy."
Marcelle Guertin (Université de Montréal). "The Question of Style in the Themes of Debussy's **Preludes for Piano**."
Richard Langham Smith (City University of London). "Debussy and the Pre-Raphaelites."
A discussion followed the session concerning recovered sources and prospective topics for research. This session is further described in item 161, **Cahiers**. At the same meeting on a session apart:
Marie Rolf (Eastman School of Music). "Debussy's Compositional Procedures: Evidence from Orchestral Manuscripts."

162. American Musicological Society. 1982 National Meeting, University of Michigan, Ann Arbor. Session on Debussy and twentieth-century music, chaired by Arthur Wenk:

Claudia Maurer Zenck (Berlin). "Debussy, prophet and seducer" [publ. item 427].
James R. Briscoe (Butler University). "Debussy's Centenary: The Early Songs of 1882" [publ. item 708].
James A. Hepokoski (Oberlin College). "Formulaic Openings in the Music of Debussy" [publ. item 000].
Roy Howat. "Dramatic Shape and Form in **Jeux de vagues**, and its relationship to **Pelléas** and later orchestral scores" [publ. item 000].
Cobb, Margaret G. Remarks on the Vasnier

relationship.

On other sessions of the same conference:

Michael L. Friedmann. "Approaching Debussy's Ondine" [publ. item 747].

David A. Grayson. "Debussy and the "Wagnerian Formula" in **Pelléas et Mélisande**" [publ. item 753].

163. American Musicological Society. 1985 National Meeting. Session on Debussy, chaired by Jann Pasler:

Marie Rolf. "The Emergence of the Symbolist Aesthetic in **En sourdine**."

Michael Nott. "A Comparative Analysis of Versions of **Fantoches**."

Douglass Green. "**Clair de lune**: An Analytical Study of its Various Versions."

William J. Peterson. "Debussy in 1914: The Composing of **Six épigraphes antiques**."

164. Concours International de Piano de Claude Debussy.

Yearly competition beginning in 1982 and organized by the city of Saint-Germain-en-Laye, France. Winners are listed in the yearly "Chroniques" of the **Cahiers Debussy**, item 123.

165. Romantic Music Festival XV (April 19-25, 1982). Butler University, Indianapolis. "The Music of Claude Debussy."

Celebrated the centenary of Debussy's debut as a performed composer (see item 165). Scholarly lectures were as follows:

Judith S. Allen. "Divers Thoughts on Debussy's **Sonates**." [rev. publ. item 614]

Thomas Warburton. "Three Bitonal Miniatures by Debussy of 1913" [publ. item 648].

Roland Nadeau. "Debussy's Chords with Deep Root."

Roy Howat. "Recent Discoveries for Piano by Debussy" [**Images oubliées**, **Morceau de concours**, **Elégie**, and **Etude retrouvée**]

Artis Wodehouse. "The Recordings of Marguerite Long: Clues to Debussy's Performance Practice [**Arabesques** I and II, **La plus que lente**, **Jardins sous la pluie**].

Arthur Wenk. "One Face, Many Masks." [Incorporated as a chapter in item 226].

William W. Austin discussed the future of Debussy research, and the above speakers and pianist Pia Sebastiani presented preconcert talks throughout the festival. Further see item 123 for 1982.

166. Society for Music Theory. National Conference, 1985. Session on Debussy and Fauré, chaired by Arthur Wenk:

Taylor Green. "**L'heure exquise**: Fauré's Use of the Whole-tone Scale in **La bonne chanson**."

Marie Rolf. "Structural Coherence in Act IV, scene 4 of Debussy's **Pelléas et Mélisande**."

Richard Parks. "Text Expression through the Use of Pitch Materials in Debussy's **Pelléas et Mélisande**."

VIII

DEBUSSY'S RELATIONSHIPS

1. Artistic Climate

167. Antoine, André. **Mes souvenirs sur le Théâtre Antoine et sur l'Odéon.** Paris: B. Grasset, 1928. LV 28-19114; PN 2636.P4 T72.

Pages 228 and 239 quote letters from D to Antoine, a prominent theater director. Of further value is Antoine's testimony as a key figure in the artistic environment.

168. ------. **Mes souvenirs sur le Théâtre-Libre.** Paris: Fayard, 1921. 324 p.; index. LC PN2636.P4T7. English translation by M. Carlson, as **Memories of the Théâtre- Libre.** Coral Gables, Fla.: University of Miami Press, 1964. xiv, 239 p.

Organizes by diary-like entries the main events concerning the progressive and frequently experimental Théâtre-Libre. On p. 218, an entry associates D with C. Mendès, O. Mirbeau, A. Silvestre, and others. Spans the period 1887-94 and provides first-hand information on the keenly innovative atmosphere of the theater.

169. Austin, William W. "Studies of Music in the 20th Century." **Journal of Musicology** 1, no. 1 (1982): 63-66.

A survey of directions for research by a foremost scholar of contemporary music. Considers the directions with which musicology has approached and might approach twentieth-century music. D and his global awareness is a cornerstone of Austin's hopes; he returns to him repeatedly, challenges the reader to assess his impact afresh, and concludes, "More and more young musicologists, I think, will be tracing connections between Debussy and young composers, connections that may skip over Schoenberg and Stravinsky, while incorporating some extra-European link."

170. Billy, André. **L'époque contemporaine, 1905-1930.** Paris: Tallandier, 1956. 365 p. LC 56-32457; PQ 305.B49.

Sees the period as one of remarkable variety, freedom of spirit, and optimism, which ends with the depression year 1930 and the rise of Nazism. Traçes the significance of and helpfully establishes the context of the related writers Paul Bourget and Catulle Mendès (at the end of their careers), Romain Rolland, Toulet, and Valéry.

171. ------. **L'époque 1900: 1885-1905.** Paris: J. Tallandier, 1951. 484 p. LC 52-20385; PQ 296.B5.

Just as R. Shattuck (item 388), takes the death of Victor Hugo in 1885 as a watershed in French culture. Traces main figures more methodically if in a less synthetic manner than Fowlie (entry 468), alongside whom the present may comment on D's literary environment.

172. Boulez, Pierre. **Points de repère.** Edited by J.-J. Nattiez. 2nd revised ed. Paris: Editions du Seuil, 1985. 588 p. ISBN 2-267-00276-0. English translation by Martin Cooper as **Orientations.** Cambridge, Mass.: Harvard University Press, 1986. ISBN 0-674-64375-5; ML60.B796P613.

A collection of all major essays written by Boulez since **Relevés** (see following). A thorough index notes many mentions of D throughout. Two articles devoted to him are "Debussy: L'Oeuvre pour orchestre" and "Miroirs pour **Pelléas et Mélisande**." The latter is especially relevant in placing **Pelléas** in the history of opera; the work is an important turning point, in Boulez's view.

173. ------. **Relevés d'apprenti**. Ed. by Paule Thévenin. Collection "Tel quel." Paris: Editions du Seuil, 1966. ML60.B796R4. English translation by H. Weinstock, as **Notes of an Apprenticeship**. New York: Knopf, 1968. 398 p. ML 60.B796 R3.

The chapter "La corruption dans les encensoirs" proposes D, Cézanne, and Mallarmé as the sources of modern art. Discusses the nature of their revolution. D defies given form and style in creating the new, which contribution Boulez relates to Musorgsky as well. The chapter "Claude Debussy," pp. 327- 47, expands on the idea of D "dreaming"--interiorizing--his revolution. These are important writings by a foremost composer and musical presence since 1950.

174. Bourne, W. "A Kindling Fever: A Study of Some Religious, Socio-Ethical and Literary Themes in Music Between 1890 and 1920, with Special Reference to Debussy, Stravinsky, and Schoenberg." Ph.D. diss., Music, Univ. of Auckland, 1969. Not examined.

175. Brody, Elaine. **Paris: The Musical Kaleidoscope, 1870-1925**. New York: Braziller, 1987. 359 p. ISBN 0-8076-1176-X; ML 270.8 P2B93 1987.

A thorough study and one of the most important in English on D's artistic milieu. Brody reveals new contacts that call for further study, as for example D's performing his music for Rodin only to have him remain silent (p. 124). Nearly all of D's major works are placed against a large background, which occasionally causes this approach to appear piecemeal. Procedes by chapter topics such as "Wagner in France and France in Wagner," Le Japonism et l'orientalisme," "The Legacy of Ida Rubinstein," and "The Spaniards in Paris" [R. Viñes, De Falla]. Most valuable if read alongside Lockspeiser (73), who focuses upon Debussy.

176. Chailley, Jacques. **40,000 ans de musique**. Paris: Plon, 1961. Translated by Rollo Myers as **40,000 Years of Music**. London: Macdonald, 1964. 229 p. LC 65-315; ML 160.C412.

A personal interpretation of music history subdivided into four sections: In Search of a

Past, of Sacred Music, of Secular Music, and of "Stars." The Epilogue is a paraphrase of Monsieur Croche, the eternal questioner of presumptions and challenger of twentieth-century habits of thought.

177. Cooper, Martin. **French Music from the Death of Berlioz to the Death of Fauré**. London and New York: Oxford University Press, 1951, rev. 1961. 239 p. ML 270.4.C7 1961.

The period of discussion is 1869-1924. Cooper's is a reasonably useful survey but is less interpretive than that by Myers (207).

178. Cope, David. **New Directions in Music**. Dubuque, Iowa: W.C. Brown, 1984. ML 197.C7 1984; ISBN 0-697-03607-3.

Observes D's challenge to traditional key structure in **Des pas sur la neige**, his reference to folk modes in **Soirée dans Grenade**, and the pentatonicism of **Pagodes (Estampes)**. D challenges Western tradition in **Prélude-faune** and **Soirée**. Relates D to non-Western influences and to Luciano Berio.

179. Dahlhaus, Carl. **Between Romanticism and Modernism: Four Studies in the Music of the Later 19th Century**. Translated and edited by M. Whittall. Berkeley: University of California Press, 1980. ML 196.D3313; ISBN 0-520-03679-4. Originally published in German as **Zwischen Romantik und Moderne**. Munich: Katzbichler, 1974.

Relationships are traced between Wagner and Schoenberg in the section "'Expanded' and 'Wandering' Tonality." Views Wagner's characteristic tonality as "wandering" (brief tonal particles in a chain), while Brahms's is "expanded" (remote regions integrated in one secure tonic). These composers represent stylistic poles. Dahlhaus's line of thought well might inform any D analysis that explores his relationship to the past.

180. ------, general ed. **Neues Handbuch der Musikwissenschaft**. Wiesbaden: Akademische

Verlagsgesellschaft Athenaion, and Laaber: Laaber-Verlag Mueller-Buscher, 1980. Complete series ISBN 3-7997-0742-5. Glossary and indexes.

Volume 6, **Die Musik des 19. Jahrhunderts**, 1980. Edited C. Dahlhaus. [ISBN 3-7997-0748-4], 360 p.
The multi-volume set **Neues Handbuch** is a highly respected collective publication of current German musicology. In volume 6 Debussy is placed in perspective of Wagnerism; attention is given to **Pelléas** as an important monument at the turn of the century.
Volume 7, **Die Musik des 20. Jahrhunderts**, 1984. Edited by Hermann Danuser. [ISBN 3- 89007-037-X], 465 p. Volume 7 views D as central in the chapter "Die Spätzeit der musikalischen Moderne," avoiding the clichés of earlier scholarship fixed on the concept "Impressionism." Relates D to Neoclassicism and to the "institutions of new music." Particular references to **Prélude-faune** and **Pelléas**, with brief discussion of the orchestral and piano music. Is current and not prejudiced but does not trace the most important trends of the century that connect to D. Particularly valuable is the discussion of music from 1950-70, which informs on current thought and might move others to probe D's artistic relations.
Volume 10, "Systematische Musikwissenschaft," 1982. Edited by C. Dahlhaus and Helga de la Motte-Haber. ISBN 3-7997-0752-2, 367 p. Discusses topics that are vital for musicology: systematic musicology, aesthetics, music and society, musical hermeneutics, and learning theory and pedagogy. D receives a number of references, with **Prélude-faune** and **La Mer** emphasized.

181. ------. **Realism in 19th-Century Music.** Translated by M. Whittall. Cambridge University Press, 1985. ISBN 0-521-261-155- 5. Originally published as **Musikalischer Realismus: Zur Musikgeschichte des 19. Jahrhunderts.** Munich: Piper, 1982.

In the chapter "The dialectics of the concept of reality," Dahlhaus compares D's compositional process to the aesthetic theories of Oscar Bie and to end developments of Realism as a movement. Views D's preference for the fluid and indefinite (the "Impressionistic") as less significant than the musical condition of stasis animated only internally. Dahlhaus argues that one must beware of analogies between D's processes and those which led 19th-century Realism to assume the form ofImpressionism.

182. [Debussy, Claude et altri.] **Pour la musique française: Douze causeries avec une préface de Claude Debussy.** Paris: Crès, 1917. vii, 342 p. LC24-615; ML270.D28.

In his preface, D speaks of Beethoven as a great musician and of Wagner rather as a creative artist. Urges that certain foreign influences be torn out of French music as if they were foul weeds, that French forms and purity be reaffirmed. Cites Offenbach and Chopin as models of good taste and naturalness. D's preface is reprinted in Lesure (47) and Langham Smith (45). The other 12 essays were lectures given in 1915 at a celebration of French music. Speaker-essayists include Romain Roland, Boucher, and others. These are largely overshadowed by D's preface, although such "period" writings as Paul Huvelin's "Musique française et musique allemande: Wagner et Bizet jugé par Nietzsche" can inform a study of D's nationalistic attitude and surroundings.

183. Devriès, Anik. "Les musiques d'Extrême-Orient à l'exposition universelle de 1889." **Cahiers Debussy** (nouvelle série) 1 (1977): 25-37.

Presents newspaper and iconograpic accounts of the Paris exposition, with a particular view toward the Javanese and Southeast Asian exhibits and corresponding musical events. Draws upon the contemporary account by ethnologist Julien Tiersot to render in concrete terms the particular events that impressed D decisively.

184. Donnay, Maurice. "Autour du Chat Noir." Paris: Bernard Grasset, 1926. 192 p.

Prose reminiscences, poems, and **tableaux vivants** descriptions relating to the Montmartre cabaret frequented by D, concerning the period 1880-1900. Important treatment of the fin-de-siècle artistic atmosphere, discussing the related figures Henri Rivière, Charles de Sivry, Maurice Vaucaire, and Jean Moréas.

185. ------. **J'ai vécu 1900.** Paris: Fayard, 1950. 294 p. PQ 2607.05Z52 1950.

Consists primarily of extracts from the author's diary covering the years 1894-1914. Donnay was a playwright of D's period and member of his close circle.

186. Edler, Arnfried. "Zur Beziehung einiger Grundfragen bei Bergson zum musikalische Denken nach 1900." In **Bericht über den Internationalen Musikwissenschaftlichen Kongress Berlin 1974**, pp. 467-70.

Discusses the relationship of Bergson's philosophy to musical thought after 1900. Bergson saw the art work as governed by organic growth, basic alogic, non-repetition, irreversibility, functionality, and fluid, interconnecting transitions. Although the whole philosophy requires careful application, the article shows how D's music parallels certain of Bergson's theories. Refers to **Jeux** and its continual variation form.

187. Faure, Michel. "L'époque 1900 et la résurgence du mythe de Cythère." **Mouvement social** 109 (Oct.-Dec. 1979): 15-34.

A sociological analysis of the nostalgia for the 18th century among French musicians around 1900. Refers in depth to D and Fauré and their works inspired by Verlaine, especially by his poems **Fêtes galantes**. Relates D's marriage to Emma Bardac to the high desirability of the elite bourgeois lifestyle in the Belle Epoque.

188. ------. **Musique et société du Second Empire aux années Vingt: Autour de Saint-Saëns, Fauré, Debussy, et Ravel.** Paris: Flammarion, 1985. 424 p. ISBN 2-08-064650-8.

Discusses the complex socio-cultural web experienced by composers, and traces their individual reactions. D relates to Monet and to the expansion of the parameters of the previous agrarian mentality. As in the preceding source, Faure refers to the ascendency of the bourgeois mentality. Observes in D a "culpability" concerning women, a bad social conscience among a bourgeoisie who have exploited the proletariat, and sees the mysticism of **Pelléas** as a manifestation of guilt escapism. A provocative book that requires careful interpretation and a reserved reading, owing to its socialist polemics.

189. Fischer, Kurt von. "Claude Debussy und das Klima des Art nouveau: Bemerkungen zur Aesthetik Debussys und J. McNeil Whistlers." In **Art Nouveau, Jugendstil und Musik**, pp. 31-46. Zurich: Atlantis, 1980. ML 55.S396 1980; ISBN 376-11-06041.

Points to parallels in the views of D and the painter Whistler, whose paintings of **Nocturnes** might have inspired D's orchestral set. Quotes widely from writings by both artists to illustrate their common attitude toward nature in art. D's music originates within the climate of Art nouveau and shares its views of art for art. A thoughtful article on aesthetics.

190. Germain, André. **Les fous de 1900**. Paris: La Palatine, 1954. 269 p. PQ PQ146.G47.

The "fous" are artists of the period, whom the author characterizes as seeking a beauty that is insolent, eccentric, and perishable. Proust is highlighted as a symbol of that sensibility. Devotes chapters to Montesquiou, Jean Lorrain, Oscar Wilde, La Princesse de Polignac, Liane de Pougy, Péladan, Maurice Barrès, Proust, Gide, and Cocteau. Each of these either relates directly to Debussy or exemplifies the period.

191. Gheusi, Pierre. **Cinquante ans de Paris: Mémoires d'un témoin (1889-1938)**. Paris: Plon, 1939. 501 p. DC 715.G45.

Helpful index of names, detailed table of contents. A valuable contemporary view of D's artistic surrounds, although superseded in ways and synthesized by Brody (item 175), Trillig (240), and Lockspeiser (73). Gheusi recalls letters to him from D regarding **Pelléas**, which were confidential and desperate and therefore "not proper to quote." D first proposed Suzanne Vorska for the role of Mélisande, according to Gheusi. Mentions the popularity of **Damoiselle élue**, **L'enfant prodigue**, and **Boîte à joujoux** in the period. D's ideas dominated the lyric stage in the early 20th century. As director of the Opéra-Comique, Gheusi was in the midst of leading musicians, although his recollections might involve imagination or faulty memory.

192. Goubault, Christian. "Modernisme et décadence." **Revue internationale de musique française** 6, no. 18 (Nov. 1985): 29-46.

D stood at the threshhold of musical modernism, even though his work was not fully appreciated until after 1950. Traces the concept of modernism as it evolved from Wagner and Nietsche to Baudelaire. Places D in artistic context (Mendès, Saint-Saëns). Describes the acceptance and rejection of modernism as it bore upon the critical reception of **Pelléas**.

193. Guichard, Léon. "Debussy et les occultistes." **Cahiers Debussy** (première série) 1 (1974): 10-14.

D was in contact with occultists around 1890 concerning the project **Les noces de Sathan**, based on an esoteric drama by Jules Bois. The project was announced for 1892 at the Théâtre d'art but later rejected. This article is the first version of one published in Lockspeiser (85). Guichard supplements Lockspeiser with his own comments and by printing a key letter of 1892 to Jules Bois.

194. ------. **La Musique et les lettres en France au temps du Wagnerisme**. Paris: Presses Universitaires de France, 1963. 354 p., index. ML 270.G853.

Discusses D along with virtually all main composers of his time, with reference to Wagnerism. Useful when following the general trend but overstates in sweeping terms Wagner's influence while understating essential, French adaptation and aesthetic differences.

195. Hodeir, André. **Since Debussy: A View of Contemporary Music**. Translated by N. Burch. London: Secker and Warburg, 1961. 256 p. ML 197.H63 1961x.

Views the 20th century as a period of transition between two civilizations, recalling Queneau and Toynbee. In "A Tribute to Claude Debussy," Hodeir notes that the deeper implications of D's music surfaced only after 1950, especially his new approaches to form and reinstatement of the power of pure sound. He thus becomes the "Mallarmé" of music, the first musician to adopt twentieth-century thought processes. D's impact is pronounced on music after 1950: "the influence...is felt on every page."

* Hoérée, Arthur. "Debussy, musicien novateur." Further see annotation, item 532.

196. Jarocinski, Stefan. **Orfeusz na rozdrozu: Eseje o muzyce i muzykach XX wieku** [Orpheus at the crossroads: Essays on music and musicians of the 20th century]. 2nd ed. Krakow: Wydawnictwo Muzyczne, 1974. 336 p. ML 197.J37 1974.

By a foremost D scholar of recent times. Discusses broad trends of the century and classifies composers as protagonists (Debussy, Schoenberg, Ives), apostles (Webern, Messiaen), or idealist-mediators (Bartók, Ravel, Britten).

197. Krenek, Ernst. **Music Here and Now.** New York: Norton, 1939. 306 p. ML 197.K92 M9.

Valuable now as an articulation of Zeitgeist by a prominent composer and thinker. Seeks to show how "new music," that from 1900-1935, relates to the past and how new music might attain a higher estimation by the audience. Observes that D's "exquisite tone marvels" have become cheapened mannerisms for popular music composers. Presses D into service when defending atonality, an idiom close to the author. Betrays a typical post-Debussy myopia in referring to "descriptive sound pictures," but more objectively refers to D's innovation of sonority as an element of compositional process.

198. Kunickaja [Kounitskaia], Raisa. **O romanticeskoj poetike v tvorcestve Debussi** [On the Romantic poetics in Debussy]. Moscow: Muzyka, 1982. 88 p.

Observes that D's sound world suggests links with Romantic ideals. Gives a stylistic and historical analysis of vocal and instrumental works and of **Pelléas**. Discusses D's ties to Symbolist poetry. Not examined.

* Laloy, Louis. **La musique retrouvée (1902-27)**. Paris, 1928. Reprinted Paris: Desclée de Brouwer, 1974. Preface by Georges Auric. 294 p. ML 423.L2.

Recalls conversations with D and remarks on Satie and Cocteau. A basic source on D's times and the period just after his death by a foremost critic and early biographer. Laloy extends the remarks of his biography (69) in ways that are quite helpful. Further see annotation, item 82.

199. Lesure, François. "Le symbolisme et les arts plastiques." **Cahiers Debussy** (nouvelle série) 8 (1984): 3-12.

Now in French, the introduction to the catalogue **Debussy e il simbolismo** (item 156). Reconsiders the label of "Impressionist" and the perception of the term by D and his contemporaries. Symbolism was central to D's aesthetic. Lesure refers in virtuoso fashion to a spectrum of related artistic figures and thought; he thus expands horizons of Debussy's milieu. He provides an excellent overview and valuable references to other writings, but necessarily his catalogue introduction is not so deep as Jarocinski (564).

200. Lethève, Jacques. **La vie quotidienne des artistes français au XIX siècle**. Paris: Hachette, 1968. Translated. by H.E. Paddon as **Daily Life of French Artists in the Nineteenth Century**. London: Geo. Allen and Unwin, 1972. 224 p. N 6847.L413; ISBN 0-04- 954015-7.

Seeks a picture of the whole class of visual artists. Considers training, lifestyle, and economic structures of a group who, within the bourgeois mindset of the times, seemed to represent an ideal. A valuable discussion of the social conditions, institutions (Villa Medici-Prix de Rome), and economics (commissions, dealers) that similarly relate to D. A similar study of musicians is needed.

201. Liess, Andreas. **Claude Debussy: Das Werk im Zeitbild.** 2 vols. in 1. Strasbourg: Heitz, 1936. 427 p. ML 410.D28L74.

A pathbreaking study of particular depth concerned with D's times from the philosophical, aesthetic, literary, and historical perspective. Replete with socialist thought typical of its time, as in the section "Das Kuntswerk und die kollektivistische Idee." D represents the era of individual sensibility. The important scholar Liess was a leader in distinguishing between Symbolist and Impressionist strains in the composer's thought.

202. Lockspeiser, Edward. "Debussy in Perspective: Portrait of Debussy 11." **Musical Times** 109 1968): 904-06.

Calls for a new vigor in D scholarship, which should explore anew his artistic environment and his personality. Points to the need for a catalogue raisonné [provided provisionally by Lesure item 51], for the publication of such important works as **Diane au bois**, **Rodrigue**, and **La saulaie**, and the publication of D's writings [see Lesure item 47 and Langham Smith 45] and letters. Further see Lesure's related assessment (540).

203. ------. "Quelques aspects de la psychologie de Debussy." In source 127.

Points to D as chief among musical Symbol ists, referring to his appreciation of Turner, Mallarmé, and Poe. Notes that a sensitive yet violent personality formed during an insecure childhood. Discusses the psychological conflict with Wagner, observing that D's interest in Musorgsky and the Russians was more for their non-Wagnerian ideals than their music. Stravinsky the eclectic is the logical outgrowth from D, whereas Schoenberg contrasts with D by Schoenberg's repression of the senses.

204. Marnold, Jean. **Musique d'autrefois et d'aujourd'hui**. Paris: Dorbon, 1912. 366 p. ML60.M18.

Contains certain of the **Chroniques** from the **Mercure de France** 1902-10. These are critical essays on contemporary performances and issues:

Russian music, Wagnerism, R. Strauss, Ravel, Liszt's oratorio **Elisabeth**, Rameau, and Weber. They complement D's critical views of these topics written in the same period. The essay on **Pelléas** (pp. 193- 97) appeared first in 1905 and pronounces the work "a victory for art over the mercantile antics [of conventional opera], of nature over routine and the materialistic." Relates **Pelléas** to Nietzsche's theory of the Unconscious.

205. Mauclair, Camille. **La réligion de la musique.** Fischbacher, 1928. vii, 350 p. ML 60.M494.

A compilation of two earlier writings, **La Réligion de la musique** (1909) and **Les Héros de l'orchestre** (1917). Mauclair, an associate of D, defines music as a spiritual substance, which is not something concrete to be "made." Essays on Franck, Chausson, Musorgsky's **Boris**, and Wagner shed light on artistic thought surrounding D. For literary relations also see Mauclair's **Servitude et grandeur littéraires**, Paris, 1922, and see item 501 Rolf.

206. Mitchell, Donald. **The Language of Modern Music.** Rev. ed. New York: St. Martin's Press, 1970. 185 p. ML 197.M55 1970; ISBN 784-01-08.

Observes that D, Stravinsky, and Webern were the points of departure for innovative thought after 1950. Notes, however, that one is becoming more conscious with links to the past as the "new music" grows older. D is termed the father of modern music, with such late works as the sonatas and etudes foreshadowing the "second Parisian school" of Boulez and others. In keeping with current thought, sees D as separate from the Impressionist aesthetic, but this study is outdated when Mitchell predicts that the new "new music" will be serial. His 1968 postscript, "Music or 'Music'?," argues that audiences lost to new music ought to be considered more seriously by composers and thus may be restored. D as a model for this purpose unfortunately is not discussed.

207. Myers, Rollo. **Modern French Music from Fauré to Boulez.** New York: Praeger, and London: Basil Blackwell and Mott [where publ. under title

Modern French Music: Its Evolution and Cultural Background from 1900 to the Present Day], 1971, pp. 61-101. ISBN [U.S. ed.] 0-631-13020-9; ML 270.5.M9M6.

Quite valuable for placing the music within a chronological and artistic context. Views the birth of modern French music occurring upon the waning of Franck's influence after 1890. Chapter 5 (pp. 61-81), "Background to Debussy's Formative Years: Symbolism and Impressionism in poetry, painting, and music," states that the spirit of Maeterlinck's **Pelléas** is reborn in D's setting. Ch. 5 maintains a literary perspective, discussing Mallarmé and Rossetti (**La damoiselle**). Chapter 6 (p. 82-101), "New Horizons in Music," views D as the central renovating force and surveys his life and achievements.

208. Nectoux, Jean-Michel. "Symbolisme et Art nouveau; Notes pour une esthétique de la musique fin de siècle." In **Art Nouveau, Jugendstil, und Musik**, pp. 13-20. Zurich: Atlantis, 1980.

Discusses the convergence of French arts in the period 1880-90. Proposes that certain music by Debussy, Fauré, Saint-Saëns, and Chabrier veers toward the Art Nouveau aesthetic. Artists of the period share an aspiration toward the unreal.

209. Pistone, Danièle. "L'impressionisme musical et l'esprit fin-de-siècle." **Revue internationale de musique française** 2, no. 5 (June 1981): 13-19.

An overview of D and such artistic figures as Franck, Verlaine, Wagner, Huysmans, and Bergson. These are united by a complex of thought incorporating the mystic, oriental, and decadent and intensely refined.

210. Pleasants, Henry. **The Agony of Modern Music.** New York: Simon and Schuster, 1955. 180 p. ML197.P5.

Pleasants does not look closely enough at particulars to see D's links to broad audiences, to world music, and to significant popular music.

One may compare Pleasants's arguments to those of Starr (see item 218).

211. Rearick, Charles. **Pleasures of the Belle Epoque: Entertainment and Festivity in Turn-of-the-Century France.** New Haven, Conn.: Yale University Press, 1985. xiii, 239 p. GV 79.R43 1985; ISBN 0-300-03230-7.

Deals with the popular culture of holidays, lifestyle, music halls, world's fairs, and other spectacles. Mentions activities directly pertinent to D, such as the cabaret Chat noir. Concludes that mass entertainment in his time was particularly creative, inexpensive, and positive. Valuable for understanding D's wider cultural background.

212. **La revue wagnérienne.** Paris, 1885-87. Repr. Geneva: Slatkine Reprints, 1968. 3 vols. ML 410.W1 A556.

A basic document of French musical and artistic Wagnerism. Includes writings by such aesthetic leaders as Edouard Dujardin (founder and director of the journal), Jules de Brayer, J.K. Huysmans, Liszt, Mallarmé, C. Mendès, Verlaine, G. Mourey, J.E. Blanche, and R. Godet. The lines of thought and possibly the particular writings helped mold D's thought, both by impressing Wagnerian values and by leading him to define personal differences with Wagner.

213. Sachs, Curt. **The Commonwealth of Art.** New York: Norton, 1946. 484 p. N 5303.S2.

A compelling study, if necessarily generalized, presenting an overview of the arts through human history. Views the arts as cycling repeatedly from classic to romantic, from ethos to pathos. Places D's **Prélude- faune** and his incorporation of oriental music on the threshhold of the contemporary age of ethos, for which harmony in the functional sense came to an end. D in **La mer** is completely personal and no mere pictorialist.

214. Salzman, Eric. **Twentieth-Century Music: An Introduction.** 3rd ed. Prentice-Hall History of Music Series. Englewood Cliffs, N.J.:

Prentice-Hall, 1988. 330 p. ML 197.S17 1988; ISBN 0-13-935057-8 paperback.

A concise and current survey of general developments, drawing upon surveys and studies by others while contributing valuable insights. For an overview of 20th-century surveys, see his Bibliographical Notes, pp. 6-7. Observes that musical France was less rooted in and broke more easily with classical tonality than Germany and Italy. D was central to such a development and drew upon the special character of the French language for his new musical discourse. While pointing to Symbolism, Impressionism, and "Debussyism," notes an absence of any real school of followers in the literal sense. D's influence nonetheless is incalculable and has not ended. Sees D as the source, for later composers, of an interest in the dissociation of the individual sound event, a heightened role of timbre, new forms free from tonal patterns and based on symmetry, and static and associative forming processes. Among the particularly excellent short surveys of D's standing, this is richer than Grout (101) but less probing than Austin (100).

215. Samazeuilh, Gustave. **Musiciens de mon temps.** Paris: La Renaissance du Livre (M. Daubin), 1947. 429 p. ML 410.S167 A3.

A compilation of essays by Samazeuilh, including those on D's **Rodrigue et Chimène** and **Pelléas** and on such contemporaries as Ysaÿe and Carré. A valuable account from one of the generation just after D.

216. Segalen, Victor. "Les synesthésies et l'école symboliste." **Mercure de France** 48 (April 1902): 57-90.

An associate and collaborator of D traces the use of the term synesthesia to Millet and quotes relevant passages from Baudelaire, Hindu writings, Rimbaud, and the Nüsbaumer brothers. Traces in the writings of Destouches two categories of sensory associations, the actual or real and the ideal or imaginative. Dwells on the association of color with sound, pointing to Wagner and Mallarmé but not D.

217. Seigel, Jerrold. **Bohemian Paris: Culture, Politics, and the Boundaries of Bourgeois Life 1830-1930.** New York: Viking Press, 1986. 453 p. DC 715.S42 1986; ISBN 0-670- 80723-0.

A detailed account of the period, although containing few references to D. He is viewed primarily in relation to Satie in a discussion apparently drawing upon Shattuck (388).

* Shattuck, Roger. **The Banquet Years [1885-1914].** See item 388.

218. Starr, Lawrence. "The 'Modern' Composer, the Conservative Audience...and Debussy." **Cahiers Debussy** (nouvelle série) 8 (1984): 13-17.

More provocative than perhaps the title suggests, the article finds that D, among all the pathmaking composers of the twentieth century, has been accepted by by the general audience. Citing **Nuages**, shows how D calls on the musical past with maturity: he employs traditional and post-traditional sounds for their sensuous potential while launching new methods of form. He differs from Schoenberg and Stravinsky, who approached the past from the vantage point of the intellect rather than that of the senses. Since 1950, music by Rochberg, Crumb, Rzewski, Bolcom, Berio, and Stockhausen has shared D's proclivity toward sensuous appeal and immediate access by the audience.

219. Stuckenschmidt, Hans Heinz. **Die Musik eines halben Jahrhunderts: 1925-1975. Essay und Kritik.** Munich: Piper, 1976. 359 pp. ISBN 3-492-02224-3.

A collection of essays and criticism. For D research, most relevant is the study "Romantik und Impressionismus in der Musik." Traces the relation of Debussy to G. Francesco Malipiero and to Berg. Is disjointed as a survey but provides valuable insights.

220. Tiersot, Julien. **Musiques pittoresques: Promenades musicales à l'Exposition de 1889.** Paris: Librairie Fischbacher, 1889. ML 3740.T43.

Concerns the oriental music and exhibits at the Paris World Exposition, which influenced D's sensibilities. Further see item 182. An invaluable, objective account.

221. ------. **Un demi-siècle de musique française: entre les deux guerres 1870-1917.** Paris: Alcan, 1918. 248 p. ML 270.4.T43.

The concluding chapter (pp. 207-28) is on D, treating him perceptively as a synthesist of extra-musical tendencies but also as an exponent of pure music, of music for its inherent processes and value. Valuable for essays on D's precursors Franck and Wagner. Makes particular reference to **Pelléas**.

222. Vander Linden, Albert. **Octave Maus et la vie musicale belge, 1875-1914.** Académie royale de Belgique, Classe des Beaux-arts, Mémoires. Tome 6, fascicule 2. 155 p. AS 242.B3416t.6, fasc.2.

See especially pp. 25-30, "Les 'XX' et la 'Libre esthétique,'" concerning artistic groups (D'Indy, Ysaÿe) and performances in Belgium. Appendices include letters of d'Indy to Maus, press accounts of performances sponsored by the "XX" and the "Libre Esthétique," including the March 1907 performance of D's **Quatuor**, **Le promenoir des deux amants**, **Pelléas**, **Prélude-faune**, and **Masques**.

223. Vogt, Hans. **Neue Musik seit 1945.** Stuttgart: Philipp Reclam jun., 1972. 538 p. ML 197.V64; ISBN 3-15-010203-0.

Discusses the influence of D on aleatoric tendencies, on Boulez, Stockhausen, and Messiaen. Sees an interaction of Debussyan thought with that of Zen-Buddhism in the minds of current composers. Notes the role of the conductor Ernest Ansermet in the promotion of D's music. Discusses D's possible influence on Boulez, Ligeti, Hindemith, Isang Yun, and Hans-Juergen von Bosc. This study complements that by Federhofer (item 275).

224. Weber, Eugen. **France, Fin de Siècle.** Cambridge, Mass.: Harvard University Press and London:

Belknap, 1986. 294 p. ISBN 0-674-31812-9. DC 33.6.W43 1986.

A concise and thoughtful discussion of D's period and its basic themes, such as decadence in the arts, "Affections and Disaffections," "The Old Arts and the New," "Theater" (including **Pelléas**), the "Best of Times" (Dreyfus Affair, economic difficulties).

225. Wenk, Arthur. "Claude Debussy and the Art Nouveau Image of Woman." **Miscellanea musicologica** (Adelaide Studies in Musicology) 13 (1984): 67-74.

Notes the constant attraction to the "femme fatale" as an art object shared by D and Rossetti (as in **La damoiselle élue**), Banville (in the **mélodies Caprice** and **Aimons-nous**), Louÿs (**La chevelure** of **Chansons de Bilitis**), Gautier (**Coquetterie posthume**), Cros (**L'archet**), and Baudelaire (**Le jet d'eau**). Points also to such feminine symbols as hair in **Pelléas**. The art image of the beautiful woman retained a creative force in D even after it lost its symbolic power in the visual arts, after 1890.

226. ------. **Claude Debussy and Twentieth-Century Music.** Boston: G.K. Hall (Twayne), 1983. 165 p. ML410/.D28 W43. ISBN 0-8057-9454-9.

Contains annotated bibliography, catalogue of musical works, discography, and index. Argues for D's importance as a central influence, if less on particular idioms than on a new way of thinking about music. His greatest impact has been felt since 1945 in the domains of the liberation of the musical moment, emphasis on timbre, and concept of rhythm not as relation but as duration. D's subtle overturning of musical conventions has been as decisive as the more celebrated revolutions of Stravinsky and Schoenberg. Contains chapters on **Pelléas**, redefining musical time, a new musical language, and "One face, many masks." The treatment of topics separately suggests that D research has not yet generated a comprehensive overview of his stylistic achievement.

2. Reception

227. Benestad, Finn. "Claude Debussy i norsk musikkliv frem til 1925: Et dokumentarisk arbeidsmateriale." [Claude Debussy in Norwegian musical life up to 1925: documentary source material]. **Studia musicologica Norvegica** 2 (1976): 15-35. In Norwegian with English summary.

Traces critical reaction to D, at first (from 1906) negative but with a turn toward the positive after 1919. Quotes from newspapers to show that critics held back D's appreciation until after World War I. Gives a chronological survey of works performed in Oslo up to 1925. Young Norwegian composers differed with the press and showed much enthusiasm for D beginning with the first performances there.

228. Caillard, C.F., and José de Bérys. **Le cas Debussy**. Paris: H. Falque, 1910. 143 p.

An invaluable document dealing with post-1900 "Debussysme," showing the intensity of debate. The authors pose the question of his importance in the evolution of musical style and the nature of his originality. They compile the responses by E. Ansermet, Maurice Barrès, Albert Bazaillas, Camille Bellaigue, Gaston Carraud, Albert Carré, Jean Chanta voine, A. Cheramy, C. Chevillard, Arthur Coquard, J. Ecorcheville, M. Faugueux, Paul Flat, Funck-Brentano, Louis Ganne, Fernand Gregh, Siegmund von Hausegger, Camille Mauclair, F. Mottl, G. de Pawlowski, Péladan, R. Hahn, R. Richard, Edouard Trémisot, Jean Udine, Siegfried Wagner, and Willy. The question leading to the essays was instigated by a negative article by Raphael Cor.

229. Gatti, Guido. "The Piano Works of Claude Debussy." **Musical Quarterly** 7 (1921): 419-60.

Long superseded by aesthetic and structural studies of the piano music. Remains a valuable source for the early reception and interpretation. To be read alongside Cortot (725) and M. Long (816). Gatti is rather vague and rarely mentions structural considerations when interpreting the music.

230. Goubault, Christian. "Les chapelles musicales françaises, ou la querelle des 'Gros-boutiens' et des 'Petits-boutiens.'" **Revue internationale de musique française** 2, no. 5 (June 1981): 99-112.

A discussion of "political parties" formed by artists and especially critics following 1900. Critics discussed are D. de Sévérac, M.-D. Calvocoressi, J. Chantavoine, and C. Mauclair. Centers on the interchange between the "Debussystes" (E. Vuillermoz, J. Marnold, L. Laloy, and M. Ravel) and the "d'Indystes" (H. Gauthiers-Villars and P. Lalo). Main journals involved were the **Mercure musical**, **Monde musical**, **Grande revue**, **Revue bleue**, **Temps**, and **Mercure de France**. The debate centered on **Pelléas**, about which further see Pasler (853).

231. ------. **La critique musicale dans la presse française de 1870 à 1914.** Geneva and Paris: Slatkine, 1984. 529 p. ISBN 2-05-100542-7; ML 3880.G68C7.

Alongside Trillig (240) a central study of D's reception in the press of his day. Emphasizes the critical views of **Pelléas**, both positive as in the writings of Paul Dukas, Louis Laloy, Jacques Rivière, and Jean Marnold, and negative criticism. Also discusses the critical reception of **La mer** and the **Images** for orchestra. Contains a useful bibliography and index.

232. Kasaba, Eiko. "La musique de Debussy au Japon." **Cahiers Debussy** (nouvelle série) 10 (1986): 28-44.

A thorough discussion of D's critical reception in Japan (beginning in 1908) and the performance of his works (beginning in 1909) by both native and foreign interpreters. The discussion covers the years until about 1920.

233. Lang-Becker, Elke. "Aspekte der Debussy-Rezeption in Deutschland zu Lebzeiten des Komponisten." **Cahiers Debussy** (nouvelle série) 8 (1984): 18-41.

The German critical reception of D's music during his lifetime. Discusses the first performance of **Pelléas** in Frankfurt in 1907. Traces significant performances by Walter Gieseking, Eugen d'Albert, Walter Niemann, and Arthur Rubinstein. Gives an exhaustive chronology from 1903 (**Prélude-faune**, Berlin) through to the 1910s. Compares D's reception to that of Mahler, Strauss, Pfitzner, Busoni, and Reger in the period. Points also to critical views of early works by Schoenberg, Berg, and Hindemith. An important study suggesting directions for D research.

234. Lebl, Vladimir. "Prozske ohlasy Debussyho tvorby v letech 1905-1921." [The Reception of D's works in Prague from 1905-1921] **HudVeda** 19, no. 3 (1982): 195-234. In Czech with summary in German.

Concerns his reception from the first performance in 1905, of **Prélude-faune**, through to that of **Pelléas** in 1921. The critical controversy is related to the orientation in Prague toward German culture and the music of Strauss, Mahler, and Schoenberg. An early admiration for D had cultural-political overtones. The public and press then turned away from him and Impressionism in general. Includes an index of D's works performed and pictures from the 1908 **Pelléas** performance.

235. Lethève, Jacques. **Impressionistes et symbolistes devant la presse**. Paris: A. Colin, 1959. 302 pp.

Reception in the press of such first showings as Manet's **Olympia**, the first Impressionist exhibition of 1874, the appearance of Mallarmé's **L'après-midi d'un faune**, and the works of Verlaine. Traces the transition from derogatory to laudatory criticism of new arts concepts. This study may be a useful point of departure for studies of D's reception. Further see Trillig (240).

236. Lorrain, Jean (pseud.). **Pelléastres: Le poison de la littérature**. Paris: Mericant, 1909. 287 p.

An adventure novel set in the period following the **Pelléas** premiere. Not flattering toward and not a responsible assessment of the artistic adventure of D. Is nonetheless one species of commentary on **Pelléas**, its time and reception.

* Pasler, Jann. "**Pelléas** and Power." See item 853.

237. Rolland, Romain. **Musiciens d'aujourd'hui.** Paris: Hachette, 1908. 278 p. Translated by M. Blaiklock as **Musicians of Today**. Freeport, New York: Books for Libraries Press, 1969. xii, 324 p. ML 390.R653 1959; ISBN 0-836-91188-1.

Focuses on **Pelléas**, the premiere of which was "one of the 3 or 4 red-letter days in the calendar of our lyric stage." Views the work as a decisively French reaction to Wagner. Ends by contrasting **Pelléas** to Bizet's **Carmen**, which works represent the 2 poles of the French aesthetic. Valuable insights into D's contemporary reception.

238. Roland-Manuel, Alexis. "Notre Debussy." **Musique** 1, no. 6 (Mar. 15, 1928): 249-52.

Chides the French public for its general lack of support of musical genius. Finds that faddish Debussysme is dead and that "Debussysme of the spirit can begin to live." Reacts to Jean Cocteau's oversimplifications of the artistic urge as it concerns Debussy.

239. Schaeffner, Georg [pseud. for Valerius Kolatchewsky]. **Claude Debussy und das Poetische (Aus Igors Papieren)**. Bern: A. Francke, 1943. 418 p. ML 410.D28 K73.

A pioneering study of D's poetic concerns, if overly imaginative and "poetic." Is cast partly in a quaint dialogue between the figures Igor and Gabriel. Perhaps of most validity at present as a document of D's reception in central Europe ca. 1940.

240. Trillig, Johannes. **Untersuchungen zur Rezeption Claude Debussys in der zeitgenössischen Musikkritik**. Diss., University of Frankfurt am Main, 1982. Published Tutzing: Hans Schneider, 1983. 496 p. ML 410.D28 T73; ISBN 3-795-20381-3.

A needed major study of D's reception in the press of his time. Preparatory chapters review musical life in the Belle Epoque, newspapers, and main journals that present music criticism. Discusses Laloy and Romain Rolland as pacesetters in Debussy criticism and general attitudes in the press concerning Impressionism, Symbolism, and nationalism in music.

241. Wellesz, Egon. "Der Stil der letzten Werke Debussys." **Melos** (Mainz) 1, nos. 166-68 (1920): 50-54.

From the perspective of 1920 Austria, Wellesz views D's neoclassic late works as a bridge to the future. In the **Six épigraphes antiques**, D opens the past to new possibilities by balancing tonality and dissonance, clarity and individuality of form. D thus relates to Mozart, who was a bridge from the **Sturm und Drang**. Also refers to the sonatas, **Etudes**, and **En blanc et noir**. Excellent particularly for D's early reception abroad.

3. Composers

242. Austin, William W. "Viewpoint: Debussy, Wagner, and Some Others." **Nineteenth-Century Music** 6, no. 1 (Summer 1982): 82-91.

A thoughtful review of Holloway's book **Debussy and Wagner** (item 308), proceeding from the perspective of Holloway's compositions. These show a conjunction of Wagner's and D's influences. Points out D's loyalties to Bach, Mozart, and Chopin, and discusses the necessity to consider such influences in order to place Wagner's in proper context.

243. ------. "Quelques connaissances et opinions de Schoenberg et Webern sur Debussy." In item 121.

Schoenberg's first contact with D's music came in 1907. His first hearing of **Ariane** by the Debussyan Dukas in 1908 reinforced the impression. The onset of complete chromaticism parallels Schoenberg's encounter with Debussy. Schoenberg later criticized D's "primitive" technique of repetition and harmonic progression, which for him paled in comparison to his own process of developing variation form. Webern was more kindly disposed toward D and admired his "new classicism."

244. Baron, Carol K. "Varèse's Explication of Debussy's **Syrinx** in **Density 21.5** and an Analysis of Varèse's Composition: a Secret Model Revealed." **Music Review** 43, no. 2 (1982): 121-34.

Includes complete score of both. The works compare along the lines of Renaissance parody procedure. Varèse requested that **Syrinx** precede **Density 21.5** in performance. He utilized D's pitch organization, whereby 2 whole-tone scales and the tritones they generate are structural. Varèse employs octatonic collections in lieu of D's pentatonic ones for bridge passages. He appears as a keen analyst of D and a reinterpreter.

245. Barricelli, Jean-Pierre and Leo Weinstein. **Ernest Chausson; The Composer's Life and Works**. Norman, Okla.: University of Oklahoma Press, 1955. 241 p. ML 410.C455 B3.

A valuable survey of Chausson, with useful references to the larger French scene in the 1890's. Quotes long passages from letters by D, Chausson, and others. The two composers were close friends and critics of each other's music in the decade of the 1890s.

246. Beaufils, Marcel. **Wagner et le wagnérisme**. Paris: Aubier, Editions Montaigne, 1946. 380 p. ML 410.W1 B25

Contains examples, table of contents, no index. Insightful analysis of Mallarmé's Wagnerism: explores the poet's understanding of Wagner as "a refuge, a harbor dangerous with certitude." For the author, both Strauss and Schoenberg remain tributary to Wagner. French music learns the important lesson of ambition from him, but D renounces Wagner's dimensions with superior courage. He returns to a truer French aesthetic of controlled sensuality in **Prélude-faune**. In **Pelléas** he joins in Mallarmé's response.

247. Boulanger, Nadia. "Lectures on Modern Music." In periodical series **The Rice Institute Pamphlet**

13, no. 2 (April 1926): 113-95. Houston: Rice Institute, 1928.

Contains three lectures: "Modern French Music," "Debussy: the Preludes," and "Stravinsky." In the discussion of the Preludes (pp. 153-77), Boulanger points to the origins of D's harmonic idiom in Liszt, Chabrier, Fauré, and Chopin. She discusses the programmatic references of each prelude, calling on "impressionistic" terminology, but her remarks always contain valuable insights.

248. Boulez, Pierre. "La corruption dans les encensoirs." **Melos** 23 (Oct. 1956): 276-82 [in French and German translation]. Also in **Nouvelle revue française** (Dec. 1956). Reprinted in item 173.

A primary writing demonstrating the interest in D among composers following 1950. Boulez links D to Cézanne and Mallarmé as originators of contemporary art. He observes **Pelléas** "emigrating to Vienna" to the post-Webern school. D has proposed a renovation of the world of sound, breaking out of conventional Western boundaries.

249. Boyd, Everett Vernon, Jr. "Paul Dukas and the Impressionist Milieu: Stylistic Assimilation in Three Orchestral Works." Ph.D. diss., Eastman School of Music, 1980. 390 p. ML 95.3 .B789.

Almost every device characteristic of D's "impressionism" is found in **L'Apprenti sorcier**, **Ariane et Barbe-bleu**, and **La Péri**.

250. Brody, Elaine. "Schumann's legacy in France." **Studies in Romanticism** 13, no. 3 (Summer 1974): 189-212.

The music and aesthetic principles of Schumann exerted a particular influence in France from 1870-1920, as it did on D. Points to influences on the accompaniment in D's songs, **Children's Corner**, **Arabesques**, and other piano music. Observes his transcription for 2 pianos of Schumann's **Am Springbrunnen**.

251. Burkholder, J. Peter. **Charles Ives, The Ideas Behind the Music.** New Haven and London: Yale University Press, 1985. 166 p. ISBN 0-300-03261-7; ML 410.I94B48.

In his **Essays before a Sonata** (1920), Ives disapproves of D's "parfume" and his emphasis on "manner" above "substance." D's (as also Wagner's and Strauss's) revolutions appear superficial to Ives in his written criticism. Burkholder follows Ives's simplifications, observing that his "literary" music emphasizes not nouns, as the pictorial music of D and Strauss might, but verbs. Discusses Ives's perception of a dichotomy of D's manner and substance. The well-documented process of active form in D's music, rather of the sort that Burkholder acknowledges in Ives, is not discussed. Whether Ives's protestations about D are smoke-screens, and whether he is indeed a follower in important regards, are questions calling for full research. For example, see Elliott Carter's observation of a link between D and Ives (items 387 and 401).

252. Bykov, B. and others. **Debussy i mouzyka XX veka** [Debussy and twentieth-century music] Leningrad: Muzyka, 1983. 247 p.

Consists of essays on Debussy by various authors. In Russian. Not examined.

253. Calvocoressi, M.-D. "Les Histoires naturelles de M. Ravel et l'imitation debussyste." **Grande revue** no. 2 (May 10, 1907): 508-15.

Views D in relation to Russian composers in his tendency to develop a given concise idea continuously. Ravel takes a broad theme and develops classically. This article is of only a general use, with both composers still evolving at the time of writing, but valuable for contemporary insight at the time of "Debussysme."

254. ------ **Modest Moussorgsky, his Life and Works.** Edited by Gerald Abraham. London: Rockliff, and Fair Lawn, New Jersey: Essential Books, 1956. 321 p. ML 410.M97 C33 1956a.

In the preface, Abraham considers this book Calvocoressi's **Magnum opus** on Musorgsky. Takes into account Musorgsky's original scores. Relates to **Pelléas**. D, Ravel, and Liadof were the earliest to exhibit an influence by Musorgsky.

255. Campbell, Lawrence. "Works for solo piano by Ned Rorem." DMus diss., Indiana University, 1983. 142 p.

The influence of D, Ravel, and Poulenc is strong in Rorem's piano music. One observes neo-Classicism with a definite tonal focus, neo-Baroque counterpoint, parallelism, and ostinato.

256. Carner, Mosco. "Debussy e Puccini." **Quaderni Pucciniani** (1982): 107-17.

A study tracing specific musical relationships in some depth. Centers on harmonic influence of D, citing examples from **Pelléas** and their parallels in **Madama Butterfly**.

257. ------. **Major and Minor**. London: Duckworth, 1980. First published 1944. 267 p. ML 60.C188; ISBN 0-8419-0600-9.

Includes the essay "Debussy and Puccini," pp. 139-147. Discusses Puccini's attraction to **Pelléas et Mélisande** as a libretto, a project abandoned only when he learned of D's work with it. Traces particularly the harmonic influence on Puccini, noting that Puccini "submitted to Debussy's spell" the longest of non-French composers. Relates **Pelléas** to **Butterfly** and **La fanciulla**, and timbral aspects of **Cathédrale engloutie** to **Il tabarro** and **Suor Angelica**.

258. ------. **Puccini: A Critical Biography**. 2nd ed. London: Duckworth, 1974. New York: Holmes and Meier, 1974, 1977. xvi, 520 p. ML 410.P89 C3 1974; ISBN 0-7156-0795-2.

Compares Puccini to Mascagni and Giordano in their reliance upon devices of D in their music after 1890. Puccini compares to D in his fin-de-siècle malaise. His French sensibility is evident especially in his orchestration. Notes D's praise of **La bohème**. A study of depth of an important successor, in ways, to D. Treats the relationship more in context if less in musical specifics than the preceding.

259. Casella, Alfredo. "Claude Debussy." **Monthly Musical Record** 63, no. 743 (Jan. 1933).

Memoirs emphasizing D's later years. Casella finds in **La mer** and **Prélude-faune** a stylistic perfection through the synchronization of imagination and means. Defends his earlier article ("Impressionismo e anti-medisimo," **Ars Nova**, March 1918), which had accused D of too great a preoccupation with simple auditory enjoyment. Quotes Pizzetti, who finds that D lacks an ardent humanity. Casella concludes that D evoked the most intense and sweetest moments in his artistic life.

260. Chechlińska, Zofia. "Chopin a impresjonizm" ["Chopin and Impressionism," in Polish]. **Szkice o kulturze muzycznej XIX wieku** 2 (1973): 21-34.

There are direct and indirect connections linking the works of Debussy to those of Chopin. Not examined.

261. Cole, Bill. **Miles Davis: A Musical Biography.** New York: Morrow Quill Paperbacks, 1974. 256 p. ML 419.D39C9 1980; ISBN 0-688-05203-7.

Notes that D was "the favorite European classical composer" of Davis. Discusses Davis's relation to the scholar André Hodeir, writer on both D and jazz. The conections of D to jazz figures such as Davis well may branch out from such biographies as this.

262. Colette et altri. **Maurice Ravel par quelques-uns de ses familiers.** Paris: Editions du Tambourine, 1939. 185 p. ML 410.R23 M38.

The article "L'oeuvre de Maurice Ravel" by E. Vuillermoz distinguishes Ravel as a "classic" and D as "impressionist," in one of the earliest writings to make the facile contrast. For an alternative view, see Rosen item 375. The present collection of essays also views others in D's extended circle, including Viñes and Fauré. Essays document the period by M. Delage, Colette, Tristan Klingsor, Roland-Manuel, and L. Fargue.

263. Curtiss, Mina. **Bizet and his World.** New York: Knopf, 1958. xvi, 477, xvii p. ML 410.B62 C87.

Little direct comment on musical relation to D, but helpful in its discussion of background, including Ernest Guiraud, Gounod, the Paris Commune, the 1871 defeat of France.

264. Daitz, Mimi Segal. "Pierre de Bréville (1861-1949)." **19th-Century Music** 5, no. 1 (Summer 1981): 24-37.

A biographical account that refers to Bréville's role as critic and composer and his friendship with D. Discusses Bréville's opera **Eros vainqueur** and his songs.

265. Davies, Laurence. **Franck.** Master Musiciens Series. London: Dent, 1973. 141 p. ISBN 0-460-03134-1; ML 410.F82D3.

Points to the relationship between D's **La plus que lente** and Franck's **Danse lente** and sees similarities between the string quartets by the two. Franck was a spirit kindred to D in his antagonism toward Saint-Saëns. Suggests a relationship between Franck's structural sense and D's, a matter inviting exploration in depth.

266. ------. **Franck and his Circle.** London: Barrie and Jenkins, 1970. 380 p. ML 410.F82 D29 19706; ISBN 0-2146-5085-5.

A more extensive study than the preceding, drawing a larger circle of relationships and referring to **C'est l'extase, Cinq poèmes de Baudelaire, Pelléas,** and **Damoiselle élue** in their connections with Franck.

267. De'Paoli, Domenico. **"Orfeo and Pelléas."** **Music and Letters** 20, no. 4 (Oct. 1939): 381-98.

Monteverdi's **Orfeo** (1602) and **Pelléas** are solitary monuments that create no school, and both exhibit remarkable prosody. D did not hear Monteverdi's music until after the composition of **Pelléas**. However, the two composers have closely related ideals of music drama.

268. Demarquez, Suzanne. **Manuel de Falla**. Paris: Flammarion, 1963. Translated by S. Attanasio. Philadelphia: Chilton, 1968. viii, 253 p. ML 410.F215D43.

Traces the relation to D in the chapter "Paris--Maturity." D coached Falla in Paris and influenced such works as **La vida breve**. D inspired a value in composition for its inherent values and resources more than in terms of novelty and picture-painting. Further see Manuel Orozeo, **Falla: Biografía ilustrada**. Barcelona: Destino, 1968, for additional commentary and iconography of Falla's Paris period.

269. Dietschy, Marcel. "Claude Debussy et André Suarès. **Revue musical de Suisse romande** 4 (Aug. 31, 1963): 14-17.

Quotes from the writer Suarès's diaries as he refers to D. Works with which Suarès was taken were **Nocturnes** and **Pelléas**. He compares D to Stravinsky, Musorgsky, and Wagner. Valuable for the observations of a fellow artist and keen observer of the times.

270. Dukas, Paul. **Correspondance de Paul Dukas**. Paris: Durand, 1971. 199 p. ML 410.D86 A3.

Views D from the vantage point of a closely associated composer-critic. One letter refers to his 1893 piano performance of the **Quatuor** "avec une agilité angélique." Includes an important letter (p. 21) referring to **Rodrigue et Chimène**. Contains a description in letters of D's illness and death, testifying to the length and value of their friendship throughout his entire maturity.

271. ------. **Les écrits sur la musique**. Paris: Société des Editions Françaises et Internationales, 1948. Repr. Paris: Stock, 1980. 691 p. ML 60.D86.

Alongside D's **Monsieur Croche**, contains among the most insightful music criticism of the period around 1900. Includes Dukas' reviews of D's **Quatuor**, **Nocturnes**, **La mer**, and **Pelléas**.

272. Dumesnil, René. "Claude Debussys und Florent Schmitts Kantaten für den Rome Preis." **Antares** (Baden-Baden) 5, no. 7 (1957): 50-51.

Compares **L'enfant prodigue** (1884) to Florent Schmitt's **Sémiramis** (1900), both having received the Prix de Rome. Observes the conservatory cantata functioning similarly in both careers, as points of departure toward early maturity.

273. Eckart-Backer, Ursula. "Claude Debussys Verhältniss zu Musikern der Vergangenheit." **Die Musikforschung** 30, no. 1 (1977): 56-63.

Relates Debussy to Rameau, Couperin, J.S. Bach, and Gluck in light of statements in **Monsieur Croche**. Sees an important relationship to all save Gluck, whom D did not appreciate. Particularly relevant to the study of **Pelléas** and D's ideal of a truly French music.

274. Falla, Manuel de. **Escritos sobre música y músicos: Debussy, Wagner, el 'cante jondo.'** Buenos Aires, 1950. Published in English as **On Music and Musicians**, translated Urman and J. Thomson, introduction by F. Sopeña. London and Boston: M. Boyars, 1979. xiv, 117 p. ISBN 0-7145-2600-2.

Includes relevant essays such as "Claude Debussy and Spain," which is a republication of Falla's article in **Revue musicale**, Dec. 1920. An important response to the "anti-Debussyan" attitude of about 1920 led by Cocteau, Les Six, and in some ways Stravinsky. Falla holds D's influence to be continuing and great. The prefatory essay by Sopeña is useful in tracing Falla's context.

275. Federhofer, Hellmut. **Neue Musik; Ein Literaturbericht.** Mainzer Studien zur Musikwissenschaft, Band 9. Tutzing: Hans Schneider, 1977. 281 p. ML 197.F43; ISBN 3-7952-0209-4.

Reviews current assessments of 20th-century music, emphasizing German writings and composers. Is thus helpful when tracing D's wider influence. Outlines research on him as an instigator of tone-color composition; his theory of music, discipline, and freedom; and his new connotations for music. Compares him to Ligeti, Penderecki, and others.

276. Fédorov, Vladimir. "Debussy vu par quelques russes." In source 121, pp. 199-211.

Valuable overview of D's Russian connections, citing the relevance of Tchaikovsky, Rimsky-Korsakov, Musorgsky, and Glazunov to the young Debussy. After D, Skriabin, Prokofiev, and Stravinsky reflect an influence. Also considers the reception of D in Russia, as by the critics and writers J. Engel, L. Sabaneyev, B. Asaf'ev, V. Karatygin, and E. Brando. The youthful relationship to Mme von Meck is noted. Also see the conference discussion recorded following Fédorov's article.

277. Fischer, Penelope Ann Peterson. "Philippe Gaubert (1879-1941): His Life and Contributions as Flutist, Editor, Teacher, Conductor, and Composer." Ph.D. diss., University of Maryland, 1982. 263 p. DA 8323616.

Gaubert is known primarily as a composer of flute and piano works. His music is influenced by D and Ravel.

278. Floros, Constantin. "Studien zur **Parsifal**-Rezeption." In **Richard Wagner: "Parsifal." Musik-Konzepte** 25 (Munich, 1982): p. 14-57. ML 3855.F639 V56.

Parsifal proclaims a private religion, mixing Christian and Buddhist ideas with those of Schopenhauer. The seminal theme of the work is the contrast between Christianity and paganism, chastity and sensuality. The author points to the traces of **Parsifal** in D's **Nocturnes**.

279. Gershwin, George. Gershwin's personal collection of D's piano and vocal music. Gift of Ira Gershwin to Library of Congress, Washington. Call no. ML30.25e.D4 Case.

Invites an exploration of the relationship to D seen in Gershwin's compositions.

280. Gervais, Françoise. **Etude comparée des langages harmoniques de Fauré et Debussy**. Paris: **La revue musicale**/Editions Richard-Masse, 1971. Published as supplement to **Revue musicale**, nos. 272-73, 1974. Volume 1 contains analyses (152 p.); volume 2 contains 566 music exx. (189 p.).

Publication of the author's 1954 dissertation, Sorbonne. Fauré's harmony is permeated by medieval modes, and his melody is linked directly to harmony. D by contrast derives from melody. His tonal language in interpenetrated by diverse aspects of rhythm, timbre, and intensities. A traditional analysis of D but an exhaustive comparison of the two composers.

281. Godet, Robert. "Chopin-Debussy." **Cahiers Debussy** (nouvelle série) 3 (1976): 11-13.

A reprint of a writing concerning a concert of Chopin's and D's music of 1918. Compares aspects of the composers.

282. ------. **En marge de Boris Godounoff**. 2 vols. Paris: F. Alcan, and London: Chester, 1926. ML 410.M88 G7.

An account of Musorgsky and the opera **Boris** as it was received in France during D's time. Godet was one of D's closest associates.

283. ------. "Weber and Debussy." **The Chesterian** 7, new series, no. 55 (1926): 220-226.

Gives in full D's critical article on Weber, centering on **Der Freischütz** and praising Weber's tone color and taste. Further see items 45-47.

284. Goebels, Franzpeter. "Klaviermusik des jungen Bartók: eine Orientierung." **Musik und Bildung** 13, no. 4 (April 1981): 237-42.

Studies Bartók's piano works up to the **Bagatelles** op. 6 (the period 1896-1900, including unpublished music). Points to the possible influence of D on the formative piano idiom the author terms "rhythmic-timbral." Recalls Bartók's judgement that D had reawakened a chordal sense.

285. Griffiths, Paul. **Bartók.** Master Musicians series. London and Melbourne: Dent, 1984. 224 p. ISBN 0-460-03182-1; ML 410.B26.

Discusses D's considerable influence on Bartók, who first encountered D's music in 1907 through Kodály. Bartok and D met in Paris, although little is known of their personal relationship. Bartók modelled his first violin sonata upon D's sonata and wrote a memorial composition after D's death. Rhythmic and harmonic innovations, encountered by Bartók in folk music, were confirmed for Bartók by D's music.

286. ------. **Modern Music: The Avant garde since 1945.** London: Dent, and New York: Braziller, 1981. ISBN 0-8076-1018- 6; ML 197.G76.

Discusses Boulez's call in the 1950's for D rather than Webern as a model for the future. Points to oriental influences on European music, especially on that by D and Mahler, although a pervasive influence has occurred more recently. Relates D to Morton Feldman, Luciano Berio, Samuel Beckett (who quotes **La mer**), and Jean Barraqué.

287. Grover, Ralph Scott. "The Influence of Franck, Wagner, and Debussy on Representative Works of Ernest Chausson." Ph.D. diss., Music, University of North Carolina, 1966. v, 336 p. UM 67-992; DA XXVII.9, pp. 3072- 73-A. ML 410.C455 G76.

D's influence is less demonstrable than that of the other two composers. It nonetheless is seen in rhythmic and harmonic blurring. Does not view Chausson as a connecting link to D, however.

288. Guillot, Pierre. "Claude Debussy et Déodat de Sévérac." **Cahiers Debussy** (nouvelle série) 10 (1986), 3-16.
Establishes the chronology of their biographical contacts, the relation of their aesthetics and style, and reciprocal influences. D's **Pelléas**, **Prélude-faune**, and **Pagodes** had an impact on Sévérac, while the latter possibly influenced **Sirènes**, the piano **Préludes**, and **Boîte à joujoux**.

289. Gut, Serge. **Franz Liszt: Les éléments du langage musical.** Paris: Klincksieck, 1975. 405 p. ML 410.L7G95; ISBN 2-2520-1771-6.

Distinguishes between the whole-tone scale that is derived harmonically (a traditional development) and that of a purely melodic conception, which is non-traditional. This distinction might be helpful for the analysis of D's stylistic evolution, as well.

290. ------. "Liszt et Debussy, comparaison stylistique." **Referate des 2. Europäischen Liszt-Symposions**, pp. 63-77. Munich: Katzbichler, 1981. ML 410.L7 E9 1978; ISBN 3-8739-7190-9.

Compares the semantic meanings for the two composers of harmonic intervals, chords, added tones, and such scales as the pentatonic. Emphasizes Liszt as a precursor of musical impressionism in general and of such uses the whole-tone scale, chords of hollow fifths, and parallel chord progressions. Refers to piano **Voiles (Preludes)** and **Cloches à travers** (Images, piano, book II) for their ambiance resembling Liszt's.

291. ------. "Skrjabin: Vermittlicher zwischen Debussy und Schoenberg." In **Alexander Skrjabin**, pp. 85-94. Graz: Universal Edition, 1980. ML 55.S92 Bd. ML 410 .S5988; ISBN 3-7024-0140-7.

Places the three composers in the trend toward the interchange of harmony and melody, considering Skriabin as the mediator between D and Schoenberg. Points to similar verticalization of horizontal events. Not examined.

292. Harding, James. **Erik Satie.** New York: Praeger, 1975. xiii, 269 p. ISBN 0-275-53720-X; ML 410.S196 H3 1975.

A standard source on Satie and his environment, including numerous references to D. Satie felt inferior to D, which colored his assessment of him. D tried to encourage Satie by orchestrating the **Gymnopédies**. Further see Pierre D. Templier, **Erik Satie**. Repr. New York: Da Capo, 1980 [c.1969]: ML 410.S196 T43 1980;ISBN 0-3067-6039-8.

293. ------. **The Ox on the Roof: Scenes from the Musical Life in Paris in the Twenties.** New York: St. Martin's Press, 1972. 261 p. ML 270.8 P2A4 1972b.

Valuable survey of Satie, Cocteau, and Les Six. Points to Satie's undercurrent of jealousy toward D, Milhaud's love of **Pelléas**, and other reactions by foremost French musicians after D. Overworks the term "Debussyste" and lumps too much of his stylistic achievements together, as if the style tendencies formed an indivisible entity. Elsewhere clarifies the dislike of the Six rather for D's imitators than for his music per se.

294. Hayner, Phillip Avery, II. "The role of the piano etude in the piano compositions of Karol Szymanowski." DMS diss., University of Cincinnati, 1982.

The 12 Etudes opus 33 of Szymanowski synthesize Debussy, Skriabin, and Max Reger. From the etude Szymanowski moved to the more complex genre of sonata.

295. Henry, Earl. "Impressionism" in the arts and its influences on selected works by Charles Martin Loeffler and Charles Tomlinson Griffes. Ph.D. diss., University of Cincinnati, 1976. vi, 389 p.

Analysis of works by these two American "Impressionists," finding Griffes to draw closer to D, Loeffler to be less innovative.

296. Hilse, Walter Bruno. "Hindemith and Debussy" [in English]. **Hindemith Jahrbuch** 2 (1972): 48-90.

Criticizes conventional Debussy analysis ("Debussy negates functional tonality") as covertly critical and not adequate in the discussion of D's positive achievement. Hindemith incorporates D's influence, as in the use of parallel chords, whole-tone scales, modes, play about a single tone, and exotic elements.

297. Hirsbrunner, Theo. "Bohuslav Martinu: Die Soloklavierwerke der dreissiger Jahre." **Archiv**

für Musikwissenschaft 39, no. 1 (1982): 64-77.

In the solo piano works of Martinu of the 1930s, Hirsbrunner finds stylistic connections to Fauré and D, particularly with regard to the melodic arabesque and its extensions harmonically. Also relates Martinu to Satie and Stravinsky.

298. ------. "Debussy--Maeterlinck--Chausson: Literary and Musical Connections." **Miscellanea musicologica (Adelaide Studies in Musicology)** 13 (1984): 57-65.

D and Chausson gained an artistic direction from Maeterlinck. Proposes the comprehensive term "Fin de siècle style" to include such artistic tendencies as Symbolism and Art Nouveau, which in any case often overlap in meaning and technique. Relates Chausson's **Serres chaudes** to D's **Proses lyriques**. Chausson remained bound to the languor of the Fin de siècle, while D evolved toward a "musique de plein air."

299. ------. "Frankreichs Opern um 1900: Auf den Spuren von R. Wagners Einfluss." **Neue Zürcher Zeitschrift** 52 (April 1979): 67.

From E. Reyer's **Sigurd** to D's **Pelléas**, the staging, scenic effects, and relationship between music and speech reflect Wagner's influence. Not examined.

300. ------. "Gabriel Fauré und Claude Debussy oder das Ende der Salonmusik." **Schweizerische Musikzeitung/Revue musicale suisse** 115, no. 2 (March-April 1975): 66-71.

Discusses the contributions of the two composers to the end of the Romantic Romance. D and Ravel transcend its conventions while preserving important impulses. Considers the role of Wagnerism, the cabaret concert and its impact on the French art song, and the salon society of the time.

301. ------. "Musik und Sprache bei G. Fauré und C. Debussy." **Melos/Neue Zeitschrift für Musik** 1, no. 5 (1975): 365-72.

Compares D's and Fauré's settings of **C'est l'extase langoureuse**. Fauré composes songs with the attitude that music is foremost; he is a master of the salon **mélodie**. D penetrates every nuance of poetry and does not yield to absolute forms and musical idioms as does Fauré.

302. ------. **Olivier Messiaen: Leben und Werk**. Bern: Laaber Verlag, 1988. ISBN 3-8900-7139-2; ML 410.M595 1988.

Contains a chapter concerning D's relationship to Messiaen. Not examined.

303. ------. **Pierre Boulez und sein Werk**. Bern: Laaber Verlag, 1985. ISBN 3-8900-7047-7; ML 410.B773 H57 1985.

Contains a section discussing the relationship to Debussy. Not examined.

304. ------. "Richard Wagners Musikdramen und ihr Fortwirken bei Debussy, Strauss, Schönberg, und Berg." In **Gattungen der Musik und ihre Klassiker**, pp. 271-285. Laaber: Laaber Verlag, 1988. ISBN 3-89007; ML 55.G25 1988.

Observes a correspondence between the manner whereby Wagner musicalizes prose in **Siegfried** and D in **Pelléas**. D's sensitivity to French takes his prosody in a further direction toward a "synthetic myth."

305. ------. "Zum Liedschaffen von G. Fauré und C. Debussy." In **Wort-Ton-Verhaltniss**, edited by Elis. Haselauer, pp. 101-08. Vienna, Cologne, and Graz: Bohlau, 1981.

Points out the extreme atomization of structure in the late songs of D, which permits the text to gain domination over the music. Argues that musical style for Fauré does not keep pace with literary developments, and the poem remains a frame for making music. Cites particular examples of **Ariettes oubliées** and **Paysage sentimental**.

306. Hirshberg, Jehoash. **Pa'ul ben-hayyim, hayyav ve-yesirato** [Paul Ben-Haim, his Life and Works]. Tel Aviv: Am Oved, 1983. 277 p. ISBN 9-6513-0134-1 (pbk.); ML 410.B449 H6 1983.

In Hebrew. Discusses the career of the German-born conductor and composer Ben-Haim (né Frankenburger, 1897-1984). Ben-Haim emigrated to Israel and helped found a national school of music. His compositions synthesize European styles (including Debussy's) and Oriental-Jewish music. Not examined.

307. Hoérée, Arthur. "Debussy et l'entre-deux-guerres, 1918-1945." In **Précis de musicologie**, new edition edited by Jacques Chailley, pp. 389-403. Paris: Presses universitaires de France, 1984. 496 p. ISBN 2-13-038457-9; ML 3797.1.P7 1984.

A valuable survey of recent French scholarship in D, if somewhat colored by conservatism. Calls for a renewed study of his orchestration, which is born of each work and foretells the **Klangfarbenmelodie** of Webern. Describes numerous, chiefly French studies of composers from 1918-1945; this précis is quite valuable concerning D's musical relations. Also see in the **Précis** the study concerned with music since 1945, which was written by P. Mari and M. Philippot.

308. Holloway, Robin. **Debussy and Wagner**. London: Eulenburg Books, 1979. 235 p. ISBN 0-903873-257 (hardcover version), 0-903873-265 (paperback); ML 410.D28H6.

Proposes to show "just how much Wagner there is in D." Surveys French Wagnerism and analyzes the Wagnerian inspiration in **La damoiselle élue**, the **Cinq poèmes de Baudelaire**, **Pelléas**, **Le martyre**, and **Jeux**. The analysis is at times remarkably insightful but sometimes stretches too far in tracing points of resemblance to the **Ring** and **Tristan**. The hyperbole of the basic premise is exposed in such findings as "[the piano works are] a non- and anti-Wagnerian development" whose "musical content is patently thin." Although Holloway must be read with caution and with a recognition of D's other important precursors, the study helps lay the groundwork for a comprehensive understanding of his complex formation. Also see item

242.

309. Holstein, Jean-Paul. "Le renouveau de la sym phonie française à la fin du XIX siècle." **Revue internationale de musique française** 2, no. 5 (June 1981): 51-60.

Symphonies by Franck, Saint-Saëns, d'Indy, and Lalo exemplify the evolution of music up to D. Also refers to Berlioz, Dutilleux, and S. de Reyer.

310. Honegger, Arthur. "Ravel et le Debussysme." **Revue musicale** 187 (Dec. 1938): 258-59.

Documents the reaction among the post-Debussy generation to him and especially to his imitators. In that regard, is perhaps as valuable a reading about Honegger as about Ravel and D. Affirms that Ravel is the classicist, while D's imitators lack form. Compares Ravel to Stravinsky in this regard and sees his lineage from Mozart and Saint-Saëns. See Rosen (375) and Howat (590) for important interpretations concerning the breadth and depth of D's formal sense.

311. Hoogerwerf, Frank W. "Willem Pijper's French aesthetic." **Tijdschrift van de Vereniging voor Nederlandse Muziekgeschiedenis** 28, no. 2 (1978): 61-80.

D decisively influenced the contemporary Dutch composer Pijper (1894-1947). Speaks of D's role at the end of the 19th century in the Dutch school's shift from a Germanic to a French artistic orientation. Describes the impact of D's cello sonata on Pijper, who credited him with inspiring composers toward a renewed interest in melody.

312. Hopkins, George William. "Debussy and Boulez." **Musical Times** 110, no. 1506 (Aug. 1968): 710-14.

Relates aspects of melody and instrumentation in Boulez's **Le soleil des eaux** to **Jeux**. D influenced post-Webern composers, although Boulez has withdrawn from certain Debussyan traits in his later music.

313. Indy, Vincent d'. **R. Wagner et son influence sur l'art musical français.** Paris: Delagrave, 1930. 92 p. ML 410.W12F695.

Underpinned by a bias in favor of Wagner, as seen in the final chapter "30 années de progrès du à l'essor wagnérien en France." With an apparently negative feeling, views **Pelléas** as "the point of closure of the Wagnerian period in France" but does not forecast the nature of the new era. Emphasizes the Wagnerian leitmotifs in **Pelléas** but ends in acknowledging its quintessentially French aesthetic. A valuable writing on Wagnerism and D's reaction to it, as seen through the eyes of Wagner's fervent adherents.

* **L'influence de Debussy.** Various essays in **Debussy et l'évolution de la musique au 20e siècle** (E. Weber, ed.), see item 127.

"Amérique (Etats-Unis)," by Virginia Raad, p. 215-32. Influence on C.M. Loeffler, C. Griffes, J.A. Carpenter, E. Whithorne, E. Hill, L. Gruenberg, Mary Howe, Marion Bauer, and jazz. Abundant bibliography.

"Amérique latine," by Luis Heitor Correa de Azevedo, 233-37. H. Oswald, Alberto Williams, H. Villa-Lobos, J. Nuñes, A. Palma, C. Pedrell, and J. Rolon.

"Angleterre," by Ed. Lockspeiser, 239-40. C. Scott, B. Britten, J. Ireland.

"Autriche et Allemande," by H.-H. Stuckenschmidt, 241-61. M. Reger, P. Graener, W. Niemann, S. Karg-Elert, A. Schoenberg, F. Schrecker, A. Berg, E. Wellesz, J. Marx.

"Espagne et Portugal," by Julia d'Almendra, 263-67. A. Fragoso, L. de Freitas Branco, F. de Freitas, C. Carneyro, M. de Falla, I. Albeniz, F. de Lacerda.

"France," by Françoise Gervais, 269-72. P. Boulez, A. Jolivet.

"Hongrie," by Dénes Bartha, 273-87. B. Bartók, Z. Kodály.

"Italie," by Alberto Mantelli, 289-90. A. Casella.

"Pays-bas (Belgique, Hollande)," by Frank Onnen, 291-99. P. Gilson, R. Moulaert, M. Poot, A. Diepenbrock, W. Pijper.

"Pays nordiques," by Poul Rovsing-Olsen, 300-11. G. Nystroem, J. Sibelius, A. Nordheim, P. Gudmundsen, B. Nilsson.

"Pologne," by Stefan Jarocinski, 313-14. K.

Szymanowski.
"Russie," by Jules Kremlev, 315-18. N. Miaskovsky, S. Prokofiev, D. Shostakovich.

314. Jarocinski, Stefan. "Grupa 'Szeŝciu' a Debussy" [The Group "Les Six" and Debussy]. **Muzyka** 24, no. 4 (1979), 35-45. In Polish.

The group, consisting of Auric, Durey, Honegger, Milhaud, Poulenc, and Tailleferre, was not consistent in aesthetics for long but early on espoused the aesthetic of Jean Cocteau's **Le coq et l'arlequin** (1918). Discusses their reaction against the immediate past, their turn to a simple and reserved expression, and their admiration of D alongside a criticism of his imitators. Jarocinski observes a simplicity in program among the Six and lack of inventiveness. They nonetheless played a key role in the development of cultural and aesthetic thought. Refers also to Satie's influence on them. This article is more extensive than the article in item 123, which nonetheless may be referred to more readily by most researchers.

315. Kaufman, Harald. "Zur Wertung des Epigonentums in der Musik (unter besonderer Berücksichtigung der Epigonen Debussys)." **Neue Zeitschrift für Musik** 129, no. 9 (Sept. 1968): 397-404.

Makes specific reference to **Les sonoritées opposées** (**Etudes** 12 for piano). Observes a gradual evolution of the motive as the basis of formal process. Discusses works by Louis Aubert, Jean Roger-Ducasse, Darius Milhaud, and Henri Büsser in comparison to D's form. A significant article showing D's impact on the evolution of musical style, which was immediate but did not form a "school."

316. Keil, Werner. "Untersuchungen zur Entwicklung des frühen Klavierstils von Debussy und Ravel." Ph.D. diss., Musicology, J.W. Goethe-University, Frankfurt, 1982. Publ. Wiesbaden: Breitkopf und Härtel, 1982. 233 p. ML724.K44 1982; ISBN 3-7651-0185-0.

Analyzes the early piano works of D from the **Danse bohémienne** to **Estampes** along with those by

Ravel. Makes a pioneering comparison of the **Images oubliées** to Ravel's **Sérénade grotesque/Entre cloches**. Seeks to determine which composer used innovative devices first. The pianist R. Viñes is central to both their development.

317. Kennedy, Michael. **The Works of Ralph Vaughan Williams.** Second edition. London: Oxford University Press, 1980. 454 p. ISBN 0-19-315454-4; ML 410.V3 K4 1980..

Works that influenced Vaughan Williams include **La mer, Prélude-faune,** and **Pelléas**. Attributes a more skillful use of woodwinds and strings to D's and Ravel's influences. Mentions other stylistic relationships but does not analyze particular links extensively. A major study of Vaughan Williams's music, this book offers a helpful starting point for discussing the relationship.

318. Keresztùry, Dezsö", ed. **Debussy: "Pelléas et Melisande"-ja.** Budapest: Zeneműkiadó, 1964. 124 p. In Hungarian.

Includes a libretto of **Pelléas** translated into Hungarian. Contains essays on D by Dénes Bartha and Kodály. The latter tells of his interest and might contribute to a study of D's impact upon him.

319. Kerman, Joseph. "Wagner: Thoughts in Season." **Score** (London) 28 (1961): 9-24.

An essay on Wagnerism that complements Kerman's book **Opera as Drama** (item 800). Views Wagner as diminishing in importance: "Wagnerism as ideology had less effect in music than in certain other fields." Relates the Wagnerian school to the serialists on the basis of the orientation to a structure and a mystique, although manifest differences are seen. This article may inform studies of **Pelléas** and D's Wagnerism.

320. Koechlin, Charles. **Correspondance.** Paris: **Revue musicale**/Editions Richard-Masse, 1982. 164 p.

Numerous references to D in the letters, from a 1905 praise of **Pelléas** for its "harmonies inquiétantes" to his 1945 remarks on Emma Debussy and Dolly de Tinan ("Il n'est pas impossible que Dolly fut la propre fille de Fauré").

321. ------. "Souvenirs sur Debussy." **Cahiers Debussy** (nouvelle série) 7 (1983): 3-6.

An article of 1947 not published previously. Koechlin remarks on the affinities of himself and his Conservatoire classmates Florent Schmitt and Ernest Le Grand toward D during the 1890s. He speaks of D's relation to the publisher Emile Baudoux and briefly describes his own work as the orchestrator of **Khamma**.

322. ------. "Souvenirs sur Debussy, la Schola, et la SMI." **Revue musicale** 15, no. 150 (Nov. 1934): 241-51.

Recalls that D was cordial with d'Indy, and that D had fought for the French school of Chausson, Chabrier, and Fauré. However, D was less enthusiastic toward d'Indy's music and teaching. Koechlin distinguishes Fauré and Saint-Saëns from Franck. The S.M.I, became the natural base for the evolution of French music after **Pelléas**, in Koechlin's view.

323. ------. "Sur l'évolution de la musique française avant et après Debussy." **Revue musicale** 16, no. 155 (1935): 264-80.

Of primary value for the study of Koechlin's thought and D's impact upon him. While he views D as a watershed, he does not discuss D's relationship to slightly later composers. Further see Koechlin, "La leçon de Debussy," **Revue musicale** 15, no. 142 (Jan. 1934): 1-19, where Koechlin finds D to be a model of naturalness and simplicity.

324. Konold, Wulf. "Karol Szymanowski." **Musica** 36, no. 5 (1982): 419-22.

In German. In discussing the life and music of Szymanowski, the article refers to the Polish situation and the upsurge of musical culture after the founding of the republic in 1920. Points out stylistic connections to D.

325. Korody, Istvan Paker. "The Influence of French Impressionism and the Essence of the Hungarian National Character in Zoltán Kodály's Piano Music." Ph.D. diss., Ohio State University, 1978. 205 p. DA 39/08, p. 4797A; UM order no. 7902060. ML 410.K732 K6 1978am.

Kodály adopted many of D's idioms as a reaction against the status quo at the turn of the century. D's example permitted Kodály to synthesize Hungarian folk elements, particularly pentatonicism. The piano music before 1920 exhibits the most pronounced influence.

326. Kurth, Ulrich. **Aus der Neuen Welt: Untersuchungen zur Rezeption afro-amerikanischer Musik in europaischer Kunstmusik des 19. und frühen 20. Jahrhunderts.** Ph.D. diss., University of Kiel, 1981. Published Goppingen: Kummerle, 1982. v, 398 p. ISBN 3-8745-2559-7; ML 3556.K95 1982.

Examines the influence of African American spirituals, ragtime, blues, and jazz on the music of D, Satie, Stravinsky, Milhaud, Dvorák, and others. The interpretations proceed from concepts of Adorno and Hauser. Considers sociologic questions of the phenomenon. Not examined.

327. Laloy, Louis. "Claude Debussy et le debussysme." **Revue S.I.M.** [Soc. Internationale de Musique, section de Paris] 6, no. 8 and 9 (Aug.-Sept., 1910): 507-19.

Defends D by contrasting him to his imitators. Notes that D was a "messenger of a new form" and expressed a greater depth than his imitators, who borrow devices singly and without integration. The succeeding article (Emile Vuillermoz, "En l'an 2012," pp. 520- 29) is a hypothetical valedictory speech for the Prix de Rome in the year 2012, which looks back to the year 1910. The historian of the future points to a prominent Debussysme in the styles of Ravel, Schmitt, Caplet, Huré, Koechlin, and others. Both articles present an important contemporaneous view of D's significance.

328. Landormy, Paul. "L'état actuel de la musique française." **La revue bleue** 14, 5e série, tome 1 (April 2, 1904).

Dukas is dramatic, Franck is not French but Belgian, and D is essentially French and "facile, élégante, sensuelle." Broaches the topic of the reception of French music in Germany. Foresees a truly popular art music emerging from D and young composers. The preceding issue of this periodical (March 26, 1904) contains section I of Landormy's article, discussing D's older compatriots Duparc, Massenet, and Chabrier.

329. ------. **Gounod.** Paris: Gallimard, 1942. 275 p. ML 410.G7L3.

Traces Gounod's contacts with prominent composers at the time of D's youth. Important references to H. Büsser but only brief remarks (pp. 261-63) regarding Gounod's influence on D, especially on melodic sensibility.

330. ------. **La musique française de Franck à Debussy.** Paris: Gallimard, 1948. 244 p. ML 270.4.L267.

Landormy's discussion has been superseded for D, but his discussion of lesser lights in the period is still useful.

331. Leibowitz, René. **Schoenberg and his School.** Translated by Dika Newlin. New York: Philosophical Library, 1949. xxvii, 305 p. ISBN 3-0671-681x; ML 390.L462 1970.

D is that point in music at which polyphony became detached from its contrapuntal origins. States that Schoenberg introduced the whole-tone scale at about the same time as D. Berg draws close to D's sonorous world in the **3 Orchestral Pieces** Op. 6. Compares D to the Second Viennese School: he threw off tradition at once with continuing certain of its processes. A path-breaking study of the Viennese and of continuing relevance, despite much scholarship since. Can become one point of departure for the much-needed, concentrated study of D's relation to Schoenberg and his school.

332. Lesure, François. "A travers la correspondance de Nadia Boulanger." **Revue de la Bibliothèque nationale** 5 (Sept. 1982): 16-23.

Announces the acquisition by the B.n. of Boulanger's correspondence and certain music manuscripts. Includes letters to D, Saint-Saëns, Ravel, Poulenc, Vierne, Valéry, and D'Annunzio.

333. ------. "'L'affaire' Debussy-Ravel." In **Festschrift Friedrich Blume zum 70. Geburtstag**, pp. 231-234. Kassel: Bärenreiter, 1963.

The personal differences between the two composers are shown to have been sensationalized by the press. A certain cordiality existed, and in fact each encouraged the other personally. Cites passages from important, unpublished letters by both.

334. ------. "Claude Debussy, Ernest Chausson et Henri Lerolle." In **Humanisme actif, I: Mélanges d'art et de littérature offerts à Julien Cain**, pp. 337-44. Paris: Hermann, 1968. AC 20.H8.

The correspondence between Chausson and the painter Lerolle in the period 1893-94 describes **Pelléas** during its genesis. Speaks of D's engagement to Thérèse Roger and D's bohemian lifestyle. Other topics of the letters include Paul Poujaud (attorney of the group), G. Moreau (painter), E. Poe, Musorgsky, D's **Proses lyriques**, R. Bonheur, Redon, Mme Escudier, d'Indy, Benoït. One remark exposes an anti-Semitic attitude of Lerolle. Lesure annotates names mentioned in the correspondence.

335. ------. "Debussy e Stravinski. **Musica d'oggi** 2, no. 6 (Milan, June 1959): 242-44.

A brief summary of the relationship, citing letters.

336. ------. "Debussy et la Belgique." **Académie Royale de Belgique, Bulletin de la Classe des Beaux Arts** 5ème série, tome LIX, nos. 2-4 (1977): 35-47.

The links to Belgium include the relationship to Franck, Ysaÿe, Maeterlinck, and other poets and painters (De Groux and A. Rassenfosse). D travelled to Brussels five times between 1893 and 1914. Gives letters of 23 Oct. 1915 to F. Poulenc on the subject of Franck; an unpublished letter of 1894 to Chausson about the performance of D's **Quatuor** in Brussels; a letter of early Oct. 1896 to Ysaÿe on **Pelléas**; and a letter to Sylvain Dupuis of 8 Jan. 1907 on **Pelléas** in Brussels.

337. ------. "Debussy et Edgard Varèse." In item 127, pp. 333-38.

A biographical study that cites and explains their correspondance. Varèse might be considered a missing, or at least unclarified, link between D and Schoenberg.

338. Lewinski, Wolf-Eberhard von. "Der Rolle der Klangfarbe bei Strauss und Debussy." **Schweizerische Musikzeitung/Revue musicale suisse** 110, no. 6 (Nov.-Dec. 1970): 357-61.

Compares the structural importance of tone color in Strauss and D. Views him as a pioneer in the emancipation of sound and relates him to Cage. Sees Strauss as the more literal interpreter of nature.

339. ------. **Musik wieder gefragt? Gedanken und Gespräche zum Musikleben von heute.** Hamburg: Claassen, 1967. 304 p. ML 60.L387 M9.

A wide range of essays on music in the 1950s and 1960s, as on the Viennese school, Penderecki in the 60s, and ballet and opera. "Das Irrtum von Impressionismus" questions the propriety of the label and stresses the view inward of the **Nocturnes**. The succeeding essay discusses Ravel as a link between D and Stravinsky; Ravel's **La valse** is a metaphor for his times.

340. Liess, Andreas. "Claude Debussy." In **Deutsche und französische Musik der Geistgeschichte des neunzehnten Jahrhunderts**, pp. 89-94. Vienna: Liechtenstein, 1950. ML 196.L719.

Views D's art as a quintessentially French expression. Symbolist aesthetic is at the heart of D and French music of his day. D and the movoment in general experienced an initial and formative influence from Wagner but reacted in a rational, classic manner, as contrasted to Wagner's German irrationality. These tendencies are the basis of D's sound world, which stands upon but reaches beyond Wagner's basis. This line of thought is expanded by Holloway (item 308). Liess is valuable still as a balanced view of D's Wagnerian relationship. Refers to the poet Baudelaire and to **Pelléas**.

341. ------. "Claude Debussy, Vater der Moderne." **Musikerziehung** 32 (June 1977): 195-98.

Discussés D's singular importance in the advent of contemporary music. His attention to Art nouveau is a microcosm and expression of nature. Relates D's "music of freedom" to **Klangfarbenmelodie** of the Viennese school, to electronic music, and to Honegger's **Pacific 231**. A useful, further commentary on his article item 567.

342. ------. "Claude Debussy und die 'Funf.'" **Neue Zeitschrift für Musik** 128, no. 2 (Feb. 1967): 69-77.

Following upon the research of A. Schaeffner, Liess traces the influence of the Russian Five on D, referring especially to Balakirev, D's **Prélude-faune**, and Rimsky-Korsakov. Notes that the relationship extended to actual borrowings from the Five.

343. Lockspeiser, Edward. "Mahler in France." **Monthly Musical Record** 90, no. 998 (March-April 1960): 52-7.

Describes Mahler's conducting in Paris during 1900-11. Mahler met D there in 1910 when conducting his 2nd Symphony. Alma Mahler's published recollections of the meeting are shown as faulty. Mahler's and D's reactions to Wagner are compared. Describes the cool reception of the **Nocturnes** in Munich in 1910.

344. ------. "Musorgsky and Debussy." **Musical Quarterly** 23, no. 4 (Oct. 1937): 421-27.

Seeks to place in perspective D's remark that "the whole of **Pelléas** is in Boris." Cites Musorgsky's remarks on aesthetics to Stassov and the role of Jules de Brayer in the discovery of Musorgsky in France. Updated by Schaeffner (384) and more-recent studies of **Pelléas**, but is an interpretation of note.

345. Macomie, Robin. **The Works of Karlhein Stockhausen.** Foreword by Karlheinz Stockhausen. London: Oxford University Press, 1976. 340 p. ISBN 0-19-315429-3; ML 410.S858 M3. Observes Stockhausen's close study of D's music.

Such elements as statistical patterning in **Jeux**, as Stockhausen saw it, made an unusually deep impression on him. The static character of much of Stockhausen's music might also be a result of his study of D. D's preludes for piano influenced Stockhausen's **Klavierstück X** (1954/1961).

346. Marschall, Gottfried. "Signes avant-coureurs des techniques impressionistes dans la musique de Jules Massenet." **Revue internationale de musique française** 2, no. 5 (June 1981): 61-72.

Massenet's melody and innovative scalar structures influenced **L'enfant prodigue** and **Pelléas**.

347. Martins, Jose Eduardo. "Quelques aspects comparatifs dans les langages pianistiques de Debussy et Scriabine." **Cahiers Debussy** (nouvelle série) 7 (1983): 24-37.

Compares sonority, dynamics, tempos and order of tempos, register, texture, and articulation. Observes a poetic musical terminology in scores that often is strikingly parallel. Numerous examples from the **Preludes** and **Etudes** and from Scriabin's piano music illustrate this.

348. ------. "La vision de l'univers enfantin chez Moussorgsky et Debussy." **Cahiers Debussy** (nouvelle série) 9 (1985): 3-16.

Considers the childhood of the two composers and notes that their compositions to be expressive of a child's view: Musorgsky's **Chambre d'enfants** and **Pictures at an Exhibition** and D's **Children's Corner** and **Boîte à joujoux**. The latter two were dedicated to D's daughter, Chouchou, whose birth seems to have awakened his sensibilities and previously shunned feelings regarding his own childhood. Approaches the difficult question of D's psychological formation as a child and provokes needed further research along psychological lines. Stimulating if speculative parallels are drawn between the two personalities and compositional processes.

349. McCalla, James. "Sea-Changes: Boulez's **Improvisations sur Mallarmé**." **Journal of Musicology** 6, no. 1 (Winter 1988): 83-106.

Boulez's cycle for voice and chamber ensemble is a setting of three sonnets by Mallarmé, whom the author views as more radical than Boulez. Refers to Boulez's insistence upon unidirectional time in music, in which he is a student of Stravinsky, the later D, and even Beethoven. Explores the concept of chance in Boulez and Mallarmé. Can elucidate further discussions of D's reference to Mallarmé as perhaps also Boulez's to D.

350. Messing, Scott. "Neo-classicism: The Origins of the Term and Its Use in the Schoenberg/ Stravinsky Polemic in the 1920's." Ph.D. diss., Musicology, Univsity of Michigan, 1986. viii, 361 p. UM 86-21,340. ML 197.M477 1986.

Distinguishes between the academic return to the past that was neo-classicism (as in the visual arts and to a degree Brahms) and the "nouveau classicisme" of the 1920s. D is a progenitor in such works as **Petite suite**, **Suite bergamasque**, **Pour le piano**, the **Images** I for piano, **Six épigraphes antiques**, and the sonatas. A useful tracing of the aesthetic in D and related composers such as Ravel, Saint-Saëns, and d'Indy. Refers to D's values as expressed in **Monsieur Croche**.

351. Mies, Paul. "Widmungsstücke mit Buchstaben-Motto bei Debussy und Ravel." **Studien zur Musikwissenschaft** 25 (1962): 363-68.

Discusses D's **Hommage à Rameau** and Ravel's **Tombeau de Couperin**. Compares the **Hommage** to Ravel's **Menuet sur le nom d'Haydn**. Stresses that Ravel is a minute structuralist. For a contrasting interpretation see Rosen, item 375.

352. Milhaud, Darius. **Notes sans musique**. Paris: R. Julliard, 1949. 336 p. Translated by D. Evans as **Notes without Music, an autobiography**. New York: Knopf, 1953. 355, xxii p. ML 410.M674 A32.

Milhaud terms D's **Quatuor**, which he heard in 1905, a revelation to him. Describes D's coaching him as performer in the premiere of the **Sonata for Flute, Viola, and Harp**. Numerous references to D throughout the autobiography.

353. Mowinckel, Laila. "Grieg og Debussy" [Grieg and Debussy]. **Norsk musiktidsskrift** 10, no. 2 (June 1973): 68-75. In Norwegian.

Discusses a Parisian performance of a Grieg work in 1903, D's negative criticism, and Grieg's response. Considers D's manner as critic and Grieg's influence on him as a composer. See also the succeeding article by the same author, "Grieg og Debussy 2." **Norsk musiktidsskrift** 10, no. 3 (September 1973): 123-29. The second article discusses the critical reception of the first concert in Norway of D's music, on Dec. 9, 1906.

354. Myers, Rollo. **Emmanuel Chabrier and his Circle**. London: Dent, 1969. 169 p. ISBN 460-03826-5; ML 410.C393 M9.

Views Chabrier as "a sworn enemy of conventions and taboos in life and art alike." Notes D's admiration for Chabrier but finds no record of direct contacts. Chabrier quipped about D's "gloomy and depressing songs" of the 1880s.

355. Nectoux, Jean-Michel. "Debussy et Fauré." **Cahiers Debussy** (nouvelle série) 3 (1979): 13-30.

Discusses biographical and aesthetic relations, drawing on various letters and unpublished documents. A thoughtful contrast of the two composers by a leading authority on Fauré. He maintains tradition while Debussy distances himself from it. Fauré has little dependence upon the timbral and cross-arts processes of D, his aesthetic being founded on the concept of pure music. The two composers thus represent two aesthetic poles.

356. ------. **Gabriel Fauré: His Life through his Letters.** Translated by J. Underwood. London and New York: Marion Boyars, 1984. 378 p. ISBN 0-7145-2768-8; M1410.F27 A413 1984. Originally published as **Gabriel Fauré, Correspondance.** Paris: Flammarion, 1980. ISBN 2-08-064259-6; ML 410.F27 A4 1980.

In his expert commentary on the letters, Nectoux sees Fauré's work along with Ravel's as representing the point of stylistic perfection preceding the break with tradition, a movement made by D. Nonetheless sees common to all three a drive toward renewal and discovery. No correspondence with D is given, although references to D abound in letters to others and in the annotations. A valuable study as well concerning D's artistic environment and times.

357. ------. "Le **Pelléas** de Fauré." **Revue de musicologie** 67, no. 2 (1981): 169-90.

D attended the 1895 Paris performance of the Maeterlinck play and considered composing a symphonic suite. Upon D's rejection of the idea, Fauré agreed to compose incidental music at the bequest of organizers for an upcoming London performance. Koechlin orchestrated Fauré's work. A thorough presentation of D's reaction to the Fauré incidental music.

358. Nestev, Izrail V. "Szergej Prokofjev és a kortársak" [Sergej Prokof'ev and his contemporaries]. **Magyar zene** (Nov. 1967): 487-500. Translated into Hungarian by E. Fono.

Discusses early 20th-century influences on Prokofiev and his relation to D, Ravel, and others. Sees a parallel with the textural uses of Ravel.

359. Nicolodi, Fiamma. "Parigi e l'opera verista: dibattiti, riflessioni, polemiche." **Nuova rivista musicale italiana** 15, no. 4 (Oct.-Dec. 1981): 577-623.

Discusses the reception of **verismo** operas by Mascagni, Puccini, Leoncavallo, and Giordano by the French press and such composers as D, Dukas, Fauré, and Bruneau. Argues that French support of **verismo** emerges.

360. Orenstein, Arbie. **Ravel: Man and Musician.** New York: Columbia University Press, 1975. 291 p. ISBN 0-231-03902-6; ML410.R23 O73.

Considers Ravel's important connections to D. This major study views him as the towering figure in French music from 1900-1918, to whom all including Ravel were obliged to react. Relates Ravel to his teacher Fauré and to the **Apaches** group of artistic radicals. Describes Ravel's reactions to such premieres as that of **Pelléas** and his personal relation to D. Qualifies D's achievements as effusive and pathbreaking, whereas Ravel's output was relatively small, innovative within tradition, and marked by an unrivalled mastery of craft. An important statement on the relation of Ravel to D and summary of contemporary judgements of the question.

361. Orledge, Robert. "Fauré's **Pelléas et Méli sande**." **Music and Letters** 51, no. 2 (Apr. 1975): 170-79.

Concerns the 1898 London production of the first staged musical version of the Maeterlinck drama. Fauré revised four numbers for the 1901 publication of the suite. His and Debussy's scores are compared briefly, a topic requiring more extensive review. Further see item 357.

362. Orlova, Alexandra. **Musorgsky's Days and Works: A Biography in Documents.** Translated and edited by Roy J. Guenther. Ann Arbor, Michigan: UMI Research Press, 1983. 697 p. ISBN 0-8357-1324-5; ML 410.M97083 1983.

A copious assemblage of biographical data and letters, arranged chronologically. Of interest concerning the genesis and contemporary reception of **Boris** and the **Nursery Songs**, which influenced D significantly.

363. Oulmont, Charles. **Musique de l'amour: E. Chausson et la "Bande à Franck."** Paris: Desclée de Brouwer, 1935. 193 p. ML 390.O93.

A valuable view of the relationship of Chausson to D. Cites relevant letters.

364. Palmer, Christopher. "Delius, Vaughan Williams, and Debussy." **Music and Letters** 50, no. 4 (Oct. 1969): 475-80.

Traces Delius's strong attraction to the culture of France, where he lived in later life. Likewise Vaughan Williams studied with Ravel and maintained affinities with French taste. D's non-functional harmony, use of timbre as an agent in structure, and love of nature relate to the two English composers.

365. Parks, Anne Florence. "Freedom, form and process in Varèse." Ph.D. diss., Cornell University, 1974. 495 p. ML 410.V27 P37 1974a.

Finds D to be one source of Varèse's ideas. D influenced his rhythm, form, instrumentation, and sonority.

366. Pasler, Jann Corinne. "Debussy, Stravinsky, and the Ballets russes: The Emergence of a New Musical Logic." Ph.D. diss., Musicology, University of Chicago, 1981. DA 42/01A, p.15. ML 3460.P37 1981a.

Compositional processes of both composers comprise an important aspect of their "revolutions." The Ballets russes gave an impetus for a new artistic synthesis, in which no one art form could dominate. Argues that both composers reversed the relationship between time in music (dynamic process) and space (overall structure): each instant of music is highly structured, while the overall shape fluctuates in the listener's perception.

367. Pinzanti, Leonardo. **Giacomo Puccini.** Turin: Edizioni RAL Radiotelevisione Italiana, 1975. 291 p. ML 410.P89 P53.

Discusses D's influence at length. Puccini was disapponited that Maeterlinck did not choose him instead of D to set **Pelléas et Mélisande.** Refers to D repeatedly in the discussion of P's style and when discusssing individual operas.

368. Pistone, Danièle. "Debussy et Wagner; Influences et réactions." **Revue musicale de Suisse romande** 32, no. 4 (Fall 1979): 10-14.

Surveys D's contacts with Wagner's music and concludes that only in his youth was the impact direct. Their musical natures were radically different. A brief but clear overview, to be supplemented by thoroughgoing analysis.

369. ------. "Les musiciens français à Rome." **Revue internationale de musique française** 5, no. 4 (June 1984): 7-28.

Quite important for establishing the context of D's Rome sojourn, even though his personal experiences are not studied in detail. Useful charts of all Prix de Rome recipients from 1803-1968. Lists compositions with a programmatic relationship to Rome. Other articles in this issue of the journal discuss the Prix de Rome, as well.

370. Poirier, Alain. "L'histoire toujours recommencée: Introduction à la pensée analytique de Jean Barraqué." **Analyse musicale** 12 (June 1988): 9-14.

A useful discussion of Barraqué's analytic conceptions. As a composer, his orientation toward serialism influences his reading of D as a precursor of the contemporary. Especially useful alongside Barraqué's articles and book on D (items 121 and 63).

371. Pound, Ezra. **Antheil and the Treatise on Harmony.** New introduction by Ned Rorem. New York: Da Capo Press, 1968. 150 p. LC card no. 67-27463 MN; ML 410.A638 P7 1968.

A reprint of the edition Chicago: Pascal Covici, 1927. Of importance for D's reception by Antheil and the writer Pound, who were leading figures in the arts just after D. Pound refers to D as "an heresy....less concerned with the mechanics of music than with using music to affect the visual imagination." Antheil finds D "a great landmark in musical composition...because of his new propulsion of time-spaces."

372. Powell, Linton E., Jr. "The piano music of Joaquin Turina (1882-1949)." Ph.D. diss., University of North Carolina, 1974. 301 p.
Compares certain of Turina's 55 published piano works to Albéniz, de Falla, and Granados. The innovations of D influenced this Spanish group decisively. Also see Powell, **A History of Spanish Piano Music**. Bloomington, Indiana: Indiana Univ. Press, 1980. viii, 213 p. ISBN 0-2531-8114-3; ML 738.P7. The book expands on the dissertation.

373. Racek, Jan. "Leos Janáceks Kompositionsprinzip in seinen Spätwerken." **Die Musikforschung** 29, no. 2 (1976): 177-83.

Examines elements of naturalism, Impressionism, and Expressionism in the late music of Janácek. Questions those who relate him to **verismo** and the 2nd Viennese school. Sees D as more closely related, although Janácek's Impressionism is personal.

374. Rolland, Romain. "Richard Strauss and **Pelléas**: from the diary of Romain Rolland, 22 May 1907." Translated from the French. **About the House** 5, no. 7 (1978): 40-43.

Strauss had vivid recollections of his first hearing of **Pelléas** in the company of Romain Rolland. He found the work "très fin" but lacking in "Schwung." Short but clear exposé of strongly differentiated aesthetics, contrasting along national lines.

375. Rosen, Charles. "Where Ravel Ends and Debussy Begins." **High Fidelity** 9 (May 1959): 117-21.
An important and provocative article that calls into question popular notions of D as post-Romantic "Impressionist" and Ravel as classicist. For Rosen, D continues the work of the great

classicists in his preoccupation with structure, while Ravel is more closely situated alongside Berlioz and Liszt. Compares the treatment of the same Haydn theme by Ravel (**Minuet on the Name of Haydn**) and Debussy (**Hommage à Haydn**). Ravel creates not a traditional minuet but a Romantic structure fixed on texture and timbre; D treats the theme classically, as a cell that gives rise to the whole structure. Reprinted in item 123.

376. Roy, Jean. **Musique française: présences contemporaines.** Paris: Debresse, 1962. ML 390.R89.

Begins with the generation following D (Satie, Koechlin, Roussel) and continues through to Jolivet, Messiaen, Dutilleux, and Boulez. Refers to D throughout in discussing contemporary French music.

377. Russell, Ross. **Bird Lives! The Life and Hard Times of Charlie (Yardbird) Parker.** New York: Charterhouse, 1973. 404 p. LC card no. 72-84214/MN/r85; ML 419.P4R9.

Mentions Parker's attraction to the music of D, Ravel, and Hindemith. That single remark is intriguing and ought to provoke further studies of depth considering the relationship of Parker to D musically.

378. Saint-Saëns, Camille. "L'anarchie musicale." **Le courrier musical** (Paris) 14, no. 1 (Jan. 1, 1911).

Includes Saint-Saëns's famous criticism of Debussy's music for its "système atonique."

379. ------. "Correspondance inédite entre Saint-Saëns et Maurice Emmanuel à propos de Debussy." **Revue musicale** no. 206 (numéro spécial 1947): 30-34.

A famous letter by Saint-Saëns (April 4, 1920) denounces D's naïveté and formlessness, concluding that he did not create a style but cultivated the absence of style. Emmanuel responds (Dec. 10, 1920) in defense of D's depth and sincerity.

Emmanuel places himself modestly as a composer in D's shadow, perhaps implying the same for Saint-Saëns. An important interchange when considering D's early reception by composers.

380. Samazeuilh, Gustave. **Musiciens de mon temps: chroniques et souvenirs.** Paris: M. Daubin, 1947. 418 p. ML 410.S167 A3.

Essays and memoirs by an early writer on D. Samazeuilh transcribed orchestral works and the **Quatuor** in their first versions for piano duo and duet. Includes an essay on **Rodrigue et Chimène**. Discusses related figures (Ysaÿe, Carré) and overall places D within context.

381. ------. **Paul Dukas.** Paris: Durand, 1913. 28 p. ML 410.D86S2.

A short but valuable, contemporary sketch of Dukas, who was in Guiraud's composition class alongside Debussy. Speaks of the influence of Musorgsky's **Boris** and **Pelléas** on Dukas.

382. Santoliquido, Francesco. **Il dopo Wagner: Claude Debussy e Richard Strauss.** Rome: Walter Modes, 1909. 94 p. ML 197.S23.

Relevant when studying the contemporary reception of both composers. Centers on their response to Wagner, a primary question of the era.

383. Satie, Erik. **Ecrits.** Edited and compiled by Ornella Volta. Paris: Editions Champs libre, 1977. Revised and enlarged 1981. 367 p. English translation by N. Wilkins as **The Writings of Erik Satie.** London: Eulenburg, 1980. 178 p. ISBN 2-8518-4073-8; ML 60.S269.

Valuable first publication of Satie's complete writings. A thorough index and lists give access to D's appearance in Satie's letters.

384. Schaeffner, André. "Debussy et ses rapports avec la musique russe." In **Musique russe**, Vol. I, edited by Pierre Souvtchinsky, pp. 95-138. Paris: Presses Universitaires de France, 1953. ML 300.S74.

Traces D's early travels to Russia with Mme von Meck. Discusses the influence of Musorgsky's **Boris** on **Pelléas**, especially on the characters Golaud and Yniold, the chant-like effects, and the speech-attuned prosody. Notes the performances of Russian music in Paris from 1872-1899. Thus Schaeffner disagrees with Dietschy (item 68), who sees Russian influence only from 1893 for D. Refers as well to the impact of Rimsky-Korsakov. Schaeffner recognizes that his research lacks certain documentation. Nonetheless, it is a pioneering study of the critical topic in depth, alongside Lockspeiser (85) and Vallas. Also see Godet and Vidal (both RM 1926, item 145), who points as well to D's enthusiasm for Borodin and Tchaikovsky.

385. ------. "Variations Schoenberg." **Contrepoint** (Paris) 7 (1951): 110-29.

The argument is the question "Why did D not set **Pierrot lunaire**?" Explores imaginatively the aesthetics of D in his later years and that of Schoenberg during his phase of atonality and serialism. Argues that D, an alert reader of the revue **S.I.M.**, must have kept abreast of Schoenberg's and Webern's development. Further considers Stravinsky's cantata **Roi des étoiles** and Cocteau's writings in the period 1911-1914.

386. Schauerte, Helga. **Jehan Alain (1911-1940), das Orgelwerk: Eine monographische Studie.** Regensburg: Bosse, 1983. vii, 231 p. ISBN 3-649-2289-3; ML 410.A29 S32.

An analysis focusing on six compositions and tracing Alain's stylistic development. Demonstrates musical and aesthetic parallels to Messiaen and D. Cites pertinent letters, diary entries, photographs, and drawings in the biographical section of the study.

387. Schiff, David. **The Music of Elliott Carter.** London: Eulenburg, and New York: Da Capo, 1983. 371 p. ISBN 0-903873-06-0; ML 410.C3293 S34 1983.

Discusses the treatment of motives in **Jeux**, which are termed "neutralized" and are fleeting aspects of the basic sound-matter; they are "epiphanies." Almost all of Carter's music is "epiphanic" in formal logic, which might relate to D's model. Also compares Carter to D in regard to orchestration, texture, and sonority. This authoritative study ought to oncourage others who will look deeply at D's relation to Carter.

388. Shattuck, Roger. **The Banquet Years: the Arts in France 1885-1914.** New York: Harcourt, Brace, 1958. DC 338.S48 Rev. ed.: **The Banquet Years: the Origins of the Avant-garde in France, 1885 to World War I.** New York: Vintage, 1968. xiv, 397 p. DC 338.S48 1968.

A highly provocative discussion of four figures who typify the era: Henri Rousseau (painter), Erik Satie (composer), Alfred Jarry (poet), and Guillaume Apollinaire (poet). Views their creative lives as windows on the Belle Epoque, the "Banquet Years" from 1885-1915. In the period the bohemian cultural underground crystallized into a self-conscious avant-garde, generating an astonishingly varied renewal and accomplishment. Places D in perspective of the times and of Satie specifically. Shattuck names D as Satie's best friend, the thorn in his flesh, and the source of his greatest sorrow.

389. Sievers, Gerd. **"Pelléas und Mélisande:** Sibelius-Debussy-Schoenberg-Fauré." **Musica** (Cassel) 15, no. 4 (Apr. 1961): 171-74.

390. ------. "Sibelius und die Komponisten seiner Zeit: Vergleich der **Pelléas und Mélisande**-Vertonungen." **Sibelius Mitteilungen** (Wiesbaden) 4 (April 1961): 7-14.

This and the preceding articles were not available to the present study. They are listed as rare sources that might foster other research into the virtually unexplored relationship of Sibelius to D.

391. Skowron, Zbigniew. "Rola i znaczenie tradycji w refleksji muzyczno-estetycznej Pierre'a Bouleza" [The Role and Meaning of Tradition in Light of Aesthetics and Music]. **Muzyka** 30, no. 3-4 (1985): 17. In Polish, with summary in English.

Considers the position of Boulez with regard to tradition, from which he draws values and standards. Boulez has noted D's independence in the posing of creative problems, his modernity of formal solutions, and his challenge to the cultural hegemony of the West. Relates Boulez to aspects of Bach and Schoenberg, as well.

392. Slattery, Thomas C. **Percy Grainger, The Inveterate Innovator**. Evanston, Illinois: The Instrumentalist Co., 1974. 308 p. LC card no. 73-87230; ML 410.G75 S55.

Grainger referred to D's music in correspondence, and he studied primary works. About 1917 he arranged **Bruyères** (prelude for piano) for 10 winds and harmonium, an arrangement not published. Responding to a survey in 1924, he named **Prélude-faune** as his example of a significant "descriptive orchestral work."

393. Smalley, Roger. "Debussy and Messiaen." **Musical Times** 109, no. 1500 (Feb. 1968): 128-31.

Refers to passages in Messiaen's **Technique de mon langage musical**, in which he notes his use of the descending major 6th as germinal and its derivation from added-tone chords. Particular chords borrowed from **Pelléas** occur in **Poèmes pour mi**. Messiaen traces certain of the modes of limited transposition and his juxtaposition of apparently unrelated sound blocks to D's influence.

* Souris, André. "Debussy et Stravinsky." **Revue belge de musicologie** 16 (1962). See item 140.

394. Spencer, Williametta. "André Caplet, aussi "musicien français" [in English]. **Revue belge de musicologie** 36-38 (1982-84): 162-74.

Explores Caplet's biography more extensively than in the following source. Notes his association with the progressive artistic activists **Les apaches**, with Ravel, and with D as conductor and confidant.

395. ------. "The Influence and stylistic heritage of André Caplet." Ph.D. diss., Musicology, University of Southern California, 1974. 404 p. DA 35/04A, p. 2329; UM no. DCJ 74-21510.

A full study of the life and music of Caplet. Précis of her findings appear in the articles listed above and below.

396. ------. "The relationship between André Caplet and Claude Debussy." **Musical Quarterly** 66, no. 1 (Jan. 1980): 112-31.

Caplet conducted the first performance of **Le martyre** and the first London and Boston performances of **Pelléas**. The article reviews Caplet's role as artistic confidant from 1907-1914. Cites their more important correspondence. See also M. Pinchard, "Debussy et A. Caplet," **Musica** 9 (Feb. 1959), 49.

397. Staempfli, Edward. "**Pelléas und Mélisande**: Eine Gegenüberstellung der Werke von Claude Debussy und Arnold Schoenberg." **Schweizerische Musikzeitung/Revue musicale suisse** 112, no. 2 (March-April 1972): 65-72.

D's setting of **Pelléas** stands in contrast to the Wagnerian tradition, which Schoenberg followed. D's opera represents a perfect musicalization of the text, whereas Schoenberg's symphonic poem is an ingenious "misinterpretation." The conclusion of both works (the death of Mélisande) demonstrates their main differences: Schoenberg is bound to an outwardly dramatic presentation of death while D is delicate and spiritual.

398. Stahnke, Manfred. "Gedanken zu Harry Partch." **Neuland** 2 (May 1982): 243-51.

Develops a notation for Partch's music and his tuning system. Discusses his distance from traditional Western music and the well-tempered system. Shows comparisons to Schumann, Wagner, Scriabin, and D.

399. Stedron, Milos. "Janácek, verismus a impresionismus." **Casopis Moravského Musea** [Journal

of Moravian Music] 53-54 (1968-69): 125-54. In Czech.

Presents a facsimile of Janácek's heretofore unknown analysis of **La mer**, an important influence on him. Deliberates whether Janácek relates more to Impressionism or to Realism and even **Verismo**. Discusses the performances of D's music that he heard in Brno. Further see the article on Janácek in **Grove VI**, which lists the contents of his personal library, including scores by D.

400. Stempel, Larry. "Not even Varèse Can Be an Orphan." **Musical Quarterly** 60, no. 1 (Jan. 1974): 46-60.

Important corollary to item 244. Discusses a newly recovered **mélodie** by Varèse and its links to tradition. Relates his melodic and harmonic configurations to **L'ombre des arbres** and **Pelléas**. Views D as the inspiration of Varèse's "liberation of sound."

401. Stone, Else, and Kurt Stone, editors. **The Writings of Elliott Carter**. Bloomington: Indiana University Press, 1977. 390 p. ML 60.C22; ISBN 0-253-36720-4.

This collection of Carter's writings contains frequent mention of D. Carter credits him with the first formulation of the 20th-century direction toward a "fresher musical psychology." He finds D's conceptions at a height in the later works such as **Jeux**. D's ideas fell on fertile ground among the Viennese school (Schoenberg, Berg, Webern) but also for Ives, who appears entirely familiar with D's music and whose conceptions frequently seem to relate to Carter's. D explored non-sequential developmental form, "a new flow of musical thought and expression," which preoccupied Carter, too.

402. Strauss, Richard and Romain Rolland. **Corres pondence; Fragments de journal**. Foreword by G. Samazeuilh. Cahiers 3 of series **Cahiers Romain Rolland**. Paris: Albin Michel, 1951. 243 p. PQ 263505 A19 vol. 3.

Rolland recalls attending a performance of **Pelléas** with Strauss, who appeared not to appreciate the work greatly. Other references throughout discuss D, the aesthetics of his times, and his artistic relationship to the German school. Further see item 374.

403. Stravinsky, Igor. **An Autobiography.** Translation of **Chroniques de ma vie** (1936) by E.W. White. London: Chalder and Boyars, 1975. x, 176 p. ISBN 0-7145-1063-7; ML 410.S932 A22 1975.

Valuable for Stravinsky's personal views and recollections of his close relationship to D. Further see the following three items.

404. ------. **Selected Correspondence.** Vol. 3. Edited and translated by R. Craft. New York: Knopf, 1985. 543 p. ML410.S932 A395; ISBN 0-394-54220-7.

Contains the principal correspondence to and from D, Stravinsky, and Emma Debussy, including eight letters from D. Valuable also for a view of Stravinsky's circle and his central role in 20th-century music from D's time onward.

405. ------. **Avec Stravinsky: lettres inédites de Claude Debussy** [et al.]. Illustrated, with a drawing by Albert Giacommetti. Commentary by R. Craft. Monaco: Editions du Rocher, 1958. 210 p. ML 410.S932 A4. See also item 404.

406. Stravinsky, Vera and Robert Craft. **Stravinsky in Pictures and Documents.** New York: Simon and Schuster, 1978. ISBN 0-6712- 4382-9; ML 410.S932 S787.

The section "Stravinsky and Debussy" surveys the personal relationship and presents important photos of the two together. Comments on Stravinsky's statement that "Debussy was my father in music." Recalls a number of excerpts from letters of D to Stravinsky and vice versa.

407. Stuckenschmidt, Hans Heinz. "Debussy or Berg?: The Mystery of a Chord Progression." **Musical Quarterly** 51, no. 3 (July 1965): 453-59.

Discusses Berg's and Schoenberg's familiarity with D's music from 1908 or earlier. Berg was particularly attracted to D's music. Points to two identical passages in D's **Pour la danseuse aux crotoles** (from **Six épigraphes antiques**) and Berg's **Vier Lieder**, Op. 2 (song 3). D must have seen the song and subconsciously grasped the progression for its expressive possibilities. An example of striking, close scholarship that provokes further exploration of D's relation to the New Viennese School.

408. Street, Donald. "The Modes of Limited Transposition." **Musical Times** 117, no. 1604 (Oct. 1976): 819-23.

Notes that not all modes in Messiaen's usage were derived by him, associating his mode 1 (whole-tone) with D. Traces other modes to D, Liszt, the Russian Five, and others.

409. Tammaro, Ferrucio. "Mélisande dai quattro volti." **Nuova rivista musicale italiana** 15, no. 1 (Jan.-March 1981): 95-119.

In discussing "Mélisande's four faces," compares the four settings of Maeterlinck's play by D, Schoenberg, Fauré, and Sibelius. Finds that D and Schoenberg plumb the psychological depths of the play, the latter preparing for the aesthetic of **Pierrot lunaire**.

410. Tawaststjerna, Erik. **Sibelius**. Vol. II, 1904-14. Translated by R. Layton. Berkeley and Los Angeles: Univ. of California Press, 1986. 302 p. ISBN 0-5200-3014-1 (vol. 1) and 0-5200-5869-0 (vol. 2); ML 410.S54T293.

During the period in question, the contacts with D's music were especially important. D and Sibelius met in London in 1909. Sibelius's letters state his belief that D would influence the course of musical development. His **Dryad** (1910) has a sense of color and texture that is Debussyian, as do portions of the 4th Symphony. The author frequently refers to aspects relating to D. This major study might be a point of departure for a thorough study of the relationship, which is absent from the literature.

411. Thomas, Werner. "Carl Orffs Skizzen zu Maeterlinck's Treibhausliedern (1913/14)." In **Bericht über den Internationalen Musikwissenschaftlichen Kongress Berlin 1974**, pp. 448-54.

Discusses Orff's 1914 draft of a "Traumspiel" based on 7 poems from Maeterlinck's **Serres chaudes**. Also treats the influence of D's **Nocturnes** on the incomplete project. Reprints the extant sketches and gives a commentary.

412. Tiénot, Yvonne. **Chabrier, par lui-même et par ses intimes**. Paris: Lemoine, 1965. 156 p. ML 410.C393T5.

Chabrier's **Gwendoline** and **Pelléas** reflect a completely differing conception of opera. This book is valuable in studying the artistic relationship.

413. Tiersot, Julien. **Un demi-siècle de musique française (1870-1919)**. 2nd revised edition Paris: Alcan, 1924. 241 p. ML 270.4.T43 1924.

Concludes his study with a chapter on D (pp. 207-228), treating him perceptively as a synthesizer of tendencies and disciple of pure music, music for its integral value. Valuable for a study of D's precursors Franck, Fauré, Chabrier, Saint-Saëns, Guiraud, Lalo, and Chausson. Finds traces of D's innovations in evidence among these. Refers to **Pelléas** and the **Nocturnes** particularly. Tiersot was among the earliest to stress that analogies between D's music and Impressionist painting are frequently too simplistic. One of the most prominent and still valid surveys of the French musical renaissance after 1870.

* ------. **Musiques pittoresques: promenades musicales à l'Exposition de 1889**. Paris: Librairie Fischbacher, 1889. ML 3740.T43.

The primary contemporaneous source on music at the 1889 Exposition in Paris, at which D encountered oriental musics with enthusiasm, and after which he began the absorbtion of non-Western elements into his music. Further see annotation, item 220.

414. Tonazzi, Bruno. "Considerazioni sull 'Omaggio a Debussy' per chitarra di Manuel de Falla." **Il fronimo** 2, no.8 (1974): 9-15.

Stravinsky, Ravel, Satie, Malipiero, Bartók, and de Falla responded to the call by the **Revue musicale** to compose works in homage to D (see item 144). This article focuses on de Falla's composition for guitar, "Le tombeau de Claude Debussy" (1920), which was also published by Chester in 1921 in an arrangement for piano.

415. Toncitch, Voya. "Impresions [sic] sur impressionisme." **Anuario musical** 36 (1981): 151-68.

Reexamines the term itself and the general procedures of the art movement, finding in the elasticity of forms rather than in pictorial quality the true relationship to D. Analyzes music by the following composers, who relate to D's sensibility: Abel Decaux, Per Noergaard (Danish), Luciano Berio, Sylvano Bussotti, Rautavaara (Finnish), M. de Falla, Bartók, Scriabin, Vladimir Rebikoff, Christian Wolff, and La Monte Young. In French.

416. "Tosca." **Avant-scène opéra** 11 (Paris, Sept.-Oct. 1977). 146 p. In French and Italian.
Contains a literal transcription [the only one to date] of the famous conversations between D and his composition teacher Ernest Guiraud. The conversations were noted down by M. Emmanuel. Commentary by A. Hoérée. Also includes excerpts of a letter of Sept. 1890 from D to Guiraud concerning Wagner's **Tristan** and the **Ring**. The youthful reaction to Wagner is made clearer.

417. Ujfalussy, József. "Kodály és Debussy" [Kodály and Debussy]. **Kodály Festschrift** [Magyar zenetörténeti tanulmányok Zoltán Kodály], ed. F. Bónis, pp. 35-42. Budapest: Zenemükiadó, 1977. In Hungarian; summaries in English and German.

Traces the decisive contacts with D during Kodály's 1907 study tour of Paris. A direct influence is seen the early works and with adaptations throughout his life. Kodály held up D as a model whereby his contemporaries could turn from the hegemony of German music, and he combined the inspiration of D with that of Hungarian folk music. Not examined.

418. Vallas, Léon. **D'Indy.** Paris: A. Michel, (vol. I) 1946, (vol. II) 1950.

Vol. I (tome I): La Jeunesse (1851-1886); vol. II (tome II): La Maturité; la vieillesse (1886-1931). Vol. II refers to D, who for d'Indy was "disquieting." Valuable documentation of d'Indy's life, works, and attitudes without, however, a deep account of the great contrasts in musical thought with that of D.

419. Van den Toorn, Pieter C. **The Music of Igor Stravinsky.** New Haven and London: Yale University Press, 1983. 512 p. ISBN 0-3000-2693-5; ML 410.S932 B6 1983.

Recounts thoroughly Stravinsky's thought about D as concerns Stravinsky's opera **The Nightingale**, his **Firebird** and **3 Pieces for String Quartet**, and about D's **En blanc et noir**. Points out obvious borrowings from D but views the two composers' language as dissimilar in important ways. D's rhythmic-metric sense is conspicuously at odds with that of Stravinsky: the former is "typically inconspicuous, vague, passive, and 'loose'" while the latter is "severe and stiff." A reexamination of the stylistic relationship in light of D's precision in both local and large-scale structure (see Howat item 590 and Parks 850) and his tendency toward controlled pitch series, including octatonic uses, might prove helpful. The author perceives D's influence as primarily philosophical. This provocatively close study of Stravinsky, particularly in its analytic probing, well might serve to inspire a similar new and comprehensive analysis of Debussy.

420. Vinay, Gianfranco. "Charles Ives e i musicisti europei: anticipazioni e dipendenze." **Nuova rivista musicale italiana** 7, no. 3-4 (July-Dec. 1973): 417-29.

Studies Ives and his independence from and dependence upon European models. Sonorities and forms suggest the influence of D on Ives, and these aspects anticipate the avant-garde. Ives is viewed as a shrewd manipulator of European models and styles. In some ways Ives anticipates the evolution of musical style in Europe. Compares Ives's **In the Night** to **La mer**. Stresses the "impressionist" idiom but does not investigate the structuralist side of Debussy.

421. Waterhouse, J.C.G. "Debussy and Italian Music," (Portrait of Debussy, 9). **Musical Times** 109, no. 1503 (May 1968): 414-18.

Observes that D influenced Pizzetti, Casella, Malipiero, and Dallapiccola, despite the Italian ambiguity toward foreign sources of inspiration.

422. Westphal, Kurt. "Die moderne Musik im Lichte Debussy's." **Die Musik** (Stuttgart) 20, no. 9 (June 1928): 633-39.

A prominent early study that documents D's reception in Germany explores systematically how key stylistic tendencies influenced others. D's creation of a new sound concept foretold Schoenberg, Stravinsky, and Hindemith. Traces D's innovations in parallel chord successions through to Wellesz and Kodály as well as to the aforementioned composers.

423. White, Eric Walter. "Stravinsky and Debussy." **Tempo** 61-62 (1962): 2-5.

A very brief survey commenting on Stravinsky's remarks about D.

424. ------. **Stravinsky, the Composer and his Works**. Berkeley and Los Angeles: University of California Press, 1966. 608 p. ML 410.S932 W47.

A basic source for Stravinsky research and important in tracing D's relationship, although stylistic connections have been reconsidered by Van den Toorn (420) and others. White records Stravinsky's reaction to **Jeux** and **Prélude-faune**. Appendix B contains letters by D and by Emma Debussy. The Register of Works lists Stravinsky's compositions connected directly with D.

425. Winking, Hans. "Klangflächen bei Bartók bis 1911: zu einigen stilistichen Beziehungen in den Orchesterwerken Béla Bartóks zur Orchestermusik des späten 19. und frühen 20. Jahrhunderts." **Studia musicologia** (Budapest) 24, no. 3-4 (1982): 549-64.

Devotes a short section to comparisons with D, whose **Nocturnes** might have influenced Bartók's **Deux images**. Refers also to **La mer** and to more thorough study in 1907 of D by both Bartók and Kodály.

426. Young, Percy M. **Elgar**. London: Collins, 1955. 447 p. ML 410.E41 Y7.

Elgar once professed a dislike for D, whom he found "lacking guts." Nevertheless, the author finds in certain works of the 1910's, such as **Owls** and **O Wild West Wind**, an influence from D.

427. Zenck, Claudia Maurer. "Debussy: Prophet and Seducer." **Cahiers Debussy** (nouvelle série) 6 (1982): 16-21.

Briefly outlines Debussy's relation to European and U.S. composers after 1950: Stockhausen, Messiaen, Dieter Schnebel, Boulez, Ligeti, Charlemagne Palestine, Giacinto Scelsi, John Cage, and Pauline Oliveros. Broad influences include tonal material and freedom in structure ("sound" composition and non-composed tendencies). This article is important for expanding scholarly horizons toward D's influence today.

4. Performers and other Musical Figures

428. Brody, Elaine. "Viñes in Paris: New Light on 20th-century Performance Practice." In **A Musical Offering: Essays in Honor of Martin Bernstein**, edited by C. Brooke and M. Clinkscale, pp. 45-62. New York: Pendragon, 1977.

The pianist Viñes (1875-1943) championed the moderns D, Ravel, Satie, the Russian school, and De Falla and fellow Spaniards. Sees Viñes as a main inspirer of D's "new" piano idiom after 1901, in effect an idiom of Ravel's communicated through Viñes to D. Performance practices as a topic is periperal in the study to biography, but the citation of Viñes's newly-recovered journal (see 441) and other unpublished material makes this article a primary contribution.

429. Büsser, Henri. **De "Pelléas" aux "Indes galantes"...de la flûte au tambour.** Paris: Librairie A. Fayard, 1955. 282 p. 410.B9816 A3.

Apparently reliable recollections of Büsser's life, touching upon circumstances surrounding **Pelléas**, Gounod, the Conservatoire, the Prix de Rome, A. Carré, A. Messager, and J. Rouché. Büsser was choral **repetiteur** for **Pelléas** and gives direct, journal-like entries dealing with its rehearsals. He also orchestrated **Printemps** and the **Petite Suite**.

430. Carré, Albert. **Souvenirs au théâtre.** Paris: Plon, 1950. 427 p. PN 2638.C31 A3.

An autobiography of Carré, who was administrative director of the Opéra-Comique at the time of **Pelléas**. Describes circumstances of the work, performers, and its reception. Places the work in perspective of other works and their performance.

431. Cuneo-Laurent, Linda. "The Performer as Catalyst: the Role of the Singer Jane Bathori (1877-1970) in the Careers of Debussy, Ravel, Les Six, and Their Contemporaries in Paris, 1904-1926." Ph.D. diss., New York University, 1982. 274 p. DA 8226746. ML 429.B28 C8 microfilm.

Bathori sang the music of the composers named and promoted new talents. She became an impresario in later years, especially in connection with Théâtre du Vieux Colombier.

432. Dietschy, Marcel. "Louis Laloy (1874-1944)." **Bulletin de la Société des Amis de Meudon** 142 (spring-summer 1977): 2276-285.

Discussion of the life of D's first biographer. Laloy was cofounder of the **Mercure musicale** with

Romain Rolland, and he wrote the libretto of Ravel's **Dolly**. Recounts his privileged relationship to D, d'Annunzio, and Rodin. Not examined.

433. Durand, Jacques. **Quelques souvenirs d'un éditeur de musique**. Paris: Durand, 1924 (Vol. I, première série) and 1925 (Vol. II, deuxième série). 136 and 161 p. ML427.D86.

Volume I covers the years from birth in 1865 to 1910. Recalls D and Guiraud, and comments on the genesis of the **Arabesques**, **Petite Suite**, **Cinq poèmes de Baudelaire**, **Quatuor à cordes**, **Pelléas**, the **Chute** and **Diable** projects, and **Martyre**. Volume II spans from 1910 to 1924 and discusses **La mer**, the **Images** for orchestra, **Jeux**, the sonatas, the **Etudes**, and D's manuscripts in general. Invaluable personal recollections that complement the letters to Durand (see item 16), who was D's editor for the music of his maturity.

434. Escher, Rudolf. **Toscanini en Debussy: magie der werkelijkheid**. Rotterdam: Van Sijn & Zonen, 1938. 55 p. In Dutch. ML422.T67.

Discusses the conductor Toscanini's interpretation of **La mer**. Escher's discussion is based on indications pencilled into a score. [This score recently has been recovered at Carnegie Hall in New York.]

435. Garden, Mary, with Louis Biancolli. **Mary Garden's Story**. New York: Simon and Schuster, 1951. ix, 302 p. ML 420.G25 A3.

Reminiscences by D's preferred Mélisande, also including valuable iconography of the opera. The chapter "D and his Mélisande" gives her recollection of the work, D's break with his first wife Lilly, and related matters. For the premiere of **Pelléas**, the Opéra-Comique "had become a cathedral." Garden also performed the **Ariettes oubliées**, **Damoiselle élue**, and **Chansons de Bilitis**. Reports that D once professed a burning love for her, which was cured in short order upon the arrival on the scene of Emma Bardac. Her story of this phase in D's life is romanticized, although her story of Lilly's carrying the torch for D is touching.

436. Inghelbrecht, Désiré-Emile. **Mouvement contraire; Souvenirs d'un musicien.** Paris, 1947. ML 410.I77 A3.

Memoirs of a prominent conductor and devoted champion of Debussy. Inghelbrecht was chorus master for the first performance of **Martyre** in 1911 and later conducted **Pelléas.**

437. Leblanc, Georgette. **Souvenirs (1895-1918).** Paris: B. Grasset, 1931. 342 p. PQ 2625.A6 L4.

Autobiography of a singer who was the wife of M. Maeterlinck, author of the play **Pelléas**. Leblanc gives her account of his conflict with D, after D chose Mary Garden over her (see item 435) to sing Mélisande in the premiere. Leblanc states that D was delighted by her singing and places another twist on their estrangement. She first sang **Pelléas** in Boston in 1912.

438. O'Connor, Garry. **The Pursuit of Perfection: a Life of Maggie Teyte.** London: Gollancz, and New York: Atheneum, 1979. 327 p. ISBN 0-689-10964-4; ML 420.T3903 19796.

Discusses the primary role of Teyte (or Tate) as interpreter of D's songs and of Mélisande in **Pelléas**. Includes her observations on D's tutelage of vocal music and an interview with D first published in **Opera Magazine** (New York) in May 1914. The interview is not reprinted elsewhere and seems not to represent Debussy correctly, probably a fault of the original publication.

439. Tetaz, Numa F. **Ernest Ansermet, interprète.** Lausanne: Payot, and Tours: Van de Velde, 1983. ISBN 2-6010-0386-3.

Discusses how the renowned conductor Ansermet, a master interpreter of D, solved problems common to conductors and players. Individual chapters deal with **La mer** and other works. Not examined.

440. Timbrell, Charles. "Walter Morse Rummel, Debussy's 'Prince of Virtuosos'." **Cahiers Debussy** (nouvelle série) 11 (1987), 24-33.

Rummel premiered the **Etudes** and gave American and English premieres of certain **Préludes**. The article reviews his important concert career in Germany and the United States before his mature life in Paris and later Brussels. Discusses four letters from Debussy to Rummel and gives a preliminary discography of his recordings.

441. Viñes, Ricardo. "Journal inédit." **Revue internationale de musique française** 2 (June 1980): 153-248.

Extracts from the pianist's diary, helpfully organized by the names of the three central figures D, Ravel, and Duparc. Offers an informative view of Parisian musical life 1888-1914 and of the genesis and first performance of D's music.

442. Ysaÿe, Antoine. **Eugène Ysaÿe: sa vie, son oeuvre, son influence.** Brussels and Paris, 1947. Translated by F. Clarkson as **Ysaÿe, by His Son Antoine**. Great Missenden, Buckinghamshire and London: Hill, 1980. 218 p. ML 418.Y8Y783.

Discusses Ysaÿe's part in the genesis of D's **Quatuor** and his relevance to **Pelléas** and the **Nocturnes**. Pages 111-18 include letters by D to Ysaÿe of 22 Sept. 1894, 13 Oct. 1896, 30 Dec. 1903, and one other not dated.

5. Dancers

443. Brody, Elaine. "The Legacy of Ida Rubinstein: Mata Hari of the Ballets Russes." **Journal of Musicology** 4, no. 4 (Fall 1985-86): 491-504.

Rubinstein figured in the composition and performance of many ballets in the early 20th century. Discusses her role in the conception and performance of **Le martyre** and D's consideration of a collaboration in Valéry's ballet-melodrama **Amphion**, later written by Honegger. Her important relationships to Diaghilev and D'Annunzio are traced.

444. Buckle, Richard. **Diaghilev.** New York: Atheneum, 1979. 616 p. ISBN 0-689-10952-0; LC 78-73084; GV 1785.D5 B79 1979b.

Contains an extensive bibliography. A current and extensive study of Diaghilev and Nijinsky and of their contacts with D. Feels that **Jeux** was "sacrificed" to Stravinsky's **Sacre** and was not thoroughly worked out by Nijinsky as choreographer. Surveys the criticism in the press. Also discusses in some detail the Nijinsky-Diaghilev ballet production of **Prélude-faune**.

445. Cherniavsky, Felix. "Maud Allan." **Dance Chronicle: Studies in Dance and the Related Arts** 6, no. 3 (1983): 189-227; and 8, no. 1-2 (1985): 1-50.

The first portion of the study points to her interest in Greek and non-Western dance. The second interprets the **Khamma** affair objectively, noting that Allan was a taskmistress for whom the project had become a costly nightmare and gained her nothing. Refers to Orledge (item 843) for biographical details.

446. Lifar, Serge. **Serge de Diaghilev: sa vie, son oeuvre, sa légende.** Paris: Rocher, 1954. 318 p. GV 1785.D5 L49.

A personal view by a prominent dancer and choreographer. Emphasizes the leadership role of the revue **Le monde de l'art** and the renaissance of culture in late 19th-century Russia. Interesting if somewhat uneven view of the Ballet russe, the "veritable tempest" surrounding its production of **Prélude-faune**, and of **Jeux** and Stravinsky's **Sacre**.

447. Nijinsky, Romola. **Nijinsky.** London: V. Gollancz, Ltd., 1933, and New York: Simon and Schuster, 1934. 447 p. GV 1785.N6 N61934a.

A biography by Nijinsky's wife, offering personal and sometimes contorted views: "D was delighted with the sensation that the **Faune** created." Like Lifar (446), interprets the production of **Jeux** virtually alongside Stravinsky's **Sacre** as shortsighted and serving D poorly. Also see Romola Nijinsky, editor, **The**

Diary of Vaslav Nijinsky. London: Gollancz, 1937. GV 1785 .N6 A3 1937.

6. Writers and Literary Movements

448. Alexander, Jean. **Affidavits of Genius: Edgar Allan Poe and the French Critics, 1847-1924.** Port Washington, New York, and London: Kennikat Press, 1971. 246 p. ISBN 0-8046-9015-4; PS 2638.A45.

An introduction surveys Poe's career. Thereafter gives in translation the major critical writings on Poe, including those by Baudelaire, Delacroix, Huysmans, Mallarmé, and Rémy de Gourmont. Baudelaire is discussed as the critic and writer at the center of Poe's active reception.

449. Bachelard, Gaston. **L'eau et les rêves.** Paris: J. Corti, 1947. 265 p. BF 411.B26 1947. Translated by E. Farrell. **Water and Dreams.** Dallas: Pegasus, 1983. x, 213 p. ISBN 0-911005-01-3; BF 411.B2613 1983.

Draws upon Freudian psychology in interpreting the dream, which is of great importance in Poe's and Mallarmé's work. A provocative source in studying D's relation to the two writers.

450. Balakian, Anna, ed. **The Symbolist Movement in the Literature of European Languages.** Budapest: Akademiai Kiado, 1982. 732 p. ISBN 963-05-2694-8; PN 761.S95 1982.

A far-reaching effort that considers the symbolist movement internationally, containing essays by prominent scholars. An invaluable approach that might be a model for tracing D's musical symbolism and its international impact.

451. Banville, Théodore de. **Oeuvres.** Geneva: Slatkine Reprints, 1972. 9 vols. PQ 1187 .A11972.

Modern edition of the poet Banville's writings, including versions of the many poems D set as songs in his youth. A few literary works and several of the particular versions D set are not included.

452. Baudelaire, Charles. **Oeuvres complètes.** Edited by Claude Pinchois, new ed., 2 vols. Paris: Gallimard, 1975-76. PQ 2191.A1 1975.

For texts in English see **Baudelaire: The Complete Verse.** Translated with introduction by F. Scarfe. London: Anvil Press Poetry, 1986. ISBN 0-85646-151-2; PQ 2191.A263 1986.

453. Bernard, Suzanne. **Mallarmé et la musique.** Paris: Nizet, 1959. 184 p. ML80.M14B4.

A detailed analysis of his texts in terms of their musical meanings and expression. Contains a helpful discussion of French literary Wagnerism and of the text **L'après-midi d'un faune.** An appendix discusses direct relationships with musicians, including Debussy.

454. Berton, Henry. **Henri de Régnier: Le poète et le romancier.** Paris: B. Grasset, 1910. 154 p.

A valuable contemporary account of the poet and literary friend of early years. Régnier had Symbolist aims.

455. Billy, André. **Les frères Goncourt: la vie littéraire à Paris pendant la seconde moitié du XIXe siècle.** Paris: Flammarion, 1954. 518 p. PQ2261.Z5B5. Translated by M. Shaw. **The Goncourt Brothers.** New York: Horizon Press, 1960. 352 p. PQ 2261.Z5 B53.

Valuable for tracing late-century literary and artistic figures from the decline of Romanticism to the predominance of Symbolism.

456. ------. **Huysmans et cie.** Paris: Nizet, 1963. 227 p. PQ 282 .B48.

Discusses the kindred spirits Chateaubriand, Sainte-Beuve, Jean Moréas, M. Jacob, and Prosper Merimée. Far more important in understanding Huysmans's private world than D's, whose wider environment still may be elucidated.

457. Blanche, Jacques-Emile. **Portraits of a Lifetime.** Translated and edited by W. Clement. London: Dent, 1937, and New York: Coward-McCann, 1938. xx, 316 p. ND 553.B56 A33.

Autobiographical discussions by a friend of D who served as intermediary between Diaghilev, Nijinsky, and D during the genesis of **Jeux**, to the scenario of which D first objected. Describes the personalities thus from the vantage point of direct observation: Nijinski was "ill-humored...puny, featureless." Recalls the inspiration of **Jardins sous la pluie** in Blanche's garden. Further describes **Damoiselle élue** in the context of the rising popularity of English letters.

458. Bonmariage, Sylvain. **Catherine [de Givré] et ses amis: Claude Debussy, Pierre Louÿs, Guillaume Apollinaire, Anna de Noailles, P.-J. Toulet, Léon-Paul Fargue.** Gap: Ophrys, 1949. 236 p. PQ 2607.E745 Z65.

Reminisces about the period 1900-1910 and includes a chapter on D, Toulet, and Louÿs. The author comments in passing on **Pelléas** as his "great musical revelation." Mixes fact with imagination but comments on the spirit of D's artistic circles.

459. Brody, Elaine. "La famille Mendès: a literary link between Wagner and Debussy." **Music Review** 33, no. 3 (Aug. 1972): 177-89.

Describes the personal relationship of Catulle Mendès and Judith Gautier, both of whom supported Wagner in France and associated with D even after their marital separation. Mendès and D collaborated on the aborted grand opera **Rodrigue et Chimène**. He served to focus the young composer on Wagner.

460. Cano, Cristina. "Victor Segalen e Claude Debussy." **Nuova rivista musicale italiana** 14, no. 2 (April-June 1980): 178-204.

The correspondence between D and Segalen from 1906-16 shows, within the context of contemporary culture, the influence D had on the writer Segalen and on his libretto (later book) **Orphée roi**.

461. Cellucci-Marcone, Silvana. **D'Annunzio e la musica.** L'Aquila: Japadre, 1972. 106 p. PQ 4804.C4.

Devotes a chapter to the relation to D. D'Annunzio came into contact with **Pelléas** early and soon began to consider a collaboration, culminating in **Le martyre**.

462. Cocteau, Jean. **Coq et l'arlequin** [Notes autour de la musique 1918]. Republished with preface by Georges Auric. Paris: Stock, 1979. ISBN 2-2340-1081-0; ML66.C64 1979.

Observes an imprecision or haziness in D's rhythmic style and prefers that of Satie in **Parade** and Stravinsky in **Sacre**. Further articulates the general aesthetic of Satie and Les Six. A basic writing concerned with aesthetics just after D.

463. Colette, Sidonie Gabrielle. **Colette: Oeuvres complètes.** Paris: Le Fleuron (Flammarion), 1948-50. PG 2605.028 1949.

Complete writings by the author, amateur musician, and famous critic of D's time. Colette was for a time the wife of Willy (Henry Gauthiers-Villars), also a writer and critic. For perhaps a more current version see **Oeuvres complètes de Colette**. Editions du centenaire. 16 vols. Paris: Club de L'Honnête Homme, 1973. PQ 2605.O28 1973.

464. Court, Raymond. "Mallarmé et Debussy." **Revue des sciences humaines** (1987, no. 1). Not examined.

465. Doherty, Thomas W. "Suarès et deux musiciens de son temps: Wagner et Debussy." **Revue des lettres modernes** 346-50 (1973): 105-23.

Traces the evolution of Suarès's thought on Wagner and D as found in his books and critical writings. Suarès begins to comment on D in 1890, finding him a painter of emotions that are excited by an external stimulus. Suarès concluded that D will prove to be one of the 3 or 4 primary composers of the past 200 years.

466. Eliot, T.S. "E.A. Poe et la France." Translated into French by H. Fluchère. **La table ronde** (Dec. 1948): 1973-92.

Explores the concepts of time and eternity and poetic purity as they concern Baudelaire and his successors, who were influenced by Poe. That circle possessed a consciousness of self, sensibility, and preoccupation with language of and for itself that has deeply influenced 20th-century poetry, in Eliot's view. May inform an analysis of D's interest in Poe.

467. Escal, Françoise. "Le debussysme de Jacques Rivière." **Revue d'histoire littéraire de la France** 5 (1985), 837-57. Not examined.

468. Fowlie, Wallace. **Climate of Violence; the French Literary Tradition from Baudelaire to the Present.** New York and London: Macmillan, 1967. xi, 274 p. PQ 145.6.V5F6.

Points to the **Quatuor** of D when discussing Proust and views **Pelléas** as a high moment in the brilliant period 1895-1914. Proposes that the theme of violence and cruelty is most significant in modern French literature. Discusses the period 1850 to the present by large movements: Baudelaire, "The Transcendence of Language" [Symbolism], "In the Wake of Symbolism" [Gide and Proust], "Picasso's Paris at Turn of Century" [Apollinaire, Jacob], "The Postwar Climate" [Existentialism, Mauriac, Antitheatre], and the "New Writers and Critics" [Camus, Sartre, Anouilh]. Helps to place D's literary tendencies within a broad perspective.

469. ------. **Jean Cocteau: The History of a Poet's Age.** Bloomington, Indiana: Indiana Univ. Press, 1966. 181 p. PQ2605.O15Z683.

Discusses D in the context of Satie's **Parade** and Cocteau's **Coq et l'arlequin**, which was an attack of sorts on Debussysme. Cocteau championed Satie as the artist who teaches the boldest lesson after those of D and Stravinsky: the lesson of simplicity.

470. ------. **Mallarmé.** London: Dobson, and Chicago: Univ. of Chicago Press, 1953. 209 p. PQ 2344.Z5F58.

Mallarmé's **L'après-midi** was understood in the poet's circle to be destined for the stage. Fowlie views the work as a metaphor for the life of the senses and that of the creative artist. (Further see Berman, item 699, and Wenk, item 898, regarding relation to D's setting). Notes D's participation in Mallarmé's "Tuesday evening" gatherings and traces in clear terms the themes and manner of Mallarmé's art.

471. Gauthier-Villars, Henry [pseud.: Willy]. See two collections of music criticism: **Bains de sons.** Paris, 1893; and **La mouche des croches.** Paris, 1894. Possible influence on the critical manner of D's **Monsieur Croche.**

472. Gide, André. **Journal.** Paris: Gallimard, 1951-54. 2 volumes. PQ 2613.I2Z528 1951 (1954).

Volume I deals with the period 1889-1939; volume II 1939-49. Gide writes perceptively upon hearing **Nuages** and observing an orchestral rehearsal attended by D. Sheds light on the period its literary leaders. Otherwise, there is no obvious indication that Gide sensed D's full achievement.

473. Goncourt, Edmond et Jules de. **Memoires de la vie littéraire.** Edited by R. Ricatte. Monaco: Imprimerie Nationale, 1956-58. PQ 2261.Z5A3.

A collection in 22 volumes of writings by the literary brothers, covering 1851-1896. A valuable lexicon indexes not names but literary terms and concepts found in the journals, which contributed to the nature of literary French in the late 19th century. Useful for tracing the particular colorations of thought and vocabulary in D's times and writing.

474. Goubault, Christian. "Colette et Debussy, 'compaignons de chaine' au **Gil blas** en 1903." **Revue internationale de musique française** 17 (June 1985): 75-86.

Colette, writer, critic, and wife of Willy, wrote her first by-line on music in **Gil Blas**, Jan. 12, 1903. D first appeared in **Gil Blas** as critic in the same issue. Compares their views and aesthetics. Reprints a March 7, 1903, critique by D for the first time, apparently, which concerns a reprise of Ernest Reyer's opera **La statue** (1861).

475. Guichard, Léon. "Bourget, Laforgue et Debussy." **Studi francesi** 19, no. 2 nuova serie 56 (May-Aug. 1975): 244-51. In French.

Discusses D's friendship with both writers and his setting of nine poems by Bourget. Inquires into the reasons why D and the poet Laforgue would take an interest in Bourget, who for Guichard is inferior. Points to the impact of Mme Vasnier's taste upon D in his youthful choice of poets, but does not account for the large number of settings of the contemporary Banville, a pacesetter. Laforgue finds in Bourget a progressive element relating to Baudelaire and the Symbolists.

476. Gullace, Giovanni. **Gabriele D'Annunzio in France: a Study of Cultural Relations.** Syracuse, New York: Syracuse University Press, 1966. 243 p. PQ 4804.G8.

Discusses the plays written in France, including **Le martyre**. Studies the reception of the play and D's extensive incidental music, for which critical reception was mixed. Recognizes certain artistic and technical misjudgements by D'Annunzio that contributed to the failure. Does not discuss D's music in depth.

477. Hertz, David M. **The Tuning of the Word: The Musico-Literary Poetics of the Symbolist Movement.** Carbondale and Edwardsville, Illinois: Southern Illinois University Press, 1987. xiv, 241 p. ISBN 0-8093-1312-x; ML 3849.H39 1987.

Observes that Symbolist poetics, which generated subsequent development of modern poetry, was born of the spirit of music. A continual cross-fertilization occurred. Chapter 1 explores Mallarmé's musico-literary aesthetic. Chapter 2 discusses the **Revue wagnérienne**, which yielded to Mallarmé's influence. D is the first major artist to appreciate Mallarmé's significance. Chapters 3 and 4 study the relationship in **Prélude-faune**; also considers the **Proses lyriques**, Baudelaire songs, **Fêtes galantes** (both sets), **Ariettes**

oubliées, and **Trois poèmes de Mallarmé**. Chapters 6 and 7 discuss the "lyric play" and Symbolist opera, with particular emphasis on **Pelléas**. D grasped both Mallarmé and Wagner with extraordinary perspicacity, although the former is viewed as the key to D's development. Wagner's "didactic manner of constructing new meanings" proved unattractive. Hertz is not probing musically but is particularly helpful concerning literary relations.

* Jarocinski, Stefan. **Debussy: Impressionism and Symbolism**. See item 564.

478. Jean-Aubry, Georges. "Laforgue et la musique." **Revue de Genève** (1921, no. 16): 443-59.

Discusses D's attraction to Laforgue in reference to **Prélude-faune**. Laforgue sojourned in Berlin for a time and communicated Wagnerian ideals to France. Quotes from Laforgue's writings, which the author relates to Baudelaire's.

479. La Jeunesse, Ernest. **Les nuits, les ennuis et les âmes de nos plus notoires contemporains**. Paris: Didier-Perrin et Cie., 1896. 402 p. PQ 2623.A4N8.

Essays on primary literary figures around D. In the preface states his purpose to "bare the soul" of literary subjects. Discusses in a romanticized manner A. France, Pierre Loti, P. Bourget, A. and L. Daudet, E. Zola, J.M. de Hérédia, H. de Régnier, C. Mendès, F. Coppée, J.K. Huysmans, M. Maeterlinck [by nature a "naïve poet"], Jean Lorrain, J. Richepin, and others in D's wider literary environment. Valuable for contemporary understanding of literary movements.

480. Langham Smith, Richard. "Debussy and the Pre-Raphaelites." **Nineteenth-Century Music** 5, no. 2 (Fall 1981): 95-109.

Centers on **La damoiselle élue**, noting an early manifestation in **Diane au bois**, and sees later occurrences of the aesthetic tendencies in **Pelléas** and **Le martyre**. Refers to the influential thought of the writers Burne-Jones, Tennyson, Bourget, and Banville. An insightful article on D's literary tastes in the 1890s.

481. Lefebvre, Louis. **Une grande figure du symbolisme, Charles Morice: le poète et l'homme.** Paris: Perrin, 1926. 254 p. PQ 2625.O76 Z58.

Discusses Morice's relationship to Laforgue, Mallarmé, Huysmans, Verlaine, and the **Revue wagnérienne**. Morice (d. 1919) was a proponent of Wagnerian thought in France in the 1880s and a key figure in the Symbolist movement. He collaborated with D on the project **Crimen amoris** (**Fêtes galantes**).

482. Lehmann, Andrew George. **The Symbolist Aesthetic in France 1885-1895.** 2nd edition. Folcroft, Pa.: Folcroft Library Ed., 1974. 328 p. ISBN 0-8414-5665-8; PQ 295.S9L4 1974b.

Observes that this first phase of Symbolism was marked by intense discussion, uncertainty, and lack of cohesiveness. Refers often to D in context and to the place of his **Prélude-faune** within the movement. Notes the general turn from Wagnerian precepts in the 1890s and points to **Pelléas** in that regard.

483. Lesure, François. "Claude Debussy et Henri Ghéon." In **Art Nouveau, Jugendstil und Musik**, pp. 67-72. Zurich: Atlantis, 1980. ISBN 3-7611-0604-1; ML 55.S396 1980.

Ghéon was the pseudonym of Henri Vangeon, a critic for **Le mercure musical** and **L'ermitage**, and later a Catholic dramatist in the circle of André Gide. His correspondence with Gide reflects upon D's music and illustrates the temper of the times. Ghéon wrote an article on **Pelléas** and referred to its subtle, non-heroic character, for which D wrote a letter of thanks. Ghéon's comments on D'Annunzio's text of **Le martyre** were less favorable.

484. ------. "Le 'Jeune Prix de Rome' de Catulle Mendès." **Cahiers Debussy** (nouvelle série) 6 (1982): 36-40.

Reprints the original article on "The Young Prix de Rome Recipient" from **Le gaulois** of 1876, which purports a Socratic dialogue between an "old Wagnerite" and the young composer, both unidentified. Debussy biographers have linked this article, which was republished with few changes in the 1884 **Revue wagnérienne**, more directly to D than Mendès originally intended.

485. Lockspeiser, Edward. **Debussy et Edgar Poe.** Preface by André Schaeffner. Monaco: Editions du Rocher, 1961 [1962]. 97 p. ML 410.D28 L82.

An essential source concerning the Poe projects **La chute de la maison Usher** and **Le diable dans le beffroi**. Views Poe as the counterpart of Wagner in D's extended preoccupation with these works and his developing aesthetic of the "inconscient." Refers to the literary influences of Swinburne and Rossetti and discusses the genesis of the Poe projects. Analyzes the existing manuscript scores and librettos. Primary sources appended (if in dim photo-reproduction) are the text of **Diable**, an extract from the libretto first version of **Chute**, the complete extant libretto of **Chute** (Bibl. nat. MS 9885), and musical sketches of **La saulaie** (on a text by Rossetti), **Chute**, and **Diable**.

486. Loncke, Joycelynne. **Baudelaire et la musique.** Paris: Nizet, 1975. 262 p. ML 80.B35 L6.

Traces Baudelaire's fascination with Wagner and his contacts with other musicians.

487. Louÿs, Pierre. **Journal intime (1882-1891).** Paris: Editions Excelsior, 1929. PQ 2623.O8Z49 1920.

A primary source concerning D's intimate friendship with the writer Louÿs and projects in common. Also see **Pierre Louÿs, Oeuvres complètes**. Geneva: Slatkine Reprints, 1973. PQ2623.O8 1973.

488. Mantelli, G.A. "Debussy e Mallarmé." **Rivista musicale italiana** 39, no. 4 (Oct.-Dec. 1932): 545-53.

An early study superseded by subsequent ones of depth. Nonetheless a valuable early interpretation of D as a Symbolist. Refers nearly exclusively to **Prélude-faune** when discussing D's music, although does project the sensibility to **La mer**, **Ibéria**, and the **Préludes** for piano book II.

489. Maurin, Mario. **Henri de Régnier, le labyrinthe et le double.** Montreal: Presses de l'Université de Montréal, 1972. 288 p. ISBN 0-8405-0166-8; PQ 2635.E34Z73.

Discusses D in connection with Régnier's "labyrinthian arabesques."

490. Michaud, Guy. **Le message poétique du symbolisme.** Paris: Nizet, 1947. 3 volumes: I, L'aventure poétique; II, La révolution poétique; III, L'univers poétique. PQ 439.M55.

An essential, extensive study of lines of thought that moved D profoundly. Volume II considers the impact of Wagner in the 1880's and the interrelation of literature with painting and Decadent thought. Volume III discusses Maeterlinck, Mallarmé, mysticism, and H. de Régnier, placing these helpfully within the broad context of Symbolism. For the broad view, may be read profitably alongside Balakian (item 450).

491. Millan, Gordon. **Pierre Louÿs ou le culte de l'amitié: essais.** Aix-en-Provence: Pandora, 1979. 306 p. ISBN 2-86371-009-5; PQ 2623.O8Z67.

A portrait of Louÿs through his friendships with Valéry, Gide, Wilde, Debussy, etc., based on original sources, many unpublished. An extended chapter (pp. 201-254) devoted to relation to D, based on Louÿs' diary and letters. Provides important insight into D's artistic circle and times, 1880-1900.

492. Oleggini, Léon. **Au coeur de Claude Debussy.** Paris: René Julliard, 1947. 219 p. ML 410.D28O45.

In effect a survey of D's life and main works, but offers thoughtful and quite pertinent interpretations and conclusions that are predominantly literary. Draws parallels with Bergson's psychological and metaphysical thought. D's reference to nature, for Oleggini, may be seen in light of Bergson.

493. Pakenham, Michael. "Un ami inconnu de Rimbaud et de Debussy: Henri Mercier." **Revue des sciences humaines** (Lille) Fasc. 111 (July-Sept. 1963): 401-07.

Mercier was a poet and the director of **Revue de monde nouveau**. D refered to their acquaintance in a letter of 1889 to R. Godet (see **Lettres à deux amis**, item 19).

494. Palmer, Christopher. "Debussy, Ravel, and Alain-Fournier." **Music and Letters** 50, no. 2 (April 1969): 267-72.

Alain-Fournier (pseudonym of Henri Alban Fournier) was a writer who tutored T.S. Eliot. In his single novel **Le grand meaulnes**, he resembles D in the preoccupation with the sea and childhood. Other elements of his writing similarly relate to D, whose music he knew well but whom he did not know personally. He was acquainted with Ravel.

495. Petitfils, Pierre. **Verlaine**. Paris: Julliard, 1981. 508 p. ISBN 2-2600-0236-6; PQ 2464.P4.

A current, extensive biography of the poet.

496. Philips, C. Henry. "The Symbolists and Debussy." **Music and Letters** 13, no. 3 (July 1932): 298-311.

Somewhat rambling but valuable as an early study that stresses Symbolist literary connections.

497. Postic, Marcel. **Maeterlinck et le symbolisme**. Paris: Nizet, 1970. 255 p. PQ 2625.A61P6.

Maeterlinck (1862-1949) represents his age and continues to exert an influence, not least through D's opera **Pelléas**. Maeterlinck is perhaps the primary exponent of Symbolism in the theater. Traces the evolution of his aesthetic and, briefly, its connections to D.

498. Praz, Mario. **The Romantic Agony**. 2nd ed. London and New York: Oxford University Press, 1970. ISBN 0-1921-2511-7; PN 755.P713 1970.

Translation of L carne, la morte e il diavolo nella letteratura romantica.

A richly informed overview of main themes and figures of literary Romanticism, from Goethe and Shelley to the post-Romantics and Symbolists D'Annunzio, Verlaine, and Swinburne. Also valuable as a source on lesser figures in D's circle, such as Toulet and Villiers de L'Isle-Adam.

499. Quinn, Patrick. **The French Face of Edgar Poe.** Carbondale, Ill.: Southern Illinois Press, 1957. 310 p. PS 2638.Q5.

A provocative discussion of what Poe meant to the French, who understood him most fully. Emphasizes the connections to Baudelaire, Mallarmé, and the Symbolist movement in general.

500. Robichez, Jacques. **Précis de littérature française du XXe siècle.** Paris: Presses universitaires de France, 1985. 467 p. ISBN 2-13-038875-2; PQ 305.P74 1985.

The first section of this comprehensive survey treats the period 1885-1914. Chapter 1 considers the novels of Paul Bourget, Huysmans, Mirbeau, and Zola and such issues as Romanticism. Chapter 2 discusses the theater of Lugné-Poe, Maeterlinck, J. Richepin, and E. Rostand. Chapter 4 discusses the prose of E. Renan and R. de Gourmont, and Chapter 5 the poetry by Régnier, Vielé-Griffin, Verlaine, Mallarmé, and Apollinaire and such issues as classicism, symbolism, violence, and the poet in the city.

501. Rolf, Marie. "Mauclair and Debussy: the Decade from **Mer belle aux îles sanguinaires** to **La mer**." **Cahiers Debussy** 11 (1987), 9-23.

The writer and critic Camille Mauclair was a close associate of Debussy in the 1890's. A chief concept of his was the fusion of the arts, inspired in part by Wagner. His 1893 short story "Mer belle aux îles sanguinaires" might have influenced the form and program of **La mer** movement I. This valuable article concludes with the entire text of the short story.

502. Schmidt-Garre, Helmut. "Rimbaud-Mallarmé-Debussy: Parallelen zwischen Dichtung und Musik." **Musik im Unterricht** 58, no. 5 (May 1967): 157-67.

The aesthetics and formal procedures of Poe, Baudelaire, Rimbaud, and Mallarmé influenced Debussy. Not examined.

503. Souffrin, Eileen. "Banville et la musique." **French Studies** (Oxford) 9 (July 1955): 238-45.

A survey only, where D is concerned, but a supplement to item 879, showing the connections of D, other musicians, and Banville. Contains a letter of 1890 by Banville to Massenet, who had suggested a collaboration.

* Souffrin-Le Breton, Eileen. "Debussy lecteur de Banville." See item 879.

504. Stimpson, Brian. **Paul Valéry and Music: A Study of the Techniques of composition in Valéry's Poetry**. Cambridge: Cambridge University Press, 1984. ISBN 0-521-25608-9; PQ 2643.A26 Z7547 1984.

Informative about literary trends in D's time and just after. Discusses Valéry's specific relation to D, beginning in 1893, and otherwise mentions D within the literary context.

505. Verlaine, Paul. **Oeuvres complètes**. Paris: Le Club meilleur du livre, 1959-60. PQ2463.A1 1959.

The complete writings of an essential poet for D. Also see Verlaine, **Oeuvres en prose**. Paris: Gallimard, 1972 (PQ 2463.A13) and **Oeuvres poétiques complètes**. Paris: Gallimard, 1962. PQ 2463.A6 1962.

* Wenk, Arthur B. **Claude Debussy and the Poets**. See item 898.

506. Woodson, Thomas, compiler. **Twentieth-Century Interpretations on "The Fall of the House of**

Usher." Englewood Cliffs, N.J.: Prentice Hall, 1969. iii, 122 p. ISBN 0-1330-1721-4; PS 2614.W6.

A useful collection of essays permitting a view of Poe criticism at present.

7. Visual Arts

507. "Debussy et les artistes au tournant du siècle." In **Eureka**, pp. 55-212. Tokyo: Seidosha, 1986. In Japanese.

Contains articles by K. Edo, A. Takahashi, I. Hashimoto, M. Moroi, A. Kanno, I. Aoyagi, Y. Kono, and F. Lesure. Not examined.

508. Denis, Maurice. **Histoire de l'art réligieux.** Paris: Flammarion, 1939. 314 p. N 7830.D35. Concerns Christian art and symbolism.

509. ------. **Nouvelles théories sur l'art moderne, sur l'art sacre, 1914-1921.** Paris: Rouart et Watelin, 1922. 290 p. N 6848.D46 1922.

A discussion by a painter and a friend of D concerning symbolism in the visual arts. Further see Denis, **Du symbolisme au classicisme: théories.** Edited O.R. d'Allones. Paris: Hermann, 1964. 181 p. ND 547.D38.

Concerns theories of Symbolism as a movement in the visual arts.

510. Jullian, Philippe. **The Symbolists.** Translated by Mary Anne Stevens. London and New York: Phaidon/Praeger, 1973. 240 p. ISBN 0-7148-1590-X; NX 549.A1J8413.

A useful introduction to Symbolism in French and Belgian art. Discusses such painters as Gauguin, Moreau, Puvis de Chavannes, Redon, and Blanche. Relates these to Verlaine, Fauré, and D (**Damoiselle élue**).

511. ------. **The Triumphe of Art Nouveau: Paris Exhibition 1900.** London: Phaidon, 1974. 216 p. Translated by S. Hardman. ISBN 0-7148-1606-x: N 6850.J8413 1974b.

At the 1900 exhibition, D's **Quatuor** was heard, although music was the least honored of the arts. Notes that D visited the oriental theaters but discusses him only in passing. Nonetheless is a valuable discussion of the Art nouveau background. Richly illustrated.

512. Lockspeiser, Edward. **Music and Painting.** London: Harper and Row, 1973. 197 p. ISBN 006-435325-7; ML 3849.L62 1973.

Traces the interaction of music and art for 19th- and 20th-century musicians, painters, poets, and critics. D's connections are shown in Lockspeiser's biography (item 85), but the present source is useful for tracing still wider relationships. Contains as an appendix an English translation of D's libretto for **La chute-Usher**, after Poe.

513. Martinotti, Sergio. "Il dialogo tra le arti." **Rassegna dell'instruzione artistica** 3, no. 1 (1968): 50-64.

Explores possible relationships between D's music and Paul Klee's paintings. Not examined.

514. Praz, Mario. **Mnemosyne: the Parallel between Literature and the Visual Arts.** Princeton, New Jersey: Princeton University Press, 1970. xv, 261 p. PN 53.P7.

Illustrated by 121 illustrations. Argues that arts media frequently exhibit a unity of taste, sense of spatial and temporal interpenetration, and even structure. Does not cite D specifically but discusses the closely related movements of Art nouveau and Pre-Raphaelitism. Remains cautious, allowing for contradictory views of interrelationships among the arts and their technical procedures. Nonetheless, the provocative arguments invite a close reading when relating D's structures and processes to those of kindred arts.

515. Redon, Odilon. **A soi-même, journal (1867-1915): notes sur la vie, l'art et les artistes.** Paris: J. Corti, 1961. 188 p. N 7454.R35A2 1961xp.

Valuable appraisal of visual arts in D's time, by his friend but curiously without direct reference to D. Further see Redon, **Lettres d'Odilon Redon, 1878-1916.** Paris and Brussels: Van Oest, 1923. 142 p.

516. Rewald, John. **Cézanne: A Biography.** New York: Abrams, 1986. 288 p. ISBN 0-8109- 0775-5; ND 553.C33 R37 1986.

Cézanne's stature as "father of modern art" is parallel to D's in music. For Cézanne's widow, "He didn't know what he was doing. He didn't know how to finish his pictures."

517. ------. **The History of Impressionism.** 4th rev. edition. New York: Museum of Modern Art, 1973. 672 p. ISBN 0-8707-0360-6; N 6465.I4 R48 1973.

A standard survey of the movement in the visual arts, from the 1855 Paris World's Fair, the Barbizon School, Salon des Refusés, Monet, Pissaro, Renoir, Sisley, and Manet, to Seurat, Gauguin, Van Gogh, and Post-Impressionism. Also see J. Rewald, **Post-Impressionism from Van Gogh to Gauguin.** 3rd ed. rev. New York: Museum of Modern Art, 1978. 590 p.

518. Schaeffner, André. "Debussy et ses rapports avec la peinture." See item 127.

Discusses D's relation to such visual arts movements as Impressionism and Neo-Impressionism (Renoir, Monet, Gauguin, Van Gogh), the Nabis, and the Fauves. The author also relates D to the figures P. Klée, Seurat, and Signac and to the "painters of the dream world" Puvis de Chavannes, Gauguin, Moreau, Redon, and Whistler. Views these latter to be closest to D in aesthetic.

A vivid discussion followed the reading of this paper that concerned connections between Impressionism, Art nouveau, and the group of **Apaches**.

519. Selz, Peter and Mildred Constantine, editors. **Art Nouveau.** Revised edition. New York: Museum of Modern Art, 1975. 192 p. ISBN 0-87070-222-x; N 6465.A7 S4 1975.

Mentions in context D's **Quatuor** and **La damoiselle élue**. Traces Art nouveau from the English "Arts and Crafts" movement of the 1880s and relates it to the quest for synthesis of the arts, Symbolism, nature, exoticism, and Japanese and other oriental art.

520. Terrasse, Antoine. **Denis: intimités**. Lausanne: IAB, 1970. 63 p. ND 553.D365T47.

Maurice Denis (1870-1943) was a painter who befriended D in the circle of the Salon des Indépendants and the **Revue blanche**. Denis was moved by Poe's and the Symbolists' writing. His painting relates to Symbolism, the Nabis, and later to "un nouveau classicisme."

521. Vaughan, Gerard. "Maurice Denis and the Sense of Music." **Oxford Art Journal** 7 (1984): 38-48.

Denis's **Definition du néo-traditionnisme** of 1890 was among the first discussions of the synthetist-symbolist aesthetic of Gauguin and his circle. Denis as a painter associated with the Nabis (Bonnard and Vuillard) and the literary Symbolists (Dujardin, Gide, Lugné-Poe). He contributed to French Wagnerism and produced the 1892 deluxe edition cover of **La damoiselle élue**. Denis's art is viewed as more formalistic than D's "Impressionist" art, a conclusion inviting reassessment in light of recent studies of D's form.

IX

STYLE AND AESTHETIC

I. General Style, Aesthetic, and Place

522. Allende-Blin, Juan. "Claude Debussy: Scharnier zweier Jahrhunderte." **Musik-Konzepte** 1-2. See item 136.

Discusses D as watershed between two centuries.

523. Ansermet, Ernest. **Ecrits sur la musique.** Edited by J.-C. Piguet. Neuchatel, Switzerland: A la Baconnière, 1971. 254 p. ML 60.A568 E3. In French and English.

By a foremost conductor of D's music. Contains a chapter "Le language de Debussy" (197-210) that relates Debussy's new tonality to phenomenology (study of human consciousness and self-awareness) and affirms the significance of the music. Terms D an "ob=jective lyricist" and not an Impressionist.

524. Byrnside, Ronald Lee. "Debussy's Second Style." Ph.D. diss., Musicology, University of Illinois, 1971. 277 p. UM 72-06,878; DA XXXII.8, p. 4647-A.

Denotes three broad stylistic phases in D's compositions. The second emerges in the 1890's, although those earliest second-style works are surrounded by early-style works. The development of his third style did not occasion the end of the second. Hence, "style" is preferred to "style period." Considers the influence of the other arts in D's eclectic aesthetic but finds the label "Impressionist" misleading.

525. Caillat, Stéphane. "Le geste du chef du choeur: Analyse gestuelle d'une chanson **a capella** de Debussy, **Dieu, qu'il fait bon regarder**." **Analyse musicale** 10 (Jan. 1988): 31-5.

Considerations by a choral conductor of tempo, approach to the beat, proper performance by the singers, and dynamics. Clear physical gestures are important to a correct rendering.

526. Coombe, Charles-Henry. "Les citations d'hymnes nationaux chez Debussy." **Revue musicale de Suisse Romande** 39, no. 1 (1986): 19-27.

D quoted national anthems in the piano prelude **Hommage à Pickwick** ("God save the king" of England), **Feux d'artifice** ("La Marseillaise" of France), **Berceuse héroïque** ("La Brabançonne" of Belgium), and in **En blanc et noir** (again La Marseillaise, along with **Ein' feste Burg** to represent Germany). The citation of anthems does not begin until 1910, perhaps reflecting D's concern for national tensions leading to the Great War. The widely varied significance of each quotation shows the breadth of Debussy's expressive palette. This is a useful summary of nationalistic quotations.

527. Dietschy, Marcel. "L'éblouissement d'amour dans l'oeuvre de Debussy." **Revue musicale de Suisse Romande** 1 (Mar. 30, 1963): 16-19.

Observes a precious moment of supreme tenderness in D's mature music. It is often marked "expressif" or "pianissimo," and it explores the beauty of the instant to the fullest. Cites passages from the **Quatuor, Children's Corner, La mer, Le martyre, Nuages (Nocturnes)**, and the **Preludes for piano**.

528. Fischer, Kurt von. "Debussy and the Climate of Art Nouveau--Some Remarks on Debussy's Aesthetics." **Miscellanea musicologica** (Ade laide Studies in Musicology) 13 (1984): 49-56. Given in German in item 189.

Points to the taste for things English in the 1890s in France, whereby Art Nouveau first was termed in the English "Modern Style" in France. The French fascination for English artistic figures Rossetti and Turner and the American-born painter Whistler is stressed.

529. Godet, Robert. "Claude Debussy." **La semaine littéraire** no. 1267: 172-74. Reprinted in **Le monde musical** 29, no. 8 (Aug. 1919).

Reflections on D's musicality and aesthetics by a close friend. Points to the fluidity of D's style, its orientation to nuance, and its naturalness. Ends with an informative account of a discussion with D following the dress rehearsal of **Pelléas**, in which D spoke of C.M. von Weber. Godet surmises that, following the rehearsal, D appeared to realize that he had dealt a death blow to Romanticism and Wagnerism.

530. Golovinskij, Grigorij. **Kompozitor i folklor: Iz opyta masterov XIX-XX vekov** [The composer and folklore: From the experiences of the artists of the 19th and 20th centuries]. Moscow: Muzyka, 1981. 279 p. ML 3845.G66 1981. In Russian.

Contains an extended essay on D as well as essays on Stravinsky and Bartók. These composers are viewed in terms of folk culture and seen to have special significance in the social context of the times. Not examined.

531. Hirsbrunner, Theo. "Der französische Wagnerismus und die Musique de Silence." **Schweizer Beiträge zur Musikwissenschaft** 2 (1974): 91-102.

Discusses d'Indy's definition of Wagnerism in France and the conception of silence in art espoused by Wagner and Mallarmé. D employs silence as a progressive element. This is a more concise explanation of ideas also expounded in Jankélévitch's **La musique et l'inneffable** (Paris 1961). The theories of a "musique de silence" of Camille Mauclair are reviewed, as is D's conception of silence as a primary element.

532. Hoérée, Arthur. "Debussy, musicien novateur." **Bulletin de la classe des beaux-arts** [Brussels, Academie royale de Belgique] 64, no. 1-2 (1982): 30-41.

Defines the innovative qualities of D's work with regard to his personal evolution and that of music history. While previous scholarship has focused on D's harmony, Hoérée recommends greater attention to his subtle but strikingly new melody. Not examined.

533. ------. "Les entretiens Debussy-Guiraud." **Avant-scène opéra** 11 (1977): 140-46.

Republishes and comments on the important dialogue with Guiraud concerned with opera and musical innovations generally, as Debussy conceived them in 1889-90. Comments on the theatrical sense and tonality of Wagner and Berlioz. The conversation was noted down by M. Emmanuel.

534. Imberty, Michel. "Il senso del tempo e della morte nell'immaginario debussiano." **Nuova rivista musicale italiano** (July-Sept. 1987), 383-409. Not examined.

535. Inghelbrecht, Germaine and Désiré-Emile. **Claude Debussy.** Paris: Costard, 1953. 310 p. ML 410.D28 15x.

A biography that cites numerous letters by D. Superseded except for aspects of style and insights into aesthetics. See especially the final chapter, "L'interprétation."

536. Jankélévitch, Vladimir. **(De la musique au silence:) Debussy et le mystère de l'instant.** Paris: Plon, 1976. 315 p. ISBN 2-2590-0000-2; ML 410.D28 J165.

Important expansion of his 1949 book **Debussy et le mystère** [Neuchâtel: Baconnière, 1949. ML 410.D28J16]. Suggests that mystery is all-encompassing mindset of D's music. Discusses aspects of mystery by sections devoted to Mystery of Destiny [states of the soul]; The Descent to the Subterranean [symbols of fall and the "néant," pessimism, the absence of clear form]; The Future Obstructed [the static, as in **Jet d'eau**; the refusal to develop ideas]; The Total Presence [natural things; the force of tonality]; The Upheaval ("Surgissement") [silence, ambiguity, "un éternel commencement"]. A personal but thought-provoking view of the psychological character of D's music.

537. ------. **La vie et la mort dans la musique de Debussy.** Neuchâtel: A La Baconnière, 1968. 140 p. ML 410.D28J18.

A recasting of the approach in the study previously cited, now exploring the relationship of Debussy to the abiding languor of the **fin-de-siècle**. The lure of the decadent and the nostalgia for light, space, and the distant are the two tendencies joining to create Debussy's aesthetic. Emphasizes the **Preludes for piano**.

538. Laloy, Louis. "Claude Debussy, la simplicité en musique." **Revue musicale, histoire et critique** 4, no. 4 (Feb. 15, 1904): 106-11.

Distinguished as among the first considerations of aesthetics marked by a comprehensive and intuitive understanding. Here D's first important biographer and in-depth critic stresses his naturalness and simplicity of style. Draws examples from **Prélude-faune**, **Pelléas**, and the **Quatuor**. D's harmony is neither new, primitive, impossible, magical, or miraculous. It is simply expressive.

539. Langham Smith, Richard. "Debussy and the Art of the Cinema." **Music and Letters** 54, no. 1 (Jan. 1973): 61-70.

Points out D's early fascination with the camera (seen in the P. Louÿs and the Gaby photos). Refers to a film-like sequence in **Ibéria** and relates **Nuages (Nocturnes)** to the pre-cinematic **ombre chinois** and its cloudscapes. D viewed the cinema as a possible renewing force for French music, one that could liberate it from the Wagnerian impasse.

540. Lavauden, Thérèse. "L'humour dans l'oeuvre de Claude Debussy." **Revue musicale** 11, no. 101 (Feb. 1, 1930): 97-105. First published in English in **The Chesterian**, April-June 1928.

Speaks of D's sensuality, languid irony, and subtle alchemy bordering on the perverse. Relates D's humor to Watteau, Musset, Shakespeare,

Musorgsky, and Schumann. Points to the Preludes for piano **General Lavine** and **Minstrels**, the song Les **Ingénus (Fêtes galantes II)**, and **Children's Corner**. Elsewhere, D holds humor "in suspense": **L'isle joyeuse** and **Soirée dans Grenade**. A rare, valuable consideration of this aspect.

541. Lesure, François (trans. Denis Stevens). "Claude Debussy after his centenary." **Musical Quarterly** 49, no. 3 (1963): 277-88.

From the vantage point of 1962, Lesure argues for D scholarship to consider form and timbre, which have influenced contemporary music decisively. Further research ought to reconsider the term "Impressionism," which for Lesure has hampered true understanding and thus proper research. Discusses the sluggishness [as of 1962] in **Pelléas** research but notes important studies of the Poe projects. The relation to Ravel is touched on, as is D's displeasure with many interpreters of his music. Lesure describes the 1962 exhibition of certain sketches (**Pelléas, Rodrigue, Nocturnes, Ibéria, sonata for violin**), the existence of which should challenge assumptions about compositional procedure. Calls for a complete edition of writings [which Lesure produced] and of the complete correspondence [which he currently is preparing]. Notes as further avenues for research D's relation to the younger musicians Francisco de Lacerda and Varèse. This is an authoritative survey of needs for Debussy research, if of course somewhat outdated now and emphasizing research to which the author is personally attracted.

542. ------. "Debussy et le XVIe siècle." In **Hans Albrecht in Memoriam**, ed. by W. Brennecke and H. Haase, pp. 242-45. Kassel: Bärenreiter, 1962. ML 55.A38.

D's interest in the Renaissance stemmed from the Conservatoire years 1880-83 and his experience of di Lasso and Palestrina in Rome (1885). Performances in Paris (1893 and later) further acquainted him with those composers and Victoria, Josquin, Le Jeune, and Clément Janequin. Mentions influences on **Le martyre** and **Trois chansons de Charles d'Orléans**. Does not explore particular musical issues, such as counterpoint, but invites further exploration of D's reaction to Dufay and Monteverdi.

543. ------. "Debussy et le syndrome de Grenade." **Revue de musicologie** 68, no. 1-2 (1982): 101-09.

Reviews the substantial number of works by D relating to Spain and suggests the date of 1880 for his brief visit to San Sebastien. Reports his reaction to Spanish music heard at the 1889 Paris World Exposition and to Bizet's **Carmen**. Survey's D's relation to Albeniz, Granados, Viñes, and de Falla; discusses in context **Lindaraja**, **Soirée dans Grenade**, **La puerta del vino**, **Ibéria**, and **En blanc et noir**. A useful survey encouraging particular, in-depth studies.

544. Lockspeiser, Edward. "Debussy's Concept of the Dream." **Royal Music Association, Proceedings** 89 (1962-63): 49-61.

The author brings the question into particular focus, although he draws upon ideas expressed in his biography (item 85). Centers on D's knowledge of the painter Turner, suggesting aesthetic parallels in their concepts of the dream. Points to the suspension of tonality and his ambiguous and enharmonic connections in **Prélude-faune**, **La mer**, and the Poe projects **Chute** and **Diable**. Lockspeiser rather overstates his point and mixes elements of thought when he observes that "Debussy had no musical antecedents in France . . . his friends were almost exclusively literary people."

545. Matsuhashi, Mari. CLAUDE DEBUSSY NO ONGAKUSHISO [The Aesthetic language of Debussy]. Dissertation, Tokyo National University of Fine Arts and Music, 1975. In Japanese. Not examined.

546. Minor, Martha D. "Hispanic Influences on the Works of French Composers of the 19th and 20th Centuries." Ph.D. diss., Musicology, University of Kansas, 1983. vii, 271 p. DA 44/08 p.2287-A; UM order no. DA 8317967.

Discusses the Spanish elements in D's music as well as in that by Ravel, Massenet, Bizet, and others.

547. Park, Raymond Roy. "The Later Style of Claude Debussy." Ph.D. diss., Music, University of Michigan, 1966. xi, 528 p. UM 67-15,699; DA XXVIII.7, p. 2718-A. ML 410.D28 P2 1974m.

Notes that the later style appeared ca. 1908 and continued through 1917 [but see Byrnside above, item 524]. Approaches the music style-critically, dealing with form, melodic materials and structure, texture, and harmony and chord succession. Remarks upon the abundance of influences that inform D's style, its improvisatory qualities, and the classicizing tendencies of the last works.

548. Pelinski, Ramon. "Musikexotismus um 1900: Claude Debussy." In **Weltkulturen und moderne Kunst**, edited by S. Wickmann, pp. 412-25. Munich: Bruckmann, 1972. ISBN 3-7654-1464-6; NX 542.07.

Deals with D's encounter of East Asian music at the Paris world exhibition of 1889. Not examined.

* Salzman, Eric. **Twentieth-Century Music: An Introduction.** See item 214 for annotation.

549. Schaeffner, André. **Essais de musicologie et autres fantaisies.** In series **Les hommes et leurs signes**. Paris: Sycomore, 1980. 371 p. ISBN 2-86262-033-5; ML 60.S275.

Contains 6 articles devoted to Debussy, including the previously unpublished writing "En peine d'un livret" concerned with **Rodrigue et Chimène**. Schaeffner had not examined the score but discusses its genesis and reception in D's circle. This collection also reprints Schaeffner's major article "Debussy et ses rapports avec la musique russe" (see item 384). Other articles on D concern the Shakespeare projects; the "Theatre imaginaire" (incomplete theater projects such as **Orphée** and **Histoire de Tristan**); his taste in painting; and Monsieur Croche. Schaeffner's views are stimulating even when he did not gain access to primary sources and falls short of the depth those would have provided.

550. Stegemann, Michael. "Ausdruck und Eindruck; Claude Debussys missverstandene Ästhetik. **Neue Zeitschrift für Musik** [or see **Melos** in some library catalogues] 147/10 (Oct. 1986), 8-12 and 147/11 (Nov. 1986), 13-18.

Part I refers to the **Nocturnes** and D's writings in relation to painting, reassessing the concept of Impressionism. Part II studies the related concepts of the Symbolists, Decadents, Mallarmé, Proust, Huysmans, Maeterlinck, and nationalism. Concludes that no one aesthetic label is proper and that D must be viewed in several, complementary lights.

551. Streletski, Gérard. "Le chef d'orchestre face à **La mer** de Claude Debussy." **Analyse musicale** 12 (June 1988): 108-12.

Urges conductors to study the score thoroughly before the first rehearsal, so that they can be the advocate of the composer. Impressionism must be an art of precision for the interpreter.

552. Vallery-Radot, Pasteur. "Claude Debussy: Souvenirs." **Revue des deux mondes** (May 15, 1938): 390-418.

An important, objective account of Debussy's personality by his physician in the years 1910 to 1917, including letters.

553. Wenk, Arthur B. "Varieties of Analysis: Through the Analytic Sieve and Beyond." In **Proceedings of the Conference on Music Bibliography.** Northwestern University, October 1986 [forthcoming].

554. Winzer, Dieter. **Claude Debussy und die franzöische musikalische Tradition.** Neue Musikgeschichtliche Forschungen Band 11. Diss., University of Frankfurt am Main, 1980. Published Wiesbaden: Breitkopf und Härtel, 1981. 164 p. ISBN 3-7651-0178-8; ML 410.D28 W5.

Argues that D's important reference to earlier French music was at once instinctive and conscious. Traces the influence of the Renaissance chanson; the suite and dance forms; the 18th-century sonata, theme, and motive; melodic parallels to Rameau; and French speech and folksong.

2. Programmaticism, Impressionism, and Symbolism

555. Ansermet, Ernest. "Debussy." **Revue musicale de Suisse Romande** 33, no. 2 (May 1980): 65-69.

An article dating from before 1960 and not included previously among Ansermet's writings. For the author, traditional music is the pure expression of feelings; that of D is the expression of feeling about something particular. But also see Barzun (following), who argues that all music expresses something beyond the notes and their relationships.

556. Barzun, Jacques. "The Meaning of Meaning in Music: Berlioz Once More." **Musical Quarterly** 66, no. 1 (Jan. 1980): 1-20.

A brilliant argument concerning Berlioz, and informative for the interpretation of D's "programmatic" intent. Concludes that both music and literature "are programmatic in the same sense of following inner experience . . . . sometimes giving, by association, reminders of the objective world." See in connection with Ansermet (source 555) the discussion of program and Impressionism.

557. Byrnside, Ronald L. "Musical Impressionism: the Early History of the Term." **Musical Quarterly** 64, no. 4 (Oct. 1980): 522-37.

The term was first applied to D's **Printemps** (orch.) in 1887. Discusses its use from 1887-1910 in reviews and other criticism. Suggests that the oversimplistic association of the general musical idiom with the visual arts may obscure a deeper understanding.

558. Crotty, John E. "Symbolist Influences in Debussy's **Prelude to the Afternoon of a Faun.**" **In Theory Only** 6, no. 2 (Feb. 1982): 17-30.

Sees rational control not abandoned but submerged in Symbolist poetry; language becomes the evocation of a dream-like state. In **Faune** the basic diatonicism is submerged by whole-tone (including tritone) usage, resulting in a musical ambiguity analogous to the poetic one. Timbral uses follow similar processes. This is a lucid essay on tonal structure relating in tangible ways to poetry. [See also the comment by D. Headlam, **In Theory Only** 6, no. 4 (May 1982), 9-11, extending Crotty's ideas with questions about harmonic versus melodic pitch centering.]

559. Durney, Daniel. "L'eau dans la musique impressioniste." **Revue internationale de musique française** 2, 5 (June 1981): 43-50.

Views the question within the larger context of Symbolism, referring to D's piano preludes **Voiles** and **Cathédrale engloutie** and to **La mer** and **Pelléas**.

560. Gervais, Françoise. "Qu'est-ce que l'Impressionisme musical?" **Revue internationale de musique française** 2, 5 (June 1981): 9-12.

A brief and traditional definition of parallel aims in the visual arts, literature, and music. Cites **La mer** to illustrate D as evocateur of visual impressions.

561. Gitter, Felix. "Die Programmatik im klavieristichen und orchestralen Schaffen von Claude Debussy." Ph.D. diss., Musicology, University of Halle-Salle, 1973. Not examined.

562. Handman, Dorel. "Psychology in Debussy's Music." **Musicology** 2, no. 3 (New York, April 1949), 243-54.

Applies "impressionist" interpretation in describing attitudes and values in the piano preludes, **Pelléas**, and **Prélude-faune**. Sees D's psychology as that of a man "eminently sensorial and sensual." Is thus an attempt to substantiate "impressionistic" analysis by pointing to psychological intent.

563. Hollander, Hans. **Musik und Jugendstil.** Zurich: Atlantis, 1975. 143 p., index, bibliog. ISBN 3-7611-0448-0; ML 3849.H53..

Traces the aesthetic of Jugendstil to **Damoiselle, Prélude-faune,** the **Proses lyriques (De reve), Chansons de Bilitis (La chevelure), Pelléas, La mer,** the **Nocturnes**, and the **Danses** for harp and orch. Points to similar style in Vaughan Williams, Mahler, Berg, Sibelius, and Strauss.

564. Jarocinski, Stefan. **Debussy: Impressionism and Symbolism**. Translated by Rollo Myers. London: Eulenburg, 1976. xv, 175 p. ISBN 0-903873-20-6 (-09-5 pbk.); ML 410.D28 J33. Originally publ. in Polish as **Debussy, a impresionizm i synmbolizm**. Krakow: Polskie Wydawnictwo Muzyczne, 1966. ML 410.D28 J33. French language translation Paris: Editions du Seuil, 1970.

Jarocinski points to Symbolism as "the artistic movement which influenced D's artistic personality most strongly." He rejects the label "Impressionism," as D had done, since it implies superficial program and insubstantial content. This study explores Symbolism in French literature and painting and in Wagner. The author analyzes **Pelléas** and many songs, D's use of sonority and harmony as symbolistic, and his influence in the twentieth century. Contains numerous bibliographic references to related arts and literature. A landmark study of D's aesthetic connections.

565. Jean-Aubry, Georges. **La musique et les nations.** Paris: Sirène; London: Chester, 1933. 265 p.

The essay "Claude Debussy, musicien français" (pp. 42-63) explores the nationalistic element in D's thought and music. Valuable as a view by a close contemporary and a document of the frequently nationalistic appreciation of D just after his death.

566. Kremlev. Jules. "Les tendences réalistes dans l'esthétique de Debussy." In source 127.

Reviews D's aesthetic tendencies toward Impressionism. neo-Classicism, constructionismformalism, and even Expressionism (as in the Poe projects). Points to the multiple levels and contradictions in his thought. If Realism is the tendency to infuse life processes into art, then D may be considered a Realist. D emphasizes music for its relevance to the senses and to life process, as do Musorgsky and other Russians.

567. Liess, Andreas. "Claude Debussy und der Art Nouveau." **Studi musicali** 4 (1975, publ. 1977), 245-76, and V (1976, publ. 1978), 143-234.

To date the most exhaustive study of this important question and a rich exploration of issues raised by Lockspeiser (item 85). Liess discusses Debussy's view of nature as symbolistic, the influence of oriental art, and the role of ornament in Debussy as related to Art nouveau. Concludes that Debussy is a supreme figure of the Art nouveau movement. This term for a movement in the related arts is proposed as more completely fit for D than either Impressionism or Symbolism.

568. Mila, Massimo. **Cent'anni di musica moderna.** Turin: EDT, 1981. 212 p. ISBN 8-8706-3020-x; ML 196.M6 1981.

Republication with a new preface of essays first published in 1944. Contains the thoughtful essay "Debussy nella recente critica tedesca" (1941). Remarks upon the beginning of German critical interest in D. Points to studies by A. Liess [who argues against the tradition of pictorial, "impressionist" analysis and for the interpretation of D as a reaction to Wagnerism], Gunther Schulz, and Jakobik.

569. Neuwirth, Gosta. "**Parsifal** und der musikalische Jugendstil." In **Richard Wagner: Werk und Wirkung**, edited C. Dahlhaus, p. 175-98. Regensburg: Bosse, 1971. 242 p. ML 410.W13 D12.

Discusses the proper application of the term Jugendstil (related to Art nouveau, from the plastic arts) to music of the late 19th and early 20th centuries. Relates aspects of Jugendstil to **Parsifal**, **Pelléas**, and Huysmans's novel **A Rebours**. Thoughtful if at times speculative, and aids in understanding D's relation to the other arts and to Wagner's influence by the agency of the related arts.

570. Orledge, Robert. "Debussy's Piano Music: Some Second Thoughts on Sources and Inspiration." **Musical Times** 122 (Jan. 1981): 21-27.

Discusses the improvements through revisions of works, D's change of order within sets, and pictorial sources of inspiration. D's refusal of the label "Impressionist" might have been a smoke-screen, for he exhibits strong tendencies toward the pictorial. Suggests that the term "Symbolist" as applied to D has been overstated and relied upon too heavily. Orledge reconsiders the manuscripts of the **Preludes for piano**, **Six épigraphes antiques**, **Suite bergamasque**, **Images 1907**, and **Etudes**.

571. Palmer, Christopher. **Impressionism in Music**. London: Hutchinson, 1973; New York: Scribner's, 1974. 248 p. ISBN 0-6841-3568-x; ML 197.P26 1974.

Debussy figures centrally, while Chopin and Liszt are seen as forerunners of Impressionism. Views a parallel between the general musical idiom and Impressionist and post-Impressionist painting. Suggests as broad, defining parameters that "Impressionism was concerned above all with sensation." Palmer's almost exclusive emphasis on the role of immediate sensation as the goal of D's music currently is out of favor, given contemporary preoccupations with structure and Symbolist interpretation. But his line of reasoning, however forced into vagueness by its aesthetic point of departure, can offer a necessary counterbalance. His analysis does help elucidate one level on which D's music functions and by which it has won many admirers.

572. Ravel, Maurice. "L'art et les hommes: à propos des **Images** de Claude Debussy." **Cahiers d'aujourd'hui** (Bruges) 3 (Feb. 1913): 135-38.

Observes two schools of composition active at the time, the "old" school of Franck's disciples and the new, of which D is the principal innovator. Observes that music critics are divided along similar lines. Suggests that a meaning far deeper than the pictorial exists in D's music. Refers to **Rondes de Printemps** and **Ibéria** from the **Images** for orchestra.

573. Schultz, Wolfgang-Andreas. **Die freien Formen in der Musik des Expressionismus und Impressionismus.** Hamburg: Verlag K.D. Wagner, 1974. 143 p. ISBN 3-921029-23-6; ML448.S387.

Traces the concept of fluctuating movement, or fluctuating form, in **Rondes de Printemps** (**Images** orch.) and **Jeux**. Analyzes works by Ravel, K. Szymanowski, and Schoenberg as well.

574. Watson, Wanda Lee. "Debussy: A Programmatic Approach to Form." Ph.D. diss., University of Texas, 1978. 295 p. DA 39: 3913A Jan. 1979; UM order no. 79-00650.

Understands **En blanc et noir**, **Le martyre**, and **Six épigraphes antiques** as translations of other art forms into music. Shows that the content of the program lends a structural basis for these. Includes a translation of the **Chansons de Bilitis** (incidental music), which becomes the point of departure for the **Epigraphes**. Goes deeper than the descriptive literary or pictorial approach that has marred certain earlier analyses, seeking the "principle of reciprocity between subject and form, the correspondence of expression and the poetic idea."

3. Structure

575. Ansermet, Ernest. "Le langage de Debussy." **Revue musicale de Suisse Romande/Feuilles musicales** 15, no. 405 (June 1962): 63-67.

Argues for a new conception of D not based upon thoughts of "Impressionism" or the "revolutionary." Instead, D ought to be appreciated for his spatial and temporal innovations and his contributions as a structuralist. His musical language thus is sure and clear, even when it explores images.

576. ------. "Le langage de Debussy." In source 127.

An expansion of the ideas in the foregoing article. Introduces the notion of the phenomenology of D's music, concerning the listener's consciousness upon hearing his music. D stands at the moment in history at which all the possibilities of tonality have been acquired: he thereupon opens the era of a completely individualized stylistic order.

577. Barraqué, Jean. "Debussy, ou l'approche d'une organisation autogène de la composition." In source 127.

D's music repudiates traditional habits of composition; a fitting analysis ought to view each work as an individual set of solutions. Each work to a common denominator, posing a new problem and offering a new solution for each composition. Refers to **Prélude-faune** to illustrate. In **La mer** the exposition and development are coexistent. D's form is conceived as perpetually open. Further see item 121, Barraqué on **La mer**.

578. Cahn, Peter. "Der Szeneaufbau in Debussys **Pelléas et Melisande**." In **Bericht über den internationalen musikwissenschaftlichen Kongress Bonn 1970**, pp. 207-12. ISBN 3-7618- 0146-7; ML 36.I6277.

Describes D's conception of structure in operatic scenes as he expressed it in conversation with his teacher Guiraud. Relates the scene structure to that of theme and variation. Finds "framing motives" that have a power relating to fate and should inform a scenic design that can overcome the passive quality of Maeterlinck's figures.

579. Canac, Henriette. "Claude Debussy: **Prélude à l'après-midi d'un faune**." In series Cahiers d'analyse et de Formation Musicale, no. 3. Paris: Leduc, 1986. 19 p.

A thematic, tonal, and formal analysis aimed at better performance. Quite thoughtful and capable of informing more extensive studies.

580. Deliège, Irène. "Le parallelisme, support d'une analyse auditive de la musique: vers un modèle des parcours cognitifs de l'information musicale: application au **Syrinx** de Claude Debussy." **Analyse musicale** 6 (Jan. 1987): 73-79.

Such parallel structural devices as repetition influence the auditive perception of a work. The first four measures of **Syrinx** present the two "networks" [motives] that give the work particular cohesion. A succinct article in the application of semiotic methods, although like many such studies it labors mightily at reinventing the wheel.

581. Denissow, Edison. "Über einige Besonderheiten der Kompositionstechnik Claude Debussys." In **Jahrbuch Peters 1978**, pp. 147-72. Leipzig: Peters, 1979. ML 5.J245.

A study of motives and intervallic procedures in the **Preludes for piano**. Traces D's montage technique, which is based upon motives, in **Minstrels** and **Nuages (Nocturnes)**. Observes a mathematical proportion among phrase lengths.

582. Dunsby, Jonathan. "Music and Semiotics: The Nattiez Phase." **Musical Quarterly** 69 (1983): 27-44.

Defines **semiotics** as applied to music as "a search to explain meaning as a relational phenomenon." Semiotics "studies the total of symbolic associations." Such an approach to total understanding of a work relates to linguistic meaning and views music as a cultural or social phenomenon. Reviews the scholarly reception of Nattiez's work (items 598, 835-36) and considers Nattiez's analysis of **Syrinx** and **Jeux**. Semiotics is viewed as a vital and necessary approach to analysis. Dunsby's article is quite important, offering an entry into the analytic-aesthetic approach of semiotics and thus a fuller appreciation of such analyses of Debussy.

583. Durney, Daniel. "Aspects du problème de la forme dans la musique instrumentale au tournant du siècle: Mahler, Schoenberg, Berg, Webern,

Debussy, 1890-1910." Diss., Doctorat 3eme cycle, Musicology, Sorbonne, 1981. 2 vol., 562 p. and 398 p. Not examined.

584. Escot, Pozzi. "Semiotics of Music." **Sonus** 6, no. 2 (Spring 1986): 11-30.

Regards semiotics in terms of a trivium: pure grammar, logic, and pure rhetoric. "Semiotics in music is the logic of the structure." A helpful reading in introducing the approach of semiotics. Is thus a companion reading to Nattiez (598), Dunsby (582), and Guertin (758).

585. Forte, Allen. "Schenker's Conception of Musical ^KStructure." **Journal of Music Theory** 3 (April 1959): 1-30. Reprinted in **Readings in Schenker Analysis**, edited Maury Yeston, pp. 3-37. New Haven, Connecticut: Yale University Press, 1984. ISBN 0-3000- 2032-5; ML 423.S33 R4.

A clear introduction by a leading analyst. See pp. 27-29 (32-33 of reprint), which provide analytic remarks on **La cathédrale engloutie**. Investigates each line as emanating from a theme rather than resulting from organum-like doubling of a monophonic idea. Illustrates Schenker's concept of polyphonic melody and applies these to such a work, which deviates from triadic norms.

586. ------. "New Approaches to the Linear Analysis of Music." **Journal of the American Musicological Society** 41, no. 2 (Summer 1988): 315-48.

A very important article that extends the basic premises and approach of Schenker, which is rooted in tonal music and is summarized in the preceding source and in Salzer (item 605). Forte now extends the process to extended- and post-tonal composition, analyzing Stravinsky's **Petrushka**, Second Tableau ("Chez Petrushka"), Wagner's Prelude to **Tristan**, and Scriabin's **Fourth Sonata** for piano. Combines the linear approach with recent tendencies of pitch-class analysis, thus uniting the large-scale horizontal dimension and the motivic structure. Illustrates by analyzing the "Tristan chord" as it extends over long spans of the Prelude. When read as Forte encourages, as guidelines and adapted sensitively, these procedures may inform the analysis of D's music.

587. Gervais, Françoise. "Structures debussystes." **Revue musicale** 258 (numéro spécial, 1962): 77-88.

D's melodies often lead to a final pitch that confirms the tonal orientation, much in the manner of Gregorian chant. Cites **Prélude-faune** and the prelude **Et la lune descend**. In the prelude **Des pas sur la neige**, one observes a quality of "eternal becoming." Relates D's structural sense to ideas of Bergson, Van Gogh, and Rodin.

588. Hepokoski, James A. "Formulaic Openings in Debussy." **Nineteenth-Century Music** 8, no. 1 (Summer 1984): 44-59.

Observes D's reliance upon syntactical models, particularly at the beginnings of works. Initial gestural patterns involve phrasing, melody, texture, and harmony, the main purpose of which is to progress from silence into motion. Types of formulaic openings include monophonic, modal/-chordal, and those involving sequence or expansion. Refers to such openings in **Printemps** (1887), **La damoiselle élue**, **Prélude-faune**, and **Pelléas**. Relates these to opening gestures by Franck, Chabrier, Saint-Saëns, and Wagner. Encourages future research to consider not merely the objective **what** but also the aesthetic questions of **how** and **why**. A clear, thoughtful study of an important aspect.

589. Howat, Roy. "Debussy, Bartók et les formes de la nature." **Revue musicale de Suisse romande** 39, no. 3 (Sept. 1986): 128-41.

Traces the Golden Section to designs in nature (plant and shell forms) and to musical structures of Bartók and D. Refers to the studies by Erno Lendvai of Bartók. Acknowledges that neither composer discussed mathematical procedures directly and that music manuscripts show no signs of numeric calculations. Provokes thinking about how the two composers arrived at such proportions intuitively and applied conscious calculation to later works.

Concerning the analysis by Lendvai of Bartók and his relation to D, further see Howat: "Bartók, Lendvai and the Principles of Proportional Analysis." **Music Analysis** 2, no. 1 (March 1983): 69-95.

590. ------. **Debussy in Proportion: A Musical Analysis.** Cambridge and New York: Cambridge University Press, 1983. xi, 239 p. ISBN 0-521-23282-1; [LC] MT 92.D3 H7 1983.

A challenging new approach to D analysis, the book suggests that a substantial number of works are structured with an attention to Golden Section ratios. Howat recognizes that D might have sensed these intuitively, although the thrust of the argument is that he planned structure consciously along geometric lines. He acknowledges that D was indeed a "thoroughly intuitive artist" but urges the view that, in the least, his proportional structures "reached their final exactitude with D's conscious assistance." D's written references to a "divin nombre" are disconcertingly few for Howat and are inconclusive, as is evidence found in sketches, marginal notes, or other outright calculations. Succeeds in raising many questions and piquing scholars' awareness that a large-scale approach to analysis of D is mandatory. Refers to important poets and painters, such as the Japanese print artists Hokusai and Hiroshige. Useful bibliography of D and of Golden Section analysis. Based upon the author's doctoral dissertation, **Proportional Structure in the Music of Claude Debussy**, Cambridge University, 1979.

Centers on **Reflets dans l'eau (Images pour piano** première série), **La mer**, and **L'isle joyeuse**. Appendices contain scores of these two piano works, **Spleen** (from **Ariettes oubliées**), and **Clair de lune (Suite bergamasque)**. The latter two works are discussed with brief analyses. Another appendix points to related structures in Schubert, Ravel, and Fauré.

591. ------. "Debussy, Ravel, and Bartók: Towards Some New Concepts of Form." **Music and Letters** 58, no. 3 (July 1977): 285-93.

Reacts to Erno Lendvai's study **Béla Bartók: an Analysis of His Music** (London, 1971), in which Bartók is shown to utilize Golden Section structures. Howat sees similar concepts in Ravel's **Miroirs** and Debussy's **Reflets dans l'eau**. This is a short study preliminary to the preceding.

592. ------. "Dramatic Shape and Form in **Jeux de vagues**, and its Relationship to **Pelléas**, **Jeux**,

and Other Scores." **Cahiers Debussy** (nouvelle série) 7 (1983): 7-23.

The structure of **Jeux de vagues** (from **La mer**) aims toward a dominating climax at 5/6s of the way through. Howat compares this to the **Images** series I, **L'isle joyeuse**, the orchestral **Images for orchestra** ("Gigues" and "Rondes de Printemps"), **Pelléas**, and **Jeux**. Points to a structure of two "waves." Extends arguments concerning Golden Section found in item 590.

593. Imberty, Michel. "**La cathédrale engloutie** de Claude Debussy: de la perception au sens." **Canadian University Music Review** 61 (1985): 90-160.

Puts aside the frequent mode of analysis emphasizing musico-pictorial description in favor of analysis of perception, considering the work as if on a first hearing not informed programmatically. Argues that such a "purely musical" analysis must join the programmatic one. The author's approach through semiology joins the studies of **Pelléas** by Ruwet (1972) and Nattiez (1975). At length orients the reader to the hierarchies of musical perception, comparing thereby an **Intermezzo** by Brahms to the prelude **La cathédrale engloutie**. If at times verbose, is a useful resume of semiology as applied to Debussy. Corroborates the current analytic emphasis upon structural depth and Symbolism.

594. ------. "De la perception du temps musical à sa signification psychologique: à propos de **La cathédrale engloutie** de Claude Debussy." **Analyse musicale** 6 (Jan. 1987): 28-37.

An extension of the preceding article. Reports on listening experiments involving 30 adult subjects with some musical background but without a specific technical orientation to the **Cathédrale engloutie**. Presents results in a graph and relates them to previous studies of Brahms and D's **Puerta del vino**. D's artistic message anticipates the dreams, enthusiasms, and soul of contemporary culture. His sense of musical time is marked by the fears of destruction and the fragmentation found throughout contemporary art.

595. ------. "Polysémie et cohérence sémantique du langage musical. I: La polysémie dans les réponses verbales associées à la musique, et la construction d'une échelle circulaire des expressivités musicales." **Sciences de l'art; Revue internationale de psychologie de l'art** 7, no. 1-2 (1970): 77-93.

Referring to the Preludes, derives a "circular scale of musical expressivity" that demonstrates the semantic ambiguity of music. Shows that the literary-pictorial, ending titles of the Preludes are of only a general nature. Not examined.

596. ------. **Signification and Meaning in Music: on Debussy's "Préludes pour le piano."** Monographies de Sémiologie et d'Analyses Musicales, III. Montreal: Faculté de Musique, University of Montreal, 1979. 96 p.

An English translation of two important writings both published under the title "Polysémie et cohérence du langage musical," in **Sciences de l'Art** 7 (1970) 77-93 [see item 595], and 8, no. 2 (1971), 65-81. These two writings here become chapters 1-2 here and lay an analytic groundwork. A new discussion, chapter 3, is entitled "Semantic Representation of the Style of Debussy." It discusses the preludes for piano.

597. Lipkis, Larry. "Aspects of Temporality in Debussy's **Jeux** and Ives's **Symphony No. 4**, Fourth Movement." Ph.D. diss. with independant composition, University of California at Santa Barbara, 1984. 100 p. DA 45/2689A Mar. 1985. ML 3850.L57 1984.

Both works date from 1912 and relate in one significant way: they make temporal demands upon the listener that are radically different from those of traditional Western art music.

598. Nattiez, Jean-Jacques and Louise Hirbour-Paquette. "Analyse musicale et sémiologie: à propos du Prélude de **Pelléas**." In **Analyse, méthodologie, sémiologie**, special vol. of **Musique en jeu** 10 (March 1973): 1-90.

Considers traditional analyses of the **Pelléas** prelude by Emmanuel, Van Appledorn, Laloy, F. Gervais, Chailley, and Leibowitz, comparing them to Ruwet's findings (603-04). Nattiez and Paquette appreciate Ruwet's account of the total perception and disinclination to stress single elements. This is a provocative reading of the **Pelléas** prelude. Can become a model for the semiotic approach to analysis of D.

599. Paja, Jadwiga. "Uwagi o formie w muzyce Debussy'ego, na przykladzie Preludiow" [Remarks on form in Debussy's music, as exemplified by his Preludes]. **Muzyka** 27, no. 1-2 (1982): 3-10. In Polish with summary in English.

Both recurring themes and sound events clarify the formal organization of D's music. His idea of mosaic form became the governing rule in Stravinsky's form, and it influenced Messiaen and Stockhausen. [not examined]

600. Pasquet, Yves-Marie. "Mouvements multiples." **Revue internationale de musique française** 2, no. 5 (Jan. 1981): 20-22.

A brief argument for a new interpretation of D, emphasizing his diversity and even discontinuity of style. The author's ideas would be welcome in an exposé of greater depth, which might permit a balanced account of D'a brand of unity.

601. Porten, Maria. **Zum Problem der "Form" bei Debussy: Untersuchungen am Beispiel der Klavierwerke.** Schriften zur Musik, Vol. 28. Munich: Katzbichler, 1974. [Diss., Univ. Zurich.] 121 p. ISBN 3-87397-034-1; ML 410.D28 P67.

Argues that each work generates its unique formal process, eschewing even personal formulae [but see Hepokoski item 588]. D's music nonetheless possesses rigorous form. Points mainly to the role of theme in D's formal process and cites examples from a variety of piano music.

602. Powers, Harold S. "Language Models and Musical Analysis." **Ethnomusicology** 24 (1980): 1-60.

D approached the composition of the Prelude to **Pelléas** by a "method" involving direct, even abrupt contrast. Powers relates to Ruwet's 1962 writing (603). Urges that, in applying the "music-as-language" metaphor, one should attend to the diversity of musical traditions, including not only the music we study but also the traditions of how we study music. An inquiry of central importance in the study of musical semantics in Debussy.

603. Ruwet, Nicolas. "Notes sur la duplication dans l'oeuvre de Claude Debussy." **Revue belge de musicologie** 16 (1962): 57-70.

Argues that immediate repetition of a phrase is not perceived as such by the listener, for repetition has a broader structural role. Sees a dialectic in D's form between the repeating and non-repeating elements. This dialectic relates to speech and thus invites the semiotic approach. An exemplary study employing semiotic thought.

604. ------. **Langage, musique, poésie.** Paris: Seuil, 1972. ISBN 2-0200-2041-6; ML 60.R98.

Analyzes several passages by Debussy, with particular reference to the Prelude of **Pelléas** and to **Nuages [Nocturnes]**. Observes that one must decompose the work analytically, according to the function of each element, and recompose these elements in terms of their relation to the whole. Ruwet seeks to identify the unity of the work in terms drawn from the semiotic analysis of poetry and language.

605. Salzer, Felix. **Structural Hearing.** Unabridged and corrected edition. 2 volumes. New York: Dover, 1962. MT 40.S2 1962.

The primary exposé of the analytic system of Heinrich Schenker for contemporary analysis, an approach that can be most helpful when adapted thoughtfully to D's new tonality. Refers to the prelude **Bruyères** and provides elaborate graphs of voice leading and tonal relations according to back-, middle-, and foreground. See especially vol. I, pp. 252-55 and vol. II, pp. 222-23.

Points to the ingenuity with which Debussy varies neighbor-tone motion.

606. Souris, André. "Poétique musicale de Debussy." In source 127.

Joins Boulez (item 173) in viewing Mallarmé and Cézanne as closely paralleling D in aesthetics and historic standing. Refers to the analysis of Mallarmé by G. Bachelard and M. Merleau-Ponty. From the **Prélude-faune** onward, D's music manifests a high unity of conception. Suggests a phenomenologic study of D. Offers the metaphor of water to explain how D's focal conception takes a particular shape: water is static but rendered dynamic by an obstacle in its course.

607. Spahlinger-Ditzig, Ursula. "Gestaltpädagogische Ansätze im Musikunterricht." **Musik und Bildung** 12, no. 10 (Oct. 1980): 608-13.

Explains Gestalt theory and therapy as they apply to music instruction, which in turn suggest new means to aural analysis. Devises a special "listening" score wherewith to teach the appreciation of the prelude **Feux d'artifice**. The "listening score" attempts a simplistic, graphic notation (such as ascending spiral lines) to aid music perception by non-specialist listeners.

608. Stirnemann, Knut. "Zur Frage des Leitmotivs in Debussys **Pelléas et Mélisande**." **Schweizer Beiträge zur Musikwissenschaft** 4 (1980): 151-70.

In thorough fashion surveys the significance of the idea of leitmotiv for Weber, Wagner, and D. Returns to Emmanuel's analysis (item 741) and to those by Van Appledorn and Van Ackere. Asserts that any adequate analysis of leitmotiv in Pelléas must consider context. Arrives at nine families, or groups, of motives that have a related dramatic function. A much-needed study of the question, clarifying D's adaptation of the leitmotiv.

609. Stockhausen, Karlheinz. "Von Webern zu Debussy: Bemerkungen zur statistischen Form." In **Texte zur elektronischen und instrumentalen Musik**,

vol. I, pp. 75-85. Cologne: Du Mont Schauberg, 1963. ML 3817.S83 v.1.

Views **Jeux** as a structure of movement and suggests a statistical analysis that will allow a comprehensive understanding.

610. Tenney, James C. and Larry Polansky. "Temporal gestalt perception in music." **Journal of Music Theory** 24, no. 2 (Nov. 1980): 205-41.

Discusses **Syrinx** in terms of temporal gestalt units. These units (motives, phrases, etc.) are internally cohesive but capable of developing meaningful hierarchies. The hierarchy of the units ranges from short ("clangs," motives), to sequences (phrases), to segments (subsections, or periods), to sections. Valuable as one explanation for listening to D, if somewhat protracted as an argument.

611. Wolff, Hellmuth Christian. "Melodische Urform und Gestaltvariation bei Debussy." **Deutsches Jahrbuch der Musikwissenschaft für 1966** 11 (1967): 95-105.

Sees traditional thematic procedures as having been replaced by variation on basic motives. These are not an Impressionistic "decay" but a conscious constructive endeavor. Refers to **Quatuor**, **La mer**, and the three sonatas and traces the approach through to Bartók.

612. Woollen, Russell. "Episodic Compositional Techniques in Late Debussy." **Journal of the American Musicological Society** 11 (1958): 79-80. [abstract of a paper].

Proposes a descriptive analysis of **Et la lune (Images II)**, which consists of alternating short episodes. D contrasts chordal with primarily linear episodes.

613. Zenck-Maurer, Claudia. **Versuch über die wahre Art, Debussy zu analysieren.** Ph.D. diss., Technische University of Berlin, 1974. Published as vol. 8 of Berliner Musikwissen schaftliche Arbeiten. Munich and Salzburg:

Musikverlag Emil Katzbichler, 1974. 147 p. ISBN 3-87397-038-4; ML 410.D28Z4.

Proposes a holistic approach to D analysis, turning from a technical one that overemphasizes one element and that avoids evaluation. Takes a literary path in analyzing the prelude **Canope**, relating the succession of sonorities to Proust's processes in **Swann's Way**. Main aspects of the proposed analysis include "Suggestion and Imagination"; the role of notation; rhythm and meter; and the arabesque. Examples are drawn from the preludes for piano. Important for pointing out main junctures of D and the New Music of the period 1954-60, as in his graphic notation.

4. Harmony and Tonality

614. Allen, Judith Shattin. "Tonal Allusion and Illusion: Debussy's **Sonata for Flute, Viola, and Harp**." **Cahiers Debussy** (nouvelle série) 7 (1983): 38-48.
Traces D's "emancipated tonality" according to its two main functions: a nostalgic reference to the past, and a structural procedure tending toward disintegration but ultimately giving "salvation." Schenkerian graphs outline the large-scale designs, which are predominantly linear.

615. Almendra, Julia d'. "Debussy et le mouvement modal de la musique du XXe siècle." In source 127.

The present article is largely a reflection upon the author's 1948 study (listed next).

616. ------. **Les modes grégoriens dans l'oeuvre de Claude Debussy**. Doctoral thesis, L'Institut Grégorien de Paris. Paris: Imprimerie G. Enault, [ca. 1948]. 192 p. ML 410.D28 A7.

The most exhaustive study to date of this important style trait. Proceeds by a survey of the modes in tradition, the functional tonal system, and Gregorian themes among D's precursors

(Berlioz, Fauré). Then discusses modality in **Pelléas** and works after it (**Martyre**, **La mer**, **Six épigraphes antiques**). Bias affects only the overstated conclusion, which implies that modality is superior to functional tonality and states that D's musical language is "Gregorian."

In their responses to the article in its form as a lecture, Jacques Chailley and Ernest Ansermet point out that all around D tonality was being expanded by modal uses, with no particular context of the Church. D referred to modality primarily later in his career, as with the **Trois bal-lades de Villon** and **Le Gmartyre**.

* Ansermet, Ernest. "Le langage de Debussy." See annotation 127.

Debussy's melodic style is enriched by modes and pentatonicism.

617. Balardelle, Geneviève. "L'exotisme extrême-orient en France au tournant du siècle." **Revue internationale de musique française** 2, no. 6 (Nov. 1981): 67-76.

Discusses D's inclination for melodic series without half steps. Relates these to his fascination with **slendro** and other oriental scales heard in the 1889 world exposition in Paris. Refers primarily to **Estampes**.

618. Berman, Lawrence David. "The Evolution of Tonal Thinking in the Music of Claude Debussy." Ph.D. diss., Music, Harvard University, 1965. 2 vols. 265 p.

Surveys 19th-century harmony and "The Legacy of Wagnerian Chromaticism" as background to D. Discusses **Le balcon** [**Cinq poèmes de Baudelaire**] as an example of Wagnerism but considers such an outright Wagnerian work an isolated phenomenon. Finds in **Damoiselle élue** the mature tendency toward balancing Wagnerian ideas with modality and other tendencies. Proposes the term "neutralization" to indicate the prominent harmonic tendency whereby D breaks down functional tonal associations by added tones, which in turn create superimposed triads when heard traditionally. Sees the decade 1890-1900 (the period of **Pelléas**'s creation) as central to the solidification of his linear harmonic style. An valuable survey of the harmonic idiom but unfortunately of difficult access. Not examined directly. See review by M. DeVoto in **Current Musicology** 9 (1969): 200-08.

619. Brailiou, Constantin. "Pentatony in Debussy's Music." In **Studia memoriae Belae Bartók sacra**, 3rd ed., pp. 377-418. London and New York: Boosey and Hawkes, 1959. ML 55.R35 1959. A second edition in French is available.

Cites a very large number of examples from D and classifies them as to the mode or other ancient scale from which they appear to derive. Stimulates further research without synthesizing the numerous examples into a cohesive overview.

620. Chailley, Jacques. "Apparences et réalités dans le langage musical de Claude Debussy." In source 127.

A study of D's harmonic style, concentrating on tones added to the triad and their function. Argues that D in his youthful music resolves such dissonances classically. However, see Briscoe (item 705) for an argument to the contrary. Chailley disputes the thesis that D's true successors are Stravinsky and Schoenberg.

621. Chew, Geoffrey. "The Spice of Music: Towards a Theory of the Leading Note." **Music Analysis** 2, no. 1 (March 1983): 35-53.

The discussion of the role of the leading note is curtailed in Schenker's writings. Its function is demonstrated here in the context of hierarchic levels. Cites examples from Haydn and Debussy.

622. Davison, Archibald Thompson. "The Harmonic Contribution of Claude Debussy." Ph.D. diss., Music, Harvard University, 1908. 131 p.

Not examined, but appears to be the first dissertation on Debussy.

623. Dickinson, A.E.F. "The Neo-Modal Style." **Music Review** 33, no. 2 (May 1972): 108-21.

Discusses the involvement of D (and Bartók, Kodály, and Vaughn Williams) in folk song. Relates pentatonicism in melody to folk music and sees new modes deriving from the pentatonic. Refers mainly to Golaud's music in **Pelléas**.

624. Doumel-Diény, A. **L'analyse harmonique en exemples.** Fascicule 16: Debussy, Quatre **Préludes**. Fascicule 17: Debussy, Trois **Etudes** et Suite **Pour le piano**. Neuchâtel: Delachaux et Niestlé, 1967.

Shenkerian analytic method here is refashioned as an aid to sensitive performance, an approach that is new and helpful. Fascicule 16 treats the preludes **Les collines d'Anacapri**, **Cathédrale engloutie**, **Canope**, and **Bruyères**. Fascicle 17 treats the etudes **Pour les tierces**, **Pour les sonoritées opposées**, and **Pour les accords**, as well as the suite **Pour le piano**.

625. Gervais, Françoise. "Debussy et la tonalité." In item 127.

Presents the concepts of rarefaction and eclipse of tonality, which are presented convincingly and ought to inform further discussion of D. Shows his expanded sense of scale and his disinclination to proceed by a rigid tonal order.

626. Geysen, Frans. "Sporen van het classicistisch modulatiemodel in muziek van deze tijd" [Traces of the Classical Modulation Model in Contemporary Music]. **Adem** 18, no. 4 (Sept.-Oct. 1982): 181-85. In Dutch with English and French summaries.

The point of reference is the modulation technique of Haydn, Mozart, and Beethoven. In the 20th century, traces of this technique are found in music by Debussy, Bartók, Prokofiev, Ligeti, Xenakis, and Stockhausen.

627. Goldbeck, Fred. "Twentieth-Century Composers and Tradition." In **Twentieth-Century Music**, pp. 23-33. New York: Orion Press, 1968. ML 197.M95 1969.

Notes that D broke with the anti-traditionalist mindset and emancipated not dissonance but consonance, which remained the basis of his static style. The music of Monteverdi and Musorgsky and the Italian comedy combine in such representative works as the sonata for violoncello.

628. Gut, Serge. "Les techniques d'harmonie impressioniste chez Debussy." **Revue internationale de musique française** 2, no. 5 (June 1981): 31-42.

Distinguishes between the static in time and the static in position or texture. Observes a static quality of harmony that is immobile and one that inclines toward immobility. This latter relates D to Impressionism in painting. Refers to the compositions **Cloches à travers** and **Mouvement** (both from **Images I** for piano) and to the piano prelude **La terrasse des audiences**.

629. Harris, Simon. "Chord-forms Based on the Whole-tone Scale in Early 20th-century Music." **Music Review** 41, no. 1 (Feb. 1980): 36-51.

Traces the derivation of whole-tone chords to the French augmented-sixth chord and to the augmented triad. Refers to **Prélude (Pour le piano)**, the prelude **Voiles**, and **La soirée (Estampes II)**. Six-note clusters in **Jeux** and **La mer** are extensions of the idea. Also refers to Berg, Bartók, Sibelius, and Wolf.

630. Hartke, S.P. "Comparative Aspects of the Treatment of the Harmonic Envelope in the First Movements of Debussy's **Quartet in G Minor** and Ravel's **Quartet in F Major**." Ph.D. diss., University of California at Santa Barbara, 1982. DA 44/2921A Apr. 1984; UM order no. DA8400037. MT 50.H294 1982a.

Static harmonic regions, or harmonic envelopes, occur in the manner of a mosaic in both compositions. Both follow the outlines of classical sonata form. D contrasts denser pitch sets to simpler sets, whereas Ravel contrasts octatonic and diatonic areas.

631. Jakobik, Albert. **Zur Einheit der neuen Musik.** Wurzburg: Konrad Triltsch Verlag, 1957. 124 p. ML 3800.J25.

Abundant examples of music. Devotes extended chapters to D, Bartók, and Hindemith. See pp. 14-44, where the author explains the concept of monistic harmony. Single, momentary sound structures are particularly rich and quasi-independent. Applies the concept to the piano prelude **Feuilles mortes**. Nonetheless, finds a tonal coherence of long range. Also observes the role of timbre in D's compositions.

632. Laloy, Louis. "Exercice analytique sur les quatres premières mesures de **Pelléas**." **Revue musicale, histoire et critique** 2, no. 11 (Nov. 1902). Reprinted in item 82, pp. 115-18.

Among the earliest studies of tonality in D. Is insightful and considers the wider meaning of the passage, eschewing the early (and unfortunately later) reliance upon talk of "color chords for sensual value." D deeply appreciated Laloy's brand of criticism.

633. Lenormand, René. **Etude sur l'harmonie modern.** Paris: Monde musical, 1913. Translated by H. Antcliffe as **A Study of Modern Harmony**, London: Williams, 1915. MT 50.L59 A7 1915. English ed. reprinted London: Wood, 1940; and New York: Da Capo 1976. MT 50.L59 A72.

The first attempt to examine systematically the element of harmony in D's music and to relate innovative features to those of his precursors. Necessarily concerns works prior to about 1910 but argues for the interpretation of D as chief among modern composers. Even so, Lenormand elicited an expression of displeasure from D.

634. Lewin, David. **Generalized Musical Intervals and Transformations.** New Haven: Yale University Press, c1987. xiii, 258 p. ISBN 0- 300-03493-8; ML 3809.L39 1987.

Comments on the opening of **Reflets dans l'eau** [**Images I**] (p. 231-44). Points to the structure of interval-motives, their generation and transformation. Observes a "private commentary" on Wagner's **Tristan** in the motive that Lewin terms "Tristan-harmony-cum-ruffle." Observes that the interrelation of harmony, motives, and dynamics require the particularly close attention of performers.

635. Meeus, Nicolas. "A propos du rôle de l'harmonie des médiantes dans l'oeuvre de Debussy." In **Mélanges de musicologie I**, pp. 27-36. Louvain: Institut Supérieur d'Archéologie et d'Histoire de l'Art, 1974. ML 55.M39.

An important article noting that D's harmony is systematically, rather than "impressionistically," structured. An expanded use of tertian relationships is a main exploration. D turns from the quintal chord relationships of traditional tonality.

636. Morgan, Robert P. "Secret Languages: The Roots of Musical Modernism." **Critical Inquiry** 10 (1983-1984): 442-61.

Musical modernism is marked by a linguistic plurality and the failure of any one language to assert a dominant position. Thus Morgan refutes Donald Mitchell (**Language of Modern Music**, London, 1963), who attempts to show serialism as "proper" to the 20th century. With D, Scriabin, Schoenberg, and Stravinsky, the tonal background breaks from the triad and its extensions. Even so, the individual solution of each composer is the outgrowth af an earlier orientation to tonality. A reading of breadth that contributes to a perspective of D's place in the twentieth century.

637. Mueller, Robert Earl. "The Concept of Tonality in Impressionist Music: Based on the Works of Debussy and Ravel." Ph.D. diss., Theory, Indiana University, 1954. 171 p. DA XIV.II, p. 2088; UM order number 19,153. ML 444.M8.

Traces three main tonal elements that figure in tonal form: 1) sonorities that obscure definite tonal function; 2) linking of sonorities in a continuous mosaic pattern; and 3) use of tonal pillars that do not define a single tonality. Refers to **Chansons de Bilitis**, **Estampes**, **Images I**, **Prélude-faune**, the **Nocturnes**, **La mer**, and

Pelléas. Unfortunately labors uselessly over the concept of "Impressionist harmony."

638. Nadeau, Roland. "Debussy and the Crisis of Tonality." **Music Educators Journal** 66 (Sept. 1979): 69-73.

Argues that D is the central figure in the development of twentieth-century tonal idioms and remains highly influential. On the other hand, the atonalists and serialists are declining in prestige and are isolated from the public. D offers an extended tonality that, with adaptations, has been an applicable model throughout the century. A concise and clear summary if somewhat biased toward tonal values. Further see Starr (item 218).

639. Parks, Richard S. **The Music of Claude Debussy**. New Haven: Yale University Press, 1989 [forthcoming]. ISBN 0-3000-4439-9; ML 410.D28 P24 1989.

Focuses on the relationship between D's pitch materials in general (from a set-theoretic perspective) and on tonality specifically, on text expression and pitch materials in the vocal and dramatic works, on form, and on register, orchestration, and meter as they contribute to structure. The book ranges widely across all genres and periods in D's career and promises to be valuable. Not examined.

640. Reiche, Jens Peter. "Die theoretischen Grundlagen javanischer Gamelan-Musik und ihre Bedeutung für Claude Debussy." **Zeitschrift für Musiktheorie** 3, no. 1 (1972): 5-15.

Observes an important parallel between the equidistant intervals of **slendro** and D's whole-tone uses. Musical procedures of gamelan, including compression and rearrangement of sections, find a counterpart in D. Makes particular reference to **Images** I no. 2 (**Hommage à Rameau**).

641. Reti, Rudolph. **Tonality-Atonality-Pantonality**. Reprinted as **Tonality in Modern Music**, New York: Collier Books, 1962. MT 40.R394 T6 1962.

A landmark study with continuing relevance. Finds that D replaces classical tonality based on harmonic progression with a melodic tonality. Cites examples from **Reflets dans l'eau (Images I)**. Argues that D is responsible for reintroducing the force of melodic tonality into Western music, such as much of the world's music observes. Traces D's achievements to his French, Spanish, and American successors in particular. Profitably could be rethought by current analysis.

642. Samson, Jim. **Music in Transition: A Study of Tonal Expansion and Atonality, 1900-1920.** London: Dent, 1977. 242 p. ISBN 0-460- 04245-9; ML 197.S184 M8.

Discusses D (together with Liszt, Busoni, and Stravinsky) as one who expands and reinterprets tonality. Studies in some detail the **Chansons de Bilitis** and **L'isle joyeuse**. Notes that D's interaction and differentiation of harmonic types is essential. Refers also to **La mer**, **Jeux**, and the **Etudes**, which prophesy the contemporary form process seen most obviously in such non-German composers as Messiaen and Stravinsky. A clear account of D's role in the history of tonality.

643. Schnebel, Dieter. "...Brouillards: Tendenzen bei Debussy." **Die Reihe** 6 (Vienna, 1960). English translation in **Die Reihe** 6, Bryn Mawr, Pennsylvania: Presser, 1961.

Serial analysis is applied to the prelude **Brouillards**. Concludes that D abandons traditional modulation and tonality altogether. His tendencies instead involve sound-structures, functional organization of intensities, and the breakup of traditional forms. Schnebel has received a challenge by Nadeau (item 834).

644. Silver, Sheila Jane. "Some Aspects of Harmonic Organization in the Music of Debussy." Ph.D. diss., Theory, Brandeis University, 1976. 134 p. UM 76-25,325; DA XXXVII.5, p. 2487- A. MT 145.D4 S55 1976.

Centers on an excerpt from **Jeux** and the preludes **Les sons et les parfums**, **La terrasse des audiences**, and **Des pas sur la neige**. Sets forth a theory of harmony in D based on the relationship of dominant 7th chords related by minor 3rd.

645. Storb, Ilse. **Untersuchungen zur Auflösung der funktionalen Harmonik in der Klavierwerken von Claude Debussy.** Ph.D. diss., University of Cologne, 1967. Published Kassel: Bärenreiter, 1971. 148 p. ML 410.D28 S7.

Describes the functional harmony of the early piano works (**Pour le piano**) and related if new devices. Discusses the outgrowth from functional harmony toward "Color-harmony," and moves to a discussion of the fully realized "Color-composition."

646. Suben, Joel Eric. "Debussy and Octatonic Pitch Structure." Ph.D. diss., Brandeis University, 1980. 59 p. DA 40:6065-66A June 1980; UM no. 80-13641. ML 410.D28 S93.

Observes that "octatonic, paratonal contrasts" play a vital role in Debussy's departures from functional tonality. Emphasizes octatonic structure as it occurs in **Prélude-faune** and **Ombre des arbres**. Not examined.

647. Trevitt, L.J.H. "The Role of the Diminished Seventh and Related Phenomena in the Development of Harmonic Dissension from Beethoven to Messiaen, with Special Reference to Debussy." Ph.D. diss., Musicology, University of East Anglia, 1975.

In his works from 1892 onward, D's establishes techniques using symmetrical series including augmented triads. These pass to Ravel,Stravinsky, and ultimately to Messiaen. Not examined.

648. Warburton, Thomas. "Bitonal Miniatures by Debussy from 1913." **Cahiers Debussy** (nouvelle série) 6 (1982): 5-15.

Discusses works that have either no key signature or a non-binding one: **Eventail** [**Trois poèmes de Mallarmé**], the **Canope**, and **Feux d'artifice** [both from **Preludes** book II]. Discusses linear tonality, bitonality, and the relation to functional tonality. Notes that two tonal levels are developed within each work. Includes graphic analyses of key passages.

649. Whittall, A. Tonality and the Whole-tone Scale in the Music of Debussy. **Music Review** 36 (1975), 261ff. Not examined.

5. Rhythm

650. Holopova, Valentina. **The Problems of Rhythm in the Work of Composers of the First Half of the Twentieth Century.** Moscow: Muzyka, 1971. 304 p. In Russian.

Provides a theoretical discussion, topology, and classification of rhythmic styles. Explores the expressive and structural role of rhythm in Debussy. Not examined.

651. Lippman, Edward A. "Progressive Temporality in Music." **Journal of Musicology** 3 (1984): 121-41.

The perception of music progressing in time is fundamental, although D appears to suspend forward motion in **Nuages [Nocturnes]**. Explores three temporal states: sheer continuity, motivation or impulsion, and structural or logical necessity. Views D's parallel motion as intensifying the effect of monophonic melody. Relates the procedure to temporal progress. Remembrance of past musical events in listening to **Nuages** governs the perception of the moment.

652. Suter, Louis-Marc. "Quelques aspects du rythme dans la musique de Claude Debussy." **Revue internationale de musique française** 2, no. 5 (June 1981): 23-30.

An important study of the rhythmic idioms. While free, D's rhythm maintains an inner symmetry. In **Etude 12**, the overall rhythm is tripartite and thus traditional, while local rhythmic schemes are highly varied. Also considers **Ibéria [Images orch.]**, **Jeux**, and **Pelléas**, discussing prosody in the latter.

653. Wilson, Lawrence A. "Ragtime: Its Roots, Style, and Significance on Twentieth-Century Music." D.Muss diss., Indiana University, 1981. 230 p.

Considers the adaptation of the ragtime idiom by contemporary composers of America and Europe. Points to rhythmic uses in D.

6. Timbre and Texture

654. Boulez, Pierre. **Musikdenken Heute-1**. Mainz: B. Schott's Söhne, 1963. ML 5.D24 Vol. 5. In French as **Penser la Musique Aujourd'hui**. Paris: Schott, 1963. In English as **Boulez on Music Today**. Translated by S. Bradshaw and R. Bennett. Cambridge, Mass.: Harvard University Press, 1971. ISBN 0-6740-8006-8; ML 197.B7213.

In a modern-day Socratic dialogue on composition, refers to Monsieur Croche and his paradox of discipline within freedom. Describes the heterophonic texture of Debussy's **Sonata for Flute, Viola, and Harp** as representative of an indispensable stage in texture between homophony and polyphony.

655. Cogan, Robert. "Claude Debussy: **Nuages**." In **New Images of Musical Sound**, pp. 85-92. Cambridge, Mass.: Harvard University Press, 1984. ISBN 0-674-61585-9; MT 6.C63N5.

Extends the concepts of item 656 by the unique application, in D research, of photographs of spectral formations (sonic wave patterns). Of direct concern is **Nuages [Nocturnes]**, where the space-color transformations unfold in three phases comprising eight stages. Relates to Berlioz. D arrives at a remarkable richness and clarity. The spectral analysis helps explain his remark about "different arrangements of a single color" in **Nuages**.

656. Cogan, Robert, and Pozzi Escot. **Sonic Design: The Nature of Sound and Music.** Englewood Cliffs, New Jersey: Prentice-Hall, 1976. xvi, 496 p. ISBN 0-1382-2726-8; MT 6.C63 S6.

Discusses the **Nocturnes (Nuages)**, the prelude **Voiles**, and **Syrinx** in terms of timbre, register, and sonority as they create form. Further see Cogan, "Tone Color: The New Understanding." **Sonus** 1, no. 1 (Fall 1980): 3-24. This latter is an articulate defense of the book **Sonic Design**, stressing the great importance of tone-color invention in music from ancient China to electronic music.

657. Covington, Katherine Russell. "A Study of Textural Stratification in Twentieth-Century Compositions." Ph.D. diss., Indiana University, 1982. 150 p. DA 8301057.

Textural stratification concerns blocks or layers of sound, which are created by timbre, register, dynamics, and type of activity. Analyzes works by D, Ives, Stravinsky, Messiaen, Varèse, and Webern.

658. Delone, Peter. "Claude Debussy, contrapuntiste malgré lui" [in English] . **College Music Symposium** 17, no. 2 (1977), 48-63.

Discuses pianistic conception and Chopin's influence in the preludes, Book I (nos. 2, 4,6, 10, 11) and Book II (nos. 5-7). These preludes exhibit a keen sensitivity toward voice leading, conter-rhythm, and spacing. Refers to R. Reti's remarks (item 641) on Debussy as a contrapuntist.

659. Gervais, Françoise. "La notion d'arabesque chez Debussy." **Revue musicale** no. 241 (1958), Carnet critique: 5-22.

Recalls D's statements in letters and critical writings concerning the arabesque in the music of Palestrina, di Lasso, and Bach. Traces the meaning of the term from the Renaissance (when it often connoted the "grotesque") to art historians of D's time (for whom as for D it connoted non-figurative, strongly linear art). Recalls its meaning for R. Schumann, Poe, Hoffmann, Balzac, Delacroix, and Gustave Moreau. Analyzes the independence of melody in Debussy's textures, his underlying linear conceptions, and his new contrapuntal uses based on superimposition of lines as well as on harmonically aloof melody. This is a major study of Debussy's "arabesque", or linearity, alongside that in Lockspeiser's **Life and Mind** (item 85). These two scholars have provoked fruitful thought but still invite further response to their ideas.

660. Gousset, Bruno. "La prééminence du timbre dans le language musical de **La mer** de Debussy." **Analyse musicale** 3 (April 1986): 37-45.

With the exception of Berlioz, before D composers orchestrated for a reinforced quartet. D is a pioneer in conceiving a universe of possibilities and combinations. In **La mer** timbre is a co-equal to theme in the process of form. Speaks of chord-timbres, in which the identity of a timbre is linked to a chord. A provocative study of timbre. Further see the entire volume III of **Analyse musicale**, which focuses on timbre as an element of form in Berlioz, Schoenberg, Messiaen, Carter, Boulez, and Stockhausen.

661. Gruber, Gernot. "Zur Funktion der 'primären Klangformen' in der Musik Debussys." In **Sym bolae historiae musicae: Hellmut Federhofer Festschrift zum 60. Geburtstag**, edited by F. Riedel, pp. 272-82. Mainz: Schott, 1972. ML 55.F32 1972.

Analyzes the primary sound groups of D's music with reference to contemporary French literary theory. Suggests that such an analysis is necessary to understanding D's compositional method. Cites examples from **Pelléas** and traces the compositional method through to Ligeti.

662. Harpole, Patricia W. "Debussy and the Javanese Gamelan." **American Music Teacher** 35, no. 3 (Jan. 1986), 8-9, 41.

Centers on **Pagodes (Estampes)**. Compares D's procedures to examples from the gamelan piece "Hudan mas." Destined for a non-specialist musical audience and illustrates how an authority may communicate specific research to that audience. D is held up as an example of one who bridges Western and oriental cultures.

663. Holdin, Calvin E. "The Organization of Texture in Selected Piano Compositions of Claude Debussy."

Ph.D. diss., Musicology, University of Pittsburgh, 1973. 101 p. UM 74-06,793; DA XXXIV.9, p. 6022-A.

Limits his discussion to the vertical and horizontal aspects of texture, the duration and continuation of textures, and the role of texture in form. Considers thirteen piano works from throughout D's career but maintains that the textural analysis of form applies generally to his music.

664. Jackson, Roland. "Polarities, Sound-masses and Intermodulations: A View of the Recent Music." **Music Review** 41, no. 2 (May 1980): 127-41.

Relates such sound masses as whole-tone clusters (in prelude **Feux d'artifice** and **Pagodes [Estampes]**) to the early music of Bartók and Stravinsky. The sound masses are prolonged structurally to result in innovative tonal designs.

665. Jarocinski, Stefan. "Quelques aspects de l'univers sonore de Debussy." In source 127.

Argues that the traditional "baggage" of anaylsis (proceeding by harmony, theme, form, etc.) no longer suffices for D or for contemporary music generally. D in the approach of traditional analysis is explained negatively. A new approach to analysis is required that appreciates his new constructive sense, and one must examine his technique of timbre, rationalization of time, horizontal structures, and successive transformation of musical elements. Timbre in the piano preludes is the focus in the body of the article.

666. Lewin, David. "Some Instances of Parallel Voice-Leading in Debussy." **Nineteenth-Century Music** 11, no. 1 (Summer 1987): 59-72.

Challenges the traditional analysis of parallel voice leading, which views the practice as organum-like doubling of a monophonic idea. Notes that such a hearing can be valid in some instances, while elsewhere such apparent parallelism is arrived at from the convergeance of independent lines. Refers to the **Sonata for Violin** and the prelude for piano **Le vent dans la plaine**, and closely examines the prelude **Canope**.

667. Mikorey, Stefan. "Klangfarbe und Composition: Besetzung und musikalische Faktur in Werken für grosses Orchester und Kammermusik von Berlioz, Strauss, Mahler, Debussy, Schönberg, und Berg." Ph.D. diss., Musicology, Ludwig-Maximilian University, Munich, 1980. Published Munich: Minerva, 1982. 263 p. ISBN 3-597-10373-1; ML 3807.M54 1982.

Studies the instrumentation for the music dramas **Pelléas** (Act III, scenes 2-3), Strauss's **Elektra**, and Schoenberg's **Erwartung**, pointing out the significance of tone color in the compositional process. Offers analytic tables outlining the structure of these according to timbre. Also refers to works for large orchestra by Strauss, Berlioz, and Mahler and to chamber orchestral works by Berg and Strauss.

668. Paja, Jadwiga. "Uwagi o formie w muzyce Debussy'ego (na przykladzie Preludiow)" [Form in Debussy's Music, with examples from the Preludes]. **Muzyka** 27, no. 1-2 (1982): 3-10. Summary in English.

Debussy creates referential sound events, or particular arrangements of texture and space, that become a structural entity. Two types of structure result: 1) a unified form consistent unto itself and deriving from the initial sound event; and 2) a mosaic-like form of seemingly unrelated sound events with certain elements nonetheless recurring, as in Stravinsky. Draws examples from the **Preludes** for piano.

669. Ringgold, John Robert. "The Linearity of Debussy's Music and its Correspondances with the Symbolist Aesthetic: Developments before 1908." Ph.D. diss., Musicology, University of Southern California, 1972. 436 p. UM 73- 00,762; DA XXXIII.7, p. 3700-A.

Linear traits relate to D's goal of intimate lyricism and connect to Wagner. In the music after 1908, however, a unique polyphony associated with the arabesque and instrumental music marks D's development. Linear considerations led to motivic variation, polymodal counterpoint, and a totally chromatic line, which would be advanced by Bartók, Schoenberg, and Stravinsky.

670. Rosing, Helmut. "Debussy und das indonesische Gamelan: eine vergleichende Klangfarben-Analyse." **HiFi Stereophonie** 7, no. 2 (Feb. 1968): 127-34.

Uses the Kay Sonograph to compare an Indonesian gamelan performance to **Le martyre**. The author uses timbral parallels to confirm the influence of gamelan on D's sound image. Somewhat overstated and mechanical but suggestive of how acoustical testing may lead to a firmer understanding of the music. Further see Cogan (item 656).

671. Souris, André. "Debussy et la nouvelle conception du timbre." **Cahiers musicaux** (Brussels) 1, no. 6 (March 1956): 23-31.

Debussy incorporates timbre as a structural element. He thus breaks with traditional, abstract processes of form, "les formes de pure rhétorique." Refers to D's response to Beethoven's formal concepts. Stravinsky and Webern build upon D's conception, as in Stravinsky's **L'histoire du soldat** and **Le sacre du printemps** and Webern's **Symphony Op. 21**. These contrast with the Beethovenian, abstract conceptions of Schoenberg and Berg.

672. Wen-Chung, Chou. "Asian Concepts and 20th-Century Composers." **Musical Quarterly** 57, no. 2 (April 1971): 211-29.

Analyzes D's perceptivity toward polyphony in the gamelan, rare for his time. Points to **La mer** for its textural affinities to gamelan and to **Jeux** for its lyric use of percussion. Considers D as the first to achieve a synthesis of oriental and Western concepts, which are traced through to Cage and Messiaen.

7. Melody and Prosody

673. Andréani, Eveline. "Texte et musique, ou les aventures du sens: A propos de **Pelléas et Mélisande**: Maeterlinck et Debussy." **Analyse musicale** 9 (Oct. 1987): 21-28.

A useful article on the relations of text and music, investigating metaphors and historical questions, the immediate background of French Symbolism, and the musical treatment of text in **Pelléas**. Sonorous color is a factor in D's prosody.

674. Hsu, Samuel. "Imagery and Diction in the Songs of Claude Debussy." Ph.D. diss., Musicology, University of California at Santa Barbara, 1972. 218 p. UM 72-26,832; DA XXXIII.5, p. 2413-A.

Seeks a perspective of the poetic-musical synthesis that D achieved in his songs, approaching the question through imagery and diction. Chapters deal respectively with the early songs (which the author relates too easily to the Parnassians), the Baudelaire songs, those on Verlaine texts, and the songs on the writers D himself, Louÿs, and Mallarmé. Musical elements respond directly to the call of Symbolist poetry.

675. Julien, Jean-Rémy. "L'influence des crieurs de Paris sur le récitatif debussyste: une hypothèse." **International Review of the Aesthetics and Sociology of Music** 15, no. 2 (1984): 141-57. Summaries in English and Serbo-Croation.

Quotes a 1900 letter revealing D's awareness of street-criers' tunes. This study refers to an 1890 source still in manuscript that documents authentic street cries in the period 1880-90. Recalls M. Proust's sensitivity to the cries and his amusing parallel of Arkel's and Golaud's singing to the cry of the escargot vendor. Admittedly hypothetical but is in a fruitful mode of thought, whereby D's recitative is closely related to natural speech contours and rhythms.

676. Large, John. "The Linguistic Problem in the Performance of Claude Debussy's Solo Song

Settings of 15th-Century Poetry (Three ballades of François Villon and two rondeaux of Charles d'Orléans)." **Journal of Research in Singing** 6, no. 1 (1982): 27-57.

Considers the original sources, modern adaptations, and D's modernized variants. Sets out the choices facing the singer: one makes the modern compromises or one attempts the Middle French as it is presumed to have been pronounced. A most helpful conclusion for singers gives the complete texts, a syllabic modern French version, and a syllabic English translation.

677. Raad, Virginia. "Les éléments folkloriques dans l'oeuvre de Claude Debussy." Diss., University of Paris, 1955. Not examined.

678. ------. "Musical Quotations in Claude Debussy." **American Music Teacher** 17, no. 3 (Jan. 1968): 22-24, 34.

A concise account and a useful point of departure for research. References to prelude for piano **Hommage à S. Pickwick Esq.**

679. Raffman, Relly. "Scalar Control." **College Music Symposium** 15 (1975): 34-51.

Discusses the positions (Dorian, etc.) of scales. In D's Preludes, the octatonic scale appears. It is symmetrical and thus apt for total scalar control. Also refers to **Prélude-faune**. Compares D's uses to Stravinsky and to jazz.

680. Spieth-Weissenbacher, Christiane. "Prosodes et symboles mélodiques dans le récitatif de **Pelléas et Mélisande**, ou place du figuralisme dans l'écriture vocale de Debussy." **International Review of the Aesthetics and Sociology of Music** 13, no. 1 (1982): 83-92. Summaries in English and Serbo-Croatian.

Describes the naturalness of the recitative as it relates to verbal rhythmic patterns and intonation. Three types of musical figures are observed in the recitative: "prosodes" (realistic transcriptions of spontaneous spoken figures); madrigalisms (realistic musical depiction of external situations); and symbols (musical features the relation of which to the abstract notion they represent is analogic).

681. ------. "Le récitatif Debussyste ou les richesses de la prosodie française." **Revuo internationale de musique française** 2, no. 5 (June 1981): 86-92.

An informative discussion of D's prosody, which springs from the French language. Among other passages, Yniold's singing in **Pelléas** is representative: it ascends by short, accented phrases that prefer the perfect intervals. Such a prosody is masterful in representing the childhood of Yniold. Recalls the prosody of Musorgsky's **Boris Godunov**.

682. Porter, L.M. "Text Versus Music in the French Art Song: Debussy, Fauré, and Verlaine in **Mandoline**." **Nineteenth-Century French Studies** (1984): 138-44.

The conceptions of D and Fauré regarding the relationship of text and music are radically different. D is imitative, programmatic, and directly interpretative, and his setting of each phrase of text is so careful as to appear fragmentary. Fauré is absolute, subordinating his text to musical ideas. Contrasts their settings of Verlaine's poem **Mandoline**.

683. Wenk, Arthur. "Parsing Debussy: Proposal for a Grammar of his Melodic Practice." **In Theory Only** 9, no. 8 (1987).

Considers the principles of cognitive science, relating these to musical style analysis and arriving at a "generative grammar." Deals with 92 melodies from D's instrumental music. Interprets pentatony as a basis for melodic practice and derives a theoretical rationale for the stasis of his melody. Refers to semiotics in analyzing melody and thus relates to studies by Guertin and Nattiez (sources 758, 598, and 835-36).

X

STUDIES OF COMPOSITIONS

684. Abbate, Carolyn. "**Tristan** in the Composition of **Pelléas**." **Nineteenth-Century Music** 5, no. 2 (Fall 1981): 117-41.

Discusses D's projects **La chute de la Maison Usher** and **Rodrigue et Chimène** as they relate to **Pelléas**. Considers the Meyer, Bréval, New England Conservatory, and Legouix manuscripts. Observes that early drafts elucidate the impact of **Tristan** upon D's composition of **Pelléas**. D appears to have manipulated the Wagner work deliberately. **Tristan** at once informs and comments on **Pelléas**. Analyzes the formal design of Act IV, scene iv, of **Pelléas**.

685. Adams, John Kenneth. "Debussy: Part I, The Early Piano Works." **Piano Quarterly** 35, no. 137 (Spring 1987): 36-40.

Surveys D's piano music of the 1880s and 1890s, placing it in the context of the Conservatory years and the period following. This and the two sequels (Parts II and III) are brief but responsible summaries for teachers and students.

"Debussy: Part II, The Later Piano Works." **Piano Quarterly** 35, no. 138 (Summer 1987): 48-53. Surveys the **Estampes**, **Images I** and **II**, and through to **La plus que lente**.

"Debussy: Part III, Sketches, Manuscripts, the **Preludes** and **Etudes**." **Piano Quarterly** 35, no. 139 (Fall 1987): 40-43. Discusses sketches for **Voiles**, **Cathédrale engloutie**, and **Fille aux cheveux de lin** (prelude).

686. Alfred, E. Maurice. "A Study of Selected Choral Works of Claude Debussy." Ph.D. diss., Fine Arts, Texas Tech University, 1980. xxiii, 392 p. UM 81-11,943; DA XLI.12, p. 4878- A.

Concerns **La damoiselle élue**, **Trois chansons de Charles d'Orléans**, and **Ode à la France**. Discusses biographical background, poets, and texts. The analysis focuses on motives, themes, and overall form. Also considers performance problems such as diction, phrasing, and rhythm.

687. Andreacchi, Peter. "An Examination of the Relation of Text to Music in Claude Debussy's **Trois poèmes de Mallarmé**." Ph.D. diss., Musicology, City University of New York, 1986. 360 p. UM DA8611321; DA 47:703A Sept. 1986.

Begins by reviewing literary Symbolism and comparing it to D's "new musical symbolism." Discusses the three songs in turn and summarizes that poetic and musical forms of necessity maintain some independence. The vocal writing shows the most direct interrelation. Mallarmé and D are closely allied in aspects of ambiguous meaning, gradual evocation of idea, sonorous beauty, and novel contexts that transform meaning.

688. Angeli, Helen Rossetti. **Dante Gabriel Rossetti, his Friends and Enemies**. London: Hamish Hamilton, 1949. PR 5246.A8.

This discussion focuses helpfully upon the aesthetics of Rossetti's **Blessed Damozel** and D's **La damoiselle élue**. Recounts a statement by Rossetti that in the **Raven**, "Poe had done the utmost in describing the grief of the lovers on earth, and so I determined to reverse the conditions...of the loved one in heaven." Traces the genesis of the poem **Blessed Damozel**.

689. Appledorn, Mary Jeanne. "A Stylistic Study of Claude Debussy's Opera **Pelléas et Mélisande**." Ph.D. diss., Theory, University of Rochester-Eastman School of Music, 1966. 452 p. UM 67-1312; DA XXVIII.2, p. 716-A.

Approaches the opera with traditional but useful style criticism. Finds that scenes and acts take well-recognized forms (ABA, ABCBA) and involve a system of 32 leitmotivs in the orchestra. Studies sonorities, root movement, and non-harmonic tones and gives a statistical analysis. Finds recurring sequences of tonal centers, relating these and other style elements to dramatic situation.

Points to modal, mixed, and functional diatonic scales, and discusses vocal writing and orchestration.

690. Austin, William W., ed. **Debussy's "Prelude to the Afternoon of a Faun."** Norton Critical Scores. New York: Norton, 1970. 167 p. SBN 0-393-02145-9 (cloth); M 1002.D28 P73 19706.

The edition is based chiefly on Debussy's 1908 revisions (collection Lang). Other sources include the Jobert MS and Lehman sketch. Contains essays by the editor and others, and includes reprints of criticism showing the work's initial reception. Austin's 30-page analysis of the work is a model by one who has devoted much thought to D and his role in the twentieth century. A complete score, notes, and bibliography are given. Further on Austin's analysis see item 100.

691. Banowetz, Joseph. "Reflections on Playing Debussy." **Piano Quarterly** 30, no. 119 (Fall 1982): 42-46.

A useful survey of main piano interpreters of D from his period and just after, including R. Casadesus, Schmitz, Viñes, Gieseking, and Cortot. The author's generalized remarks reflect high artistry and provoke research in depth into performance practice of the piano works.

692. Barbag-Drexler, Irena. "Debussy, der Impressionist." **Musikerziehung** 32, no. 6 (June 1979): 198-204.

Emphasizes the central place of piano music in D's oeuvre. Makes particular references to the **Estampes**, **Arabesques**, and **Suite bergamasque**. Observes and discusses briefly the depth of structure and meaning beneath the decorative surface, thus saving the article from clichés.

693. Barraqué, Jean. "**La mer** de Debussy, ou la naissance des formes ouvertes." **Analyse musicale** 12 (June 1988): 15-62.

Cites **La mer** as an early example of "open form" in the twentieth century, in which D departs from traditional archetypes of form. Ideas are exposed and developed by D in an uninterrupted surge, as co-existents. The proper analysis of his music thus should view harmony, orchestration, and articulation as co-adjacent forces. Despite the theory of a new analysis, in practice Barraqué has recourse to traditional formal parlance: **Jeux de vagues** is analyzed as to introduction, exposition, development, and so on. In the end, the reader perceives from the analysis that D worked with traditional boundaries while revitalizing these at lower levels of form. "Forming" is seen within "form." This text by Barraqué was unpublished at the time of his death and appears here for the first time. See item 121, **Analyse musicale** 12, of which this is the centerpiece.

694. Barraud, Henri. **Les cinq grands opéras**. Paris: Seuil, 1972. 301 p.

Provides a synopsis of the libretto and music of **Pelléas**. Is a worthy aid to preparing a general study such as program annotation. Also discusses **Don Giovanni**, **Tristan**, **Boris Godunov**, and **Wozzeck**.

695. Bathori, Jane [pseud. of Jeanne Marie Berthier]. **Sur l'interprétation des mélodies de Claude Debussy**. Introduction by Darius Milhaud. Paris: Les Editions Ouvrières, 1953. 38 p. MT145.D4 B4.

Bathori sang many of D's songs to his piano accompaniment and later recorded certain of those (see Cobb item 55). She met him in 1904 but encountered the music as a performer when Ravel introduced her to the **Proses lyriques** in 1898. Her advice to singers emphasizes precision along with delicacy of nuance. Works discussed are the **Chansons de Bilitis**, **Fêtes galantes** books I and II, **Le Son du cor**, **L'échelonnement**, **Ariettes oubliées**, **Mandoline**, **Chansons de Charles d'Orléans**, **Cinq poèmes de Baudelaire**, **Trois poèmes de Mallarmé**, **Trois ballades de Villon**, **Proses lyriques**, and **Noël des enfants**. A thoughtful book by an important contemporary, and thus important to performers.

696. Bein, Joseph H. "Debussy's Orchestral **Images**: Other Features of the Style." Ph.D. diss., University of Rochester, 1970. 234 p. UM 70-4456; DA XXX.9, p. 3965-66-A.

Views the Images for orchestra as a landmark in the evolution of structure and as a prime example of programmatic representation. Traces the occurrence of tertian sonority and root movement and both traditional and innovative cadences. Harmonic progression involves linear thinking such as parallelism. **Gigues** and **Rondes de Printemps** gain formal unity by motivic and thematic development; **Ibéria** does so by thematic transformation and cyclic form. Discusses the counterpoint of rhythmic cells, which attains a high level of complexity at times.

697. Benedetto, Renato di. "Congetture su **Voiles**." **Rivista italiana di musicologia** 13, no. 2 (1978): 312-44.

In the "conjectures about **Voiles**" from the preludes for piano, finds a correspondence between formal and linguistic organization, which sheds light on the title. Points to parallels with the Symbolist poets, to tonal structures based on the whole tone scale, and to the thematic and textural form ABA'. An important article relating D's musical symbolism to Mallarmé's literary symbolism. Includes a full score of the work.

698. Berman, Laurence D. "Claude Debussy: **Piano Trio in G Minor**." **Nineteenth-Century Music** 11, no. 3 (Spring 1988): 291-94.

An extended review calling into question the editorial policies of the recently published trio, but also noting that major problems are present when editing Debussy. Comments as well on the musical significance of the piece. Further see Derr, item 732.

699. -----. "**Prelude to the Afternoon of a Faun** and **Jeux**: Debussy's Summer Rites." **Nineteenth-Century Music** 3, no. 3 (March 1980): 225-38.

The **Prelude** is traditional formally and does not follow the formal design of Mallarmé's poem. **Jeux** relates more closely to Mallarmé's novel conceptions in its play of changing intensities and open structures. This is a strong article that helps define Symbolism in its musical manifestations, which especially in **Jeux** reach to great psychological depth.

700. Billeter, Bernhard. "Debussy trahi par lui-même?" **Schweizerische Musikzeitung** (July-Aug. 1979): 214-15.

A response to Dietschy (item 735). Maintains that D himself departed from his expressive indications in the scores when he recorded **Danseuses de Delphes**, **Cathédrale engloutie**, and **Danse de Puck** from the **Preludes** book I. Interesting interchange about performance practice in the piano works.

701. Blumenthal, Daniel Henry. "Four Early Original Works for Piano 4-Hands by Claude Debussy." Volume I, Discussion and Analyses (xi, 42 p.); Volume II, Editions and Commentary (vii, 109 p.). DMA diss., Juilliard School of Music, New York, 1987.

A useful commentary on and publication of the **Symphonie en si mineur** (in both the 1933 and the 1965 Soviet editions); **Triomphe de Bacchus**, first movement (including both a reprint of the 1928 Choudens ed. and a new edition based on the manuscript); the **Triomphe de Bacchus**, second movement (Andante) in its first edition; and the **Andante cantabile** (a manuscript that surfaced recently and then was resold, becoming unavailable). The critical commentary appears thoughtful and the editions reliable.

702. Boll, André. "Le drame lyrique, sa présentation décorative." **Revue musicale** 4, no. 4 (Feb. 1923): 21-28.

The art of the stage set is one of abnegation, such that the **metteur-en-scène** must seek to complement the music. Discusses the sets for **Pelléas** as well as for works by Dukas and Wagner. In Boll's view, the set for **Pelléas** must not be too literal, a shortcoming of many settings.

703. ------. "**Pelléas** et sa présentation décorative." **Revue musicale** 9, no. 1 (Nov. 1927): 94-96.

Boll designed sets for the 1927 Amsterdam performance, two of which are illustrated. He describes Jusseaume's original stage designs and terms them "minutie," for they sought to crowd in too many visual symbols at once.

704. Boris, Siegfried. "Claude Debussy: **Syrinx für Soloflöte.**" **Musik und Bildung** 1, no. 4 (1969): 173-75.

Emphasizes the mythological and allegorical significance and programmatic intent. While tonality is ambiguous, certain tones nonetheless are guides. Not examined.

* Boulez, Pierre. **Orientations**. Cambridge, Mass.: Harvard University Press, 1986.

Two particularly relevant essays by this leading composer are "Reflections in **Pelléas et Mélisande**," pp. 306-17, and "Debussy: Orchestral Works," pp. 318-22. Both were published previously as recording liner notes. See further annotations 172-73.

* ------. **Points de repère**. second edition. Paris: Editions du Seuil, 1985. ISBN 2-2670-0276-0; ML 60.B796 P6 1985.

In "Benchmarks," a major figure of 20th-century music discusses orchestral works by D and **Pelléas**. See the annotation, item 172.

705. Briscoe, James R. "The Compositions of Claude Debussy's Formative Years (1879-1887)." Ph.D. diss., Musicology, University of North Carolina, 1979. xiv, 448 p. UM 79-25,888; DA XL.8, p. 4290-A. ML 410.D28 B85 1979a.

Considers 21 unpublished and 20 published works (at time of writing) of the 62 completed compositions of the period. Discusses biography and salient features of melody, rhythm, tonality, structure, and texture. Considers the young D's relation to French and Russian precursors, to Wagner, and to his coming mature style. Concludes that his early idiom is pivotal between the 19th and 20th centuries and has its origins primarily in French 19th-century music. Works discussed in depth include **Diane au bois**, **Printemps**, **Apparition**, **Zéphyr**, and **Enfant prodigue**.

706. ------. "Debussy **d'après** Debussy: The Further Resonance of Two Early **Mélodies**." **Nineteenth-Century Music** 5, no. 2 (Fall 1981): 110-16.

Describes the early **mélodie Fête galante** (1882) as the first version of the **Menuet** from the Petite **suite**, and the **mélodie La fille aux cheveux de lin** (ca. 1882-84) as the predecessor of the prelude for piano with the same title. Considers these early songs as evidence of a personal evolution that began with with the first works.

707. ------. "Debussy, Janus, and **Diane au bois**." **Musical Quarterly**, forthcoming 1990.

The unpublished opera scene **Diane au bois** is the most important and extended musical conception of D's youth. Considers the unpublished works **Diane--Ouverture** and the duo **Ode bachique** from the pre-operatic project **Hymnis**, which prepares for **Diane**. Discusses D's life at the time and the role of Banville's play that was adapted as the libretto of **Diane**. Analyzes the structure, which calls upon Wagnerian leitmotives but also adopts the procedures of lyric opera found in Massenet. In **Diane au bois**, D refers to his French past and aesthetic inclinations, seeks a revitalization through Wagner's ideas, and anticipates the synthesis of both idioms which would be achieved in **Pelléas**.

708. ------. "Debussy's Earliest Songs." **College Music Symposium** 24, no. 2 (Fall 1984): 81-95.

Discusses D's biography in the period surrounding 1882. Traces the innovative aspects of **Les roses**, **Fête galante**, **Rondel chinois**, and **Apparition**, citing specific passages and relating the innovations to his precursors Duparc and Chopin. Aspects that look to the future are new dissonance levels and tonality, sensitive prosody, and form involving melodic transformation. Concludes that Wagner's and the Russians' influence came after important tendencies had already set in. D's innovations appear to be inspired by late 19th-century French vocal music.

709. Brunel, Pierre. "Claude Debussy interprète d'Edgar Poe: **La chute de la maison Usher**." **Revue de littérature comparée** 3 (1987), 359-68.

Surveys D's unfinished theater projects before centering on **La chute**. Finds that D is sensitive to Poe's intent, judging by the musical and literary manuscripts of the work that remain. Relates to E.T.A. Hoffmann's **Rat Krespel**. A succinct account to be augmented by other analyses of the music and text in depth.

710. Buck, Charles Henry III. "Structural Coherence in the Preludes for Piano by Claude Debussy." Ph.D. diss., Musicology, University of California at Berkeley, 1975. xiii, 211 p. [Not examined or found in DA. See RILM 76/15508dd.66.] ML 410.D28 B8255.

711. Bugeanu, Constantin. "La forme musicale dans le **Pelléas** de Debussy." **Revue roumaine d'histoire d'art** 6 (1969): 243-60.

In French. An analysis centering on Act II, final scene, demonstrating that bar form is the framework. Further suggests that bar form is the structural basis of the entire opera.

712. Burge, David. Articles in **Keyboard Magazine**.

A series of pedagogic discussions of Debussy's piano music, by a contemporary composer and teacher. Aims to introduce the music to the popular audience and performers of the piano. A model accomplishment in clarity and pleasurableness of writing without condescension.

Vol. 11, no. 12 (Dec. 1985): 28. The sources of D's inspirations. Discusses the **Suite bergamasque**.

Vol. 12, no. 1 (Jan. 1986): 113. Harmonic daring and visionary episodes in D's piano music.

Vol. 12, no. 2 (Feb. 1986): 34-35. Observes striking harmonic juxtapositions in **Reflets dans l'eau [Images I]**. Noteworthy for thoughtful analysis.

Vol. 12, no. 3 (Mar. 1986): 26. Evocative titles and performance directions. Reference to **Children's Corner**.

Vol. 12, no. 4 (Apr. 1986): 27. Debussy's **Preludes**, Book I.

Vol. 12, no. 5 (May 1986): 30-31. Debussy's **Preludes**, Book II.

Vol. 12, no. 6 (June 1986): 28-29. Explores the virtuosic requirements of D's **Etudes**.

713. Burkhart, Charles. "Debussy Plays La **Cathédrale engloutie** and Solves Metrical Mystery. **Piano Quarterly** 65 (Fall 1968): 14-16.

D's 1913 Welte-Mignon recording clarifies the ambiguous meter, 6/4=3/2, which begins the prelude. In passages in which quarter-notes are the basic motion, they receive the beat, as does the half note in passages clearly in 3/2 (m. 7-12, 22-83, 86-end). Identifies recordings of performers who do interpret (George Copland, Cortot, Gina Bachauer) and those who do not interpret D's intentions instinctively (Schmitz, Gieseking, R. Casadesus).

714. Cahn, Peter. "Der Szenenaufbau in Debussys **Pelléas et Mélisande**." In **Bericht über dem International Musikwissenschaftliches Kongress Bonn 1970**, p. 207-12. Kassel: Bärenreiter, 1975.

The structure of scenes and acts in **Pelléas** reflects D's 1889 aesthetic, expressed to Guiraud, of "short, mobile scenes without long and heavy acts." Such a conception also guided D's work on **La chute de la maison Usher**.

715. Caillat, Stéphane. "Le geste du chef du choeur. Analyse de sa mise en oeuvre dans l'interprétation d'une chanson a capella de Debussy, **Dieu! qu'il la fait bon regarder!**" **Analyse musicale** 10 (Jan. 1988): 31-35.

Discusses the gestures appropriate to the performance practice of the chanson. Of direct concern are textual and musical nuances. Reproduces the entire chanson in miniature score.

716. Chailley, Jacques. "Le symbolisme des thèmes dans **Pelléas et Mélisande**." **L'information musicale** 64 (April 3, 1942): 889-890.

Not available to the present study, but a commentary (on leitmotives?) by a prominent scholar that is worth pursuing for serious analysis of **Pelléas**.

717. Charru, Philippe. "**La Cathédrale engloutie**, prélude de Claude Debussy; Le mouvement au

rhythme de la forme." **Analyse musicale** 4 (3ème trimestre 1986): 72-77.

The prelude is based upon immobile harmonies. However, the nuances of sonorous material open up an immense musical space. Finds a structure of 2 main parts (m. 1-46 and 47-71) and a coda (72-89).

718. ------. "Une analyse des 24 **Préludes pour piano** de Debussy: le mouvement musical au rhythme de la forme." **Analyse musicale** 12 (June 1988): 63-88.

The preceding article is preliminary to the present, more extensive study. Centers on **Cathédrale engloutie** and **Voiles** (from **Preludes** Book I) and **La terrasse des audiences** and **Tierces alternées** (from Book II). Analyzes in detail the structural cells (in essence, pitch sets), the longer themes, and the harmonic variants of the themes that result in structural motion. At the end, presents the structure of all 24 preludes in charts.

719. Chimènes, Myriam. "**La mer**, les **Préludes pour piano**, le **Prélude à l'après-midi d'un faune**: orientation bibliographique et discographique." **Analyse musicale** 12 (June 1988): 103-07.

A briefly annotated and selective bibliography of the works named. Also indicates a selective discography that is up-to-date.

720. ------. "Les vicissitudes de **Khamma**." **Cahiers Debussy** (nouvelle série) 2 (1978): 11-29.

Reveals MS sources concerning the Canadian dancer Maud Allan, who commissioned **Khamma** in 1910 but never danced it. Gives in full the original contract, pertinent letters, and newspaper accounts. Chimènes's dissertation at the University of Paris is entitled "**Khamma**, Ballet de Claude Debussy: Histoire et Analyse." Dissertation not examined.

721. Chirico, T. "Gli **Studi** de Debussy." **Rivista italiana di musicologia**, Quaderni, 19, no. 4 (Oct.-Dec. 1985): 665-80.

A study of the **Etudes**, plentifully illustrated by musical examples. The discussion centers on motivic, timbral, and registral processes of form. The Etudes are viewed as the summit of D's harmonic art, in which classic tonality and purely sonorous, new uses are coordinated.

722. Chun, Edna Breinig. "Debussy's piano music 1903-1907." DM diss., Piano Pedagogy, Indiana University, 1980. x, 217 p.

Discusses the aesthetics of his critical writings and the influences on Debussy. Analyzes **Estampes**, **Masques**, **L'isle joyeuse**, **Images** I and II, and **D'un cahier d'esquisses**.

723. Cnattingius, Claes M. "Notes sur les oeuvres de jeunesse de Claude Debussy. **Svensk tidskrift för musikforskning** (Uppsala) 44 (1962): 31-53.

Centers on the phase 1878-1888. Discusses certain of the works available in 1962 in chronological order, mentioning general traits of D's maturity already evident in his youth. Further see Briscoe (item 705) for style analysis and updating of bibliographic details and the works list of the present study.

724. Cobb, Margaret G. "The Several Versions of **Trois mélodies de Claude Debussy**." **Cahiers Debussy** (nouvelle série) 10 (1986): 24-27.

Considers the early (1883-4), 1891, and 1902 versions of **Paysage sentimental** and the versions of **Romance** ("Voici que le printemps"). Observes as well the ballade text and quotation from the French folksong "Nous n'irons plus au bois" in the song **La belle au bois dormant**. Indicates recordings and calls for an analysis.

725. Cortot, Alfred. **Cours d'interprétation.** Volume 1. Edited by Jeanne Tiéffry. Paris, 1934. Translated into English by R. Jacques. London: Harrap, 1937. 278 p. MT 140.C7.

Includes an extended discussion of the **Preludes for piano**, interpreting the titles and giving performance practice suggestions. Offers advice of continuing, high relevance. Also discusses performance considerations in **Pour le piano** and **Danse bohémienne**. Invaluable commentary by a renowned interpreter of the generation after Debussy.

726. Cox, David. **Debussy: Orchestral Music**. BBC Music Guides. London: British Broadcasting Corp., 1974. ISBN 0-563-12678-7; MT 130.D4 C7 1974.

States the premise that D's new musical landscape is conveyed most explicitly by his orchestral works. Is addressed to general audiences but conveys current thought since Lockspeiser (item 85) about structure, the structural and not merely "Impressionistic" role of sonority, and the new tonality. Does not condescend to its audience and discusses certain well-chosen examples. A model of its type, informative for general discussion and program annotation.

727. Dawes, Frank. **Debussy's Piano Music**. BBC Music Guides. London: British Broadcasting Corp., 1969. ISBN 0-563-08577-0; MT 145.D4D4. Reprint. Seattle: University of Washington Press, 1971. MT 145.D4 De 1971.

Very short but useful summary provoking further research. Particularly relevant to pianists, who will require a look at other studies for in-depth analysis. Reviews D's aesthetics and connections to Tchaikovsky and Ravel. Up to 1896, the piano was less important and his writing related to the accompaniment of the songs. Full maturity was achieved in 1903 (**Estampes**). Includes a particularly thoughtful survey of the preludes.

728. De Simone, Robert A. "The University of Washington's Production of 'The Turn of the Screw' [Britten] and a New English Translation of "**L'enfant prodigue**." DMA diss., University of Washington, 1981. 258 p.

Of importance here for the translation.

729. Debussy, Claude. **Sketches for the "Prélude à l'après-midi d'un faune**. Washington: Lehman Foundation, 1963. ML 96.5 D28 P7.

A facsimile of the particelle, the definitive draft of 1892-94 from which the orchestration was made. In his preface Roland-Manuel suggests that a comparison of the particelle with the orchestral score offers much insight into D's technique of orchestration. Such a study of this landmark work is still awaited.

730. Demuth, Norman. **French Piano Music: A Survey with Notes on its Performance.** London: Museum Press, 1959. 179 p. MT140.D45.

Encourages performers to regard the French piano idiom as one of clarity; one should not infuse an excessive romanticism or whim. Addresses both amateurs and advanced students. Is useful in that regard, although a shortcoming for scholarship is the tendency toward oversimplification: "D's piano music is expressed in terms of sound rather than line" (p. 98). Previous to the lesson of Ravel's **Jeux d'eaux,** D mostly reflected both the clavecin school and the salon tradition. Demuth is fixed on Impressionism as D's end goal in aesthetics, against which all is judged. The piano **Preludes** book II, for example, is heard as less successful than the first. The **Etudes** for piano are barely mentioned.

731. Denisov, Edison. "Über einige Besonderheiten der Kompositionstecknik Claude Debussys." In **Jahrbuch Peters 1978: Aufsätze zur Musik**, ed. E. Klemm, pp. 147-72. Leipzig: Peters, 1978. ML 5.J245.

Points to vigorous if veiled construction of the **Preludes**. Motives are key to both vertical and horizontal forms. Emphasizes **Danseuses de Delphes, Voiles, Les sons,** and **Le vent dans la plaine.**

732. Derr, Ellwood. "Sein erstes überliefertes Instrumentalwerk zur Erstveröffentlichung von Claude Debussys frühen **Klaviertrio.**" **Melos/Neue Zeitschrift für Musik** 11 (Dec. 1985): 10-16.

Considers the style and editorial problems of the **Trio in G Minor** (1882), which Derr recovered and edited for publication.

733. Dietschy, Marcel. "Adieu, Pelléas! (lettre ouverte à Mme de Tinan, héritière de Debussy)." **Revue musicale de Suisse romande** 33, no. 5 (1980): 225-26.

Concerns a proposal by filmmaker Pierre Jourdan, who had approached D's heirs for permission to write a script and to film **Pelléas**. Although the Maeterlinck heirs accepted the idea, D's did not. Dietschy argues in his open letter that the film could win innumerable admirers throughout society for D. Points out a root problem that has vexed D research and appreciation: over-protection among certain principals such as publishers, heirs, collectors, and even manuscript librarians.

734. ------. "Debussy, interprète de ses propres oeuvres." **Schweizerische Musikzeitung/Revue musicale suisse** 120, no. 1 (Jan.-Feb. 1980): 12-14.

Accepts the challenge of B. Billeter concerning D's recorded piano performances [see 700 and the following item]. While D betrayed his own performance ideals, the circumstances of his illness prevented him from performing as he would have preferred in the few recordings he left.

735. ------. "Debussy trahi par les virtuoses de piano." **Schweizerische Musikzeitung/Revue musicale suisse** 116, no. 1 (Jan.-Feb. 1976): 48-52.

An analysis of eleven modern recordings of **Children's Corner**. None of the pianists, according to Dietschy, presented accurately the text as notated. This review, written by a devoted student of D, might serve as a model for other studies of performance practice and, given his close attention to the scores, for criticism of the performance of D in general. It is not, however, without personal biases.

736. ------. "Wagner et le Quatuor de Debussy." **Schweizerische Musikzeitung/Revue musicale suisse** 121, no. 4 (1981): 243-47.

Reviews the evolution of D's appreciation of Wagner, citing a passage from an unpublished letter. Makes a somewhat tenuous parallel between the beginning theme of the **Quartet** and the sea motive in **Tristan** Act I. The Wagner theme seems to have imprinted itself, only to be modified within D's new tonal idiom.

737. Dille, D. "Inleiding tot het vormbegrip bij Debussy." In **Hommage à Charles Van den Borren: Mélanges,** pp. 175-96. Antwerp: De Nederlandsche Boekhandel, 1945. ML 55.B665 H6.

Centers on **Prélude-faune**, tracing the evolution of the flute theme and its bearing on the larger form. Finds that the faun's psychology is the driving force behind the thematic transformation.

738. Domling, Wolfgang. **Claude Debussy: "La mer."** Munich: Fink, 1976. 36 p. MT 130.D4 D6.

An analysis of **La mer** and discussion of its genesis, relating to programmaticism, Impressionism, its first performance, and different versions. Is a short but useful analysis, to be augmented by Rolf (868) and Barraqué (121). Gives detailed tables and charts of musical elements as they figure in the form. Avoids the pitfalls of popular, "pictorial" analysis but speaks more of the succession of parts than the organic whole.

739. Eimert, Herbert. "Debussys **Jeux**." **Die Reihe** vol. 5. Vienna, 1959.

Jeux is shown as an organism of melodic cells, which grow to become larger sections. Seeks to illuminate the process of form and not only the materials themselves. A main analysis of the particular composition and of form in late Debussy in general, which has influenced and still might inform further research.

740. Elst, Nancy van der. "**Printemps**, een jeugdwerk van Claude Debussy." **Mens en melodie** (Utrecht) 19, no. 4 (April 1964): 110-13.

Traces the genesis of the work as a Prix de Rome envoi. Discusses the official censure of its "vague impressionism." Observes an influence of Franck on the cyclicism of its structure.

741. Emmanuel, Maurice. **"Pelléas et Mélisande" de Debussy: Etude et Analyse.** Paris: Editions Mellottée, 1926, 1950. 224 p. MT 100.D44 P28.

Still valuable analysis of leitmotives and other aspects of structure, tonality, and melody. Chapter 2, "La genèse de l'oeuvre," contains a valuable, eye-witness account of 1889 theorizing by D on opera and aesthetics. Also contains a letter to André Messager. In his conclusion Emmanuel relates the innovations of **Pelléas** to French tradition.

742. Enix, Margery Ann. "The Dissolution of the Functional Harmonic Tonal System: 1850-1910." Ph.D. diss., Indiana University, 1977. ML 240.4.E54 1977am.

Analyzes **Pelléas** as a key work in the dissolution of tonality, along with Wagner's **Tristan**, Mahler's **Das Lied von der Erde**, and Strauss's **Elektra**.

743. Escher, Rudolf. "Debussy and the Musical Epigram." **Key Notes** (Amsterdam) 10, no. 2 (Dec. 1979): 59-63.

Concerns the **Six épigraphes antiques**, which Escher orchestrated in 1977. Compares to E. Ansermet's orchestration (Paris: Durand, 1939). Escher in his orchestration has sought to capture the atmosphere of "Eros the distant."

744. Estrade-Guerra, Oswald d'. "Les manuscrits de **Pelléas et Mélisande** de Debussy." **Revue musicale**, numéro special no. 234, **"Le martyre de St.-Sébastien,"** carnet critique 5-24.

Discusses D's lengthening (but not new composition) of the interludes in the opera, which permitted scene changes and continuity between scenes. Quotes pertinent letters, and reviews the Meyer, Lerolle, and Bréval manuscripts. This article is updated and extended by Grayson (753).

745. Fischer, Kurt von. "Bemerkungen zu den zwei Ausgaben von Debussys **Ariettes oubliées**." In **Symbolae historiae musicae: Hellmut Federhofer zum 60. Geburtstag**, ed. by F. Riedel, pp. 283-89. Mainz: Schott, 1971. ML 55.F37 S9.

Comments on the differences between the 1888 and 1903 editions of **Ariettes**, which clarify a changing style, form, and prosody. From the first to the later version, one may observe stylistic change that reflects personal maturity, at the time when D ceased to prefer the forename Achille (for the 1888 **Ariettes**) and took up Claude (before the 1903 version).

746. Freundlich, Irwin. "Random Thoughts on the **Preludes** of Claude Debussy." **Current Musicology** 13 (1972): 48-54.

Remarks emphasizing clarity and simplicity of performance to communicate Debussy's rigorous craftsmanship and unity of detail. The programmatic footnote-titles are generally reflected in the music but do not explain the rightness of D's choices, which relate to a unifying, purely musical conception. Especially valuable for performance practice of the piano music.

747. Friedmann, Michael L. "Approaching Debussy's **Ondine**." **Cahiers Debussy** (nouvelle série) 6 (1982): 22-35.

Outlines the six parts of the "mosaic form" in the prelude, which suggest D as a true precursor of Stravinsky in form. Fluid interactions between vertical and horizontal events and flexible linkages foretell innovations in music after 1950. Charts and graphs illustrate tetrachord and trichord use and strata of textural activity.

748. Genest, Emile. **L'opéra-comique, connu et inconnu**. Paris: Fischbachler, 1925. 351 p. ML 1727.8.D2 G32.

Documents the origins of the Opéra-comique from the Middle Ages to the 18th century. Centers on the period 1713-1925. Helps establish the larger context of **Pelléas**.

749. Gilman, Lawrence. **Aspects of Modern Opera: Estimates and Inquiries**. New York: Lane, 1908. 215 p. ML 1705.G45.

Extended essays on Wagner, Puccini, Strauss, and "A Perfect Music-Drama: **Pelléas et Mélisande**."

See also Gilman's **Debussy's "Pelléas et Mélisande," a Guide to the Opera** (New York: Schirmer, 1907; MT 100.D44 P3). Both are valuable when considering the contemporary reception of **Pelléas** and still valuable for insights into analysis. The analysis of leitmotives may be studied alongside that by Emmanuel (item 741) and more recent studies.

750. Godet, Robert. "Le lyrisme intime de Debussy (II)." **Revue musicale** 2, no. 3 (1 Jan. 1921): 43-60.

A general overview of the songs and larger vocal works. By a close friend, these views are relevant to any consideration of D as his times viewed him. Recalls conversations with D and quotes passages from letters that expose his aesthetics.

751. Gousset, Bruno. "La pré-éminence du timbre dans le langage musical de **La mer** de Debussy." **Analyse musicale** 3 (April 1986): 37-45.

Composers before D orchestrated in essence for a reinforced quartet, with the notable exception of Berlioz. **La mer** manifests timbre as a new parameter of structure, equal in relevance to theme, tonality, and so on. Discusses the ideas of "sound-note" and "chord-timbre" in **De l'aube à midi**. Timbre "modulates," predominates over harmony in the structure, and joins forces with local rhythm, large-level time, and dynamics. An excellent and clear synopsis of this major aspect of style. Further see Jarocinski (item 127) and Barraqué (63 and 121).

752. Grayson, David. "Debussy in the Opera House: An Unpublished Letter Concerning Yniold and Mélisande." **Cahiers Debussy** (nouvelle série) (1985): 17-28.

Gives in its entirety a previously unpublished letter from D to Pierre Gheusi of Spring 1914. Concerns D's continuing involvement with further productions of **Pelléas** and the casting of roles. Sheds light on D as a man of the theater.

753. ------. **The Genesis of Debussy's "Pelléas et Mélisande."** Ann Arbor, Michigan: UMI Research Press, 1986. 342 p. ISBN 0-8357-1674-0; ML 410.D28G7 1986.

A revision of a quite significant doctoral dissertation. Evaluates the manuscripts and early editions and includes an account of the opera's history and reception. Reviews pertinent correspondence quite thoughtfully, serving other scholars as a model interpretation of D's letters and their clues to the genesis of works. Examines musical sources in the direction of a critical edition, which the author is completing for the Debussy **Oeuvres complètes**. Considers aesthetics and the composition of **Pelléas** in light of Wagner. Suggests a need for further studies of **Pelléas**, specifically in the areas of vocal style and form. The extensive bibliography suggests numerous studies pertinent to **Pelléas**, supplementing the present listings. Grayson's Catalogue of Sources (manuscripts and early editions) is similarly detailed and explanatory. He helpfully has reviewed the present catalogue entry on **Pelléas** and has updated details of manuscript sources indicated here.

754. ------. "The Libretto of Debussy's **Pelléas et Mélisande**. **Music and Letters** 66, no. 1 (1985): 34-50.

Discusses the complex transformation of **Pelléas** from play to libretto, discussing Maeterlinck's revisions of his original play, D's cuts (especially as illustrated in Act IV/iv), and changes of wording and the timing of phrases. Points to D's alterations of stage setting. Although Maeterlinck had authorized and even suggested cuts, he nonetheless objected in a **Le figaro** letter that D had treated the play like "conquered territory."

755. Grout, Donald J. **A Short History of Opera.** 2nd ed. New York: Columbia University Press, 1965. 852 p. ISBN 0-231-02422-3; ML 1700.G83 1965.

In the chapter "Old Bottles, New Wine," Grout views Impressionism as the most radical influence on musical style from 1900-1915, and **Pelléas** is the pacesetter. A somewhat generalized view ("**Pelléas** is Debussy's only work for the stage, with the exception of **Le martyre**...") and out of date, makes no mention of the Poe projects or **Diane au bois**. In these regards is updated by Orledge (item 843) and others. Of importance to D research is Grout's placement of him within the larger context of opera. Points to D's relation to Puccini, Déodat de Sévérac, Bloch, Schrecker, Bartók, Poulenc, and Berg as opera composers.

756. Guck, Marion A. "One Path Through Debussy's ...**des pas sur la neige**: Insights into the Methodology of Sketch Rejection." **In Theory Only** 1, no. 5 (Aug. 1975): 4-8.

Presents a Schenkerian analysis of the extant sketches, relating them sketches to the completed prelude. A useful if technically obscure source in the application of Schenkerian analysis to Debussy. Also see the same author's article "Tracing Debussy's ...**des pas**.... **In theory only** 1, no. 6 (Nov. 1975): 4-12.

757. Guenther, Ulrich and Rudolf Frisius. "Musik und Bewegung. Neue Verbindungen zwischen Musik und Sport." **Musik und Bildung** 3, no. 1 (Jan. 1971): 16-21.

Relates musical rhythm to that of sport, referring to two compositions concerning tennis: D's **Jeux** and Kagel's **Match**. Music suggests movement in sound, producing psychic stimulation.

758. Guertin, Marcelle. "Différence et similitude dans les **Préludes pour piano** de Debussy." **Canadian University Music Review/Revue de musique des universités canadiennes** 2 (1981): 56-83.

Understands a dialogue between the fugitive and the durable in the **Preludes** book I. Seeks to clarify their thematic processes and discusses a "technique of paradigm" in D's form, whereby inner unities such as theme are established, reacted to, and contrasted with.

759. Gulke, Peter. "Musik aus dem Bannkreis einer literarischen Aesthetik: Debussys **Prélude à l'après-midi d'un faune**." **Jahrbuch Peters**

1978. Aufsätze zur Musik I, ed. E. Klemm, p. 103-146. Leipzig: Peters, 1979, 103-46.

D's music is under the "spell" of a literary aesthetic. Thoughtfully relates his approach to form to the **art pour l'art** principle of Mallarmé's poetry. Linguistic symbols help mold the musical material. Observes that D no longer followed Mallarmé's ideas in his later works, and points out that Symbolism was considered a failure by 1914. Studies the psychological processes reflected in the work. A parallel study is that by Berman (item 699) as regards the subconscious and dream imagery. Lists several matters of editorial detail concerning the editions by M. Pommer (Peters, 1970) and W. Austin (Norton, 1970). See Austin (690) for a complementary analysis.

760. Gurkov, Vladimir. "Liriceskaja drama K. Debjussi i opernye tradicii" [The lyric drama of Claude Debussy and operatic tradition]. In the collection **Ocerki po istorij zarnbeznoj muzyki XX veca** [Historical essays on foreign music of the twentieth century]. Compiled by Sergej Bogojavlenskij. Leningrad: Muzyka, 1983. 120 p. In Russian. Not examined.

761. Gut, Serge. "Analyse musicale de la Sonate pour violoncelle et piano de Debussy." **Education musicale** 257 (April 1979): 221-25. Not examined.

762. ------. "**Canope** de Debussy: Analyse formelle et structure fondamentale." **Revue musicale de Suisse Romande** 33, no. 2 (May 1980): 60-65.

The tonal structure of the prelude derives from a superposition of fifths. Three motives are discussed, which determine a tripartite structure.

763. ------. "**La cathédrale engloutie**, prélude de Claude Debussy: Interférences entre le matériau, la structure et la forme. **Analyse musicale** 4 (3ème trimestre 1986): 78-81.

The first theme (m. 7 ff.) is less important structurally than the second (m. 28 ff.). Analyzes traditionally (theme, tonality, sections) and then proposes a "synthetic view" that considers the long-range auditory experience. D explores the confluence of the individual and the anonymous, large world.

764. ------. "Un grand indépendant: Claude Debussy." **Education musicale** 248 (May 1978): 283-87.

Contains an analysis of the **Sonate pour flûte, alto, et harpe**. Not examined.

765. ------. "Konstante und bewegliche Elemente in **Jeux** von Claude Debussy." In **Bericht über den Internationalen Musikwissenschaftlichen Kongress Berlin 1974**, pp. 395-98.

Finds three constant elements lending cohesion in **Jeux**: a short chromatic motive, a refrain-like melody, and a waltz-like rhythmic motive. There also is a polyphonic continuity. Divides the form into three sections according to the emphasis upon and distribution of the three elements.

766. Gut, Serge and Danièle Pistone. **La musique de chambre en France de 1870 à 1918**. Musique-Musicologie 5. Paris: Champion, 1978. 239 p. ISBN 2-8250-3038-9; ML 1127.G9.

An extensive and valuable survey of chamber music in France, observing its revival, forms, and place in concert life. Situates D's chamber music within that revival and general environment.

767. Haché, Reginald. "The Legendary Cathedral of Brittany." **Journal of the American Liszt Society** 19 (June 1986): 67-76.

Concerns the prelude **La cathedrale engloutie**, visual sources of its inspiration, and primary stylistic traits. Addressed to piano teachers and students but of interest to scholars of performance questions as well.

768. Haino, Ethan. "Generated Collections and Interval Control in Debussy's Preludes." **In Theory Only** 4, no. 6 (Feb.-March 1979): 3-15.

Suggests that intervals of generation (2nds, 3rds, and 7ths) create pitch classes in a number of preludes. The author finds this approach useful in relating D to broad currents of the twentieth century. Affirms with many others the prominence of motivic structure in D. See Rahn (item 861).

769. Hamoen, Dirk Jacob. "The **Chansons de Bilitis**: Fiction, Fact, and a New Face." **Key Notes Donemus** 21, no. 1 (1985): 18-24.

Questions the edition of the **Chansons de Bilitis** incidental music by A. Hoérée (Editions Jobert 1971). Prefers the unpublished edition by the composer Rudolf Escher (d. 1980), which leans more heavily upon the piano **Six épigraphes antiques**. The Escher version takes into consideration D's further maturity by the time of the incidental music.

770. Hang, Wiltrud. **Claude Debussy, historische Einordnung: Analyse "Prélude à l'après-midi d'un faune."** Ravensburg: Holzschuh, 1977. 74 p.

Discusses the late 19th-century artistic context, analyzes the work, and describes D's historical place. Proceeding from the biographies by Vallas and Strobel, discusses D in the traditional manner as Impressionist and analyzes traditionally.

771. Hardeck, Erwin. "Debussys **Jeux**: Struktur-Stellung im Gesamtwerk." In **Bericht über den Internationalen Musikwissenschaftlichen Kongress Bonn 1970**, pp. 424-26.

Disputes H. Eimert's thesis (item 739) that the ornamentation in **Jeux** is not motivic and denies a special significance to this composition in D's output. Acknowledges its important loosening of traditional form.

772. ------. **Untersuchungen zu den Klavierliedern Claude Debussys.** Diss., University of Cologne. Published in Regensburg: Bosse, 1967. v, 244 p. ML 410.D28 H28.

Analyzes the structure of songs individually and considers them in related groups. Refers to youthful songs; the role of Symbolism, Impressionism, and Realism; and the relationship of the song sets to the tradition of the song cycle. Useful but not fundamental as is Ruschenburg (872) when studying the songs.

773. Harding, James. **Folies de Paris: The Rise and Fall of French Operetta.** London: Chappel and Co., 1979. 183 p. ISBN 0- 903443-28-7; ML 1900.H33.

Popular in style but valuable for placing **Pelléas** within the larger context of the Opéra-Comique. Explores the many associations of the first conductor of **Pelléas**, A. Messager, and those of the principal singers.

774. Headland, David. "Comment on Crotty, 'Symbolist Influences in Debussy's **Prélude à l'après-midi d'un faune**.'" **In Theory Only** 6, no. 4 (May 1982): 9-11.

Harmonic events are more closely identified with the pitch center **e**, while melodic events generally emphasize **c-sharp**. Analyzes aspects of the opening theme. Also see Crotty (item 558).

775. Hirsbrunner, Theo. "Claude Debussy und Pierre Louÿs: zu den **Six épigraphes antiques** von Debussy." **Die Musikforschung** 31, no. 4 (1978), 426-42.

Reviews the close personal relationship between poet and composer and their five projects planned jointly. Discusses the only completed project, **Chansons de Bilitis** incidental music, and the **Epigraphes antiques** partly drawn in turn from the incidental music. The present compositions synthesize the oriental influence and certain aspects of Renaissance music.

776. ------. "Debussy, **Le martyre de Saint Sébastien** und der Geist des Fin de siècle. **Oesterreichische Musikzeitschrift** 39 (May 1984): 230-36.

Views **Le martyre** in light of Fin-de-siècle currents in literature and the other arts. A thoughtful assessment of the work as related to Art nouveau, Symbolism, and Orientalism. Refers to the first performance, Bakst's stage design, and Fokine's choreography. Outlines the action of the five acts and assesses D's music.

777. ------. "Debussys Ballett **Khamma**." **Archiv für Musikwissenschaft** 36, no. 2 (1979): 105-21.

Model scholarship in its overview of past studies and argument for a fresh view. Disputes the assumption that **Khamma** was a failure, which conclusion derived from the extra-artistic conflict between Maud Allan and D. Nor are D's derogatory judgements entirely reliable. Revises the view of Koechlin's role in orchestration, which now appears limited and under D's supervision. Relates **Khamma** to **Jeux**, **Le martyre**, and Strauss's **Salome**, to staged set pieces by W. Rihm and M. Trojahn, and to the machine music of the 1920s.

778. ------. "Debussys **Le martyre de Saint-Sébastien**: Wandlungen der Wiedergabe. In **Werk und Wiedergabe**, pp. 320-325. Thurnauer Schriften zur Musiktheater 5. Bayreuth: Mühl'scher Universitätsverlag Fehr, 1980. ISBN 3-921-73323-5; MT 955.W4.

Traces various productions subsequent to the 1911 premiere: those with Ida Rubinstein remaining as lead dancer in the 1920s, under André Cluytens, and those at La Scala and the Paris Opéra. Relates to other multi-media presentations such as Milhaud's **Christophe Colombe**.

779. ------. "Frankreichs Opern um 1900: Auf den Spüren von R. Wagners Einfluss." **Neue Zürcher Zeitschrift** 52 (April 1979): 67.

From E. Reyer's **Sigurd** to D's **Pelléas**, the stage action in French opera, many scenic effects, and the relationship between music and speech reflect Wagner's influence. Not examined.

780. ------. "Musik und Dichtung im französischen Fin de Siècle am Beispiel der **Proses lyriques** von Claude Debussy." In **Dichtung und Musik**, pp. 152-74. Stuttgart: Klett-Cotta, 1979. ISBN 3-1293-6920-1; ML 3849.D5.

D's **Proses lyriques** realize the inherent musicality of speech and reflect the influences of writers (Verlaine, Mallarmé, and Laforgue) and painters (G. Moreau, Puvis de Chavannes, and the Pre-Raphaelites). Written in a rhythmicized prose, the texts also show a religious strain relating to the Prosas of the Middle Ages. Suggests aesthetic and particular musical influences from Wagner.

781. ------. "Musik und Sprache bei G. Fauré und C. Debussy." **Melos/Neue Zeitschrift für Musik** 1, no. 5 (Sept.-Oct. 1975): 365-72.

A comparative analysis of Verlaine's **C'est l'extase**, set by Fauré and D, reveals that in prosody and harmony Fauré is bound to the past of Romance and salon, while D represents the new. D's treatment is a modern, psychological search into the text.

782. ------. "Zu Debussys und Ravels Mallarmé-Vertonungen." **Archiv für Musikwissenschaft** 35, no. 2 (1978): 81-103.

Discusses the aesthetic relation between composers and poet in the settings by both of **Soupir** and **Placet futile**, in Debussy's **Apparition** and **Eventail** [**Mallarmé Songs**], and in Ravel's **Sainte** and **Surgi de la croupe**. Ravel emphasizes the poet's formal rigor, while Debussy extends Mallarmé's inner ambiguity. Both composers anticipate aspects of Boulez.

783. "Hommage à Amy Dommel-Diény (1894-1981)." **Cahiers de l'harmonie vivante** 10 (March 1983). 56 p.

An entire number of the periodical. Brings together reminiscences by students, lecture notes, and an analysis of D's étude **Pour les tierces** by Mlle Dommel-Diény.

784. Howat, Roy. "Debussy: **Masques**, **L'isle joyeuse**, and a Lost **Sarabande**." **Journal of the Musicological Society of Australia** 10 (1987). Not examined.

785. ------. "A Thirteenth Etude of 1915: The Original Version of **Pour les arpèges composés**." **Cahiers Debussy** (nouvelle série) 1 (1977): 16-24.

Describes the manuscript sketch of another D étude "retrouvé", **Pour les arpèges**, which is only partly fleshed out by the composer. The etude relates to certain finished works and might have been preserved by D for future use. A clear exposé of Howat's thought when he reconstructed the work for publication.

786. Imberty, Michel. "**La cathédrale engloutie** de Debussy: de la perception au sens." **Canadian University Music Review/Revue de musique des universités canadiennes** 6 (1985): 90-160.

Seeks a new analysis not dependent upon the program. Is concerned with the musical signification that is recognized spontaneously and on a purely musical basis by listeners not oriented to the program. Discusses the prelude **Puerta del vino** and the **Intermezzo** in E-flat minor, Op. 118/6, by Brahms. Also see Imberty, "De la perception du temps musical à sa signification psychologique: à propos de **La cathédrale engloutie** de Debussy." **Analyse musicale** 6 (Jan. 1987): 28-37.

787. Indy, Vincent d'. "A propos de **Pelléas et Mélisande**: essai de psychologie du critique d'art." **L'occident** (Brussels) (June 1902).

Not available to the present study but probably informative concerning the contemporaneous reception of **Pelléas**.

788. Inghelbrecht, D.-E. **Le chef d'orchestre et son équipe**. Paris: 1949. 206 p. Translated into English by G. Prerauer and S. Kirk. New York: Library Publ., 1954. MT 85.I6.

Makes few references to D except regarding rehearsal techniques. Because Inghelbrecht is an important interpreter, his ideas for **La damoiselle élue** are of interest.

789. ------. **Le chef d'orchestre parle au publique.** Paris: Julliard, 1957. 227 p. ML 60.I6 1957.

Discusses his purposes as performer. Includes a chapter "A travers **Pelléas et Mélisande**." Further cites D within the context of musical life in the early twentieth century.

790. ------. **Comment on ne doit pas interpréter "Carmen," "Faust," "Pelléas."** Paris: Au Ménestrel (Heugel), 1933. 75 p.

Seeks to correct improper interpretations by conductors of D, which derive from a lack of comprehension of his artistic message. Stresses balance and subtlety and points to particular passages. Recalls the early performances of **Pelléas**. Valuable for the question of orchestral performance.

791. Jacobs, Paul. "On Playing the Piano Music of Debussy." **Cahiers Debussy** (nouvelle série) 3 (1979): 39-44.

Stimulating thoughts by an experienced performer. Reprinted from **Keynote Magazine**, September 1979.

792. Jarocinski, Stefan. "Debussy and his Poets" [introductory essay accompanying the complete recording of D's songs]. Laid in phonograph recording EMI 2C 165-16.371-4. 4-record set.

The recordings were made in 1971 and 1977-79. 60 songs are contained, not including a number of the early songs that were unpublished or unrecorded at the time. The liner notes also provide an excellent, poetic translation of the texts by Béatrice Vierne, which fruitfully may be considered alongside Cobb (item 48) and Rohinski (867). Jarocinski's is a masterful survey of the songs, referring to the important influences from movements in literature. Quotes from D's letters and critical writings as regards poetry and from authorities as they view his achievements in song composition. Concludes that D's "entire imagination...is steeped in poetry." Further see Cobb, Meister (823), and Wenk (898).

793. John, Nicholas, ed. and compiler. **"Pelléas et Mélisande": Claude Debussy.** London: Calder, and New York: Riverrun Press, 1982. 96 p. ISBN 0-7145-3906-6; ML 410.D28.

A collection of essays on aspects of Pelléas by Hugh Macdonald, Roger Nichols, A. Raitt, and N. John. Contains a valuable new translation into English by Macdonald, illustrations from early performances, and a helpful if general thematic guide. An excellent, current opera guide for audiences who are not necessarily experts, with much of value for the researcher.

794. Joseph, Charles M. "The Original Version of Debussy's **Sarabande**." **The Piano Quarterly** (Summer 1982), 48-50.

Discusses the variants between the known version (from **Pour le piano**, 1901) and the original version, which is the 2nd movement in the 1894 **Images oubliées**, there titled **Souvenir du Louvre**. Finds over 100 differences between the two versions. Notes performance considerations.

795. **Journal of Music Theory** 22, no. 2 (Fall 1978). Analysis symposium on Debussy's Etude **Pour les sixtes**.

All of the following apply Schenkerian analysis. Further on the Schenkerian analysis to post tonal music see Forte (586).

Barkin, Elaine. "Notes in Progress," pp. 291-312. Describes the 6th as the generative interval and sees it moving "irruptively, fluctuantly, and disjunctively."

Benjamin, William E. "**Pour les sixtes**: An Analysis," pp. 253-90. Discovers a tetradic tonality relating significantly to tradition. Examines registral choices, interruptions, motives, and the rhetorical significance to structure of repetition.

Gauldin, Robert. "An Analysis," pp. 241-51. Focuses on tonal organization and voice leading. Suggests a mode of analysis perhaps more pertinent to D's tonal language than the pitch-class approach of Haino (768).

796. Kasaba, Eiko. "A propos des deux préludes orchestraux du **Martyre de Saint Sébastien**." **The Waseda Journal of General Sciences** 32 (Tokyo, October 1987), 15-42. Not examined.

797. ------. "Debussy no kakyoku kenkyu, Miyabiyaka na utage dai isshu" [A Study of Debussy's **Fêtes galantes**, set I]. **Ongaku gaku** 22, no. 3 (Feb.1976): 121-38. In Japanese and French.

Based on the 1975 M.A. thesis of the author. Not examined.

798. ------. "**Le martyre de Saint Sébastien**: Etude sur la gènese." **Cahiers Debussy** (nouvelle série) 4-5 (1980-81): 19-37.

Authoritative overview of the composition and related documents. Considers the chronology of composition, the relation of libretto to music, editions, and the autograph MS.

799. Keil, Werner. **Untersuchungen zur Entwicklung des frühen Klavierstils von Debussy und Ravel.** Wiesbaden: Breitkopf, 1982. 233 p. ISBN 3-7651-0185-0; ML 724.K44 1982.

Provides a traditional analysis of the piano music from the **Danse bohémienne** through to **Pour le piano**, **Images oubliées**, and **Estampes**. Regards the latter as D's first masterpiece for piano. Discusses only the known, published works and does not consider the newly-recovered works, about which see Blumenthal (701). Compares D's and Ravel's styles as composers for piano.

800. Kerman, Joseph. **Opera as Drama.** New York: Vintage Books (Random House), 1956. 269, iv p. ML 3858.K4 1956x.

Chapter 6, "Opera as Sung Play," observes that the play is "enveloped whole into the opera." D's music for **Pelléas** is not a transformation but a clarification of Maeterlinck. Wagner's ideal in **Tristan** is contrasted: for him opera is symphonic poem and not literary in essence. Whereas Wagner has the true dramatic instinct, in Kerman's opinion and following his thesis, Maeterlinck (and thereupon Debussy) allows a fixation on fate to stultify action. D's reticent method could not do enough to transform the play into operatic drama as Kerman conceives it. One might explore further alongside Kerman's how well D's own conception of a fitting musical treatment was realized. Essential reading for the study of dramaturgy in **Pelleas**, which study may also be informed by studying D's conception in **Diane**, **Rodrigue**, and the Poe projects **Chute de la maison Usher** and **Diable dans le beffroi**. A revised edition of the book is available.

801. Kono, Yuki. "Debussy no ongakusoao ni kansuru bigakuteki kosatsu 'Proses lyriques' o chushnin ni" [An Aesthetic Contemplation on Debussy's Musical Creation, with Particular Focus on the 'Proses lyriques']. MA diss., Musicology, Tokyo Gakugei University, 1983. 237 p.

D's unusually keen sense of hearing explains his emphasis on the "mystery of the moment." Considers the **Proses lyriques** and other vocal music to illustrate the point. Not examined.

802. Kopcevskij, Nikolaj. "**Childrens Corner** von Claude Debussy: stilistische Parallelen und Probleme der Interpretation." Translated from Russian into German. **Jahrbuch Peters 1978**. Aufsatz zur Musik, I, edited by E. Klemm, pp. 173-209. Leipzig: Peters, 1979. ML 5.J245.

Children's Corner (1906-08) marks a change in piano writing as regards timbre, from the transparent and Impressionistic to the more concise and resolute. Discusses the genesis, use of borrowed and closely related themes from Tchaikovsky, Borodin, Musorgsky, and D's own **Mandoline**. Refers to the pianist Cortot's interpretations (see item 725) and relates to **Jardins (Estampes)**. Concludes that the **Children's Corner** joins the **Préludes**, **Images**, and **Estampes** in inaugurating a new era of piano composition.

803. Kramer, Lawrence. **Music and Poetry: The Nineteenth Century and After.** Berkeley and Los Angeles: The University of California Press, 1984. xii, 251 p. ISBN 0-5200-4873-3; ML 3849.K7 1984.

Centers on the mechanics whereby music and poetry converge. Discusses lyric, non-dramatic forms rather than opera. Correlates a given composer and poet in their common perception of structural rhythm, as for example in repetition. Refers to D only in passing (**Prélude-faune** and the prelude Les **sons et les parfums**), but Kramer's approach can enrich the discussion of D's song settings and other works.

804. Kunze, Stefan. "Der Sprechgesang und das Unsagbare zu **Pelléas et Mélisande** de Debussy." In **Archiv für Musikwissenschaft**, suppl., vol. 23: **Festschrift für H.H. Eggebrecht zum 65. Geburtstag**, pp. 338-60. Stuttgart: Steiner, 1984. ISBN 3-515-03662-8; ML 5.A63 Suppl.

Stresses the proximity of D's lyric recitative to the French language. Analyzes Act I, scene 2 and Mélisande's tower song (III/1). Considers the flexibility of rhythms and prosody.

805. Laloy, Louis. "La dernière oeuvre de Claude Debussy: l' **Ode à la France.**" **Musique** (Mar. 15, 1928): 245-49 and 254.

Recalls D's attitude in 1916 toward the war, as manifest in his **Noël des enfants**. D attempted two versions of the **Ode à la France**. Laloy reconstructed D's sketches of the second version. The orchestration of Laloy's piano-vocal score was made by Marius-François Gaillard with the consent of Laloy and Emma Debussy. The facsimile of D's sketch (p. 254 of the present article) reveals the considerable extent of Laloy's contribution.

806. Lang-Becker, Elke. **Claude Debussy: "Nocturnes."** Meisterwerke der Musik. Munich: Fink, 1982. 52 p. In German. ISBN 3-7705-2074-2; MT 130.D4 L36 1982.

Analyzes the Nocturnes, discusses the origins of the composition, and considers its genre and title. Provides documentary evidence pertaining to the title. A useful study relevant first to the general, German-speaking audience but also to scholars.

807. Langham Smith, Richard. "La genèse de **La damoiselle élue**" [in English]. **Cahiers Debussy** (nouvelle série) 4-5 (1980-81): 3-18.

Important article on the relation of the work to the literary figures D.G. Rossetti and other Pre-Raphaelites. Discusses that movement as an aesthetic focus for D before his turn toward Symbolism. See also Langham Smith's article, item 481.

808. Leibowitz, Marian. "Debussy's **Pelléas et Mélisande**: Monteux Score No. 40." M.A. thesis, Smith College, 1980.

Discusses post-publication changes of the orchestration as they were noted in a score owned by the conductor Pierre Monteux. Not examined.

809. Leibowitz, René. **Les fantômes de l'opéra: essais sur le théâtre lyrique.** Paris: Gallimard, 1972. 393 p. ML 1700.1.L43.

Devotes a chapter to the aesthetics and problems of interpreting **Pelléas**, "**Pelléas et Mélisande** ou les fantômes de la réalité" (pp. 291-326). Comments on the "scandals" surrounding the premiere and the political struggle between partisans and adversaries. Observes that **Pelléas** is at the heart of the repertory without qualifying as a rousing favorite.

810. ------. "**Pelléas et Mélisande** ou le No man's land de l'art lyrique." In **Histoire de l'Opéra**. Paris: Buchet/Chastel, 1957. ML 1700.L525h.

Finds D's impass with the Poe projects related to the central problem of **Pelléas**; no opera since has penetrated the rare domain of the work. D deliberately distanced himself from the broad stream of opera, and **Pelléas** has made no mark on later opera. A provocative viewpoint that provokes a response from scholars of the **Pelléas** reception.

811. Lesure, François, ed. **Claude Debussy: Esquisses de "Pelléas et Mélisande."** Facsimile publication with introduction. Publications du Centre de Documentation Claude Debussy II. Geneva: Editions Minkoff, 1977.

The introduction outlines the stages in the composition of **Pelléas**, refers to the two sketches that are reproduced, and gives relevant passages from letters. Gives facsimiles of the 63-page sketch formerly of the André Meyer Collection (June-July 1895) and the 29-page "Bréval" MS (Oct. 1893, May 1895), also at the B.n. Does not reproduce the 12-page "Legouix" sketch (Sept.-Oct. 1893). Facsimiles are printed in black ink, obscuring the various colors of ink and pencil essential to a thorough account of layers of composition.

812. ------. "**Crime d'amour** ou **Fêtes galantes**: un projet Verlainien de Debussy (1912-1915)." **Cahiers Debussy** (nouvelle série) 10 (1986): 17-23.

Augments the discussion by Orledge (source 843) of the dramatic project. The original scenario was by Charles Morice, based upon the text of Verlaine. Later, Louis Laloy was drawn into the collaboration. Gives two letters by D of 1912 concerning the project, which previously have not been published. A scenario remains in a MS sketchbook but apparently no musical sketch was made. D abandoned the collaboration when preoccupied with **Jeux** and **Preludes** book II.

813. Lidov, David. "Debussy's Formal Procedures in **Voiles**." In **On Musical Phrase**, pp. 87-98. Monographies de sémiologie et d'analyses musicales I. Montreal, 1975. MT 75.L5.

Analyzes a 3-part division of the structure, which involves a prominent use of the whole-tone scale. Observes a discourse of the active and the static that is reminiscent of functional tonality.

814. Lockspeiser, Edward, compiler. **Debussy et Edgar Poe**. Preface by André Schaeffner. Monaco: Editions du Rocher, 1961 [1962]. 97 p. ML 410.D28.L82.

The leading source on the development of the Poe operatic projects **La chute de la maison Usher** and **Diable dans le beffroi**. Has not been surpassed as a study of primary documents by later studies, which are nonetheless important. Views Poe's aesthetic as the counterpart of Wagner's in

D's stylistic development. Notes D's extended preoccupation and cultivation of the aesthetic of the unconscious. Refers to the literary influences of Swinburne and Rossetti, as well.

Unpublished sources appended are the text of **Diable**, an extract of the libretto (1st version) of **La chute**, the complete libretto of **La chute** (Bibl. nat. ms. 9885), Debussy's sketches for **La saulaie** (after Rossetti), and musical sketches from **Diable** and **La chute**. Facsimiles of the three scores are reproduced in white on black but unfortunately are not very legible.

815. ------. "**Frères en art**: pièce de théâtre inédite de Debussy." **Revue de musicologie** 56, no. 2 (1970): 165-76.

Analysis of the work, which was composed from 1895-99. The play concerns the aesthetic and practical problems confronting both English and French artists in the period. Both D and his collaborator René Peter considered the project amateurish when judged beside the contemporaneous **Pelléas**. Refers to inspiration by Ruskin, Turner, Delacroix, and Proust. Also see Orledge item 843.

816. Long, Marguerite. **At the Piano with Debussy.** Translated by Olive Senior-Ellis. London: Dent, 1972. ISBN 0-460-03821-4. 112 p. The original is **Au Piano avec Debussy**. Paris: Julliard, 1960. 170 p.

At times derivative and perhaps based on hear say, the study nonetheless contains important insights into the piano music. Long cites coaching with D in 1914 on **L'isle joyeuse** and continuing later with the **Etudes**. Contains remarks about the pianism of Francis Planté, also a protégé of Debussy, and Long's personal commentary on the **Preludes** and other works. Invaluable views of a pianist who knew D and was a pacesetter in French piano playing at the time.

817. Maeterlinck, Maurice. **Pelléas et Mélisande.** Brussels: Labor, and Paris: Nathan, 1983. 111 p. ISBN 2-8259-0272-1; PQ 2625.A5 P4 1983.

An easily accessible, current edition of Maeterlinck's original play, which with a few revisions D set as the opera.

818. Mahlert, Ulrich. "Die 'göttliche Arabeske': zu Debussys **Syrinx**." **Archiv für Musikwissenschaft** (1986), 181-200. Not examined.

819. Mallard, Betty Parker. "Performance Instructions in the Preludes and Etudes of Claude Debussy." Ph.D. diss., University of Texas, 1979. 144 p.

Performance indications reflect structural considerations of tempo and rhythm. Such indications direct proper dynamics, tone quality, and pedaling, and they inform the presentation of successive melodic ideas and simultaneous textural elements.

820. Mataigne, Viviane. "Une analyse du **Prélude à l'après-midi d'un faune**. **Analyse musicale** 12 (June 1988): 89-102.

A clear review of prior analyses: Austin (item 690), Dille, Decsey, and Howat (item 590). Recalls Austin's statement that the several analyses of the work differ more in language than in substance. Outlines with musical examples the main themes and generative cells; discusses harmony, counterpoint, and orchestration; and sees conjunctions with Mallarmé's poem. A final chart outlines an ABA' form. Concludes that continuity and the links between melody and accompaniment are the dominant features of the score.

821. McKay, James R. "The Bréval Manuscript: New Interpretations." **Cahiers Debussy** (nouvelle série) 1 (1977): 5-15.

Discusses the compositional approach and chronology of this early sketch of **Pelléas**, currently B.n. MS 1206. The sketch is preparatory to Act IV, scenes 1, 2, and 4. Transcribes passages of the Bréval manuscript and compares to relevant passages of the published version.

822. Meeus, Jean. "Le **Prélude à l'après-midi d'un faune**: une analyse harmonique." **Analyse musicale** 13 (scheduled for Oct. 1988).

Not examined. Discusses harmonic innovations, especially less-used scalar degrees.

823. Meister, Barbara. **Nineteenth-Century French Song: Fauré, Chausson, Duparc, and Debussy.** Bloomington: Indiana University Press, 1980. xiii, 402 p. ISBN 0-253-34075-6; ML 2827.M36.

Discusses all solo songs with piano published by 1980, with the aim of increasing performers' and listeners' understanding. Does not plumb literary depths as does Wenk, or give consistent translations such as those by Rohinsky or R. Miller in Cobb (Items 867 and 48). It nonetheless is readily accessible and useful to performers; it can complement Wenk, Rohinsky, and Cobb in the study of the songs.

824. Mellers, Wilfred. "The Final Works of Claude Debussy, or 'Pierrot faché avec la lune.'" **Music and Letters** 20, no. 2 (1939): 168-76.

The final works reflect a beauty-filled inner life, the expression of which is traced from the early songs and their reference to the figure Pierrot of the Commedia dell'arte. D's music shows the vision of one as if exiled and possessing an "ineffable melancholy." Relates this theme most thoughtfully to the sonatas but skirts the importance of the etudes. Mellers' approach well could join hands with the highly technical recent analyses of the late music in the direction of a holistic view.

825. Meylan, Pierre. "Un manuscrit inédit de Debussy: **Scherzo pour violoncelle et piano**, 1882." **Revue musicale de Suisse romande** (Lausanne) 19, no. 1 (March 1966): 8-9.

The first direct study of this work, which the author finds to be "a laboratory experiment" in a conventional style. Does not indicate that the middle, lyric section is probably the **Nocturne** listed in the 1882 concert program on which the work was premiered [see items 145 and 705]. These sources point out that the cello part bears the title "Nocturne et Scherzo."

826. Michel, André. **La sirène dans l'élément musical.** Paris: Editions de la Diaspora française, 1970. 19 [ii] p. ML 410.D28 M5.

Discusses the mythological Siren as it relates to D's **Nocturnes** and to works by some 50 composers, including Haydn, Roger-Ducasse, Durey, Chopin, and Wagner. Centers on Debussy, using a psychoanalytic approach concerned with the subconscious, the libido, etc. Perhaps worthwhile insights into D's psychology if superficial musical analysis. Also refers to D's project **Orphée**.

827. Moe, Orin, and William B. Chappell. "Debussy and Baudelaire: **Harmonie du soir.**" **Bonnes feuilles** 4, no. 1-2 (Spring 1975): 122-48.

Shows the relationship of form and expressive content in the poetry and its musical setting. D's musical score, from the **Cinq poèmes de Baudelaire** comments upon the poet's dialectic of time, which literary commentaries have neglected to consider. Melodic materials follow the linear organization of the poem, musical rhythm derives from that of the poem, and both the vocal part and the accompaniment suggest psychological innuendoes. A model study of D's sensitivity toward poetry in the songs.

828. Moevs, Robert. "Intervallic Procedures in Debussy: **Sérénade** from the **Sonata for Cello and Piano**, 1915. **Perspectives of New Music** 8, no. 1 (Fall-Winter 1969): 82-101.

Stylistic procedures derive from a common germ, the major or minor harmonic 9th. Pentatonic and whole-tone aspects relate to the 9th as well. Views D's compositional approach as broad but sufficiently cohesive. Suggests that the nontonal style of the contemporary must evolve along the lines of D, to include the triadic sound without, however, a "concomitant stylistic disorientation and disruption."

829. Mooser, Robert Aloys. "Sur une prétendue 'symphonie' de Debussy." **Dissonances** (Geneva) 5, no. 12 (Dec. 1932): 358-61.

Reports on the 1932 Russian publication of the **Symphonie en si mineur**, which was still forthcoming at the time of writing. Mistakenly Mooser locates Mme von Meck and her entourage at Chenonceaux, where Debussy is said to have composed the **Symphonie** in 1879. Questions the authenticity of the work, notwithstanding such "evidence" and the author's not having seen the score. An interesting document that illustrates the obscurities and half-knowledge too often shrouding D's early music and biography. Further see Blumenthal item 701.

830. Milnar, Antal. "Debussy budapesti hangversenyerol" [A Concert by Debussy in Budapest]. **Muzsika** 11, no. 10 (Oct. 1968): 31-32. In Hungarian.

Recollections of the violist in the Waldbauer-Kerpelz string quartet, who performed D's string quartet in 1910. At the same concert D performed his piano music with clarity and precision but also with an extemporaneous quality.

831. Monnard, Jean-François. "Claude Debussy: **La mer**: des fautes de copie à l'interprétation." **Schweizerische Musikzeitung/Revue musicale suisse** 121 (Jan.-Feb. 1981): 11-16.

The Durand and Eulenburg editions contain significant departures from D's intentions. An authentic interpretation must also take his tempos and tempo relationships into account and must avoid the customary but excessive ritardandos. Further see Rolf, item 868.

832. Mueller, Richard. "Javanese Influence on Debussy's **Fantaisie** and Beyond." **Nineteenth Century Music** 10, no. 2 (Fall 1986): 157-86.

To date the study of greatest focus on the **Fantaisie** for piano and orchestra. Discusses D's even earlier pentatonic use and experiences of the Paris Conservatoire gamelan. Reveals the Javanese theme upon which the cyclic theme of the Fantaisie is based. Argues that Debussy fully assimilated the ostinato procedures of gamelan; his later revisions of orchestration and texture show, however, that he was dissatisfied with his earlier, too literal dependence upon gamelan. Suggests that the orchestral work **Printemps**, the works **Clair de lune** and **Et la lune descend** (piano **Images** 1907), and the sketches for the ballet **No-ja-li** exhibit the Javanese influence, as well. An appendix concerns the Javanese theme Wani-wani.

833. Myers, Rollo. "The Opera that Never Was: Debussy's Collaboration with Victor Segalen in the Preparation of **Orphée**." **Musical Quarterly** 64, no. 4 (Oct. 1978), 495-506.

Reconsiders D's literary talents as observed in his active reshaping of the libretto **Orphée**. The play was written by Segalen in conformity with D's wishes. See also the letters to Segalen, item 35.

834. Nadeau, Roland. "**Brouillards**: A Tonal Music." **Cahiers Debussy** (nouvelle série) 4-5 (1980-81): 38-50.

Challenges D. Schnebel (item 643) and argues that D's prelude for piano possesses a loyalty to tonic despite its "extraordinary diffusion of tonal force." Sees the broadening of tonality by D as anticipating the new uses of Stravinsky, Hindemith, and Prokofiev.

835. Nattiez, J.J. "From Taxonomic Analysis to Stylistic Characterization." In **Actes du premier Congrès International de Sémiotique Musicale**. Edited by G. Stefani, pp. 83-110. Pesaro: Centro di Iniziativa Culturale, 1975. Published with corrections in J.J. Nattiez et al. **Three Musical Analyses**. Toronto: Toronto Semiotic Circle (Monographs, Working Papers, and Prepublications No. 4), 1982, pp. 1-35. P 99 M65 fol. 1982, no. 4.

An exhaustive, semiotic analysis of **Syrinx**. Further see the following entry.

836. ------. "**Syrinx** de C. Debussy." In **Fondements d'une sémiologie de la musique**, pp. 330-54. Paris: Union Générale d'Editions, 1976. ISBN 2-2640-0003-1; MT 6.N198 F7.

A thoughtful approach to Debussy analysis applying musical semiotics. Considers the various levels of structure, motives, and overall perception of shape. Nattiez's analytic thought, here and in the other articles mentioned in this book, can help invigorate Debussy analysis.

837. Nestrovski, Arthur Rosenblat. **Debussy e Poe**. Porto Alegre and Sao Paulo, Brazil: L & PM

Editores, 1986. 126 p. In Brazilian Portuguese. ML 410.D28 N45 1986.

Discusses the Poe-Baudelaire connection in French artistic culture. Treats in detail the two Poe projects by D, **La chute-Usher** and **Diable**. Considers the original writings by Poe in their entirety, projecting their aesthetics through to Debussy.

838. Nichols, Roger. "Debussy's Two Settings of **Clair de Lune**. **Music and Letters** 47, no. 3 (July 1967): 229-35.

Compares the 1882-84 and the 1892 settings, which reveal the growth toward maturity in prosody, formal balance, and rhythm as a unifying agent. The 1892 setting exhibits the syllabic style that would climax with **Pelléas**.

839. Nichols, Roger and Richard Langham Smith. **Pelléas et Mélisande**. Cambridge Opera Handbooks. Cambridge: Cambridge University Press, 1989. ISBN 0-5213-0714-7; ML 410.D28.

Contains a chapter on the sources of the opera by David Grayson. Otherwise, it is a joint writing by the two authors named, who are eminent authorities. Not examined, but promises to be a valuable guide to the opera.

840. Nygren, Dennis Quentin. "The Music for Accompanied Clarinet Solo of Claude Debussy: An Historical and Analytical Study of the **Première rhapsodie** and **Petite pièce**." DM diss., Northwestern University, 1982. 183 p. UM order number DA8400759; DA 44:2922A Apr. 1984.

Shows certain similarities between the form-giving melodic cells of the **Rapsodie** for clarinet and those of other works by D. Includes suggestions for performers and describes textual discrepancies among the six editions of the **Rapsodie**.

841. Okada, Akiko. "Piano kyoiku o chushin ni Dobisshi o mite" [A Study of Debussy Through his Piano Music]. **Memoirs of Kinitachi** m. col. VI

(Sept. 1970), pp. 37-50. In Japanese with an English summary.

Considers the new range of D's harmony, which is termed "unique, mysterious, and sensual." As Mallarmé's, D's expression is suggestive and restrained, translating elements of nature into music. Not examined.

842. Orledge, Robert. "Another Look Inside Debussy's 'Toybox.'" **Musical Times** 117, no. 1606 (Dec. 1976), 987-89.

Discusses the genesis of **La boite à joujoux** (1913), referring to the collaboration with Caplet on its orchestration. Discusses the plan for a marionette production and elements influenced by Stravinsky. Suggests that those elements in the scenario, which is by Hellé, might have first interested D in the project.

843. ------. **Debussy and the Theatre.** Cambridge: Cambridge University Press, 1983. xvii, 383 p. ISBN 0-5212-2807-7; ML 410.D28 O74 1982.

States the purpose "to give as full and varied a picture of Debussy's theatrical experiences as possible" and to collate scattered accounts into a single source. Orledge first discusses opera (**Pelléas**, **Diane au bois**, **Rodrigue et Chimène**, the Poe projects); ballet (**Jeux**, **Khamma**), and works not conceived for ballet but later choreographed (**Prélude-faune**) and incidental music for the theater (**Le martyre**, **Chansons de Bilitis**). Part IV treats theater projects left incomplete or never begun, and Part V seeks an overview, "In Perspective," of the 11 completed stage works and 54 unfinished projects. Deals thoroughly with biography, literary sources, correspondance, and criticism, and usually so with sources. Orledge is less searching in musical and dramatic analysis. Is a compilation of findings in the foregoing and succeeding articles by Orledge, where fuller discussion is offered.

844. ------. "Debussy et la Girl anglaise: The Legend of **Khamma**." **Musical Times** 127, no. 1717 (March 1986), 135-40.

Describes the first conception of **Khamma** as Isis in 1910 and the irresistably large commission from Maud Allan, who teamed with William Courtney to produce the scenario. Views the music as functioning both on the cinematographic level and purely musically, by four interrelated themes. Gives a rather brief account of thematic processes, which require further study. Observes Stravinsky's influence.

845. ------. "Debussy's **House of Usher** Revisited." **Musical Quarterly** 62, no. 4 (Oct. 1976): 536-53.

Discusses the three versions of the libretto of **La chute de la maison Usher**. Cites passages, and explains D's steps toward the final version, which contains two scenes (B.n. Ms 9885, of 1916). Refers to important differences between the artistic conception of the two operas, while seeing relationships between the characters Pelléas and Usher. A probing study by Orledge.

846. ------. "Debussy's Orchestral Collaborations, 1911-13, I: **Le martyre de Saint-Sébastien.**" **Musical Times** 115, no. 1582 (Dec. 1974): 1030-35.

An account of the 1911 collaboration with Caplet and the orchestration by three assistants of portions of **Le martyre**. Studies the extant sketches and concludes that, apart from the "unimaginative" chorus parts in the last act, the music was composed solely by Debussy. Traces the portion Caplet orchestrated through handwriting analysis.

847. ------. "Debussy's Orchestral Collaborations, 1911-13, II: **Khamma.**" **Musical Times** 116, no. 1583 (January 1975): 30-35.

Investigates the role of Koechlin in the orchestration of **Khamma** and D's troubles with Maud Allan. D's rash request of Koechlin to "write **Khamma** yourself and I will sign it" did not come to pass. Koechlin viewed **Khamma** as superior to **Jeux**; the former perhaps owed a debt to Stravinsky's Russian ballets.

848. ------. "Debussy's second English Ballet: Le **palais du silence** or **No-ja-li**." **Current Musicology** 22 (1976): 73-78.

Describes plans for an exotic oriental play of 1913-14 for A. Charlot's revue **Not Likely!** The theater project was abandoned, and D's newly orchestrated **Printemps** was substituted for new music. Provides an analysis of and examples from the extant sketches, which are incomplete ideas.

849. ------. "The Genesis of Debussy's **Jeux**." **Musical Times** 128, no. 1728 (Feb. 1987): 68-73.

Comments on the earliest known draft, at the Stadtbibliothek in Winterthur, Switzerland. Also considers two other primary sources. These give proof of D's struggle with the final climax, the proximity in time of the initial to the final conception, a structure based heavily upon 8-measure gestures, and motivic planning. In later stages D was concerned with the scenario and orchestration. The several stages testify to the importance and complexity of **Jeux** and dispute the common notion that it was written in haste.

850. Parks, Richard S. "Organizational procedures in Debussy's **Douze Etudes**." Ph.D. diss., Musicology, Catholic University of America, 1973. 597 p. UM no. DA74-7663.

Centers on thematic and tonal resources and the manipulative procedures applied to them. Texture, rhythm, registration, and counterpoint are considered to be related to pitch organization. The analysis of each etude relies upon Schenkerian approaches and considers three perspectives: the overall formal plan, the tonal organization, and the basic shape. Finds all the etudes to be "emphatically tonal" and respectful of broad principles of the common practice. This dissertation is valuable unto itself and as a basis for the two analyses cited below. Also see item 639.

851. ------. "Pitch Organization in Debussy: Unordered Sets in **Brouillards**." **Music Theory Spectrum** 2 (1980): 119-34.

The etude **Brouillards** well represents the later style with its nontraditional voice leading, harmony, and tonality. Parks suggests that set theory illuminates the compositional process when traditional tonal analysis does not. Argues against the unqualified, simplistic characterization of D's innovations as "foreign to tradition," because such a characterization implies arbitrary choice. The author shows that pitch sets functioning along motivic lines lend coherence and are grasped by the listener. The compositional process in **Brouillards** is markedly different from that elsewhere, even when an analysis of sets is applied. No over-arching system or formula for producing compositions is seen, and "each piece is its own master."

852. ------. "Tonal Analogues as Atonal Resources and their Relation to Form in Debussy's **Chromatic Etude**." **Journal of Music Theory** 29, no. 1 (Spring 1985): 33-60.

Complements the study of **Brouillards** listed above. States that the **Chromatic Etude** contains atonal contexts, deploying pitch materials as lines and sonorities without tonal reference in any traditional sense. However, tonal analogues (such as an inherently tonal tetrachordal motive) are in evidence and remain D's preferred pitch resources. These become sets, are transposed chromatically, and otherwise are developed according to atonal procedures. While only vestigial in this work, tonality nonetheless is an organizing force at both structural and superficial levels. The most remarkable feature of the piece is its "utter lack of affectation"; it gives proof of consummate mastery.

This study relates specifically to analyses of the late music but also offers exciting possibilities for analysis of the earlier music, for which traditional analysis falls short as well.

853. Pasler, Jann. "**Pelléas** and Power: Forces Behind the Reception of Debussy's Opera." **Nineteenth-Century Music** 10, no. 3 (Spring 1987): 243-64. Translated as "Opéra et Pouvoir: Forces à l'oeuvre derrière le scandale du **Pelléas** de Debussy." In **La Musique et le Pouvoir**, edited by Joel-Marie Fauquet, pp. 147-77. Paris: Librairie aux Amateurs, 1987.

The premiere was greeted by reactionaries with surprise and hostility, and by the Debussystes with shows of excessive enthusiasm. Heated discussions of the work's merits extended even beyond the 100th performance in 1913. Pasler illustrates by charts the ticket receipts of contemporaneous operas and the critical reviews of **Pelléas**. Discusses relevant aesthetic, social, and political issues operative among groups who figured in the early audiences. Considers the debate over D as "anarchist." While noting that certain critics assessed the work on its inherent terms, Pasler argues persuasively that the clash of extra-musical values affected the reception of **Pelléas** decisively. A model for the study of D's reception.

854. ------. "Debussy, **Jeux**: Playing with Time and Form." **Nineteenth-Century Music** 6, no. 1 (Summer 1982): 60-75.

Maintains that the structure of **Jeux** involves not only timbre and motive but also the overall rhythm of meters, tempos, and large sectional change. Relates D's conception to the "process" form of the philosopher Henri Bergson and to cinematography. Views the underlying continuity of **Jeux** in terms of purposeful movement and change.

855. Pecerskij, Petr. "Tragiceskaja tarantella" [A tragic tarantella]. **Sovetskaja muzyka** (Feb. 1977, no. 2): 105-07. In Russian.

Traces the origins of the project **Masques et bergamasques** and discusses various interpretations of meaning. Reviews archival materials and gives an analysis, concluding that the work belongs to the category of tragedy.

856. **Pelléas et Mélisande**. Issue of **l'Avant-scène--opéra**, no. 9, March-April 1977.

Special issue devoted to the opera. Contains complete libretto, list of important performances in leading opera houses, bibliography, and discography. Particular essays are:

Macherey, Pierre. "Debussy et Maeterlinck," 4-12.

Clément, Catherine. "Mélisande à la question,

ou le secret des hommes," 15-19.
Goléa, Antoine. "Genèse de l'oeuvre," 20-24.
[Plot synopsis], 25.
Original libretto, with musical commentary by Henry Barraud, 27-82.
Fogel, Susan Lee. "L'originalité de Pelléas et **Mélisande**: les inventions orchestrales," 84-89.
Dutronc, Jean-Louis. "Jacques Jansen: 30 ans de Pelléas," 90-93.
Macherey, Pierre. **Proust et "Pelléas**," 94-95.
Cadieu, Martine. "**Pelléas et Mélisande**: peinture visionnaire ou fait-divers?" 97-98.
Terrasson, René. "L'alchimie d'une oeuvre," 100-03.
Lanceron, Alain. "Jorge Lavelli: 'pour échapper à la loi du château,'" 104-07.
Pouget, François. "Discographie comparée," 108-09.
Letellier, Charles. "**Pelléas** et les 78 tours [78 rpm discography]," 110-11.
"L'oeuvre à l'affiche," 111-25.
Samama, Guy. "V. Jankélévitch: Debussy," 131-45.

Also contains bibliography and many illustrations concerning **Pelléas**.

* Peter, René. "Ce que fut la "générale" de **Pelléas et Mélisande**." See item 132.

857. Peterson, William John. "Debussy's **Douze études**: A Critical Analysis." Ph.D. diss., Musicology, University of California at Berkeley, 1981. 271 p. UM 82-00-236; DA XLII.7, p. 2927-A. ML 410.D28 P4 1981a.

The etudes reflect D's interest in "la musique pure" toward the end of his life, as also do the three sonatas. Discusses the genesis of the Etudes and the editorial work by D on Chopin's piano works. Treats continuity of structure as the central question. Considers the fair copy (B.n. MS 993), which allows insight into compositional procedure, and the Morgan Library MS of **Pour les arpèges composés [Etude retrouvée]**, which although different might have informed the etude of that title. While ABA and AA' form is employed in the etudes, contrapuntal motion is more decisive than traditional dominant resolution in the innovative conclusions. Views D as discovering his new voice, turning from programmatic to pure-music procedures. These involve classic economy of means and the integration of design with fantasy.

858. Photiadès, Constantin. "M. Claude Debussy et la centième de **Pelléas et Mélisande**. **La revue de Paris** 20, no. 2 (Mar.-Apr. 1913): 513-38.

An expression of passionate enthusism is followed by a brief biography. Recalls the reception of **Pelléas** in 1902 and anticipates the 1913 performance that was the 100th of the work. Of some interest in the reception and general appreciation of the work.

859. Raad, Virginia. "The Cathedrals of Monet and Debussy." **Clavier** 25, no. 3 (March 1986): 11-14.

Describes aspects of performing the prelude for piano **La cathédrale engloutie**, relating it to painting and D's biography. The author overstates the point when she notes that neither D nor Monet was preoccupied with form. This article seeks to relate D vividly to the other arts in terms immediately accessible to a wide public. Even for the general audience, it might be expanded by the argument that D was a musical structuralist of great range, for whom the programmatic was only one of multiple layers of perception.

860. Rafols, Alberto. "Debussy and the Symbolist Movement: The Preludes." D.M.A. diss., University of Washington, 1975. 195 p. UM 76-17,594; DA 37/02A, p.683. ML 410.D28 R27 1978x.

Relates structural and aesthetic procedures of Symbolist poets to the preludes for piano. Leans upon the programmatic subtitles as point of departure for analysis and finds comparisons with songs of related titles. The author notes that his approach is speculative but related to the compositional process. Includes a detailed analysis of **Les sons et les parfums**, which the author holds as the best example of the connection with Symbolist literature. Not examined.

861. Rahn, Jay. "Comment on Haino 'Generated Collections.'" **In Theory Only** 5, no. 2 (May-June 1979): 19-22.

Criticizes the concept of cyclic collections and proposes a theory of scales instead. Rahn's analysis allows for tonal tendencies in D rather than referring to pitch-class (order-determinate) uses. See Haino (768).

862. Rauss, Denis-François. "Ce terrible finale." **Cahiers Debussy** (nouvelle série) 2 (1978): 30-62.

Discusses thoughtfully the MS sources and the genesis of the sonata for violin, movement three. Considers the sketches of the former de Tinan collection (now at the B.n.) and relevant B.n. manuscripts 992, 15380, 17678, 17716, 17726, and 17732.

* **Revue musicale** 234 (1957). Numéro special illustré, "Le martyre de Saint-Sébastien." See annotation, item 147.

863. Riessauw, Anne-Marie Rodolf. "Musico-literaire verhoudingen in de Verlaine-liederen van Fauré en Debussy. Een stijlkritisch onderzoek gevolgd door een catalogus van vocale werken van europese componisten op gedichten van Verlaine." [Text-music Relations in the Verlaine Songs by Fauré and Debussy. A Stylistic Study with a Catalogue of Vocal Works on Verlaine Poems by European Composers.] Ph.D. diss., Musicology, University of Ghent, 1978. 7 volumes. xxxi, 2316 p.

Not examined, but appears to be the longest single study to date concerned with Debussy.

864. Ringger, Rolf Urs. "**Gymnopédies**: Zu Debussys Orchestrierung zweier Stücke von Satie" **Neue Zürcher Zeitschrift** 82 (April 1980): 69- 70.

Considers the personal relationship of the two composers and the genesis of D's setting, and analyzes the original and the orchestration. Not examined.

865. Rivière, Jacques. . . . **Etudes** . . . 7th edition. Paris: Gallimard, 1925. LC: PQ2635.I87E8.

Essays on compositions by D, including those on **Pelléas** and the major orchestral works. Gives contemporaneous insights and reception. Not examined.

866. Robichez, Jacques. **Le Symbolisme au théâtre: Lugné-Poe et les débuts de L'Oeuvre.** Paris: L'Arche, 1957. 568 p. PN 2636.P3 R62.

Discusses the role of the Théâtre de L'Oeuvre in the performance of Symbolist drama. Describes the "discovery" of Maeterlinck by O. Mirbeau in 1890 and the 1893 performance of the play **Pelléas**. Cites criticism of **Pelléas**, including that by H. Céard, that forecast an operatic setting.

867. Rohinsky, Marie-Claire, ed. and trans. **The Singer's Debussy.** New York: Pelion Press, 1987. ML 54.6 D42R62 1987; ISBN 0-8239-0671-X.

Contains notes, bibliography, indexes of titles, first line, and general aspects; chronology, pronunciation guide, and catalogue of songs. Proposes to give background information relevant to the singer, as well as translation and pronunciation of song texts. Considers songs published only through about 1982 and thus does not list the 13 songs of the Recueil Vasnier (those published in 1982) and the **Sept poèmes de Banville** (published 1985). Most successful in the highly useful, expert information about French pronunciation in general and the phonetic guide to each song. Each is given a word-for-word translation and a smoother one. The translations, when coupled with the pronunciation guide, recommend this book over Cobb (see item 48). However, it does not match Cobb's helpfulness as regards sources of poetry and biographical and artistic background.

868. Rolf, Marie. "Debussy's **La mer**: A Critical Analysis in the Light of Early Sketches and Editions." Ph.D. diss., Theory, University of Rochester, 1976. x, 367 p. UM 77-08,315; DA XXXVII.11, p. 6833-A. MT 130.D4 R644 1976a.

Focuses on the only sketch of **La mer**, at the University of Rochester-Eastman, Sibley Music Library, and dating to 1903-05. Places the work in historical perspective, discusses its genesis, and reviews the critical reception. The compositional process from sketch to score is studied, whereby D continually transformed his ideas through to the fair copy. That continual transformation finds an analogue in the formal procedure of **La mer**, in which the musical fabric is subject to continual variation of melody, harmony, and rhythm. The author relates the manuscript and musical forming procedures to the sea itself. A model study analyzing a sketch and its development into a composition.

869. ------. "Debussy's Settings of Verlaine's **En sourdine**." In **Perspectives on Music**, pp. 205-33. Austin, Texas: Humanities Research Center, University of Texas, 1985.

Considers the five versions of 1882 and the two of 1892. Helpfully distinguishes the various stages in the evolution of the conception. Music examples show variants in the work, which is from the song set **Fêtes galantes I**. Discusses changes in prosody from one stage to the next.

870. ------. "Orchestral Manuscripts of Claude Debussy: 1892-1905." **Musical Quarterly** 70, no. 4 (1984): 538-66.

Reviews the extant manuscripts of **Prélude-faune, Nocturnes**, and **La mer** in their short score versions. Also remarks on the only extant sketches among the group, which are of **La mer**, movement 1. These relate at instances to the **Pelléas** manuscripts. D's manuscript handwriting [at this stage] is precise. Changes from short score to final version reveal his penchant for simplicity and motivic unity, with notable changes at the end of **La mer**.

871. Rolland, Romain. **Musiciens d'aujourd'hui**. 5th ed. Paris: Hachette, 1912. 278 p. ML 390.R655. Translated into English by M. Blaiklock, with title **Musicians of Today**. New York: Holt, 1915. 324 p. English translation reprinted Freeport, N.Y.: Books for Libraries Press, 1969. ISBN 0-8369-1188-1; ML 390.R653 1969.

Includes a chapter "Claude Debussy: **Pelléas et Mélisande**," pp. 234-45. Relates the importance of the premiere to premieres by Lully, Rameau, and Gluck. Observes that D's success is due to translation into art of European fatalism and to his pathbreaking opposition to Wagner. The preceding essay, "French and German Music" (pp. 207-33), refers to works by Franck and Mahler. A foremost commentator of his day, Rolland can inform the question of nationalist artistic thought in D, as in the composer's written criticism.

872. Ruschenburg, Peter. "Stilkritische Untersuchungen zu den Liedern Claude Debussys." Doctoral diss., University of Hamburg, 1966. 177 p. MT 115.D418 R9.

Reviews thoroughly the poetry, small- and large-scale structures, melody and prosody, rhythm, whole-tone use, and influences on the songs. This is a basic source in the structural analysis of D's songs, if not in the analysis of their musico-poetic relations. An appendix contains the first publication of the **mélodies Caprice** and **Jane**.

* Salzer, Felix. **Structural Hearing: Tonal Coherence in Music.** Analyzes **Prélude-faune** and prelude for piano **Bruyères**. See item 605.

* Samazeuilh, Gustave. "La première version inédite de **En sourdine** [**Fêtes galantes I**], avec fac-similé." See item 132 for full citation.

873. Sauguet, Henri. "French Song: Some Notes." **Parnassus** 10, no. 2 (Fall-Winter 1982): 251-55.

Compares treatments of text by 20th-century song composers. For D, text and music possessed an equal emotional content. The approaches to prosody varied widely among the composers Ravel, Fauré, Satie, Milhaud, Poulenc, and Messiaen. A short, subjective article that perhaps is of most value for revealing the interests of the composer Sauguet.

874. Schaeffner, André. "Claude Debussy et ses projets shakespeariens." **Revue d'histoire du théâtre** 15, no. 4 (1964): 446-53.

Discusses D's attraction to Shakespeare, as also that of Mallarmé and Maeterlinck. Traces the parallels between the play **Hamlet** and **Pelléas**, and observes D's interests dating from as early as 1886. D might have known Verdi's **Otello**, and the two composers shared an interest in **King Lear**. D must have seen Parisian performances such as Sarah Bernhardt's **Hamlet** in 1893. Shortly after that, D and Toulet began to collaborate on **As You Like It**. This brief survey helps put the Shakespearian projects in perspective of D's whole development.

875. Scherliess, Volker. "Hanns Eislers Bearbeitung von Debussys **Prélude à l'après-midi d'un faune**." **Neue Zeitschrift für Musik** 141, no. 2 (March-April 1980): 130-32.

A brief account of Eisler's arrangement of **Prélude-faune**, of about 1920. The instrumentation was for chamber orchestra and now is preserved at the Arnold Schoenberg Institute, Los Angeles. Contains a musical example of Eisler's score.

876. Schmitz, E. Robert. **The Piano Works of Claude Debussy**. Foreword by Virgil Thompson. New York: Duell, Sloan, and Pierce, 1950. Reprint, New York: Dover, 1966. 234 p. ISBN 0-486-21567-9.

The author was a pupil of D. His book, an analytic commentary, remains of interest to performers and teachers, but they must also read sources that are more current.

877. Seraphin, Hellmut. "Debussys Kammermusikwerke der mittleren Schaffenzeit: analytische und historische Untersuchung in Rahmen des Berücksichtigung des Ganztongeschlechts." Doctoral diss., Erlangen-Nurnberg, Friedrich Alexander-University, 1962. 144 p. ML 410.D28 S481 1962z.

Discusses the chamber music of D's middle period: **Première rapsodie** for clarinet, **Petite pièce**, **Syrinx**. The **Quatuor** and the **Sonatas** are referred to in comparison. Proceeds by an analysis of themes, form, tonality, and harmony. Does not consider the youthful works that preceded the **Quatuor**.

878. Shand, David A. "The Sonata for Violin and Piano from Schumann to Debussy (1851-1917)." Ph.D. diss., Music, Boston University, 1948. 403 p. Not examined.

879. Souffrin-Le Breton, Eileen. "Debussy lecteur de Banville." **Revue de musicologie** 46, no. 122 (Dec. 1960): 200-22.

A quite significant writing on D's early vocal music, which most often sets the poetry of Banville. Traces D's works published as of 1960 and certain ones in manuscript. Considers the songs written for Mme Vasnier as well as **Hymnis** and **Diane au bois** in light of the personal relationship. Views Banville as an important precursor of Verlaine, Mallarmé, and Symbolism as a literary movement. He thus was an important figure in D's development.

880. Spence, Keith. "Debussy at Sea." **Musical Times** 120, no. 1638 (Aug. 1979): 640-42.

Investigates little-known biographical details surrounding the composition of **La mer**, including an account by a local historian in St. Malo.

881. Spieth-Weissenbacher, Christiane Elisabeth. "Le récitatif mélodique dans **Pelléas et Mélisande** de Claude Debussy." Diss., Doctorat 3, Musicology, University of Strasbourg, 1979. Not examined.

882. Stefani, Gino. "Musica e titoli: i preludi di Debussy." **Nuova rivista musicale italiana** 10, no. 4 (Oct.-Dec. 1976): 596-616.

Considers the relationship of the prelude for piano titles to the music itself, as related to general semiotic theory. Urges the interpretation of the titles as metaphors for larger experience. **La Puerta del vino**, for example becomes a metaphor for all that is Spanish. A thoughtful analysis of the elusive programs of the prelude titles.

883. Stirnemann, Knut. "Zur Frage des Leitmotivs in Debussys **Pelléas et Mélisande**." In **Schweizer Beiträge zur Musikwissenschaft, IV, ed. Jürg Stenzl**. Studien zur Musik des 19. und 20.

Jahrhunderts. Bern and Stuttgart: Haupt, 1980. 266 p. ISBN 3-2580-2934-2; ML 5.S32 Bd. 4 ML193.

An outstandingly clear analysis of leitmotives in **Pelléas**, extending Emmanuel (item 741). Families of themes are the proper concept to trace, since themes are transformed. The identification of themes upon any single occurrence is not helpful or proper to a discussion of long-range thematic structure.

884. Storb, Ilse. "Untersuchungen zur Auflösung der funktionalen Harmonik in den Klavierwerken von Claude Debussy." Doctoral diss., University of Cologne, 1971. ML 410.D28 S7.

A helpful if at times tedious survey, from the nearly functional harmony in the early works, to the tonal outreach of the middle phase, to the composition by timbre and sonority rather than by tonal system in the last phase. Stresses the piano works with many examples therefrom.

885. Street, William Henry. "Elise Boyer Hall, America's First Female Concert Saxophonist." D.M. diss., Northwestern University, 1983. UM no. 85-04819.

Discusses the genesis of the **Rapsodie** for saxophone. Not examined.

886. Suter, L.M. "Claude Debussy: **Pour les accords**, Etude no. 12 pour piano." **Revue musicale de Suisse Romande** 36, no. 3 (Sept. 1983): 105-24.

Sees in the **Etudes** proof of Debussy's statement that he was "relearning music," that is, rediscovering his classicizing urge toward pure music. Points out important variants between the autograph MSS and the Durand edition. The twelfth Etude is a structural coda for the set. The first 3 eighth-note chords of Etude 12 form a motive fundamental to the particular ABA' structure, which springs from Golden Section planning.

887. Serbescu, Silvia. "12 studii pentru pian de Debussy" [Debussy's 12 piano Etudes]. **Muzicka** 19, no. 11 (Nov. 1969): 9-13. In Rumanian.

An analysis of interpretive problems and piano technique. Not examined.

888. Tammaro, Ferruccio. "Mélisande dai quattro volti." **Nuova rivista musicale italiana** 15, no. 1 (Jan.-March 1981): 95-119.

The play **Pelléas** by Maeterlinck was set by four composers, D, Schoenberg, Fauré, and Sibelius. D and Schoenberg represent two cultural poles, while the other two composers are seen in the middle and bear the influence of both aesthetics. Seeks reasons why all four focused their interest on the play at the same time.

889. Terrasson, René. **"Pelléas et Mélisande," ou l'initiation.** Paris: EDIMAF: 1982. 205 p. ISBN 2-9038-4610-6-3; ML 410.D28T44 1982.

Investigates the occult and the complex of symbols in **Pelléas**, pointing to 36 melodic cellules that give musical and poetic meaning. Then comments virtually line by line on the libretto, interpreting D's vision as unified with Maeterlinck's, and points to symbolic meanings.

890. Tiersot, Julien. "Oeuvres de première jeunesse de Berlioz et de Debussy." **Le ménestrel** 95 (Paris, Jan. 6, 1933).

By a foremost scholar. Concerns the cantata **Daniel**. Not examined.

891. Tosi, Guy. "D'Annunzio et Debussy: La genèse musicale du **Martyre de Saint Sébastien**." **Il Verri** (Milan) Ser. 7, no. 7-8 (Sept.-Dec. 1985): 7-34.

Describes a proposal by Roger-Ducasse, in collaboration with Nadia Boulanger and before D took an interest, to write music for **Le martyre**. Thereafter, d'Annunzio approached Henry Février. Traces the biographical context, associations, and reception **Le martyre**. D'Annunzio attributed the finer inspiration to D's score rather than to his own writing. Does not treat drama or music at great length but is helpful on the genesis of the project.

892. Tovey, Donald Francis. "Debussy: **The Blessed Damozel**." In **Essays in Musical Analysis**. 7th ed. Vol. V: Vocal Music, p. 242-47. London: Oxford Univ. Press, 1937. MT 90.T58.

Contrasts D's **Damoiselle élue** to Berlioz's **Mort de Cléopatre**, the parallels between which are only superficial. D's work was truly revolutionary, especially in chord progressions that deny polyphonic principles. Shows that D's setting follows the original 1850 text by Rossetti, rather than the later and awkward revision. There follows a useful if somewhat cursory tracing of themes and their appropriateness to text. Further see Langham Smith (item 481) for a richer interpretation of literary associations and meaning.

893. Trevitt, John. "Debussy inconnu: an Enquiry I and II." **Musical Times** 114, no. 1568 (Sept., Oct. 1973): 881-86 and 1001-05.

Part I treats the earliest vocal music; II treats the slightly later vocal and instrumental works. Calls for a new edition of **Printemps** (1887) that respects Debussy's intention to include a choir. A responsible overview but updated by Briscoe (705) and subsequent studies.

894. Vallas, Léon. "En feuilletant les partitions musicales de Debussy." **Musique** (Nov. 15, 1927): 68-73.

Gives a facsimile of p. 50 and 58 of **Le gladiateur**. Among the earliest manuscript studies, this article attempts to chronologize the youthful works for the first time. Considers manuscripts originally owned by the publishers Durand and Jobert, which since Vallas's article have passed to the B.n. As a source study, has been updated substantially, but is of interest for a first assessment of the early works.

895. Vital, Cla. "Studien zu Debussys Skizzen zu **Rodrigue et Chimène** und **Pelléas**." Ph.D. diss., Musicology, University of Zurich, 1981. Not examined.

896. Watson, Lorne. "Cadences in Debussy's **Preludes, Books I and II**." DMA Diss., Indiana University, 1976. 80 p.

Discusses traditional cadences based on diatonic harmony; chromatic cadences; modal, pentatonic, and whole-tone materials at cadences; and implied cadences.

897. Wenk, Arthur B. "Checklist of Errors in Debussy's Piano Music." **Piano Quarterly** 68 (Summer 1969): 18-21.

Deals with most manuscripts at the Bibliothèque nationale save those of the preludes. Cites discrepancies between these and the first French editions, almost always by Durand. One anticipates that the editors of the complete works of D, currently being issued by Durand, will seek to resolve the discrepancies.

898. ------. **Claude Debussy and the Poets.** Berkeley: University of California Press, 1976. x, 345 p. ISBN 0-5200-2827-9; ML 410.D28 W4.

A reworking of a dissertation by the same title [Cornell University 1970, UM 70-23,094], this book is a primary source on Debussy's songs and their literary basis. Looking through the poetic lens, Wenk analyzes songs on poetry by Banville, Verlaine (**Ariettes, Fêtes galantes**), Baudelaire (**Cinq poèmes**), Louÿs (**Chansons de Bilitis**), and Mallarmé (**Trois poèmes**). Also considers the composer as poet (**Proses lyriques**) and the integration of poetry into **Prélude-faune**. Appendix containing thoughtful translation of poems cited; useful bibliography on related poets and literary movements not found elsewhere in Debussy sources.

899. White, David A. "Echoes of Silence: The Structure of Destiny in Debussy's **Pelléas et Mélisande**." **Music Review** 41, no. 4 (Nov. 1980): 266-77.

Silence symbolizes destiny and is a sonorous link in the structure, culminating with the emphasis on silence in the final scene. Identifies three types of silence: silence of drama (unresolved enigma), of language (both actual silence and vague statement), and silence of nature (human and divine). A highly personal interpretation that nonetheless illuminates one meaning of the opera.

900. Williams, Bernard. "L'envers des destinées: Remarks on Debussy's **Pelléas et Mélisande.**" **Universities Quarterly** 29, no. 4 (Fall 1975): 389-97.

An interpretation of the opera's central theme of destiny. D interprets the inner life of the characters with great depth, which early critics and certain of the audience failed to see. This article is a concise, helpful statement of dramatic theme.

901. Wilson, Eugene Norman. "Form and Texture in the Chamber Music of Debussy and Ravel." Ph.D. diss., Theory, University of Washington, 1968. iv, 272 p. UM 68-12,723; DA XXIX.3, p. 927-A. MT 140.D28 W54 1968a.

Traces salient features of both composers' early styles as represented in their string quartets, which exhibit adapted "ternary-sonata" forms, coloristic textures, and a late-Romantic tonal idiom. Describes the expansion of harmonic criteria in D's late sonatas, involving tonality, modality, "pentatonality," and special tonal sets. Ravel develops in contrasting fashion: he retains his basic gestures while attempting to change the outer surface of his style.

902. Wolff, Stéphane. **Un demi-siecle d'Opéra-comique, 1900-50.** Paris: Editions A. Bonne, 1953. 338 p.

An alphabetical list of works performed and operatic casts, including **Pelléas**. Describes the 1902 first performance and the reprises of 1906 and others through 1952, giving singers cast in main roles and conductors.

903. ------. **L'Opéra au Palais Garnier (1875-1962).** Paris: [déposé au journal] **"Entracte,"** 1962. 565 p. ML 1727.8.P2W8.

A catalogue of all works performed at the Opéra, listing first performances, performers, reprises, and administrators. Details operas, oratorios, ballets. Catalogues **Le martyre**, **Petite suite**, and **Prélude-faune** as regards their performance and choreography at the Opéra.

904. Youens, Susan Lee. "Debussy's setting of Verlaine's **Colloque sentimental**: From the Past to the Present." **Studies in Music** (Australia) 15 (1981): 93-105.

Shifting textures are viewed as principal determinants of structure in the work [from **Fêtes galantes II**]. The ghost characters of the poem represent in one case the Romantic past, in the other the modern nihilistic spirit. Debussy employs two musical languages as metaphors for the two characters. Sees the diminished 7th chord at the conclusion, which does not "progress," as representing both D's new "linear" style at once with the dismantling of the late-Romantic harmonic vocabulary.

905. ------. "From the Fifteenth Century to the Twentieth: Considerations of Musical Prosody in Debussy's **Trois ballades of François Villon**." **Journal of Musicology** 2, no. 4 (1983): 418-33.

Provides an articulate introduction to matters of prosody in D, with thought and sensitivity recognizing the absence of rigid rhythmic patterns in French poetry. Considers prosody in Berlioz and Duparc and briefly surveys D's prosody up to the Villon songs of 1910. Points out corruptions of the original Villon in D's text and the composer's lack of fidelity to Villon's somewhat regularized verse, citing D's proclivity toward prose and prose-poetry, such as in his setting of Maeterlinck.

906. ------. "A Gradual Diminuendo: Debussy and the **Trois Ballades de François Villon**." In **Perspectives on Music**, pp. 69-99. Austin: Humanities Research Center, University of Texas, 1985. ISBN 0-87959-102-1; ML 55.P478 1985. First appeared in **The Library Chronicle** nos. 25/26 (Univ. of Texas) (Special issue, Feb. 1984), 68-99.

Concerns the orchestral version with voice made by D. The published copy given by him to A. Messager, including his manuscript corrections, is in the holdings of the Humanities Research Center. The corrections, made in 1915, concern subtleties of orchestration and dynamics.

907. ------. "Music, Verse, and 'Prose Poetry': Debussy's **Trois Chansons de Bilitis**." **Journal of Musicological Research** (Fall 1986), 69-94. Unavailable to this study.

908. ------. "To Tell a Tale: Symbolist Narrative in Debussy's **Fêtes galantes II**." **Nineteenth-Century French Studies** 16, nos. 1 and 2 (Fall-Winter 1987-88): 180-91.

Observes that D followed the tradition of composer as "Poet's Editor" in the **Baudelaire Songs**, the **Chansons de Bilitis**, and **Fêtes Galantes II**. Unlike set I, set II is a cohesive narrative, a distilled triptych of the birth, history, and death of love conveyed in the terms of Symbolism. Aside from atmosphere, no particular musical unity is found. In this article, the analysis of poetry is keen but not technical musically, in keeping with the journal.

909. ------. "The Unseen Player: Destiny in **Pelléas et Mélisande**." In **Reading Opera**, edited by R. Parker and A. Groos, pp. 60-91. Princeton: Princeton Uiversity Press, 1988. ISBN 0-691-09132-3 (cloth); ML 2110.R4.

Views the opera as a rare instance of the fundamental interdependency of words and music. D's musical achievement is seen in relation to Schopenhauer; his treatment clarifies the premise that Destiny is the most important player. A valuable, full exploration of a concept often mentioned as basic to **Pelléas** but not proved.

910. Zenck-Maurer, Claudia. "Form- und Farbenspiele: Debussys **Jeux**." **Archiv für Musikwissenschaft** 33, no. 1 (1976): 28-47.

Reviews the reception of **Jeux** by Stockhausen and Eimert [739], whose interpretations of form are questioned. Discusses the musical and psychological motivations for the structure, stating that it may be viewed from the traditional perspective of repetition and contrast. **Jeux** utilizes timbres, speech idioms, and dance forms to convey the quickly changing psychological situations. Charts each "psychological moment" in the scenario and score.

XI

ADDRESSES: SCHOLARS, LIBRARIES, AND PUBLISHERS

1. Scholars and Other Persons

The following scholars are actively involved with research on Debussy, his music, and his times. Scholars listed have lectured and published on Debussy on multiple occasions. They have indicated an interest in exchanging ideas and information with other Debussy scholars. The aim of this listing is to bring together students of Debussy whose interests are extensive. It is not intended for short-ranged inquiries.

Each entry indicates the name, area of interest within Debussy scholarship, and current mailing address.

Abravanel, Prof. Claude
Bibliography of Debussy
Director of the Library
Jerusalem Rubin Academy of Music and Dance
Givat Ram Campus, Jerusalem 91904

private address:
55 Ramban Street
92268 Jerusalem, Israel (tel. (02) 633354)

Austin, Prof. William W.
Debussy's relationship to the 20th century
Prélude à l'après-midi d'un faune
Department of Music, Lincoln Hall
Cornell University
Ithaca, New York 14853 USA

Blumenthal, Dr. Daniel H.
Early piano duos and duets
116, rue des Confédérés
B-1040 Bruxelles, Belgium tel. (032) 736.06.46

Briscoe, Prof. James R.
The early music (1879-1888); primary and secondary sources
Jordan College of Fine Arts
Butler University
Indianapolis, Indiana 46208 USA 317/283-9231

Chimènes, Mlle Myriam
Khamma, Jeux
13, rue du Cherche-Midi
75006 Paris, France

Fischer, Prof. Dr. Kurt von
Form; aesthetics; Art nouveau relationship
Laubholzstrasse 46
CH-8703 Erlenbach, Switzerland

Goubault, Prof. Christian
c/o Editions Champion
7, quai Malaquais
75006 Paris, France

Grayson, Prof. David
Pelléas; sources for Debussy study
School of Music
University of Minnesota
Minneapolis, Minnesota 55455 USA tel. 612/624-5740

Gut, Prof. Serge
Chamber music; preludes; comparison to Liszt; structure
Directeur, Département de Musicologie
Université de Paris-Sorbonne (Paris IV; Place de la Sorbonne)
1, rue Victor Cousin
75230 Paris Cedex 05,
France

Hepokoski, Prof. James
Aesthetics and analysis
School of Music
University of Minnesota
Minneapolis, Minnesota 55455 USA

Hirsbrunner, Prof. Theo
D's relation to artistic climate and to other composers.
Optingenstrasse 53
CH-3013 Bern, Switzerland

Howat, Dr. Roy
Piano music; sources; editorial matters; structure
26 Morden Court
London Road
Morden, Surrey SM4 5HN
United Kingdom

Langham Smith, Mr. Richard
Lecturer in Music
Rodrigue et Chimène; D's critical writings; biography and artistic climate, including the Pre-Raphaelites
Department of Music
The City University
Northampton Square
London EC1V 0HB tel. 01-253 4399
United Kingdom

Lesure, Mr François
Former Conservateur-en-chef, Département de Musique, Bibliothèque Nationale; Editor-in-chief of the **Oeuvres complètes** de Debussy; Editor of the **Cahiers Debussy**; concerned with Debussy and his artistic relations.
Ecole Pratique des Hautes Etudes
4e section
45-47 rue des Ecoles
75005 Paris, France

Lundgren, Mr. Stephen E.
Discography of Debussy
West Queen Anne
2123 10th Avenue West
Seattle, Washington 98119 USA

Mueller, Dr. Richard
D and the Orient; cultural milieu; Debussyism in America
Department of Music
University of Chicago
5845 South Ellis Avenue
Chicago, Illinois 60637 USA

Nattiez, Prof. J.J.
Semiotic analysis to Debussy
Faculté de Musique
Université de Montréal
C.P. 6128, succursale A
Montréal, Québec, Canada H3C 3J7

Nectoux, Dr. Jean-Michel
D's relationship to Fauré
51, Boulevard de Charonne
75011 Paris, France

Nichols, Mr. Roger
Letters; D's biography; **Pelléas**
West End, Docklow
Leominster, Herefordshire HR6 ORU
United Kingdom

Orledge, Prof. Robert
Debussy and the theater; orchestral and other source studies
Department of Music
University of Liverpool
80 Bedford Street South
Liverpool L69 3BX tel. 051-709-6022 X2490
United Kingdom

Parks, Prof. Richard S.
Tonality, form, timbre; how D understood his compositional resources; D and esotericism
Faculty of Music, Talbot College
The University of Western Ontario
London, Ontario, Canada N6A 3K7

Pasler, Prof. Jann
Pelléas; D's reception; social and political forces; the **Apaches**
Department of Music B-026
University of California, San Diego
La Jolla, California USA 92093

Peterson, Prof. William
Piano music and analysis
Department of Music
Pomona College
Claremont, California 91711-6341 USA

Rolf, Prof. Marie
Orchestral works; songs; editorial procedures; analysis
University of Rochester
Eastman School of Music
26 Gibbs Street
Rochester, New York 14604 USA

Suter, Prof. Dr. Louis-Marc
Université de Berne
1, route du Pré-de-l'Ile
CH 1752 Villars-sur-Glâne
Switzerland

Thieullent, Maitre Henri
Heir and representative of Debussy's estate
17, avenue Foch
76600 Le Havre, France

Wenk, Dr. Arthur B.
Relationship between text and music, especially in the songs and **Pelléas**; a musical grammar of D's melodic and general style.
The Sedbergh School
Montebello, Québec
Canada J0V 1L0

Youens, Prof. Susan
Vocal music
Department of Music
University of Notre Dame
Notre Dame, Indiana 46556 USA

2. Libraries and Institutions
Current addresses as of summer 1989.

Bibliothèque Nationale
Département de la Musique

Location:
58, rue de Richelieu, Paris 2e

Correspondence:
2, rue Vivienne
75084 Paris Cedex 02
France tel. (1) 47.03-81.26

The British Library
The Manuscript Collections
Great Russell Street
London WC1B 3DG tel. 01-323 7510
United Kingdom

Centre de Documentation Claude Debussy
Mlle Miriam Chimènes, Conservateur
C.I.D.M.
IRCAM/CNRS
Centre Pompidou, 1er étage, Poste 60 50
31, rue St. Merry
75004 Paris, France tel. 42.77-12.33
[If no response is forthcoming, write to the Centre in care of the Bibliothèque nationale, Département de la musique, at the above address.]

Fondation Martin Bodmer
Dr. Hans Braun, Directeur
19-21 Route de Guignard
CH 1223 Cologny-Genève, Switzerland
tel. 022/36 23 70

The Newberry Library
Curator of Music Special Collections
60 West Walton Street
Chicago, Illinois 60610 USA
tel. 312-943-9090

New York Public Library
Special Collections in Music
Lincoln Center
111 Amsterdam Avenue
New York, New York 10023 USA

The Pierpont Morgan Library
Mr. J. Rigbie Turner, Curator of Music Manuscripts
29 East 36th Street
New York, New York 10016 USA
tel. 212-685-0008

Stanford University
Memorial Library of Music
Department of Special Collections, Green Library
The Knoll
Stanford, California 94305 USA

Stiftelsen Musikkulturens Fraemjande
Mr. Goeran Grahn, Curator
Riddargatan 35-37
S-11457 Stockholm, Sweden

University of Texas at Austin
Harry Ransom Humanities Research Center
Ms. Cathy Henderson, Research Librarian
P.O. Drawer 7219
Austin, Texas 78713-7219 tel. 512/471-9119

3. Publishers

Associated
Associated Music Publishers
24 E. 22nd St.
New York, New York 10010 USA

Choudens
Editions Choudens
Directeur, Monsieur André Chevrier
38, rue Jean-Mermoz
75008 Paris, France tel. 42.66-62.97 or 43.59- 31.51
US agent: Peters Corporation
British agent: United Music Publishers

Costallat
Editions Costallat/Erato
50 rue des Tournelles
75003 Paris, France tel. 48.04-98.07

<u>Durand</u>
Editions Durand S.A.
Mr Jean-Manuel de Scarano, Directeur
Mme Odette Vidal, Secrétaire
215 rue du Faubourg St. Honoré
75008 Paris, France tel. 42.89-17.13
US agent: Theodore Presser
British agent: United Music Publishers

<u>Eschig</u>
Editions Max Eschig
48, rue de Rome
75008 Paris, France tel. 45.22-66.64
US agent: Associated Music Publ.
British agent: Schott and Co. (London)

<u>Henle</u>
G. Henle USA Inc.
P.O. Box 1753
2446 Centerline Industrial Drive
St. Louis, Missouri 63043 USA

<u>Heugel</u>
Editions Heugel-Leduc
175, rue Saint Honoré
75040 Paris Cedex 01 tel. 42.96-89.11
France

<u>Jobert</u>
Société des Editions Jobert
Mme Denise Jobert-Georges, Directrice
76, rue Quincampoix
75003 Paris, France tel. 42.72-83.43
US agent: Theodore Presser
British Agent: United Music Publishers

<u>Leduc</u> (see Heugel)

<u>Peters</u>
Peters Corporation
373 Park Avenue South
New York, New York 10016 USA

<u>Revue musicale</u>
La Revue musicale
Editions Richard-Masse
7, place Saint-Sulpice
75006 Paris, France tel. 43.26-28.36

<u>Salabert</u>
Editions Salabert
22 rue Chauchat
75009 Paris, France tel. 48.24-55.60
US agent: G. Schirmer
British agent: United Music Publishers

<u>Schirmer</u>
G. Schirmer, Music Publishers
24 E. 22nd St.
New York, New York 10010 USA

<u>Schott</u>
Schott and Company
48, Great Marlborough Street
London W1V 2BN, United Kingdom

<u>Presser</u>
Theodore Presser, Publishers of Music
Mr. Arnold Broido, President
Presser Place
Bryn Mawr, Pennsylvania 19010 USA
tel. 215/525-3636

<u>United</u>
United Music Publishers
42 Rivington Street
London EC2A 3BN, United Kingdom

XII

INDEX OF DEBUSSY'S WORKS

Underlined page numbers indicate the main entry in the Catalogue of Works.

See titles of sets as well as titles of particular pieces in sets. Further see the Index of Letters and Writings.

Acquarelles, 48
  Also see Ariettes oubliées
Aimable printemps, L'. See Printemps (L'aimable)
Aimons-nous et dormons, 5, 47, 271
Amphion, 9
Andante Cantabile, 6, 78, 400
Andante cantabile (4 hands L. 36 bis), 77
Andante cantabile (4 hands), 77
Angélus, 8, 47
Apparition, 6, 47, 48, 239, 401, 402 421
Après-midi. See Prélude à l'après-midi d'un faune
Arabesques, Deux, 7, 8, 65, 250, 278, 290, 326, 387, 390, 397
Archet, L', 6, 20, 48, 271
Ariettes oubliées, 6, 7, 11, 47, 48, 210, 232, 291, 326, 336, 368, 398, 411, 453
As You Like It, 11, 15, 97, 448
Auprès de cette grotte sombre, 59. Also see Trois chansons de France and Promenoir des deux amants
Axel, 7, 20
Baisers, Les, 6, 49
Balcon, Le, 51, 234
  See Cinq poèmes de Ch. Baudelaire
Ballade slave (piano), 65
Ballade à la lune, 5, 49
Ballade de Villon à s'amye, 63, 206. Also see Trois ballades de Fr. Villon
Ballade des femmes de Paris, 63. Also see Trois ballades de Fr. Villon
Ballade que Villon feit, 63. Also see Trois ballades de Fr. Villon
Ballade slave, 65
Ballet, 79. Also see Petite suite
Barcarolle, 6, 50
Beau soir, 5, 6, 8, 47, 50
Belle au bois dormant, La, 8, 47, 50, 406
Berceuse héroïque, 14, 37, 66, 350
Berceuse pour "La tragédie de la mort", 10, 28
Boîte à joujoux, 14, 26, 260, 287, 304, 437
Brouillards, 75, 194, 220. Also see Préludes pour piano Livre II
Bruyères, 75. Also see Préludes pour piano Livre II

Cahier d'esquisses, D'un. See D'un cahier d'esquisses
Calmos dans le demi-jour (En sourdine, which also see), 47, 53
Canope, 75. Also see Préludes pour piano Livre II
Caprice, 5, 50, 187, 271, 447
Caprices en blanc et noir See En blanc et noir
Cathédrale engloutie, 74, 366, 369. Also see Préludes pour piano Livre I
Ce qu'a vu le vent d'ouest, 74. Also see Préludes pour piano Livre I
Chanson espagnole, 6, 22, 50, 60
Chanson triste, 6, 50
Chansons de Bilitis, 9, 10, 11, 14, 47, 51, 78, 93, 245, 271, 326, 360, 381, 383, 398, 418, 419, 437, 453, 456
Chansons de Bilitis (incidental music), 10, 28, 363
Chansons de Charles d'Orléans. See Trois chansons de Ch. d'Orléans
Chevalier d'or, 9
Chevaux de bois (Ariettes), 6, 48. Also see Ariettes oubliées
Chevelure, La, 51, 271. Also see Chansons de Bilitis
Children's Corner, 12, 13, 66, 90, 94, 278, 304, 350, 354, 403, 409, 426
Choeur des brises, 40
Chute de la maison Usher, La, 12, 13, 14, 15, 20, 84, 87, 205, 219, 220, 231, 326, 339, 345, 355, 395, 402, 404, 426, 429, 438
Cinq poèmes de Charles Baudelaire, 7, 8, 47, 51, 241, 282, 292, 326, 376, 398, 433, 453
Clair de lune, 5, 47, 60, 76, 238, 250, 434, 436
Clair de lune (1st version), 52. Also see the preceding.
Clair de lune (2nd version), 52, 54
Cloches, 47. Also see Deux romances
Cloches à travers les feuilles, 71. Also see Images set II
Cloches ("Les feuilles s'ouvraient"), 53. Also see Deux romances
Collines d'Anacapri, 74. Also see Préludes pour piano Livre I
Colloque sentimental, 55, 228. Also see Fêtes galantes série II
Coquetterie posthume, 6, 52, 60, 271
Crime d'amour. See the following:
Crimen amoris, 14, 222, 338, 429
Crois mon conseil, chère Climène, 59. Also see Promenoir des deux amants
C'est l'extase langoureuse, 48, 282, 291. Also see Ariettes oubliées

Damoiselle élue, La, 7, 8, 9, 10, 40, 220, 260, 266, 271, 282, 292, 326, 332, 337, 344, 347, 360, 367, 376, 396, 423, 428, 452
Daniel, 5, 41, 451
Dans le jardin, 8, 47, 52
Danse, 76
Danse bohémienne, 5, 67, 295, 407, 425
Danse pour piano, 67. Also see Tarentelle styrienne

Danse de Puck, 74. See Préludes pour piano Livre I
Danse sacrée et danse profane (pour harpe et cordes), 11, 30, 360
Danseuses de Delphes, 73. Also see Préludes pour piano Livre I
Daphnis et Khloé, 9
De fleurs, 8, 59. Also see Proses lyriques
De grève, 59. Also see Proses lyriques
De l'aube à midi sur la mer, 30, 33. Also see Mer, La
De rêve, 59. Also see Proses lyriques
De soir, 9, 59. Also see Proses lyriques
Des pas sur la neige, 74, 256. Also see Préludes pour piano Livre I
Deux danses pour harpe. See Danse sacrée
Deux romances, 8, 47, 53
Diable dans le beffroi, Le, 11, 12, 13, 14, 15, 21, 72, 84, 87, 205, 326, 339, 355, 426, 429
Dialogue du vent et de la mer, 31, 33. Also see Mer, La
Diane au bois, 6, 7, 21, 264, 337, 401, 402, 415, 426, 437, 449
Diane-ouverture, 5, 21, 22, 402
Dieu! qu'il la fait, 43, 350, 404. Also see Trois chansons de Charles d'Orléans
Divertissement, 6, 77
Doctor Gradus ad Parnassum, 66. Also see Children's Corner
Duos and Duets for Piano, 77
D'un cahier d'esquisses, 13, 67, 406

Echelonnement des haies, L', 47, 64. Also see Trois mélodies
Eglogue, 6, 53, 187
Elégie, 15, 67, 250
En bateau, 79. Also see Petite suite
En blanc et noir, 15, 78, 276, 322, 350, 355, 363
En sourdine, 6, 54, 60, 229, 250
En sourdine (early version, 47, 53
Enfant prodigue, L', 6, 11, 41, 47, 234, 260, 284, 303, 401
Epigraphes antiques, Six, 14, 28, 67, 78, 250, 276, 304, 319, 362, 363, 376, 411, 418, 419
Esquisse, 68
Estampes, 11, 68, 70, 210, 256, 295, 379, 381, 388, 389, 395, 397, 406, 407, 425, 426
Esther et la maison de fous, 29
Et la lune descend sur le temple qui fut, 71. Also see Images (deuxième série)
Etude "retrouvée." Pour les arpèges composés, 68, 250, 422, 442
Etudes (piano), 15, 68, 206, 223, 233, 243, 245, 249, 265, 276, 295, 303, 326, 328, 362, 378, 383, 385, 395, 403, 406, [cont.] 408, 421, 422, 424, 430, 431, 432, 439, 440, 442, 450
Eventail, 64. Also see Trois poèmes de S. Mallarmé
Exercises for the Paris Conservatory, 80

Fanfare d'ouverture, 30
Fantaisie pour piano et orchestre, 7, 8, 31, 434
Fantoches, 5, 49, 54, 60, 250. Also see Fêtes galantes, first set
Fantoches (early version), 54

Faune, Le, 55, 329. Also see Fêtes galantes, second set
Fées sont d'exquises danseuses, Les, 75, 235. Also see Préludes pour piano Livre II
Fête galante [single song], 5, 54, 402
Fêtes, 31, 34. Also see Nocturnes
Fêtes galantes, sets I and II, 222, 259, 336, 398, 453. Also see the following.
Fêtes galantes
first set, 8, 47, 54, 425, 446, 447
second set, 11, 47, 55, 354, 455, 456
Fêtes galantes (originally titled Crimen amoris), 26, 429
Feuilles mortes, 75. Also see Préludes pour piano Livre II
Feux d'artifice, 75, 350. Also see Préludes pour piano Livre II
Fille aux cheveux de lin, La (piano prelude), 74
Fille aux cheveux de lin, La, (song), 5, 55, 402
Fleur des blés, 5, 47, 55
Fleur des eaux, 6, 20, 55
Flots
palmes, sables, 5, 56
Flûte de Pan, 29, 51. Also see Chansons de Bilitis
Frères en art, 8, 11, 29, 237, 430.

General Lavine--eccentric, 75. Also see Préludes pour piano Livre II
Gigues, 14, 31. Also see Images pour orchestre
Gladiateur, Le, 6, 42, 452
Golliwogg's Cake-walk, 66. Also see Children's Corner
Green, 48, 250. Also see Ariettes oubliées
Gymnopédies, 9, 40, 288, 444

Harmonie du soir, 7, 51. Also see Cinq poèmes de Ch. Baudelaire
Herbe tendre, 10
Hélène, 42
Histoire de Tristan, 12, 84, 199, 356
Hommage à Haydn, 13, 69
Hommage à Rameau, 70, 305. Also see Images, première série
Hommage à S. Pickwick, 75, 350. Also see Préludes pour piano Livre II
Hymnis, 6, 22, 402, 449

Ibéria, 12, 13, 19, 31, 194, 210, 228, 339, 353, 354, 355. Also see Images pour orchestre
Il dort encore, 22. Also see Hymnis
Il pleure dans mon coeur, 48, 91. Also see Ariettes oubliées
Images, 13, 28, 87, 199, 426
Images
piano, set I, 11, 12, 70, 304, 368, 369, 379, 380, 381, 382, 403
piano, set II, 12, 71, 288, 362, 374, 434
both sets, 395, 406
Images for orchestra, 14, 19, 31, 273, 326, 363, 369, 385, 399
Images oubliées (piano), 9, 70, 232, 250, 296, 424, 425
Intermezzo pour violoncelle solo et orchestre, 6, 32, 44
Intermezzo (composition for four hands), 78
Invocation, 6, 42
Isle joyeuse, L', 11, 12, 71, 354, 368, 369, 383, 406, 422, 430

Jane, 5, 56, 447

Jardins sous la pluie, 68, 250, 332. Also see Estampes
Jet d'eau, Le, 7, 38, 51, 271. Also see Cinq poèmes de Ch. Baudelaire
Jeux, 14, 26, 87, 193, 197, 206, 221, 224, 231, 232, 243, 248, 259, 292, 293, 303, 313, 317, 323, 326, 329, 332, 363, 365, 368, 369, 370, 374, 379, 383, 385, 391, 399, 410, 415, 417, 418, 420, 429, 437, 438, 439, 441, 456
Jeux de vagues, 33, 221, 368. Also see Mer, La
Jimbo's Lullaby, 66. Also see Children's Corner

Khamma, 13, 27, 220, 232, 248, 297, 329, 405, 420, 437, 438
King Lear. See Roi Lear.

Légende de Tristan, 12
Lent, 70
Lilas, Le, 5, 6, 56, 58
Lindaraja, 10, 79, 355
Little Nigar
The, 71
Little Shepherd, 66. Also see Children's Corner

Madrid
princesse des Espagnes, 5, 57
Mais il ton chant son luth, 22
Mandoline, 5, 47, 57, 60, 394, 398, 426
Marche des anciens comtes de Ross. See the following:
Marche écossaise, 8, 38, 79
Martyre de Saint Sébastien, Le, 13, 14, 29, 86, 87, 194, 205, 220, 222, 237, 239, 240, 241, 244, 292, 316, 326, 327, 328, 333, 336, 337, 338, 350, 354, 363, 376, 391, 411, 415, 419, 420, 425, 437, 438, 444, 451, 455
Masques, 11, 12, 72, 270, 406, 422
Masques et bergamasques, 13, 27, 441
Matin d'un jour de fête, Le, 31. Also see Ibéria and Images pour orchestre
Mazurka, 8, 72
Menuet, 76, 79. Also see Petite suite
Mer, La, 11, 33, 84, 193, 197, 199, 205, 210, 216, 222, 227, 228, 257, 267, 273, 281, 283, 287, 296, 317, 323, 324, 326, 327, 339, 342, 350, 355, 357, 359, 360, 364, 368, 369, 374, 376, 379, 381, 383, 388, 391, 397, 405, 410, 413, 434, 445, 446, 449
Mer belle aux îles sanguinaires, 33, 342
Mer est plus belle, La, 47, 64. Also see Trois mélodies
Minstrels, 38, 74, 91. Also see Préludes pour piano Livre I
Morceau de concours (clar.), 21, 44, 72, 250
Morceau de concours (piano), 72. Also see Pièce pour piano
Mort des amants, La, 52. Also see Cinq poèmes de Ch. Baudelaire
Musique, 6, 57, 60

Noces de Sathan, Les, 261
Nocturne (piano), 8, 72
Nocturne et scherzo [cello], 6, 44, 432
Nocturnes (orch.), 9, 10, 11, 12, 34, 37, 98, 197, 204, 206, 210, 227, 228, 231, 260, 283, 285, 301, 302, 320, 324, 328, 350, 353, 354, 357, 360, 365, 372, 381, 385, 386, 387, 427, 433, 446
Noël des enfants, 15, 47, 57, 398, 427

No-ja-li (Le palais du silence), 14, 19, 20, 28, 434, 439
Nuages, 34, 200, 206, 269, 335, 350. Also see Nocturnes (orch.)
Nuit d'étoiles, 5, 47, 58
Nuits blanches, 10, 58, 187

O floraison divine des lilas. See Lilas, Le.
Ode à la France, 15, 42, 396, 427
Ode Bachique, 22
Oeuvres complètes de Debussy, 221, 222, 226, 245
Ombre des arbres, 48, 317. Also see Ariettes oubliées
Ondine, 75, 221. Also see Préludes pour piano, Livre II
Orchestral Works, 227, 254, 257, 315, 401, 407, 445
Orphée, 22, 96, 332, 356, 435

Page d'album, 73
Pagodes, 68, 287. Also see Estampes
Palais du silence. See No-ja-li
Pantomime, 5, 47, 58, 238
Par les rues et par les chemins, 31. Also see Images (orch.) and Ibéria
Parfums de la nuit, 31. Also see Images (orch.) and Ibéria
Paysage sentimental, 6, 8, 47, 58, 60, 291, 406
Paysages belges, 48. Also see Ariettes oubliées
Pelléas et Mélisande, 8, 9, 10, 11, 12, 13, 14, 22, 23, 87, 93, 97, 193, 194, 196, 197, 199, 201, 204, 205, 207, 210, 218, 219, 220, 221, 222, 223, 227, 229, 232, 233, 235, 238, 239, 241, 243, 244, 246, 248, 251, 254, 257, 260, 261, 263, 265, 266,
[Pelléas cont.]268, 270, 271, 273, 274, 275, 277, 278, 280, 282, 283, 284, 287, 289, 290, 291, 292, 294, 296, 297, 300, 301, 302, 303, 306, 307, 309, 312, 313, 314, 315, 316, 317, 320, 325, 326, 327, 328, 332, 333, 334, 337, 338, 341, 351, 353, 354, 359, 360, 361, 364, 367, 368, 369, 370, 372, 373, 376, 378, 380, 382, 385, 388, 390, 392, 394, 395, 398, 400, 401, 402, 403, 404, 409, 411, 412, 413, 414, 419, 420, 422, 423, 424, 425, 427, 428, 430, 431, 436, 437, 438, 440, 441, 442, 443, 445, 446, 448, 449, 451, 452, 453, 454, 456
Petite pièce (clar.), 44, 436, 448. Also see Morceau à déchiffrer
Petite suite, 7, 79, 304, 325, 326, 402, 455
Piano works in general, 216, 220, 224, 227, 237, 244, 249, 257, 272, 278, 292, 295, 303, 362, 371, 384, 388, 395, 397, 400, 403, 406, 407, 408, 412, 423, 425, 430, 434, 436, 442, 448, 450, 453
Pièce pour piano, 65, 72
Pièce pour piano (Pour le vêtement du blessé), 15. Also see the preceding.
Pièce pour Psyché. See Syrinx
Pierrot, 5, 47, 59, 238
Placet futile, 64. Also see Trois poèmes de S. Mallarmé
Plus que lente, La, 13, 38, 73, 250, 282, 395
Poe projects, 205. Also see Chute de la maison Usher and Diable dans le beffroi
Poissons d'or. See Images pour piano, set II

Pour ce que plaisance, 64. Also see Trois chansons de France
Pour invoquer Pan, 78. Also see Epigraphes antiques.
Pour la danseuse aux crotales, 78. Also see Epigraphes antiques
Pour le piano, 10, 11, 70, <u>73</u>, 204, 210, 304, 378, 379, 384, 407, 422, 424, 425
Pour l'égyptienne, 78. Also see Epigraphes antiques
Pour les accords, 68. Also see Etudes
Pour les agréments, 68. Also see Etudes
Pour les arpèges composés, 68, 219. Also see Etudes
Pour les cinq doigts, 68. Also see Etudes
Pour les degrés chromatiques, 68. Also see Etudes
Pour les huit doigts, 68. Also see Etudes
Pour les notes répétées, 68. Also see Etudes
Pour les octaves, 68. Also see Etudes
Pour les quartes, 68. Also see Etudes
Pour les sixtes, 68. Also see Etudes
Pour les sonorités opposées, 68. Also see Etudes
Pour les tierces, 68. Also see Etudes
Pour que la nuit soit propice, 78. Also see Epigraphes antiques
Pour remercier la pluie au matin, 78. Also see Epigraphes antiques
Pour un tombeau sans nom, 78. Also see Epigraphes antiques
Prélude à l'après-midi d'un faune, 8, 9, 12, 10, 13, <u>34</u>, 79, 84, 193, 197, 210, 229, 231, 239, 248, 256, 257, 267, 270, 274, [Prélude-faune]281, 287, 296, 302, 315, 323, 329, 331, 336, 337, 338, 339, 353, 355, 358, 359, 360, 364, 367, 373, 381, 384, 393, 397, 399, 405, 407, 410, 415, 418, 419, 427, 431, 437, 446, 447, 448, 453, 455
Prélude à l'après-midi d'un faune (2-piano arr.), 79
Prélude (from Pour le piano, which also see), 73
Prélude (from Suite bergamasque, which also see), 76
Préludes pour piano (both books; various), 19, 217, 227, 249, 278, 287, 288, 303, 315, 328, 339, 350, 353, 354, 359, 362, 365, 367, 370, 371, 372, 373, 375, 378, 379, 380, 383, 384, 387, 389, 390, 393, 395, 399, 400, 402, 403, 404, 405, 406, 407, 408, 412, 415, 416, 417, 422, 426, 427, 430, 431, 435, 443, 447, 449, 453
Préludes pour piano
Livre I, 12, 13, <u>73</u>
Préludes pour piano
Livre II, 14, <u>75</u>, 429
Première rapsodie (clar.), 13, 35, 36, <u>38</u>, 44, 45, 436, 448
Première suite d'orchestre, 6, <u>35</u>
Prince porté soit des serfs Eolus, 78. Also see En blanc et noir
Printemps (1887/orch.), 7, 14, <u>36</u>, 199, 325, 358, 367, 401, 410, 439, 452
Printemps (L'aimable printemps), 6, <u>42</u>
Printemps (Salut Printemps), 5, 6, <u>43</u>
Promenoir des deux amants, Le, 13, 47, <u>59</u>, 64, 270
Proses lyriques, 8, 9, 47, 58, <u>59</u>, 300, 336, 360, 398, 421, 426, 453

Puerta del Vino, 75, 194, 355. Also see Préludes pour piano, Livre II

Quant j'ai ouy le tabourin, 43. Also see Trois chansons de Charles d'Orléans
Quartet. See Quatuor
Quatre chansons de jeunesse, 48
Quatuor à cordes, 8, 9, 10, 11, 45, 98, 228, 270, 283, 301, 305, 312, 326, 328, 334, 345, 347, 350, 353, 374, 379, 409, 448, 454
Quelques aspects de 'Nous n'irons plus au bois, 70. Also see Images oubliées pour piano

Rapsodie
Première [clar.]. See Première rapsodie
Rapsodie pour saxophone, 11, 12, 36, 45, 50
Recueil Vasnier, 60, 445
Recueillement, 7, 51. Also see Cinq poèmes de Ch. Baudelaire
Reflets dans l'eau, 70, 383. Also see Images set I
Regret, 6, 60, 61
Rêverie (song), 61
Rêverie (piano), 8, 75
Rodrigue et Chimène, 7, 8, 25, 204, 223, 229, 237, 264, 268, 283, [cont.] 312, 332, 354, 356, 395, 426, 437, 452
Roi Lear, Le, 11, 30, 99
Romance d'Ariel, 6, 60, 61
Romance "L'âme évaporée", 47, 53. Also see Deux romances
Romance "Musique pour éventail." See Romance "Voici"
Romance "Silence ineffable", 6, 60, 61
Romance "Voici que le printemps", 6, 47, 60, 61, 406
Rondeau "Fut-il jamais", 5, 47, 62
Rondel, 64. Also see Trois chansons de France
Rondel chinois, 5, 62, 402
Rondes de printemps, 13. Also see Images (orch.)
Roses, Les, 5, 6, 62, 402

Salut printemps. See Printemps (Salut)
Sarabande, 70, 73, 422. Also see Pour le piano
Saulaie, La, 9, 43, 92, 199, 264, 430
Scènes au crépuscule, 20. Also see Nocturnes
Séguidille, 5, 62
Sept poèmes de Banville, 62, 445
Sérénade, 6, 56, 62
Serenade for the Doll, 66. Also see Children's Corner
Sérénade interrompue, La, 74, 231. Also see Préludes pour piano Livre I
Siddharta, 12
Sirènes, 34, 287. Also see Nocturnes
Six épigraphes antiques. See Epigraphes antiques
Snow is Dancing, 66. Also see Children's Corner
Soirée dans Grenade, 68, 256, 354, 355. Also see Estampes
Son du cor, 47, 64. Also see Trois mélodies
Sonatas in general, 19, 197, 232, 234, 245, 265, 276, 287, 293, 304, 326, 374, 375, 432, 442, 448, 454
Sonate [1ère] pour violoncelle et piano, 15, 46, 379, 416, 433
Sonate [2ème] en trio pour flûte, alto, et harpe, 15, 45, 221, 305, 386, 417
Sonate [3ème] pour violon et piano, 15, 19, 45, 187, 354, 389, 444, 449

Songs in general, 46, 216, 224, 227, 237, 290, 291, 305, 392, 398, 402, 413, 419, 423, 426, 432, 433, 443, 445, 447, 449, 452, 453
Souhait, 5, 56, 63
Soupir, 64, 421. Also see Trois poèmes de S. Mallarmé
Suite bergamasque, 8, 11, 76, 304, 362, 368, 397, 403
Symphonie en si mineur, 5, 37, 400, 433
Syrinx, 14, 29, 30, 206, 277, 365, 374, 387, 401, 431, 435, 448

Tarentelle styrienne, 8, 67, 76
Temps a laissié, Le, 64. Also see Trois chansons de France
Terrasse des audiences, La, 75. Also see Préludes pour piano Livre 2
Theater compositions in general, 227, 228, 356
Tierces alternées, 75. Also see Préludes pour piano Livre II
Toccata, 73. Also see Pour le piano
Tombeau des naïades, 51. Also see Chansons de Bilitis
Tragédie, 5, 63
Trio en sol, 5, 46, 222, 399, 408
Triolet à Philis. See Zéphyr
Triomphe de Bacchus, Le, 6, 37, 77, 78, 400
Trois ballades de François Villon, 13, 47, 63, 376, 393, 398, 455
Trois chansons de Charles d'Orléans, 10, 12, 43, 78, 354, 396, 398
Trois chansons de France, 11, 47, 59, 64, 393
Trois mélodies [Verlaine], 8, 47, 64, 222
Trois mélodies de Claude Debussy, 406
Trois poèmes de Stéphane Mallarmé, 14, 47, 64, 245, 337, 384, 396, 398, 421, 453
Trois scènes au crépuscule, 8, 37. Also see Nocturnes

Valse romantique, 8, 77
Vent dans la plaine, Le, 73. Also see Préludes pour piano Livre I
Vocal music, 224, 402, 413, 426, 449, 452. Also see Songs
Voici des fruits, 48. Also see Ariettes oubliées
Voici que le printemps. See Romance "Voici"
Voiles, 73. Also see Préludes pour piano Livre I

Yver vous n'estes qu'un villain, 43, 78. Also see Trois chansons de Charles d'Orléans

Zéphyr, 5, 47, 65, 401
Zuleima, 6, 7, 44

XIII

GENERAL INDEX

Further see the Index of Letters and Writings.

Abbate, Carolyn, 21, 248, 395
Abraham, Gerald, 208
Abravanel, Claude, 187, 218
Académie de France, 222
Académie des Beaux Arts, 7, 41, 44
Adams, John Kenneth, 395
Added-tone, 315
Adorno, Theodor, 298
Aesthetics, 85, 193, 200, 206, 215, 225, 244, 245, 246, 247, 250, 257, 260, 261, 263, 264, 265, 266, 267, 272, 275, 277, 278, 287, 293, 294, 295, 302, 303, 304, 305, 306, 310, 313, 318, 319, 333, 336, 338, 339, 341, 346, 347, 343, 349, 350, 351, 352, 353, 355, 357, 360, 362, 365, 367, 373, 390, 393, 396, 402, 404, 406, 407, 408, 411, 414, 416, 421, 426, 428, 429, 430, 436, 441, 443, 451
African American, 298
Alain, Jehan, 313
Alain-Fournier [pseud. of H.A. Fournier], 341
Albéniz, Isaac, 294, 310, 355
Albert, Prince of Belgium. 66
d'Albert, Eugen, 274
Aleatoric, 245, 270
Alexander, Jean, 330
Alexandre, [?], 76
Alexandrescu, Romeo, 193
Alfred, E. Maurice, 395
Allan, Maud, 13, 27, 329, 405, 420, 438
Allen, Judith S., 221, 250, 375
Allende-Blin, Juan, 21, 231, 349
Alliance Française, 242
Almendra, Julia d, 225, 226, 375
Alvarez, A.M., 132
Ambrière, Francis, 86
America, North and South, culture and music, including Debussy's relation to, 208, 226, 351
American Musicological Society, 248
Amsterdam, 14
Analysis, 194, 197, 203, 217, 256, 263, 277, 286, 288, 289, 292, 295, 309, 313, 321, 322, 357, 360, 363, 364, 365, 366, 368, 369, 370, 371, 372, 373, 374, 375, 377, 378, 380, 383, 385, 387, 388, 389, 390, 391, 394, 396, 397, 398, 400, 402, 403, 404, 405, 407, 410, 411, 413, 415, 416, 417, 418, 419, 421, 422, 424, 425, 430, 431, 432, 433, 435, 437, 439, 440, 443, 444, 446, 447, 448, 449, 450, 451, 456, 470
Anarchism, 441
Andreacchi, Peter, 396
Andréani, Eveline, 392
Andrée, Jeanne, 58
Angeli, Helen Rossetti, 396
Annamite theater, 7

Annunzio, Gabriele d', 29, 86, 201, 229, 240, 242, 244, 300, 326, 328, 333, 336, 338, 342, 451
Anouilh, Jean, 334
Ansermet, Ernest, 13, 225, 226, 228, 270, 272, 327, 349, 358, 363, 376, 411
Antheil, George, 309
Antiquity, Classical, 197
Antoine, André, 253
Antoni, Eric, 244
Aoyagi, Y., 344
Apaches, Les, 307, 315, 346
Apollinaire, Guillaume, 314, 332, 334, 342
Appledorn, Mary Jeanne van. See Van Appledorn
Arosa, Achille, 3
Art nouveau, 215, 260, 266, 271, 290, 302, 345, 346, 347, 350, 361, 420
Articulation, 398
"Arts and Crafts" movement, 347
Asaf'ev, V., 285
Ashbrook, William, 195
Asian music, 7, 197, 219, 228, 245, 255, 258, 266, 267, 270, 287, 292, 320, 345, 347, 361, 376, 382, 388, 391, 356, 419, 420, 434, 439
Astrological signs, 245
Astruc, Gabriel, 13, 29, 86
Atonality, 262, 313, 382, 440
Aubert, Louis, 295
Audiences, Debussy and, 221, 265, 269, 443
Augmented triads, 379, 384
Auric, Georges, 263, 295, 333
Austin, William W., 205, 226, 248, 251, 253, 276, 397
Austria, 226. Also see Vienna
Autograph materials, 248. Further see Catalogue of Works
Avant-garde, 245, 287, 314, 322
Babaïan, Marguerite, 63
Bach, J.S., 15, 39, 276, 284, 315, 387
Bachauer, Gina, 404
Bachelard, Gaston, 330, 373
Bachelet, Alfred, 49
Bagès, 49
Bakst, Léon, 27, 86, 420
Balakian, Anna, 330
Balakirev, Mily, 302
Balardelle, Geneviève, 376
Ballets Russes, 13, 14, 27, 35, 308, 328, 329
Balzac, Honoré de, 387
Balzer, Jurgen, 193
Banowetz, Joseph, 397
Banville, Théodore de, 21, 22, 37, 47, 49, 50, 54, 56, 58, 59, 61, 62, 63, 65, 244, 271, 330, 336, 337, 343, 402, 449, 453
Barbag-Drexler, Irena, 397
Barbier, Jean-Joel, 241
Barbier, Jules, 42
Barbizon School, 346
Bardac, Emma. See Debussy, Emma
Barkin, Elaine, 424
Baron, Carol K., 277
Baron, Emile, 86, 92
Barraqué, Jean, 193, 216, 224, 225, 246, 287, 309, 397
Barraud, Henri, 398, 442
Barrès, Maurice, 260, 272
Barricelli, Jean-Pierre, 277
Bartha, Denès, 226
Bartók, Béla, 206, 224, 231, 233, 238, 245, 262, 286, 287, 294, 321, 324, 351, 367, 368, 374, 378, 379, 380, 389, 391, 415
Barzun, Jacques, 358
Baschet, Marcel, 15, 36
Batchelder Collection, 109
Bathori, Jane, 12, 59, 325, 398
Baudelaire, Charles, 6, 74, 210, 216, 230, 231, 239, 261, 268, 271, 302, 330, 331, 334, 336, 337, 339, 342, 343, 392, 433, 453, 456

Baudoux, Emile, 297
Bauer, 67, 131, 218, 294
Bayle, François, 245
Bazaillas, Albert, 272
Bazille, August, 5
Bâton, Rhené, 36
Beaufils, Marcel, 277
Beckett, 287
Beethoven, Ludwig van, 4, 258, 304, 378, 391
Belgium, 14, 226, 237, 270, 299, 300, 344, 350
Bellaigue, Camille, 272
Belle Epoque, 259, 267, 275, 314
Beltrando, Marie-Claire, 236
Benedetto, Renato di, 399
Benestad, Finn, 272
Benjamin, William E., 424
Benoït, 300
Ben-Haim, Paul, 292
Berg, Alban, 48, 269, 274, 291, 294, 299, 317, 318, 360, 365, 379, 415
Bergson, 259, 266, 340, 367, 441
Berio, Luciano, 256, 269, 287, 321
Berlioz, Hector, 6, 237, 293, 311, 352, 358, 376, 386, 388, 390, 413, 451, 452, 455
Berman, Laurence D., 248, 376, 399
Bernard, Robert, 242
Bernard, Suzanne, 331
Bernhardt, Sarah, 448
Berton, Henry, 331
Bérys, José de, 272
Biancolli, Louis, 326
Bibliography of Debussy, 187, 188, 194, 195, 198, 217, 219, 232, 236, 368, 414, 453
Bibliothèque de l'Opéra Paris, 116
Bibliothèque nationale Département des manuscrits, 108
Bie, Oscar, 257
Billy, André, 254, 331
Biography, 193, 232, 402, 437
Bitonality, 221, 384
Bizet, Georges, 244, 258, 275, 282, 355
Blanc-Audra, Mme, 54, 61
Blanche, J.-E., 68, 267, 332, 344
Blancpain, Marc, 242
Bloch, Ernest, 27, 415
Blues, 298
Blumenthal, Daniel Henry, 37, 400
Bohemian lifestyle, 300, 314
Bois, Jules, 261
Bolcom, 269
Boll, André, 241
Bondeville, E., 241
Bonheur, Raymond, 34, 59, 239, 300
Bonmariage, Sylvain, 332
Bonnard, 347
Bonnaure, Jacques, 244
Bonniot, Mme E., 64
Borgeaud, Henri, 92, 93, 95, 235
Boris, Siegfried, 401
Borodin, Alexander, 7, 313, 426
Bos, Charles du, 216
Bosc, H.-J. von, 270
Boschot, Henriette, 237
Botticelli, 36
Boucher, Maurice, 193, 216, 258
Boucherle, Alain, 228
Bouchor, Maurice, 50
Boucourechliev André, 194, 243
Boulanger, Nadia, 277, 300, 451
Boulez, Pierre, 28, 193, 197, 208, 229, 230, 231, 242, 243, 245, 254, 265, 270, 278, 287, 291, 293, 294, 304, 311, 315, 324, 373, 386, 388, 401, 421
Bourgeois, 259, 263, 269
Bourgeois lifestyle, 259
Bourget, Paul, 8, 50, 53, 57, 58, 61, 254, 336, 337 342
Bourne, W., 255
Boyd, Everett Vernon, Jr., 278

Boyer, Georges, 44
Brahms, Johannes, 256, 304, 369, 422
Brailiou, Constantin, 235, 377
Brando, E., 285
Brayer, Jules de, 267, 303
Bréval Manuscript, 24, 219, 431
Bréville, Pierre, 282
Briscoe, Anna, 54
Briscoe, James R., 22, 83, 221, 249, 377, 401, 406
Britten, Benjamin, 262, 294
Brody, Elaine, 255, 260, 278, 324, 328, 332
Bruneau, Alfred, 307
Brunel, Pierre, 402
Brussel, Robert, 238, 239
Bruyr, José, 228
Bryckaert, Raymond, 228
Buck, Charles Henry III, 403
Buckle, Richard, 329
Budapest, 13, 218
Buddhism, 270, 285
Buenzod, Emmanuel, 228
Bugeanu, Constantin, 403
Burkhart, Charles, 404
Burkholder, J. Peter, 233, 279
Burne-Jones, 247, 337
Busoni, Ferruccio, 130, 274, 383
Bussotti, Sylvano, 321
Butler Univ. Romantic Music Festival, 54
Büsser, Henri, 14, 36, 247, 295, 299, 325
Bykov, Viktor, 224, 279
Byrnside, Ronald, 349, 358

Cadences, 453
Cadieu, Martine, 442
Cage, John, 301, 324, 391
Cahiers Debussy, 188, 189, 217
Cahn, Peter, 364, 404
Caillard, C.F., 272
Caillat, Stéphane, 350, 404
Cain, Julien, 242, 247
Calvocoressi, M.-D., 273, 279
Campbell, Lawrence, 280
Camus, Albert, 334
Canac, Henriette, 364
Cano, Cristina, 332
Caplet, André, 12, 13, 26, 29, 36, 41, 67, 86, 87, 92, 212, 298, 315, 316, 437, 438
Carnegie Hall, 326
Carner, Mosco, 231, 280
Carneyro, C., 294
Carpenter, J.A., 294
Carraud, Gaston, 272
Carré, Albert, 10, 235, 268, 272, 312, 325
Carrière, Eugène, 194
Carter, Elliott, 279, 313, 317, 388
Cary Collection, 110
Cas Debussy, Le, 12, 272
Casadesus, Robert, 397, 404
Casafuerte, Marchese di, 94, 201
Casella, Alfredo, 94, 201, 238, 294, 281, 323
Castaldi, Paolo, 216
Casts of premieres, 186
Catalogue of Debussy's works, 3, 17, 185, 186, 195, 203, 204, 223, 264, 414
Catalogues of Important Sales, 248
Catholic, Roman, 338
Cell, Structural, 451
Céard, H., 445
Cellucci-Marcone, Silvana, 333
Centenary of Debussy's birth, 234, 240, 242, 246, 247, 250, 354
Centre de Documentation Claude Debussy, 191, 215, 222, 223
Cercle musical, 67, 71
Cerutti, Jean, 4
Cézanne, Paul, 229, 255, 278, 346, 373
Chabrier, Emmanuel, 11, 266, 278, 297, 299, 305, 320, 367
Chailley, Jacques, 225, 255, 376, 377, 404

Chamber music, 206, 227, 228, 417, 448, 454
Chamfray, Claude, 228
Chance as musical phenomenon, 304
Chansarel, René, 31, 88, 220
Chantavoine, 272, 273
Chappell, William B., 433
Charlot, A., 78, 439
Charpentier, Gustave, 71
Charru, Philippe, 217, 404
Chat Noir cabaret, 8, 267
Chateaubriand, 331
Chausson, Ernest, 8, 45, 59, 64, 84, 87, 92, 216, 235, 238, 265, 277, 287, 290, 297, 300, 301, 308, 320, 432
Chechlińska, Zofia, 281
Chennevière, Daniel, 194
Chenonceaux, Château de, 5
Cheramy, A., 272
Cherniavsky, Felix, 329
Chesterian, The, 90
Chevalier de la Légion d'Honneur, 11
Chevillard, Camille, 33, 34, 38, 272
Chew, Geoffrey, 377
Childhood. See Debussy, childhood of
Chimènes, Myriam, 215, 217, 220, 221, 223, 405
Chion, Michel, 245
Chirico, T., 405
Chopin, Frédéric, 4, 15, 39, 69, 219, 258, 276, 278, 281, 286, 362, 387, 402, 442
Choral Works by Debussy, 227
Chord, Debussy's approach to in composition, 288, 379, 381, 452, 455
Choreography, 240, 455
Chou Wen-Chung, 391
Chouchou. See Debussy, Claude-Emma
Christianity, 285, 344
Chromaticism, 276, 376, 391, 440, 453
Chronology of Debussy's Life, 3, 198, 209, 228, 246, 247
Chun, Edna Breinig, 406
Cicile, Emile, 41
Cinematography, 353, 438, 441
Clark, Charles W.,39
Classicism, Debussy and, 234, 281, 293, 310, 311, 342, 344, 347, 356, 378, 406, 442, 450
Clavecin, 408
Clément, Catherine, 441
Cluytens, André, 420
Cnattingius, Claes M., 406
Cobb, Margaret G., 83, 88, 185, 189, 191, 195, 217, 218, 219, 223, 249, 406, 432
Cocteau, Jean, 193, 244, 247, 260, 263, 275, 284, 289, 295, 313, 333, 334
Coduti, C. Leonard, 43
Coeuroy, André, 242
Cogan, Robert, 386
Cognitive science, 394
Cohen, Gustave, 240
Cohen Levinas, Danielle, 243
Cole, Bill, 281
Colette, Sidonie Gabrielle, 281, 333, 335
Collaer, Paul, 216
Collection Comoedia Charpentier, 229
Collection Jacques Rouché, 116
Collection Lang, 397
Collection musicale André Meyer, 185
Collection musicale François Lang, 109, 397
Color [Tone color], 319, 380, 386, 387
Color-harmony, 384
Comédie des Champs-Elysées, 14
Commedia dell'arte, 432
Commune, Paris, 282
Compositional procedure, 249, 257, 262, 304, 308, 354, 390, 440, 442, 443, 446
Comte de Ségur, 43
Concerts Colonne, 27, 31, 33, 38, 44, 52

Concerts Colonne-Lamoureux, 38
Concerts Lamoureux, 10, 33, 34
Concerts Pasdeloup, 30, 38
Concerts Séchiari, 39, 41
Concordia amateur choral society, 5, 92, 219
Concours International de Piano de Claude Debussy, 222, 250
Conductors [including Debussy as], 349, 350, 357, 423, 454
Conservatoire de Paris, 4, 5, 6, 41, 42, 43, 44, 196, 212, 297, 325, 354, 395
Consonance, 379
Constantine, Mildred, 347
Contemporary culture, 194, 332, 369
Contemporary music, 224, 242, 302, 311, 354, 389
Coombe, Charles-Henry, 350
Cooper, Martin, 208, 256
Cope, David, 256
Copland, George, 404
Coquard, Arthur, 272
Cor, Raphael, 272
Corbiot, O., 228
Coronio, N., 73
Correa de Azevedo, Luiz Heitor, 226
Correspondence. See Letters
Cortot, Alfred, 31, 228, 229, 237, 243, 272, 397, 404, 406, 426
Costallat, Editions, 226
Costumes in theater works, 240
Counterpoint, 299, 354, 366, 387, 391, 386, 399, 417, 431, 439, 442, 452
Couperin, François, 224, 284
Courrier musical de France, 224
Court, Raymond, 333
Courtney, W.L., 27, 438
Covington, Katherine Russell, 387
Cox, David, 407
Craft, R., 96, 318
Craftsmanship, 412
Critic, Debussy as. See Debussy as critic
Critical views, 237
Critics and Criticism, 85, 199, 201, 205, 237, 273, 283, 285, 330, 3 34, 3 35, 358, 445, 447, 454. See also Press and Reception
Croche, Monsieur. See Monsieur Croche
Croix, Thierry de la, 243
Croiza, Claire, 56, 63
Cros, Charles, 48, 271
Cross, Anthony, 231
Crotty, John E., 358, 419
Crumb, George, 269
Cuneo-Laurent, Linda, 325
Curtiss, Mina, 282
Cusenier, S., 228
Cuttoli, Raphael, 240
Cyclic form, 399, 410
Cytovic, Vladimir, 224
Czechoslovakia, 274, 276, 317

Dahlhaus, Carl, 256
Daitz, Mimi Segal, 282
Dallapiccola, Luigi, 242, 323
Danckert, Werner, 188, 194, 202
Daudet, L., 337
Davies, Laurence, 282
Davis, Miles, 281
Davison, Archibald Thompson, 377
Dawes, Frank, 407
De Groux, 301
De Schloezer, B., 217
De Simone, Robert A., 407
De Tinan, Mme Gaston [Hélène (Dolly)], 89, 212, 222, 297, 409
Debussy, Adèle-Clémentine, 3
Debussy, Alfred, 3
Debussy, Claude-Emma [Chouchou], 11, 15, 66, 86, 87, 89, 96, 107, 212, 235, 304
Debussy, Concours de piano, 222, 250
Debussy, Emma [Mme Claude], 11, 12, 15, 31,

[cont.] 45, 46, 55, 59, 64, 73, 80, 86, 89, 92, 96, 107, 195, 211, 212, 213, 248, 259, 297, 318, 323, 326
Debussy, Emmanuel, 3
Debussy, Eugène-Octave, 4
Debussy, Manuel-Achille [composer's father], 3, 13
Debussy, Rosalie Texier [Lilly], 9, 10, 11, 20, 90, 211, 213, 326
Debussy, Victorine [née Manoury, composer's mother], 3, 14
Debussy as critic, 83, 84, 86, 130, 282, 283, 333, 335, 338, 380
Debussy as pianist, 235
Debussy, Centenary of birth, 234, 240, 242, 246, 247, 250, 354
Debussy, childhood of, 211, 264, 304, 341
Debussy Edition, 227. Also see Oeuvres complètes
Debussy et l'évolution de la musique au XXe siècle, 225
Debussy Festivals. See Festivals, Debussy
Debussyism, 12, 90, 196, 199, 201, 213, 229, 239, 245, 268, 272, 273, 275, 279, 289, 293, 298, 334
Debussy's letters, 86
Debussy's manuscripts, 83. Also see Catalogue of Works
Decadence, 266, 271, 340, 353, 357
Decaux, Abel, 321
Declamation, 231
Dedicatees, 186. Also see Catalogue of Works
Deguingand, Mme Emile, 55
Delacroix, Eugène, 63, 64, 330, 387, 430
Delage, Maurice, 217, 281
Delibes, Léo, 238
Deliège, Célestin, 234
Deliège, Irène, 365
Delius, Frederick, 308
Delone, Peter, 387
Demarquez, Suzanne, 283
Demus, Jörg, 70
Demuth, Norman, 408
Denis, Maurice, 344, 347
Denisov, Edison, 365, 408
Densities, 224
Depecker, Th., 77
Derr, Ellwood, 46, 408
Destiny, 453, 454, 456
Destouches, 268
Development procedures, 352
Devillez, Hubert, 240
Devriès, Anik, 219, 258
De'Paoli, Domenico, 282
Diaghilev, Serge, 14, 26, 35, 201, 328, 329, 332
Diatonicism, 359, 379
Dickinson, A.E.F., 377
Diction, 396
Diepenbrock, A., 294
Dietschy, Marcel, 130, 195, 196, 197, 199, 200, 203, 204, 211, 213, 218, 220, 222, 228, 283, 313, 325, 350, 400, 409
Dilé, Léo, 200
Dille, D., 410
Discography of Debussy, 186, 188, 189, 194, 217, 218, 223, 224, 232, 328, 405
Dissonance, 276, 379, 402
Doherty, Thomas W., 333
Domling, Wolfgang, 410
Donnay, Maurice, 258
Doret, Gustave, 35, 40, 89
Doumel-Diény, A., 378, 421
Doyen, Jean, 56
Dream, Debussy's concept of, 355, 359
Dreyfus Affair, 271
Dubois, 82
Ducarsin, François, 243
Dufay, Guillaume, 354
Dujardin, Edouard, 267, 347
Dukas, Paul, 7, 12, 40, 90, 197, 238, 239, 244, 273, 276, 278, 283, 299, 307, 312, 400
Dumesnil, Maurice, 70, 195
Dumesnil, René, 284
Dunsby, Jonathan, 365
Dunton-Green, L., 238

Duparc, Henri, 299, 328, 402, 432, 455
Dupin, Etienne, 7, 51
Dupont, Gabrielle [Gaby], 8, 9, 10, 25, 201, 213, 353
Dupuis, Sylvain, 301
Durand, Emile, 46, 81
Durand, Jacques [also Editions Durand], 4, 11, 15, 26 [Mme Jacques], 33, 79, 89, 92, 186, 189, 326
Durand and Costallat, Editions [jointly], 226
Duration of works, 186
Durey, Louis, 295
Durney, Daniel, 236, 359, 365
Dutilleux, Henri, 243, 293, 311
Dutronc, Jean-Louis, 442
Dvorák, Antonin, 298
Dynamics, 303, 381, 387, 413, 431, 456
D'Annunzio. See Annunzio, d'.

Earlier composers, 205
Early music of Debussy, 204, 434, 440, 452
East Asian music. See Asian music
Echo de Paris, 10
Echo musical (Paris), 227
Eckart-Backer, Ursula, 284
Economic structures, 263, 271
Ecorcheville, Jules, 272
Edition Peters Leipzig, 233
Editorial questions concerning Debussy, 226, 233, 399, 434
Edler, Arnfried, 259
Edo, K., 344
Education musicale (Paris), 228
Eimert, Herbert, 410, 418, 456
Eisler, 448
Electronic music, 302, 373, 387
Elgar, Edward, 208, 324
Eliot, T.S., 334, 341
Elst, Nancy van der, 410
Emmanuel, Maurice, 7, 229, 238, 239, 241, 311, 321, 352, 373, 411, 413
Engel, Emile, 12, 285
England, culture, music, and Debussy's trips to, 11, 14, 226, 230, 231, 238, 308, 332, 347, 350
Epoque. See Period and Debussy's relation to
Ermitage, L', 338
Escal, Françoise, 334
Escher, Rudolf, 326, 411, 418
Escot, Pozzi, 366, 386
Escudier, Léon, 300
Esthetics. See Aesthetics
Estrade-Guerra, Oswald d', 203, 411
Ethnology, 235
Existentialism, 334
Exoticism, 347
Exposition of themes, 246
Exposition, Debussy, catalogues [various], 191, 247
Exposition, Paris, of 1889, 7, 219, 228, 258, 270, 320, 355, 356, 376
Exposition, Paris, of 1900, 10, 345
Expressionism, 236, 310, 361

Fabiani, François, 245
Facsimiles of Debussy manuscripts, 194, 246, 408, 428, 447, 452. Also see Catalogue of Works
Falla, Manuel de, 12, 197, 212, 238, 255, 283, 284, 294, 310, 321, 324, 355
Fargue, Léon-Paul, 216, 247, 281, 332
Fatalism, 447
Fate, role of in Debussy, 244, 364
Faugueux, M., 272
Fauré, Gabriel, 9, 15, 90, 206, 208, 212, 216, 220, 235, 236, 251, 259, 266, 278, 281, 286, 290, 291, 297, 305, 306, 307, 314, 319, 320, 344, 368, 376,

[cont.] 394, 421, 432, 444, 447, 451
Faure, Michel, 244, 259
Fauves, Les, 346
Faye, Jean Pierre, 231
Féart, Rose, 64
Federhofer, Hellmut, 270, 284
Fédorov, Vladimir, 225, 285
Feldman, Morton, 287
Ferchault, Guy, 195
Ferrari, Luc, 245
Feschotte, Jacques, 228
Festivals and Conferences, including early "Festival Debussy," 12, 14, 75, 248, 250
Feuilles musicales (Lausanne), 228
Feure, Georges de [Georges van Sluijters], 28
Février, Henry, 451
Filenko, Galina, 224
Film. See Cinematography
Fin-de-siècle, 197, 215, 233, 236, 258, 266, 280, 290, 293, 353, 419, 421. Also see Period
Final Works, 432
First performances, 187. Also see Catalogue of Works
Fischer, Kurt von, 219, 232, 260, 350, 411
Fischer, Penelope Ann Peterson, 285
Five, The Russian. See Russia, music and culture
Flat, Paul, 272
Fleury, Louis, 29, 30
Floros, Constantin, 285
Fogel, Susan Lee, 442
Fokine, Michel, 420
Folklore and folk music, 287, 298, 322, 351, 358, 378, 393, 406
Fontaine, 10, 43, 54, 59
Form, 193, 205, 208, 210, 217, 221, 224, 225, 231, 234, 240, 241, 243, 248, 249, 255, 259, 262, 268, 269, 276, 279, 291, 293, 295, 298, 308, 311, 314, [cont.] 315, 317, 321, 322, 342, 343, 347, 352, 354, 356, 358, 363, 364, 365, 379, 381, 382, 383, 387, 388, 389, 390, 391, 396, 397, 399, 402, 403, 405, 406, 408, 410, 412, 414, 415, 416, 417, 418, 421, 431, 433, 436, 439, 440, 441, 442, 443, 448, 454, 456. Also see Structure
Forte, Allen, 233, 366
Fourestier, L., 240
Fournier, Alain, 217
Fourrier, Mme Camille, 52, 55, 64
Fowlie, Wallace, 254, 334
Fragoso, A., 294
France, culture and music, 85, 205, 226, 231, 237, 239, 241, 243, 254, 256, 258, 266, 270, 275, 277, 278, 280, 284, 290, 292, 293, 294, 297, 299, 302, 303, 307, 308, 311, 314, 320, 330, 332, 334, 336, 338, 344, 350, 351, 353, 355, 357, 401, 402, 408, 411, 417, 420, 427, 436
France, Anatole, 337
Franck, César, 5, 87, 88, 216, 239, 265, 266, 270, 282, 287, 293, 297, 299, 301, 308, 320, 362, 367, 410, 447
Frankenburger, 292
Freitas Branco, L. de, 294
Freud, Sigmund, 330
Freundlich, Irwin, 412
Friedmann, Michael L., 221, 250, 412
Frisius, Rudolf, 415
Fromont, Editions, 9, 10, 8[illegible]
Fubini, Enrico, 216
Fuchs, Henriette, 92, 97, 219, 235
Funck-Brentano, 272
Fusion of the arts, 342

Gabriel Marie, 41
Gaillard, M.F., 42, 43

Gala Claude Debussy. See Debussy, Festivals
Gamelan, 7, 228, 258, 382, 388, 391, 434. Also see Asian music
Ganne, Louis, 272
Garden, Mary, 10, 11, 41, 48, 232, 326, 327
Gasco, Alberto, 84
Gatti, Guido, 272
Gaubert, Philippe, 285
Gauguin, Paul, 204, 344, 346, 347
Gauldin, Robert, 424
Gaulois, Le, 338
Gauthiers-Villars, Henry, 273. Also see Willy
Gauthier, André, 190
Gautier, Théophile, 52, 62, 271, 332
Gál, György Sándor, 196
Genealogy, 211
Genest, Emile, 412
Genre, concept of 224
Germain, André, 260
Germany, culture and music, including Debussy's views of, 243, 268, 273, 274, 276, 284, 292, 293, 299, 302, 318, 321, 323, 350. Also see War, World, I
Gershwin, George, 285
Gervais, Françoise, 225, 226, 236, 241, 286, 359, 367, 378, 387
Gestalt, 373, 374
Geysen, Frans, 378
Ghéon, Henri, 338
Gheusi, Pierre, 260, 413
Giacommetti, Albert, 318
Gide, André, 8, 260, 334, 335, 338, 340, 347
Gieseking, Walter, 212, 274, 397, 404
Gil Blas, 11, 335
Gilman, Lawrence, 412
Gil-Marchex, Henri, 216
Gilson, 234, 294
Giordano, 280, 307
Gitter, Felix, 359
Giubertoni, Anna, 215
Glazunov, Alexander, 7, 285
Glinka, Mikhail, 7
Global awareness in Debussy, 253
Gluck, Christoph, 11, 39, 284, 447
Godet, Robert, 7, 54, 64, 90, 92, 212, 213, 219, 225, 226, 235, 237, 238, 239, 241, 242, 267, 286, 313, 341, 351, 413
Goebels, Franzpeter, 286
Goethe, Johann Wolfgang von, 342
Goldbeck, Fred, 378
Golden Section, 367, 368, 450
Goléa, Antoine, 196, 442
Golovinskij, Grigorij, 351
Goncourt, Edmond et Jules de, 239, 335
Goossens, Eugene, 238
Gorog, André, 236
Goubault, Christian, 3, 84, 189, 196, 237, 261, 273, 335
Gounod, Charles, 5, 81, 235, 282, 299
Gourdet, Georges, 197
Gourmont, R. de, 330, 342
Gousset, Bruno, 388, 413
Graener, P., 294
Grainger, Percy, 315
Granados, Enrique, 310, 355
Grand, 297
Grande revue, 273
Graphology. See Handwriting
Gravollet, Paul, 52
Grayson, David A., 23, 222, 250, 411, 413, 436
Green, Taylor, 251
Gregh, Fernand, 272
Gregorian chant, 375
Grieg, Edvard, 244, 305
Griffes, Charles T., 289, 294
Griffiths, Paul, 287
Grout, Donald Jay, 206, 414
Grover, Ralph Scott, 287
Gruber, Gernot, 388
Gruenberg, L., 294
Gubisch, Nina, 236
Guck, Marion A, 415
Gudmundsen, P., 294
Guenther, Ulrich, 415

Guéritte, T.J., 90, 230
Guertin, Marcelle, 249, 394, 415
Gueulette, Alain, 224
Guézer, Jean-Pierre, 224
Gui, Vittorio, 90, 94, 201
Guichard, Léon, 218, 261, 336
Guillot, Pierre, 222, 287
Guinand, Edouard, 41, 50
Guiomar, Michel, 228
Guiraud, A., 197
Guiraud, Ernest, 5, 6, 7, 22, 41, 81, 97, 229, 235, 238, 282, 312, 320, 321, 326, 352, 364, 404
Gulke, Peter, 415
Gullace, Giovanni, 336
Gurkov, Vladimir, 224, 416
Gut, Serge, 236, 288, 379, 416, 417

Haché, Reginald, 417
Hague, The, 14
Hahn, Reynaldo, 215, 232, 272
Haino, Ethan, 417
Halbreich, Harry, 200
Hall, Elisa, 36, 450
Hamilton, D., 218
Hamoen, Dirk Jacob, 418
Handman, Dorel, 359
Handwriting, Debussy's, 211, 237, 246
Hang, Wiltrud, 418
Hardeck, Erwin, 418
Harding, James, 288, 419
Harmony in Debussy's music, 234, 236, 242, 267, 278, 280, 286, 287, 288, 290, 297, 308, 309, 356, 359, 360, 367, 375, 380, 381, 383, 384, 398, 403, 405, 406, 419, 431, 437, 450, 453, 454, 455
Harpole, Patricia W., 388
Harris, Simon, 379
Harry Ransom Humanities Research Center, 83, 117, 219, 241
Hartke, S.P., 379
Hartmann, Arthur, 48, 91
Hartmann, Georges, 9, 10, 14, 23, 34, 74, 83
Hashimoto, M., 344
Hauel, Sylvie, 245
Hausegger, Siegmund von, 272
Hauser, 298
Haydn, Franz Josef, 69, 311, 377, 378
Hayner, Phillip Avery, II, 289
Headland, David, 419
Hegel, Georg, 194
Heifetz, Jascha, 66
Heine, Heinrich, 32, 44, 63
Helffer, Claude, 227
Hellé, André, 14, 26, 437
Henderson, Robert, 231
Henry, Earl, 289
Hepokoski, James A., 249, 367
Hérédia, J.M. de, 337
Hermeneutics, 257
Hertz, David M., 336
Hill, E., 294
Hill, James N.B., 241, 294
Hilse, Walter Bruno, 289
Hindemith, Paul, 270, 274, 289, 311, 323, 380, 435
Hindu religion, 268
Hirashima, M., 218
Hirbour-Paquette, 370
Hiroshige, Ando, 368
Hirsbrunner, Theo, 3, 197, 201, 203, 245, 289, 351, 419
Hirshberg, Jehoash, 292
Hocquet, Vital, 59
Hodeir, André, 261, 281
Hoérée, Arthur, 28, 229, 232, 262, 292, 321, 351, 418
Hoffmann, E.T.A., 387, 403
Hokusai, 247, 368
Holdin, Calvin E, 388
Holland. See Netherlands
Hollander, Hans, 360
Holloway, Robin, 276, 292
Holopova, Valentina., 385
Holstein, Jean-Paul, 236, 293
Homage to Debussy, Compositions of, 238

Honegger, Arthur, 293, 295, 302, 328
Hoogerwerf, Frank W., 293
Hooreman, Paul, 235
Hopkins, George William, 231, 293
Horoscope, 245
Hottinguer, Mme Ph., 65, 76
Howat, Roy, 219, 221, 223, 227, 249, 250, 293, 367
Howe, Mary, 294
Hsu, Samuel, 392
Hugo, Victor, 254
Humanities Research Center. See Harry Ransom
Humor in Debussy's music, 353
Hungary, 226, 296, 298, 306, 322
Huré, 298
Huvelin, Paul, 258
Huysmans, K.J., 266, 267, 330, 331, 337, 338, 342, 357, 361
Hyspa, Vincent, 50

Iconography of Debussy, 190, 191, 194, 195, 198, 202, 223, 247, 248, 283
Imberty, Michel, 369, 422
Impressionism, 7, 197, 199, 201, 205, 206, 207, 208, 209, 210, 224, 228, 229, 230, 236, 245, 257, 263, 264, 265, 266, 268, 269, 274, 276, 278, 281, 288, 289, 298, 301, 303, 310, 316, 320, 321, 323, 346, 347, 349, 354, 357, 358, 359, 360, 361, 363, 374, 379, 381, 382, 397, 407, 408, 410, 414, 418, 419, 426
Improvisation, 229, 245, 356
Incipits for vocal works, 186
Incontrera, Carlo de, 215
Indy, Vincent d', 8, 208, 270, 273, 293, 294, 297, 300, 304, 322, 351, 422
Inédits sur Claude Debussy, 229
Inghelbrecht, Désiré-Emile, 26, 38, 327, 422
Germaine and Désiré-Emile, 352
Institut de France, 15, 41
Instrumentation, 186, 293, 308, 352, 390, 448
Interpretation of Debussy, 217, 244, 272, 423, 426, 434, 451
Interpreters, 189, 354, 357, 397, 407, 423
Intervallic procedures, 365, 424, 433
Interviews with Debussy, 84, 218, 222
Ireland, J., 294
Isang Yun, 270
Israel, nation of, culture and music, 218, 292
Italy, culture and music [including Debussy's views of], 13, 90, 226, 231, 238, 268, 323
Ives, Charles, 130, 233, 262, 279, 317, 322, 370, 387

Jackson, Roland, 389
Jacob, Maxime, 217, 331, 334
Jacobs, Paul, 70, 220, 248, 423
Jacquemont, Maurice, 240
Jakobik, Albert, 197, 380
Jameux, Dominique, 245
Janáček, Leoš, 248, 310, 316
Janequin, Clément, 354
Jankélévitch, Vladimir, 216, 241, 351, 352, 442
Japan, culture and music, 218, 222, 255, 273, 344, 347, 355. Also see Asian music
Jarocinski, Stefan, 3, 198, 207, 218, 219, 220, 225, 226, 236, 242, 262, 263, 295, 360, 389, 423
Jarry, Alfred, 314
Javanese gamelan. See Gamelan
Jazz, 210, 294, 298, 393

Jean-Aubry, Georges, 30, 90, 91, 92, 230, 235, 237, 337, 360
John, Nicholas, 424
Jolivet, André, 294, 311
Joly-Segalen, Annie, 96. Also see Segalen, Victor
Joseph, Charles M., 424
Josquin Desprez, 227, 354
Jourdan, Pierre, 409
Journal, Le, 29
Jugendstil, 360, 361
Julien, Jean-Rémy, 392
Jullian, Philippe, 344
Jusseaume, 246, 400

Kagen, Sergius, 46
Kanno, A., 344
Karatygin, V., 285
Karg-Elert, Sigfrid, 294
Kasaba, Eiko, 220, 222, 273, 425
Kaufman, Harald, 295
Kay Sonograph, 391
Kecskemeti, Istvan, 234
Keil, Werner, 295, 425
Kennedy, Michael, 296
Keresztùry, Dezső, 296
Kerman, Joseph, 296, 425
Klee, Paul, 345, 346
Klemm, E., 132
Klingsor, Tristan, 281
Koch Foundation Collection, 110
Kodály, Zoltán, 224, 287, 294, 296, 298, 321, 323, 324, 378
Koechlin, Charles, 14, 27, 221, 231, 238, 239, 296, 297, 298, 306, 311, 420, 438
Kono, Yuki, 344, 426
Konold, Wulf, 297
Kopcevskij, Nikolaj, 426
Kopff, René, 228
Korody, Istvan Paker, 298
Kounitskaia, Raisa Ivanova, 198, 262
Koussevitsky, Sergey, 14, 78
Kramer, Lawrence, 233, 426
Kremlev, Jules, 225, 226, 360
Kremlev, T.A., 198
Krenek, Ernst, 262
Kunze, Stefan, 427
Kurth, Ulrich, 298
Kushner, David Z., 84

La Jeunesse, Ernest, 337
La Mure, Pierre, 198
Labisse, F., 240
Lacerda, Francisco de, 246, 294, 354
Laforgue, Jules, 336, 337, 338, 421
Laichterova, Marie, 84
Lalo, Edouard, 5, 293
Lalo, Pierre, 12, 273
Laloy, Louis, 12, 14, 26, 42, 71, 91, 92, 199, 212, 234, 235, 237, 263, 273, 276, 298, 325, 353, 380, 427, 429
Lamartine, Alphonse de, 42, 238
Lanceron, Alain, 442
Landormy
Paul, 235, 299
Lang, Collection, 109
Lang, Paul Henry, 207
Lang-Becker, Elke, 221, 273, 427
Langdon Davies, 130
Langham Smith, Richard, 25, 131, 196, 200, 220, 249, 337, 353, 428, 436
Large, John, 392
Lassus, Orlande de, 6, 354, 387
Late music, 201, 439, 440
Laul, Rudolph, 224
Lavauden, Thérèse, 353
Lavelli, Jorge, 442
Lavignac, Albert, 4
Le Jeune, Claude, 354
Learning theory and pedagogy, 257
Lebeau, Narcisse, 8, 59
Lebl, Vladimir, 274
Leblanc, Georgette, 10, 244, 327
Leconte de Lisle, 42, 53, 55, 56
Lee, Noël, 70

Lefebvre, Louis, 338
Legouix Manuscript, 23
Lehmann, Andrew George, 338
Leibowitz, Marian, 428
Leibowitz, René, 299, 428
Leitmotives, 373, 396, 402, 404, 411, 413, 449
Lelouch, Emile, 236
Lendvai, Ernö, 367, 368
Lenoir-Fischer, Jeanne, 242
Lenormand, René, 380
Leoncavallo, Ruggero, 307
Lerolle, Henri [and family], 8, 9, 23, 70, 73, 232, 300
Lesbroussart, Henri, 237
Lestang, Paul de, 63
Lesure, François, 84, 88, 90, 91, 92, 93, 94, 95, 131, 132, 185, 186, 188, 190, 215, 217, 218, 219, 221, 222, 223, 226, 232, 233, 234, 235, 242, 245, 246, 247, 249, 263, 300, 338, 344, 354, 428
Letellier, Charles, 442
Lethève, Jacques, 263, 274
Letters by Debussy and to him, 83, 84, 133, 185, 201, 202, 205, 219, 222, 226, 230, 232, 234, 235, 238, 240, 241, 248, 253, 260, 264, 277, 300, 301, 305, 306, 308, 311, 312, 313, 318, 319, 321, 323, 326, 328, 340, 341, 352, 357, 409, 411, 413, 414, 423, 429, 435
Lewin, David, 233, 380
Lewinski, Wolf-Eberhard von, 301
Lewis, Christopher, 233
Lhermite, Tristan, 59, 64
Liadof [Lyadov], Anatol, 280
Liane de Pougy, 260
Librairie de l'art indépendant, 51, 238
Library of Congress, 109
Lidov, David, 429
Liebich, Franz and Louise, 12, 199
Liess, Andreas, 223, 242, 264, 301, 361
Lifar, Serge, 240, 329
Ligeti, György, 197, 270, 285, 324, 378, 388
Linear structural and tonal sense, 375, 384, 387, 390, 399, 433, 440, 455
Linguistics, 392, 399, 416
Lippman, Edward A., 385
Lisbon. See Portugal
Liszt, Franz, 6, 91, 233, 265, 267, 278, 288, 311, 319, 362, 383
Literary concerns and influences, 185, 210, 239, 244, 254, 255, 264, 266, 279, 290, 291, 330, 337, 339, 340, 355, 358, 359, 360, 363, 370, 375, 388, 416, 425, 428, 432, 433, 435, 437, 449, 453
Lockspeiser, Edward, 20, 22, 86, 87, 92, 93, 196, 197, 200, 203, 204, 208, 218, 225, 226, 231, 232, 235, 255, 260, 261, 264, 302, 313, 339, 345, 355, 429
Loeffler, Charles Martin, 289, 294
Loncke, Joycelynne, 339
London. See England
Long, Marguerite, 79, 250, 272, 430
Lorrain, Jean, 260, 274, 337
Loti, Pierre, 30, 337
Louÿs, Pierre, 8, 9, 10, 11, 28, 43, 51, 68, 80, 84, 92, 93, 201, 235, 239, 271, 332, 339, 340, 353, 392, 419, 453
Lugné-Poe, 342, 347, 445
Lully, Jean-Baptiste, 447
Lundgren, Stephen E., 189
Lyon, Gustave, 30
Lyric opera, 402
Lyricism, 201, 390

Macdonald, Hugh, 424
Mâche, François-Bernard, 245
Macherey, Pierre, 441, 442
Machlis, Joseph, 207
Machuel, D., 228
Macierakowski, Jerzy, 243
Macomie, Robin, 303

MacReady, Alexandra, 242
Maeterlinck, Maurice, 8, 9, 10, 23, 66, 229, 244, 266, 290, 301, 306, 309, 319, 320, 327, 337, 340, 341, 342, 357, 364, 392, 409, 414, 425, 430, 441, 445, 448, 451, 455
Mahler, Gustav, 13, 201, 274, 302, 360, 365, 390, 411, 447
Mahlert, Ulrich, 431
Malipiero, G. Francesco, 269, 321, 323, 238
Mallard, Betty Parker, 431
Mallarmé, Stéphane, 8, 34, 48, 64, 194, 197, 216, 229, 231, 239, 244, 245, 255, 262, 264, 266, 267, 268, 274, 277, 278, 304, 330, 331, 333, 334, 336, 338, 339, 340, 342, 343, 351, 357, 373, 392, 396, 399, 416, 421, 431, 437, 448, 449, 453
Manet, Edouard, 274, 346
Mantelli, Alberto, 226
Mantelli, G.A., 339
Manuscripts, Debussy's, including studies of, 98, 217, 218, 223, 227, 247, 248, 249, 326, 395, 411, 414, 446, 452
Marnold, J., 273
Mari, P., 292
Marmontel, Antoine, 4, 5
Marnat, Marcel, 216
Marnold, Jean, 264, 273
Marot, Blanche, 51
Marschall, Gottfried, 236, 303
Martin, Auguste, 216, 229, 247
Martineau, Henri, 96
Martinotti, Sergio, 345
Martins, Jose Eduardo, 221, 222, 303
Martinu, Bohuslav, 289
Marx, J., 294
Mascagni, Pietro, 280, 307
Mason, Daniel Gregory, 207
Massenet, Jules, 236, 299, 303, 343, 355, 402
Mataigne, Viviane, 217
Matsuhashi, Mari, 355
Mauclair, Camille, 222, 265, 272, 273, 342, 351
Maurer, Philippe, 244
Mauriac, François, 334
Maurin, Mario, 340
Maus, Octave, 234, 270
Mauté "de Fleurville," Mme, 4
Mayeur [saxophonist], 36
McCalla, James, 304
McKay, James R., 219, 431
Meck, von, family, 37, 62, 97, 198, 285, 313
Meecham, Paul, 21
Meeus, Jean, 431
Meeus, Nicolas, 381
Meister, Barbara, 432
Mellers, Wilfred, 432
Melody, aspects of, 243, 286, 288, 293, 299, 303, 352, 356, 358, 359, 367, 376, 378, 383, 385, 387, 392, 394, 401, 410, 411, 417, 446, 447
Melos, 229
Mendès, Catulle, 8, 25, 221 253, 254, 261, 267, 332, 337, 338, 339
Ménestrel, Le, 10
Mercier, Henri, 341
Mercure de France, 11, 264, 273
Mercure Musical, 12, 273, 325, 338
Merimée, Prosper, 331
Merleau-Ponty, M., 373
Messager, André, 23, 25, 41 66, 92, 93, 235, 239, 241 325, 419, 456
Messiaen, Olivier, 193, 231 262, 270, 291, 311, 313, 315, 319, 324, 371, 383, 384, 387, 388, 391, 447
Messing, Scott, 304
Metaphysics, 340
Meter, 382, 404
Metropolitan Opera of New York, 12
Metzger, Heinz-Klaus, 232
Meylan, Pierre, 228, 432

Miaskovsky, 295
Michaud, Guy, 340
Michel, André, 432
Middle Ages, 421
Mies, Paul, 304
Mikorey, Stefan, 390
Milhaud, Darius, 244, 289, 295, 298, 305, 398, 420, 447
Millan, Gordon, 340
Miller, Richard, 185
Millet, Jean-François, 268
Milnar, Antal, 434
Mimart, P., 38, 44
Minardi, Gian Paolo, 215
Minor, Martha D., 355
Mirbeau, O., 253, 342, 445
Mise en scène. See Stage design.
Mitchell, Donald, 265
Modality, 196, 225, 256, 286, 289, 367, 375, 376, 377, 397, 453, 454
Modern music and culture, including Modernism, 255, 257, 261, 262, 265, 269, 287, 375, 381, 412
Modrowska, Maria, 243
Modulation, 378, 383
Moe, Orin, 433
Moevs, Robert, 433
Molinari, Bernardino, 94, 201
Mollat du Jourdin, Guy, 241
Monde de l'art, 329
Monde musical, 273
Monet, Claude, 194, 247, 259, 346, 443
Monistic harmony, 380
Monjovet, Jane, 58
Monnard, Jean-François, 434
Monsieur Croche, 10, 130, 201, 243, 244, 256, 283, 284, 304, 335, 356, 386
Montesquiou, Robert, 260
Monteux, Pierre, 27, 428
Monteverdi, Claudio, 282, 354, 379
Montmartre, 258
Mooser, Robert Aloys, 433
Moréas, Jean, 8, 258, 331
Moreau, Emile, 42, 300, 344, 346, 387, 421
Moreau-Sainti, Mme, 5, 58
Morgan, Robert P., 381
Morgan Library, Pierpont, 83, 110, 187
Morice, Charles, 14, 26, 338, 429
Morin, S., 228
Moroi, M., 344
Morse, Peter, 190
Mortier, Jane, 75
Mosaic structure, 371, 379, 381, 390, 412
Moscow, 5, 14, 220. Also see Russia
Motives, 295, 313, 365, 373, 374, 380, 381, 391, 408, 416, 417, 418, 424, 435, 439, 440, 441, 446, 450
Mottl, F., 272
Moulaert, R., 294
Mourey, Gabriel, 12, 14, 30, 248, 267
Mowinckel, Laila, 305
Mozart, Wolfgang Amadeus, 6, 276, 293, 378
Mueller, Richard, 434
Mueller, Robert Earl, 381
Musée Debussy at St. Germain-en-Laye [prospects for], 222, 242
Music after 1950, 262, 412. Also see Modern music
Music drama, 282
Musical education, 85
Musical greetings by Debussy, 80
Musical life 1880-1900, 232
Musical Times. Portrait of Debussy, 230
Musicien français, Debussy as. See France, culture and music
Musik-Konzepte, 231
Musorgsky, Modest, 7, 12, 202, 206, 227, 232, 255, 264, 265, 279, 283, 285, 286, 300, 303, 304, 307, 312, 313, 354, 361, 379, 394, 426
Musset, Alfred de, 49, 50, 57, 62, 353

Mycielski, Zygmunt, 242
Myers, Rollo, 208, 231, 256, 265, 305, 435
Mystery, sense of in Debussy, 352, 426
Mysticism, 244, 260, 266, 340
Mythological references, 401

Nabis, Les, 346, 347
Nadeau, Roland, 220, 250, 382, 383, 435
National anthems, 350
National schools, 231
Nationalism, 85, 193, 196, 200, 201, 234, 237, 258, 276, 357, 360, 447
Nattiez, Jean-Jacques, 249, 365, 369, 370, 394, 435
Nature, 194, 199, 224, 301, 302, 308, 310, 340, 347, 367, 437, 454
Nectoux, Jean-Michel, 215, 220, 266, 305
Neo-Baroque, 280
Neo-Classicism [including "New Classicism"], 206, 209, 257, 276, 277, 280, 304, 360
Neo-Impressionism, 346
Neo-Romantic, 234
Nestev, Izrail V., 306
Nestrovski, Arthur Rosenblat, 435
Netherlands, The, 14, 226
Neue Zürcher Zeitung, 232
Neuwirth, Gosta, 361
New England Conservatory MS, 24
New music. See Modern music
New York Public Library, 116
Newman, Ernest, 230
Nichols, Roger, 93, 201, 208, 218, 436
Nicolodi, Fiamma, 307
Niemann, Walter, 274, 294
Niemeyer, Laura, 54
Nietzsche, Friedrich, 258, 261, 265
Nihilism, 455
Nijinsky, Romola, 329
Nijinsky, Vaslav, 13, 14, 26, 35, 329, 332
Nilsson, B., 294
Nineteenth-Century Music, 232
Noailles, Anna de, 332
Noble, Jeremy, 231
Noergaard, Per, 321
Non-Western music and influences, 206, 210, 320
Nordheim, A., 294
Norway, 226, 272, 305
Notation, 375
Nott, Michael, 250
Nuance, 351
Nuñes, J., 294
Nüsbaumer brothers, 268
Nygren, Dennis Quentin, 436
Nystroem, Göstra, 294

Occultism, 218, 261, 451
Octatonicism, 277, 322, 379, 384, 393
Offenbach, Jacques, 258
Ohana, Maurice, 243
Okada, Akiko, 436
Oleggini, Léon, 340
Oliveros, Pauline, 324
Ombre chinois, 353
Onnen, Frank, 226, 239
"Open air" music, 231, 290
Open form, 397
Opera, composers and tradition, 352, 364, 415, 416
Operetta, 419
Opéra [theater in Paris], 8, 14, 26, 116, 240, 420, 428, 454
Opéra-Comique, 9, 10, 13, 14, 23, 25, 93, 241, 261, 325, 326, 412, 419, 454
Orchestration, 292, 314, 382, 388, 397, 398, 408, 411, 413, 420, 431, 437, 438, 439, 444, 456
Orenstein, Arbie, 307
Orff, Carl, 320
Organization, 225, 249. Also see Form
Oriental music and culture. See Asian music

Orléans, Charles d', 43, 64, 78
Orledge, Robert, 208, 248, 307, 329, 362, 437
Orlova, Alexandra, 307
Ornamentation, 418
Orozeo, Manuel, 283
Ostinato procedures, 434
Oswald, 294
Oulmont, Charles, 87, 308
O'Brien, Maire and Grace, 204
O'Connor, Garry, 327
O'Loughlin, Niall, 231

Paja, Jadwiga, 371, 390
Pakenham, Michael, 341
Palache, John G., 85
Palestine, Charlemagne, 324
Palestrina, Giovanni, P. da, 6, 354, 387
Palisca, Claude, 206
Palma, A., 294
Palmer, Christopher, 308, 341, 362
Pantonality, 382
Paoli, Rodolfo, 94, 200, 201
Parallel chord progressions and voice leading, 288, 289, 323, 385, 389, 399
Parallel structural devices, 365
Paris Expositions. See Expositions, Paris.
Park, Raymond Roy, 356
Parker, Charlie "Yardbird," 311
Parks, Anne Florence, 308
Parks, Richard S., 249, 251, 439
Parnassians, 392
Partch, Harry, 316
Pasler, Jann, 233, 250, 275, 308, 440
Pasquet, Yves-Marie, 236, 371
Passerieu [friend in youth], 57
Paulet, G., 52
Pawlowski, G. de, 272
Paye, L., 241
Pecerskij, Petr, 224, 441
Pedagogy, 403
Pedaling, 431
Pedrell, C., 294
Péladan, 260, 272
Pelinski, Ramon, 356
Pelouze-Wilson, Mme, 5
Penderecki, Krzysztof, 197, 285, 301
Pentatonicism, 256, 277, 288, 298, 376, 377, 378, 394, 433, 434, 453, 454
Performance Practice, 248, 250, 324, 350, 364, 378, 396, 397, 400, 404, 406, 409, 412, 417, 423, 431, 455
Performers, 215, 324, 381, 398, 403, 404, 408, 409, 423, 436, 448
Period, Debussy's relation to, 237, 238, 239, 256, 258, 259, 260, 263, 264, 266, 269, 283, 294, 299, 301, 306, 313, 314, 318, 332, 334, 335, 338, 340, 342, 349, 402, 413, 430. Also see Fin-de-siècle
Periodicals, 215
Personality of Debussy, 200, 202, 205, 211, 212, 224, 264, 357, 360
Petazzi, Paolo, 216
Peter, René, 8, 10, 11, 28, 29, 94, 202, 229, 237, 430, 442
Peters Edition Leipzig, 233
Peterson, William John, 249, 250, 442
Petit, Françoise, 224
Petitfils, Pierre, 341
Pfitzner, Hans, 274
Phenomenology, 349, 364, 365, 373
Philippot, M., 292
Philips, C. Henry, 341
Philosophy, 264, 322
Photiadès, Constantin, 443
Photos of Debussy. See Iconography
Phrase, 365, 367, 374
Pianists, 409

Piano writing, 324, 426
Picasso, Pablo, 334
Pierné, Gabriel, 27, 32, 239
Pierpont Morgan Library. See Morgan Library, Pierpont
Pijper, Willem, 293, 294
Pincherle, Marc, 227
Pinzanti, Leonardo, 309
Pissaro, Camille, 346
Pistone, Danièle, 236, 266, 309, 417
Pitch classes, 418, 444
Pitch materials, 251, 382
Pizzetti, Ildebrando, 281, 323
Planté, Francis, 430
Pleasants, Henry, 266
Plein air. See "Open air music"
Pociej, Bohdan, 243
Poe, Edgar Allan, 7, 11, 13, 20, 21, 84, 201, 218, 230, 231, 264, 300, 330, 334, 339, 342, 343, 344, 347, 354, 361, 387, 396, 402, 415, 426, 428, 429, 435, 437
Poetic concerns and influences, 93, 224, 275, 291, 303, 334, 336, 363, 368, 392, 396, 423, 426, 433, 447, 449, 451, 453, 455, 456
Poirier, Alain, 216, 309
Poland, 226, 297
Polansky, Larry, 374
Polignac, Princesse de, 215, 260
Political issues, 441
Polyphony. See Counterpoint
Polytonality, 194
Poniatowski, André, 8, 95
Poot, M., 294
Popelin, Gustave and Claudius, 117
Popular culture, 266, 267
Porebrowiczowa, Anna, 243
Porten, Maria, 371
Porter, L.M., 394
Portugal, 226, 246
Postic, Marcel, 341
Post-Impressionism, 346
Post-tonal composition, 366
Pouget, François, 442
Poujaud, Paul, 300
Poulenc, Francis, 243, 247, 280, 295, 300, 301, 415, 447
Poulet, Gaston, 46
Pound, Ezra, 309, 310
Pour la musique française, 258
Powell, Linton E., Jr., 310
Powers, Harold S., 371
Prague. See Czeckoslavakia
Praz, Mario, 341, 345
Pre-Raphaelites, 249, 337, 345, 421, 428
Press, 223, 227, 229, 230, 234, 240, 242, 272, 273, 275, 300, 307, 329. See also Critics and Criticisms
Primoli, Giuseppe, 6
Prince Albert 1er de Belgique. See Albert, Prince
Prix de Rome, 6, 41, 81, 221, 234, 238, 247, 263, 284, 298, 309, 325, 338, 410. Also see Rome and Conservatoire
Prix Debussy, 218
Program (in sense of programmaticism), 278, 358, 360, 363, 369, 394, 399, 401, 410, 412, 422, 442, 443, 449
Prokofiev, Sergey, 220, 285, 295, 306, 378, 435
Proletariat, 259
Pronunciation, 445
Prosodes, 393
Prosody, 244, 291, 313, 392, 394, 402, 412, 421, 427, 436, 446, 447, 455
Proust, Marcel, 201, 215, 232, 245, 260, 334, 357, 392, 430, 442
Prunières, Henry, 211, 239, 242
Psychology [of and in Debussy], 200, 201, 225,

[cont.] 264, 304, 319, 330, 340, 353, 359, 399, 410, 416, 421, 422, 433
Public and its sensibilities, 199
Puccini, Giacomo, 231, 280, 307, 309, 412, 415
Pure music, 270, 306, 320, 358, 442, 450
Puvis de Chavannes, Pierre, 247, 344, 346, 421

Quatuor Ysaÿe, 8
Queen's Hall Orchestra, 95
Queneau, 262
Quinault, R., 26
Quinn, Patrick, 342
Quotations, 393

Raad, Virginia, 226, 393, 443
Racek, Jan, 310
Rackham, Arthur, 235
Raff, Joachim, 39
Raffman, Relly, 393
Rafols, Alberto, 443
Ragtime, 298, 386
Rahn, Jay, 443
Rameau, Jean-Philippe, 11, 12, 39, 205, 239, 265, 284, 358, 447
Ramuz, C.F., 239
Rassenfosse, A., 301
Rattalino, Piero, 215, 244
Raunay, Jeanne, 10, 52
Rauss, Denis-François, 216, 220, 444
Rautavaara, Einojuhani, 321
Ravel, Maurice, 9, 10, 13, 34, 67, 73, 76, 95, 197, 206, 216, 220, 236, 238, 245, 262, 265, 273, 279, 280, 281, 285, 293, 296, 298, 300, 301, 304, 306, 307, 308, 310, 311, 315, 321, 324, 325, 326, 328, 341, 354, 355, 362, 363, 368, 379, 384, 398, 407, 408, 421, 425, 447, 454
Rayon, Jean-Paul, 236
Read, General Meredith, 38, 79
Realism, 225, 257, 317, 361, 419
Rearick, Charles, 267
Rebikoff, Vladimir, 321
Reception, Critical and popular, 90, 188, 193, 196, 200, 202, 205, 233, 234, 237, 240, 261, 275, 276, 285, 299, 302, 307, 308, 312, 323, 325, 336, 356, 361, 365, 397, 413, 422, 428, 441, 443, 445, 446, 451, 456. See also Critics and Criticism.
Recitative, 236, 393, 394, 449
Recordings. See Discography.
Redon, Odilon, 194, 247, 300, 344, 346
Reference books, 185
Reger, Max, 274, 289, 294
Register of instruments and voices, 303, 382, 387, 424, 439. Also see sonority
Régnier, Henri de, 8, 238, 239, 331, 337, 340, 342
Reiche, Jens Peter, 382
Relationships, 247, 253
Religion, 255, 265, 285
Renaissance period, 277, 354, 357, 387, 419
Renan, E., 342
Renard, Jules, 244
Renoir, Pierre-Auguste, 232, 346
Repetition, 234, 276, 365, 372, 427
Reti, Rudolph, 382
Revolution in music, 225, 255
Revue belge de musicologie, 233
Revue blanche, 10, 347
Revue bleue, 273
Revue de monde nouveau, 341
Revue de musicologie, 234
Revue internationale de musique française, 236
Revue musicale, 237, 238, 239, 240, 242

Revue musicale de Suisse romande, 228
Revue wagnérienne, 267, 336, 338
Rewald, John, 346
Reyer, 290, 293, 336, 420
Reynold's Bar, 9
Rhythm, 196, 236, 245, 271, 286, 287, 308, 322, 333, 375, 385, 392, 396, 401, 413, 415, 417, 427, 431, 433, 436, 439, 441, 447, 455
Richard, R., 272
Richard, Albert, 241
Richepin, J., 337, 342
Riehn, Rainer, 232
Riessauw, Anne-Marie Rodolf, 444
Rihm, W., 420
Rimbaud, Arthur, 268, 343
Rimsky-Korsakov, Nikolay, 7, 232, 285, 302, 313
Ringger, Rolf Urs, 444
Ringgold, John Robert, 390
Rivière, Jacques, 217, 258, 273, 334, 444
Robichez, Jacques, 342, 445
Rochberg, George, 269
Rodin, Auguste, 255, 326, 367
Roger, Thérèse, 8, 59, 219, 300
Roger-Ducasse, Jean, 15, 30, 36, 78, 79, 212, 295, 451
Rohinsky, Marie-Claire, 432, 445
Roland-Manuel, Alexis, 225, 275, 281, 408
Rolf, Marie, 222, 249, 250, 251, 342, 445
Rolland, Romain, 201, 254, 258, 275, 276, 310, 317, 326, 446
Rolon, J., 294
Romantic era, 263, 269, 290, 310, 311, 341, 454, 455
Romantic Music Festival. See Festivals, Debussy
Romanticism, 331, 342, 351
Rome, 14, 220, 222, 247. Also see Prix de Rome
Romilly, Mme Gérard de, 95, 216, 220
Rootzen, Kajsa, 202
Rorem, Ned, 280
Rosen, Charles, 220, 281, 293, 305, 310
Rosenstiel, Léonie, 209
Rosing, Helmut, 391
Rossetti, Dante Gabriel, 6, 40, 43, 92, 247, 266, 271, 339, 396, 428, 430, 452
Rosso, François, 244
Rostand, E., 342
Rouard, Isabelle, 243
Rouart, Mme E., 73
Rouché, J., 325
Roudier, Patrick, 245
Rousseau, Henri, 314
Rousseau, Jean-Jacques, 243
Roussel, Albert, 227, 238, 311
Roussilhe, Jean-Paul, 189
Rovsing Olsen, Poul, 226
Roy, Jean, 47, 241, 311
Royal Philharmonic Soc., 31
Royaumont, 109
Rubinstein, 255, 274, 328, 420
Ruch muzyczny (Warsaw), 242
Rudyar, Dane, 194
Rummel, Walter, 69, 223, 327
Ruschenburg, Peter, 419, 447
Ruskin, John, 430
Russell, Henry, 87, 92
Russell, Ross, 311
Russia, culture and music, and Debussy's voyages there, 5, 7, 14, 202, 220, 225, 226, 238, 264, 265, 279, 285, 302, 313, 319, 324, 329, 356, 361, 401, 402
Rutz, Hans, 202
Ruwet, Nicolas, 234, 369, 372
Rzewski, Frederic, 269

S.I.M. [revue], 313
Sabaneyev, Leonid, 202, 285
Sadie, Stanley, 209
Saint-Germain-en-Laye, 3, 223, 242

Saint-Marceaux, Mme de, 219
Saint Petersburg, 14
Saint-Saëns, Camille, 39, 216, 261, 266, 282, 293, 297, 300, 304, 311, 320, 367
Sainte-Beuve, 331
Salle Erard, 75
Salle Gaveau, 32, 46, 56
Salle Laurent, 45
Salmon, Joseph, 46
Salon [as social phenomenon], 290, 421
Salon des Indépendants, 347
Salon des Refusés, 346
Salon music, 197
Salon tradition, 408
Salzer, Felix, 372, 447
Salzman, Eric, 267, 356
Samama, Guy, 442
Samazeuilh, Gustave, 98, 229, 268, 312, 317, 447
Saminsky, Lazare, 238
Samson, Jim, 383
Santoliquido, Francesco, 312
Sarrazin, G., 40
Sartor, Michel, 244
Sartre, Jean-Paul, 334
Satie, Erik, 8, 9, 10, 15, 40, 95, 193, 206, 210, 212, 215, 228, 232, 235, 238, 244, 246, 263, 269, 288, 289, 290, 295, 298, 311, 312, 314, 321, 324, 333, 334, 444, 447
Sauguet, Henri, 225, 241, 447
Scala, La, in Milan, 222, 420
Scale, Debussy's concept of, 377, 378, 393
Scandinavian music, 226
Scelsi, Giacinto, 324
Scenic design. See Stage design
Schaeffer, Boguslaw, 243
Schaeffer, Pierre, 245
Schaeffner, André, 96, 217, 220, 225, 302, 312, 339, 346, 356, 429, 447
Schaeffner, Georg, 275
Schauerte, Helga, 313
Schelle, Michael, 37
Schenker, Heinrich, 366, 372, 375, 377, 376, 415, 424, 439
Scherer, Colette, 237
Scherliess, Volker, 448
Schiff, David, 313
Schmidt-Garre, Helmut, 343
Schmitt, Florent, 238, 284, 297, 298
Schmitz, E. Robert, 397, 404, 448
Schnebel, Dieter, 231, 324, 383
Schoenberg, Arnold, 206, 225, 226, 230, 231, 232, 233, 243, 244, 254, 255, 256, 262, 264, 269, 271, 274, 276, 277, 288, 291, 294, 299, 301, 304, 313, 314, 315, 316, 317, 318, 319, 323, 363, 365, 377, 381, 388, 390, 391, 451
Schola Cantorum, 11
Schopenhauer, Arthur, 285, 456
Schrecker, F., 294, 415
Schubert, Franz, 233, 368
Schuh, Willi, 232
Schuler, Mme R., 211
Schultz, Wolfgang-Andreas, 363
Schumann, Robert, 4, 40, 278, 316, 354, 387
Scott, C., 294
Scriabin. See Skryabin
Sebastiani, Pia, 251
Second Parisian School, 265
Segalen, Victor, 12, 22, 96, 268, 332, 435
Seigel, Jerrold, 269
Selz, Peter, 347
Semantics, 370, 372
Semiotics, 249, 365, 366, 369, 370, 371, 372, 394, 435, 449
Semitic, 300
Sensation in Debussy, 246
Sensuous appeal, 269
Seraphin, Hellmut, 448
Serbescu, Silvia, 450
Serialism, 265, 296, 309, 313, 381, 382, 383

Seroff, Victor, 97, 205
Set theory, 382, 440, 454
Seurat, Georges, 346
Sévérac, Déodat de, 222, 273, 287, 415
Shakespeare, William, 6, 11, 353, 356, 448
Shand, David A., 449
Shattuck, Roger, 254, 269, 314
Shaw, George Bernard, 84
Shelley, Percy Bysshe, 342
Shostakovich, Dmitry, 295
Sibelius, Jean, 294, 314, 319, 360, 379, 451
Sievers, Gerd, 314
Signac, Paul, 346
Signatures, 246. Also see handwriting
Silence (as element of time in music), 351, 352, 367, 453
Silences [journal], 243
Silver, Sheila Jane, 383
Silvestre, A., 253
Simplicity, 353
Singers, 398, 419, 445, 454
Siohan, Robert, 212
Sisley, Alfred, 346
Sivry, Charles de, 258
Six, Les, 220, 284, 289, 295, 325, 333
Skowron, Zbigniew, 314
Skryabin, Alexander, 221, 285, 288, 289, 303, 316, 321, 366, 381
Slattery, Thomas C., 315
Slonimsky, Nicolas, 210
Smalley, Roger, 231, 315
Smith, Richard Langham. See Langham Smith, Richard
Social context and sociology, 201, 244, 246, 255, 257, 259, 263, 298, 351, 365, 393, 441
Socialism, 264
Société Musicale Indépendante, 45, 74, 216
Société Nationale de Musique, 7, 8, 10, 35, 36, 41, 45, 49, 51, 59, 68, 69, 73, 74, 75, 76
Society for Music Theory, 251
Somfai, Laszlo, 233
Sonic wave patterns, 386
Sonority, 225, 244, 262, 299, 303, 308, 314, 322, 360, 381, 382, 387, 392, 405, 406, 407, 424, 439, 440, 450. Also see Sound and Timbre
Sopeña, F., 284
Souffrin-Le Breton, Eileen, 343, 449
Sound, 268, 278, 315, 317, 323, 324, 371, 383, 389, 390, 391. Also see Sonority and Timbre
Sound archives, 189
Sources, 439, 444. Also see Catalogue of Works
Souris, André, 225, 233, 315, 391
Southeast Asian. See Asian
Spahlinger-Ditzig, Ursula, 373
Spain, culture and music, 5, 226, 238, 284, 310, 324, 355, 449
Spectral formations, 386
Speech patterns, 358, 372, 392
Spence, Keith, 449
Spencer, Williametta, 315
Spies, Markus, 231
Spieth-Weissenbacher, Christiane, 236, 393, 449
Spirituals, 298
Staempfli, Edward, 316
Stage design, 241, 290, 400, 414, 420
Stahnke, Manfred, 316
Starr, Lawrence, 221, 269
Stasis, 394
Stassov [Stasov], Vladimir, 303
Static element in music, 303, 379
Stedron, Milos, 316
Stefani, Gino, 449
Stempel, Larry, 317
Stevens family, 8, 9, 53, 54
Stiftelsen Musikkulturens Främjande, 117

Stimpson, Brian, 343
Stirnemann, Knut, 373, 449
Stockhausen, Karlheinz, 243, 269, 270, 303, 324, 371, 373, 378, 388, 456
Stoianova, Ivanka, 244
Stone, Else Kurt, 317
Storb, Ilse, 384, 450
Stralet Rostand, Claude, 230
Strauss, Richard, 12, 201, 208, 265, 274, 277, 279, 291, 301, 310, 312, 317, 360, 390, 411, 412, 420
Stravinsky, Igor, 13, 14, 78, 84, 96, 201, 202, 204, 206, 212, 230, 231, 232, 233, 235, 238, 248, 254, 255, 264, 265, 269, 271, 278, 283, 284, 285, 290, 293, 298, 300, 301, 304, 308, 313, 315, 318, 321, 322, 323, 329, 333, 334, 351, 366, 371, 377, 381, 383, 384, 387, 389, 390, 391, 393, 412, 435, 437, 438
Stravinsky, Vera, 318
Street, Donald, 319
Street, William Henry, 450
Street-criers' tunes, 392
Streletski, Gérard, 357
Strobel, Heinrich, 202, 230, 232
Structure, 193, 208, 209, 224, 234, 240, 241, 248, 251, 256, 272, 277, 282, 291, 296, 301, 303, 305, 308, 311, 322, 323, 324, 345, 356, 359, 362, 363, 366, 380, 381, 382, 389, 397, 399, 401, 402, 403, 404, 405, 407, 410, 411, 413, 416, 418, 424, 427, 429, 435, 439, 440, 443, 447, 450, 453, 457. Also see Form
Stuckenschmidt, Hans Heinz, 226, 269, 318
Style, 225, 230, 246, 255, 271, 349
Stylistic phases, 349
Suarès, André, 237, 242, 283, 333
Surrealism, 208
Survey of life and works, 197, 201, 228
Suter, Louis-Marc, 236, 385, 450
Sweden, 226
Swinburne, Algernon Charles, 339, 342, 430
Symbolism, 194, 199, 206, 208, 210, 215, 221, 245, 250, 263, 264, 266, 268, 276, 290, 302, 330, 331, 334, 336, 338, 339, 340, 341, 342, 344, 347, 357, 358, 359, 360, 361, 369, 390, 392, 396, 399, 404, 416, 419, 420, 428, 443, 445, 449, 456. Also see Literary concerns
Symposium Claude Debussy in Milan, 243
Synesthesia, 268
Systematic musicology, 257
Szánto, Theodore, 109
Szymanowski, Karol, 289, 295, 297, 363

Tableaux vivants, 258
Tailleferre, Germaine, 295
Takahashi, 344
Tammaro, Ferruccio, 319, 451
Taruskin, Richard, 233
Taverne Pousset, 8
Taverne Weber, 9
Tawaststjerna, Erik, 319
Tchaikovsky, Pyotr, 7, 40, 285, 313, 407, 426
Tcherina, Ludmilla, 240
Templier, Pierre, 288
Tempo, 303, 431, 434
Temporality, 385
Temps, Le, 12, 273
Tenney, James C., 374
Tennyson, Alfred, 337
Terrasse, Antoine, 347
Terrasson, René, 442, 451
Tetaz, Numa F., 327
Texas, University of. See Harry Ransom Humanities Research Center

Text, 392, 394, 445, 447
Text expression, 382
Texts of all songs, 185
Texture, 224, 303, 311, 314, 319, 356, 367, 379, 386, 401, 412, 431, 439, 454
Teyte, Maggie, 327
Théâtre Antoine, 253
Théâtre d'art, 261
Théâtre de l'Odéon, 253
Théâtre de L'Oeuvre, 9, 445
Théâtre des Champs-Elysées, 27, 32, 38, 75
Théâtre du Châtelet, 29, 35
Théâtre du Vieux Colombier, 325
Théâtre-Libre, 253
Théâtre Lyrique du Vaudeville, 26
Théâtre Royal de la Monnaie, 234
Theatrical sense, 352
Theme, 234, 243, 249, 364, 366, 371, 374, 388, 404, 405, 410, 413, 415, 416, 419, 431, 438, 439, 450
Thieberg [violinist], 6, 44
Thomas, Werner, 320
Thompson, Oscar, 203
Thompson, Virgil, 448
Tiénot, Yvonne, 203, 228, 320
Tiersot, Julien, 258, 269, 320, 451
Timbre, 197, 209, 224, 244, 245, 268, 271, 280, 284, 286, 301, 306, 308, 311, 354, 359, 380, 386, 387, 388, 390, 413, 426, 441, 450, 457. Also see both Sonority and Sound
Timbrell, Charles, 223, 327
Time in music, (sense of) 217, 286, 304, 308, 333, 389
Times, Debussy's. See Period and Fin-de-siècle
Tinan, Mme de. See De Tinan
Tokyo. See Japan 222
Tonality, 221, 225, 229, 233, 256, 268, 276, 286, 289, 324, 349, 352, 355, [cont.] 359, 364, 366, 372, 375, 378, 381, 383, 384, 389, 396, 399, 401, 402, 406, 407, 411, 413, 416, 424, 429, 433, 435, 439, 440, 444, 448, 450, 454
Tonazzi, Bruno, 321
Toncitch, Voya, 321
Tone color. See Timbre
Toscanini, Arturo, 13, 326
Toscanini Memorial Archives, 116
Tosi, Guy, 451
Toulet, Paul-Jean, 9, 11, 92, 96, 130, 212, 254, 332, 342, 448
Tovey, Donald Francis, 452
Toynbee, Arnold, 262
Translations of Debussy's songs, 185
Trevitt, John, 452
Trevitt, L.J.H., 384
Trémisot, Emmanuel, 272
Trillat, Ennemond, 69
Trillig, Johannes, 260, 273, 275
Trojahn, M., 420
Turina, Joaquín, 310
Turner, J.M.W., 247, 264, 355, 430
Turner, J. Rigbie, 187
Twentieth century, culture and music, 210, 221, 224, 253, 256, 262, 267, 269, 271, 279, 356, 360, 378, 381, 382, 385, 397, 416, 418. Also see Period

Udine, Jean, 272
Ujfalussy, József, 203, 245, 321
United States of America, 8, 12, 13, 14. Also see America, North and South
University of Texas at Austin. See Harry Ransom Humanities Research Center

Valade, Léon, 63
Valéry, Paul, 9, 131, 254, 300, 328, 340, 343

Vallas, Léon, 20, 85, 132, 195, 197, 200, 201, 202, 203, 204, 205, 208, 211, 212, 230, 242, 313, 322, 452
Vallery-Radot, (Joseph) Pasteur, 89, 97, 204, 213, 241, 242, 357
Vallin, Ninon, 65
Van Ackere, 373
Van Appledorn, Mary Jeanne, 373, 396
Van den Toorn, Pieter C., 322
Van Gogh, Vincent, 346, 367
Vander Linden, Albert, 234, 270
Vangeon, Henri, 338
Varèse,Edgard, 212, 225, 226, 277, 301, 308, 317, 354, 387
Vasnier family, including Blanche, Eugène, and Marguerite, 5, 6, 22, 48, 50, 52, 53, 54, 55, 56, 57, 58, 59, 60, 61, 62, 63, 80, 92, 97, 198, 213, 222, 235, 238, 239, 249, 336, 449
Vaucaire, Maurice, 258
Vaughan, Gerard, 347
Vaughan Williams, Ralph, 296, 308, 360, 378
Verdi, Giuseppe, 448
Verismo (opera), 307, 310, 317
Verlaine, Paul, 4, 10, 14, 26, 53, 54, 55, 58, 64, 204, 259, 266, 267, 274, 338, 341, 342, 343, 344, 392, 394, 421, 429, 444, 446, 449, 453, 455
Vial, Mireille, 245
Victoria, Tomás Luis de, 354
Vidal, Paul, 5, 57, 97, 220, 235, 239, 313
Vielé-Griffin, 342
Vienna, 13, 218
Viennese School [Schoenberg et al.], 299, 301, 302, 310, 317, 319
Vierne, Louis, 300, 423
Villa Médicis, 239. Also see Prix de Rome
Villatico, Dino, 216
Villa-Lobos, Heitor, 294
Villiers de L'Isle-Adam, P.A.M., 20, 342
Villon, François, 63, 78, 455
Vinay, Gianfranco, 322
Viñes, Ricardo, 11, 12, 32, 59, 68, 70, 71, 72, 73, 74, 75, 212, 236, 255, 281, 296, 324, 328, 355, 397
Virtuosic effects, 403
Visual arts, 263, 271, 304, 310, 344, 359
Vital, Cla, 452
Vladimirova, Anna, 224
Vocal style and writing, 396, 397, 414
Vogt, Hans, 270
Voice leading, 233, 372, 424, 439
Volta, Ornella, 215
Von Meck. See Meck
Vorska, Suzanne, 260
Vuillard, 247, 347
Vuillermoz, Emile, 83, 205, 213, 237, 240, 244, 273, 281, 298

Wagner, Richard, 6, 7, 8, 12, 40, 85, 91, 197, 200, 203, 210, 227, 228, 229, 237, 239, 244, 255, 256, 257, 258, 261, 264, 265, 266, 267, 268, 270, 272, 275, 276, 277, 279, 283, 284, 285, 287, 290, 291, 292, 294, 296, 302, 309, 312, 316, 321, 331, 332, 333, 337, 338, 339, 340, 342, 347, 351, 352, 353, 360, 361, 366, 367, 373, 376, 381, 390, 395, 400, 401, 402, 409, 411, 412, 414, 420, 425, 429, 447
Wagnerism. See the preceding
Waldbauer-Kerpelz string quartet, 434

War, World, I, 14, 91, 201, 350, 427
Warburton, Thomas, 221, 250, 384
Waterhouse, J.C.G., 231, 323
Watkins, Glenn, 210
Watson, Lorne, 453
Watteau, Antoine, 353
Weber, Edith, 205, 225, 226, 241, 265, 286, 294, 351, 373
Weber, Eugen, 270
Webern, Anton, 225, 226, 230, 243, 262, 265, 276, [cont.] 278, 287, 292, 293, 313, 317, 365, 373, 387, 391
Weinstein, Leo, 277
Wellesz, Egon, 276, 294, 323
Welte-Mignon recording, 232, 404
Wenk, Arthur B., 220, 221, 248, 249, 250, 271, 343, 357, 394, 453
Western concepts and tradition, 256, 278, 315, 316, 370, 383, 388, 391
Westphal, Kurt, 323
Whistler, James A. McNeill, 194, 204, 260, 346, 351
White, David A., 453
White, Eric Walter, 323
Whithorne, E., 294
Whittall, A., 385
Whole-tone use, 277, 288, 289, 299, 319, 359, 379, 382, 385, 399, 429, 433, 447, 453
Widor, Charles-Marie, 5, 15
Wilde, Oscar, 9, 260, 340
Williams, Alberto, 294
Williams, Bernard, 454
Willy [pseud. of H. Gauthiers-Villars, which also see], 272, 333, 335
Wilson, Eugene Norman, 454
Wilson, Lawrence A., 386
Winking, Hans, 324
Wodehouse, Artis, 250
Wolf, Hugo, 233, 379
Wolff, Albert, 30
Wolff, Hellmuth Christian, 321, 374
Wolff, Stéphane, 454
Wood, Henry J., 95
Woodson, Thomas, 343
Woollen, Russell, 374
World exposition. See Exposition, Paris
World music, 266. Also see Asian music
World War I. See War
Worms de Romilly, 73
Wu Yiwei, 213
Wurmser-Delcourt, 31, 76

Xenakis, Yannis, 242, 378

Youens, Susan, 233, 455
Young, Percy M., 321, 324
Ysaÿe, Antoine, 328
Ysaÿe, Eugène, 37, 45, 92, 98, 204, 268, 270, 301, 312, 328

Zeller, Hans Rudolf, 231
Zenck, Claudia Maurer, 221, 249, 324, 374, 456
Zimmermann, Rainer, 233
Zola, Emile, 337, 342